Turbo Pascal 7:
The Complete Reference

Turbo Pascal 7:
The Complete Reference

Stephen O'Brien
and
Steven Nameroff

Osborne **McGraw-Hill**

Berkeley   New York   St. Louis   San Francisco
Auckland   Bogotá   Hamburg   London   Madrid
Mexico City   Milan   Montreal   New Delhi   Panama City
Paris   São Paulo   Singapore   Sydney
Tokyo   Toronto

Osborne McGraw-Hill
2600 Tenth Street
Berkeley, California 94710
U.S.A.

For information on translations or book distributors outside of the U.S.A., please write to Osborne **McGraw-Hill** at the above address.

Turbo Pascal 7: The Complete Reference

1234567890 DOC 99876543

ISBN 0-07-881793-5

To Micah Meredith,
who kindly let us work even when you wanted to play

Publisher
Kenna S. Wood

Acquisitions Editor
William Pollock

Associate Editor
Vicki Van Ausdall

Technical Editor
Joe LaRosa

Editor
Janis Paris

Proofreaders
Carol Burbo
Theo Crawford

Computer Designer
Stefany Otis

Cover Design
Bay Graphics Design, Inc.

Ilustrator
Marla Shelasky

Contents
at a Glance

Part I   The Language   **1**

  1   Turbo Pascal Program Structure   3
  2   Primitive Data Types   41
  3   Complex Data Types   59
  4   Subprograms   83
  5   Program Control Structures   117
  6   Pointers, Dynamic Memory, and Polymorphism   153
  7   Files   181
  8   External Procedures and Inline Code   205

Part II   The Environments   **227**

  9   The Development Environments: The DOS and
       Windows IDEs   229
 10   The Object Browsers in DOS and Windows   259
 11   The Resource Workshop   277
 12   Debugging in DOS and Windows   301

Part III   Standard Turbo Pascal Libraries   **327**

13   The System Unit   329
14   The Crt and WinCrt Units   363
15   Dos and WinDos Units   403
16   Graphics in DOS and Windows   435
17   Turbo Vision   499
18   Using Object Windows   573

Part IV   Writing Applications in Turbo Pascal   **625**

19   Procedure and Function Library   627
20   Complex Data Structures   665
21   Merging, Searching, and Sorting   687
22   Interrupts, Telecommunications, and
         Memory-Resident Programs   713
23   Optimizing Turbo Pascal Programs   739

Part V   Appendixes   **765**

A   Turbo Pascal Error Codes   767
B   ASCII Codes for the PC   775
C   The PC Keyboard   779
D   Turbo Pascal Reserved Words   783

      Index   795

Contents

Acknowledgments	xvii
Introduction	xix

Part I
The Language

1
Turbo Pascal Program Structure — 3

Elements of All Programs	3
Headings	5
Declarations	5
Constants	7
Types	8
Variables	9
Labels	10
Blocks	11
Input and Output	14
Using Variables for Input	15
Units	17
Using Units	17
Creating Units	18
Includes	19
Overlays	20
OvrInit	24
OvrInitEMS	25
OvrSetBuf	25
OvrGetBuf	25
OvrClearBuf	25
Compiler Directives	25
Switch Directives	26
Parameter Directives	35
Conditional Directives	37

2
Primitive Data Types — 41

Numeric Types	41
Integer Types	41
Real Types	42
80×87 Data Types	42
Non-Numeric Scalar Types	43
Enumerated Types	43
Type Casting	45
Arithmetic Operators	46
Integer and Real Expressions	47
Hierarchy of Arithmetic Operators	48
Integer Versus Real Arithmetic	49
Logical Operators	57

3
Complex Data Types — 59

Arrays	59
Strings	60
Null-Terminated Strings	61
Multidimensional Arrays	62

Records	63
Variant Records	67
Substitute for Multidimensional Arrays	71
Objects	71
Code + Data = Object	72
Inheritance	74
Encapsulation	76
Public and Private Areas	77
Sets	78
Numeric Sets	78
Character Sets	79
Sets of User-Defined Elements	79
Sets and Memory Allocation	79

4

Subprograms   **83**

Procedures and Functions	83
Defining Procedures in Pascal	83
Passing Parameters to a Procedure	84
Functions versus Procedures	87
Nesting and Precedence of Subprograms	89
Subprograms and the Scope of Variables	92
More on Parameters	94
Passing Parameters of Different Types	94
Open Parameters	96
Passing Set Parameters	98
Untyped Parameters	99
Passing Literal Values	102
Methods	103
Implementing Methods	103
Methods and Private Areas	106
Static Methods	107
Virtual Methods	109
Inside Virtual Methods	111
Methods and Object Type Compatibility	112
Recursion	114

5

Program Control Structures   **117**

Condition Statements	119
Boolean Functions in Control Structures	121

Decision Making and Conditional Branching	122
The If-Then Statement	122
The If-Then-Else Statement	124
Nested If-Then Statements	128
Conditional Branching with the Case Statement	132
Repetitive Control Structures	136
For-Do Loop	137
Repeat-Until Loop	140
While-Do Loop	141
Modifying Control Structures	142
Using Break	142
Using Continue	144
Using Exit	146
Using Goto	148

6

Pointers, Dynamic Memory Allocation, and Polymorphism   **153**

The Memory Model	153
DOS Memory Mapping Conventions	154
Segments and Offsets	154
Pointers	160
The Pointer Variable	160
New and Dispose	162
Mark and Release	163
GetMem and FreeMem	165
Using the @ Operator	165
The PChar Type	167
Pointers with Complex Data Structures	169
Pointers in Objects	174
Objects That Contain Pointers	174
Pointers to Objects	175
Polymorphism	176

7

Files   **181**

Text Files	182
Text-File Identifiers	182
Reading Strings from Text Files	185
Reading Multiple Strings per Line	186

Reading Numbers from Text
Files   186
Errors in Numeric Input   189
Writing Text Files   189
File Buffers   190
Flushing a File   191
Typed Files   191
Records and Typed Files   192
Strings and Typed Files   193
More Complex Typed Files   195
Untyped Files   197
Procedures for Typed and Untyped
Files   199
Devices as Files   202
The Standard Input and Output
Devices   203
Printer Devices   204
Serial Devices   204
The NUL Device   204

8

External Procedures and Inline Code   205

Extending Turbo Pascal   205
Inline Code   206
Inline Directives   208
External Procedures   210
An External Function   210
Using Global Data and
Procedures   212
Using the Turbo Assembler   214
Using the Asm Statement   218
Debugging Assembler   221

Part II
The Environments

9

The Development Environments: The DOS and Windows IDEs   229

Getting Started in the DOS IDE   230
The Desktop   231

Dialog Boxes   232
Getting Started in the Windows IDE   233
The Main Menus in DOS and
Windows   233
The File Menu   234
The Edit Menu   237
The Search Menu   239
The Run Menu   242
The Compile Menu   244
The Debug Menu   245
The Tools Menu   247
The Options Menu   247
The Window Menu   254
The Help Menu   257
Local Menus   257

10

The Object Browser in DOS and Windows   259

The DOS Object Browser   259
Browsing Units   260
Browsing Objects   263
Browsing Globals   265
Searching for a Symbol   266
Browser Options   266
The Windows Object Browser   268
The Local Menu   268
The Speed Bar   270
Browsing Units   270
Browsing Objects   272
Browsing Globals   275
Browsing a Symbol   275
Browser Options   276

11

The Resource Workshop   277

What is a Resource?   277
Creating a Project   278
Adding an Identifier Unit   278
Saving your work   280
Creating a Menu   281
Changing Items   281
Creating Items   283
Testing the Menu   285
Creating Accelerators   285
Changing an Accelerator   285
Adding an Accelerator   286
Creating a Dialog Box   286

The Dialog Window 287
Adding a Push Button 288
Adding More Controls 290
Aligning the Controls 291
Setting the Order 293
Setting the Tabs 293
Setting the Groups 294
Common Operations 294
The File Menu 294
The Edit Menu 296
The Resource Menu 298
The View Menu 299
The Window Menu 300
The Help Menu 300

12

Debugging in DOS and Windows 301

The Integrated Debugger 301
Getting Ready to Debug 302
Debugger Features 302
The Execution Bar 303
Go to Cursor 303
Trace Into 304
Step Over 304
Evaluate and Modify 306
Call Stack Window 308
Watch Expressions 308
Breakpoints 312
CTRL-BREAK 313
A Debugging Example 313
Starting Up 314
Adding Watch Variables 315
More on the Watch Window 316
Display Format 317
Programming for Debugging 320
Memory Requirements and Limitations 321
The Stand-Alone Debugger for Windows 322
Controlling Program Execution 323
Watch Expressions 323
Breakpoints 323
Evaluating and Modifying Expressions 325

Part III
Standard Turbo Pascal Libraries

13

The System Unit 329

String Routines 329
Using Standard Routines 330
Direct Manipulation of Characters 338
Manipulating the Length Byte 339
String Routines/System Unit 341
I/O Routines 343
I/O Routines/System Unit 344
Math Routines 349
Math Routines/System Unit 351
Pointer Routines 354
Pointer Routines/System Unit 354
Other Routines 357
Other Routines/System Unit 357

14

The Crt and WinCrt Units 363

PC Text Display 363
The Video Adapter and Display Memory 364
The Attribute Byte 364
PC Text Modes 365
Controlling Color with Turbo Pascal 365
Using Screen Coordinates 366
Text Display Routines Crt Unit 369
Using Video Memory 370
Simple Windows 373
Pop-Up Windows 374
Multiple Logical Screens and Pop-Up Windows 376
Screen Control Routines Crt Unit 383
Avoiding Vertical Retrace 384
Other Crt Subprograms 397
Miscellaneous Crt Routines Crt Unit 397

Using WinCrt Unit 398
Using WinCrt Windows 399
WinCrt Subprogram Reference 400
Routines Unique to WinCrt 401

15

The Dos and
WinDos Units 403

Date and Time Routines 404
Date and Time Routines
DOS Unit 406
Disk and File Routines 408
Disk and File Routines
DOS Unit 411
Process Routines 414
Process Routines
DOS Unit 417
System Services Routines 419
The 8088 Registers 419
Setting the Cursor Size 423
Reporting Key State 425
System Services Routines
DOS Unit 427
The WinDos Unit 428
Routines Unique to WinDos
The WinDos Unit 432

16

Graphics in DOS
and Windows 435

Setting Up the BGI 436
Graphics Adapters and
Coordinate Systems 438
Set-up Routines/Graph Unit 440
Drawing Shapes 445
Lines 445
Circles 450
Drawing Routines/Graph Unit 453
Using Colors and Patterns 456
Color and Pattern Routines
Graph Unit 461
Working with Images 466
Image Routines/Graph Unit 470

Graphical Text 471
Graphical Text Routines
Graph Unit 474
Graphics in Windows 476
Introducing Object Windows 476
Drawing Lines and Shapes 478
Patterns in Windows 482
Drawing Graphical Text 488
Selected Graphics Routines
WinProcs unit 493

17

Turbo Vision 499

Creating and Using Flash Cards 500
Creating an Application Object 501
TApplication Object Summary
APP.TPU 503
Creating Event Commands 504
Creating a Menu Bar 505
TMenuBar Object Summary
MENUS.TPU 506
TMenuBox Object Summary
MENUS.TPU 509
kbXXXX Constant Summary
DRIVERS.TPU 510
TRect Object Summary
OBJECTS.TPU 510
Creating a Status Line 511
TStatusLine Object Summary
MENUS.TPU 512
Creating the Event Handler 514
TProgram Object Summary
APP.TPU 519
TDeskTop Object Summary
APP.TPU 521
TGroup Object Summary
VIEWS.TPU 522
Writing Support Code 523
TObject Object Summary
OBJECTS.TPU 525
Creating Collections 526
TCollection Object Summary
OBJECTS.TPU 529
TSortedCollection Object
Summary/OBJECTS.TPU 532

TStringCollection Object
Summary/OBJECTS.TPU   533
Creating a Simple Dialog Box   534
    TDialog Object Summary
    DIALOGS.TPU   535
    TView Object Summary
    VIEWS.TPU   536
Creating More Complex Dialog
Boxes   537
    TButton Object Summary
    DIALOGS.TPU   543
    TInputLine Object Summary
    DIALOGS.TPU   545
    TLabel Object Summary
    DIALOGS.TPU   547
    TStaticText Object Summary
    DIALOGS.TPU   548
    TCheckBoxes Object Summary
    DIALOGS.TPU   549
    TRadioButtons Object Summary
    DIALOGS.TPU   549
    TCluster Object Summary
    DIALOGS.TPU   550
    TListBox Object Summary
    DIALOGS.TPU   553
    THistory Object Summary
    DIALOGS.TPU   554
    TFileDialog Object Summary
    STDDLG.TPU   555
Using Streams   557
    TBufStream Object Summary
    OBJECTS.TPU   562
    TEmsStream Object Summary
    OBJECTS.TPU   564
    TStream Object Summary
    OBJECTS.TPU   565
Other Turbo Vision Objects   566
    TWindow Object Summary
    VIEWS.TPU   567
    TScroller Object Summary
    VIEWS.TPU   569
    TScrollBar Object Summary
    VIEWS.TPU   571
    TResourceFile Object Summary
    OBJECTS.TPU   571

18

Using Object Windows   573

Creating an Application Object   573
Defining Menu Commands   575
Creating and Loading a Menu Bar   576
Creating and Loading Accelerators   579
Completing the Skeletal Application   580
    TApplication Object Summary
    OWindows Unit   584
    TWindow Object Summary
    OWindows Unit   585
    TWindows Object Summary
    OWindows Unit   587
Writing Support Code   588
    Strings Unit Summary   594
Creating Dialog Boxes   598
    Add Card Dialog Box   598
    Question Dialog Box   602
    Answer Dialog Box   605
    File Dialogs   607
    Putting It All Together   608
    TDialog Object Summary
    ODialogs Unit   612
    TControl Object Summary
    ODialogs Unit   613
    TButton Object Summmary
    ODialogs Unit   614
    TCheckBox Object Summary
    ODialogs Unit   614
    TRadio Button Object Summary
    ODialogs Unit   615
    TStatic Object Summary
    ODialogs Unit   616
    TEdit Object Summary
    ODialogs Unit   617
    TListBox Object Summary
    ODialogs Unit   618
    TComboBox Object Summary
    ODialogs Unit   619
    TScrollBar Object Summary
    ODialogs Unit   620
    TGroupBox Object Summary
    ODialogs Unit   621

TDlgWindow Object Summary
  ODialogs Unit   622
TFileDialog Object Summary
  OStdDlg Unit   623

Part IV
Writing Applications
in Turbo Pascal

19
Procedure and
Function Library   627

String Routines   627
  Replacing Strings   628
  Personalizing Messages   629
  Error-Free Data Entry   630
  Removing Blanks   631
  Big Strings   633
Math Routines   636
  Real_To_Frac   637
  Frac_To_Real   639
  Bit Manipulation   640
  An Interactive Calculator   643
I/O and File Routines   650
  Fast Write   651
  Generating Sound   652
  InKey   652
  InputStringShift   653
  File Encryption   659

20
Complex Data Structures   665

Doubly Linked Lists   665
Stacks as Reusable Objects   671
Binary Trees as Abstract Objects   675
  Implementing the Tree Structure   676
  Using the Tree Structure   681

21
Merging, Searching,
and Sorting   687

Merging   687
Searching Methods   691
  Sequential Search   691
  Binary Search   693
Sorting Methods   696
  General Sorting Principles   697
  Bubble Sort   697
  Shell Sort   700
  Quick Sort   705
  Comparing Sorting Algorithms   708
Using Sorted Collections   709

22
Interrupts,
Telecommunications, and
Memory-Resident Programs   713

Using Interrupts   713
  Hardware and Software
    Interrupts   714
  The Interrupt Vector Table   714
  Replacing Interrupts   715
Writing the Interrupt Handler   717
  Restoring the Data Segment   717
  Turbo Pascal Interrupt Support   717
  PC Telecommunications   718
  The Telecommunications
    Program   719
  The Circular Input Buffer   730
Memory-Resident Programs   731
  The Reentrance Issue   731
  Going Resident   732
  Activating the TSR   732
  Blanking the Screen   735
  How the TSR Works   735
  The Interrupt Handlers   735

23
Optimizing Turbo Pascal
Programs   739

Optimization: Perfection Versus
  Excellence   739
Approaches to Optimization   740
Timing Program Execution   740
Optimizing Control Structures   743
  Nested If-Then Statements   743
  Testing Values in Boolean
    Expressions   749
Optimizing Arithmetic   752

Optimizing File Operations 754
Optimizing String Operations 756
Compiler Directives 759
   Range Checking 759
   Stack Checking 760
   Boolean Evaluation 761
Procedures and Functions 762
Reference Parameters Versus Value
   Parameters 763

Run-time Error Messages 772
   DOS Errors 772
   I/O Errors 773
   Critical Errors 773
   Fatal Errors 773

Part V
Appendixes

A

**Turbo Pascal
Error Codes** **767**
   Compiler Error Messages 767

B

ASCII Codes for the PC **775**

C

The PC Keyboard **779**

D

**Turbo Pascal Reserved
Words** **783**

Index **795**

Acknowledgments

Many people deserve credit for helping make this book possible. Special thanks are offered to the following people.

To Joe LaRosa, who kept the technical content of the book on track, and to Janis Paris, who kept the grammar in line.

To Nan Borreson at Borland, who withstood our constant nagging.

To the wonderful staff at Osborne/McGraw-Hill, especially Bill Pollock, Vicki Van Ausdall, and Jeff Pepper, who kept us on our toes.

Finally, to Michael Ann Nameroff, for technical assistance with the index and emotional support throughout.

Introduction

Turbo Pascal has come to dominate the Pascal market. The little compiler that changed the way people program has gone through many changes over the years. Today it is still the best deal in the business. Turbo Pascal combines the benefits of structured programming in Pascal with a vast array of additional tools, including object-oriented programming and Turbo Vision. Whether you are just learning about PC programming or are a serious software developer, Turbo Pascal offers every powerful feature you could ask for in one friendly package.

Today there are also two additional products: Turbo Pascal for Windows and Borland Pascal. Turbo Pascal for Windows includes a Windows development environment as well as the tools to create actual Windows applications. Windows programming is quickly growing in popularity, especially with the introduction of tool support such as ObjectWindows.

Borland Pascal is for the professional developer—it contains all of Turbo Pascal (for DOS), Turbo Pascal for Windows, as well as several stand-alone tools. These tools include Turbo Assembler, Turbo Debugger, Turbo Profiler, WinSight, WinSpector, and more.

Structured Programming

Two of the most widely used programming languages today, Pascal and BASIC, started out as teaching tools. There the similarity between the two languages ends. Comparing the two will help you understand what Pascal is all about.

In the early 1970s, a major movement in programming began. Known as *structured programming,* this approach stressed breaking a program down into manageable pieces and then assembling those pieces into a program with a coherent, logical flow.

Pascal, developed by Niklaus Wirth, was designed to teach structured programming skills to future programmers. By enforcing a strict set of rules regarding the declaration of variables, program structure, and flow of control, Pascal steered the aspiring programmers toward good programming habits. In addition, Pascal provided a wide range of programming tools that made writing good, clear code much easier than was possible with COBOL or FORTRAN.

BASIC, on the other hand, was developed as an easy-to-learn language for nonprogrammers. It lets nontechnical people quickly learn to write simple programs. Unfortunately, BASIC encourages poor programming habits and unreadable code. It is significant that many new versions of BASIC resemble Pascal.

Contemporary students of programming, who are generally taught structured programming from the outset, might be surprised at just how pervasive the **goto** command was and, to a great extent, still is. This simple command allows programmers to jump anywhere within a program regardless of consistency in the program flow. Debugging and maintaining programs full of **gotos** is very difficult.

Structured programming, sometimes known as "goto-less programming," sought to eliminate the **goto** command by providing a rich set of program control structures. Pascal, a direct result of the structured programming philosophy, provided these control structures, which both increased program readability and helped eliminate unforeseen errors created by unstructured program flow. As a result, by learning to program in Pascal, students were almost forced into learning good programming habits.

Turbo Pascal and Standard Pascal

While standard Pascal had many strong points, it was never fully developed for use in commercial applications. It lacked useful input and output functions and sorely needed string types. Nonetheless, this version of Pascal was considered the standard for the world.

Borland recognized both the strengths and the weaknesses of standard Pascal and updated the language substantially. The result is a rich language that provides the programmer with the logical structure of standard Pascal plus an extensive set of tools.

In making these additions, Borland broke away from the Pascal standard, a move that prompted criticism from some quarters. Despite this, Turbo Pascal and its extensions have become the international standard for Pascal on microcomputers.

About This Book

This book is intended for almost all Turbo Pascal programmers, from beginners who have some experience to advanced Pascal programmers. It covers all aspects of the compiler, with extensive examples. Designed primarily as a reference guide, the book provides quick access to concise information on a broad range of topics.

If you are a Turbo Pascal programmer who wants to transition to Windows programming, this book is also for you. It demonstrates how to write programs in DOS, then rewrites those programs so they work in Windows. Also covered are many Windows functions that are unavailable in the DOS environment. Included in this book is coverage of the Windows IDE, the Resource Workshop, the standard units for Windows, and ObjectWindows.

The additional tools included in Borland Pascal, such as Profiler, WinSight, and WinSpector, as well as Turbo Assembler, are beyond the scope of this book.

Turbo Pascal is one of the leading programming environments for personal computers. *Turbo Pascal 7: The Complete Reference* is the resource you need to get the most from Borland's premier product.

How This Book Is Organized

This book is divided into five parts to help you find what you need quickly and easily. Part I introduces the Turbo Pascal language, from program syntax to standard functions and procedures. Part II covers the programming environments, including both IDEs and the Resource Workshop. Part III is a reference for the standard units, including Turbo Vision and Object Windows. Part IV shows you how to write better applications including complex data structures and memory-resident programs. Finally, Part V contains material, such as ASCII and error codes, in an easily referenced group of appendixes.

Style Conventions

The style of the text is designed to make it easy for you to distinguish among the elements of Turbo Pascal. Reserved word and standard types, such as **procedure** and **boolean,** are in boldface text. Procedures, functions, variables and objects defined in the Turbo Pascal units are in initial caps. For example, if you see TextColor or TWindow, you know that those identifiers are somewhere in a standard unit.

Identifiers defined by programs in this book are also initially capitalized, but they are also in italics. Thus *TextDemo* and *MyString* are identifiers from a listing.

Getting the Programs on Disk

Every program in this book is listed in its entirety, allowing you to type them into your computer and see them work. If you'd rather not take the time (or risks) to do it all yourself, you can obtain a copy of the programs on disk from the authors.

For as little as $19.00, you can receive a floppy disk in MS-DOS format. On that disk are all the programs and units found in this book. You'll also get a cross-reference of program names to page numbers. Just fill in the order blank that follows and mail it with your check to the address shown.

Please allow 2-3 weeks for delivery of domestic orders, 4-6 weeks for overseas orders. Osborne McGraw-Hill assumes no responsibility for this offer.

Please send me the programs and units from *Turbo Pascal 7: The Complete Reference* on a floppy disk. I have enclosed the proper amount with a check drawn from a U.S. bank.

Name: _____

Address: _____

_____

Basic price (5 1/4" disk):	$19.00	$19.00
For 3 1/2" disk, add:	$ 1.00	_____
For overseas orders, add:	$ 2.00	_____
TOTAL enclosed:		_____

Send payment to:

Starry Software
Box 131
Big Canoe, GA 30143

Part *I*

The Language

Chapter 1

Turbo Pascal Program Structure

A place for everything and everything in its place. This saying accurately describes Pascal, an orderly language consisting of well-defined sections, each of which serves a specific purpose. This chapter will provide a "road map" which lays out each of the sections and its relationship to the other sections.

A *program* is a set of Turbo Pascal instructions that can execute as a separate application. All programs can be broken down into three major sections: the *heading*, the *declarations*, and the *block*.

As your programs grow in size, you will need to partition them into smaller, more manageable pieces. Turbo Pascal provides three mechanisms for this: *units, include files*, and *overlays*.

This chapter starts with a brief discussion of the basic elements in Turbo Pascal. Then it describes each of the major sections in detail, as well as the partition mechanisms. Also included are discussions of simple input and output and compiler directives.

Elements of All Programs

At the extreme lowest level, all high-level programming languages consist of ASCII characters: letters, numbers, symbols, carriage returns, and spaces. At a more useful level, you can define a language as a series of *elements*, the smallest parts of the program that have separate, identifiable meaning. In Turbo Pascal, there are four classes of elements: reserved words, identifiers, constants, and symbols.

Reserved words are those used exclusively by a language; they cannot be used for any other purpose. The complete set of reserved words for Turbo Pascal appears in Appendix D. You should never attempt to create an identifier with the same name as a reserved word. For example, the declaration

```
procedure Do;
```

will fail with a compiler error because **do** is a reserved word.

 For technical reasons Borland subdivides reserved words into reserved words and standard directives. Since you should not create identifiers that match the names of standard directives, this book will consider them to be included in the set of reserved words.

An *identifier* is a word that you use to reference a location in memory. Practically speaking, an identifier is the name of a variable, type, subprogram, parameter, and so on. All identifiers must start with a letter or underscore, and can be followed by any number of letters, numbers, and underscores. Only the first 63 characters are used to determine uniqueness. The following declarations demonstrate valid identifiers:

```
procedure My_Procedure;
procedure This_Is_An_Excessively_Long_Identifier_Indeed;
procedure _Starts_With_An_Underscore;
procedure A;
procedure _;
procedure __;
```

Of course, there's a big difference between valid identifiers and useful identifiers. The last three identifiers may be legal, but they score no points for readability. Here are two examples with invalid identifiers:

```
procedure AnEmbedded$ymbol;
procedure 1NiceName;
```

In the first, a symbol ($) is part of the identifier. The second one starts with a number. Neither example will compile.

Neither reserved words or identifiers are *case sensitive,* which means it doesn't matter whether the letters in the word are uppercase or lowercase. The words **Begin, begin, BEGIN,** and **bEgIn** all refer to the same reserved word.

Identifiers defined by Borland are part of the standard units, and are described in Part III. Identifiers defined in programs within this book will appear in italics.

A *constant* is a value that never changes. Constants in Turbo Pascal are either numbers or strings. Numbers can be **integers**, like 45 and -2, or **reals**, like 2.1 and 4E+10. Numeric constants are defined in detail in Chapter 2, "Primitive Data Types."

String constants are any values enclosed in single quotes ('). The null string is denoted as '', which indicates an empty string. Turbo Pascal also lets you define your own constants, as covered later in this chapter.

A *symbol* is a character, or sequence of characters, that has special meaning in a high-order language. The symbols defined in Turbo Pascal are summarized in Table 1-1.

The order in which you combine symbols, constants, identifiers, and reserved words is the *syntax* of a language. The remainder of Chapters 1 to 8 are dedicated to detailing the syntax of Turbo Pascal.

Headings

The heading for a program consists of the word "Program" followed by the program name. In Standard Pascal, this is a mandatory line that identifies the name of the program and whether it will be using input, output, or both. A typical Standard Pascal heading would look like this:

```
Program ProgName(Input, Output);
```

Turbo Pascal supports the syntax required by Standard Pascal, but it actually ignores it. You will find it useful to include a heading for the sake of program documentation.

The heading for a subprogram includes, at a minimum, the type of the subprogram (procedure or function) and its name. Functions also require a return type. Here are some examples:

```
procedure DisplayMenu;

function GetOption : char;
```

You can also include a parameter list in a subprogram heading, as you'll see in Chapter 4 "Subprograms".

Units also have headings, consisting of the word **unit** followed by the unit name. Units will be covered later in this chapter.

Declarations

The declaration section of a Turbo Pascal entity includes definitions for variables, constants, labels, types, and subprograms. The fact that subprograms are also entities is what allows you to nest subprograms within other subprograms.

Symbol	Purpose
(space)	Separate elements
#	Identify ASCII characters
$	Define hexademical numbers
'	Start and end strings and character constants
(	Start expressions, various lists
(*	Start a comment
(.	Same as [
)	End expressions, various lists
*	Multiply
*)	End a comment
+	Add numbers, concatenate strings, or join sets
,	Separate various list elements
−	Subtract numbers, negate values, or intersect sets
.	Qualify identifiers; separate elements; decimal point for real numbers
..	Separate ranges of arrays
.)	Same as]
/	Divide
:	Define identifiers
:=	Assign values
;	Separate statements, terminate declarations
<	Less than
<=	Less than or equal to
<>	Not equal to
=	Equal to
>	Greater than
>=	Greater than or equal to
@	Retrieve the address of an identifier
[	Start an array index
]	End an array index
^	Retrieve the value of a pointer
{	Start a comment
}	End a comment
(CR)	Carriage return (does not display on screen)

Table 1-1.   *Symbols defined by Turbo Pascal*

In Standard Pascal, the declaration section must be in a specific order: first the constants, then the types, then the variables. In Turbo Pascal, you can use whatever order you choose. The only restriction is that you must declare an identifier before you use it.

Constants

Turbo Pascal does not initialize variables when a program starts. As a result, there is no way of telling what value a variable contains until you assign one.

Constants, on the other hand, are assigned values specified by the programmer when the program starts. To illustrate the importance of constants, consider the example of a program that computes interest on loans. The program uses a fixed interest rate of 7%, which appears about 100 times within the program. At the same time, a variable interest rate of 7% also appears frequently in the program. To change all the fixed-rate values from 7% to 8% would require checking each occurrence of the number 7, deciding if the number is a fixed or a variable rate, and changing the value manually.

If, on the other hand, a constant named *FixedRate* (or some other appropriate name) is declared, changing the value throughout the program would be accomplished simply by changing the declaration.

The Turbo Pascal reserved word **const** signals the beginning of a constant-definition area. You have two choices of constants in Turbo Pascal: untyped and typed. An untyped constant is declared with the following syntax: an identifier followed by an equal sign, a literal value (numeric or text), and a semicolon, as shown in this example:

```
const
  DaysPerWeek = 7;
  HoursPerDay = 24;
  Message = 'Good Morning';
```

These constants are called *untyped* because you do not specify their type definition. Untyped constants are in fact true constants, that is you cannot change their value anywhere in your program.

Typed Constants

Typed constants are defined similarly, except that the type definition is inserted between the identifier and the equal sign, as shown in the following example.

```
const
  DaysPerWeek : integer = 7;
```

```
Message : string[20] = 'Good Morning';
Interest : real = 0.14;
```

If you are concerned about memory utilization, you should use typed constants rather than untyped constants. Untyped constants take up more space because the constant identifier is replaced by the literal value when the program is compiled. In the preceding example of untyped constants, Turbo Pascal would replace every identifier *Message* with the string literal 'Good Morning.'

Typed constants, on the other hand, are defined in the data segment one time and take up only as much memory as the data type requires. Anytime your program uses a typed constant, it refers to that single copy.

Another characteristic of typed constants is that you can change their values. In a sense, typed constants are not constants at all, but are initialized variables. If you want to be absolutely certain that a constant's value remains the same throughout a program, use an untyped constant.

Consider using typed constants to initialize any or all variables to specific values when a program starts. This will avoid the unpredictable results that can occur when a variable is not properly assigned.

Types

In the type-definition area, denoted by the Turbo Pascal reserved word **type,** you can define your own data types and later use them to declare variables. The general form for type definitions is an identifier followed by an equal sign, the data type, and a semicolon, as shown here:

```
type
  PayType = (Salary, HourlyRate);

  Customer = record
    Name : string[30];
    Age : integer;
    Income : real;
  end;

  MaxString = string[80];
  NameList = array [1..100] of string[30];
```

The first data type, *PayType,* is an enumerated scalar with two legal values. The second, *Customer,* is a **record** data type containing three fields. *MaxString* denotes a **string** variable with 80 characters, and *NameList* is an **array** of 100 strings, each 30 characters long. The ability to create customized data types is one of Pascal's most powerful features and is discussed at length in Chapter 3 as well as used throughout this book.

Variables

Variables are locations in memory to which you assign names. To begin a variable-declaration area, type the reserved word **var** followed by the variable identifier (the name you give the variable), a colon, and the data type (for example, **var I : integer;**).

You can declare variables by using standard Turbo Pascal data types (for example, **boolean, real, integer**) or user-defined data types created in the **type** section. The format for variable declarations is nearly the same as that used for type definitions, but the identifier is followed by a colon rather than an equal sign.

```
var
  I, J, K : integer;
  X, Y, Z : real;
  BeyondLimit : boolean;
  Ad : AdType;

  Book : record
    Title : string[20];
    TotPages : integer;
    TheText : array [1..1000] of string[50];
  end;
```

The declaration of the variable *Book* is an example of a type definition within a variable definition. The major disadvantage of this kind of declaration is that the data type has no name, and therefore cannot be used in parameter lists. Instead, consider creating separate type and variable declarations:

```
type
  BookRec = record
    Title : string[20];
    TotPages : integer;
    TheText : array [1..1000] of string[50];
  end;

var
  Book : BookRec;
```

Strong Typing

Pascal is often called a *strong-typed* language. This means that you must declare the type of each variable, and you cannot mix different types of variables. In assignment statements, the values on the right must be compatible in type with the corresponding variable on the left. For example, if the variable *I* is defined as an integer, the following statement would be illegal:

```
I := 1.0 + 2;
```

The value 1.0 is a real value and cannot be used in an assignment statement for an integer because using a real value to evaluate an integer variable goes against the properties of a strong-typed language. (See Chapter 2 for a thorough discussion of integer versus real values.) Observing the strong-typing rules helps avoid errors in programming. Turbo Pascal is less picky about strong typing than Standard Pascal, but you still have to follow these rules:

- A real cannot be used directly in an assignment statement for an integer. The real must first be converted to an integer by using the Trunc or Round standard functions.

- An array can be assigned to another array only when the two have the same range and type.

- A variable that is passed to a procedure (or function) must be defined as the same type as the variable defined in the procedure heading.

Strong typing as implemented in Turbo Pascal is relatively unrestrictive, yet it still helps programmers avoid unnecessary errors.

Labels

Labels are used to mark points in a program. By using the **goto** statement together with a label, you can force the program flow to jump from place to place. Many programmers consider the use of the **goto** statement bad programming technique because it leads to messy, unstructured programs. To help keep you from abusing the **goto** statement, Turbo Pascal limits the scope of a label to a single procedure block.

The label-declaration area begins with the reserved word **label.** The declarations themselves consist simply of identifiers that are separated by commas and terminate with a semicolon, as shown next:

```
label
   EndOfProgram, NextStep;
```

When used in your program, the label is followed by a colon (for example, *EndOfProgram:*). Statements following the label are executed whenever a **goto** statement branches to that label. The following program demonstrates a valid use of a label and **goto** statement.

```
Program GoToTest;

var
```

```
  I, J : integer;
  A : array [1..100, 1..100] of integer;

{ ********************************************************}

function Found : boolean;
label
  JumpOut;
begin
  for I := 1 to 100 do
    for J := 1 to 100 do
      if A[I, J] < 0 then
        begin
          Found := True;
          goto JumpOut;
        end;
  Found := False;
JumpOut:
end;

{ ********************************************************}

begin
  FillChar(A, SizeOf(A), 0);
  A[50,50] := -1;
  Writeln(Found);

  Readln;
end.
```

The function *Found* searches through a matrix of integers looking for a negative value. If a negative value is found, the function should return True; if not, False. However, as you will learn in Chapter 5, "Program Control Structures," use of the Exit procedure is much cleaner than the **goto** statement.

Blocks

Once you have completed the heading and declarations of a Turbo Pascal entity, you can create the block. For programs and subprograms, a block starts with the reserved word **begin,** and finishes with the reserved word **end.** Blocks contain the instructions that assign values to variables, create logical branching, call other procedures and functions, and so on. In Turbo Pascal, the part of the program that executes first, the program block, is defined at the end of the program, as shown in Figure 1-1.

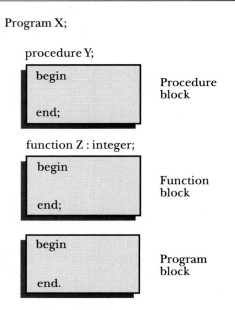

Program X;

procedure Y;

> begin
>
> end;

Procedure block

function Z : integer;

> begin
>
> end;

Function block

> begin
>
> end.

Program block

Figure 1-1.   *Block organization*

To help review the fundamental characteristics of a Pascal program, study the following listing:

```
Program Payroll;

const
  BonusRate = 0.07;
  Employees = 60;

type
  EmployeeType = record
    Name : string[30];
    Id : integer;
    HourlyRate : real;
    HoursWorked : integer;
    GetsBonus : boolean;
    TotalPay : real;
  end;

  MaxStr = string[255];

var
```

```pascal
  Employee : array [1..Employees] of EmployeeType;
  I : integer;
  S : MaxStr;

Label
  EndOfProgram;

{**************************************************}

procedure CalcPay(var Employee : EmployeeType);

  function CalcBonus(Pay : real) : real;
  begin
    CalcBonus := Pay + (Pay * BonusRate);
  end;

begin
  with Employee do
    begin
      TotalPay := HoursWorked * HourlyRate;
      if GetsBonus then
        TotalPay := CalcBonus(TotalPay);
    end;
end;

{**************************************************}

procedure WriteReport(Employee : EmployeeType);
begin
  with Employee do
    begin
      Writeln('Name: ', Name);
      Writeln('Total pay: ', TotalPay:0:2);
    end;
end;

{**************************************************}

begin
  for I := 1 to Employees do
    begin
      CalcPay(Employee[I]);
      if Employee[I].TotalPay < 0 then
        begin
          Writeln('Error: Total pay less than zero!');
          goto EndOfProgram;
        end;
      WriteReport(Employee[I]);
    end;
```

```
    EndOfProgram:
end.
```

The program heading is the top line. The declaration section defines constants, data types, variables, labels, procedures and functions. Each procedure and function, as well as the main program, has a block that goes from **begin** to **end.**

At the heart of this program is the user-defined record type *EmployeeType.* This record, containing basic information about an employee, contains all the desired information for an employee. The *Employee* array contains 60 elements, each of which is a record of type *EmployeeType.* The constant *Employees* defines the maximum size of the array. If the number of employees changes, all you need to do is change the definition of this constant.

The main program block in the *Payroll* program consists of a loop that executes once for every employee. Each iteration, or execution, of the loop calls the procedure *CalcPay,* which calculates the pay for the employee. After this procedure executes, the main program block tests to make sure that the result, *TotalPay,* is not less than zero, since clearly no one should (or could) be paid a negative amount. If the result is less than zero, the program jumps to the *EndOfProgram* label and terminates. If, however, the amount of *TotalPay* is in the correct range, the program calls the procedure *WriteReport,* which writes the employee's name and the total amount paid.

Turbo Pascal's program structure is straightforward and logical, but requires the programmer to understand the concepts of structured programming. Some programmers see this imposition of structure as a limitation, an unnecessary attempt to tell them how to program. In time, however, you will come to appreciate the strict nature of Turbo Pascal and will learn from it good programming habits that apply to any language.

Input and Output

Up to now you have learned the structure of a Turbo Pascal program, without regard to functionality. In this section you will learn how to do the most essential piece of any program—retrieving and displaying information.

Consider the following program:

```
Program Prog1;

begin
  WriteLn('This is my first program.');
  ReadLn;
end.
```

When you execute this program in the Integrated Development Environment (IDE), your monitor will show this message:

```
This is my first program.
```

When you are ready to return to the IDE, you would press ENTER.

A Turbo Pascal program always starts execution at the **begin** statement of the main block and continues until it reaches the **end** statement. (A program will also stop when it encounters the Halt command or a fatal error, but these are exceptions.)

The WriteLn statement in the previous program displays a string, and ReadLn makes the computer wait until you press ENTER. Whenever you run a program in the IDE, you should use the ReadLn statement to stop a program before the screen switches back to the editor screen.

WriteLn is a Turbo Pascal standard procedure that displays numbers and strings of characters to the screen, prints them on a printer, or writes them to a disk file. It also adds two special characters, carriage return and line feed (ASCII codes 13 and 10), to the end of the line. These special characters, often referred to in programming shorthand as CR/LF, signal that the end of a line of text has been reached, and that any additional text should start on the next line.

Inside the parentheses of the WriteLn statement are the items to be printed. While in this case the WriteLn procedure prints only one line, it is capable of printing more than one item at a time. The following listing is an example of a WriteLn statement that prints three separate strings.

```
WriteLn('This is one string.', '  ', 'This is another.');
```

A *string* is any combination of characters that is enclosed in single quotation marks. You will learn more about strings in Chapter 3. In the example WriteLn procedure, commas separate one string from another. Note that the second string consists of two blank characters, thus creating a space between the first and third strings. When this statement is executed, the result looks like the following.

```
This is one string. This is another string.
```

Like WriteLn, the procedure Write also displays strings and numbers; but Write does not add CR/LF characters to the end of the line. When you use Write, the cursor remains on the same line as the information written, while WriteLn moves the cursor to the beginning of the next line.

Using Variables for Input

Programs that merely write messages are not very interesting. To be truly useful, a program must process data, and that requires the use of variables.

To define a variable, you must give it a name and a type. You can give a variable almost any name you want, but it is best to choose a name that describes the information the variable holds. For example, you might call a variable that holds the name of a customer *CustomerName* and define it as follows:

```
var
  CustomerName : string[50];
```

The type **string[50]** identifies the variable as a string and indicates that the length of this string cannot exceed 50 characters.

The ReadLn statement gets a value from a source outside the program, such as the person using the program or a disk file. When a program encounters a ReadLn statement, it stops and waits until the user types in the data and presses ENTER. ReadLn then takes the input and assigns it to a variable named in the ReadLn statement. For example, the statement

```
ReadLn(CustomerName);
```

waits for the user to type in a string of characters, accepts a string, and stores it in the variable *CustomerName*.

The following sample program demonstrates how ReadLn obtains input and stores it in variables.

```
Program Prog2;

var
  I : integer;
  S : string[20];

begin
  Write('Enter a number: ');
  ReadLn(i);"
  WriteLn('Your number is ',i);

  Write('Enter a string: ');
  ReadLn(s);
  WriteLn('Your string is ',s);

  ReadLn;
end.
```

When you execute this program, it will display **Enter a number:** on your monitor. If you type the number 9 and press ENTER, The program will display **Your number is 9**. It will then skip one line on the screen, and display **Enter a string:**. If you type in

ABC and press ENTER, the program would display **Your string is ABC**. The program uses the ReadLn statement to obtain a number and a string from the user.

If the ReadLn statement detects an error in the input, it notifies you and halts the program. For example, suppose you run *Prog2* again, but when it asks for a number, you type ABC and press ENTER. Turbo Pascal would detect an *input/output error* and display this message:

```
Runtime error 106 at 0000:008F
```

Error 106 indicates an invalid numeric format. In short, Turbo Pascal was expecting a number, and it got something else, ABC, which is not a valid integer. The value 0000:008F is the location in the program at which the error occurred. If you are running the program from within the IDE, Turbo Pascal will automatically locate the error in the source code and highlight that part of the program on the screen.

Prog2 also demonstrates the use of the WriteLn statement when used with no parameters. When executed, this statement simply writes a CR/LF combination to the computer monitor, which places the cursor on the first position of the next line.

Units

As the programs you write get larger and larger, they become much more difficult to manage. One way to help break up large programs is to use units. A *unit* is a logical grouping of declarations that is compiled separately, and is accessible by programs and other units. Units can contain types, constants, variables, and subprograms.

A unit has three primary advantages:

- Modularity—since units are compiled separately, they break a program into manageable pieces.

- Reuse—declarations are available to any other program or unit, so units act as libraries for reusable components.

- Information hiding—units are structured so that a program using that unit is insulated from the details of its implementation.

These advantages will become much more evident once you start using standard units and eventually create your own.

Using Units

Borland Pascal 7.0 comes with over twenty standard units. One of them, the System unit, is automatically used when compiling your program. If you need to access a declaration or subprogram in any other standard unit, you must include a **uses** clause. This clause is simply a list of the units to be searched during compilation.

 Part III, "Standard Turbo Pascal Libraries," covers each of the standard Turbo Pascal and Borland Pascal units in detail.

Syntactically, the **uses** clause is part of the program heading—it must appear before any program declarations. The heading

```
Program MyProgram;

uses Crt;
```

tells the compiler that the types, variables, constants, or subprograms implemented by the Crt unit may be referenced by the *MyProgram* program.

When working with units, you usually start with the need for a particular capability, such as clearing the screen. You search the index to find that the Crt unit contains a ClrScr procedure. Then you add the Crt unit to the **uses** clause, and call ClrScr in the program. It's that simple!

Creating Units

Creating your own units is a little more complicated. You start by determining which declarations will be accessed by other units and programs. These declarations constitute the **interface** section of the unit. Then you complete the declarations, including local procedures and variables, in the **implementation** section. Finally you can include a *unit block,* which contains any required initialization code. These sections are illustrated by this syntax description:

```
Unit (Unitname);
interface
{
visible declarations
}
implementation
{
hidden declarations and blocks
}
{
unit block
}
```

When you compile the unit to disk, a .TPU file will be created which contains the object code for that unit.

To help clarify the details of creating a unit, study the following example:

```
Unit MATH;

interface

function Square(X : integer): integer;

implementation

function Square;
begin
  Square := X * X;
end;

end
```

The MATH unit (capitalized here to denote that it was created) currently contains one function called *Square*. The procedure heading is in the **interface** section of the unit. In the implementation section, the name of the function is repeated (but not the rest of the heading), and the function block is included.

To call the *Square* function in a program, you add a **uses** clause with the MATH unit. Then you call *Square* as if it was implemented in the program itself. Here's an example:

```
Program MathTest;

uses MATH;

var
  I : integer;

begin
  I := 4;
  Writeln(Square(I));
end.
```

You will see more complex examples of units throughout the book, especially in the latter chapters.

Includes

The Turbo Pascal editor cannot hold more than 62K of text at any time. Normally, of course, this should not be an issue. If you are using good programming techniques, then you are using units to break your program into meaningful pieces. If for some reason, however, your program exceeds the 62K limit, you have to break it into multiple files. When you compile the program, the Include File directive pulls all the pieces together from these multiple files. The Include File directive is also useful when you have standard libraries of frequently used routines.

To include a file in a Pascal program, create a comment with the compiler directive $I and the name of the file to be used. For example, the sample directive {$I PROCS.INC} tells Turbo Pascal to read the include file PROCS.INC as if the text were written in the program. For example, consider this procedure as the contents of file LISTFILE.INC:

```
procedure ListFiles;
var
  I : integer;
begin
end;
```

Now add this code as the contents of **MAIN.PAS**:

```
Program Main;

{$I LISTFILE.INC}

begin
  ListFiles;
end.
```

Here, the main program file (MAIN.PAS) makes a call to the procedure *ListFiles,* yet *ListFiles* is defined not in the file MAIN.PAS but in the file LISTFILE.INC. The include statement in MAIN.PAS tells the compiler to read in LISTFILE.INC at that point and use its code as part of the program.

If you do not specify an extension with the filename, the .INC extension is assumed.

Overlays

To support overlays, Turbo Pascal supplies a standard unit, aptly named Overlay. By including this unit in your program's **uses** clause, you can overlay your program's units to minimize the amount of memory your program requires. Using overlays is quite easy as long as you follow some simple rules:

- Enable the Force Far Calls compiler directive ({$F+}) for the program and all units.

- Name the Overlay unit first in your program's **uses** clause.

- Compile overlaid units with the {$O+} compiler directive.

- List the overlaid units using the {$O *filename*} compiler directive.

- Make sure that your program uses OvrInit to initialize the overlay before any statements execute, including initialization sections of overlaid units.

When writing Windows applications, you do not need to use overlays—the Windows memory manager handles overlays automatically.

The use of overlays is best described by example. The following listing includes the code for two units (OVR1 and OVR2) and a main program *TestOvr*. Both the units are to be overlaid and, therefore, include the {$O+,F+} compiler directive.

```
{$O+,F+}
Unit OVR1;

interface

procedure Message1;

implementation

procedure Message1;
begin
  Writeln('Message 1');
end;

end.

{*********************************}

{$O+,F+}
Unit OVR2;

interface

procedure Message2;

implementation

procedure Message2;
begin
  Writeln('Message 2');
end;
```

```
end.

{***********************************}

{$O+,F+}
Program TestOvr;

uses
  Overlay, OVR1, OVR2;

{$O OVR1}
{$O OVR2}

begin
  OvrInit('TESTOVR.OVR');
  Message1;
  Message2;
  Readln;
end.
```

The program declares the Overlay unit as the first unit in the **uses** clause and also declares the units to be overlaid using the {$O *filename*} directive. The first line of the program performs the necessary initialization of the overlay.

As you can see, the overlay process is extremely simple. Complications arise, however, when the overlaid units contain initialization code. Consider the following listings, which are similar to the previous unit, except that initialization code has been added to the units to be overlaid. Turbo Pascal always executes initialization code before it executes the first statement in the main program. This means that the overlaid units will execute before the overlay manager is initialized. How can you overcome this problem?

Fortunately, the answer is not so difficult. Instead of initializing the overlay manager in your main program, place the initialization code in a unit and include this unit in the **uses** clause *before* any of the overlaid units. This ensures that the overlay manager will be installed before any of the overlaid files execute. Here is the working program:

```
{$O+,F+}
Unit OVR1;

interface

procedure Message1;

implementation

var
  S : string;
```

```
procedure Message1;
begin
  Writeln(S);
end;

begin
  S := 'Message 1';
end.

{********************************}

{$O+,F+}
Unit OVR2;

interface

procedure Message2;

implementation

var
  S : string;

procedure Message2;
begin
  Writeln(S);
end;

begin
  S := 'Message 2';
end.

{********************************}

{$O+,F+}
Unit OVRSTART;

interface

uses Overlay;

implementation

begin
  OvrInit('TESTOVR.OVR');
  if OvrResult = OvrNotFound then
    begin
      WriteLn('File TESTOVR.OVR not found.');
```

```
      Halt;
   end;
end.


{*********************************}


{$O+,F+}
Program TestOvr;

uses
  Overlay, OVRSTART, OVR1, OVR2;

{$O OVR1}
{$O OVR2}

begin
  Message1;
  Message2;
  Readln;
end.
```

The Turbo Pascal overlay system includes five routines (discussed in the following sections) for initializing the overlay manager and controlling the program's use of memory. When they execute, these routines set the global variable OvrResult to indicate if any problems occurred. The Overlay unit defines the following constants to help you interpret the value of OvrResult:

```
const
  OvrOk           =  0;  { No error }
  OvrError        = -1;  { Nonspecific error }
  OvrNotFound     = -2;  { Overlay file not found }
  OvrNoMemory     = -3;  { Not enough memory }
  OvrIOError      = -4;  { Error reading .OVR file }
  OvrNoEMSDriver  = -5;  { EMS driver not loaded }
  OvrNoEMSMemory  = -6;  { Insufficient EMS memory }
```

Your program should take care to test the value of OvrResult every time you use one of the five overlay routines.

OvrInit

This procedure initializes the overlay manager and prepares overlaid units for use. OvrInit takes a single string parameter containing the name of the overlay file, which is usually the name of the main program file with the .OVR suffix. This procedure is called only once and must be called before any of the overlaid units.

OvrInitEMS

While overlays save memory, they slow down your program due to frequent disk reads. The Turbo Pascal overlay manager is capable of loading the entire overlay file into expanded memory, which greatly reduces access time to overlaid procedures. To load an overlay into expanded memory, simply execute the procedure OvrInitEMS. If the computer has enough expanded memory available, the overlay file will be loaded into it; if not, the overlay will execute from disk as it normally would.

OvrSetBuf

When you initiate OvrInit, the overlay manager captures the minimum amount of memory needed to run the overlaid procedures. You can expand this amount of memory with OvrSetBuf, a procedure that takes a **longint** parameter (see Chapter 2) which represents the size, in bytes, of the overlay buffer you wish to use. For example, the statement OvrSetBuf(100000) reserves 100,000 bytes for use as an overlay buffer. The size of the buffer must be at least as large as the minimum buffer size and less than MemAvail. Also, OvrSetBuf must be called only when the heap is clear of dynamic variables.

OvrGetBuf

This function returns a **longint** representing the current size of the overlay buffer. You can use this value as a guide when increasing the size of the buffer with OvrSetBuf.

OvrClearBuf

This procedure removes all overlaid units from the overlay buffer. Doing this ensures that any subsequent call to an overlaid procedure will require a disk read. You will normally never need to clear the overlay buffer. One circumstance where you might is when you want to reclaim, for other purposes, the memory used by the overlay buffer.

Compiler Directives

The Turbo Pascal compiler offers many options that you can use to make programming and debugging easier. These options, which perform tasks such as error checking, are called *compiler directives* because they direct the compiler in its work. You have been introduced to some of these directives earlier in this chapter. The format of a compiler directive is a comment that has a dollar sign as its first character. Here are some example of valid compiler directives:

```
{$F+}
(*$R-*)
{$O MYOVR}
```

Most directives are defined by a single letter followed by a plus sign, a minus sign, or an expression. Compiler directives can be broadly classified into three groups: *switch directives*, *parameter directives*, and *conditional directives*.

Switch Directives

Switch directives turn on or off Turbo Pascal's special features, such as input/output error checking, stack checking, and data alignment. They are called switch directives because they can have only two conditions: on or off.

Switch directives are identified by single letters (uppercase or lowercase). For example, the $S directive controls stack checking, $R sets up range checking, $I specifies input/output error checking, and so on. The format for enabling or disabling a compiler directive is a dollar sign followed by the directive and either a plus sign (to enable) or a minus sign (to disable); these characters are enclosed in comment delimiters (either parentheses with asterisks or braces). The following are examples of valid compiler directive statements:

```
{$I-}
```

```
{$i-}
```

```
{$s+,v-,r+,a+}
```

The first two statements are the same; both disable input/output error checking. As you can see from the examples, either type of comment delimiter (braces or parentheses with asterisks) can be used; the case of the directive (upper or lower) is unimportant. The third example specifies four compiler directives at once. It enables Stack-Overflow Checking, disables Var-String Checking, and enables Range Checking and Align Data by Word. Note that in this statement, the dollar sign appears before the first directive only.

Turbo Pascal lets you set compiler directives in two ways. The easier way is to set the directives from the Options|Compiler menu. The directive settings in this menu become the global default values for all programs and units. In other words, Turbo Pascal will use the settings in the Options|Compiler menu for all compiler directives not specified in the source code. The disadvantage of using the menu is that your code is less portable. In other words, if you gave your source code to someone else, they would have to change their menu settings to match yours.

Switch directives are of two types: global and local. Global directives, as the name implies, affect the compilation of an entire program, from beginning to end, and must be declared at the very beginning of your program or unit (before the first **uses**,

label, **const**, **type**, **procedure**, **function**, **interface**, or **begin** keyword). Local directives can appear at any point in a program and only affect that portion of the program that follows the directive. For example, you can turn on range checking, a local directive, at the beginning of a procedure and then turn it off at the end of the procedure.

Align Data (Global)

The 8086 family of microprocessors can access memory faster when datum are aligned on even-numbered addresses, also known as *word boundaries.* When the Align Data compiler directive is active ({$A+}), Turbo Pascal makes sure that every variable and typed constant larger than one byte begins at an even address. Aligning data on word boundaries makes data access faster, but also increases the amount of memory required for data storage because "dead" bytes are inserted where necessary to make sure that variables begin on word boundaries. If you are concerned about the amount of memory your program requires, you may want to disable this directive ({$A-}).

Boolean Evaluation (Local)

Turbo Pascal supports two types of Boolean evaluation—complete and short-circuit. To understand the difference between the two, consider the following example:

```
if (A < B) and (B > C) then
  begin
    .
    .
    .
  end;
```

The preceding Boolean statement consists of two separate tests connected with **and**. Under complete boolean evaluation, Turbo Pascal will test both comparisons before branching. But, if *A* is greater than or equal to *B,* there is really no need to test if *B* is greater than *C.* Under short-circuit evaluation, Turbo Pascal will only test so far as is necessary to determine the result of the entire expression. Under certain circumstances, short-circuit evaluation can speed up a program appreciably. To turn on short-circuit evaluation, use {$B-}; to select complete evaluation, use {$B+}.

Debug Information (Global)

Enabling the Debug Information directive ({$D+}), instructs Turbo Pascal to generate information needed to match executable instructions to locations in source files. This is the information that allows you to step through a program one line at a time or to locate the source of a run-time error when it occurs. Turbo Pascal adds debugging information to the end of .TPU files, making the files larger than they otherwise would be. This does not, however, affect the speed of the executable code.

Disabling this directive will gain you very little (for example, a little extra disk space, slightly shorter compile time) at the cost of not being able to step through a program. Generally speaking, Debug Information should always be enabled.

Emulation (Global)

The 80x87 math coprocessor chip offers significant computational advantages over the 8088/80x86. Unfortunately, not every computer has the 80x87 installed. When enabled, the Emulation compiler directive, $E, gives you access to the 80x87's data types whether or not the math chip is present.

Let's say you are distributing a statistics program that requires the mathematical precision of the 80x87. But you also want to sell the program to people without the coprocessor installed. When Emulation is enabled, Turbo Pascal checks to see if the 80x87 chip is installed. If it is, your program will use the power of the math chip; if not, your program will perform all the 80x87 computations using the main microprocessor. Naturally, your computations will take much longer without the 80x87 chip. Even so, it is better to have one program that everyone can use than to have separate versions for 80x87 and non-80x87 machines. Unless you are going to need extremely precise mathematical results, you are better off leaving Emulation disabled.

 The $E switch has no effect on Windows applications.

Force Far Calls (Local)

Turbo Pascal supports multiple code segments—one code segment for each unit and an additional one for the main program. Function and procedure calls that take place within a unit or program file are known as *intrasegment* or *near* calls because the code that executes the call and the called procedure both reside in the same code segment. When, however, a statement in one unit calls a procedure in another unit, this is an *intersegment* or *far* call because the call crosses code segment boundaries.

Near calls require less work than far calls because the code segment does not change. Far calls, by virtue of the fact that more than one code segment is involved, require more work and execute more slowly. Fortunately, Turbo Pascal is smart enough to know when to use a near call and when to use a far call. There are times, however, when you will want to override Turbo's judgment and force a procedure to be called as a far call, even though it would normally be considered a near call.

The circumstances under which you would need to force a far call are generally very advanced and uncommon. Suffice it to say that when necessary, you can force a procedure to be a far call by enabling the $F compiler directive as demonstrated here:

```
Program TestFarCall;

{*******************************************}

{$F+}procedure FarCall;{$F-}
begin
end;

{*******************************************}

begin
  FarCall; { This would normally be a near call }
end.
```

The procedure *FarCall* is clearly in the same code segment as the call made at the end of the program, which means that the procedure would be executed as a near call. The $F compiler directive alters the situation by forcing the procedure to be a far call.

Generate 80286 Code (Global)

The 80286 microprocessor introduced new machine code instructions that can make programs run more efficiently. With the Generate 80286 Code compiler directive set using {$G+}, the compiler will use the new instructions. The disadvantage of setting this option is that your programs will no longer run on 8088 machines.

Input/Output Checking (Local)

The $I compiler directive, which is used to check for I/O errors in your program, is enabled with the statement {$I+}. Perhaps the most common type of Turbo Pascal error, an I/O error, is also among the most dangerous. Undetected, I/O errors can produce unpredictable results in a program that appears to be operating normally.

When Input/Output Checking is enabled, an I/O error produces a run-time error and halts your program. However, enabling the $I compiler directive is not the best way to handle I/O errors. A more effective method is to disable the $I directive with the statement {$I-} and trap I/O errors yourself.

Smart Callbacks (Global)

A *callback* routine is a subprogram written for Windows that is called outside an application, often by Windows itself. When you include {$K+}, the default, in your program, the compiler will automatically create the proper return code; hence the name Smart Callbacks. Without this option, you must use the functions

MakeProcInstance and FreeProcInstance. Only a Windows guru could find a need to disable this option.

The $K switch has no effect on DOS applications.

Local Symbol Information (Global)

Local Symbol Information refers to information about variables and constants that are local to a unit or procedure. Normally, Turbo Pascal does not save information about these symbols, making it impossible to view or change their values in a debugging session. By enabling the Local Symbol Information compiler directive, {$L+}, Turbo Pascal generates and saves information about all local variables so that you can use them as you debug your program.

The Local Symbol Information compiler directive works with the Debug Information directive in the following ways. When Debug Information is disabled ({$D-,L-} or {$D-,L+}), Turbo Pascal saves no information for debugging purposes and the $L compiler directive has no effect. When $D is enabled but $L is disabled ({$D+,L-}), Turbo Pascal stores debugging information only for global variables and constants. When both $D and $L are enabled ({$D+,L+}), Turbo Pascal saves debugging information for both global and local symbols.

Numeric Processing (Global)

Turbo Pascal offers two types of floating-point numeric processing: Normal mode and 80x87 mode. The Normal mode supports the 6-byte **real** data type and does not use the 80x87 match coprocessor, even if it is available. The 80x87 mode offers four additional floating-point data types as well as access to the power of the 80x87 math chip. Use the {$N-} compiler directive to select the Normal mode and {$N+} to select the 80x87 mode.

The $N compiler directive is used in conjuction with the $E (Emulation) compiler directive. When both are enabled ({$N+,E+}), your program can use the 80x87 mode even when the math chip is not installed. If the chip is installed, your program will use it for floating-point operations; if not, your program will use emulation routines that provide the same level of precision, but at a lower speed. When Emulation is not enabled in the 80x87 mode, ({$N+,E-}), your program will run only on machines with the math chip installed.

Overlay Code Generation (Global)

If you want to include a unit in an overlay file, you must enable the Overlay Code Generation compiler directive ({$O+}). This tells Turbo Pascal to generate the code necessary to manage this unit as an overlay. Note, however, that enabling the $O compiler directive does not require you to overlay the unit, it only makes overlaying possible. On the other hand, you cannot overlay a unit unless you have enabled the $O compiler directive.

Open Parameters (Global)

Version 7.0 of Turbo Pascal introduces several extensions to the Pascal syntax. One of the most useful is the concept of *open parameters*. An open parameter is an array or string whose upper and lower bounds are left undefined. See Chapter 4, "Subprograms," for details on this new feature.

The $P directive enables or disables the ability to create open parameters. The only reason for leaving it in its default state ({$P-}) is if you are need to write programs that are portable to other compilers. Otherwise you should enable Open Parameters.

Overflow Checking (Local)

Turbo Pascal has always supported Range Checking with the $R directive. However, try to guess the result of the following program:

```
Program Overflow;

{$Q-,R+}

var
  SI1, SI2, SI3 : shortint;
  I1, I2, I3 : integer;

begin
  I1 := 20000;
  I2 := 20000;
  I3 := I1 + I2;
  Writeln ('Integer sum is ', I3);

  SI1 := 100;
  SI2 := 100;
  SI3 := SI1 + SI2;
  Writeln ('Shortint sum is ', SI3);

  Writeln ('Press ENTER...');
  Readln;
end.
```

If you guessed a run-time error computing *I3,* you're wrong—Range Checking does not check for overflow of **integer** and **word** variables.

In version 7.0 of Turbo Pascal the Overflow Checking switch has been added. If you change the program so that $Q is enabled, you will see the run-time error computing *13*.

Like Range Checking, Overflow Checking can slow down program execution significantly. If you have debugged your program thoroughly, you might wish to recompile it with {$Q-}.

Range Checking (Local)

Most data types in Turbo Pascal have limitations. For example, a byte cannot hold a value greater than 255. An array of five elements cannot hold a sixth element. A string defined as **string[20]** cannot hold 21 characters. Any attempt to violate these limitations creates a range error—a value or condition that does not fit within the limits of the variable.

When Range Checking is enabled ({$R+}), Turbo Pascal generates code that checks that all indexing and assignments are within proper range. When a range error is found, Turbo Pascal generates a run-time error and halts the program. If, on the other hand, Range Checking is disabled, all out-of-bounds assignments and indexing operations go unreported. The results could be disastrous.

Range errors never occur in a properly functioning program, but they can be common during early stages of program development. To protect yourself against them, always enable the $R compiler directive while developing a program and then disable it when compiling the final version.

One final point about Range Checking: when enabled, it significantly increases the size of your compiled program and slows its execution. If you find your program is poking along where it should be flying, make sure that you did not inadvertently leave Range Checking enabled somewhere in your program.

Stack-Overflow Checking (Local)

When your program calls a procedure or function, Turbo Pascal allocates memory from the stack for local variables. Enabling the Stack-Overflow Checking compiler directive ({$S+}) tells Turbo Pascal to generate the code needed to make sure that enough memory is available on the stack to hold these local variables. If there is not enough memory, your program will terminate with a run-time error. If the $S compiler directive is disabled ({$S-}), no checking will be done, and your computer will probably crash when it runs out of stack memory. Stack checking takes time and increases your program's executable code, so you should only enable the $S directive when you are developing and debugging your program.

Typed @ Operator (Global)

Another new feature of Turbo Pascal 7.0 is the ability to verify compatibility of pointers. In previous versions of Turbo Pascal, or when the $T option is disabled, the result of @MyVar would always be of type **pointer**. With the Typed @ Operator switch, the result of an @ operation would be a pointer to the type of its operand. Pointers are discussed in detail in Chapter 6.

To help clarify this option, consider the following program:

```
Program Check_Pointers;

var
  I : ^byte;
  C : char;

begin
  C := 'A';
  I := @C;

  Writeln('I is ', I^);
  Readln;
end.
```

This program compiles and runs as long as the Typed @ Operator option is disabled. If you insert {$T+}, however, the compiler will fail with a "Type Mismatch" error.

Var-String Checking (Local)

When Var-String Checking is enabled, Turbo Pascal performs strict type checking on string parameters passed to procedures and functions. To understand how Var-String Checking works and why it is important, consider the following program:

```
Program TestVarStr;

type
  Str30 = string[30];

var
  S : String[20];

{***************************************************}

procedure ChangeS(var S : Str30);
var
  I : integer;
begin
  for I := 1 to 30 do
    S[I] := Chr(Ord(S[I]) + 1);
end;
```

```
{************************************************}

begin
  S := 'abc';
  ChangeS(S);
  Writeln(S);
  Readln;
end.
```

In this program, *S,* a variable declared to be **string[20]**, is passed to procedure *ChangeS* whose parameter type is **string[30]**. If Var-String Checking were enabled ({$V+}), this program would not compile because the variable type and the parameter type do not match. You might think that forcing string variables to match procedure parameters is unnecessary, but consider what could happen.

In the preceding program, procedure *ChangeS* alters each character in a 30-character string. The variable *S,* however, is declared to be only 20 characters long. What happens when *ChangeS* tries to modify 30 characters when the variable has only 20? The answer is that the program will alter memory beyond the limit of string *S.* In short, you will be trashing memory and not know it. By now you should realize just how important Var-String Checking is and how insidious Var-string errors can be if they go undetected. If you do decide to disable Var-String Checking, make certain that there is no chance that your program will create undesired havoc.

Windows Stack Frames (Local)

The $W compiler switch controls the machine code instructions used to enter and exit a subprogram. You need not be concerned with the details of the differences; simply follow these rules:

- If you want your program to support all Windows modes, or if you are debugging your program, use $W+.

- If your program will always run in DOS mode, you can speed up execution by using $W-.

Extended Syntax (Global)

When Turbo Pascal for Windows was created it extended the syntax of Pascal to simplify calls to the Windows API (written in C). These extensions are now available with both Turbo Pascal and Borland Pascal. If you enable Extended Syntax with {$X+}, you will be able to

- Set the value of a PChar variable to a string constant. See Chapter 3, "Complex Data Types," for more details.

- Call a function as if it was a procedure, ignoring the return value. See Chapter 4 for more details.

If you are not writing your program for Windows, you probably have no need for either of these features, so you may want to disable this switch.

Symbol Reference Information (Global)

There are three compiler directives that work together to provide information to the debugger. The first is $D, which provides the line numbers and source code. The second is $L, which provides local symbols of the main program. The final directive is $Y, which adds symbol information to each unit in the application. The $Y switch is ignored unless both $D and $L are enabled.

When you are finished debugging your program, you can speed up program execution by disabling $Y (as well as $D and $L).

Parameter Directives

Unlike switch directives, parameter directives do not have clearly defined on/off states. Instead, these directives indicate names of files that are to be used during compilation and the size of memory to be allocated to the program.

Code Segment Attributes (Global)

Windows gives you some control over several aspects of your program's code segment. Borland lets you change these aspects by specifying one or more of these words in the $C directive:

- MOVEABLE (the default) or FIXED—determines whether the code segment can be moved in memory.

- PRELOAD (the default) or DEMANDLOAD—determines when the code segment is loaded (at program start or on demand).

- PERMANENT (the default) or DISCARDABLE—determines whether the code segment can be removed when no longer needed.

Executable File Description (Global)

For programs written for Windows, the $D directive lets you add a description to the executable file. This directive can apply either to a .DLL or .EXE file.

This directive has no effect on DOS applications.

Include File (Local)

An *include file* is a source file that is compiled as part of another source file. The $I directive is used followed by the name of the file with the source code. If you do not specify a file extension for the $I directive, Turbo Pascal will assume the .PAS extension.

To understand how this works, look at the following listing. The procedure *ProcA* is contained in a file named MAININC.INC. The main program file uses the Include compiler directive to insert the code in MAININC.INC into the program.

```
{ Contents of file MAININC.INC }
procedure ProcA;
begin
  Writeln('ProcA');
end;

{ Program including MAININC.INC }
Program Main;
{$I MAININC.INC}
begin
  ProcA;
  Readln;
end.
```

Include files were primarily used when a program became too large to fit into the Turbo Pascal editor, but for the most part have been replaced by units.

Link Object File (Local)

If you write routines in assembler for use in your Pascal programs, you will need to link the assembler object files with your Pascal program. This is done with the Link Object File compiler directive ($L) followed by the name of the object file.

Memory Allocation Sizes (Global)

The Memory Allocation Sizes ($M) compiler directive gives you complete control over the amount of memory your program uses for its stack and heap. The directive is followed by three numbers, separated by commas, representing the amount of memory for the stack, and the minimum and maximum memory sizes for the heap. For example, the directive {$M 30000,1000,5000} allocates 30,000 bytes to the stack and a minimum of 1000 and a maximum of 5000 to the heap. The amount of memory you allocate to the stack must be from 1024 to 65520. The heap can have from 0 to 655360 bytes allocated to it.

Overlay Unit Name (Local)

The Overlay Unit Name compiler directive ($O) is followed by the name of a unit and instructs Turbo Pascal to include that unit in the overlay file. The unit named in this directive must be compiled with the {$O+} compiler directive to allow it to be overlaid. The Overlay Unit Name compiler directive must be placed after the program **uses** clause, as shown here:

```
Program OvrTest;

uses
  UNIT1, UNIT2, UNIT3;

{$O UNIT1}
{$O UNIT2}
```

In this program's declaration section, *UNIT1* and *UNIT2* are named to be included in the overlay file; *UNIT3* will not be overlaid.

Conditional Directives

Turbo Pascal's conditional compilation directives allow you to maintain different versions of a program in the same source file. By changing certain definitions, you can compile some sections of code and hide others. At the heart of conditional compilation is the *condition symbol,* a symbol defined by you to control the conditional compilation process. The program listed here demonstrates how the conditional symbol is defined and used to control compilation.

```
Program ConditionExample;
{$DEFINE TEST}                    { Define symbol }

{$IFDEF TEST}                     { If symbol defined, do this... }
{$R+,S+}

{$ELSE}                           { If symbol not defined, do this... }
{$R-,S-}

{$ENDIF}                          { End of conditional compilation. }

begin
  {$UNDEF TEST}                   { Undefine the symbol }

  {$IFDEF TEST}                   { If symbol defined, do this... }
  Writeln('TEST DEFINED');
```

```
  {$ELSE}                        { If symbol not defined, do this... }
  Writeln('TEST NOT DEFINED');

  {$ENDIF}                       { End of conditional compilation. }

  Readln;
end.
```

The program begins by defining the symbol TEST. The first use of TEST enables the $R and $S compiler directives if TEST is defined (as it is in this case) and disables them if TEST is not defined. After the **begin** keyword, TEST is undefined, a process that nullifies the previous {$DEFINE TEST} directive. Since TEST is no longer defined, the line

```
Writeln('TEST NOT DEFINED');
```

is compiled. The conditional compilation directives offered by Turbo Pascal are described next.

$DEFINE

Use this directive to define a conditional symbol. Any code that depends on the symbol defined will be compiled, *but only in the file in which the DEFINE directive appears.* Consider the case of a program that uses a main source file, an include file, and a unit file. In each file, conditional compilation directives are used. If you use the $DEFINE directive in the main source file, and not in the include and unit files, only the main source file will be affected; the other files will compile without the $DEFINE directive. The only way to globally define a compilation symbol is to use the Conditional Defines feature on the Options/Compiler menu.

$UNDEF

This directive negates the $DEFINE directive. Once a symbol has been used with $UNDEF, any code that depends on that symbol will not be compiled.

$IFDEF

This directive instructs Turbo Pascal to compile code if a named conditional symbol is defined.

$IFNDEF

This directive instructs Turbo Pascal to compile code if a named conditional symbol is not defined.

$IFOPT

You can also control compilation based on another compilation directive. For example, you can compile code only when the $R compile directive is enabled by writing {$IFOPT R+}.

$ELSE

Use this directive after any of the IF... directives ($IFDEF, $IFNDEF, $IFOPT) as a branch when the first condition is untrue.

$ENDIF

This directive marks the end of a conditional compilation sequence. All code appearing after the $ENDIF statement will be compiled regardless of conditional symbols.

Using compiler directives effectively is an important step in becoming a productive programmer. You must understand how to use these directives to get the most out of Turbo Pascal.

Chapter *2*

Primitive Data Types

Turbo Pascal provides programmers with a rich set of *primitive* data types, those types which cannot be broken into simpler types. Examples are **integer**, **word**, **byte**, **shortint**, and **longint** for numbers without decimal places; **real**, **single**, **double**, **extended**, and **comp** for numbers with decimal places; **boolean** for true and false conditions; and **char** for characters. You can also create your own primitive types, known as *enumerated* types. This chapter discusses the primitive data types offered by Turbo Pascal and how they can be used.

Numeric Types

Turbo Pascal has a range of numeric data types, including integer, real, and a third category called **80×87** data types, which are described in the sections that follow.

The terms "integer" and "real" will be used throughout this book to represent the class of integer types and the class of real types, respectively. You will see **integer** and **real** in boldface type when referring to those specific data types.

Integer Types

A variable of type **byte** occupies one byte. A *byte* is an unsigned numeric value that can range from 0 to 255. The **shortint** type stores signed, one-byte values, ranging from -128 to 127. **Integer** variables also hold numerical values that have no decimal places. Because they are two bytes (16 bits) long, **integers** can range in value from -32,768 to 32,767 (without the commas). The **word** data type is two bytes long, like

integer, but is unsigned, giving it a range of 0 to 65,535. **Longint** variables are signed numbers that occupy four bytes in memory and have a range of -2,147,483,648 to 2,147,483,647.

In arithmetic expressions, all integer types are *type compatible,* meaning the compiler lets you use the types interchangeably. For example, a **byte** variable can be assigned a value from a **longint** variable as long as the value does not exceed the **byte** type's numeric range.

Real Types

For numbers with fractional portions, or with magnitudes that exceed 2,147,483,647 (the maximum value of **longint**), Turbo Pascal provides the **real** data type, also known as the *floating-point* type. A **real** variable requires six bytes of storage and can range in value from 2.9 x 10E-39 to 1.7 x 10E38. Because of their complex structure, arithmetic operations involving **reals** take far longer to execute than do operations on integer types, which are stored in their binary numerical equivalents.

A common problem encountered with **real** variables is the overflow condition. This occurs when you try to assign too large a number to a **real** variable and may cause a run-time error in the program. You will find, however, that this is not always true. For example, if 1 is added to a **real** variable with the maximum value of 1.7 x 10E38, the value remains unchanged and no execution error is detected. Even though an overflow condition logically should exist, the program does not detect one. This is because a **real** can store only 11 to 12 significant digits. That means that adding small numbers to a large **real** value will not change the value of the **real.**

On the other hand, an overflow condition can occur unexpectedly. If a **real** variable with the maximum value of 1.7 x 10E38 is multiplied by 1.0, the value should not change and there should be no overflow error. However, Turbo Pascal detects an overflow condition and halts execution.

Admittedly, you are unlikely to encounter such extreme conditions regularly; in most cases you will never come close to the limit of **reals** in Turbo Pascal.

80×87 Data Types

In addition to the **byte, integer, shortint, word, longint,** and **real** data types, Turbo Pascal supports four other numerical data types: **single, double, extended,** and **comp.** These are the data types supported by the 8087 family of processors.

The **single** data type is a "short real" in the sense that it requires only 4 bytes of storage and has only 7 to 8 significant digits. You would need this type only if you were desperate for memory space. The **double** data type is a "long real," requiring 8 bytes and giving 15 to 16 significant digits. For those who need the ultimate in precision, there is the "really, really long real," the **extended** data type, which uses 10 bytes and provides 19 to 20 significant digits with a range in value of 3.4 x 10E-4932 to 1.1 x 10E4932.

The 80×87 data types also include the **comp** type, which is actually an integer type. This data type uses 8 bytes, contains 19 to 20 significant digits, and ranges from -2E63 + 1 to 2E63 − 1. This data type can be useful for calculations requiring very large integer values.

With Turbo Pascal's range of numerical data types, you should be able to select the one that precisely fits your needs. Best of all, Turbo Pascal's Emulation mode gives you access to the full range whether or not your computer has the 8087 math coprocessor installed.

Non-Numeric Scalar Types

The term *scalar* refers to those types that are countable. All of the integer types are scalar because all of their values can be identified. This section describes those scalar types that are not numeric.

The data type **char** represents a single ASCII character. Like the **byte** type, the **char** (character) data type occupies one byte of storage in memory. Unlike the **byte** variable, however, a **char** variable cannot be used directly in arithmetic expressions. It is used instead for manipulating and comparing text, as well as in string-assignment statements. Constants of type **char** are single characters enclosed in single quotes, such as 'a' and '1.' When you use two single quotes with no character inside, such as '', then you have the *null character.*

The **boolean** data type is the simplest of all types, since it consists of only two values: True and False.

Enumerated Types

One of the most powerful aspects of Turbo Pascal is its ability to define customized data types. By tailoring data structures to a program's specific algorithms, you can increase your program's readability and simplify its maintenance. The simplest of user-defined types is the enumerated scalar.

An enumerated scalar (or user-defined scalar) requires one byte of memory and can have up to 256 elements. The power of user-defined scalars is that the programmer names the values, allowing easier programming and debugging. The following are examples of enumerated scalars:

```
Income : (High, Moderate, Low);
Sex : (Male, Female);
Occupation : (Doctor, Teacher, Other);
```

The following code excerpt demonstrates the readability of user-defined scalars:

```
if Occupation = Doctor then
   Income := High
else if Occupation = Teacher then
   Income := Moderate
else
   Income := Low;
```

Without user-defined scalars, the programmer must develop coding schemes to represent the values (for example, 1 = Doctor, 2 = Teacher, 3 = Other). When the number of coded variables is large, it is difficult to keep track of the meanings of different values.

Each element of a user-defined scalar equates to a byte value according to its position in the enumerated set, with the first element having a value of 0. In the preceding examples of enumerated sets, the High income has the value 0, while Low income has the value 2. To determine the current value of *Income,* use the Turbo Pascal standard function Ord (which returns the integer value of any scalar variable). If *Income* is currently High, then the statement **Ord(Income)** returns the value 0; if it is Low, it returns 2. If you wish, you can assign this value to a numeric variable, as is done next, where the variable *I* will be equal to 1 after the assignment statement:

```
var
   I : integer;
   Color : (Black, Brown, Blue, Green, Red, Yellow, White);

begin
   Color := Brown;
   I := Ord(Color);
end.
```

Since *Brown* is the second value in the **Color** type, *I* will be set to 1 (ordinarily starts with 0).

While transforming a user-defined scalar to a numeric value is easy, the opposite is untrue. In the following example, the statement **Color := I** is illegal:

```
var
   I : integer;
   Color : (Black, Brown, Blue, Green, Red, Yellow, White);

begin
   I := 1;
   Color := I;
end.
```

To resolve this illegal statement simply, you can use the Turbo Pascal standard function FillChar, which is discussed in Chapter 13, "The System Unit." The following example shows one way to assign a numeric value (**integer** or **byte,** not **real**) to an enumerated set.

```
var
  I : integer;
  Color : (Black, Brown, Blue, Green, Red, Yellow, White);

begin
  I := 1;
  FillChar(Color, 1, I);
end.
```

The use of FillChar forces *Color* to be assigned to *Brown.*

Type Casting

In the Introduction you learned that Pascal is known as a strongly-typed language. Strong typing has its advantages, there are times when a programming problem can be solved best by relaxing type checking. This can be done with *type casting,* a technique in which a variable of one type is temporarily treated as another type. For example, you cannot normally assign a character variable to an integer variable because the types are incompatible. You can, however, use the following type cast to achieve the same result,

```
I := integer(Ch);
```

where *I* is an **integer** variable and *Ch* is a character (**char**) variable. This statement treats the binary value of *Ch* as if it were an **integer** value. The program below demonstrates more ways to use the type cast technique:

```
{$R-}
Program TestTypeCast;

uses Crt;

var
  I : integer;
  W : word;
  C : char;
  B : boolean;
  P : pointer;
  R : real;
  S : string;
```

```
begin
  ClrScr;
  C := 'A';
  Writeln('C = ', C);

{ Convert character to integer }
  I := integer(C);
  Writeln('I = ', I);

{ Convert integer to boolean }
  B := boolean(I);
  Writeln('B = ', B);

{ Convert pointer value to real }
  P := @C;
  R := Real(P^);
  Writeln('R = ', R);

{ Convert pointer value to a string }
  S := string(P^);
  Writeln('S = ', S);

  Readln;
end.
```

Note how the pointer variable is interpreted as both a **real** variable and a **string** variable. When used with type casts, pointers are particularly powerful, since they can take on any data type.

Arithmetic Operators

Logic and the power to crunch numbers are characteristics long associated with computers, an association reinforced by the names of such computer languages as FORTRAN (from Formula Translator) and ALGOL (from Algorithmic Logic). Pascal continues in this vein: it is named after Blaise Pascal, a 17th-century mathematician, and provides powerful arithmetic functions and extensive logic commands.

Turbo Pascal arithmetic is based on the concept of an *expression* or equation. An expression consists of a combination of identifiers, numeric values and functions, and operators, all of which result in a specific numeric value. If that sounds too complicated, consider this well-known expression:

$2 + 2$

This has all the elements of a mathematical expression—numeric values and an operator (the plus sign)—but it is not a Pascal statement. In Pascal, a mathematical expression must be part of either an assignment statement or a logical statement. A numerical assignment statement computes a value from an expression and stores the value in a numeric variable. An example of an arithmetic assignment statement is

```
Result := 2 + 2;
```

When this statement is executed, Turbo Pascal calculates the right-hand side of the statement and assigns the result to the variable *Result*.

An arithmetic expression in a logical statement is similar, except that the expression does not result in a numerical value but in a True or False condition. For example, the logical statement

```
if Result = (2 + 2) then ...
```

does not change the value in the variable *Result*. Rather, Turbo Pascal adds the two numbers and compares them to the value that is already in *Result*. In this case, if *Result* is equal to 4, then the expression is True; if **not**, it is False. Logical structures are discussed more fully later in this chapter.

Note that the assignment operator in Pascal is :=, while the logical operator is =. This might seem to be a trivial distinction, but there is a rationale behind it: an assignment statement does not imply equality. In arithmetic, a statement such as $X = X + 1$ is simply incorrect. In Pascal, however, the statement $X := X + 1$ is perfectly legal. Remember, this assignment statement does not say, "X is equal to $X + 1$"; it says, "Take the value of $X + 1$ and assign it to the variable X."

Integer and Real Expressions

In Turbo Pascal, arithmetic expressions result in either an integer value or a real value. For an expression to yield an integer result, two conditions must be met. First, all the operands in the expression must be integers (or floating-point variables converted to integers with the Trunc or Round function). Second, if division is performed, the **div** operator must be used instead of the / character. (The standard mathematical functions are described in Chapter 13.)

Any expression that is not an integer expression is, by default, a real expression. Even if an expression has 50 integer operands and only 1 real operand, the expression results in a real value. The following illustration shows examples of both integer and real expressions:

```
Program Math1;

var
  I, J, K : integer;
  X, Y, Z : real;

begin
  J := 2;

  I := 1 + J;
  J := 3 div I;
  K := (I + J) div (3 * J);

  Writeln(I, ' ', J, ' ', K);

  J := 2;

  X := 1.5 + J;
  Y := 3 / I;
  Z := (I + J) div (3 * J);

  Writeln(X:2:2, ' ', Y:2:2, ' ', Z:2:2);
  Writeln;
  Writeln('Press ENTER...');
  Readln
End.
```

Hierarchy of Arithmetic Operators

The order of precedence dictates that multiplication and division are performed before addition and subtraction and that any operation in parentheses is done first. Turbo Pascal follows these rules: it has four hierarchical levels of arithmetic operators, as shown here:

Operator	Priority
Unary Minus, Unary Plus	1 (Highest)
Parentheses	2
Multiplication, Division	3
Addition, Subtraction	4 (Lowest)

A *unary* minus is the sign that directly precedes a number and indicates that the number is negative. For example, the minus sign in the number –3 is a unary minus. When used in arithmetic expressions, the unary minus can lead to statements such as

```
Result := 1 - -3;
```

in which case, *Result* is equal to 4.

Turbo Pascal also supports the unary plus. While the unary plus has absolutely no impact on the value of the number, the fact that it is supported means that a statement such as

```
Result := 1 - +2;
```

is compilable. In this case, *Result* is equal to –1.

Please note, however, that the unary plus operator is not an indicator of absolute value (the absolute value of a negative number is its positive equivalent). If a unary plus precedes a variable with a negative value, the variable remains negative.

The second level in the hierarchy of Turbo Pascal arithmetic operators is parentheses. Following the order of precedence, operations within parentheses are executed before operations outside parentheses. To clarify this rule, consider the following two expressions:

```
A := 3 * 4 + 5;
A := 3 * (4 + 5);
```

In the first case, the multiplication operator takes precedence, so that 3 * 4 is evaluated first, yielding 12, and 5 is added to 12 for a final result of 17. In the second case, the operation within the parentheses takes precedence over the multiplication operator, so that 4 + 5 is evaluated first, yielding 9, and 9 is multiplied by 3 for a final result of 27.

You should use parentheses to increase clarity, even when they are not strictly necessary. For example, the following two expressions yield the same result, yet the parentheses in the latter make it more readable.

```
R := A + B * C * D + X + Y / R;
R := A + (B * C * D) + X + (Y / R);
```

Integer Versus Real Arithmetic

The last two levels in the hierarchy of arithmetic operators are multiplication and division (level 3) and addition and subtraction (level 4). Here Turbo Pascal uses strong typing, forcing a separation between integer arithmetic and real arithmetic.

Integer Arithmetic

The rules of integer arithmetic apply when an expression is assigned to an integer variable. All operators in an integer expression must be either integers or reals converted to integers using the Turbo Pascal standard functions Round or Trunc. The program shown next provides examples of both legal and illegal integer arithmetic statements.

```
Program IntegerMath;

var
  I, J, K : integer;
  X, Y, Z : real;

begin

{Legal Statements}
  I := 10 + J;
  J := I div K;
  K := J + Round(X) + Trunc(Y/Z);

  Writeln('I = ', I);
  Writeln('J = ', J);
  Writeln('K = ', K);
  Writeln;

  Write('Press ENTER...');
  Readln;

{Illegal Statements}
{
  I := 10.0 + J;
  J := I / K;
  K := J + X + Y / Z
}

end.
```

Round and Trunc are Turbo Pascal standard functions that convert real values into integer values, but in slightly different ways. The Round function rounds a real value to the nearest integer. If the decimal portion is below 0.5, the real value is rounded down; otherwise, it is rounded up. For example, the result of **Round(10.49)** is the integer value 10, while **Round(10.5)** returns the value 11.

The Trunc standard function truncates a real value, chopping off any decimal places. Therefore, the result of **Trunc(10.99)** is 10. With the Round and Trunc standard functions, you can freely mix reals within integer expressions. However, it is important that the value of the real does not exceed the limits of an integer.

Note that integer expressions cannot contain numeric constants that have decimal places.

Special Integer Operators

The integer-division operator **div** is replaced by the slash character for floating-point arithmetic. The following integer operators, however, have no counterpart for floating-point operations: **mod, and, or, xor, shl,** and **shr.**

The **mod** operator returns the remainder of integer division. For example, 7 **div** 2 yields 3; the remainder of 1 is lost. The **mod** operator, however, discards the integer part of the quotient and returns the remainder. Therefore, 7 **mod** 2 returns 1.

The remaining integer operators—**and, or, xor, shl,** and **shr**—are familiar to anyone who has used Assembler. These are also known as bit-manipulation operators since they are usually used not for arithmetic but to alter the values of specific bits in a **byte** or **integer** variable. To understand how these operators work, it is necessary to know what a **byte** and **integer** look like in memory.

A **byte** consists of eight bits, each bit capable of storing one of two values: 0 and 1. Because bits can store only two numbers, they are base-two numbers. Consider the equivalent binary and decimal numerical values in Table 2-1. (Binary numbers are typically indicated by a lowercase "b" appended to the digits.) Note that the highest value a **byte** can hold is 255.

Integers consist of two bytes. As a result, their numerical range extends far beyond the limit of 255 that a single byte can hold. The largest possible two-byte integer value is 65,535, or 11111111 11111111b. In Turbo Pascal, however, the left-most bit in an **integer** determines the sign of the number; 0 indicates a positive number, 1 a negative number. As a result, the largest **integer** value in Turbo Pascal is 32,767, or 01111111 11111111b, and the smallest **integer** value is -32,768, or 11111111 11111111b. For simplicity, the bit-manipulation operators are illustrated with **byte** values rather than **integers**; the general concepts apply equally to both.

The And, Or, and Xor Operators

The **and, or,** and **xor** operators compare each bit in two different byte variables and return a third byte variable as the result. The value of the resulting byte depends on the type of the comparison.

Decimal	Binary
0	00000000b
1	00000001b
2	00000010b
3	00000011b
10	00001010b
100	01100100b
255	11111111b

Table 2-1.   *Binary and Decimal Equivalents*

The **and** operator compares each bit in two bytes one by one and stores the result in a third byte. If the comparison finds both bits are on, the corresponding bit in the third byte is also turned on (that is, set to a value of 1). If the bits compared are not both on, the corresponding bit in the third byte is turned off.

Figure 2-1 gives an example of the **and** command. Byte1 is operated on Byte2 using **and**, yielding Byte3. Bit 0 in Byte1 is on, but it is off in Byte2. Because only one, and not both, of these bits is on, bit 0 in Byte3 is turned off. Bit position 2 is different in that it is on in both Byte1 and Byte2. Therefore, bit 2 in Byte3 is turned on.

Like the **and** operator, the **or** operator compares each bit in two bytes and stores the result in a third byte. However, the bit in the third byte is turned on if the comparison finds either bit or both bits in Byte1 and Byte2 are on. The corresponding bit in the third byte is turned off only if both of the bits compared are off.

In Figure 2-2, Byte1 is operated on Byte2 using **or**, yielding Byte3. Bit 0 in Byte1 is on, but in Byte2 it is off. Because the **or** operator requires only one of the bits to be on, bit 0 in Byte3 is turned on. In this example, the only bit position that fails the or test is bit 7. Because bit 7 is off in both Byte1 and Byte2, bit 7 in Byte3 is also turned off.

The **xor** comparison is True if one bit, and only one bit, is on between two bytes. If both bits are on or both bits are off, the comparison fails and the corresponding bit in the third byte is turned off.

In Figure 2-3, Byte1 is operated on Byte2, using **xor**. Bit 0 is on in Byte1 and off in Byte2. Because only one of the bits is on, the comparison is True, and bit 0 in Byte3 is turned on. On the other hand, bits 2 and 7 are turned off in Byte3 because bit 2 is on in both Byte1 and Byte2 and bit 7 is off in both bytes.

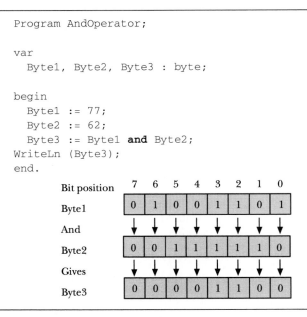

```
Program AndOperator;

var
  Byte1, Byte2, Byte3 : byte;

begin
  Byte1 := 77;
  Byte2 := 62;
  Byte3 := Byte1 and Byte2;
WriteLn (Byte3);
end.
```

Figure 2-1.   *Bit manipulation using the **and** operator*

```
Program OrOperator;

var
  Byte1, Byte2, Byte3 : byte;

begin
  Byte1 := 77;
  Byte2 := 62;
  Byte3 := Byte1 or Byte2;
WriteLn (Byte3);
end.
```

Bit position	7	6	5	4	3	2	1	0
Byte1	0	1	0	0	1	1	0	1
Or								
Byte2	0	0	1	1	1	1	1	0
Gives								
Byte3	0	1	1	1	1	1	1	1

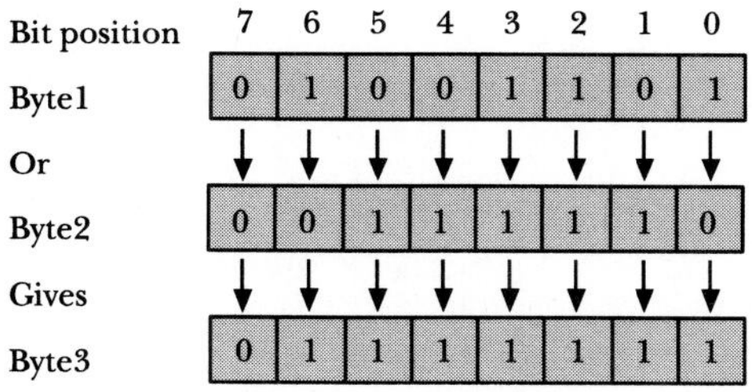

Figure 2-2.   *Bit manipulation using the **or** operator*

```
Program XorOperator;

var
  Byte1, Byte2, Byte3 : byte;

begin
  Byte1 := 77;
  Byte2 := 62;
  Byte3 := Byte1 xor Byte2;
WriteLn (Byte3);
end.
```

Bit position	7	6	5	4	3	2	1	0
Byte1	0	1	0	0	1	1	0	1
Xor								
Byte2	0	0	1	1	1	1	1	0
Gives								
Byte3	0	1	1	1	0	0	0	1

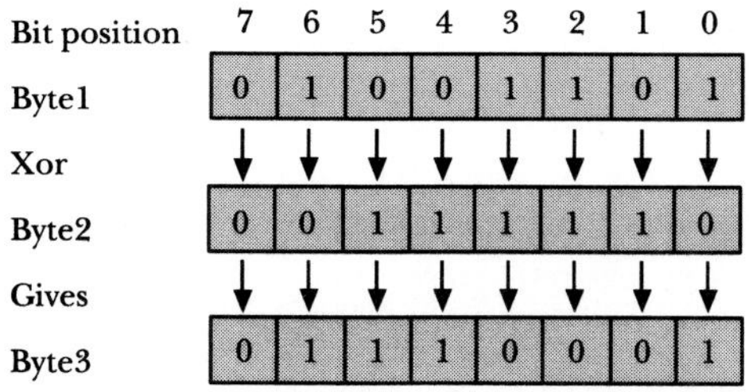

Figure 2-3.   *Bit manipulation using the **xor** operator*

The Shl and Shr Operators

As their names suggest, the operators *shift-left* (**shl**) and *shift-right* (**shr**) shift the bits in a byte left or right. A byte can be shifted left or right a maximum of eight times, at which point all the bits are set to zero. When a byte is shifted left by 1, each bit in the byte moves one position to the left. The left-most bit is lost, and a zero appears in the right-most position, as follows:

```
Program ShiftLeft;

var
  I : byte;

begin
  I := 255;              {I equals 11111111b}
  Writeln('I = ', I);
  I := I shl 1;          {I equals 11111110b}
  Writeln('I = ', I);
  I := I shl 1;          {I equals 11111100b}
  Writeln('I = ', I);
  I := I shl 1;          {I equals 11111000b}
  Writeln('I = ', I);
  I := I shl 1;          {I equals 11110000b}
  Writeln('I = ', I);
  I := I shl 1;          {I equals 11100000b}
  Writeln('I = ', I);
  I := I shl 1;          {I equals 11000000b}
  Writeln('I = ', I);
  I := I shl 1;          {I equals 10000000b}
  Writeln('I = ', I);
  I := I shl 1;          {I equals 00000000b}
  Writeln('I = ', I);

  Writeln;
  Write('Press ENTER...');
  Readln;
end.
```

Shift-right (**shr**) operates in the same way as shift-left, but it works in the opposite direction. When a byte is shifted to the right, the right-most bit is lost and the left-most bit is set to zero.

*If you have an **integer** or **byte** variable, you can use **shl** and **shr** as a very fast way to multiply and divide by two, respectively.*

Real Arithmetic

An arithmetic expression yields a floating-point result under two conditions: when the expression contains any floating-point operands and when division is executed with the slash (/) operator. Floating-point operands are any identifiers defined as **real** or any numeric literal with decimal places (for example, 10.2). The following program, which comprises examples of both integer and floating-point expressions, highlights the small differences between the two expression types.

```
{$N-,E-}
Program Math1;

uses CRT;

var
  I, J, K : integer;
  X, Y: real;

begin
  ClrScr;
  I := 1;
  K := 3;
  Y := 3.324;

  J := I div K;    {integer expression}
  X := I / K;      {floating-point expression}
  Writeln('Integer math. I div K = ', J);
  Writeln('Real math.   I / K   = ', X:0:4);
  Writeln;

  J := I + 3;      {integer expression}
  X := I + 3.0;    {floating-point expression}
  Writeln('Integer math. I + 3 = ', J);
  Writeln('Real math.   I + 3.0 = ', X:0:4);
  Writeln;

  J := I + K;      {integer expression}
  X := I + Y;      {floating-point expression}
  Writeln('Integer math. I + K = ', J);
  Writeln('Real math.   I + Z = ', X);
  Writeln;
  Writeln;

  X := 10 * 10;
  Writeln('Valid conversion to real. 10 * 10 = ', X:0:2);
  Writeln;

  I := 10000;
```

```
  J := 10000;
  X := I * J;
  Writeln('I = 10000');
  Writeln('J = 10000');
  Writeln('Invalid conversion to real. I * J = ', X:0:2);
  Writeln;

  I := 10000;
  J := 10000;
  X := 1.0 * I * J;
  Writeln('I = 10000');
  Writeln('J = 10000');
  Writeln('Valid conversion to real. 1.0 * I * J = ', X:0:2);
  Writeln;

  Write(Press ENTER...);
  Readln;
end.
```

The preceding listing points out a potential source of error in programs. Consider the assignment statement

```
X := 10 * 10;
```

The right side of the statement, which is an integer expression, is evaluated as an integer before being converted into a floating-point value.

A problem arises when the result of the integer expression exceeds the maximum integer value of 32,767. In the following statements

```
I := 10000;
J := 10000;
X := I * J;
```

the integer expression overflows the maximum integer value before being converted to a **real**. As a result, X is incorrectly assigned the value -7936. To eliminate this error, include a floating-point operand in the expression. The expression is then evaluated as a floating-point expression.

In the preceding program listing, the solution is to multiply the expression by 1.0, like this:

```
X := 1.0 * (I + J);
```

This forces the expression to be evaluated as a floating-point value, thereby producing the correct result.

Logical Operators

Turbo Pascal supports the logical operators: = (equal), <> (not equal), < (less than), > (greater than), <= (less than or equal), >= (greater than or equal), **and, or,** and **not.** The first six operators are valid for any primitive data type. The last three will operate on any non-real primitive type.

Logical operators are generally used in **if-then** statements, which test to determine whether adjacent statements should be executed. This is an example of an **if-then** statement:

```
if A > B then
  Writeln('A is greater than B');
```

In this example, *A* and *B* are **integer** variables. If *A* equals 5 and *B* equals 2, then the test **A > B** will be True, and the line following the statement will execute.

The **not** operator negates the result of a logical test. For example, if **A > B** is evaluated as True, then **not (A > B)** will be False. For any test using the **not** operator, there is an equivalent test without it. For example, **not (A > B)** is the same as **A <= B.**

An **if-then** statement can control the execution of more than one statement by using **begin** and **end** to create a block of code. In the following example, if *A* is greater than *B*, all the statements between the **begin** and **end** statements will execute:

```
if A > B then
  begin
    Writeln('A is greater than B');
    B := A;
  end;
```

The **if-then** statement can be extended with the Turbo Pascal reserved word **else**. If the condition tested fails, the program executes the code following the **else** clause, as shown in this example:

```
if A > B then
  begin
    Writeln('A is greater than B');
    B := A;
  end
else
  begin
    Writeln('A is not greater than B');
    A := B;
  end;
```

Note that the statement preceding the **else** clause is not terminated with a semicolon. Turbo Pascal considers the **else** clause to be a continuation of one long statement, so a semicolon indicating the end of a statement is inappropriate. The **if-then-else** structure is covered in greater detail in Chapter 5, "Program Control Structures."

Chapter *3*

Complex Data Types

In Chapter 2 you studied the primitive types—types that can store only one piece of data. This chapter will show you ways to group data into more complex data types, such as arrays, records, objects, and sets.

Arrays

Any data type, whether standard or user defined, can be extended into an array. An *array* is a variable that stores multiple pieces of data, each of the same type. To define an array, follow this general format:

ArrayType = array [*lower limit .. upper limit*] of BaseType;

The lower limit and the upper limit are any legal scalar values in which the upper limit is greater than the lower limit.

Arrays are usually used when a program includes a list of recurring elements. For example, to hold a year's worth of stock prices, define the array as follows:

```
type
  Prices = array [1..365] of real;

var
  Price : Prices;
```

To refer to a specific price, indicate which element in the array you want. For example, to set the price on the tenth day in the year, you would use

```
Price[10] := 34.50;
```

The lower limit on an array does not have to be 1. It makes more sense to start the array at a value that corresponds to the context of your data. If you were measuring the conductivity of a metal with a temperature range of –100 to +100 degrees Celsius, you would define the array as

```
type
  Conductivity = array [-100..100] of real;
```

The range of the array now matches the functional range of temperatures (assuming that the measurements will be taken at whole-number intervals).

Another example of an array that matches its data is one that stores the average income of people aged 35 to 65. An array defined as the following would do the trick.

```
type
  AverageIncome = array [35..65] of real;
```

The lower and upper bounds of the array must be the same type, known as the *index type.* Although **integer** values are used most often, other scalar types are allowed. For example, the following array could be used to help count letters in a file:

```
type
  Frequencies = array ['A'..'Z'] of word;
```

This type uses **char** values to index the array.

 *When defining an array type, don't force the index type to be **integer.** If another type makes more sense, use it!*

Strings

The **string** data type stores text information. Internally, a string is actually an array, with this definition:

```
type
  string = packed array [0..255] of char;
```

The [0] element of a string is used to store the current length of the string, and is often called the *length byte*.

When you declare a variable of type **string,** it uses the above definition. You can restrict a string to fewer characters by including the maximum length in the definition. Here is an example:

```
var
  S : string[10];
```

The variable *S* actually occupies 11 bytes in memory (including the length byte). If this variable contains the word 'HELLO', the first byte in memory holds the binary value 5, indicating that the variable contains five characters. In this case, the last five bytes of the variable are ignored by Turbo Pascal's string-manipulation procedures. The memory allocated to the **string** variable would look like this:

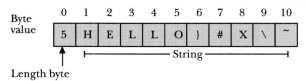

Note that the first byte is not the character '5' but the number 5 in binary (00000101), and that the last five bytes contain random data.

Maintaining a length byte requires quite a bit of overhead. As a result, string-manipulation statements tend to be among the slowest in Turbo Pascal. Yet the alternative implementation of strings, such as in C, is even less efficient. In C, the character array (the equivalent of the Pascal **string** type) has no length byte. Consequently, any time a program needs to know the length of a string, it has to calculate it by counting every character until a delimiter is reached.

One of the reasons that the **string** type is so powerful is that it can be processed in two different ways: by directly manipulating its individual elements or by using one of the Turbo Pascal standard functions and procedures for strings. Both methods have advantages, depending on the circumstances. See Chapter 13, "The System Unit," for a complete discussion on functions and procedures for strings.

Null-Terminated Strings

Borland Pascal 7 defines a new type of string called a *null-terminated string*. A null-terminated string is unique because its length is determined by the first occurrence of a null (#0) character in the string. These strings are primarily used to access Windows functions.

To declare a null-terminated string, you define an array of characters with 0 as the lower bound, such as

```
type
  FileNameStr = array [0 .. 12] of char;
```

This definition creates a null-terminated string of up to 12 characters. Although there are 13 locations in the array, at least one must hold the null character.

Null-terminated strings are primarily used in conjunction with the pointer type PChar, which will be covered in more detail in Chapter 6.

Multidimensional Arrays

Any arrays defined to have more than one dimension are considered to be *multidimensional* arrays, although they rarely exceed three dimensions. Two-dimensional arrays, sometimes called *matrices,* are quite common, especially in multivariate statistics. For example, when measuring the conductivity of a metal, the following two-dimensional arrays could be used, assuming that the temperature intervals are whole numbers:

```
var
  Temp_Conductivity : array [1..200, 1..2] of real;
```

The best way to think about this array is to visualize a table of columns and rows: the first dimension in the array (1..200) provides the rows, and the second dimension (1..2) provides the columns. Going row by row, all you need to do is put the temperatures in one column and the matching conductivity ratings in another, as shown in Table 3-1.

First Index	[,1] Temperature	[,2] Conductivity
1	99.34	12.3
2	97.76	12.2
3	96.01	11.9
.	.	.
.	.	.
.	.	.
100	99.01	2.9

Table 3-1. *Sample Temperature and Conductivity Readings*

To assign a value in a multidimensional array, specify both dimensions, as shown in the following two statements:

```
Temp_Conductivity[1,1] := -99.34;
Temp_Conductivity[1,2] := 12.3;
```

To refer to an observation pair, specify both the row and the column. In this example, the first temperature reading is *Temp_Conductivity[1,1]*, while the corresponding conductivity rating is *Temp_Conductivity[1,2]*.

Records

A *record* is a combination of other data types into a new data type. The syntax of a record definition looks like this:

RecordType = record
  Field1Name : Field1Type;
  Field2Name : Field2Type;
  .
  .
  .
end;

Each record field can be either a primitive type or a complex type. The following example exhibits a typical record definition:

```
type
  TCustomer = record
    Name    : string[30];
    Address : string[60];
    Age     : integer;
    Income  : real;
    Married : boolean;
  end;
var
  Customer : TCustomer;
```

Using records has two advantages. First, all data elements for a single record are logically connected to each other. This makes it easier to keep track of things. Second, some operations, such as assignments and file operations, can be performed on an entire record, eliminating the need to refer to each element in the record.

Using records in assignment statements is straightforward. You can access elements in a record in two ways: by explicit reference or implicit reference using the reserved word **with,** as shown in Figure 3-1. To create an explicit reference, you use the record name followed by a period which is then followed by the element name. The statement

```
Rec1.B := 1;
```

is an example of an explicit reference. In an implicit reference, using the reserved word **with,** you do not need to repeat the record name in each assignment statement.
The assignment statement

```
Rec2 := Rec1;
```

assigns every element in *Rec1* to the corresponding element in *Rec2*.
Implicit references can be nested so that one **with** statement refers to more than one record, as shown in Figure 3-2. The statement

```
with Rec2, Rec1 do
```

allows the programmer to reference elements in both records implicitly. Problems can arise, however. In Figure 3-2, *Rec1* and *Rec2* both have an element *A*. This ambiguous reference does not tell Turbo Pascal which record element is being referred to. Thus, the compiler assumes that the ambiguous element belongs to the last record that contains that element. In Figure 3-2, the assignment statement

```
A := A;
```

assumes that both elements are from *Rec1*. In short, it assumes that the statement means

```
Rec1.A := Rec1.A;
```

```
Program WithDemo;

uses Crt;

type
  RecType = record
    A : string[20];
    B : integer;
    C : real;
  end;

var
  Rec1, Rec2 : RecType;

begin
  ClrScr;

  Rec1.A := 'sss';
  Rec1.B := 1;
  Rec1.C := 123.23;

  with Rec1 do
    begin
      A := 'sss';
      B := 1;
      C := 123.23;
    end;

  Rec2 := Rec1;

  with Rec2 do
    begin
      Writeln(A);
      Writeln(B);
      Writeln(C);
    end;

  Writeln;
  Write('Press ENTER...');
  Readln;
end.
```

These segments do exactly the same thing

Record-to-record block assignment

Output using the **with** option

Figure 3-1.   *Using the **with** statement with records*

```
Program NestedWithDemo;

uses Crt;

type
  Rec1Type = record
    A : string[20];
    B : integer;
    C : real;
  end;

  Rec2Type = record
    A : string[20];
    R1, R2 : real;
  end;

var
  Rec1 : Rec1Type;
  Rec2 : Rec2Type;

begin
  ClrScr;

  with Rec1 do
    begin
      A := 'sss';
      B := 1;
      C := 123.23;
    end;

  with Rec2 do
    begin
      A := 'xxx';
      R1 := 20.0;
      R2 := 10.0;
    end;
```

Figure 3-2.   *Nested **with** statements*

```
    with Rec2, Rec1 do
      begin
        A := A;
        C := R1 * R2;
      end;

    with Rec2 do
      with Rec1 do
        begin
          A := A;
          C := R1 * R2;
        end;

    with Rec1 do
      begin
        Writeln(A);
        Writeln(B);
        Writeln(C);
      end;

    Writeln;
    Write('Press ENTER...');
    Readln;
  end.
```

These segments do exactly the same thing

Figure 3-2.   *Nested* **with** *statements (continued)*

Variant Records

Turbo Pascal supports a special kind of record type called a *variant record*. These records give you the ability to create data structures that more precisely reflect the entities they represent. As a side effect, they can conserve more memory space than standard records. The syntax of the variant record uses the reserved word **case**:

    RecordType = record
      Field1Name : Field1Type;

```
      Field2Name : Field2Type;
      .
      .
      .
    case {TagField :} TagType of
      TagValue1 :
        (Variant1Field1Name : Variant1Field1Type;
         Variant1Field2Name : Variant1Field2Type;
        ...);
      TagValue2 :
        (Variant2Field1Name : Variant2Field1Type;
         Variant2Field2Name : Variant2Field2Type;
        ...);
      .
      .
      .
  end;
```

Each variant section is enclosed in parentheses and terminated with a semicolon. The reserved word **end** denotes completion of both the variant part and the record definition.

For example, consider the use of the variant record in the following listing:

```
Program VariantRecord;

uses Crt;

type
  VehicleType = (Car, Boat, Plane);
  VehicleRec = record
    IDnumber : integer;
    Price    : real;
    Weight   : real;
    case Kind : VehicleType of
      Car : (MilesPerGallon : integer;
             Odometer : real);
      Boat : (Displacement : real;
              Length : integer);
      Plane : (Engines : integer;
               Seats : integer);
  end;

var
  Vehicle : VehicleRec;
```

```
begin
  ClrScr;
  with Vehicle do
    begin
      IDnumber := 123;
      Price := 12000;
      Weight := 1200;
      Kind := Car;
      MilesPerGallon := 21;
      Odometer := 75000.0;

      case Kind of
        Car:
          begin
            Writeln('Kind = Car');
            Writeln('Miles per gallon = ', MilesPerGallon);
            Writeln('Odometer = ', Odometer:0:1);
          end;
        Boat:
          begin
            Writeln('Kind = Boat');
            Writeln('Displacement = ', Displacement);
            Writeln('Length = ', Length);
          end;
        Plane:
          begin
            Writeln('Kind = Plane');
            Writeln('Engines = ', Engines);
            Writeln('Seats = ', Seats);
          end;
      end;
    end;
  Writeln;
  Write('Press ENTER...');
  Readln;
end.
```

Notice how the record contains separate sections pertaining to different types of transportation. Because of this flexibility, variant records can cover broad classes of categorical data, yet still retain specific detailed information.

The fields under Car, Boat, and Plane comprise a total of four **integers** and two **reals**—20 bytes in total. But the variant portions of the records share the same memory. Since the largest single block of memory used by a variant portion of the record is eight bytes (a **real** and an **integer**), only eight bytes are allocated to the variant part of the record.

The field named Kind is known as the *tag field.* The tag field helps keep track of which part of the variant record is in use. When a tag field is used, the variant record is known as a *discriminated union* because the tag field can discriminate which portion of the variant record should be used.

Another type of variant record is the *free union,* or a variant record that does not have a tag field. COBOL programmers will feel at home with free unions because they resemble COBOL's redefined fields.

The following program example presents an example of a free-union variant record.

```
Program FreeUnion;

uses Crt;

type
  CharByte = record
    case Integer of
      1 : (Characters : array [1..10] of char);
      2 : (Numbers : array [1..10] of byte);
  end;

var
  CB : CharByte;

begin
  ClrScr;
  CB.Characters[1] := 'A';
  Writeln('Numeric value of character A is: ', CB.Numbers[1]);

  Writeln;
  Write('Press ENTER...');
  Readln;
end.
```

Notice that the variant record definition has no tag field; only a data type, **integer**, is specified. The lack of a tag field means no tag value is stored and that you can refer to any of the variant elements without restriction.

This example program is special because the variant record defines one array in two different ways. The 10-byte array in one line is defined as an array of characters, while in the next line it is defined as an array of bytes. Since these arrays share the same memory (because they are the variant part of the record), you can refer to the elements in the arrays as either characters or numbers. This is demonstrated in the program block. Notice where a character is assigned to the first element in the array using the identifier *Characters,* and then the element is written out as a number using the identifier *Numbers.*

Substitute for Multidimensional Arrays

The examples of multidimensional arrays shown earlier in this chapter should make one thing clear—it is hard to keep track of what values are in which column. There is simply no clue given in the array itself. Because it is preferable to deal with variables that have meaningful names, Turbo Pascal provides an alternative to multidimensional arrays: arrays of records. The following example shows why these arrays are better than the multidimensional ones:

```
type
  ObservationRec = record
    Temperature : real;
    Conductivity : real;
  end;
  ObservationArray = array [1..200] of ObservationRec;
var
  Observation : ObservationArray;
```

Arrays of records create clear definitions; it is immediately apparent that the **record** and **array** definitions in the preceding illustration defines a series of observations consisting of temperatures and conductivities. These can be referred to by name in the following manner:

Observation[1].Temperature
Observation[1].Conductivity

Whenever you use multidimensional arrays, consider the possibility that you may be able to substitute an array of a record type that does the job, yet improves program clarity.

Objects

By now, almost all programmers have heard the term OOP. Object-oriented programming is the hottest method of software development today. Ever since version 5.5, objects and OOP have been an integral part of Turbo Pascal. Now with version 7, OOP is even better.

If you have never used OOP techniques, do not fear. Once you learn the new terms and map those concepts that you already know, you will be well on your way to mastering OOP. Contrary to popular belief, you need not relearn programming to understand OOP.

As its name implies, object-oriented programming relies heavily on the concept of the object. In our daily lives, we are familiar with all kinds of objects—televisions, lamps, checkbooks, and so on. But when we turn on a television, we don't distinguish between its physical elements (the tuning dial, the picture tube, the antenna) and its behavior (providing an image and sound). We simply turn it on and select a channel.

Like the television, objects make programs more accurately conform to the way we deal with the real world. To gain this quality, objects depend on three main concepts: (1) combining code and data, (2) inheritance, and (3) encapsulization.

Code + Data = Object

As a Pascal programmer, you are accustomed to defining data structures to hold information and defining procedures and functions to manipulate information. In OOP, data and procedures are combined into objects. An object contains both the characteristics of an entity (its data) and its behavior (its procedures). By melding these characteristics and behaviors, an object knows everything it needs to do its work.

To understand objects, it is useful to think in terms of metaphors. An airplane can be described in physical terms—the number of passengers it can hold, the amount of thrust it generates, its drag coefficient, and so on. Alternatively, an airplane can be described in functional terms—it takes off, it ascends and descends, it turns and lands, and so on. Yet neither the physical description nor the functional description alone captures the essence of what the airplane is—you need both.

In traditional programming, you would define an airplane's physical characteristics as a data structure, such as this:

```
type
  Airplane = record
    AirSpeed : word;
    Altitude : word;
    Flaps    : (Up, Down);
  end;
```

You would define the airplane's behaviors separately as procedures and functions:

```
procedure Accelerate;
begin
  {...}
end;
procedure Decelerate;
begin
  {...}
end;
```

```
procedure FlapsUp;
begin
  {...}
end;
procedure FlapsDown;
begin
  {...}
end;
```

In OOP, characteristics (data) and behaviors (procedures) are combined into a single entity known as an object. The object just given contains declarations for both data and procedures. In the language of OOP, procedures and functions declared within an object are known as *methods*. Notice that the object defines only the methods header; the actual code for the methods is specified separately. See Chapter 4, "Subprograms," for more details on methods.

Thus, an airplane defined as an object might look like this:

```
type
  Airplane = object
    AirSpeed : word;
    Altitude : word;
    Flaps    : (Up, Down);
    procedure Init;
    procedure Accelerate;
    procedure Decelerate;
    procedure Ascend;
    procedure Descend;
    procedure FlapsUp;
    procedure FlapsDown;
  end;
```

Once an object has been defined, you can declare variables using the object's name, as shown here:

```
var
  A : Airplane;
```

In your program, you can now write statements like these:

```
with A do
  begin
    Init;
    FlapsUp;
    Accelerate;
    Ascend;
  end;
```

Now you can begin to see the advantages of OOP—all actions affecting an object can be made by referring to the object itself. There can be no confusion about which data structure procedure *FlapsUp* will use. Given the previous definition of the Airplane object, you are allowed to access the object's fields directly. For example, it is perfectly legal to write

```
A.Flaps := Up;
```

however, calling *A.FlapsUp* is the better alternative.

As you become better acquainted with OOP, you will learn that accessing an object's fields directly is both unnecessary and undesirable. In fact, Turbo Pascal 7 enables you to prevent access to an object's fields, as you will see later in this chapter.

Inheritance

Although objects contain data and procedures of their own, they can also inherit the same from other objects. Inheritance in OOP has as its roots a concept that is familiar to Turbo Pascal programmers: nesting records. Consider the following record definitions:

```
type
  Ages = 0..150;
  PersonInfo = record
    LastName  : string[30];
    FirstName : string[20];
    Age       : Ages;
  end;
  Grades = 0..12;   { 0 is K }
  StudentInfo = record
    Person  : PersonInfo;
    Grade   : Grades;
    Teacher : string[30];
  end;
```

The record *PersonInfo* contains fields used to describe any person. The second record, *StudentInfo,* declares *Person,* which contains the fields in the *PersonInfo* record. This type of nesting allows you to build increasingly complex record structures.

In OOP, you use this same concept to build increasingly complex objects. The following listing shows how to use objects to replace nested record declarations:

```
type
  Ages = 0..150;
  Person = object
    LastName  : string[30];
    FirstName : string[20];
```

```
   Age        : Ages;
   procedure Init;
   procedure SetName(NewFirst, NewLast : string);
 end;
 Grades = 0..12;   { 0 is K }
 Student = object(Person)
   Grade   : Grades;
   Teacher : string[30];
   procedure Init;
 end;
```

Notice how the declaration of *Student* includes a reference to the *Person* object:

```
Student = object(Person)
```

By this declaration, *Student* inherits everything contained in *Person*—data and methods. You can refer to the data field *Student.LastName* just as if you had declared it explicitly. In OOP terminology *Person* is an ancestor type and *Student* is a descendant type. An object can have more than one ancestor type. In the example just given, *Person* is the immediate ancestor of *Student* and *Student* is the immediate descendant of *Person*. The overall lineage of ancestors and descendants is known as the *object hierarchy*.

Not only do objects inherit data, but they also inherit methods. In the previous example, the *Person* object included the method *SetName,* which presumably assigns a name to the person. Since the *Student* object is a descendant of *Person,* it inherits the *SetName* method. This is reasonable because you would assign a name to a student the same way you assign a name to a person. With inheritance you avoid writing the same method to support two objects.

You might have noticed that both *Person* and *Student* contain a method called *Init,* which presumably initializes each data field. You would use a duplicated name in the case where you don't want to inherit the method of an ancestor. In this particular example, you probably need to do more initializing for *Student* objects than you would for *Person* objects. The two *Init* procedures might look something like this:

```
procedure Person.Init;
begin
  LastName := '';
  FirstName := '';
  Age := 0;
end;
procedure Student.Init;
begin
  inherited Init;
  Teacher := '';
  Grade := 0;
end;
```

Notice that the first step in initializing an object of type *Student* is to call the *Init* method of its immediate ancestor, *Person*. This helps to avoid duplication of code by saving *Student.Init* from initializing data fields defined by *Person*. The reserved word **inherited,** new to Turbo Pascal 7, allows you to call the ancestor's *Init* method without knowing the name of the ancestor.

Although method names can (and probably will, as you will see with virtual methods) be duplicated for inherited objects, data field names cannot. Once an object's data field is named, no data field in any descendant object can share that field's name. You cannot override data fields like you can methods.

Since data fields and methods exists all the way down an object's hierarchy, it is often difficult to determine all of the fields and methods included with an object. You must carefully trace through the hierarchy, noting which methods are overridden and which are not. The Object Browsers, part of the version 7 IDE, make this task much easier (see Chapter 10).

Inheritance is a complex subject with many ramifications, which will be dealt with in detail over the remainder of this chapter and the next. While at first these complexities make OOP appear difficult to use, with practice you will find that it are easily mastered.

Encapsulation

One of the overriding goals of OOP is *encapsulation,* the creation of objects that function as complete entities. One of the rules of encapsulation is that the programmer need never directly access the data fields within an object. Instead, methods should be defined within the object to handle all data manipulation. Consider the following object definition:

```
type
  Person = object
    LastName  : string[30];
    FirstName : string[20];
    Age       : Ages;
    procedure Init;
    procedure Display;
    function GetLastName  : string;
    function GetFirstName : string;
    function GetAge       : Ages;
    procedure SetLastName(NewLastName : string);
    procedure SetFirstName(NewFirstName : string);
    procedure SetAge(NewAge : Ages);
  end;
```

This expanded form of the *Person* object contains the same three data fields you saw in a previous example: *LastName, FirstName,* and *Age.* To provide access to these three fields, the object defines all the possible methods to either report or alter the value of a field.

Your first reaction to encapsulation is probably to notice its drawbacks: it's fairly code intensive and appears to be much more cumbersome than simple field access. The primary benefit of encapsulation is that by limiting access to just the methods, you are free to change the fields without any side effects. Suppose you discover that memory space is a problem with your application. You are forced to shorten the size of the name fields by several characters. If you used encapsulation properly, you can make the change without affecting other code.

One way to help provide encapsulation is to use units. If you have been writing any large programs, you probably already use units to help break your code into manageable pieces. Objects and OOP lend themselves very easily to units. You place the object declarations in the **interface** section of the unit, and you place the bodies of the methods in the **implementation** section. The number of objects you have in a unit is up to you. Many programmers define only one object per unit.

Public and Private Areas

Version 6.0 of Turbo Pascal introduced a new reserved word: **private.** Now Turbo Pascal 7 has added the reserved word **public.** Together these words enable you to divide an object declaration into *public areas* and *private areas*. A public area contains the data and methods that you are making available to all other modules. A private area contains fields and methods that are available only to subprograms in the same module. Any definitions prior to **public** or **private** are considered to be public.

Consider this simple object definition:

```
type
   Positions = (On, Off);
   LightSwitch = object
      Position : Positions;
      function GetPosition : Positions;
      procedure TurnOn;
      procedure TurnOff;
   end;
```

Since methods provide complete functionality for the *LightSwitch* object, the data field can be moved into the private area:

```
type
   Positions = (On, Off);
   LightSwitch = object
      function GetPosition : Positions;
      procedure TurnOn;
      procedure TurnOff;
```

```
private
  Position : Positions;
end;
```

Moving *Position* to the private area prevents other modules from accessing the field directly. Since the methods are defined in the same module as the object declaration, they have complete access to the private fields.

If you want to keep the data declarations before the method declarations, you would need to create an explicit public area:

```
type
  Positions = (On, Off);
  LightSwitch = object
    private
      Position : Positions;
    public
      function GetPosition : Positions;
      procedure TurnOn;
      procedure TurnOff;
  end;
```

Sets

In Turbo Pascal, a *set* is a group of related numbers or characters. Sets are primarily used to see if a character or number belongs to the set. For example, you might define a set that consists of the capital letters from 'A' to 'Z' and then use the set to check if other characters in the program are included in it. If a character is included in the set, you know it is uppercase. A discussion of numeric and character sets follows.

Numeric Sets

Numeric sets can consist only of integers (actually byte values). The sets include any integers from 0 to 255; such numbers as -1 and 256 exceed the range established by Turbo Pascal. Here are two examples of numeric set definitions.

```
var
  Zero_Through_Nine : set of 0..9;
  FullRange : set of byte;
```

In the first line, *Zero_Through_Nine* can include any combination of integers (byte values) from 0 to 9, but the number 10 cannot be included because it is outside the range of the set.

In the second line, no range is specified for the set *FullRange*; the definition specifies only that the set consists of bytes. Later in the program, the programmer can define *FullRange* to be any numeric subset with a statement such as this:

```
FullRange := [0..9];
```

Now, the set *FullRange* has the same elements as *Zero_Through_Nine*.

Character Sets

Character sets can consist only of characters. Like numeric sets, the maximum range of character sets is from 0 (00h) to 255 (FFh). The major difference between numeric sets and character sets is that character sets can be directly compared with character variables. Here are two examples of character-set definitions:

```
var
  UpperCase : set of 'A'..'Z';
  AllChars : set of char;
```

The set *UpperCase* can include any combination of uppercase characters from 'A' (ASCII code 65) to 'Z' (ASCII code 90). Thus, the character 'a' (ASCII code 97) could not be included in this set.

The second set, *AllChars,* is defined as a **set of char.** This means that this set can include any combination of characters from 0 to 255.

Sets of User-Defined Elements

Finally, a set can consist of elements defined by the user. These elements are neither numeric nor character and must be listed individually. The maximum number of elements allowed is 255. Here is an example of a user-defined set:

```
var
  Ingredients : set of (Eggs, Milk, Butter, Flour);
```

All operations on sets of user-defined elements follow the same rules as all other sets.

Sets and Memory Allocation

Sets can use a maximum of 32 bytes of storage—the equivalent of 256 individual bits. This is what limits the scope of a set to the range 0 to 255. If your set has only a few elements, it uses only a few bytes, and allocating the full 32 bytes would be wasteful. Therefore, sets are automatically reduced in size. For example, a set defined as

```
X : set of 1..5;
```

needs only one byte, so Turbo Pascal allocates just one byte for the set. The values in the byte are allocated as follows:

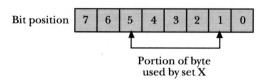

The arrows indicate the part of the byte used to store the set. When an element is present in a set, the appropriate bit is turned on (that is, set to 1). To illustrate how the memory would represent the presence of elements in a set, consider the following set assignment:

```
X := [1..3, 5];
```

This statement assigns the elements 1, 2, 3, and 5 to set *X*. In memory, this assignment creates the following bit pattern:

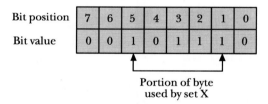

The 1s in the bit value portion of this illustration indicate the presence of an element in the set. They are found in the 1, 2, 3, and 5 positions of the byte, which correspond precisely to the assignment statement.

Since Turbo Pascal needs only one byte to store set *X*, the remaining 31 bytes are used for other purposes. Only three bits of memory (the 0, 6, and 7 positions) are wasted. To further illustrate the storage of sets, consider the following set definition:

```
X : set of 7..8;
```

This set comprises only two elements, but requires two bytes of storage. Why? Because the set straddles a byte boundary, as shown in this illustration:

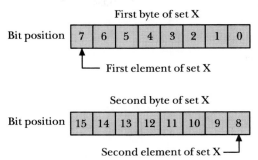

The first element (7) is in the first byte, while the second element (8) is in the second byte. Two bytes are used (but 14 of the 16 bits are ignored), and the remaining 30 bytes are available for other data.

It is possible to create a compiler that eliminates this kind of wasted memory, but such a compiler would increase the size of the compiled programs and slow down execution. Wisely, Borland decided to accept a minimal amount of waste in return for faster execution and smaller code.

Chapter *4*

Subprograms

Subprograms have always been part of the Pascal language in the form of procedures and functions. With object-oriented methods and Version 7's enhancements, however, subprograms are not as simple as they used to be. This chapter will help you sort out all the new features, as well as the old.

Procedures and Functions

The logic of modular programming states that it is easier to write a good program if you break it down into small chunks. In Pascal, these chunks are called procedures or functions. Modular programs are easier to write and maintain because each procedure and function can be written and tested independently of the main program. Once you are sure it is functioning correctly, you can integrate it into the main program with confidence. In addition, Pascal allows you to pass variables into the function or procedure, further increasing the modularity of the program.

Defining Procedures in Pascal

To define a procedure in Pascal, you need at least two things: a name for the procedure, and a block of code. The example shown here presents a simple procedure definition that provides both ingredients.

```
Program ProcDemo;

var
```

```
  X, Y : integer;

procedure Subtract;                  {procedure name (heading)}
begin
  X := X - 1;                        {procedure block}
  Y := Y - 1;
end;


begin
  X := 5;
  Y := 10;
  Subtract;                          {procedure call}
end.
```

The Pascal reserved word **procedure** tells the compiler that a procedure is about to be defined. The next identifier is the name of the procedure, *Subtract*. When you want to execute a procedure in your program, you will call it by the name you gave it in the procedure definition.

The procedure *Subtract* decrements the value of variables *X* and *Y* by 1. In the example, *X* and *Y* are initialized to 5 and 10, respectively. Upon returning from *Subtract, X* is equal to 4 and *Y* is equal to 9. Note that *Subtract* can use variables *X* and *Y* because they are *global* variables—variables that are declared at the main program level and can be used by any procedure in the program.

Passing Parameters to a Procedure

The preceding example works for global variables *X* and *Y* only. If you want to decrement any other pair of variables, you are out of luck. You can expand the usefulness of this procedure by defining parameters. Then you can use the same procedure for any two **integer** variables. The following example shows the revised procedure with the *Subtract* parameters.

```
Program ProcDemo2;

var
  X, Y, Q, W : integer;

{*****************************************************}

procedure Subtract(A : integer; var B : integer);
begin
  A := A - 1;
  B := B - 1;
```

```
end;

{*********************************************************}

begin
  X := 5;
  Y := 10;
  Q := 1;
  W := 4;
  Subtract(X, Y);
  Subtract(Q, W);
end.
```

Note that the procedure name is now followed by a list of two variables—*A* and *B*—both of which are **integer** parameters. When *Subtract* is called, the program passes two integer values to the procedure. In the statement **Subtract(X, Y)**, *X* supplies the value for parameter *A*, and *Y* supplies the value for parameter *B*. Thus, *X* and *Y* are the parameters being passed to the procedure. Once inside the procedure, *A* takes the value of *X*, and *B* takes the value of *Y*. The same logic applies to the second call to *Subtract,* where *Q* and *W* are passed as parameters.

While the procedure *Subtract* decrements each parameter by one, the effect on *X* will be different than on *Y*. In the procedure definition, parameter *B* is preceded by the Pascal reserved word **var,** while *A* is not. Parameters preceded by **var** are called *reference* parameters; those without it are called *value* parameters. In Turbo Pascal 7, there is a hybrid form of parameters, called *constant* parameters. The different types are discussed in the following sections.

Reference Parameters

When a variable is passed to a procedure as a reference parameter, changes made to that variable within the procedure remain even after the procedure has ended. Changes to reference parameters are permanent because Turbo Pascal passes to the procedure not the variable's value, but the variable's address in memory. In other words, the variable inside the procedure and the variable passed to the procedure as a reference parameter share the same address. Therefore, a change in the former is reflected in the latter.

In the preceding example, the global variable *Y*, with a value of 10, is passed to the procedure as parameter *B*. The procedure subtracts 1 from *B*, giving a value of 9. When the procedure ends, *Y* is passed back to the main program, where it retains the value of 9.

In short, the reference parameter and the actual variable passed to the procedure are the same; that is, they share the same position in memory. Therefore, any change made to the reference parameter is stored as a permanent change in the actual variable.

Value Parameters

Value parameters are different from reference parameters. When a value parameter is passed to a procedure, a temporary copy of the variable is placed in memory. Within the procedure, only the copy is used. When the value of the parameter is changed, it only affects the temporary storage; the actual variable outside the procedure is never touched.

In the preceding illustration, *A* is a value parameter because it is not preceded by the reserved word **var.** When the program starts, it initializes *X* to 5. Upon calling *Subtract,* the program makes a copy of *X* in temporary storage and passes the copy to the procedure. Within *Subtract,* parameter *A* refers to the temporary storage location, not to the actual location of *X*. Therefore, when *A* is decremented, only the value in temporary storage is affected. At the end of the procedure, the value in temporary storage is discarded, and the global variable *X* retains the original value of 5.

Constant Parameters

Value parameters are beneficial because they prevent a subprogram from changing variables unexpectedly. The major drawback of value parameters, however, is that they pass a complete copy of the parameter to the subprogram. For large data structures this can mean a lot of additional overhead in both time and stack space. Constant parameters, new with Turbo Pascal 7, give you the protection of value parameters with the speed of reference parameters.

To demonstrate constant parameters, consider the following example:

```
Program ValueParameter;

uses Crt, Dos;

const
  ArraySize = 5000;

type
  BigArray = array [1..ArraySize] of integer;

var
  MyArray : BigArray;
  I : integer;

procedure DisplayLast(TheArray : BigArray);
begin
  Writeln('Last = ', TheArray[ArraySize]);
  TheArray[1] := 0;
end;

begin   {main program}
```

```
  for I := 1 to ArraySize do
    MyArray[I] := I;

  DisplayLast(MyArray);
  Writeln('First = ', MyArray[1]);

  Writeln('Press ENTER...');
  Readln;
end.
```

Notice that a very large array is being passed to procedure *DisplayLast*. After displaying the last value, however, the procedure modifies the array. Since the parameter is a value parameter, the actual array *MyArray* is unaffected.

Knowing that passing such a large array is inefficient, you might be tempted to change the parameter to a reference parameter:

```
procedure DisplayLast(var TheArray : BigArray);
```

Making this change will speed up execution, but it will also yield an unwanted side effect: the first value of *MyArray* will be changed.

The best solution is to create a constant parameter. To accomplish this, simply add the reserved word **const** in front of the parameter declaration:

```
procedure DisplayLast(const TheArray : BigArray);
```

With this change, the compiler will catch the unwanted side effect and generate an "Invalid Variable Reference" error. This would force you to eliminate the second statement in the *DisplayLast* procedure block.

Functions versus Procedures

Both procedures and functions provide modularity to your programs. Both are self-contained blocks of code and both can accept data through parameters. The difference between functions and procedures, illustrated by the following examples, is in how they return values.

```
procedure Square(X : real; var X2 : real);
begin
  X2 := X * X;
end;

function Square(X : real) : real;
begin
  Square := X * X;
end;
```

The procedure *Square* passes two parameters. The first parameter, *X*, is the number to be squared, and the second, *X2,* is the result. The procedure multiplies parameter *X* by itself and assigns the result to the parameter *X2.* Because *X2* is a reference parameter, its new value is retained when the procedure ends.

The function *Square* produces basically the same result as the procedure. However, the function does not store the result in a parameter, but passes it back through the function itself.

The major difference between functions and procedures is the way they are called. A call to a procedure is its own statement, such as

```
Square(X, X2);
```

or

```
Square(X, X2);
if X2 > 100 then . . .
```

A function call, on the other hand, must be part of an expression. Here are two examples:

```
X2 := Square(X);
```

or

```
if Square(X) > 100 then . . .
```

Another way of looking at it is that functions are like variables whose value depends on the parameters you pass to them. Procedures, on the other hand, cannot be used in assignment, comparison, or arithmetic expressions. At most, a procedure can return a variable that can be used in expressions.

Both functions and procedures have their strong points. Functions are generally preferred when one clearly identifiable result is desired. In the preceding example, a function makes more sense than a procedure since obtaining the squared value is the objective. A procedure, rather than implying a specific result, performs an operation that may return many or no results. In the end, experience is the best guide in deciding between functions and procedures.

Calling Functions as Procedures

Turbo Pascal 7 has added a new feature that allows you to call a function in the same manner you call a procedure. When you turn a function call into its own statement, you lose the value returned by the function. Therefore, this feature would not be useful when calling any functions in Turbo Pascal's standard units. This capability is primarily useful when calling C functions, such as those in the Windows API.

Here is a declaration of a function in the WinProcs unit:

```
function DestroyMenu(Menu : HMenu): Bool;
```

If you've programmed Windows applications for a long time, and you understand that this function never fails as long as you have a menu, you may call it as if it were a procedure:

```
DestroyMenu(TheMenu);
```

When you run this call, the return value is simply discarded.

In order to use this feature, you must enable the Extended Syntax with the {$X+} compiler directive.

Nesting and Precedence of Subprograms

Pascal is known as a block-structured language, that is, a language in which every statement in a program belongs to a specific block of code. A simple program can consist of only one block, as shown here:

```
Program Sample;

begin
  Writeln('Hello');
end.
```

The program block is the lowest level in the program: it is the foundation upon which you can build more layers. In the preceding example, the entire program exists at the program-block level. When you add procedures and functions to a program, you add more levels, as shown in Figure 4-1. This program consists of three blocks— one program block and two procedure blocks—but has only two levels. Because both procedures are nested within the program block, they are both level-2 procedures, as the indentation suggests.

By nesting procedures within other procedures, you can add even more levels to the program. In Figure 4-2, for example, procedure *Proc1A* is nested inside procedure *Proc1* to form a third level in the program.

Nesting procedures creates "privacy" among procedures. A procedure that is nested inside another is private to that procedure. Keeping procedures private can decrease programming errors by limiting the use of a procedure to a specific section of your program.

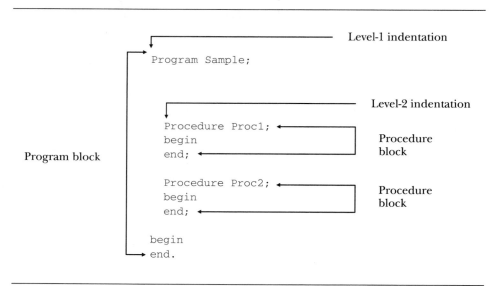

Figure 4-1.   *Adding levels to a Turbo Pascal program*

Procedural Scope

Note that Figure 4-2 contains three procedures named *Proc1A*: the first is at level 2; the other two are at level 3, nested within the procedures *Proc1* and *Proc2*.

Although these three procedures have the same name, each is treated as a distinct entity. A call to *Proc1A* in the program block executes the level-2 procedure, while calls made within Proc1 and Proc2 refer to their respective nested procedures.

Two rules govern the scope of procedures:

- A program may call a procedure within the block where it is declared and within any subblock nested in that block.

- The exception to Rule 1 occurs when the program declares another procedure of the same name in a higher-level subblock.

In Figure 4-2, the level-2 procedure *Proc1A* would normally extend its scope into *Proc1* and *Proc2*. But because the program declares the same procedure name in *Proc1* and *Proc2*, the scope of the level-2 procedure is limited to the first level.

 Seldom does it make sense to use the same procedure name in more than one location in your program. These examples should be used only to understand the concept of scope.

Procedural Precedence

In some languages (notably C), the order in which you declare procedures makes no difference. In Turbo Pascal, a language far more orderly than C, you cannot call procedures until you have declared them. (The only exception to this is when you use **forward** declarations, which are discussed in the next section.) For example, in Figure 4-2, *Proc2* can call *Proc1,* but *Proc1* cannot call *Proc2.*

The rule of procedural precedence is based on the logic that a complex idea is best built from simple ideas. In other words, a program should be built from small, simple procedures that are combined to form increasingly complex procedures. A programmer should see a continual evolution from the beginning to the end of a Turbo Pascal program, culminating in the program block, which may well consist of only a few procedure calls.

```
Program Sample;  ←——————————— Level 1

    procedure Proc1A;  ←——————————— Level 2
    begin
    end;

    procedure Proc1;  ←——————————— Level 2

      procedure Proc1A;  ←——————————— Level 3
      begin
      end;

    begin
    end;

    procedure Proc2;  ←——————————— Level 2

      procedure Proc1A;  ←——————————— Level 3
      begin
      end;

    begin
    end;

  begin
  end.
```

Figure 4-2. *Nesting procedures within procedures*

Forward Declarations

While procedural precedence enforces a desirable order in a program, there are times when you simply need to refer to a procedure before you declare it. For these cases, Turbo Pascal provides the **forward** declaration, which informs the compiler that a procedure exists before it specifies what the procedure does. A **forward** declaration consists of the normal procedure heading followed by the word **forward** and a semicolon. The body of the procedure is declared later, at which point only the name of the procedure, and not the entire program heading, is declared. The following listing shows an example of a **forward**-declared procedure.

```
Program EndlessLoop;

var
   I : integer;

procedure Step2(I : integer); forward;
procedure Step1(I : integer);
begin
   I := I + 1;
   Writeln(I);
   Step2(I);
end;

procedure Step2;
begin
   I := I + 1;
   Writeln(I);
   if I > 100 then Halt;
   Step1(I);
end;

begin
   I := 1;
   Step1(I);
end.
```

In this case, *Step2* and *Step1* both call each other—something not allowed by procedure precedence, but overcome by the **forward** declaration of *Step2*.

Subprograms and the Scope of Variables

In BASIC and some other programming languages, all variables are global, that is, all variables can be referred to at any point throughout the program. Pascal supports global variables, but also provides local variables. These are variables that exist within a limited portion of the program, also known as the scope of a variable. By limiting the scope of variables within subprograms, you can eliminate unwanted side effects.

The term "subprogram" is used throughout this book to mean either a procedure or a function.

The scope of a variable is determined by the block in which it is declared, as illustrated in Figure 4-3.

Because it is defined within the program block, variable *X* is global in scope, meaning it can be accessed throughout the program. The variable *Y*, defined within procedure *A*, is limited in scope and can only be referred to within the scope of procedure *A*.

Finally, variable *Z*, defined within procedure *B*, is even more limited in scope: it can only be referred to within the body of procedure *B*. Therefore, procedure *B* can use variables *X*, *Y*, and *Z*; and procedure *A* can use both variable *X* and variable *Y*, but not variable *Z*. The main program, the most limited of all, can refer only to variable *X*.

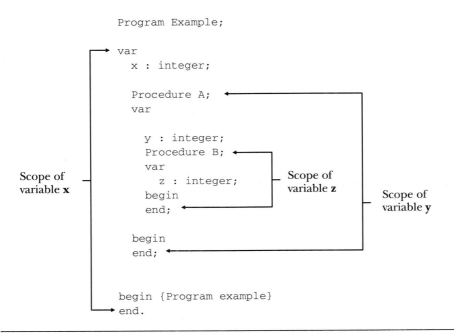

Figure 4-3.   *Determining the scope of a variable*

Variables at different levels can share the same name. However, giving variables the same name limits the scope of one of the two. This is demonstrated in the program listed here:

```
Program DoubleName;

var
  X : integer;

procedure Proc1;
var
  X : string[20];

  procedure Proc2;
  begin
    X := 'Mac';
  end;

begin
  X := 'Jones';
end;

begin
  X := 1;
end.
```

This program contains two variables named *X*. In the program block, *X* is an **integer** variable, while in *Proc1* it is a **string** variable. *Proc1* cannot access the global variable *X* because it has already defined its own variable with the same name. When *Proc2* refers to *X*, it uses the variable defined in *Proc1* because *Proc2* is declared within *Proc1*.

More on Parameters

Earlier in this chapter you learned the basic rules for passing data to and from subprograms using parameters. In this section you will see more detail on the rules governing parameters: matching the types, passing sets, using untyped parameters and literal values as parameters.

Passing Parameters of Different Types

The variables that you pass to a procedure or function must match the type declaration of their respective parameters. If, for example, a parameter is declared to be an

integer, you cannot pass a **real** type through it. A procedure declaration that includes the standard Turbo Pascal scalars follows.

```
procedure Example (I : integer;
                   R : real;
                   B : boolean;
                   X : byte);
```

User-defined types, including strings, can also be used to define parameters, as follows.

```
Program StringDemo;

type
  Str255 = string[255];
  Str80 = string[80];

var
  St1 : Str255;
  St2 : Str80;

{ ************************************************** }

procedure Blank(var S : Str255);
begin
  S := '';
end;

{ ************************************************** }

begin
  Blank(St1); (* legal *) {
  Blank(St2); (* not legal *) }
end.
```

Note that the parameter *S* is defined by using the type definition supplied by the user. Note also that you can pass **strings** to the procedure as reference parameters only if the parameter and the variable have been defined as the same **string** type. In the example just given, variable *St2* cannot be passed as a parameter because it is defined as **string[80],** while the procedure heading defines the parameter as **string[255].** This is an example of Pascal's strong typing.

You can also override Turbo Pascal's strict checking on **string** reference parameters by using the {$V–} compiler directive, which turns off string-type checking. With the $V directive disabled, Turbo Pascal allows you to pass any type of **string** variable through any type of **string** parameter. However, a better solution is to use open parameters, which is discussed in the next section.

Open Parameters

One of the benefits of using subprograms is that more of your code becomes reusable across multiple applications. Turbo Pascal 7 has added a new feature called *open parameters* that will make many subprograms even more reusable. An open parameter is an array parameter where the upper and lower bounds are defined by the caller instead of the declaration.

To declare an open parameter you use the form

VariableName : array of TypeName

To access the bounds of the array, you use the standard functions Low and High.

Suppose you wanted to write a program that computed the average of a group of numbers. Before Version 7, you would probably write a program like this:

```pascal
Program NoOpenParameter;

type
  RealArray = array [1..20] of real;

var
  MyArray : RealArray;
  I : integer;

function Mean(AnyArray : RealArray):real;
var
  I : integer;
  Sum : real;
begin
  Sum := 0.0;
  for I := 1 to 20 do
    Sum := Sum + AnyArray[I];
  Mean := Sum / 20.0;
end;

begin
  for I := 1 to 20 do
    begin
      MyArray[I] := Random * 20.0;
      Writeln (MyArray[I]:7:2);
    end;

  Writeln ('Mean is ', Mean(MyArray):7:2);
  Writeln ('Press ENTER...');
  Readln;
end.
```

Although the code to compute the mean is a subprogram, it can only compute the mean for arrays of type *RealArray*; which makes the function far from reusable.

Now study the following unit. Notice that the new function *Mean* will now compute the average of any **real** array.

```
Unit STATS;

{$P+}

interface

function Mean(AnyArray : array of real):real;

implementation

function Mean(AnyArray : array of real):real;
var
  I : integer;
  Sum : real;
begin
  Sum := 0.0;
  for I := Low(AnyArray) to High(AnyArray) do
    Sum := Sum + AnyArray[I];
  Mean := Sum / (High(AnyArray) - Low(AnyArray) + 1);
end;

end.
```

You can see how open parameters allow you to create complete libraries of reusable code.

The next program uses the STATS unit to compute the average of the values in a specific array.

```
Program TestStats;

uses STATS;

var
  MyArray : array [1..20] of real;
  I : integer;

begin
  for I := 1 to 20 do
    begin
      MyArray[I] := Random * 20.0;
      Writeln (MyArray[I]:7:2);
```

```
   end;

  Writeln ('Mean is ', Mean(MyArray):7:2);
  Writeln ('Press ENTER...');
  Readln;
end.
```

Since a string is actually an array, you can use a string as an open parameter. To do this, enable open parameters by including the {$P+} compiler directive. Then change the type in parameter declaration so that it is just **string.** The program that blanked different strings, shown earlier in this chapter in the StringDemo program, would then look like this:

```
Program OpenStringDemo;

{$P+}

type
  Str255 = string[255];
  Str80 = string[80];

var
  St1 : Str255;
  St2 : Str80;

{*************************************************}

procedure Blank(var S : string);
begin
  S := '';
end;

{*************************************************}

begin
  Blank(St1); { both legal }
  Blank(St2); { with $P+ }
end.
```

If needed you can use the Low and High functions to determine the size of the actual string.

Passing Set Parameters

Sets, another user-defined type, follow the same rules that apply to strings. An example of a set used as a parameter is shown in the following illustration:

```
Program SetDemo;

type
  CharSet = set of char;

var
  Ch : char;
  UpCaseChar : CharSet;

(*****************************************************)

function TestChar(Ch : char; TestSet : CharSet) : boolean;
begin
  TestChar := Ch in TestSet;
end;

(*****************************************************)

begin
  Ch := 'A';
  UpCaseChar := ['A'..'Z'];
  if TestChar(Ch, UpCaseChar) then
    Writeln(Ch);
end.
```

The user-defined type *CharSet* is used to define a parameter in *TestChar.* When the function is called, the variable *UpCaseChar* is passed to the function as parameter *TestSet.*

Untyped Parameters

Parameters defined using a data type (such as **real, integer,** and so on) are appropriately called *typed* parameters. Turbo Pascal also allows you to use *untyped* parameters. The advantage of untyped parameters is that you can pass variables of any type of data into them—**strings, reals, integers, booleans,** and any other data type are all legal.

How is it that an untyped parameter can accept any data type? To understand this, think about typed parameters. When you define a typed parameter, you tell Turbo Pascal what type of data to expect. Thus, Turbo Pascal can easily determine if a mismatch exists between the variable type and the parameter type. When you use untyped parameters, however, the procedure or function has no idea what it is you are passing to it. The procedure accepts whatever is passed to it and expects the programmer to know how to handle it. Because of this, untyped parameters must be used carefully. Consider the example shown here:

```
procedure Example(var X);
var
```

```
   Y : integer absolute X;
begin
   Writeln(Y);   { Legal: Y is of type integer }
   Writeln(X);   { Illegal: X has no type }
end;
```

Parameter *X* (a reference parameter) has no type associated with it. Therefore, *X* is an untyped parameter. The reserved word **var** is necessary because all untyped parameters must be reference parameters.

While *X* is clearly a parameter, it cannot be used directly by the procedure. Why not? The procedure does not know what *X* is, so it cannot handle the parameter.

Instead of using *X,* you must declare a variable in the procedure that is **absolute** at *X.* This means that the variable you declare will reside at exactly the same address as *X.* In the example, *Y* is defined as an **integer** variable that is located at the same place in memory as *X.* Now you can use variable *Y* in place of *X.*

When this procedure is called, any type of variable can be passed to this procedure, and the procedure will treat the variable as an **integer.** What does that mean? Suppose you pass a **string** into the procedure. Since *Y* is an **integer,** and an **integer** is two bytes long, the procedure will take the first two bytes of the **string** and treat them as an integer value. Of course, the integer value will have absolutely no relation to the value of the string. If you pass a string with the value "TEXT" into the procedure, the integer value will be 21,500—a totally meaningless value.

So why use untyped parameters? In certain and very few instances, untyped parameters are useful. One example, a procedure that compares two variables to see if they are equal, is shown in the following illustration:

```
{$V-}
Program CompareData;
var
   I1, I2 : integer;
   R1, R2 : real;
   S1, S2 : string;

{*************************************************}

function Compare(var X, Y;
                 Kind : char) : integer;
var
   AString : string[255] absolute X;
   BString : string[255] absolute Y;
   AReal : real absolute X;
   BReal : real absolute Y;
   AInteger : integer absolute X;
   BInteger : integer absolute Y;

begin
```

```
  case Kind of
    'R' : { Real }
      begin
        if AReal > BReal then
          Compare := 1
        else if AReal < BReal then
          Compare := -1
        else
          Compare := 0;
      end;

    'I' : { Integer }
      begin
        if AInteger > BInteger then
          Compare := 1
        else if AInteger < BInteger then
          Compare := -1
        else
          Compare := 0;
      end;

    'S' : { String }
      begin
        if AString > BString then
          Compare := 1
        else if AString < BString then
          Compare := -1
        else
          Compare := 0;
      end;

  end; { of case }
end;

{************************************************}

begin
  R1 := 10000.0;
  R2 := -33.0;
  Writeln(Compare(R1, R2, 'R'));

  I1 := 100;
  I2 := 200;
  Writeln(Compare(I1, I2, 'I'));

  S1 := 'Neder';
  S2 := 'Ballard';
  Writeln(Compare(S1, S2, 'S'));
```

```
end.
```

This example passes two variables at a time into the function *Compare.* The variables are passed as untyped parameters and are subsequently redefined as **real, integer,** and **string** variables. The third parameter, *Kind,* is a character denoting the type of the first two parameters. An 'S' indicates **string,** 'R' indicates **real,** and 'I' indicates **integer.**

By checking the value of *Kind,* the procedure knows whether to compare **strings, reals,** or **integers.** The final result, then, is a generalized procedure that can compare any two variables of type **integer, real,** or **string.** The only restriction is that you must tell the procedure what type of variable you are comparing.

Passing Literal Values

In the examples so far, only variables have been passed as parameters to functions. You can also pass literal values, such as a number or a string, to a procedure, but only as value parameters. The example here shows how the numeric literal 3.0 is passed to the function *Square.* The function performs just as it would if a variable had been passed to it.

```
Program SquareTest;

function Square(X : real) : real;
begin
  Square := X * X;
end;

begin
  Writeln(Square(3.0));
end.
```

String literals are groups of characters enclosed in single quotation marks. The following example illustrates how a string literal is passed to a procedure:

```
Program StringTest2;

{*******************************************}

procedure WriteUpCase(St : string);

var
  I : integer;
begin
  for I := 1 to Length(St) do
```

```
    St[I] := UpCase(St[I]);
  Writeln(St);
end;


{*********************************************}


begin
  WriteUpCase('This is a string literal');
end.
```

This procedure takes the string passed to it, converts it to all uppercase characters, and writes it out. In the preceding example, the string passed is a literal, but the procedure would accept a string variable as well.

You can pass literal values and string literals to value parameters only, not to reference parameters.

Methods

One of the frustrating aspects of object-oriented programming (OOP) to an unfamiliar reader is the new terminology. Inheritance, polymorphism, and constructor are just of few of the new terms you must tackle before using OOP. Even the word "method" seems out of place—if it's just a procedure included in a record, why call it a method? Well, the point is that it's *not* just a procedure!

Think of an object that is part of our everyday world, such as a ball. Now consider each *method,* or way, you can manipulate the ball: throw it, roll it, inflate it, and so on. The same thought process must take place when doing OOP.

The remainder of this section discusses how to write both static and virtual methods. Polymorphic methods are covered in Chapter 6, "Pointer, Dynamic Memory, and Polymorphism."

Implementing Methods

In Chapter 3, "Complex Data Types," you studied this object definition:

```
type
  Airplane = object
    AirSpeed : word;
    Altitude : word;
    Flaps    : (Up, Down);
    procedure Init;
    procedure Accelerate;
    procedure Decelerate;
```

```
    procedure Ascend;
    procedure Descend;
    procedure FlapsUp;
    procedure FlapsDown;
  end;
```

Notice that the object defines only the methods header; the actual code for the methods is specified later in the program or unit. Here is the implementation of two of the methods:

```
procedure Airplane.Init;
begin
  Flaps := Down;
  AirSpeed := 0;
  Altitude := 0;
end;

procedure Airplane.FlapsUp;
begin
  Flaps := Up;
end;
```

When a method is implemented, its header identifies both the object name (such as *Airplane*) and the subprogram name (such as *FlapsUp*), similar to the way you refer to a field in a record.

Within a method, all data fields are referred to without specifying the object name. Specifying *Airplane.* in the declaration acts like a **with** statement for the body of the method.

As mentioned in Chapter 3, units provide the perfect mechanism to enforce the concepts of OOP. Take a look at the initial implementation of the *Person* object, in unit form:

```
Unit PERSONS;

interface

type
  Ages = 0..150;
  Person = object
    LastName  : string[30];
    FirstName : string[20];
    Age       : Ages;
    procedure Init;
    procedure Display;
    function GetLastName  : string;
    function GetFirstName : string;
```

```
   function GetAge        : Ages;
   procedure SetLastName(NewLastName : string);
   procedure SetFirstName (NewFirstName : string);
   procedure SetAge (NewAge : Ages);
 end;

implementation

procedure Person.Init;
begin
  LastName := '';
  FirstName := '';
  Age := 0;
end;

procedure Person.Display;
begin
  Writeln('Person: ', FirstName, ' ', LastName);
  Writeln('Age: ', Age);
end;

function Person.GetLastName : string;
begin
  GetLastName := LastName;
end;

function Person.GetFirstName : string;
begin
  GetFirstName :=  FirstName;
end;

function Person.GetAge : Ages;
begin
  GetAge := Age;
end;

procedure Person.SetLastName(NewLastName : string);
begin
  LastName := NewLastName;
end;

procedure Person.SetFirstName(NewFirstName : string);
begin
  FirstName := NewFirstName;
end;

procedure Person.SetAge(NewAge : Ages);
begin
  Age := NewAge;
```

```
end;

end.
```

You will see several examples throughout this chapter and Chapter 6 that build on this unit, so study it carefully. Notice how placing all of the code associated with the *Person* object into one unit reduces confusion and enforces encapsulation.

Methods and Private Areas

The addition of public and private areas to objects allows you to enforce the concepts behind encapsulation. Study the following unit, the complete definition of the *Student* object:

```
Unit STUDENTS;

interface

uses PERSONS;

type
  Grades = 0..12;  { 0 is K }
  Student = object(Person)
    procedure Init;
    procedure Display;
    function GetGrade   : Grades;
    function GetTeacher : string;
    procedure SetGrade(NewGrade : Grades);
    procedure SetTeacher(NewName : string);
  private
    Grade    : Grades;
    Teacher  : string[30];
  end;

implementation

procedure Student.Init;
begin
  inherited Init;
  Grade := 0;
  Teacher := '';
end;

procedure Student.Display;
begin
  Write('Student: ', GetLastName, ', ', GetFirstName);
  Writeln ('; Age ', GetAge);
```

```
   Writeln('Grade: ', Grade);
   Writeln('Teacher: ', Teacher);
end;

function Student.GetGrade : Grades;
begin
   GetGrade := Grade;
end;

function Student.GetTeacher : string;
begin
   GetTeacher := Teacher;
end;

procedure Student.SetGrade(NewGrade : Grades);
begin
   Grade := NewGrade;
end;

procedure Student.SetTeacher(NewName : string);
begin
   Teacher := NewName;
end;

end.
```

Just like the previous example, the methods provide complete access to the data fields, so the fields are placed in the private area. If you needed to change the fields in any way, you could do so without fear of unwanted side effects.

Look closely at the method *Student.Display.* This method was written assuming that the fields defined in *Person* object were also moved to the private section. It had to call the *GetAge* method to output the age instead of using the *Age* field directly. Since the two objects were declared in different units, the descendent object loses access to the fields in its own ancestor.

There may also be cases where you want to place methods in the private area. For example, you may want to maintain a sorted list as part of an object. For that you will probably write a *Sort* method. But since the data is always sorted, you don't want to allow other modules to call *Sort,* so you place that method in the private area.

Static Methods

Methods in OOP actually come in two varieties: static and virtual. The examples you have seen thus far in this chapter have all been *static* methods. These methods are simple to understand, and execute almost exactly like normal procedures and functions. They are called static methods because when they call other methods, they always call the same ones. The calls are bound at compile time. This process is known as *early binding.*

Virtual methods, on the other hand, act much differently. When you call a virtual method, the actual call is bound at run time, when the call is made. This is called *late binding*. To make these terms clearer, and to understand the advantages of virtual methods, let's study a comprehensive example.

Earlier in this chapter you studied the implementation of the units PERSONS and STUDENTS. Given those two object declarations, suppose you want to add the following method to the *Person* object:

```
procedure Person.HappyBirthday;
begin
  Age := Age + 1;
  Writeln('The following record has been updated:');
  Display;
end;
```

This method automatically updates the person's age, then calls the *Display* method to display the update.

Since the *Student* object is a descendent of *Person,* it inherits this new method. Now you write a short program to create a student, assign all the proper values, then call the *HappyBirthday* method to update the student's age. Here is that sample program:

```
Program Static_vs_Virtual;

uses PERSONS, STUDENTS, Crt;
var
  AStudent : Student;

begin
  ClrScr;
  with AStudent do
    begin
      Init;
      SetLastName('Judd');
      SetFirstName('Jessica');
      SetAge(5);
      SetGrade(1);
      SetTeacher('Mr. Spillman');
      Display;
      Writeln;
      HappyBirthday;
    end;
  Readln;
end.
```

When you run this program, you get the output shown in Figure 4-4. Notice that when the age is updated, the program displays the record as though it was just a person, not a full-fledged student. How did this occur?

```
Student: Judd, Jessica; Age 5
Grade: 1
Teacher: Mr. Spillman

The following record has been updated:
Person: Jessica Judd
Age: 6
```

Figure 4-4.   Output from Static_vs_Virtual using static methods

The problem is caused by the use of static methods. The method *HappyBirthday* resides in the *Person* object, so a call to *AStudent.HappyBirthday* causes Turbo Pascal to trace up the hierarchy from the *Student* object to the *Person* object to locate the method. Once *HappyBirthday* executes, it encounters a call to a method named *Display*. With static methods, this call was automatically bound to the *Display* method that resides in the *Person* object (see Figure 4-5). So instead of displaying a student, it displays a person.

Virtual Methods

One way to overcome this problem would be to redefine the *HappyBirthday* method within the *Student* object. But that solution runs counter to the philosophy of OOP, which strives to reduce redundant code. The OOP solution is to use virtual methods. As introduced earlier, virtual methods use late binding, which determines the exact path of execution at run time.

There are two steps to turn a static method into a virtual one. The first step is to create a *constructor* method. The constructor tells Turbo Pascal that virtual methods will be used for that object. To create a constructor, you simply substitute the word **constructor** for **procedure** in both the object declaration and the method definition.

The second step is just as simple: you add the reserved word **virtual** to the method heading in the object declaration. Here are the revised declarations of the *Person* and *Student* objects:

```
type
  Ages = 0..150;     (* in years *)
  Person = object
    constructor Init;
    procedure Display; virtual;
    function GetLastName  : string;
    function GetFirstName : string;
    function GetAge       : Ages;
    procedure SetLastName(NewLastName : string);
    procedure SetFirstName(NewFirstName : string);
    procedure SetAge(NewAge : Ages);
```

```
   procedure HappyBirthday;
private
   LastName   : string[30];
   FirstName  : string[20];
   Age        : Ages;
end;


Grades = 0..12;   (* 0 is K *)
Student = object(Person)
   constructor Init;
   procedure Display; virtual;
   function GetGrade    : Grades;
   function GetTeacher  : string;
   procedure SetGrade(NewGrade : Grades);
   procedure SetTeacher(NewName : string);
private
   Grade      : Grades;
   Teacher    : string[30];
end;
```

The method *Display* is now a virtual method for both objects, and the method *Init* is now a constructor for both objects. Once these changes are made, the call to *AStudent.HappyBirthday* traces up to *Person.HappyBirthday* as before. But, when *Person.HappyBirthday* encounters a call to *Display,* it knows to execute the version in *Student,* not *Person* (see Figure 4-6). If you make these few changes, the output of the previous program will change from that shown in Figure 4-4 to the output pictured in Figure 4-7.

Three rules govern the declaration of virtual methods. First, you must call a constructor method for an object before calling any virtual methods. (The internal reasons for this will be discussed in the next section.) Second, once a method has been declared virtual in an object, the same method in any descendent object must

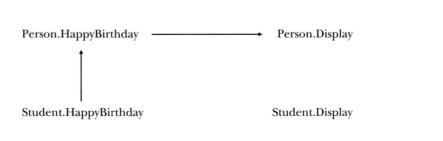

Figure 4-5.   *Path of static method calls*

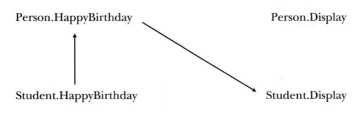

Figure 4-6.   *Path of virtual method calls*

also be declared virtual. And third, once a virtual method has been declared, its header cannot change in any descendents. This means you cannot add, change, or delete parameters or change between a function and a procedure.

Inside Virtual Methods

The primary structure that supports virtual methods is the VMT, or *virtual method table*. As the name implies, a VMT is a table of addresses that point to virtual methods. Turbo Pascal sets up a VMT for every object type that contains or inherits a virtual method. By maintaining a table of addresses for each object type, Turbo Pascal can determine a path of execution that would be impossible to determine at compile time.

The structure of the VMT begins with two words. The first word contains the size of the object. The second word contains the negative value of the first word and is used to validate that the VMT has been properly initialized. The compiler directive {$R+} enables VMT validation. When it is enabled, Turbo Pascal tests to see if the sum of the first two words of the VMT is zero. If it does not, Turbo Pascal generates run-time error 210.

The role of the constructor method is to initialize the VMT. This is why you must call a constructor of an object before you can call any of its virtual methods.

```
Student: Judd, Jessica; Age 5
Grade: 1
Teacher: Mr. Spillman

The following record has been updated:
Student: Judd, Jessica; Age 6
Grade: 1
Teacher: Mr. Spillman
```

Figure 4-7.   *Output from Static_vs_Virtual using virtual methods*

If you are using objects with virtual methods, be sure to initialize the object by calling its constructor at the beginning of your program.

The other fields in the VMT contain the addresses of the proper virtual methods for that object. All variables of the same object type point to the same VMT. Given the declarations of the *Person* and *Student* objects from the previous example, the VMT would contain only one other entry: the address of the proper *Display* method. The entire structure for the two objects is given in Figure 4-8.

When a virtual method is called, Turbo Pascal places the address of the calling variable on the stack of the virtual method. Thus, when calling *AStudent.Display,* the address of the variable *AStudent* is placed on the stack. This address in known as the **self** parameter, and it is always the last item placed on the stack. Using this address, the method picks up the VMT address of the variable and executes the appropriate method by using the address found in the VMT. In other words, the variable places a pointer to itself to the method, the method uses that pointer to locate the VMT, and the VMT tells the method which code to execute.

Methods and Object Type Compatibility

Object variables follow slightly different compatibility rules than do normal Turbo Pascal variables. The primary difference is that an ancestor type is compatible with a descendent type, but the reverse is not true. For example, given the variables defined in a previous program, the statement

```
APerson := AStudent;
```

would be legal, but

```
AStudent := APerson;
```

would generate a compiler error. The reasoning is that, through inheritance, *AStudent* contains everything in *APerson,* but *APerson* does not (or probably does not) contain everything in *AStudent.* The valid statement just listed assigns to *APerson* all values that it shares in common with *AStudent.* The other fields are ignored.

Similarly, a procedure that accepts a *Person* object variable as a **var** parameter can also accept a variable of type *AStudent.* Thus a procedure declared

```
procedure ChangeValue(var AnyPerson : Person);
begin
  {...}
end;
```

could be called as

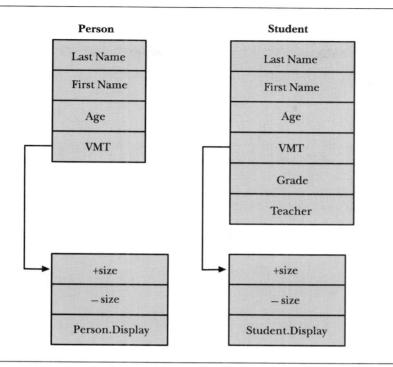

Figure 4-8. *Internal structure of object variables*

```
ChangeValue(AStudent);
```

The flexibility of object type compatibility may seem unimportant at first, but it is the simpler form of an extremely powerful OOP concept: *polymorphism*. Polymorphism is just a fancy way of saying that a procedure is willing to accept a wide range of object types, even if it is unaware of them at compile time. As long as the parameter variable is a descendent of the **var** parameter type, the procedure will accept it. You could define 10 (or 100) different ancestors to *Person,* and the *ChangeValue* procedure would not only accept them, but would use them as you intended.

Polymorphism has another important implication. If the procedure that accepts the object gets its information about that variable at run time, you will be able to define compatible objects without recompiling the unit that contains the procedure. This adds the important quality of *extensibility.* You can compile a unit of routines that accept polymorphic variables, distribute the compiled unit without the source code, and the users will be able to create their own objects to work with the compiled procedures. In other words, you don't have to think of everything in advance—the end users can add what they want!

Although the passing of objects as **var** parameters gives you both polymorphism and extensibility, it still has its limitations. The code inside the *ChangeValue* procedure, for instance, only knows about *Person* objects, and therefore cannot modify any fields other than the ones contained in *Person*. The real power of polymorphism comes when you combine virtual methods with dynamic objects, as you will see in Chapter 6.

Recursion

Recursion is a technique wherein a procedure, in the process of performing its tasks, makes calls to itself. How can a procedure make calls to itself? It is a difficult concept to grasp, even for experienced programmers. Recursion can best be described by the classic example, the factorial function. The factorial of integer *N* is the cumulative product of all integers from 1 to *N*. For example, the factorial of 2 is 1 * 2, while the factorial of 3 is 1 * 2 * 3. The nonrecursive factorial function would be coded as follows:

```
function Factorial(N : integer) : longint;
var
  F : longint;
  I : integer;
begin
  F := 1;
  for I := 2 to N do
    F := F * I;
  Factorial := F;
end;
```

The calculation in this nonrecursive example is straightforward: *F*, originally set equal to 1, is repeatedly multiplied by successive **integer** values up to and including *N*. Compare this to this recursive version:

```
function Factorial(N : integer) : longint;
begin
  if N = 0 then
    Factorial := 1
  else
    Factorial := N * Factorial(N-1);
end;
```

The recursive version works by repeatedly multiplying *N* by the factorial of the number just preceding it. While the recursive version is more elegant and intellectually appealing, most programmers find the nonrecursive version easier to understand and code. Which is better? That depends on several things.

On the negative side, recursive procedures have a major weak point: each time a procedure calls itself, Turbo Pascal must set up space on the stack for temporary storage. This not only slows a procedure's execution, but also increases the danger of using up the program's stack space, which could cause the program to crash.

On the other hand, some algorithms are so naturally adapted to a recursive structure that forcing them into a nonrecursive form just does not make sense. A good example of such an algorithm is a function that evaluates a mathematical expression stored in a string. The Calculator program, explained in Chapter 19, Procedure and Function Library," shows how the recursive process follows the flow of the underlying algorithm. Study it carefully.

Chapter *5*

Program Control Structures

This chapter discusses the various control structures Pascal provides, the ways they are used, and their good and bad points.

The least complicated Turbo Pascal program starts at the first **begin** statement of the program block, executes each statement in order, and stops when it hits the final **end** statement. This straightforward program structure is illustrated in the following program:

```
Program PayRoll;

uses Crt;

var

  TotalPay,
  HourlyRate,
  HoursWorked : real;

begin
  ClrScr;
  Write('Enter your hourly rate: ');
  Readln(HourlyRate);
  Write('Enter the number of hours you worked: ');
  Readln(HoursWorked);

  TotalPay := HourlyRate * HoursWorked;
```

```
  Writeln('Your total pay is: $', TotalPay:0:2);
  Writeln;
  Write('Press ENTER...');
  Readln;
end.
```

Programming tasks can rarely be expressed in such simple terms, however. The preceding program, for example, does not take into account that people often work more than 40 hours per week, entitling them to overtime pay.

You can express additional complexity by using *control structures*. Control structures give programs the ability to act differently under different situations. Adding a control structure (in this case, the **if-then** statement) to the preceding program gives it the ability to compute overtime pay:

```
Program PayRoll2;

uses Crt;

var
  TotalPay,
  HourlyRate,
  HoursWorked,
  OvertimeHours : real;

begin
  ClrScr;
  Write('Enter your hourly rate: ');
  Readln(HourlyRate);
  Write('Enter the number of hours you worked: ');
  Readln(HoursWorked);
  OvertimeHours := 0.0;
  if (HoursWorked > 40.0) then
    begin
      OvertimeHours := HoursWorked - 40.0;
      HoursWorked := 40.0;
    end;

  TotalPay := (HourlyRate * HoursWorked) +
              (1.5 * HourlyRate * OvertimeHours);

  Writeln('Your total pay is: $', TotalPay:0:2);
  Writeln;
  Write('Press ENTER...');
  Readln;
end.
```

Here, the **if-then** statement tests whether an individual put in any overtime by comparing the number of hours worked to 40. If the number of hours is greater than 40, overtime pay is clearly due. The expanded equation includes the calculation of overtime pay at 1.5 times the standard rate.

Condition Statements

All Turbo Pascal control structures, with the major exception of the **goto** statement, have one thing in common: they do something based on the evaluation of a condition statement. A *condition statement*, also known as a boolean statement, is any expression that results in either a True or False condition. In **for-do** statements, explained later in this chapter, the condition is implied, but for all other control structures (**if-then**, **while-do**, **repeat-until**), the condition statement is explicitly defined.

Condition statements can consist of direct comparisons:

```
Age > 12
Name = 'Jones'
X < Y
```

or they can include calculations:

```
X > (Y * 12)
(X–15) <> (Y * 12) + Sqr(Z)
```

or they might have multiple conditions:

```
(Age > 12) and (Name = 'Jones');
```

All boolean expressions have a common element: they have a left side that is compared with a right side using a logical operator. Logical operators have already been discussed in this book, but are presented here again:

```
>   Greater than
<   Less than
>=  Greater than or equal to
<=  Less than or equal to
=   Equal to
<>  Not equal to
```

These operators can be used to compare any two expressions when the operands are compatible. For example, it is illegal to compare a **real** with a **string,** or a **string** with an **integer.** You can, however, mix **reals, integers,** and **bytes** in boolean expressions because they are all numeric types.

Simple boolean expressions, those that use only one operator, are easy to understand. For example, the boolean expression **I > 0** is clearly understood to mean "I is greater than 0." Complications arise, however, when you combine multiple expressions with the **and** or **or** operator. The following program illustrates the kind of unexpected results that can occur:

```
Program IntegerOr;

uses Crt;

var
  I, J : integer;

begin
  ClrScr;
  I := 9;
  J := -47;
  Writeln('I or J > 0  = ', I or J > 0);
  Writeln;
  Writeln('(I > 0) or (J > 0)  = ', (I > 0) or (J > 0));

  Writeln;
  Write('Press ENTER...');
  Readln;
end.
```

This program writes out the result of two boolean expressions. Both expressions are legal and appear to test if either *I* or *J* is greater than zero. Since *I* is assigned a value greater than zero, you might expect both expressions to be True. Appearances can be deceiving, however: the result of the first boolean expression is False.

To understand why the first expression is False, you must understand Turbo Pascal's hierarchy of operators. Arithmetic operators (+, −, *, /, **div**) are always executed before logical operators (**and, or, xor**). The **and** and **or** operators, however, can serve as either arithmetic or logical operators, depending on how they are used. In the preceding example, the **or** operator is positioned between two integers, which tells Turbo Pascal to treat it as an arithmetic **or.** When *I* equals 9 and *J* equals −47, the arithmetic result of **I or J** is −39 (using bit arithmetic). Since −39 is less than 0, the result of the boolean expression is False.

The program's second boolean expression, on the other hand, separates the tests of *I* and *J* into two distinct boolean expressions and clarifies the separation with parentheses. (In general, parentheses make boolean expressions more readable and less prone to error.) In this case, the **or** operator is treated as a logical operator. First *I* is compared with 0, which results in True. Then *J* is compared with 0, resulting in

False. Finally, the two results are combined with the **or** operator, giving an overall True result.

Boolean Functions in Control Structures

If a control statement requires an especially complex boolean expression or if the same boolean expression is used in many control statements throughout your program, you should create a boolean function that contains the expression. Using the boolean function in place of the expression decreases your coding and reduces errors. For example, the following program uses the boolean function *Qualifies* to determine whether a potential site for a store is a good candidate.

```
Program SiteEvaluation;

uses Crt;

var
  CarsPerHour,
  PopulationDensity,
  TaxRate,
  LandCostPerSquareFoot,
  LaborCostPerHour : real;

{***************************************************}

function Qualifies : boolean;

begin
  Qualifies := (CarsPerHour > 1000) and
               (PopulationDensity > 5000) and
               (TaxRate < 0.10) and
               (LandCostPerSquareFoot < 150) and
               (LaborCostPerHour < 6.50)
end;

{***************************************************}

begin
  ClrScr;
  Write('Enter number of cars per hour: ');
  Readln(CarsPerHour);
  Write('Enter population density per square mile: ');
  Readln(PopulationDensity);
  Write('Enter Tax Rate: ');
  Readln(TaxRate);
  Write('Enter land cost per square foot: ');
  Readln(LandCostPerSquareFoot);
```

```
  Write('Enter labor cost per hour: ');
  Readln(LaborCostPerHour);
  Writeln;

  if Qualifies then
    Writeln('Good site!')
  else
    Writeln('Forget it.');

  Writeln;
  Write('Press ENTER...');
  Readln;
end.
```

The following boolean expression is complex:

(CarsPerHour > 1000) and (PopulationDensity > 5000) and
(TaxRate < 0.10) and (LandCostPerSquareFoot < 150) and
(LaborCostPerHour < 6.50)

By isolating it in a function, you can substitute the identifier *Qualifies* wherever the full boolean statement would normally go. This reduces the possibility of error (and the amount of typing) and makes it easier to modify the program since all changes can be done in the function itself; these modifications are automatically reflected throughout the program.

Decision Making and Conditional Branching

Based on information it receives, a program can choose between different courses of action. However, if you want your program to make decisions, you must specifically tell it what information it will use, how to evaluate the information, and what course of action to follow. This type of programming is often called *conditional branching* because programs that use this method branch in different directions based on a condition (that is, the evaluation of data).

The If-Then Statement

The simplest form of conditional branching is the **if-then** statement, which causes a program to execute a block of code if a condition is True. This process is described schematically in Figure 5-1.

The first thing an **if-then** statement does is to evaluate the information provided to it in the form of a boolean statement. If, for example, the boolean statement is

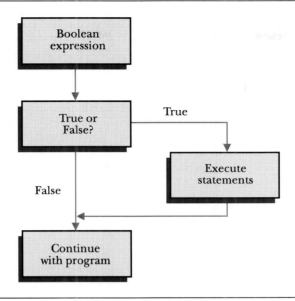

Figure 5-1. *Flowchart of **if-then** statement*

(*Age* > 21), the information is contained in the variable *Age*, which is compared with the test value 21.

The evaluation produces one of two possible results—True or False. If the statement is True, the program executes the block of code that immediately follows the **if-then** statement. If the result is False, the program skips the block. Consider the following example.

```
Program TestAge;

uses Crt;

var
  Age : integer;

begin
  ClrScr;
  Write('Enter Age: ');
  Readln(Age);
  if Age >= 21 then
    Writeln('This person is not a minor.');

  Writeln;
  Write('Press ENTER...');
  Readln;
end.
```

The program asks the user to enter a number (an age), and then the **if-then** statement tests to see if *Age* is greater than or equal to 21. If the result of the test is True, the program executes the statement

```
Writeln('This person is not a minor');
```

The program executes the second Writeln statement regardless of the result of the **if-then** statement. In this example, only one statement follows the **if-then** test. If you want to conditionally execute more than one statement, use **begin** and **end** to indicate what statements are included. For example, the expanded version of *TestAge*, shown here, writes two lines when *Age* is greater than or equal to 21:

```
Program TestAge;

uses Crt;

var
  Age : integer;

begin
  ClrScr;
  Write('Enter Age: ');
  Readln(Age);

  if Age >= 21 then
    begin
      Writeln('This person is not a minor.');
      Writeln('This person is ', Age, ' years old.');
    end;

  Writeln;
  Write('Press ENTER...');
  Readln;
end.
```

The **begin** and **end** statements tell Turbo Pascal to execute both of the enclosed Writeln statements when *Age* is greater than or equal to 21. Although the **begin** and **end** statements are not required when only one statement is to be executed conditionally, you might want to include them for the sake of program clarity and consistency.

The If-Then-Else Statement

The **if-then** statement provides just one branch, which executes when the boolean statement is True. Many times, a program requires two branches: one that executes

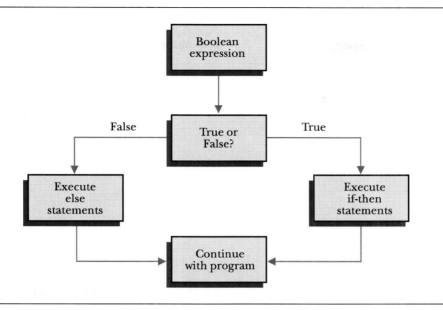

Figure 5-2.   *Flowchart of **if-then-else** statement*

if True, the other if False. This situation is shown in Figure 5-2, where a program executes different blocks of code depending on the outcome of an evaluation.

To express this situation in Turbo Pascal code, you must use the control structure of an **if-then-else** statement. This statement works as follows: if an evaluation is True, the block of code that follows the **then** statement executes; if False, the block of code that follows the **else** statement executes. In either case, when the selected block of code terminates, program control skips to the end of the **if-then-else** statement, as depicted here:

```
Program TestAge;

uses Crt;

var
  Age : integer;

begin
  ClrScr;
  Write('Enter Age: ');
  Readln(Age);

  if Age >= 21 then
```

```
    begin
      Writeln('This person is not a minor.');
      Writeln('This person is ', Age, ' years old.');
    end
  else
    begin
      Writeln('This person is a minor.');
      Writeln('This minor is ', Age, ' years old.');
    end;

  Writeln;
  Write('Press ENTER...');
  Readln;
end.
```

As in the earlier examples, the following statements are executed when *Age* is greater than or equal to 21:

```
Writeln('This person is not a minor');
Writeln('This person is ', Age, ' years old');
```

If age is less than 21, the program executes these two statements:

```
Writeln('This person is a minor');
Writeln('This minor is ', Age, ' years old');
```

 *When writing code that uses if-then-else statements, do not terminate the **end** that precedes the **else** with a semicolon. Turbo Pascal considers the entire if-then-else structure to be one continuous statement, and semicolons appear only at the end of a statement.*

Extending the If-Then-Else Statement

The **if-then** structure provides one branch, and the **if-then-else** structure provides two. But what happens when you need to express a series of conditions? In such cases, you can extend **if-then-else** with the **else-if** statement. **Else-if** statements allow you to chain boolean statements, giving your program the ability to multiple branch (see Figure 5-3). The key element of this figure is the path that the program takes when it finds the first boolean expression to be False. Instead of executing a block of code, the program evaluates a second boolean expression; it is here that the **else-if** statement comes into play. If this expression is also False, the program executes the final block of code.

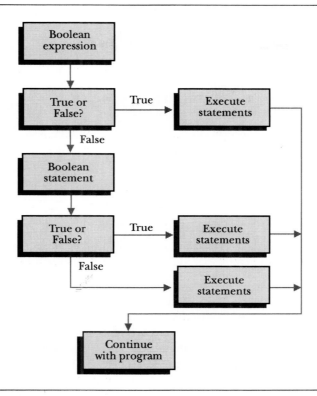

Figure 5-3.   *Multiple branching*

The following sample program demonstrates how **else-if** can create multiple branches:

```
Program PrintGradeMessage;

uses Crt;

var
  Grade : char;

begin
  ClrScr;
  Write('Enter your Grade: ');
  Readln(Grade);
```

```
Grade := UpCase(Grade);
if Grade = 'A' then
  Writeln('Excellent.')
else if Grade = 'B' then
  Writeln('Getting there.')
else if Grade = 'C' then
  Writeln('Not too bad.')
else if Grade = 'D' then
  Writeln('Just made it.')
else if Grade = 'F' then
  Writeln('Summer school!')
else
  Writeln('That''s not a Grade.');

Writeln;
Write('Press ENTER...');
Readln;
end.
```

This program asks the user to enter a grade (A, B, C, D, or F) and prints a message that comments on the grade entered. The program's five boolean expressions result in a total of six branches. (The sixth branch is the statement that follows the final **else**.)

As you can see by now, the **if-then-else** structure is extremely powerful, allowing you to build a tremendous amount of intelligence into your programs.

Nested If-Then Statements

One way to allow your program to consider two or more separate conditions before embarking on a course of action is to nest the **if-then** statements. Figure 5-4 depicts the flow of a nested **if-then** statement.

A nested **if-then** statement can produce very complex branching schemes. Consider this problem: you are running a game of chance using a box full of black and white marbles. A player takes two marbles from the box at random, and, depending on the combination of colors chosen, he or she is paid at the following rate:

First Marble	Second Marble	Payoff
White	White	0:1
White	Black	2:3
Black	White	1:1
Black	Black	2:1

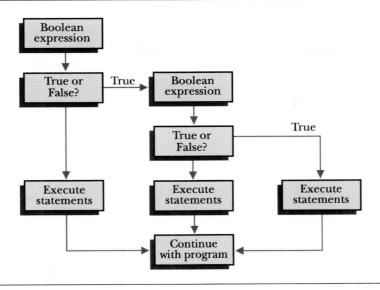

Figure 5-4. *Nested if-then statements*

If the first marble is white and the second is white, the gambler loses everything. If white is first and black is second, he or she loses one-third of the bet. If black is followed by white, the gambler breaks even. Two black marbles doubles the bet.

To code this game in Turbo Pascal, use the **if-then-else** statement, as shown here:

```
Program BetTest;

uses Crt;

type
  MarbleValues = (Black, White);
var
  FirstMarble,
  SecondMarble : MarbleValues;
  I   : integer;
  Bet : real;

begin
  ClrScr;
  repeat
```

```
  I := Random(2);
  FillChar(FirstMarble, 1, I);
  I := Random(2);
  FillChar(SecondMarble, 1, I);

  Write('Enter amount of bet (zero to quit): ');
  Readln(Bet);
  if Bet = 0 then
    Halt;

  if (FirstMarble = White) and (SecondMarble = White) then
    begin
      Bet := Bet * 0.0;
      Writeln('First Marble is White; Second Marble is White');
    end
  else if (FirstMarble = White) and (SecondMarble = Black) then
    begin
      Bet := Bet * (2 / 3);
      Writeln('First Marble is White; Second Marble is Black');
    end
  else if (FirstMarble = Black) and (SecondMarble = White) then
    begin
      Bet := Bet * 1.0;
      Writeln('First Marble is Black; Second Marble is White');
    end
  else { (FirstMarble = Black) and (SecondMarble = Black) }
    begin
      Bet := Bet * 2.0;
      Writeln('First Marble is Black; Second Marble is Black');
    end;

  Writeln('You get $', Bet:0:2, ' back.');
  Writeln;
  Writeln;
  until I > 100;
end.
```

The program explicitly refers to each of the four possible combinations of black and white marbles. It will work just fine, but it could be coded more efficiently in this format:

```
Program BetTest2;

uses Crt;

type
  MarbleValues = (Black, White);
var
```

```
    FirstMarble,
    SecondMarble : MarbleValues;
    I   : integer;
    Bet : real;

begin
  ClrScr;
  repeat
    I := Random(2);
    FillChar(FirstMarble, 1, I);
    I := Random(2);
    FillChar(SecondMarble, 1, I);

    Write('Enter amount of bet (zero to quit): ');
    Readln(Bet);
    if Bet = 0 then
      Halt;

    if (FirstMarble = White) then
      begin
        Write('First Marble is White; ');

        {*****************************************}
        { Beginning of nested if-then statement. }
        {*****************************************}

        if (SecondMarble = White) then
          begin
            Bet := Bet * 0.0;
            Writeln('Second Marble is White');
          end
        else { SecondMarble = Black }
          begin
            Bet := Bet * (2 / 3);
            Writeln('Second Marble is Black');
          end
      end

    else { FirstMarble = Black }
      begin
        Write('First Marble is Black; ');

        {*****************************************}
        { Beginning of nested if-then statement. }
        {*****************************************}

        if SecondMarble = White then
          begin
            Bet := Bet * 1.0;
```

```
            Writeln('Second Marble is White');
         end
      else { SecondMarble = Black }
         begin
            Bet := Bet * 2.0;
            Writeln('Second Marble is Black');
         end;
   end;


   Writeln('You get $', Bet:0:2, ' back.');
   Writeln;
   Writeln;
  until I > 100;
end.
```

The preceding program's first-level **if-then** statement tests for the color of the first marble, and its second-level, or nested, statement tests for the color of the second marble. Rather than testing both marbles in each **if-then** statement, the nested **if-then** structure separates the tests.

The first example evaluates up to three boolean statements before it finds the correct branch. Since each boolean statement contains two comparisons, the program may execute as many as six comparisons before coming to a result.

If you use nested **if-then** statements, however, you do not need to test more than two comparisons at any time. Thus, your program does less work and gives results more quickly than it would otherwise. While the time saved by the sample program is too small to be noticeable, it can be significant in programs with nested **if-then** statements that are repeated many times.

Conditional Branching with the Case Statement

If you need to branch based on the value of ordinal data types (that is, integer types, **char,** and enumerated types) in your programs, you can use the Turbo Pascal **case** statement in place of the **if-then** statement. **Case** provides a logical and clear structure for multiple branching. Here is a typical use of the **case** statement:

```
Program CaseExample;

uses Crt;

var
  Number1,
  Number2  : real;
  Operator : char;
  St, St1, St2 : String[80];
```

```
    P,
    Code : integer;

{*******************************************************}

procedure Compute;
begin
  St1 := '';
  St2 := '';
  P := 1;

  Write('Enter a formula with two numbers (e.g. 1+2): ');
  Readln(St);

{ Pick up the first number }

  while (St[P] = ' ') and (P <= Length(St)) do
    P := P + 1;
  while (St[P] in ['1'..'9', '.']) and (P <= Length(St)) do
    begin
      St1 := St1 + St[P];
      P := P + 1;
    end;

{ Pick up the Operator }

  while (St[P] = ' ') and (P <= Length(St)) do
    P := P + 1;
  Operator := St[P];
  P := P + 1;

{ Pick up the second number }

  while (St[P] = ' ') and (P <= Length(St)) do
    P := P + 1;
  while (St[P] in ['1'..'9', '.']) and (P <= Length(St)) do
    begin
      St2 := St2 + St[P];
      P := P + 1;
    end;

{ Convert number strings to reals }

  Val(St1, Number1, Code);
  Val(St2, Number2, Code);

{ Perform computations }

  case Operator of
```

```
     '+' : Writeln('Answer is: ', Number1 + Number2:0:3);
     '-' : Writeln('Answer is: ', Number1 - Number2:0:3);
     '*' : Writeln('Answer is: ', Number1 * Number2:0:3);
     '/' : Writeln('Answer is: ', Number1 / Number2:0:3);
  end;
end;


{*******************************************************}


begin
  ClrScr;
  repeat
    Compute;
  until St = '';

end.
```

This program asks for a string that contains a simple formula (for example, 1 + 2). It extracts the numbers and the operator from the string, converts the extracted strings into **real** values, and then uses the **case** statement to perform the correct calculation.

Although you primarily think of using a **case** statement when there are many options, the **case** statement is also more readable than the **if-then** statement even for only a few options. For instance, consider this rewrite of the *BetTest2* marble program:

```
Program BetTest3;

uses Crt;

type
  MarbleValues = (Black, White);
var
  FirstMarble,
  SecondMarble : MarbleValues;
  I   : integer;
  Bet : real;

begin
  ClrScr;
  repeat
    I := Random(2);
    FillChar(FirstMarble, 1, I);
    I := Random(2);
    FillChar(SecondMarble, 1, I);

    Write('Enter amount of bet (zero to quit): ');
    Readln(Bet);
    if Bet = 0 then
```

```
      Halt;

   case FirstMarble of
     White:
       begin
         Write('First Marble is White; ');
         case SecondMarble of
           White:
             begin
               Bet := Bet * 0.0;
               Writeln('Second Marble is White');
             end;
           Black:
             begin
               Bet := Bet * (2 / 3);
               Writeln('Second Marble is Black');
             end;
         end;
       end;

     Black:
       begin
         Write('First Marble is Black; ');
         case SecondMarble of
           White:
             begin
               Bet := Bet * 1.0;
               Writeln('Second Marble is White');
             end;
           Black:
             begin
               Bet := Bet * 2.0;
               Writeln('Second Marble is Black');
             end;
         end;
       end;
   end;

   Writeln('You get $', Bet:0:2, ' back.');
   Writeln;
   Writeln;
 until I > 100;
end.
```

Although the logic is exactly the same as the previous version, this **case** statement version is much simpler to understand.

An especially powerful feature of the **case** statement is its ability to interpret ranges, as shown here:

```
Program CaseWithRanges;

uses Crt;

var
  Key : char;

begin
  ClrScr;
  repeat
    Writeln;
    Write('Press a Key (q to quit): ');
    Key := ReadKey;
    Writeln;
    if Key = 'q' then halt;

    case Key of
      'A'..'Z' : Writeln('You pressed an uppercase letter');
      'a'..'z' : Writeln('You pressed a lowercase letter');
      '0'..'9' : Writeln('You pressed a numeric key');

    else
      begin
        Writeln('You pressed an unknown key');
        Writeln('Try again');
      end;
    end;
  until False;
end.
```

When the user of this program presses a key, the **char** variable *Key* stores the character. The **case** statement then evaluates the character according to the ranges specified; if the character falls between "A" and "Z," the program knows it must be an uppercase letter. The last statement in the **case** structure is preceded by **else,** which provides a default branch for variables that do not fit into any of the specified categories. Any time a character is not in one of the ranges A . . Z, a . . z, or 0 . . 9, the program executes the statement that follows **else.**

Repetitive Control Structures

Most programs require a method of repeating a block of code. One way is simply to write as many statements as you need, as in the following program, which reads in five numbers and writes out the sum.

```
Program NoLoop;

uses Crt;

type
  NumberArray = array [1..5] of real;

var
  Numbers : NumberArray;
  Sum : real;

begin
  ClrScr;
  Write('Enter a number: ');
  Readln(Numbers[1]);
  Write('Enter a number: ');
  Readln(Numbers[2]);
  Write('Enter a number: ');
  Readln(Numbers[3]);
  Write('Enter a number: ');
  Readln(Numbers[4]);
  Write('Enter a number: ');
  Readln(Numbers[5]);

  Sum := Numbers[1] + Numbers[2] + Numbers[3] +
         Numbers[4] + Numbers[5];

  Writeln('The sum is: ', Sum:0:2);
  Writeln;
  Write('Press ENTER...');
  Readln;
end.
```

All those Readln statements are not only inefficient, but they also produce a very limited program, one that must have five numbers entered, no more, no less. To improve this program, you can use one of Turbo Pascal's three looping control structures.

For-Do Loop

The **for-do** loop is a particularly powerful looping structure. Nearly every programming language provides some form of this structure, but Turbo Pascal's implementation of it is superior to that of most other languages.

When coding a **for-do** loop, you must specify a starting point, an ending point, and a scalar variable, known as the *control variable,* to be used as a counter. A typical **for-do** loop statement might look like the following.

```
for I := 1 to 100 do
  begin
   {
   statements
   }
  end;
```

The first time Turbo Pascal executes this **for-do** loop, it sets *I* equal to 1 and executes the block of code following the loop statement. When it has executed the last statement in the block, it increases *I* by one. When *I* exceeds the upper limit (in this case, 100), the loop terminates, and control passes to the next line in the program. But as long as *I* is less than or equal to 100, Turbo Pascal continues to execute the block of code.

The following listing is an updated version of the *NoLoop* program. Adding **for-do** loops to a program substantially increases readability and reduces the amount of code needed.

```
Program ForDoLoop;

uses Crt;

type
  NumbersArray = array [1..5] of real;

var
  I : integer;
  Numbers : NumbersArray;
  Sum : real;

begin
  ClrScr;
  for I := 1 to 5 do
    begin
      Write('Enter a number: ');
      Readln(Numbers[I]);
    end;

  Sum := 0;
  for I := 1 to 5 do
    Sum := Sum + Numbers[I];

  Writeln('The sum is: ', Sum:0:2);
  Writeln;
  Write('Press ENTER...');
  Readln;
end.
```

Obviously this code is not as efficient as it could be—you could do it all in one loop with no array (try it). The intent is to show you examples of loops without getting bogged down in the example itself.

*After you complete a **for-do** loop, you cannot rely on the value of the control variable. Officially, its value is undefined.*

One of the secrets to better programming is the use of constants. In the previous listing, the number 5 is used throughout the program. What happens when you decide to change the program to add 10 numbers? To avoid having to change numbers all through the code, use a constant at the beginning of the program. Here is the revised program:

```
Program ForDoLoop2;

uses Crt;

const
  TotalValues = 5;

type
  NumbersArray = array [1..TotalValues] of real;

var
  I : integer;
  Numbers : NumbersArray;
  Sum : real;

begin
  ClrScr;
  for I := 1 to TotalValues do
    begin
      Write('Enter a number: ');
      Readln(Numbers[I]);
    end;

  Sum := 0;
  for I := 1 to TotalValues do
    Sum := Sum + Numbers[I];

  Writeln('The sum is: ', Sum:0:2);
  Writeln;
  Write('Press ENTER...');
  Readln;
end.
```

Repeat-Until Loop

While the **for-do** loop clearly improves the program, it still must read a predetermined number of values. One way you can eliminate this restriction is by using the **repeat-until** loop.

Following is the general format for the **repeat-until** loop.

```
repeat
  {
  statements
  }
until boolean condition;
```

The word **repeat** tells Turbo Pascal to execute statements until it reaches the **until** instruction. Turbo Pascal then evaluates the boolean expression or function in the **until** instruction, and if it is False, the program goes back to the **repeat** instruction and continues executing the block of code.

The main advantage of the **repeat-until** loop is that it does not require you to specify a set number of iterations in advance: it continues to repeat until the boolean expression is True.

The following sample program is a refined version of the previous example. This program allows you to enter from one to five numbers, which are then summed:

```
Program RepeatUntilLoop;

uses Crt;

const
  TotalValues = 5;

type
  NumbersArray = array [1..TotalValues] of real;

var
  I,
  Count : integer;
  Numbers : NumbersArray;
  Sum : real;

begin
  ClrScr;
  Sum := 0;
  Count := 0;
  repeat
    Write('Enter a Number: ');
    Count := Count + 1;
```

```
   Readln(Numbers[Count]);
 until (Count = TotalValues) or (Numbers[Count] = 0);

 for I := 1 to Count do
   Sum := Sum + Numbers[I];

 Writeln('The sum is: ', Sum:0:2);
 Writeln;
 Write('Press ENTER...');
 Readln;
end.
```

In this example, the **repeat-until** loop terminates under two conditions: when *Count* equals 5 or the number entered is zero. For example, if you enter the numbers 1, 3, and 0, the program exits from the **repeat-until** loop without asking for the fourth and fifth numbers. The **for-do** loop that calculates the sum is the same as the one in the previous program, but in this program the upper limit is set to the **integer** variable *Count,* which counts the number of values the user enters. Therefore, the **for-do** loop executes once for each number entered.

While-Do Loop

The **while-do** loop is similar to the **repeat-until** loop, except the **while-do** loop tests a boolean condition *before* it executes any statements in a block. The following code shows the sample program with a **while-do** loop:

```
Program WhileDoLoop;

uses Crt;

const
  TotalValues = 5;

type
  NumbersArray = array [1..TotalValues] of real;

var
  I, Count : integer;
  Numbers : NumbersArray;
  Sum : real;

begin
  ClrScr;
  Sum := 0;
  Count := 1;
  Write('Enter a Number: ');
```

```
    Readln(Numbers[Count]);

    while (Numbers[Count] <> 0) and (Count < TotalValues) do
      begin
        Write('Enter a Number: ');
        Count := Count + 1;
        Readln(Numbers[Count]);
      end;

    for I := 1 to Count do
      Sum := Sum + Numbers[I];

    Writeln('The sum is: ', Sum:0:2);
    Writeln;
    Write('Press ENTER...');
    Readln;
end.
```

If the **while-do** loop finds that the boolean expression is False, Turbo Pascal does not execute the block of code that follows the **while-do** block. Notice how cumbersome the **while-do** loop is in the cases where you want to execute the loop body at least once. This program works around the problem by repeating the Write and Readln statements just before the loop.

Modifying Control Structures

While modifying control structures is never strictly necessary, there are a number of situations where it can yield an elegant solution. Turbo Pascal 7 includes four different ways to change normal program control: the standard procedures Break, Continue, and Exit, and the **goto** statement. This section will show you when each of these is appropriate.

Using Break

The purpose of the Break procedure is to terminate execution of a loop. When your program executes a Break, it exits the loop (or the innermost loop if nested) and moves to the next statement in the program.

In the previous program the while-do loop had a fairly complex boolean condition controlling the program. You can simplify the code by using a Break for one of the conditions, as shown in the following listing:

```
Program WhileWithBreak;

uses Crt;
```

```pascal
const
  TotalValues = 5;

type
  NumbersArray = array [1..TotalValues] of real;

var
  Count, I : integer;
  Numbers : NumbersArray;
  Sum : real;

begin
  ClrScr;
  Sum := 0;
  Count := 1;

  while Count < TotalValues do
    begin
      Write('Enter a Number: ');
      Readln(Numbers[Count]);
      if Numbers[Count] = 0 then
        Break;
      Count := Count + 1;
    end;

  for I := 1 to Count do
    Sum := Sum + Numbers[I];

  Writeln('The sum is: ', Sum:0:2);
  Writeln;
  Write('Press ENTER...');
  Readln;
end.
```

Using Break in this case makes it obvious that you normally expect the user to enter all five values, but you give them an alternative of entering a zero.

Another common use of the Break procedure is in error handling. Study this program:

```pascal
Program DivideWithBreak;

uses Crt;

const
  TotalValues = 100;
```

```
type
  NumberArray = array [1..TotalValues] of real;

var
  Divisors,
  Dividends,
  Quotients : NumberArray;
  I : integer;

begin
  ClrScr;
  Randomize;

  for I := 1 to TotalValues do
    begin
      Dividends[I] := Random(10);
      Divisors[I] := Random(10);
      Write (I:4, Dividends[I]:7:2, Divisors[I]:7:2);
      if Divisors[I] = 0 then
        begin
          Writeln;
          Writeln('Error: Division by zero');
          Break;
        end;
      Quotients[I] := Dividends[I] / Divisors[I];
      Writeln(Quotients[I]:7:2);
    end;

  Writeln;
  Write('Press ENTER...');
  Readln;
end.
```

This program relies on three arrays of integers. The main loop divides the elements in one array by the elements in another and assigns the result to an element in a third array. Whenever you divide in Turbo Pascal, you risk a run-time error if the divisor is zero, so the program first tests the divisor to see if it is zero, in which case the Break procedure is used to get out of the loop.

Using Continue

If you have FORTRAN programming experience, you're already familiar with a Continue command. In Turbo Pascal, you use Continue to mean "Go back to the start of the loop." One of the most popular uses of Continue is verifying user input. In this next listing, Continue is used to handle the situation where the user accidently types a non-numeric entry:

```
Program WhileWithBreakAndContinue;

uses Crt;
const
  TotalValues = 5;

type
  NumbersArray = array [1..TotalValues] of real;

var
  Count, I : integer;
  Numbers : NumbersArray;
  Sum : real;

begin
  ClrScr;
  Sum := 0;
  Count := 1;

  while Count < TotalValues do
    begin
      Write('Enter a Number: ');
      {$I-}
      Readln(Numbers[Count]);
      {$I+}
      if IOResult > 0 then
        begin
          Writeln ('You must enter a number.');
          Continue;
        end;
      if Numbers[Count] = 0 then
        Break;
      Count := Count + 1;
    end;

  for I := 1 to Count do
    Sum := Sum + Numbers[I];

  Writeln('The sum is: ', Sum:0:2);
  Writeln;
  Write('Press ENTER...');
  Readln;
end.
```

Without Continue, you would need another loop inside the first that loops until the user enters a valid number. The Continue procedure simplifies this effort.

Consult Chapter 7, "Files," if you are unfamiliar with the use of the IOResult function.

Using Exit

The Exit procedure is very similar to Break, except it works for entire subprograms rather than loops. Consider the following program. In it, a three-dimensional array is searched until an element with the value of 1 is found. This first approach uses a series of nested **while-do** statements:

```
Program FindUsingWhile;

uses Crt;

type
  ThreeDArray = array [1..25, 1..25, 1..25] of byte;

var
  I, J, K : integer;
  TheArray : ThreeDArray;

begin
  ClrScr;
  FillChar(TheArray, SizeOf(TheArray), 0);
  TheArray[20,20,20] := 1;

  I := 1;
  J := 1;
  K := 1;

  while (I <= 25) and (TheArray[I, J, K] <> 1) do
    begin
      while (J <= 25) and (TheArray[I, J, K] <> 1) do
        begin
          while (K <= 25) and (TheArray[I, J, K] <> 1) do
            K := K + 1;
          if K > 25 then
            begin
              K := 1;
              J := J + 1;
            end;
        end;
      if J > 25 then
        begin
          J := 1;
```

```
        I := I + 1;
      end;
   end;

  Writeln('Found at: ', I, ', ', J, ', ', K);

  Writeln;
  Write('Press ENTER...');
  Readln;
end.
```

As you can see, there is a lot of extra logic included to ensure that the processing stops once the value is found.

A better solution is to use the standard procedure Exit. This procedure causes the program to return out of the current subprogram. The following program is the other implementation of the search program. This one uses Exit to gracefully return from a procedure once the value is found:

```
Program FindUsingExit;

uses Crt;

type
  ThreeDArray = array [1..25, 1..25, 1..25] of byte;

var
  I, J, K : integer;
  TheArray : ThreeDArray;

procedure FindIt;
begin
  for I := 1 to 25 do
    for J := 1 to 25 do
      for K := 1 to 25 do
        if TheArray[I,J,K] = 1 then
          Exit;
end;

begin
  ClrScr;
  FillChar(TheArray, SizeOf(TheArray), 0);
  TheArray[20,20,20] := 1;

  FindIt;
  Writeln('Found at: ', I, ', ', J, ', ', K);

  Writeln;
  Write('Press ENTER...');
```

```
  Readln;
end.
```

The Break procedure would not work in this situation because there are several nested loops.

 If Exit is used in the main program, it halts the entire program.

Using Goto

The term *unstructured branching* describes what happens when a program jumps directly from one point to another. This process is also known as direct transfer or unconditional branching. The latter term is misleading because unstructured branching can and usually is used with a boolean condition statement. Turbo Pascal allows unstructured branching through the **goto** statement, which is used with a label identifier. The label identifier marks the position in the program to which control is to be transferred.

As you learned in Chapter 1, "Turbo Pascal Program Structure," labels are declared with the Turbo Pascal reserved word **label,** followed by the label identifiers, which are separated by commas and terminated with a semicolon.

```
label
  Point1,
  Point2;
```

You can place the label identifiers in the program at locations to which you wish to transfer control. To do this, simply type the label identifier followed by a colon, as shown here:

```
I := 1;
Writeln(I);

Point1:
B := J / 3;
```

To execute a **goto** statement, simply specify the label to which the code is to branch. For example, the instruction

```
goto Point1;
```

tells Turbo Pascal to skip directly to the point in the program where the label *Point1* is located. The following program shows an example of unstructured branching:

```
Program GoToExample;

uses Crt;

var
  I : integer;
  Ch : char;

label
  Retry,
  Stop,
  DoLoop,
  Next,
  Male,
  Female;

begin
  ClrScr;
  Retry:
  Write('What is your sex: ');
  Readln(Ch);
  Ch :=UpCase(Ch);

  if not (Ch in ['F', 'M']) then
    goto Retry;

  if Ch = 'M' then
    goto Male
  else
    goto Female;

  Male:
    Writeln('Sex is Male');
    goto DoLoop;

  Female:
    Writeln ('Sex is Female');

  DoLoop:
  I := 1;

  Next:
  I := I + 1;

  if I > 10 then
    goto Stop;

  Writeln('I = ', I);
  goto Next;
```

```
 Stop:
 Writeln;
 Write('Press ENTER...');
 Readln;
end.
```

If you have been programming in FORTRAN 4, you may be comfortable with the
previous listing. However, you must admit that it is extremely difficult to follow.
Compare it with the following listing, which is the same program using proper control
structures:

```
Program NoGotoExample;

uses Crt;

var
  I : integer;
  Ch : char;

begin
  ClrScr;

  repeat
    Write('What is your sex: ');
    Readln(Ch);
    Ch := UpCase(Ch);

    if Ch = 'M' then
      Writeln('Sex is Male')
    else if Ch = 'F' then
      Writeln('Sex is Female');

  until Ch in ['F', 'M'];

  for I := 1 to 10 do
    Writeln('I = ', I);

  Writeln;
  Write('Press ENTER...');
  Readln;
end
```

As discussed in the introduction, the Pascal language was developed to do away
with the **goto** statement. Turbo Pascal supports the **goto** statement, but with one
major restriction that attempts to keep it from being misused: Turbo Pascal will not
let you transfer control to a label that is outside the current program block. In other

words, you can jump to a point within a program or procedure block, but you cannot jump from one procedure into another. The advantage of using Exit, Break, and Continue over **goto** is that you know exactly where the next statement will be—no more searching for labels.

Turbo Pascal offers both structured and unstructured methods for creating clear, concise applications. This variety of tools makes programming in Turbo Pascal especially rewarding, allowing you to develop a personal programming style while encouraging you to learn good programming habits.

Chapter *6*

Pointers, Dynamic Memory Allocation, and Polymorphism

Turbo Pascal uses different segments, or parts, of your computer's memory for different purposes. Some segments hold the instructions your computer executes, while the others store data. Although most of memory management in Turbo Pascal is "behind the scenes," an understanding of these segments and their roles will lead to better use of memory.

This chapter begins by introducing you to how Turbo Pascal manages RAM. Then it explains pointer variables and the procedures that manipulate them. Finally it applies pointer concepts by describing code that implements linked lists, using both records and objects. Also included in this chapter is a detailed discussion of polymorphism.

The Memory Model

Turbo Pascal divides your computer's memory into four parts—the code segment, the data segment, the stack segment, and the heap. Programs that use units have a code segment for each unit as well as for the main program. All programs, however, have only one data segment, which contains typed constants and global variables.

Although the data segment is clearly dedicated to data storage, data also can be stored in other locations. The stack and heap hold dynamic data, allocating memory as it is needed. While the stack is critically important, its operation is controlled automatically by Turbo Pascal—you can't do much with the stack yourself. The heap, on the other hand, is especially important for advanced programming techniques. This chapter discusses the role of the heap and how you can use *dynamic memory allocation* in your programs.

DOS Memory Mapping Conventions

The first step in understanding how Turbo Pascal manages memory is to learn something about the internal workings of your microcomputer. A computer has a certain amount of RAM (random access memory). Let's say yours has 640 kilobytes. A kilobyte represents 1024 bytes, so your 640K computer really has a total of 655,360 bytes of RAM.

When your program first starts, it sets up a segment that holds the program's instructions (the code segment or segments), a segment to hold the program's data (the data segment), and a segment to hold temporary data (the stack segment). As the instructions in the code segment execute, they manipulate data in both the data segment and the stack segment.

How does the program know at which byte these three segments begin? For that matter, how does a program locate any particular byte in memory? By using addresses. Every byte has an *address,* a 20-bit value that uniquely identifies that location. When a program needs to access a particular byte, it uses the address to find the byte's location in memory.

If a computer's address consisted of a single word (two bytes), it could not address more than 64K (65,536 bytes) of RAM. This was the case for the early 8-bit microprocessors.

The advent of 16-bit processors, particularly the Intel 8086/88 family, ushered in a new memory-addressing scheme, known as *segmented addressing*. Segmented addressing combines two word values—a segment and an offset—to form a 20-bit address. Think of segments as blocks on a street and offsets as the houses on each block.

Each segment holds 64K of RAM. The 8086/88 processors have 16 segments, resulting in 1,048,560 bytes (1 *megabyte*) of addressable memory. However, in real mode, the DOS operating system limits the amount of memory your computer can use to 640K. In protected mode, you are only limited by the amount of available RAM on your machine.

Segments and Offsets

Turbo Pascal provides two standard functions, Seg and Ofs, that make it easy to explore memory addressing on your PC. Seg provides the segment in which a variable resides, and Ofs provides its offset. The following program uses these functions to display the addresses of four variables:

```pascal
Program Addresses;
uses Crt;
type
  St4 = string[4];
var
  I : word;
  S : string[5];
  R1 : real;
  Ch : char;

{**********************************************}

function WordToHex(W : word) : St4;
var
  HexStr : St4;

  {**********************************************}

  function Translate(B : byte) : char;
    begin
      if B < 10 then
        Translate := Chr(B + 48)
      else
        Translate := Chr(B + 55);
    end;

  {**********************************************}

begin
  HexStr := '';
  HexStr := HexStr + Translate(Hi(W) shr 4);
  HexStr := HexStr + Translate(Hi(W) and 15);
  HexStr := HexStr + Translate(Lo(W) shr 4);
  HexStr := HexStr + Translate(Lo(W) and 15);
  WordToHex := HexStr;
end;

{**********************************************}

begin
  ClrScr;
  Writeln('word:    ', WordToHex(Seg(I)), ':', WordToHex(Ofs(I)));
  Writeln('string:  ', WordToHex(Seg(S)), ':', WordToHex(Ofs(S)));
  Writeln('real:    ', WordToHex(Seg(R1)), ':', WordToHex(Ofs(R1)));
  Writeln('char:    ', WordToHex(Seg(Ch)), ':', WordToHex(Ofs(Ch)));

  Writeln;
  Write('Press ENTER...');
```

```
   Readln;
end.
```

This program defines four variables of different types and then displays the addresses of each of the variables. For example, the statement **Seg(I)** finds the segment of variable *I,* while **Ofs(I)** returns the offset.

The function *WordToHex* accepts a **word** parameter and returns the hexadecimal value as a string of four characters. Segments and offsets are customarily shown in hexadecimal format.

When you run the previous program, your screen will show the following messages, though you will see different numbers because your computer may be configured differently.

```
word :    8766:005C
string:   8766:005E
real :    8766:0064
char :    8766:006A

Press ENTER...
```

As you can see, all the variables, which are global, have the same segment. (Global variables all reside in the data segment.) Furthermore, the distance between offsets exactly matches the number of bytes needed to store each variable type. For example, a **word** starts at offset 5Ch and requires two bytes of storage; the next variable in line (a **string**) starts at offset 5Eh.

Turbo Pascal typed constants are stored in the data segment, while untyped constants exist in the code segment. Actually, untyped constants simply become part of the computer code. For this reason, untyped constants do not have addresses.

Variables that are declared in procedures and functions are stored on the stack, a dynamic data storage area. When a program calls a procedure, Turbo Pascal allocates space on the stack for the procedure's local variables. As Turbo Pascal adds variables to the stack, the stack grows downward in memory. When the procedure ends, Turbo Pascal discards these variables and frees the memory to be used again.

The fourth segment in Turbo Pascal memory, the heap, is a dynamic data area that you control. The heap allows efficient use of memory because it eliminates the need to preserve all the data structures throughout a program; instead, you can create a variable on the heap at one point, remove it from the heap at another, and then reuse the space for another variable at still another place.

The following program demonstrates how data can exist in any of the four Turbo Pascal segments:

```
Program Segments;

uses Crt;

type
  St4 = string[4];
```

```
var
  X : word;
  P : ^word;

{**********************************************}

function WordToHex(W : word): St4;
var
  HexStr : St4;

  {**********************************************}

  function Translate(B : byte) : char;
  begin
    if B < 10 then
      Translate := Chr(B + 48)
    else
      Translate := Chr(B + 55);
  end;

  {**********************************************}

begin
  HexStr := '';
  HexStr := HexStr + Translate(Hi(W) shr 4);
  HexStr := HexStr + Translate(Hi(W) and 15);
  HexStr := HexStr + Translate(Lo(W) shr 4);
  HexStr := HexStr + Translate(Lo(W) and 15);
  WordToHex := HexStr;
end;

{**********************************************}

procedure ShowCodeSegment;
begin
  Writeln;
  Writeln('The code segment is ', WordToHex(Cseg));
end;

{**********************************************}

procedure ShowDataVariable;
begin
  Writeln;
  Writeln('The location of global variable X is ',
      WordToHex(Seg(X)), ':',
      WordToHex(Ofs(X)));
  Writeln('This is in the data segment.');
end;
```

```
{*********************************************}

procedure ShowStackVariable;
var
  I : word;
begin
  Writeln;
  Writeln('The location of variable I is ',
          WordToHex(Seg(I)), ':',
          WordToHex(Ofs(I)));
  Writeln('This is in the stack segment.');
end;

{*********************************************}

procedure ShowHeapVariable;
begin
  Writeln;
  Writeln('The location of pointer variable P is ',
          WordToHex(Seg(P^)), ':',
          WordToHex(Ofs(P^)));
  Writeln('This is on the heap.');
end;

{*********************************************}

begin
  ClrScr;
  Writeln('Addresses are shown in the format Segment:Offset.');
  New(P);
  ShowCodeSegment;
  ShowDataVariable;
  ShowHeapVariable;
  ShowStackVariable;

  Writeln;
  Write('Press ENTER...');
  Readln;
end.
```

When you run this program, your terminal will display output that looks something like Figure 6-1.

Each of the four variables in this example resides in a different segment. The first location, that of the code segment, is 8711. The variable *X* is located in the data segment (87A1). Pointer variable *P*, placed on the heap with the statement **New(P),** is located in segment 8BCF.

```
Addresses are shown in the format Segment:Offset.

The code segment is 8711

The location of global variable X is 87A1:005C
This is in the data segment.

The location of pointer variable P is 8BCF:0000
This is on the heap.

The location of variable I is 87CF:3FF8
This is in the stack segment.

Press ENTER...
```

Figure 6-1.   *Sample output of program segments.*

The last variable listed is a local variable declared within a procedure. All local variables get stored on the stack, and in this example the stack segment begins at 87CF.

Figure 6-2 provides a schematic diagram of Turbo Pascal's memory. The lines separating the segments are matched with the hexadecimal values from the sample program. The code segment occupies lowest memory followed by the data and stack

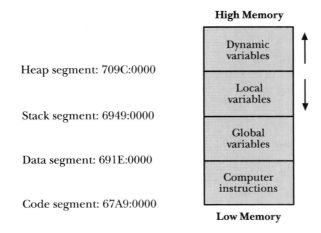

Figure 6-2.   *Turbo Pascal memory allocation*

segments. The heap occupies all the high memory that is left over, up to the maximum you set with the $M compiler directive. The diagram also demonstrates that the stack grows downward and the heap grows upward.

Pointers

Most variables you declare in Turbo Pascal are *static*, that is, memory is allocated to them from the time the program starts until it ends. The heap, on the other hand, uses dynamic data types known as *pointers*. Pointer variables are dynamic because you can create them and dispose of them while a program is running. In short, different pointer variables can use and reuse memory on the heap.

Using pointer variables on the heap offers two main advantages. First, it expands the total amount of data space available to a program. The data segment is limited to 64 kilobytes, but the heap is limited only by the amount of RAM in your computer.

The second advantage of using pointer variables on the heap is that it allows your program to use less memory. For example, a program might have two very large data structures, but only one of them is used at a time. If these data structures are declared globally, they reside in the data segment and occupy memory at all times. However, if these data structures are defined as pointers, they can be put on the heap and taken off as needed, thus reducing your program's memory requirements.

The Pointer Variable

A pointer variable does not hold data in the same way that other variables do. Instead, it holds the address that points to a variable located on the heap. Suppose you have a pointer variable named *Px* that holds the address of an **integer.** Now, you can use *Px* to point to the **integer,** but *Px* itself is not the **integer.** If you are confused, this example, which demonstrates the simple use of a pointer variable, may help. The following program listing demonstrates the simple use of a pointer variable:

```
Program PointerDemo;

uses Crt;

type
  St4 = string[4];
var
  I : ^integer;
{*********************************************}
function WordToHex(W : word) : St4;
var
  HexStr : St4;
{*********************************************}
```

```
  function Translate(B : byte) : char;
  begin
    if B < 10 then
      Translate := Chr(B + 48)
    else
      Translate := Chr(B + 55);
  end;
{***********************************************}
begin
  HexStr := '';
  HexStr := HexStr + Translate(Hi(W) shr 4);
  HexStr := HexStr + Translate(Hi(W) and 15);
  HexStr := HexStr + Translate(Lo(W) shr 4);
  HexStr := HexStr + Translate(Lo(W) and 15);
  WordToHex := HexStr;
end;
{***********************************************}
begin
  ClrScr;
  New(I);
  I^ := 100;
  Writeln('The value of I is: ', WordToHex(Ofs(I)));
  Writeln('The value that I points to is: ', I^);
  Dispose(I);
  Writeln;
  Write('Press ENTER...');
  Readln;
end.
```

The ^ placed before the data type in the definition tells Turbo Pascal to define *I* as a pointer variable:

```
I : ^integer;
```

When the program starts, the heap is a blank slate. Before you can use pointer *I,* you must use the statement **New(I)** to tell Turbo Pascal to assign an address on the heap to the pointer *I.* **Dispose(I),** which appears near the end of the program, is the opposite of New. Dispose effectively takes a variable off the heap, allowing memory to be used for other variables.

Once you place it on the heap, you can use the variable in assignment and arithmetic statements by adding the ^ symbol to the identifier:

```
I^ := 100;
```

The ^ tells Turbo Pascal that you are referring to the variable on the heap and not to the pointer itself. What would happen if the statement were **I := 100**? This

```
Type
  St10 = string[10];
var
  I : ^integer;
  R : ^real;
  S10 : ^St10;
  W : ^word;
```

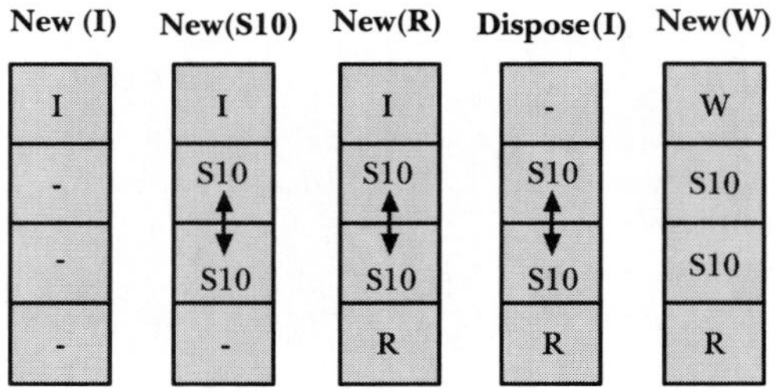

New (I)	New(S10)	New(R)	Dispose(I)	New(W)
I	I	I	-	W
-	S10 ↕	S10 ↕	S10 ↕	S10
-	S10	S10	S10	S10
-	-	R	R	R

Figure 6-3.   *Dynamic allocation using New and Dispose*

statement changes the value of the pointer, not the value of the variable on the heap. Now, *I* points to memory location 100 rather than to its proper location.

When you run the preceding program, your terminal displays the following messages:

```
The value of I is: 005C
The value that I points to is: 100

Press ENTER...
```

The first line displays the address that the pointer is holding. In this case the address is 005C. The second line is the value of *I*, the variable at address 005C on the heap.

New and Dispose

When you allocate and dispose of dynamic variables, what actually happens in the heap? Figure 6-3 describes the process of allocation and deallocation. In the figure, Turbo Pascal declares four pointer variables: one **integer,** one **real,** one **string,** and one **word**. The columns represent memory on the heap. Turbo Pascal always allocates memory on the heap in exact amounts. Thus, when the program executes the New statement, the heap provides 2 bytes, just enough to store the **integer** variable.

In the second column, Turbo Pascal allocates a **string** of 10 characters to the heap. Because this **string** requires 11 bytes of storage (10 characters plus the length byte), Turbo Pascal allocates 11 bytes on the heap. In short, the heap always provides as many bytes of memory as are necessary to contain the data structure put on the heap.

The third column in Figure 6-3 shows the additional allocation of a **real** variable, requiring 5 bytes of memory. The next column demonstrates the impact of the Dispose statement. When Turbo Pascal disposes *I*, the 2-byte chunk that *I* was using is released for use by other dynamic variables. This creates a "hole" in the heap. To use this portion of memory again, the data structure must fit into this hole. If not, Turbo Pascal must allocate memory elsewhere on the heap.

In the fifth column, Turbo Pascal allocates a **word** variable to the heap. Because this variable fits into the hole left by *I*, Turbo Pascal reuses that memory.

Using New and Dispose requires careful planning and rigorous testing. One common error is to reallocate the same variable on the heap. For example, the two following statements

```
New(I);
New(I);
```

both allocate an **integer** on the heap, but only one of the **integers** can be accessed as a variable. You not only cannot access the first **integer,** you cannot even get rid of it. Since the *I* pointer points to the second **integer,** it cannot be used to Dispose the first variable. Always make sure that each New is matched by a Dispose.

Mark and Release

Turbo Pascal offers an alternative to using New and Dispose to dynamically allocate memory: Mark and Release. Instead of leaving holes in the heap the way New and Dispose do, Mark and Release lop off an entire end of the heap from a particular point onward. This process is demonstrated in the following program:

```
Program HeapRelease;

uses Crt;

type
  Atype = array [1..100] of char;

var
  HeapTop : ^word;
  A1, A2, A3 : ^Atype;
```

```
begin
  ClrScr;
  Mark(HeapTop);
  Writeln('Initial free memory: ', MemAvail);
  Writeln;
  Writeln('-------------');
  Writeln;

  New(A1);
  Writeln('Free memory after allocating A1: ', MemAvail);
  New(A2);
  Writeln('Free memory after allocating A2: ', MemAvail);
  New(A3);
  Writeln('Free memory after allocating A3: ', MemAvail);
  Writeln;
  Writeln('-------------');
  Writeln;

  Release(HeapTop);
  Writeln('Free memory after release: ', MemAvail);
  Writeln;
  Write('Press ENTER...');
  Readln;
end.
```

This program allocates three pointer variables—*A1, A2,* and *A3*—and uses the MemAvail standard function to display the amount of free memory left over. MemAvail returns the total amount of memory in bytes available on the heap returns. For example, if MemAvail returns a value of 20, that means there are 20 bytes of memory left on the heap for use in dynamic allocation.

```
Initial free memory: 83888

--------------

Free memory after allocating A1: 83784
Free memory after allocating A2: 83680
Free memory after allocating A3: 83576

--------------

Free memory after release: 83888

Press ENTER...
```

Figure 6-4.   *Sample results after freeing memory*

The previous program uses a pointer variable named *HeapTop* to keep track of the point from which you release memory. The statement **Mark(HeapTop);** stores the current address of the top of the heap to the pointer *HeapTop*. The program calls the Mark procedure prior to placing any variables on the heap. As a result, when it calls Release, it deallocates all the variables on the heap, freeing the memory for another use. Running the program results in the messages shown in Figure 6-4.

As you can see, each time a variable is placed on the heap, the amount of available memory decreases. When **Release(HeapTop);** is called at the end of the program, the amount of free memory reverts to the initial amount. If you had marked the *HeapTop* pointer after *A1* was allocated, only the memory for *A2* and *A3* would be released.

Dispose and Release are incompatible methods of recovering memory. You can choose to use one or the other, but never use both in the same scope of your program.

GetMem and FreeMem

A third method of dynamic memory allocation is GetMem and FreeMem. These are much like New and Dispose in that they allocate and deallocate memory one variable at a time. The special value of GetMem and FreeMem is that you can specify how much memory you want to allocate regardless of the type of variable you are using. For example, you can allocate 100 bytes to an **integer** variable *I* with the statement

```
GetMem(I, 100);
```

Variables allocated with GetMem are deallocated with FreeMem, as shown by the following:

```
GetMem(I, 20);
I := X + Y;
Writeln(I);
FreeMem(I, 20);
```

The number of bytes specified in the FreeMem statement must match that in the GetMem statement. Do not use Dispose in place of FreeMem; if you do, the heap will become hopelessly unsynchronized.

Using the @ Operator

When performing address operations, it is often necessary to assign the address of a variable or procedure to a pointer. This is accomplished with the @ operator, which returns the address of the identifier that follows it. For example, if *A* is an **integer,** then **@A** is the memory address of the **integer** variable. The following code demonstrates how you might use the @ operator with a pointer variable:

```
Program AddressTest;

type
  B_Type = array [1..2] of byte;

var
  I : word;
  B : ^B_Type;

begin
  I := $FFFF;
  B := @I;
  Writeln(B^[1], ' ', B^[2]);
  Writeln;
  Write('Press ENTER...');
  Readln;
end.
```

In this example, *B* is a pointer to an array of two bytes, and *I* is a **word** variable. The program initializes *I* to FFFFh and then assigns the address of *I* to pointer *B*. Now, using the pointer variable, it is possible to treat the two bytes in the **word** variable as separate entities.

The type of the pointer returned by the @ operator depends on the setting of the $T compiler directive (new to Turbo Pascal 7). With $T disabled, all addresses returned by @ are of type **pointer**. This would mean that it would be compatible with any pointer type. Study the following listing:

```
Program PointerChecks;

var
  I : integer;
  WPtr : ^word;

begin
  I := -1;
  Wptr := @I;        {valid only with $T-}
  Writeln ('WPtr^ = ', WPtr^);
end.
```

If you enable pointer type checking, either with the compiler options or a directive, this listing will not compile. If you disable the switch, the program will compile, but you will be doing a type conversion, possibly unintentionally.

The PChar Type

Version 7 of Turbo Pascal includes a new standard type called PChar. If you are accustomed to Pascal naming conventions, you could correctly guess the implementation of this type:

```
type
  PChar = ^char;
```

Although this type is not very exciting on its own, Turbo Pascal has combined it with an extended syntax called null-terminated strings.

The standard **string** type uses the first byte (index 0) to store the length of the string. For example, if you have this program:

```
Program StandardString;

var
  AnyString : string[10];

begin
  AnyString := 'ABC';
end.
```

The variable *AnyString* will be stored like this:

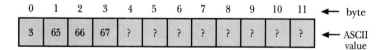

Notice that a variable of type **string[10]** actually uses 11 bytes to store the string.

A *null-terminated string,* in contrast, uses the null character (Chr(0)) to determine the length of the string. In other words, in this similar program,

```
Program NullTerminatedString;

{$X+}

var
  NTString : PChar;

begin
  GetMem(NTString, 11);
  NTString := 'ABC';
end.
```

The variable *NTString* will be stored in this manner:

0	1	2	3	4	5	6	7	8	9	10	11	← byte
65	66	67	0	?	?	?	?	?	?	?	?	← ASCII value

This is how strings are stored in the C programming language. Since the Windows API is written in C, Turbo Pascal uses null-terminated strings to make the interface smoother.

As a more useful example, consider the following definition for GetCurDir in the WinDos unit:

```
function GetCurDir(Directory : PChar; Drive : byte) : PChar;
```

This is a typical windows interface for two reasons:

1. Although it is declared as a function, the return value is basically meaningless, so you will use Turbo Pascal's extended syntax to call it as though it were a procedure.

2. Although Directory is a value parameter, it's contents can and will be changed by the function (the function will only change the character array, not the pointer to it).

Therefore it may be more useful to think of the declaration like this:

```
procedure GetCurDir(Directory : var PChar; Drive : byte);
```

The following program demonstrates the typical way to call GetCurDir:

```
program PCharExample;

uses WinCrt, WinDos;

var
  Dir: PChar;

begin
  GetMem(Dir, 80);
  GetCurDir(Dir, 0);
  Writeln('The current directory is ', Dir);
end.
```

The WinDos unit is covered in detail in Chapter 15, "Dos and WinDos Units."

Pointers with Complex Data Structures

Since the heap is generally used to access large data spaces, pointer variables are generally used with large, complex data structures. Defining a complex data structure including a pointer is a two-step process.

```
type
  CustPtr = ^CustRec

  CustRec = record
    Name : string[25];
    Address : string[40];
    City : string[20];
    State : String[2];
    Next : CustPtr;
  end;
```

Here, the declaration **CustPtr = ^CustRec;** defines *CustPtr* as a pointer to *CustRec*. Note that *CustRec* has not yet been defined. Declaring pointers is the one case in which Turbo Pascal allows you to refer to a data structure before it is defined.

The easy way to manage a group of objects is to define an array. One problem with arrays, however, is that you always have to allocate enough space for the maximum possible number of elements. As a result, you either define very large arrays and waste memory or define small arrays and limit the power of your program. Pointers provide an alternative to arrays—*linked lists*.

Data items in a linked list have pointers that keep track of the order of the list. Singly linked lists use one pointer that points to the record that comes next. The previous listing shows an example of the structure required for a singly linked list. Doubly linked lists have pointers in both directions, so that each data item is linked to the one before it and the one after it. The latter is covered in detail in Chapter 20, "Complex Data Structures."

Figure 6-5 shows the structure of a singly linked list. Each record contains data and a pointer. The pointers indicate which record comes next in the list. The pointer of the last record is set to **nil**, indicating there are no more records in the list.

To change the order of the list, only the pointer values need to be changed. In Figure 6-5, the pointer in Data 1 is changed to point to Data 3, and Data 3 is made to point to Data 2. Now, the pointer in Data 2 points to **nil**, indicating that this is the last record in the list.

Building a linked list in a Turbo Pascal program requires considerable effort. Even so, it is a skill worth learning since many advanced sorting and searching routines use linked lists to increase their speed and maximize memory usage.

You, not Turbo Pascal, are responsible for maintaining pointers correctly, and this takes a bit of doing. First, you must keep track of where your list begins and ends. You must also know which record the program currently is processing in the list and where the next data record is located.

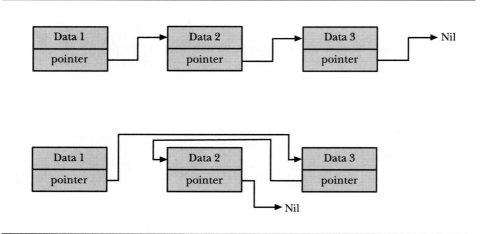

Figure 6-5.   *A singly linked list*

A typical singly linked list requires at least three pointers: one to point to the beginning of the list, one to point to the current record, and one to point to the previous record. The following definition shows how these pointers might be defined:

```
var
  FirstCust,
  PrevCust,
  CurrentCust : CustPtr;
```

If you want to process the list sequentially from beginning to end, you must know the location of the first link in the list. *PrevCust,* which points to the link preceding the current link, makes the pointer called *Next* point to the next record.

A new link in a linked list must be connected to the previous link. The very first link, however, has no previous link and is, therefore, an exception. How does a program know if it is creating the first link or some other link? When the program begins, you must initialize the pointer *FirstCust* to **nil**:

```
FirstCust := nil;
```

The procedure that creates new links tests *FirstCust* to see if it is equal to **nil.** If it is, the program knows this is the first link in a linked list and processes it appropriately. The following program segment demonstrates how these pointers create a linked list.

```
if FirstCust = nil then
  begin
    New(CurrentCust);
    FirstCust := CurrentCust;
    CurrentCust^.Next := nil;
  end
else
  begin
    PrevCust := CurrentCust;
    New(CurrentCust);
    PrevCust^.Next := CurrentCust;
    CurrentCust^.Next := nil;
  end;
```

The **if-then-else** statement checks to see if this is the first link in the list (*FirstCust* = **nil**). If so, the program creates a *CurrentCust* record and sets *FirstCust* equal to *CurrentCust*. It sets the *Next* field in *CurrentCust* equal to **nil** because there is no next link in the chain at this time.

The second time through, *FirstCust* is not equal to **nil** since it was previously set equal to *CurrentCust*. Therefore, the program skips to the **else** branch, where it sets the pointer *PrevCust* equal to *CurrentCust* and creates a new *CurrentCust*. At this time, the program is using all three position pointers: *CurrentCust* points to the newly created link, *PrevCust* points to the preceding link, and *FirstCust* points to the first link in the list. After it creates the new *CurrentCust,* the program sets the *Next* field in *PrevCust* to point to the new link. The elements of these lists are linked by the connection of one record to another with a pointer field.

The following program shows how a singly linked list creates and manipulates a list of customer names and addresses:

```
Program SimpleLink;

uses Crt;

type
  CustPtr = ^CustRec;
  CustRec = record
    Name : string[20];
    Address : string[40];
    City : string[20];
    State : string[2];
    Next : CustPtr;
  end;

var
  FirstCust,
  PrevCust,
  CurrentCust : CustPtr;
```

```
  Ch : char;
{**************************************}
procedure AddRecord;
{**************************************}
procedure EnterData;
begin
  with CurrentCust^ do
    begin
      Write('Enter customer name: ');
      Readln(Name);
      Write('Enter address: ');
      Readln(Address);
      Write('Enter city: ');
      Readln(City);
      Write('Enter state: ');
      Readln(State);
    end;
end;
{**************************************}
begin
  ClrScr;
  if FirstCust = nil then
    begin
      New(CurrentCust);
      EnterData;
      FirstCust := CurrentCust;
      CurrentCust^.Next := nil;
    end
  else
    begin
      PrevCust := CurrentCust;
      New(CurrentCust);
      EnterData;
      PrevCust^.Next := CurrentCust;
      CurrentCust^.Next := nil;
    end;
end;
{**************************************}
procedure ListRecords;
var
  Cust : CustPtr;
begin
  Cust := FirstCust;
  while Cust <> nil do
    begin
      with Cust^ do
        Writeln(Name, ', ', Address, ', ', City, ', ', State);
      Cust := Cust^.Next;
    end;
```

```
  Writeln;
  Write('Press ENTER...');
  Readln;
end;
{*************************************}
begin
  FirstCust := nil;
  repeat
    ClrScr;
    repeat
      Write('A)dd a customer, L)ist customers, Q)uit: ');
      Ch := ReadKey;
      if Ch = #0 then
        Ch := ReadKey;
      Writeln;
      Ch := Upcase(Ch);
    until Ch In ['A', 'L', 'Q'];

    if Ch = 'A' then
      AddRecord
    else if Ch = 'L' then
      ListRecords;

  until Ch = 'Q';
end.
```

The procedure *ListRecords* demonstrates how to process a linked list sequentially. The essential parts of the code are as follows:

```
CurrentCust := FirstCust;
while CurrentCust <> nil do
  begin
    { Statements }
    CurrentCust := CurrentCust.Next;
  end;
```

The procedure sets pointer *CurrentCust* equal to *FirstCust,* the first item in the list. Next, a **while-do** loop repeats a block of code until the pointer *CurrentCust* is **nil,** indicating that the program has reached the end of the list. Within the block of code, the last statement

```
CurrentCust := CurrentCust.Next;
```

causes *CurrentCust* to point to the next item in the list.

Even a cursory review of the previous program illustrates the added complexity of using a linked list instead of a standard array. Every time the program needs a new record, it must create it and set up all the appropriate links. And if you want to move backward through a singly linked list, you simply cannot do it. Chapter 20 contains the code for doubly linked lists.

Pointers in Objects

When you talk about dynamic allocation of objects, you must understand that there are two kinds of dynamic objects. There are objects that contain pointers as data fields, and there are variables that are pointers to objects. You could also have a third kind, which is the combination of the first two. Let's look at the first two in more depth. The third kind needs no further elaboration once you've mastered the others.

Objects That Contain Pointers

When an object includes a pointer field, the **constructor** method gets an additional purpose—it is responsible for allocating the memory for the dynamic field. Consider the following object definition:

```
type
  BufferType = array[1..1000] of byte;
  Buffer = object
    Buff : ^BufferType;
    constructor Init;
    procedure SetB(NewBuff : BufferType);
    procedure WriteToFile(var TheFile : file); virtual;
    destructor Done;
  end;
```

The *Buffer* object contains a dynamic data field, so the **constructor** *Init* will allocate the memory:

```
constructor Buffer.Init;
begin
  New(Buff);
end;
```

Since the *Buffer* object contains a virtual method, the **constructor** serves its second function of initializing the VMT.

When working with dynamic data fields, you also use a **destructor** method. The following is the simple code required to perform the deallocation:

```
destructor Buffer.Done;
begin
  Dispose(Buff);
end;
```

Pointers to Objects

Turbo Pascal also supports creating variables that are pointers to objects. The following is a simple example of using a dynamic variable that allocates a *Person* object:

```
Program Dynamic_Objects;

uses PERSONS;

var
  APersonPtr : ^Person;

begin
  New(APersonPtr, Init);
  APersonPtr^.SetLastName('Lederman');
  Writeln('The Last name is ', APersonPtr^.GetLastName);
  Dispose(APersonPtr);
  Readln;
end.
```

Unlike the previous kind of dynamic objects, this kind requires no changes to the unit that defined the object.

You may have noticed a strange syntax in the call to New in the above listing. Turbo Pascal extends the traditional use of the New and Dispose standard procedures. Now both routines can take two parameters—a dynamic variable and a procedure name. The call

```
New(APersonPtr, Init);
```

performs the same task as these two calls:

```
New(APersonPtr);
APersonPtr^.Init;
```

By combining the syntax, you help to ensure that you remember both steps. You also guarantee that they're in the right order.

Dynamic deallocation is a mirror image of allocation. The Dispose command can also include a call to a **destructor** method. This would be the equivalent of calling the **destructor**, then doing a traditional Dispose.

Since the use of pointer variables is very common in OOP, you should include a pointer type for every object declaration. For the units discussed in this chapter, the type

```
PPerson = ^Person;
```

should be added to the PERSONS unit, and the type

```
PStudent = ^Student;
```

should be added to STUDENTS. The remainder of this chapter assumes that these additions were made.

Polymorphism

In Chapter 4 you learned about how polymorphism is applied to **var** parameters in methods. In this section, you will see how dynamic objects and virtual methods combine to give you an even more powerful form of polymorphism.

One of the rules of Turbo Pascal is that all pointer types are *assignment-compatible*. This means that you can pass a pointer to any variable to a subprogram. If you pass a pointer to an object variable to a method, that method can in turn call a virtual method, which gives you extremely powerful polymorphism. Confused? Let's look at a detailed example.

Setting Ourselves Up

Suppose we want to keep track of a list of people. We start with the PERSONS unit, which contains the declaration of the *Person* object. This unit is shown in Chapter 4. We can then build a dynamic linked-list object that stores pointers to variables of type *Person*. Here is the interface section of the PERSLIST unit:

```
Unit PERSLIST;

Interface

uses PERSONS;

type
  PPersonNode = ^PersonNode;
  PersonNode = record
    PersonPtr : PPerson;
    Next : PPersonNode;
  end;
```

```
PersonList = object
  constructor Init;
  procedure AddPerson(ThisPerson : PPerson);
  procedure DisplayList;
private
  First : PPersonNode;
end;
```

Notice there is a record type to represent each node in the linked list. The nodes contain only pointers to objects—this is critical.

The second structure is an object that is the linked list. To initialize that list, we need a **constructor**. The *Init* **constructor** is very simple and looks like this:

```
constructor PersonList.Init;
begin
  First := nil;
end;
```

To add an object to the end of this list, we need code similar to the algorithm described earlier in this chapter:

```
procedure PersonList.AddPerson(ThisPerson : PPerson);
var
  TempNode,
  NewNode : PPersonNode;
begin
  New(NewNode);
  New(NewNode^.PersonPtr, Init);
  NewNode^.PersonPtr := ThisPerson;
  NewNode^.Next := Nil;
  if First = nil then
    First := NewNode
  else
    begin
      TempNode := First;
      while TempNode^.Next <> nil do
        TempNode := TempNode^.Next;
      TempNode^.Next := NewNode;
    end;
end;
```

Note that although the method accepts a pointer to a *Person* object, it allocates no space for the object (only for a new pointer to that object). Therefore, any module that calls this method must have already allocated memory for that object.

The final part of the implementation is the code to display the entire list:

```
procedure PersonList.DisplayList;
var
  Current : PPersonNode;
begin
  Current := First;
  while Current <> nil do
    begin
      Current^.PersonPtr^.Display;
      Writeln;
      Current := Current^.Next;
    end;
end;
```

This method accomplishes the display by calling *Person.Display*. Remember, *Display* is a virtual method (this will be important soon).

Now let's look at a program that tests the linked-list program. This program generates some simple names just to validate the code:

```
Program TestList;

uses PERSLIST, PERSONS, Crt;

var
  APerson : PPerson;
  AList : PersonList;
  Count : integer;

begin
  ClrScr;
  AList.Init;
  for Count := 1 to 4 do
    begin
      New(APerson, Init);
      with APerson^ do
        begin
          SetLastName('Last' + Chr(Count+48));
          SetFirstName('First' + Chr(Count+48));
          SetAge(Count);
          AList.AddPerson(APerson);
        end;
    end;

  AList.DisplayList;
  Readln;
end.
```

If you were to run this program, with all of its supporting units, you would see the output shown in Figure 6-6.

```
Person: First1 Last1
Age: 1

Person: First2 Last2
Age: 2

Person: First3 Last3
Age: 3

Person: First4 Last4
Age: 4
```

Figure 6-6.   *Output from the TestList program*

Where Polymorphism Comes In

At this point, assuming you've understood the example, you're probably thinking of several simpler ways to accomplish the same task. The complexity is required for one critical reason: we can now use the same code for inherited objects, even different objects in the same list. This is polymorphism at its finest—using the same methods to support objects of "many forms." (The term polymorphism comes from combining the Latin word for "many" with the Latin word for "form.")

In case you find this hard to swallow, study the following example. It is a slight change to the previous test program:

```
Program Polymorphism;
uses PERSLIST, PERSONS, STUDENTS, Crt;

var
  AStudent : PStudent;
  APerson : PPerson;
  AList : PersonList;
  Count : integer;

begin
  ClrScr;
  AList.Init;
  for Count := 1 to 4 do
    if Odd(Count) then
      begin
        New(APerson, Init);
        with APerson^ do
          begin
            SetLastName('Last' + Chr(Count+48));
            SetFirstName('First' + Chr(Count+48));
            SetAge(Count);
          end;
        AList.AddPerson(APerson);
      end
```

```
   else
     begin
       New(AStudent, Init);
       with AStudent^ do
         begin
           SetLastName('Last' + Chr(Count+48));
           SetFirstName('First' + Chr(Count+48));
           SetAge(Count);
           SetGrade(Count+5);
           SetTeacher('Teacher' + Chr(Count+48));
         end;
       AList.AddPerson(AStudent);
     end;

  AList.DisplayList;
  Readln;
end.
```

In this program, the object type alternates between *Person* objects and *Student* objects. Since the linked list is storing only pointers, it can handle objects of different types and different sizes. And, since the *DisplayList* method calls the virtual method *Display,* it can display objects of any type that is a descendant of *Person.* The output of this program appears in Figure 6-7.

If you are still confused, type in the code you see in this section and experiment with it. You should be warned that almost all of the objects in Turbo Vision and Object Windows are polymorphic. This means that you must understand polymorphism to take full advantage of the structures that these tools provide. Once you have mastered the concepts in this chapter, you are ready for Turbo Vision and Object Windows.

This chapter gives only a hint at the usefulness of pointers and dynamic allocation. While it is a difficult topic to master, the rewards can be great in terms of program efficiency and flexibility.

```
Person: First1 Last1
Age: 1

Student: Last2, First2; Age 2
Grade: 7
Teacher: Teacher2

Person: First3 Last3
Age: 3

Student: Last4, First4; Age 4
Grade: 9
Teacher: Teacher4
```

Figure 6-7.   *Output from Polymorphism program*

Chapter 7

Files

A computer that does not store programs and data is little more than a powerful calculator. People who bought early microcomputers without disk drives soon found this out—when they turned their computers off, their work disappeared. Of course, your computer does have at least a floppy disk drive and possibly a hard disk drive. This allows you to take advantage of Turbo Pascal's powerful disk file operations. Learning to use disk files is vital to producing useful programs, and Turbo Pascal helps by supporting three basic types of disk files: *text, typed,* and *untyped*. This chapter discusses how you create and use these kinds of files.

All Turbo Pascal files, regardless of type, share common characteristics. First, all files are used for either input or output. Input is when a program takes data from a file and uses it in the program; output stores the results of a program in a file or sends the results to a *device* such as a terminal or printer. As you will see, it is also possible for certain files to be used for both input and output.

Files can be stored on floppy disks and hard disk drives. There are, of course, other storage media (tape, optical disks, RAM disks, and so on), but they are less common. DOS requires that every file have a name of one to eight characters. Filenames can also include a three-letter *extension* that usually helps describe the contents of a file. For example, the Turbo Pascal program file is named TURBO.EXE. The .EXE filename extension tells DOS that this is a program file that can be executed from the DOS prompt. Turbo Pascal source files (the files you create with the Turbo Pascal editor) generally have the .PAS filename extension (for example, PROG1.PAS).

If a file is stored in a DOS directory, the directory path is also part of the filename. If, for example, the file PROG1.PAS is in the Turbo directory on drive C, the full description or *pathname* of the filename is C:\TURBO\PROG1.PAS. DOS filename conventions are discussed in detail in your DOS user's manual. You should be thoroughly familiar with these conventions before using Turbo Pascal files.

Text Files

Text files consist of lines that are terminated by a carriage return and linefeed (CR/LF) and which contain characters, words, and sentences, as shown in Figure 7-1. The CR/LF combination (ASCII codes 10 and 13) is known as a delimiter. A delimiter marks the end of some element, such as a field, record, or in this case, the end of a line.

You can tell if a file consists of text by using the DOS TYPE command. For example, your Turbo Pascal disk comes with a text file called README. If you enter **TYPE README** at the DOS prompt and press ENTER, the file is displayed on the screen in a readable form. If, however, you try to display a nontext file (such as TURBO.EXE) in the same way, you will see only gibberish.

Text-File Identifiers

Before you work with text files, you must declare a text-file identifier in your program. Text-file identifiers are declared just like variable identifiers, except that the Turbo Pascal reserved word **text** is used. An example of a text-file declaration is as follows:

```
Program TextFile;

var
  TxtFile : text;
```

Filename: TEXT.DAT

Line 1	⟶	This is an example of a line of text.[CR/LF]
Line 2	⟶	Every line in a text file ends with a[CR/LF]
Line 3	⟶	carriage return and linefeed.
Line 4	⟶	[CR/LF]
Line 5	⟶	Even empty lines, like the one above.[CR/LF]
Line 6	⟶	50 12.23 0.23 40343 332324[CR/LF]

Figure 7-1. *A typical text file*

In this illustration, *TxtFile* is a variable identifier of type **text.** Before using *TxtFile* for input or output, you must assign it to a disk file. A typical Assign statement looks like this:

```
Assign(TxtFile, 'TEXT.DAT');
```

Once *TxtFile* is assigned to TEXT.DAT, the disk file is never referred to by name again: all file operations refer to the identifier *TxtFile*.

After you assign a file identifier to a disk file, prepare the disk file with one of three Turbo Pascal commands—Reset, Rewrite, or Append. Reset opens the disk file and prepares it as an input file. Only input commands can be used on a file that has been reset. Any attempt to write to a Reset text file generates an I/O (input/output) error.

The Reset command also positions the *file pointer*, a counter that keeps track of a program's position in a file, at the beginning of the file. This causes all input to start at the very beginning of the file and move forward from there.

An attempt to Reset a file that does not exist generates an I/O error. You can override the I/O error, if desired, by disabling the $I compiler directive with the statement {$I-}. Here is an example:

```
Assign(TxtFile, 'TEXT.DAT');
{$I-}
Reset(TxtFile);
{$I+}
if IOResult <> 0 then
  begin
    Writeln ('Input file not found.');
    Halt;
  end;
```

When I/O checking is turned off with {$I-}, any errors are detected by a call to the IOResult function. A value of 0 means the Reset was successful.

Notice how $I is turned off just before the call to Reset, and turned back on just after. You want to disable I/O checking only when you verify the I/O with IOResult.

Rewrite and Append both prepare a text file for output, but they function in different ways. When an existing file is prepared with Rewrite, its contents are erased and the file pointer is placed at the beginning of the file. If the file identifier is assigned to a nonexisting file, the Rewrite command creates a file with the name given in the Assign statement. The Append command, on the other hand, preserves the contents of a file and positions the file pointer at the very end of the file. As a result, any data added to the file is appended to what is already there.

As with the Reset statement, should you attempt to use Append on a file that does not exist, Turbo Pascal generates an I/O error.

When you are finished using a file for either input or output, you must close the file. The Close command performs this task and performs several other tasks in the process. Close makes sure that all data in temporary buffers is stored to disk. This is known as *flushing* the buffers and is discussed in detail later in this chapter.

The Close command also frees up a DOS *file handle*. A file handle is a mechanism that DOS provides to programs, which helps manage file operations. When you Reset or Rewrite a file, DOS allocates a file handle to Turbo Pascal. Because DOS limits the number of file handles, you should always use Close to keep the supply of file handles plentiful. Finally, the Close command updates the DOS file directory to reflect the file's size, time, and date.

Once closed, a file cannot be used for input or output until it is opened again with Reset, Rewrite, or Append. The link between the file identifier and the disk file, however, remains in force even after the file is closed. Therefore, to reopen a file, it is not necessary to repeat the Assign command. This process is illustrated in Figure 7-2.

```
Program FileTime;
var
  TxtFile : Text;

begin
Assign(TxtFile, 'TEXT.DAT');  ◄─── Links TxtFile to the file TEXT.DAT.

Reset(TxtFile);  ◄───────────── Prepares TxtFile to be read.

Rewrite(TxtFile);  ◄─────────── Prepares TxtFile to be written to.

Close(TxtFile);  ◄───────────── Closes TxtFile, updates DOS directory.

Append(TxtFile);  ◄──────────── Reopens TxtFile for additional output.

Close(TxtFile);  ◄───────────── Final closing ensures
                                 that all output is saved.

end.
```

Figure 7-2.   *Opening text files*

Reading Strings from Text Files

Once a text file is reset, you can extract information from it with the Read and Readln procedures. Examples of text-file input can be seen in the following program, in which the disk file TEXT.DAT is linked to the file identifier *TxtFile*.

```
Program Text1;

var
  TxtFile : text;
  S : string[80];

begin
  Assign(TxtFile, 'TEXT.DAT');
  Reset(TxtFile);

  Readln(TxtFile, S);
  Writeln(S);

  Read(TxtFile, S);
  Writeln(S);
  Close(TxtFile);
end.
```

Subsequently, *TxtFile* is prepared for reading with the Reset command. The first input operation in this program example is the statement

```
Readln(TxtFile, S);
```

which tells Turbo Pascal to read characters from the current line in the file and place them into the string variable *S*. After the characters are read, the file pointer moves to the beginning of the next line in the file.

When reading in a string from a text file with the Readln procedure, three possible situations can occur:

- There are exactly enough characters left in the line to fill the string to its maximum length.

- There are not enough characters left in the line to fill the string to its maximum length.

- There are more characters left in the line than are needed to fill the string to its maximum length.

In the first two cases, Turbo Pascal reads in all the characters left in the line, assigns them to *S*, and then moves the file pointer to the beginning of the next line. The string length is set equal to the number of characters read.

In the third case, Turbo Pascal reads in as many characters as necessary to fill the **string** variable and then moves the file pointer to the next line. Any characters between the end of the string and the end of the line are ignored.

The Read procedure operates much like the Readln procedure, but after it reads in a string, Read places the file pointer just after the last character read; it does not move the file pointer to the beginning of the next line. If the Read procedure encounters a CR/LF (or just a simple carriage return), indicating the end of the line has been reached, it stops reading characters and also does not advance the file pointer until a Readln procedure is used.

Reading Multiple Strings per Line

A single Readln procedure can read in several strings at one time. For example, the statement

```
Readln(TxtFile, S1, S2, S3)
```

reads characters from the current line and fills the **string** variables *S1, S2,* and *S3* in order. If the line being read is

This is a line of characters

and the string variables are all of type **string[5],** the strings would be assigned values as follows:

Reading Numbers from Text Files

Text files can store not only words and sentences, but also numeric data. Numbers, however, are not stored in their binary form but as characters. For example, in RAM, the **integer** value 20545 (20,545) is stored as two bytes with a binary value of 0101000001000001. But in a text file, the number is stored as the characters 2, 0, 5, 4, 5, requiring a total of five bytes. When reading the number 20545 from a text file, Turbo Pascal translates the number from a string of characters into binary **integer** format.

As it reads a number from a text file, Turbo Pascal skips the blank characters in a line until it finds a nonblank character. It then reads in characters until it encounters either a blank character, a letter (or other non-digit), or a CR/LF. When the characters are read in, Turbo Pascal combines the characters into an alphanumeric string and converts the string into either an **integer** or a **real** value, depending on the type of variable being used. If the conversion is successful, the number is assigned to the variable; if it is not successful, Turbo Pascal generates an I/O error.

To learn how numbers are read from text files, examine the numeric text file TEST.DAT in Figure 7-3. This file contains three columns of numbers. The first column is integers, the second real numbers in decimal format, and the third real numbers in scientific notation. You can read the three numbers on each line of the file by employing the following statements:

```
Read(TxtFile, I);
Read(TxtFile, R1);
Readln(TxtFile, R2);
```

or by using the equivalent single statement:

```
Readln(TxtFile, I, R1, R2);
```

Turbo Pascal assigns the first number found in a line to the **integer** variable *I* and the next two numbers to **real** variables *R1* and *R2*.

The following program contains a routine that reads the numerical file TEST.DAT and calculates the average of each column of figures.

```
Program ComputeAverages;

var
  F : text;
  I, Count : integer;
```

11	27.53	6.4144900000E+02
21	50.83	1.1843390000E+03
31	74.13	1.7272290000E+03
41	97.43	2.2701190000E+03
51	120.73	2.8130090000E+03
61	144.03	3.3558990000E+03
71	167.33	3.8987890000E+03
81	190.63	4.4416790000E+03
91	213.93	4.9845690000E+03
101	237.23	5.5274590000E+03

Figure 7-3.   *TEST.DAT, a numeric text file*

```
    Imean,
    R1, R2,
    R1mean,
    R2mean : real;

begin
    Assign(F, 'TEST.DAT');
    Reset(F);

    Count := 0;
    Imean := 0;
    R1mean := 0;
    R2mean := 0;

    while not Eof(F) do
      begin
        Readln(F, I, R1, R2);
        Writeln(I:10, ' ', R1:10:3, ' ', R2:10:3);

        Count := Count + 1;
        Imean := Imean + I;
        R1mean := R1mean + R1;
        R2mean := R2mean + R2;
      end;

    Imean := Imean / Count;
    R1mean := R1mean / Count;
    R2mean := R2mean / Count;

    Writeln;
    Writeln(Imean:10:3, ' ', R1mean:10:3, ' ', R2mean:10:3);
    Close(F);
    Writeln;
    Write('Press ENTER...');
    Readln;
end.
```

This program introduces the Turbo Pascal standard function Eof, which stands for end-of-file. Eof is a boolean function that is true only when the file pointer is at the end of your file. It can be used to repeat input commands so that an entire file is processed from beginning to end. In the previous example, the statement

```
while not Eof(F) do
```

tells Turbo Pascal to execute the next block of code until **Eof(F)** returns True, that is, until the last character in the file is read.

Errors in Numeric Input

If the format of a number read from a text file is incorrect, the program produces an I/O error. For example, reading the number 50000 into an **integer** variable would cause an error because the largest integer allowable is 32767. Similarly, reading the number 32.1 into an **integer** variable could potentially cause an error because of the decimal point, which would terminate the input of the integer. The next call to Read would pick up the decimal point, resulting in an I/O error if a numeric value was expected. **Real** variables pose fewer restrictions since numbers can be read with or without a decimal place or in scientific notation.

Writing Text Files

A text file can be used for output after being prepared with the Rewrite or Append procedures, as discussed earlier in this chapter. Once prepared, the Write or Writeln procedures output the file. The first parameter in these procedures, the text-file identifier, tells Turbo Pascal where to send the data. It is followed by any number of variable identifiers or literal values to be output. For example, the following statements write the line "Jones 21" to the text file identified as *TxtFile*.

```
Name := 'Jones';
I := 21;
Writeln(TxtFile, Name, ' ', I);
```

Write and Writeln normally output values without any special formatting. Adding a colon and a number after the parameter, however, specifies that the value is to be right-justified in a space defined by the number. For example, these statements

```
Name := Johnson;
Writeln(Name)
Writeln(Name:20);
Writeln(Name:4);
```

result in the following output:

```
Johnson
             Johnson
Johnson
```

The first Writeln statement is unformatted, so the value is written left-justified. The second statement tells Turbo Pascal to create a field 20 characters wide and to right-justify the value within this field. Since the name "Johnson" is seven characters long, Turbo Pascal right-justifies the name by preceding it with 13 blanks. The third statement is also formatted, but the field width of 4 is less than the length of the value itself. When this occurs, the formatting has no effect. **Integers** follow the same output formatting as **strings**: a single colon followed by the number of spaces to right-justify the number. **Reals,** however, can be formatted with either one or two parameters. The first parameter determines the width of the field in which the number will be right justified, and the second determines the number of decimal places. The following program demonstrates various formats for **real** numbers and shows their results:

```
Program RealFormat;

var
  R : real;

begin
R := 123.23;
  Writeln(R);           { Result:  1.2323000000E+02  }
  Writeln(R:0);         { Result:  1.2E+02            }
  Writeln(R:10);        { Result:  1.2323E+02         }
  Writeln(R:10:2);      { Result:  123.23             }
  Writeln(R:0:0);       { Result:  123                }

  Writeln;
  Write('Press ENTER...');
  Readln;
end.
```

File Buffers

Reading from and writing to a disk file are two of the slowest operations a computer performs. The time it takes for a disk drive to locate data seems like years to a microprocessor. Small chunks of memory called *buffers* are set aside for data to be used in disk operations. Buffers speed up processing by reducing the number of disk reads and writes. For example, suppose a program reads five characters from a text file with the following statements (assuming each variable is of type **char**):

```
Read(TxtFile, Ch1);
Read(TxtFile, Ch2);
Read(TxtFile, Ch3);
Read(TxtFile, Ch4);
Read(TxtFile, Ch5);
```

If the input is not buffered, the program must go to the disk for each character read. If, however, the program picks up all five characters with the first Read statement and stores them in a buffer, the buffer can distribute the characters to the next four Read statements without having to access the disk.

Turbo Pascal provides text files with a standard 128-byte buffer. Every time a program reads data from a text file, the buffer is filled with 128 bytes, even if you only ask for 10. Of course, you will never know the extra bytes are in memory since Turbo Pascal takes care of all that for you.

When you process large text files, the standard 128-byte buffer can cause noticeable speed deterioration. Turbo Pascal allows you to expand a text file's buffer with the SetTextBuf procedure, in which you specify a variable to use as the buffer, for example:

```
var
  F : Text;
  Buffer : array [1..512] of byte;

begin
  Assign(F, 'TEST.DAT');
  SetTextBuf(F, Buffer);
  Reset(F);
```

This code assigns a buffer of 512 bytes to text file F, though you could have made the buffer larger. Be careful, however, not to call SetTextBuf once you have opened a file, or you will probably lose some data. Also, make sure that the buffer is declared globally; if you use a local buffer, you might lose data if the local variable is discarded.

Flushing a File

When writing to a buffered file, Turbo Pascal actually sends the data to an output buffer. When the buffer is filled, the entire contents are written to the disk at one time.

To force Turbo Pascal to empty an output buffer before it is filled, use the Flush procedure. The statement **Flush(F)** forces any data in the *F* buffer to be saved to disk immediately, thus eliminating any possibility that the data will be lost. Closing an output file automatically flushes the output buffer.

Typed Files

Typed files are files that contain data of a particular type, such as **integers, reals, records,** and so on. These valuable files can make your programming easier and more efficient. In fact, typed files provide far faster input and output than do text files.

Unlike text files, which are unstructured, typed files have a rigid structure that is dependent on, and defined by, the type of data they hold. In the following example, the file identifier *F* is declared as a typed file called **file of real.**

```
Program TypedFile;

var
  F : file of real;
```

This declaration tells Turbo Pascal that this file will be used to store only **real** numbers. In fact, this file will store **real** numbers in the same format in which they are stored in RAM. Herein lies the reason that typed files are fast: because they bypass all the translation and conversion processes that data undergoes within text files, they can transfer the data directly to memory.

For example, a file that is declared to be of type **integer** knows that it is to store only integers; the data within it does not have to be converted into integer before it can be processed.

Records and Typed Files

Because they are not made up of lines, as are text files, typed files cannot use the Readln and Writeln statements. But if typed files are not organized into lines, how are they organized? Typed files are organized into records, each data item representing one record. The length of a record corresponds to the number of bytes required to store the data type. In the previous example, the file stores numbers of type **real.** Since a **real** number requires six bytes in Turbo Pascal, the record length for the file is six bytes: the first six bytes of the file contain the first record (**real** number), the next six contain the second record, and so on. For **integers,** numbers that require just two bytes, a typed file is organized into two-byte records.

The following program shows how a typed file is declared, used for output, and then used for input:

```
Program RealFile;

uses CRT;

var
  R : real;
  F : file of real;

begin
  ClrScr;
  Assign(F, 'REAL.DAT');
  Rewrite(F);

  R := 100.234;
  Write(F, R);

  R := 32.23;
```

```
   Write(F, R);

   R := 9894.40;
   Write(F, R);

   Reset(F);
   while not Eof(F) do
     begin
        Read(F, R);
        Writeln(R:0:3);
      end;

   Writeln;
   Write('Press ENTER...');
   Readln;
end.
```

This program writes out three **real** numbers. Since each **real** number requires six bytes, the size of the file is 18 bytes. You can confirm this with the DIR command at the DOS prompt.

Notice the following characteristics of the program just listed:

- A call to Read or Write advances the file pointer.

- The call to Reset moves the file pointer to the beginning of the file.

- Reading or writing to a typed file is done sequentially, unless you use the Seek procedure, described later in this chapter.

Strings and Typed Files

Typed files can also be of a **string** type, but this is very different from a text file. Even though both methods are designed to hold strings, the way they store strings is what separates them. Consider the following example:

```
Program OutputCompare;

type
  Str10 = string[10];

var
  TxtFile : text;
  StringFile : file of Str10;
  S : Str10;

begin
  Writeln('Rewriting OUTPUT.TXT');
```

```
Assign(TxtFile, 'OUTPUT.TXT');
Rewrite(TxtFile);

Writeln('Rewriting OUTPUT.STR');
Assign(StringFile, 'OUTPUT.STR');
Rewrite(StringFile);

S := 'ABCD';

Writeln('Writing to OUTPUT.TXT');
Write(TxtFile, S);
Writeln('Writing to OUTPUT.STR');
Write(StringFile, S);

Writeln('Closing files.');
Close(TxtFile);
Close(StringFile);

Writeln;
Write('Press ENTER...');
Readln;
end.
```

The program declares two files, one **text** and the other type **file of** *Str10*. Both files are prepared for output, and the string 'ABCD' is written to both. This is where the similarity ends.

In the case of the **text** file, Turbo Pascal writes the letters A, B, C, and D and nothing more, as shown here:

In the typed file, however, Turbo Pascal stores the string in its full form: the length byte, the legitimate characters in the string (ABCD), and any garbage characters that fill out the remaining six bytes of storage, as shown here:

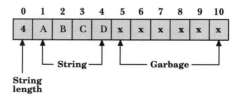

This example demonstrates that **string** files require more space than text files because each file record includes the string length byte as well as any garbage bytes.

The data stored in a typed file has exactly the same form that it has when it is stored in RAM. This fact leads to a huge increase in input/output performance when compared to text-file processing. Why? Because every time Turbo Pascal uses a text file, some time is wasted while numbers are converted into characters and back again and strings are stripped of their length byte and any unused bytes. Data from typed files, on the other hand, can be read directly into RAM without any transformation. That means less work for the computer and, as a result, faster processing.

More Complex Typed Files

Just as you can define your own data types, you can also define a file to hold these data types. For example, a record of data type *CustomerRec* with fields *Name, Address,* and *Telephone* could be stored in a file as defined in the following program:

```
Program RecordFile;

uses CRT;

type
  CustomerRec = record
    Name : string[30];
    Address : string[40];
    Telephone : string[15];
  end;

var
  Customer : CustomerRec;
  CustFile : file of CustomerRec;

{***********************************************************}

procedure CreateFile;
begin
  Assign(CustFile, 'CUST.DAT');
  Rewrite(CustFile);

  with Customer do
    begin
      Name        := 'Tim Freeman';
      Address     := 'Lowell, MA';
      Telephone   := '(123) 456-7890';
    end;
  Write(CustFile, Customer);

  with Customer do
    begin
      Name        := 'S. Cunningham';
      Address     := 'Balboa, CA';
      Telephone   := '(714) 555-4321';
```

```
      end;
   Write(CustFile, Customer);

   with Customer do
     begin
       Name       := 'Sarah Lederdog';
       Address    := 'Big Canoe, GA';
       Telephone  := '(111) 222-3333';
     end;
   Write(CustFile, Customer);

   Close(CustFile);
end;

{*******************************************************}

procedure DisplayFile;
begin
   Assign(CustFile, 'CUST.DAT');
   Reset(CustFile);

   while not Eof(CustFile) do
     begin
       Read(CustFile, Customer);
       with Customer do
         Writeln(Name, ' ', Address, ' ', Telephone);
     end;
   Close(CustFile);
   Writeln;
end;

{*******************************************************}

begin
   ClrScr;
   CreateFile;
   DisplayFile;

   Write('Press ENTER...');
   Readln;
end.
```

Because the file is declared to be of the same type as the record *Customer*, it is possible to read and write a complete record at a time. This increases speed because you do not have to read or write each item of the record separately.

Untyped Files

Untyped files are an especially powerful tool provided by Turbo Pascal. While text files assume that a file consists of lines terminated with CR/LF, and typed files assume that a file consists of a particular type of data structure, untyped files make no assumptions about the structure of the data in a file. You can read data from an untyped file into any data type you want.

Because Turbo Pascal makes no assumptions about the format of the data, the transfer from disk to your data structure is immediate. This is why untyped files are used for applications requiring high-speed input and output.

The following example, which copies the contents of one file to another, demonstrates a typical use of untyped files. As you can see, two file identifiers, *SourceFile* and *DestFile,* are declared to be of type **file.** Untyped files get their name from the fact that the reserved word **file** is not followed by a type specification, as is the case with typed files.

```
Program CopyFile;

uses CRT;

var
  SourceFile,
  DestFile : file;
  RecordsRead : integer;
  Buffer : array [1..1000] of byte;

begin
  ClrScr;
  if ParamCount <> 2 then
    begin
      Writeln('CopyFile [FromFile] [ToFile]');
      Halt;
    end;

  Assign(SourceFile, ParamStr(1));
  {$I-}
  Reset(SourceFile, 1);
  {$I+}
  if IOresult <> 0 then
    begin
      Writeln(ParamStr(1), ' not found.');
      Halt;
    end;

  Writeln('. = 1,000 bytes copied.');
```

```
  Assign(DestFile, ParamStr(2));
  Rewrite(DestFile, 1);
  BlockRead(SourceFile, Buffer, SizeOf(Buffer), RecordsRead);

  while RecordsRead > 0 do
    begin
      Write('.');
      BlockWrite(DestFile, Buffer, RecordsRead);
      BlockRead(SourceFile, Buffer, SizeOf(Buffer), RecordsRead);
    end;

  Close(SourceFile);
  Close(DestFile);
  Writeln;
  Write('Press ENTER...');
  Readln;
end.
```

Unlike text and typed files, the Reset and Rewrite statements for untyped files can take a second parameter, the record size. For example, the statement

```
Reset(SourceFile, 1);
```

prepares the file to be read and specifies that the record length is 1 byte. This makes sense since the data structure is an array of **bytes.** If the data structure were an array of **integers,** you could set the record length to 2, because integers require two bytes of storage. While Turbo Pascal does not require you to match the record length to the size of the data type you are using, doing so makes programming easier. Note that if you do not specify a record length in the Reset or Rewrite statements, Turbo Pascal assigns a default record length of 128 bytes. If you read and write to untyped files, it requires two special Turbo Pascal standard procedures, BlockRead and BlockWrite. In the previous example, the statement

```
BlockRead(SourceFile, Buffer, SizeOf(Buffer), RecordsRead);
```

takes four parameters. The file identifier *SourceFile* is first. The second parameter specifies the data structure into which the data will be placed. In the example, the data structure is the array of bytes *Buffer.*

The third parameter specifies the number of records to read. In the example, the record size was set to 1 byte by the Reset statement. The data structure *Buffer,* however, is 1000 bytes in length. To completely fill *Buffer,* then, you have to read in 1000 records. You could simply write in the number 1000 as the third parameter, but the Turbo Pascal standard function SizeOf offers a better alternative. SizeOf returns the number of bytes used by a specific data structure. For example, if *I* is an **integer,** then **SizeOf(I)** returns the value 2. In the example, the statement **SizeOf(Buffer)** returns 1000 because that is the number of bytes *Buffer* uses. By using the SizeOf function, you can change the size of the buffer without having to change BlockRead statements.

The fourth and last parameter in the BlockRead statement is the **integer** variable *RecordsRead*. When the BlockRead statement executes, it attempts to read in the number of records specified (1000 in the example). However, if the file pointer is close to the end of the file, you may actually read fewer than 1000 records. *RecordsRead* tells you exactly how many records were read by the BlockRead statement. Any time *RecordsRead* is less than the number of records specified, the end of the file has been reached.

BlockWrite operates much the same as BlockRead, except that there are only three parameters. The file identifier comes first, followed by the data structure used for the output. The third parameter is the number of records to write to the file. In the example program, *RecordsRead* specifies the number of records to write because you want to write out exactly what was read in.

Procedures for Typed and Untyped Files

Nontext files (that is, typed and untyped files) are also known as *random access files,* meaning that records in a file can be accessed in nonsequential order. If you want to, you can read the third record first, then the tenth record, and the first record after that. This is done in a two-step process: first position the file pointer at the correct record, and then read the record. This is demonstrated in the following program, which creates a typed data file and then reads the records back in nonsequential order.

```
Program DataBaseFile;
{$v-}
uses CRT;

type
  MaxStr  = string[255];
  CustRec = record
    Name : string[30];
    Age  : integer;
    Income : real;
  end;

var
  Cust : CustRec;
  CustFile : file of CustRec;

{*****************************}

procedure AddRec(NameIn : MaxStr;
```

```
                         AgeIn : integer;
                         IncomeIn : real);
begin
  with Cust do
    begin
      Name := NameIn;
      Age := AgeIn;
      Income := IncomeIn;
    end;
  Write(CustFile,Cust);
end;

{****************************}

procedure DumpRec;
begin
  Writeln;
  with Cust do
    begin
      Writeln('Name:    ', Name);
      Writeln('Age:     ', Age);
      Writeln('Income: ', Income:0:0);
    end;
end;

{*****************************}

begin
  ClrScr;
  Assign(CustFile, 'CUSTFILE.DAT');
  Rewrite(CustFile);

  AddRec('G. Jones', 30, 43000.0);
  AddRec('T. Smith', 37, 94000.0);
  AddRec('G. Stechert', 23, 28000.0);

  Reset(CustFile);
  Writeln('The number of records in the file is: ',
          FileSize(CustFile));
  Writeln;
  Write('Press ENTER...');
  Readln;

{*************************************************************}
{ Write out the contents of the third record in the file. }
{ Because the first record in a file is number 0, the third }
{ record is number 2.                                       }
{*************************************************************}
```

```
  Seek(CustFile, 2);
  Writeln;
  Writeln;
  Writeln('This is record number: ', FilePos(CustFile)+1);
  Read(CustFile, Cust);
  DumpRec;
  Writeln;
  Write('Press ENTER...');
  Readln;

{***********************************************************}
{ Write out the contents of the first record in the file. }
{***********************************************************}

  Seek(CustFile, 0);
  Writeln;
  Writeln;
  Writeln('This is record number: ', FilePos(CustFile)+1);
  Read(CustFile, Cust);
  DumpRec;
  Writeln;
  Write('Press ENTER...');
  Readln;

{************************************************************}
{ Write out the contents of the second record in the file. }
{************************************************************}

  Seek(CustFile, 1);
  Writeln;
  Writeln;
  Writeln('This is record number: ', FilePos(CustFile)+1);
  Read(CustFile, Cust);
  DumpRec;
  Writeln;
  Write('Press ENTER...');
  Readln;

{******************************************}
{ Change the contents of the first record }
{******************************************}

  Seek(CustFile, 0);
  AddRec('E. Wilkins', 85, 99999.0);
  Seek(CustFile, 0);
  Writeln;
  Writeln;

  Writeln('This is record number: ', FilePos(CustFile)+1);
```

```
    Read(CustFile, Cust);
    DumpRec;
    Writeln;
    Write('Press ENTER...');
    Readln;

    Close(CustFile);
 end.
```

The Seek statement moves the file pointer to the beginning of the third record. Note that the third record is referred to as number 2 in the Seek statement because Turbo Pascal typed files begin with record 0. When the file pointer is in place, you can read the record as you normally would. After the Read is executed, the file pointer is automatically moved to the beginning of the next record. In this case, the third record is the last record in the file. Any attempt to read beyond the end of the file results in an I/O error.

An example of a nonsequential Read is shown by the following two statements:

```
Seek(CustFile, 2);
Read(CustFile, Cust);
```

Two other standard functions, FileSize and FilePos, are also used. FileSize returns the total number of records in the file; FilePos returns the current position of the file pointer.

An especially powerful feature of random access files is the ability to update records at any point in the file. This is demonstrated at the end of the previous example program (titled *DataBaseFile*), where the information in the first record is changed and then displayed. What is particularly noteworthy is that the Write procedure is used without a preceding Rewrite statement. This seems to go against the rule that a file must be prepared with Rewrite before you can add data to it. For nontext files, the Rewrite command is only necessary to create the file. Once the file exists, the Reset command allows you to both read and write to the file.

Devices as Files

In Turbo Pascal, all input and output are performed using devices such as a keyboard, a monitor, or a disk file. To make things easier, Turbo Pascal lets you treat all devices as files. This allows you to treat all input and output uniformly, making your programming much easier.

All input and output in a program normally are performed using DOS devices. A DOS device is an input or output device that DOS is designed to handle. This includes keyboards, disk drives, and video monitors. Some devices, such as optical disks, tape backup units, mice, and other specialized equipment, are not supported by DOS and require their own *device drivers* to make them work with DOS. Writing device drivers is an advanced topic outside the scope of this book, but every programmer should know how to use DOS devices.

The Standard Input and Output Devices

While all input and output in Turbo Pascal are performed through devices, you are not always aware of it. For example, the statement **Readln(S)** tells Turbo Pascal to accept input from the *standard input* device. Likewise, the statement **Writeln(S)** indicates output using the *standard output* device.

The name of the standard output device is CON, as in console, and refers to the video display. The standard input device is also CON, but refers not to the screen, but to the keyboard. The following program demonstrates how the CON device can be used for input and output much like a disk file.

```pascal
Program DeviceTest;

uses CRT;

var
  F : text;
  S : string;

Begin
  ClrScr;
  Assign(F, 'CON');
  Rewrite(F);
  Writeln(F, 'Output to CON');
  Writeln;

  Writeln('Enter string using Readln(S)');
  Write('Type a string. Press ENTER when done: ');
  Readln(S);
  Writeln('>', S);

  Assign(F, 'CON');
  Reset(F);
  Writeln('Enter string from CON using Readln(F, S)');
  Write('Type a string. Press ENTER when done: ');
  Readln(F, S);
  Writeln('>', S);

  Writeln;
  Write('Press ENTER...');
  Readln;
end.
```

Notice that the CON device can be used with the Reset or Rewrite procedures, just like a disk file. In fact, the standard input and output devices use the same file handles used by disk files.

Printer Devices

DOS supports various printer devices: PRN, LPT1, LPT2, and LPT3. (LPT1 and PRN refer to the same device.) Most people use only one printer, and so use only LPT1 and PRN devices. Naturally, printers are used for output only. If you try to use Reset on a printer device, Turbo Pascal will generate an immediate end of file (the Eof function will return True).

Turbo Pascal also offers another way to route output to the printer: the Printer unit. This unit declares a text-file variable name Lst, which directs output to the printer. This brief program demonstrates how the Lst variable is used:

```
Program TestPrt;

uses Printer;

begin
  Writeln(Lst, 'ABC');
end.
```

Serial Devices

Most computers have serial ports, which they use for printers, modems, local area networks, and other communications purposes. Turbo Pascal supports two DOS serial devices: COM1 and COM2. In addition, Turbo Pascal supports an AUX (for auxiliary) device, which is the same as COM1.

While these devices make it easy to send and receive data through serial ports, they are far too limited for most purposes. Communications programs, for example, usually need to bypass DOS devices and go directly to the serial port.

The NUL Device

Turbo Pascal recognizes one more device; the NUL device. This device is special because it ignores everything you send to it. You might wonder what use such a device could possibly have. Generally, you will use the NUL device when you are programming an output function, but don't actually want to send out any data.

Chapter *8*

External Procedures and Inline Code

When the first computers were developed, no programming languages existed. Every program had to be entered directly into the computer in the form of machine language, which consists of numeric codes that represent instructions. Writing and maintaining programs in machine language was extremely difficult; assembler language was developed in response to this need.

Assembler uses mnemonic labels rather than numeric codes, which makes it easier both to write and maintain programs. Even so, assembler programming is still tedious and error prone. Many lines of code are needed to execute even simple tasks. In the early days, each type of computer had its own assembler language, which made it impossible to transfer a program from one computer to another.

High-level languages, such as COBOL and FORTRAN, are the next step up from assembler. Because one high-level statement does the job of many assembler statements, programs can be written faster. Another advantage is that programs written in high-level languages can be moved from one computer to another with only small modifications. So as time went on, assembler was relegated to special-purpose programs, while general applications, with few exceptions, were written in high-level languages.

Extending Turbo Pascal

As a high-level language, Turbo Pascal provides a great deal of power and exceptional speed. Yet procedures written in assembler run much faster and give you control over

every aspect of your computer. Fortunately, you can extend the power of Turbo Pascal
by incorporating assembler routines into your programs, thereby combining the logic
and structure of Turbo Pascal with the speed of assembler.

There are three ways to incorporate assembly language into Turbo Pascal programs: *external procedures, inline code,* and the **asm** statement. External procedures are
assembly-language routines that you assemble to .OBJ files and link to your Turbo
Pascal program when you compile it. Inline code consists of machine-language
instructions that you insert directly into your Turbo Pascal program. The **asm**
statement lets you include assembly language instructions as part of your Pascal code.
Turbo Pascal will not catch errors with code from any of these methods, so you must
take great care to see that your assembler or machine code is fully debugged.

Inline Code

Using inline code is much like regressing to the earliest days of computers because
you are dealing with the numeric codes that represent machine-language instructions. Writing inline code is no easy task—it requires a solid knowledge of both
assembler and Turbo Pascal.

To use inline code, you must begin with the **inline** statement, which tells Turbo
Pascal to interpret the parenthetic expression as machine-language instructions. The
instructions themselves are hexadecimal numbers preceded by a dollar sign and
followed by a slash, as shown here:

```
inline($8B/$46/<I/      { MOV AX,I       }
       $03/$46/<J/      { ADD AX,J       }
       $89/$46/$FE);    { MOV [BP-2],AX  }
```

In this example, the comments show the assembler mnemonics that correspond
to the inline code. This inline code moves variable *I* into the AX register, adds *J* to
the value in AX, and then moves the contents of AX to a position on the stack. While
it is not obvious from the code, both *I* and *J* are value parameters that are located on
the stack. If these were global variables, different inline code would be required,
similar to the methods discussed in the section "Using Global Data and Procedures"
later in this chapter.

Notice the use of the size operators < and >. For lack of a better name, let's refer
to < as the byte-size operator and > as the word-size operator. These operators are
used to reference variables. In the preceding example, the variables are value
parameters of type **word.** The byte-size operator is used because the variables are
located using single-byte offsets to the BP register. Using the correct size operator is
vitally important. The only way to be absolutely sure you have done so is to use a
debugger, like Turbo Debugger, to view your inline code in unassembled form.

Discussion of the use of DOS special registers is beyond the scope of this book. For more information, refer to Kris Jamsa's DOS: The Complete Reference (Berkeley: Osborne/McGraw-Hill, 1992).

In the example just given, all inline code is included in a single statement that spans three lines. Another approach is to declare each line as a separate inline statement, as shown here:

```
inline($8B/$46/<I);      { MOV AX,I        }
inline($03/$46/<J);      { ADD AX,J        }
inline($89/$46/$FE);     { MOV [BP-2],AX   }
```

While this approach is more cumbersome, it is also easier to debug with Turbo Debugger. If you were to code all three lines as a single statement, Turbo Debugger would only show the first line as part of the unassembled listing. But if you have made each line a statement, Turbo Debugger will show each line with its unassembled code, making debugging much easier.

The following listing demonstrates a simple inline function that adds two integers:

```
Program TestInline;

uses Crt;

{**************************************************}

function Sum(I, J : integer) : integer;
begin
    inline($8B/$46/<I);      { MOV AX,I        }
    inline($03/$46/<J);      { ADD AX,J        }
    inline($89/$46/$FE);     { MOV [BP-2],AX   }
end;

{**************************************************}

begin
  ClrScr;
  Write('1 + 2 = ');
  Writeln(Sum(1,2));

  Writeln;
  Write('Press ENTER...');
  ReadLn;
end.
```

Notice that the function heading is the same as it would be for a Turbo Pascal function. The function block starts with **begin** followed by the **inline** statement and open parenthesis, which tells Turbo Pascal that machine code follows. Each byte of machine code is entered in hexadecimal format and separated by a slash. The **inline** statement ends with a close parenthesis. The assembler mnemonics, added as comments, have no effect on the program, but help explain what the code is doing.

Now that you have coded the inline procedure, you might be interested to see what the machine-level instructions look like. Here is the unassembled code for the function *Sum*:

```
PUSH    BP
MOV     BP,SP
SUB     SP,+02

MOV     AX,[BP+06]
ADD     AX,[BP+04]
MOV     [BP-02],AX

MOV     AX,[BP-02]
MOV     SP,BP
POP     BP
RETF    0004
```

The three lines in the middle of the listing are the inline statements. To these, Turbo Pascal has added seven instructions. The first three lines set up the stack on entry to the procedure. Of these, the first two lines are standard to any procedure or function call. The third line, "SUB   SP,+02", is used for functions that return one-byte or two-byte results. In other words, Turbo Pascal reserves two bytes on the stack as a temporary holding place for the function result.

The last four lines in the listing move the function result from the stack into the AX register, restore the SP and BP registers to their original values, and make a far return while popping the parameters off the stack.

Returning function results in inline procedures can be tricky. Turbo Pascal expects to find the function result at a specific location on the stack. You must make sure the function result gets placed on the stack before the procedure ends.

Notice that a far return is used to terminate the function because the $F+ compiler directive was enabled when the program was compiled. As you can see, writing inline procedures and functions is not easy. Not only do you need to work in machine language, but you also need to know how Turbo Pascal works at the assembler level.

All in all, it is far easier and more productive to use the **asm** statement (covered later) instead of **inline.** There is one place, however, where inline code is indispensable—inline directives.

Inline Directives

An *inline directive* is like an inline procedure or function, except that Turbo Pascal adds no code to set up or clear the stack. An inline directive is declared much like an inline procedure or function, except that the **begin** and **end** reserved words are omitted. The following listing demonstrates the difference between an inline function and an inline directive:

```
{ Inline Function }
function Sum(I, J : integer) : integer;
begin
  inline($8B/$46/<I);       { MOV AX,I        }
  inline($03/$46/<J);       { ADD AX,J        }
  inline($89/$46/$FE);      { MOV [BP-2],AX   }
end;


{**************************************************}

{ Inline Directive }
function SumD(I, J : integer) : integer;
inline($58/        { POP AX - moves j into AX }
       $5B/        { POP BX - moves i into BX }
       $03/$C3);  { ADD AX,BX - sums values }
```

When you compile this code, function *SumD* produces the following instructions:

```
POP AX
POP BX
ADD AX,BX
```

As you can see, Turbo Pascal has not added a single instruction. With inline directives, what you see is what you get. Notice, however, that the inline directive cannot access variables by name. And because Turbo Pascal did not set up the stack, you can't refer to the parameters as offsets of BP (unless, of course, you set up the stack yourself). The inline directive accesses the parameters by popping them off the stack directly into registers.

As the example just given illustrates, procedures and functions written as inline directives are not easy to program. Generally speaking, inline directives are best used for short segments of code that perform a special function. For example, this inline directive stores the value of SP in *WordVar,* a variable of type **word.**

```
inline($89/$26/WordVar);   { MOV WordVar,SP }
```

Naturally, you aren't going to need to obtain the value of the SP register very often, but when you do, the most efficient way of doing this is through an inline directive. As your programming tasks become more advanced, you will find many uses for this special programming technique.

External Procedures

External procedures are routines that you write in assembler, assemble to an .OBJ file, and then link to your Turbo Pascal program when you compile it. Compared with inline code, assembler routines have many advantages. Assembler code is far easier to write, interpret, and maintain than is the machine language used in inline procedures. In fact, when programmers write an inline procedure, they usually code it as an external procedure and then convert it to inline code. Since inline procedures have no major advantages over external procedures, there is little reason to go that extra step.

More important, external routines give you direct access to Turbo Pascal global variables, local variables, parameters, procedures, and functions. In other words, you can access Turbo Pascal data and functions just as easily in assembler as in Turbo Pascal. These powerful features make writing external assembler routines an attractive alternative to Turbo Pascal when extra speed is required.

An External Function

Earlier you saw inline code for a function that adds two integers. The following assembler listing, written as an external routine, performs the same function:

```
CODE      SEGMENT BYTE PUBLIC
          ASSUME CS:CODE


PUBLIC SUM


SUM           PROC FAR

              PUSH   BP
              MOV    BP,SP

              MOV    AX,[BP+08]
              ADD    AX,[BP+06]

              POP    BP
              RET    4

SUM           ENDP
CODE          ENDS
              END
```

While it is small, this example routine demonstrates the essential aspects of assembler routines. It begins by defining the CODE segment and declaring the procedure *Sum* as a public procedure. (While assembler lets you use any code segment name, Turbo Pascal recognizes only two: CODE and CSEG.) The PUBLIC designation is important since it tells the assembler that this routine must be made available to other program modules. If you do not declare a routine PUBLIC, you will not be able to access it from Turbo Pascal.

The remainder of the assembler code defines the *Sum* routine. The procedure begins, as all external procedures should, by saving the base pointer (BP) and setting the stack pointer. The next two statements take the integer parameters from the stack, add them, and leave the result in the AX register. For functions that return scalars (for example, bytes, integers, words, and so on), Turbo Pascal will expect to find the result in the AX register. Notice that the procedure ends with the **RET 4** instruction. The value 4 refers to the four bytes (two integers) that Turbo Pascal pushed onto the stack when the routine was called. You must make sure that all parameters are removed from the stack when your procedure returns.

To use the external routine just given in a program, first assemble it to an .OBJ file. For the sake of example, assume the assembler code is in ADD.ASM and the object file is ADD.OBJ. Inside your Turbo Pascal program, you declare the external routine as follows:

```
{$F+}
{$L ADD}
function Sum(I, J : integer): integer; external;
```

The first statement is a compiler directive that forces far calls. Since our external routine is declared a FAR PROC and terminates with a RETF command, we must ensure that Turbo Pascal treats it as a far call. The next line is a compiler directive that tells Turbo Pascal to look in the ADD.OBJ file to resolve any external references. Since the procedure *Sum* is contained in ADD.OBJ, the external reference will be resolved by the linker.

The final statement is the function declaration, which concludes with the **external** directive, which tells Turbo Pascal that the code for this procedure will be found in an object file. The complete program, using the external routine, is shown here:

```
Program TestExternal;

uses Crt;

{************************************************}

{$F+}
{$L ADD}
function Sum(I, J : integer) : integer; external;

{************************************************}

begin
  ClrScr;
```

```
   Write('1 + 2 = ');
   Writeln(Sum(1,2));

   Writeln;
   Write('Press ENTER...');
   Readln;
end.
```

Using Global Data and Procedures

One of the most valuable features of Turbo Pascal's assembler interface is the ability to use global procedures, variables, and typed constants in your assembler routines. This feature makes your code much easier to maintain because you can intersperse Pascal and assembler code with much greater flexibility.

As an example of how an assembler routine might use global data and procedures, consider a routine designed to change a string from lowercase to uppercase. The procedure takes a string as a variable parameter and returns it with all uppercase letters. In our example, however, a limitation states that passing a string of more than a certain number of characters is illegal and should cause the program to stop executing. Your assembler routine needs to know what the maximum number of characters is, and how to transfer control when an error is detected.

The following assembler code meets these criteria. The Turbo Pascal global variable *MaxStrLen* holds the number that signals an error. Of course, you could hard-code a number into the procedure, or pass a number as a parameter, but these solutions make the program more clumsy and difficult to maintain.

```
DATA      SEGMENT BYTE PUBLIC

          EXTRN MaxStrLen : BYTE;

DATA      ENDS

CODE      SEGMENT BYTE PUBLIC
          ASSUME CS:CODE, DS:DATA

          EXTRN       StrLenError : FAR

          PUBLIC      UPCASESTR

UPCASESTR    PROC FAR

          PUSH        BP
          MOV         BP,SP

          LDS         SI,[BP+6]        ; Move string length byte
          MOV         AL,BYTE PTR [SI] ; into AL.
```

```
        XOR        CX,CX              ; Move string length
        MOV        CL,AL              ; into CL.
        CMP        CL,MaxStrLen       ; If the string is less than
        JL         LOOP1              ; the maximum length, go on.
        CALL       StrLenError        ; If not, call StrLenError.

LOOP1:  INC        SI                 ; Point to character.
        MOV        AL,BYTE PTR [SI]   ; Load char into AL.
        CMP        AL,97              ; Compare to 'a'.

        JB         NOTLOW             ; If lower, jump.
        CMP        AL,122             ; Compare to 'z'.
        JA         NOTLOW             ; If higher, jump.
        SUB        AL,32              ; Uppercase char.
        MOV        BYTE PTR [SI],AL   ; Move char to string.

NOTLOW: LOOP       LOOP1

        POP        BP
        RET        2

UPCASESTR     ENDP

CODE    ENDS
        END
```

Part of the CODE segment refers to an external procedure named *StrLenError*, a global Turbo Pascal routine that is called when an illegally long string is passed to the assembler routine. When the procedure starts, it looks at the length byte of the string parameter. If the length is greater than or equal to the test value (*MaxStrLen*), control is passed to Turbo Pascal procedure *StrLenError*, which prints a message and halts execution. The program listed here shows how this routine can be tested:

```
{$F+}
Program TestAsm;

uses Crt;

const
  MaxStrLen : Byte = 100;

var
   S : string;

{$L UPCASE}
procedure UpCaseStr(var S : string); external;

{**************************************************}
```

```
procedure StrLenError;
begin
  Writeln('String length error encountered.');
  Writeln;
  Write('Press ENTER...');
  Readln;
  Halt;
end;

{**************************************************}

begin
  ClrScr;
  S := 'abcdef';
  Writeln('Lower case = ', S);

  UpCaseStr(S);
  Writeln('Upper case = ', S);
  Writeln;
  Writeln('Force a string-length error condition.');
  Writeln;
  Write('Press ENTER...');
  Readln;

  S[0] := Chr(101);
  UpCaseStr(S);
end.
```

Make sure the $F compiler directive is enabled when you compile this program because the external routine was defined as a far call. If you do not enable the $F compiler directive, your program will crash when it attempts to return from the external procedure.

Using the Turbo Assembler

In the previous examples of external routines, all references to parameters were made using an offset to the base pointer (for example, [BP+6]). Using offsets is time consuming and error prone. Fortunately, Borland has introduced a solution in Turbo Assembler.

Turbo Assembler is a full-fledged, high-performance assembler, with additional capabilities that make linking to Turbo Pascal easy. Consider the following example assembler routine—a procedure called *Switch* that swaps the values of two variables. The procedure requires three parameters—two pointers (one to each of the variables to be swapped), and a **word** parameter that indicates the size of the parameters to be swapped (for example, integers would have a size of two). Normally, your assembler routine would need to define data and code segments and include entry and exit code to set up the stack and pop the correct number of parameters. With Turbo Assembler, much of the work is done for you.

```
.MODEL TPASCAL
.DATA

BUFFER DB 256 DUP(?)     ; Buffer to hold value during switch

.CODE
PUBLIC SWITCH

Switch  PROC FAR A : DWORD, B : DWORD, Dsize : WORD

; MOVE A INTO BUFFER

        LDS     SI,A      ; Load address of A into DS:SI
        LEA     DI,BUFFER ; Load address of Buffer in ES:DI
        MOV     CX,Dsize  ; Move Dsize into CX


        ; Move contents of A into Buffer
        REP     MOVS BYTE PTR ES:[DI],DS:[SI]

; MOVE B INTO A

        LDS     SI,B      ; Load address of B into DS:SI
        LES     DI,A      ; Load address of A in ES:DI
        MOV     CX,Dsize  ; Mov  Dsize into CX

        ; Move contents of B into A
        REP     MOVS BYTE PTR ES:[DI],DS:[SI]

; MOVE BUFFER INTO B

        LEA     SI,BUFFER ; Load address of Buffer into DS:SI
        LES     DI,B      ; Load address of B in ES:DI
        MOV     CX,Dsize  ; Move Dsize into CX

        ; Move contents of Buffer into B
        REP     MOVS BYTE PTR ES:[DI],DS:[SI]

        RET

SWITCH  ENDP
        END
```

The first line of the assembler routine, .MODEL TPASCAL, tells Turbo Assembler to generate code for linking to a Turbo Pascal program. The .DATA and .CODE directives replace the more cumbersome pseudo operation codes required by other assemblers. The procedure prototype

```
Switch  PROC FAR A : DWORD, B : DWORD, Dsize : WORD
```

tells Turbo Assembler the name of the procedure (*Switch*), that it is a far call, and that the procedure will take three variables—two addresses (*A* and *B*) and one numeric value parameter (*Dsize*).

Note that the procedure in the assembler listing given earlier does not include any entry or exit code. In fact, the RET instruction, at the end, does not even specify the number of bytes to pop off the stack—Turbo Assembler fills in the correct number for you. Moreover, Turbo Assembler lets you refer to parameters and global variables by their Turbo Pascal names. As you can see, writing external routines in Turbo Assembler is far easier than using standard assemblers.

The program listed here shows how to use the assembler routine just given. The $L compiler directive names the object file to link with. The program contains two switching procedures: *Switch,* the external routine, and *Switch1,* a routine written in Turbo Pascal. The Pascal procedure is offered as a comparison and, surprisingly, runs nearly as fast as the assembler routine—a testimony to the efficiency of Turbo Pascal.

```
{$F+}
Program SwitchTest;

uses Crt;

var
  A, B : integer;
  C, D : real;
  E, F : string;

{$L SWITCH}
procedure Switch(var A, B;
                 C : integer); external;

procedure Switch1(var A, B;
                  C : integer);
var
  Buf : string;

begin
  Move(A, Buf, C);
  Move(B, A, C);
  Move(Buf, B, C);
end;

begin
```

```
ClrScr;

A := 1;
B := 2;
C := 12.34;
D := 45.67;
E := 'ABCDEFG';
F := 'HIJKLMN';

Writeln('Using assembler');
Writeln;
Writeln(A, ' > ', B);
Switch(A, B, SizeOf(A));
Writeln(A, ' < ', B);
Writeln;

Writeln(C:0:2, ' > ', D:0:2);
Switch(C, D, SizeOf(C));
Writeln(C:0:2, ' < ', D:0:2);
Writeln;

Writeln(E, ' > ', F);
Switch(E, F, SizeOf(E));
Writeln(E, ' < ', F);
Writeln;
Writeln;

A := 1;
B := 2;
C := 12.34;
D := 45.67;
E := 'ABCDEFG';
F := 'HIJKLMN';

Writeln('Using Pascal');
Writeln;
Writeln(A, ' > ', B);
Switch1(A, B, SizeOf(A));
Writeln(A, ' < ', B);
Writeln;

Writeln(C:0:2, ' > ', D:0:2);
Switch1(C, D, SizeOf(C));
Writeln(C:0:2, ' < ', D:0:2);
Writeln;

Writeln(E, ' > ', F);
Switch1(E, F, SizeOf(E));
Writeln(E, ' < ', F);
```

```
   Writeln;
   Writeln;

   Readln;
end.
```

The example just given merely touches on the power of Turbo Assembler. If you are serious about writing external routines for Turbo Pascal, you should consider the advantages Turbo Assembler can offer.

Using the Asm Statement

In most circumstances, the **asm** statement is the best way to include assembler with your programs. The **asm** statement lets you put assembly language instructions almost anywhere in your Turbo Pascal program. Turbo Pascal has a built-in assembler, and when it encounters the **asm** statement it automatically converts the instructions to machine code.

Remember the *Sum* function in the previous two sections? Here it is again, only using an **asm** statement:

```
Program BuiltInAssembler;

uses Crt;

{************************************************}

function Sum(I, J : integer) : integer;
begin
  asm
    MOV    AX, I
    ADD    AX, J
    MOV    @Result, AX
  end;
end;

{************************************************}

begin
  ClrScr;
  Write('1 + 2 = ');
  Writeln(Sum(1,2));

  Writeln;
  Write('Press ENTER...');
  Readln;
end.
```

As you can see, the asm statement starts with the reserved word **asm,** followed by a series of assembly language instructions, followed by the reserved word **end.**

Immediately, you can see the advantages of the **asm** statement over its **external** counterpart:

- First, all of the preliminary work, like setting up the BP register, and the final cleanup, like the RET statement, are done for you.

- Second, you can use the formal parameter names in the instructions, instead of BP offsets.

- Third, you can use special names, like @Result for the result of a function.

If your entire subprogram will be implemented using the built-in assembler, you can add the **assembler** clause to the subprogram declaration. This eliminates the need for the extraneous **begin** and **end** clauses. Here is the same function *Sum* implemented with the **assembler** clause:

```
function Sum(I, J : integer) : integer; assembler;
asm
   MOV    AX, I
   ADD    AX, J
   MOV    @Result, AX
end;
```

You should also see the readability advantage that **asm** has over **inline,** with no added overhead.

The built-in assembler uses local labels to eliminate the need for label declarations. To reference a local label, start the label name with an @ character. The following listing is the **asm** implementation of the uppercase converter given earlier as an external procedure:

```
Program TestAsm;

uses Crt;

const
  MaxStrLen : Byte = 100;

var
   S : string;

procedure StrLenError;
begin
  Writeln('String length error encountered.');
  Writeln;
```

```
  Write('Press ENTER...');
  Readln;
  Halt;
end;

{***********************************************}

procedure UpCaseStr(var S : string); assembler;
asm
        LDS        SI,S                 { Move string length byte }
        MOV        AL,BYTE PTR [SI]     { into AL. }

        XOR        CX,CX                { Move string length }
        MOV        CL,AL                { into CL. }
        CMP        CL,MaxStrLen         { If the string is < }
        JL         @LOOP1               { the max length, go on. }
        CALL       StrLenError          { If not, it's an error. }

@LOOP1: INC        SI                   { Point to character. }
        MOV        AL,BYTE PTR [SI]     { Load char into AL. }
        CMP        AL,97                { Compare to 'a'. }

        JB         @NOTLOW              { If lower, jump. }
        CMP        AL,122               { Compare to 'z'. }
        JA         @NOTLOW              { If higher, jump. }
        SUB        AL,32                { Uppercase char. }
        MOV        BYTE PTR [SI],AL     { Move char to string. }

@NOTLOW:LOOP       @LOOP1
end;

{***********************************************}

begin
  ClrScr;
  S := 'abcdef';
  Writeln('Lowercase = ', S);

  UpCaseStr(S);
  Writeln('Uppercase = ', S);
  Writeln;
  Writeln('Force a string-length error condition.');
  Writeln;
  Write('Press ENTER...');
  Readln;

  S[0] := Chr(101);
  UpCaseStr(S);
end.
```

Again, if you compare this implementation to the previous one, you can see how much more streamlined you can make **asm** statements. This can improve readability and maintainability as well.

Debugging Assembler

You can't program in assembler without a debugger. Whether you use the venerable DEBUG.COM or a more advanced program, there is no substitute for tracing through your code one step at a time. Borland's Turbo Debugger is an invaluable tool for programmers who write assembler routines. With Turbo Debugger you can execute your program one machine instruction at a time, seeing exactly what happens to every register and location in memory. You will also learn a lot about the internal workings of Turbo Pascal—how parameters are passed to the stack, how arithmetic is performed, what registers are saved at certain points, and much more.

To see how Turbo Debugger works, let's use a program, given earlier in this chapter, that contains inline code:

```
{$D+,L+}
Program TestInline;

uses Crt;

{**************************************************}

function Sum(I, J : integer) : integer;
begin
  Inline($8B/$46/<I);      { MOV AX,I        }
  Inline($03/$46/<J);      { ADD AX,J        }
  Inline($89/$46/$FE);     { MOV [BP-2],AX   }
end;


{**************************************************}

begin
  ClrScr;
  Write('1 + 2 = ');
  Writeln(Sum(1, 2));

  Writeln;
  Write('Press ENTER...');
  Readln;
end.
```

When you compile this program, you must be sure that Standalone Debugging is On and that the $D and $L compiler directives are enabled. Doing this gives Turbo Debugger the information it needs to match your program's source code to its executable code.

When you have compiled this program to disk, start Turbo Debugger by typing **TD** followed by the name of the program (type **TEST**) you want to examine. Assuming the program file is named TEST.PAS, the command would be

    C>TD TEST

Turbo Debugger loads the TEST.EXE file and reads the TEST.PAS and TEST.MAP files. Using debugging information appended to the .EXE file, Turbo Debugger can display a line of source code along with the underlying machine-language instructions. Figure 8-1 shows how the TEST.PAS program looks in Turbo Debugger. Notice that an arrow is pointing to the first **begin** statement in the program. As you trace through your program, this arrow will always point to the next statement to be executed.

You can trace through your program by using the F7 and F8 keys. Either key executes one line at a time, but the F8 key skips over function calls, while F7 traces into function calls. Using the cursor keys on the numeric pad, you can scroll the program up and down to see different parts of your program. If you scroll down a

```
 ≡  File  Edit  View  Run  Breakpoints  Data  Options  Window  Help      READY
╔[■]═Module: TESTINLINE File: TEST.PAS 18══════════════════════════1═[↑][↓]═╗
║                                                                            ║
║    function Sum(I, J : integer) : integer;                                 ║
║    begin                                                                   ║
║      Inline($8B/$46/<i);        { MOV AX,I      }                          ║
║      Inline($03/$46/<j);        { ADD AX,J      }                          ║
║      Inline($89/$46/$FE);       { MOV [BP-2],AX }                          ║
║    end;                                                                    ║
║                                                                            ║
║                                                                            ║
║    {*************************************************}                     ║
║                                                                            ║
║ ► begin                                                                    ║
║      ClrScr;                    █                                          ║
║      Write('1 + 2 = ');                                                    ║
║      Writeln(Sum(1, 2));                                                   ║
║                                                                            ║
║      Writeln;                                                              ║
║      Write('Press ENTER...');                                             ║
╚═══Watches══════════════════════════════════════════════════════2═════════╝
║                                                                            ║
╚════════════════════════════════════════════════════════════════════════════╝
 F1-Help F2-Bkpt F3-Mod F4-Here F5-Zoom F6-Next F7-Trace F8-Step F9-Run F10-Menu
```

Figure 8-1.   *Pascal program in Turbo Debugger*

few statements and press F4, Turbo Debugger will execute all previous statements leading to the current position.

To get the most from Turbo Debugger, you have to get down to the machine-level instructions. This is easy to do—simply press F10 to activate the main menu, select the View option, and then press C for CPU (see Figure 8-2). This will open the CPU window, which consists of four "panes." The upper-left pane shows your unassembled code (see Figure 8-3); to the right is the register frame, which displays the contents of the CPU's registers. The bottom-right pane keeps track of the stack, and the bottom-left pane displays a portion of RAM. You will be primarily concerned with the code and register frames. Look in the code pane for the following Pascal statement:

```
TESTINLINE.20: WriteLn(Sum(1,2));
```

This is line 20 in your source file, which writes out a function result. Below this line, Turbo Debugger lists the machine instructions that carry it out:

```
cs:0059 BF5001          mov     di,0150
cs:005C 1E              push    ds
cs:005D 57              push    di
cs:005E B80100          mov     ax,0001
cs:0061 50              push    ax
```

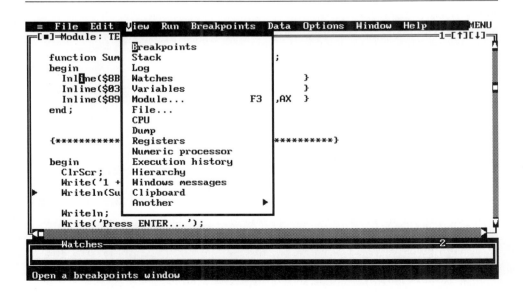

Figure 8-2.   *Selecting the CPU screen from the View menu*

```
cs:0062 B80200          mov     ax,0002
cs:0065 50              push    ax
cs:0066 E897FF          call    TESTINLINE.SUM
cs:0069 99              cwd
cs:006A 52              push    dx
cs:006B 50              push    ax
cs:006C 31C0            xor     ax,ax
cs:006E 50              push    ax
cs:006F 9A7807264C      call    4C26:0778
```

Each line consists of three parts—the location of the instruction in the code segment (for example, cs:0059), the machine-language instructions in hexadecimal (for example, BF5001), and the assembler code (for example, "mov di,0150"). As you can see, the single line of source code produced 14 machine-language instructions, two of which are calls to other routines. In the middle of the code is the call to the procedure *Sum,* which contains inline code. Keep pressing F7 until Turbo Debugger traces into *Sum.* The screen will look like the one in Figure 8-4. Notice that the procedure begins with

```
cs:0000 55              push    bp
cs:0001 89E5            mov     bp,sp
cs:0003 83EC02          sub     sp,0002
```

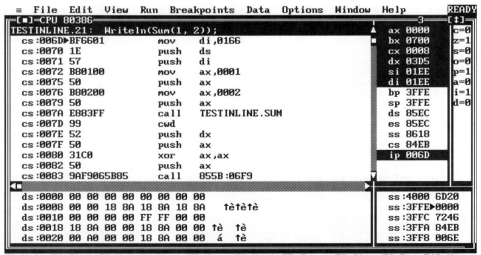

Figure 8-3.   *Turbo Debugger's CPU screen*

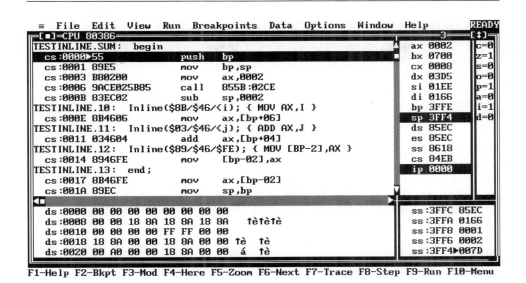

Figure 8-4. *Inline code in Turbo Debugger*

Turbo Pascal added this code to the inline function to set up the stack before your procedure executes. The next three lines consist of inline code:

```
TESTINLINE.10: Inline($8B/$46/<i); { MOV AX,I }
  cs:0006 8B4606          mov     ax,[bp+06]
TESTINLINE.11: Inline($03/$46/<j); { ADD AX,J }
  cs:0009 034604          add     ax,[bp+04]
TESTINLINE.12: Inline($89/$46/$FE); { MOV [BP-2],AX }
  cs:000C 8946FE          mov     [bp-02],ax
```

Notice how the inline code compares with the machine instructions in the unassembled lines. By using Turbo Debugger, you can check your inline code to make sure it is doing what you expected.

The procedure ends with code that moves the function result into the AX register, cleans up the stack, and returns to the originating point in the program:

```
cs:000F 8B46FE           mov     ax,[bp-02]
cs:0012 89EC             mov     sp,bp
cs:0014 5D               pop     bp
cs:0015 C20400           ret     0004
```

Inline code is particularly difficult to debug because it consists of nothing but numeric machine instructions. Turbo Debugger lets you see the assembler instructions that your inline statements represent, and executes each statement individually so you can isolate problem areas. But Turbo Debugger is not restricted to use with inline code—it works equally well for external routines and straight Pascal code. It is also a great way to learn about assembler programming. With Turbo Debugger, you can inspect the handiwork of some of the best programmers around.

Turbo Pascal produces extremely efficient code, but there are times when you want or need to do even better. Assembler routines and inline code can make your programs faster and more powerful. Compared with inline code, external routines tend to be easier to develop and maintain. Whichever approach you take, Turbo Assembler will make assembler programming easier, and Turbo Debugger will aid in tracking down errors in your assembler code.

Part *II*

The Environments

Chapter *9*

The Development Environment: The DOS and Windows IDEs

One of the reasons Turbo Pascal is so enjoyable to use is its integrated development environment (IDE). Once you are in the Turbo Pascal IDE, you can edit, compile, run, and debug your programs without having to go back to the DOS prompt. Borland pioneered the concept of the IDE and, through constant refinement, has produced the most efficient programming system available.

With the introduction of Turbo Pascal 7.0, the IDE now offers even more features, including syntax highlighting, local menus, and tool access. Each of these new features is covered in this chapter.

Borland is currently marketing five different versions of the IDE:

1. The Turbo Pascal IDE, which runs under DOS and can create DOS applications only.

2. The Turbo Pascal protected-mode IDE, which runs under DOS in protected mode and can create DOS applications only.

3. The Borland Pascal DOS IDE, which runs under DOS in protected mode and can create DOS, protected-mode DOS, or Windows applications.

4. The Turbo Pascal for Windows IDE, which runs under Windows and can create Windows applications only.

5. The Borland Pascal for Windows IDE, which runs under Windows and can create DOS, protected-mode DOS, or Windows applications.

Fortunately the IDEs themselves are very similar. This chapter will refer to the IDEs primarily as the DOS IDE, which covers the first three, and the Windows IDE, which covers the last two. It will also point out any subtle differences between the different versions of each.

Getting Started in the DOS IDE

To start Turbo Pascal, type **TURBO** at the DOS prompt and press ENTER. For protected-mode Turbo Pascal, use the **TURBOX** command. For Borland Pascal, use **BP.** Whichever command you use, you will enter the integrated development environment, shown in Figure 9-1.

At the top of the screen is the main menu, which contains ten choices: File, Edit, Search, Run, Compile, Debug, Tools, Options, Window, and Help. The simplest way to select a menu is to click on the name with the left mouse button. You can also press F10 and the arrow keys and then press ENTER, or type ALT and the first letter of the option (for example, press ALT-F for File).

The bottom line of the screen is the *status bar*. The status bar keeps you informed about your various options at any given time. Most of the time the status bar will contain hot keys, or shortcuts to menu items. The hot keys for the standard screen are summarized in Table 9-1.

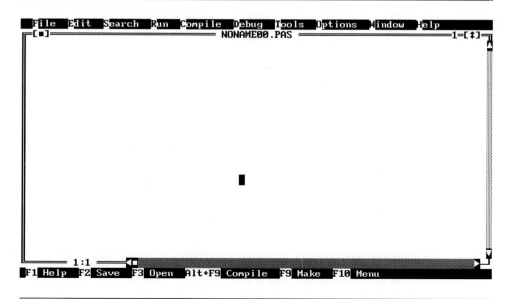

Figure 9-1.   *The DOS IDE at startup*

Hot Key	Equivalent Menu Option
F1 Help	Help|Help
F2 Save	File|Save
F3 Open	File|Open
ALT-F9 Compile	Compile|Compile
F9 Make	Compile|Make
F10 Menu	n/a

Table 9-1.   *Hot Keys on the Status Bar*

The Desktop

The rest of the screen is the *desktop,* which can contain one or more *windows.* Each window is a work area, either for editing a file, watching debug information, or examining the output area. The window that appears in the initial screen is an editor window for the file NONAME00.PAS. Inside the window you would enter all the text for a Pascal program or unit.

If you have a mouse, you can use the controls around the border of each window to manipulate the display. In the upper-right corner of the window, next to the window number, is the *zoom box.* This box contains either an arrow pointing up (↑) or an arrow pointing up and down (↕). By clicking your left mouse button on this character, you can toggle between the window filling the desktop and the window filling only a portion of the desktop. You can accomplish the same thing using the Window\|Zoom menu command.

In the upper-left corner is a solid square (■), called the *close box.* When you click the left mouse button over this box, you close the window and the file it contains. This is the same as the Window\|Close menu command.

Along the right and bottom edges of the window are *scroll bars.* Each scroll bar has an arrow at the top (or left), an arrow at the bottom (or right), and a light bar in between. Somewhere on that bar will be a darker square, which indicates the relative position of the cursor in the file. The scroll bar along the bottom is not nearly as useful as the one on the right, since most people limit their programs to the first 80 characters. If you click on the up arrow, you'll move up one row in the file. If you click on the scroll bar below the darker square, you'll move down one page. Finally, if you drag the darker square along the scroll bar, you can move the cursor position to any page in the file.

The lower-right corner is usually a different color than the rest, which indicates that it's the *resize corner.* If you hold down the left mouse button, you can drag that corner to alter the size of the window. To move the entire window, drag the top line of the window.

The desktop can contain many windows. One of them is the *active window,* which most commands act upon. Whenever you type a character, it goes into the active window.

Dialog Boxes

Whenever the IDE gives you a choice before executing a command, it displays a *dialog box.* A dialog box looks very similar to a window, in that it appears in the desktop with a rectangular frame. However, several things distinguish a dialog box from a window:

- You cannot type freely in a dialog box, only in certain fields.

- You cannot resize a dialog box, although you can move it around the desktop.

- You cannot access any other window, or the main menu, until you finish with the dialog box.

A dialog box always contains one or more *controls,* or areas of input/output. There are five types of controls; each is described here.

Push Buttons   A *push button* is a word or phrase in a box. Push buttons have a three-dimensional look to them, so that you can tell when they are "pushed." To close a dialog box, you usually need to select one of the push buttons. One push button often acts as a default, and appears in a different color. If you press ENTER, it's as if you selected the default push button.

Input Boxes   An *input box* is an area where you can enter text. For example, when you save a new program, you enter the name of the file in an input box. You will often find default text in an input box, which appears in reverse video; when you start entering new text, the default text disappears.

Check Boxes   A *check box* is a set of square brackets, with or without an "X". When you click on a check box, you are toggling an option on or off. The "X" indicates that the option is on.

Radio Buttons   The term *radio button* comes from car stereos, where there are a series of buttons that select stations, but only one button can be active at any given time. In the DOS IDE, radio buttons appear as sets of parentheses. One set will contain a dot, which indicates the active option. When you click on a radio button, the dot will move from its current position to the option you clicked.

List Boxes   A *list box* is a multiline control that offers a list of options. List boxes that have many options usually have scroll bars to let you move through the options. When you click on a line, you select that option.

Getting Started in the Windows IDE

One of the main goals of the Windows environment is that all applications written for Windows have the same look and feel. The Windows IDE is no exception—if you are familiar with Windows programs, you will have no problems using the Windows IDE. You invoke the IDE in the normal fashion, by double-clicking the icon from the Program Manager. When you do this, you'll see a window like the one in Figure 9-2.

The one major difference between the DOS IDE and Windows IDE is the speed bar, a group of icons along the top or left side of the window. Many programmers prefer to place it on the left side so they can see more lines of their programs. For some of the icons it is difficult to determine what they do from their picture, so use Table 9-2 for assistance. Also the IDE sets some of them to gray when they don't apply, such as pasting when the clipboard is empty.

The Main Menus in DOS and Windows

If you have been using modern programs for awhile, even if not for programming, you should be able to "explore" through the IDEs and accomplish any tasks. This section is provided as a reference, in case you would like more information on a particular menu option.

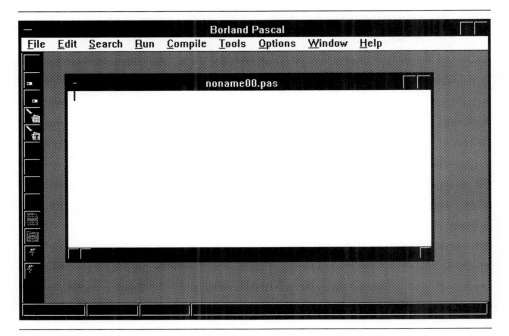

Figure 9-2. *The Windows IDE at startup*

Order	Icon Description	Equivalent Menu Option
1	Question mark	Help|Using Help
2	Floppy and right arrow	File|Open
3	Right arrow and floppy	File|Save
4	Flashlight	Search|Find
5	Flashlight with T	Search|Search again
6	Scissors	Edit|Cut
7	Paper, arrow, paper	Edit|Copy
8	Clipboard, arrow, paper	Edit|Paste
9	Arrow going up and left	Edit|Undo
10	Page with folded corner	Compile|Compile
11	Manila folder	Compile|Make
12	Lightning bolt	Run|Run
13	Lightning bolt and bug	Tools|Turbo Debugger
3*	Closed door	File|Exit

* Only when no files are open

Table 9-2.   *Speed Bar Icons and Their Menu Equivalents*

The File Menu

The File menu contains the commands and dialog boxes that control files.

New

The File|New command creates a new editor window, and gives the file a default name, NONAME00.PAS. Future new files will be NONAME01.PAS and so on. When you save any NONAME*nn* file, the IDE executes the Save As option forcing you to change the name to something more meaningful.

Open

The File|Open dialog box assists you in selecting a file to open to browse or edit. Included in this box is a scrollable box with names of all .PAS files in the current directory. In most cases all you need to do is double-click your mouse on the file you want to open. You can also change directories by double-clicking on the directories in the box. If you don't have a mouse, it's usually fastest to type the name of the file in the Name field, and then press ENTER. The IDE assumes a .PAS extension if you omit it.

In the Windows IDE, the directories appear in a separate box, along with the disk letters, as you can see in Figure 9-3. The method for changing directories is the same—double-click on the directory you wish to move to.

The Replace option lets you open the file without creating a new window. Suppose you are finished editing a file in edit window #1. If you open the next file using Replace, it will become the file in window #1. If you use Open instead, it will go in window #2. There is no Replace option in the Windows IDE.

The File|Open dialog box can be also be accessed through the status line, speed bar (in Windows), or hot key (F3).

Save

The File|Save command writes the contents of the active window to disk. If the name of the file is still NONAME*nn*.PAS, this option will display the File|Save As dialog box.

You can call this function from the status line, speed bar (in Windows), or by pressing the F2 key.

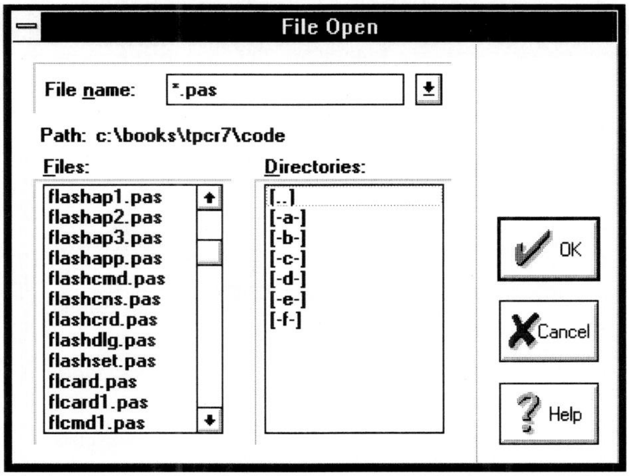

Figure 9-3. The File|Open dialog box in the Windows IDE

Save As

The File|Save As dialog box lets you change the name of the active file before you save it. The DOS IDE includes a box with the names of the existing Pascal files in the current directory. The Windows IDE includes a box that lets you use the mouse to change directories.

If you try to save a file using a name that already exists, you will see a message box asking you to confirm that you wish to overwrite the existing file. You can cancel the save at that time if you like.

Save All

When you select the File|Save All command, the IDE saves all changed files, regardless of which one is active.

Change Dir

The DOS IDE includes a File|Change Dir dialog box, shown in Figure 9-4. This box provides a visual display of the directory tree. The best way to change directories is to double-click the mouse on the directory you wish to move to.

In the Windows IDE there is no File|Change Dir dialog box, since the File|Open and File|Save As boxes have directory boxes in them.

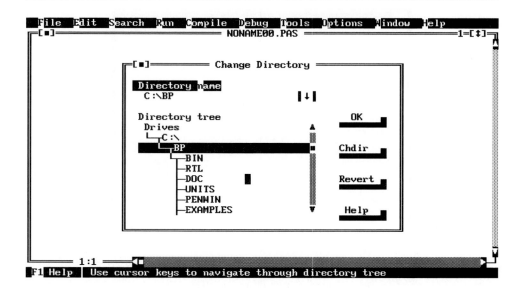

Figure 9-4.   *The File|Change Dir dialog box*

Print

The File|Print command sends the entire contents of the active window to the printer. You cannot print Output windows or Help windows with this command.

Printer Setup

If the File|Print command does not work properly, select the File|Printer Setup dialog box. This box will let you change print drivers, as well as direct the printer to print the file based on syntax highlighting.

DOS Shell

The File|DOS Shell command temporarily suspends Turbo Pascal, clears the screen, and displays the DOS prompt, from which you can run other programs or DOS commands. You must remember, however, that Turbo Pascal is still resident, so your computer will not have as much memory as it would normally. To return to Turbo Pascal from the DOS shell, simply type Exit at the DOS prompt. This option is not available in Windows—to get to DOS use the MSDOS icon in the Program Manager.

Exit

When you want to leave the integrated development environment, select File|Exit or press ALT-X to return to DOS. In the Windows IDE, you can also use the Close command in the control box.

If you have files that have changed but are not saved, the IDE displays a message box allowing you to save or cancel your changes.

Recalling Files

As you edit different files, the IDE remembers the previous five files you worked with and includes their names as options in the File menu. When you select one of these files, the IDE will reopen the file in a new window.

The Edit Menu

The IDE enables you to have multiple source files open in different windows at the same time. The options in the Edit menu let you operate on blocks of text and transfer them from one edit window to another via the *clipboard*, a special buffer set up to hold the text that you want to move or copy. In the Windows IDE, the clipboard is the Windows clipboard, which means you can actually transfer blocks of data between Turbo Pascal and other applications.

You can select text blocks in a number of ways. The simplest way is to use the mouse. Position the mouse at the beginning of the desired text, hold down the left button, and drag the mouse to the end of the text. If the text extends beyond the limits of the window, the text will scroll as you drag the mouse.

The other way to select a block is with the SHIFT key. Move the cursor to the beginning of the block, hold down the SHIFT key, and move the cursor to the end of the text.

Undo

The Edit|Undo command is new to the IDE. With Version 7.0, the IDE remembers every character you add, delete or change. Every time you execute Edit|Undo, or press ALT-BACKSPACE, the IDE backs up to a previous state. Through the editor options, you can group the Undo's so that sets of characters are undone, rather than one at a time.

Redo

The Edit|Redo command works only after an Undo—its function is to restore the file as though the Undo was never executed. You can run this command as many times as you ran Undo.

Cut

The Edit|Cut command removes a selected block of text from the active edit window and moves the block to the clipboard. The removed block of text is now ready to be pasted into another place in either the same window or another window.

The SHIFT-DEL hot key combination will also execute the Cut command. In the Windows IDE, the Cut command can be selected from the speed bar.

Copy

The Edit|Copy command works like Edit|Cut except that it does not remove the selected block from the source file. A copy of the block is placed in the clipboard, from which it can be pasted elsewhere.

The CTRL-INS hot key combination will also execute the Copy command. In the Windows IDE, the Copy command can be selected from the speed bar.

Paste

The Edit|Paste command copies text from the clipboard into the active window at the current cursor location. The Paste command always uses the block of text that was most recently placed in the clipboard.

The SHIFT-INS hot key combination will also execute the Paste command. In the Windows IDE, the Paste command can be selected from the speed bar.

Clear

The Edit|Clear command removes a block of text, but does not place it in the clipboard. The CTRL-DEL hot key combination will also execute the Clear command.

Show Clipboard

The DOS IDE allows you to view and even alter the contents of the clipboard with the Edit|Show Clipboard command. When you execute this command, you will see a new window with the contents of the clipboard. The DOS IDE maintains a history of all clipboard contents, which will also appear in the window. The current clipboard contents will be selected in the window. You can view the window or make changes; then close the window to return to your file.

The Search Menu

The Search menu is smaller for the Turbo IDE than for protected-mode IDE or the Windows IDE. This is because the other IDEs support the new Object Browser tool. See Chapter 10 for details on how to use this tool.

Find

The Search|Find dialog box, shown in Figure 9-5, lets you locate a text pattern in a source file. In the Windows IDE, this box is accessible from the speed bar. The box includes several options that alter the way the search is performed. These options are defined below.

Case sensitive Check this option if you want the IDE to distinguish between lowercase and uppercase letters.

Whole words only If you check this option, the IDE will match only those strings that are surrounded by blanks or symbols.

Regular expression Checking this box enables the IDE's extended expression matching, which provides for the use of the special characters described in Table 9-3. Some programmers will recognize these wildcards as those used in Borland's Grep utility.

Scope The scope of the search can be either global (the entire file) or just the selected block of text.

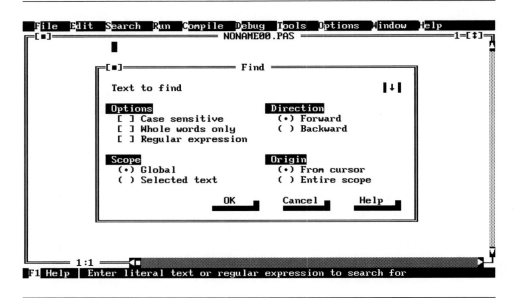

Figure 9-5.   *The Search\Find dialog box*

Direction   The search can proceed either forward (to the end of the file) or backward (to the start of the file).

Origin   The search can begin from the current cursor position, or it can encompass the entire scope of the file.

Replace

The Search|Replace dialog box is very similar to the Search|Find box, but the former allows you to replace one text string with another. There are three additions in the Replace dialog box. Beneath the "Text to find" field there is a "New text" field, where you type the text that will replace the old. There is also a "Prompt on replace" field that, when selected asks you to confirm each replacement before it is made. Finally, there is a "Change All" command, which will replace all occurrences instead of just the first one it finds.

Search Again

This command simply repeats the most recent find or replace operation. The CTRL-L hot key combination will execute the same command. In the Windows IDE, this command is accessible from the speed bar.

Wildcard	Description
^ (Caret)	Match only at the start of a line. ^ABC matches ABC, ABCX, ABCYY, and so on.
$ (Dollar sign)	Match only at the end of a line. ABC$ matches ABC, XABC, YYABC, and so on.
. (Period)	Match any character. AB. matches ABA, ABB, ABC, and so on.
* (Asterisk)	Match any number of occurrences of the specified characters, including no occurrences. ABC* matches AB, ABC, ABCD, ABD, and so on.
+ (Plus sign)	Match any number of occurrences of the specified characters, excluding no occurrences. ABC+ matches ABCD, ABCL, and so on.
[] (Square brackets)	Match includes any of the characters in the brackets. AB[CD] matches ABC or ABD.
[^] (Bracketed caret)	Match excludes any of the characters in the brackets following the caret. AB[^CD] matches ABX, ABF, and so on.
[-] (Bracketed minus)	Match includes a range of characters specified by using the minus sign. AB[C-G] matches ABC, ABD...ABG.
\ (Backslash)	Indicates that the next character is to be treated as part of the string and not as a special character. AB\^ matches AB^.

Table 9-3.   *Special Characters Used in Extended Expression Matching*

Go To Line Number

The Search|Go To Line Number dialog box asks you to enter a line number. Assuming you enter a valid number, the IDE moves the cursor to the first column of the desired line.

Show Last Compiler Error

Every time you attempt a compile, the IDE stores the line number of the most recent compiler error. When you select Search|Show Last Compiler Error, the IDE moves the cursor to that line and redisplays the error message. If you have added lines of code in front of the error since your last compile, the cursor will be placed on a line other than the one that caused the error.

Find Error

Sometimes, while a program is being run from the DOS prompt, the program will encounter a run-time error that looks like this:

Runtime error 200 at 0000:0099.

Code 200 is the run-time error caused by division by zero. The numbers 0000:0099 are the address (segment) and offset, at which the error occurred. To locate the error, you select the Search|Find Error dialog box, and enter the address. The IDE will locate the error in the source code and display the location on the screen. Note that to use this feature, you must have Debug information enabled with {$D+}, which is the default.

Find Procedure

If you have ever written a large program with many procedures and functions, you know how hard it is to remember how each works. The Search|Find Procedure dialog box helps by quickly locating the source code where a procedure or function was defined. Now you can locate a procedure or function in just seconds, even when your source code consists of thousands of lines in 20 different units. This option, however, is available only during debugging sessions.

If you are using the protected-mode IDE or the Windows IDE, you will not have this option. Instead, you will see the options Units, Globals, and Symbols. These options are part of a new IDE feature, the Object Browser, which is described in Chapter 10.

The Run Menu

The options on the Run menu are used to execute a program from within the IDE. Most of the selections are used for debugging programs by executing portions and then stopping. The Windows IDE does not have any of the debugging options because it uses Turbo Debugger for debugging.

Run

The Run|Run command compiles and runs your program in one command. If the file being compiled depends on other files that have changed, those files will also be recompiled. The Run|Run command executes either the file in the active window or the primary file (see the Compile|Primary File option in the next section for more information). The program will run normally until it encounters a run-time error or a break point that you have set.

This command is available using the hot-key combination CTRL-F9. In the Windows IDE, this command is accessible from the speed bar.

Step Over

The Run|Step Over command executes a single line of code. If that line is a procedure or function call, Step Over executes the entire procedure in one step. You can also initiate the Step Over feature by pressing F8. Use this feature when you are confident that a subprogram works and you don't want to see the process line by line.

Trace Into

The Run|Trace Into command also executes a single line of code. However, if that line is a procedure or function call, it jumps to the source code for that routine and continues to execute one line at a time. With this feature you can see how your program works, line by line, from start to finish. Trace Into, also available as F7, will trace only into programmer-defined units, not to standard Turbo Pascal units.

Go To Cursor

To use this feature, place the cursor on any line in a program, and then select Go To Cursor from the Run menu (or just press F4). The IDE will execute your program normally, but when it encounters the line on which you placed the cursor, it stops the program and returns you to the editor. At that point you can continue debugging or reset the program and start from the beginning.

Program Reset

While debugging a program, you might want to reset the program to start from the beginning. To do this, simply select Run|Program Reset or press CTRL-F2. This command closes all open files and returns the program pointer to the first statement in the program.

Parameters

Programs often depend on command-line parameters that are passed to the program when it is executed from the DOS prompt. The Run|Parameters dialog box lets you specify parameters that will be passed to the program while it is running in the IDE.

The Compile Menu

The Compile menu contains the commands you need to create linkable object modules or complete executable programs.

Compile

When you select the Compile|Compile command, the IDE compiles the source file that is in the active window. If the source file is a unit, the IDE creates a file with the proper extension (.TPU for DOS units, .TPW for Windows units, and .TPP for protected-mode units). Program files, on the other hand, are compiled to executable code that is stored either in memory or on disk in an .EXE file. If the source file in the editor uses any other units, those units must be compiled first.

You can call the Compile command by pressing ALT-F9 or by clicking the mouse on the command in the status line or speed bar.

Make

The Compile|Make command is more powerful than the Compile|Compile command; it compiles not only the code in the active window, but also any source files that the program depends upon that have changed since the last time the entire program was compiled. The result of the Make process is an executable program that can be run and debugged.

You can also execute Compile|Make by pressing F9. In the Windows IDE, this command is accessible from the speed bar.

Build

The Compile|Build command operates just like Compile|Make, except that all units are recompiled, regardless of whether they are out of date. For example, when developing a program, you might have Range Checking ({$R+}) turned on. When your program is final, however, you want to turn Range Checking off to maximize speed. To do this, you can change the setting of the global compiler directive (assuming the units don't have their own embedded directives) and use the Build command to recompile all the units. The new units will reflect the changed compiler directive.

Destination

The Compile|Destination command will toggle between Memory and Disk. When compiling, making, or building a program, you can store the resulting code either on disk (in a file with the .EXE or .TPU extension) or in memory. Compiling to memory is slightly faster than to disk, but requires more memory and does not create a permanent copy of the executable code.

Primary File

If your program includes multiple files, you may want to specify the main program file with the Compile|Primary File dialog box. When no file is specified as the primary file, the Make and Build process will begin with the file that is in the active window. Once you specify a primary file, however, the Make or Build process will always begin with that file, no matter what file is in the active window.

Clear Primary File

This command clears the primary file name so that Build or Make commands act on the file in the active window.

Information

After you have compiled a program, you can get information about it by selecting Compile|Information dialog box. This box tells you how much memory your program requires, the memory available to run the program, the number of lines compiled in your program, and more.

Target

In the Borland Pascal IDEs there is an additional menu item, the Compile|Target dialog box. This box lets you change the target where the application will run, from DOS, to protected-mode DOS, to Windows.

The Debug Menu

The Debug menu gives you access to powerful commands and windows for testing a program for errors. From this menu you can evaluate equations that use variables in the program, alter the value of variables to test the effect of the change, and more. Chapter 12 covers each Debug menu item in greater detail.

This menu appears in the DOS IDE only; the Windows IDE uses Turbo Debugger for debugging.

Breakpoints

The Debug|Breakpoints dialog box lets you add, delete, and edit *breakpoints*. A breakpoint is a line of your program or an expression that causes the program to halt temporarily. There are two types of breakpoints: when you set an *unconditional* breakpoint, you tell the IDE to stop execution at a certain line in your program; when you set a *conditional* breakpoint, you tell the IDE to stop when a given expression evaluates to True.

Call Stack

When you select the Debug|Call Stack command, the IDE brings up the Call Stack window. In this window you can see the current *call stack*—the hierarchy of procedure and function calls that have been made to get to the current location.

Watch

The Debug|Watch command activates the Watch window. In this window you can track the values of variables throughout your program. You can also enter expressions in the Watch window.

Output

The Debug|Output command activates the Output window. This window is the same as the user screen, except you can scroll through it like any other edit window.

User Screen

When you are debugging in the IDE, you cannot see what your program is displaying on the screen. If you want to see what your program is displaying (from the user's point of view), use the Debug|User Screen command or press ALT-F5. Once the screen appears, pressing any key will return you to the IDE.

Evaluate/Modify

The Debug|Evaluate and Modify dialog box serves two useful purposes. First, it is a powerful calculator that can use variables from a program in expressions. In this dialog box you can test the validity of expressions before their results are used by other parts of the program.

The second use of the Evaluate and Modify box is to give variables new values. The ability to evaluate expressions and change the values of variables is important because it allows you to simulate a wide range of situations without repeatedly recompiling the entire program.

Add Watch

The Debug|Add Watch dialog box lets you add a watch expression to the Watch window. The default variable in the watch expression is the variable at the current cursor location. This dialog box is a subset of the functionality provided by the Watch window.

Add Breakpoint

The Debug|Add Breakpoint dialog box lets you add a new breakpoint. The default breakpoint is the current cursor location. This dialog box is a subset of the functionality provided by the Debug|Breakpoints dialog box.

The Tools Menu

The Tools menu is new to Turbo Pascal 7.0, and gives you access to other programs.

The Options Menu

The IDE offers many options that let you customize your programs and programming environment. The Options menu gives you complete control over these options so that the compiler, linker, and environment work the way you want them to.

Compiler

The Options|Compiler dialog box lets you set various options that change the way the IDE compiles a program. Each check box in the dialog box corresponds to a compiler directive. Table 9-4 gives you a cross-reference between the check boxes and the compiler directives. The explanation for each directive is found in the last section of Chapter 1.

The remaining controls in this dialog box are for conditional defines and multitarget options.

Conditional Defines   Many programmers use conditional compilation directives to make their programming easier. Programmers control these directives, which include or exclude portions of code, by defining compiler directive constants. These constants can be defined in the program itself or in the Conditional defines section of the Options/Compiler menu.

Compiler Settings For...   The Borland Pascal IDEs, which support multiple targets, maintain separate options for each target. For instance, you may want strong typing of @ operations for DOS programs, but not for Windows programs. As you can see in Figure 9-6, these IDEs include an additional control to specify the target for which the current settings apply.

Memory Sizes

The Options|Memory Sizes dialog box lets you set the amount of memory your program will use for its heap and stack. Note that the heap is defined as a minimum

Dialog Box Field	Equivalent Compiler Directive
Force far calls	$F
Overlays allowed	$O
Word align data	$A
286 instructions	$G
Range checking	$R
Stack checking	$S
I/O checking	$I
Overflow checking	$Q
Debug information	$D
Local symbols	$L
Symbol information	$Y
Strict var-strings	$V
Complete boolean eval	$B
Extended syntax	$X
Typed @ operator	$T
Open Parameters	$P
8087/80287	$N
Emulation	$E
Smart callbacks	$K
Windows stack frame	$W

Table 9-4.   *Compiler Options and Their Equivalent Directives*

and maximum amount. If you set a minimum heap limit, the IDE will check to see if that much memory is available before your program begins. When you set a maximum heap limit, the IDE will use no more than that amount of memory for your program. The default values are 64K for the stack size, 0K for the minimum heap size, and 640K for the maximum heap size. If you use the $M compiler directive, the values in the directive will override those in the dialog box.

Linker

From the Options|Linker dialog box you can control the use of map files and link buffers:

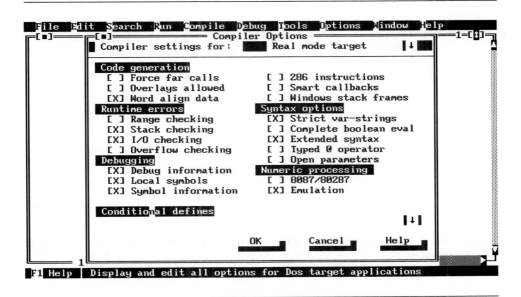

Figure 9-6.   *The Options|Compiler dialog box in the protected-mode DOS IDE*

Map File   The linker can produce three types of map files: Segments, Publics, and Detailed.

The Segments map file contains only the location, size, and name of each segment created by Turbo Pascal. A typical program uses several code segments, one data segment, one stack segment, and one heap segment.

The Publics map file contains all the segment information and adds the memory location of every public procedure, function, and variable.

Finally, the Detailed map file contains all the Segments and Publics information plus line number information that links specific memory locations to specific source code lines. For large programs, the detailed map file can be quite large.

Link Buffer   The location of the link buffer depends on how much memory your program needs—putting the link buffer in memory speeds things up, but requires more RAM. For large programs, you may need to assign the link buffer to disk.

Debug Info in EXE   The Windows IDE includes an additional option in the Linker dialog box, called Debug Info in EXE. If you check this box, debug information will be included in the .EXE file, which means you can debug it with Turbo Debugger. If you remove the check, the .EXE file will be smaller, but you can't debug it.

Debugger

The Options|Debugger dialog box gives you control over the type of debugging and the frequency of display swaps. This dialog box is not available in the Windows IDE.

Debugging   If you wish to perform debugging while in the integrated development environment, you must enable Integrated debugging. (You must also enable Debug information in the Options|Compiler dialog box.) Enabling Integrated debugging tells Turbo Pascal to add debugging code to object modules.

You can also use Borland's stand-alone debugger, which can be accessed automatically from the IDE.

Display swapping   When you are debugging a program, you see only the Edit and Watch windows—the display that the user would see is hidden. To keep your program's screen output from interfering with the Edit and Watch windows, Turbo Pascal uses screen swapping. For a split second, Turbo switches from the Edit window to the output screen, executes the line of code, and returns to the Edit window. The process is too fast for you to see what your program wrote to the screen. To see what the display screen looks like, press ALT-F5.

Turbo Pascal provides three types of screen swapping—Smart, Always, and None. When Display swapping is set to None, Turbo Pascal will not swap the display as you trace through a program. This feature removes the annoying flash you see on your display as it is swapped, allowing your program to write over the Edit and Watch windows. When a program overwrites your display, you can restore it by using the Refresh display feature. At the other extreme, you can set screen swapping to Always, which means that Turbo Pascal will swap screens with every statement, even when your program is not writing to the screen.

In between Always and None is Smart screen swapping, which means that Turbo Pascal will swap screens only when the code affects the screen, or a procedure or function is called.

Directories

The Options|Directories dialog box lets you tell the IDE where to look for files that don't exist in the current directory.

EXE & TPU Directory   This entry is the directory in which Turbo Pascal will store any .EXE or .TPU files.

Include Directories   Turbo Pascal will search the directories named here if it cannot find an Include file in the current directory.

Unit Directories   If your program calls for a unit that does not exist in the current directory, Turbo Pascal will search in directories specified under Unit directories.

Object Directories   The directories entered here contain .OBJ files used for external routines declared in your programs.

Resource Directories   The Windows IDE also includes an area to contain the directories to be searched for resource files.

Tools

The DOS IDEs give you the ability to modify the set of programs in the Tools menu. To add a new tool, select the New button in Options|Tools dialog box. This will bring up another dialog box, where you can enter the name, parameters, and hot key combination for the tool. When you press OK you will return to the Options|Tools dialog box. The next time you access the Tools menu you will see your new tool.

The Options|Tools dialog box also provides controls to modify and delete tools from the Tools menu. You can even remove any of the default set of tools.

The Windows IDE provides none of this flexibility. In its Options|Tools dialog box, you can only alter the locations of the four tools included in the Tools menu.

Environment|Preferences

The Environment option in the Options menu is actually a submenu, with access to five dialog boxes. The first is the Options|Environment|Preferences dialog box. The groups of options available in this dialog box vary with each IDE. Here are explanations of all of them:

Screen Size   Turbo Pascal supports the 25-line standard display, the 43-line EGA text display, and the 50-line VGA text display. You can select the display you want with the Screen Size radio buttons. This option is not available in the Windows IDE.

Auto Save   All the settings you make in the Turbo integrated development environment can be saved to a configuration file so that you do not have to reset everything each time you start Turbo Pascal. When you enable Config auto save, Turbo Pascal automatically saves the current configuration for you, so you do not lose any changes you made during your programming session.

When you run a program or use the File|DOS Shell command, you risk losing your editing changes if you should crash the computer. To avoid this risk, you can enable Editor Files auto save, which saves your changes to disk before transferring control to DOS or your program.

Desktop File   In the DOS IDE, you can specify whether you want one desktop file for all directories, or one desktop file for each directory where you invoke the IDE. In the Windows IDE, there is always only one desktop file.

Options   The Options group contains a few miscellaneous options, most of which affect the Object Browser, and are described in Chapter 10. The last option is called Change Dir On Open, which applies when you open a file. If you open a file from a different directory other than the default directory, and this option is checked, the default will be updated. If the option is not checked, the only way to change the default directory is with the File|Change Dir dialog box. This option is not available in the Windows IDE.

Source Tracking   In the Borland Pascal IDEs, there is a Source Tracking set of options. These affect the Object Browser only, and are covered in Chapter 10.

Desktop File Options   The IDE automatically saves file and window information in the desktop. For a small cost in additional disk space, the Borland IDEs will also save symbol information as part of the desktop.

Command Set   The Windows IDE is caught in a dilemma—should it support commands that act more like the DOS IDE, or should it act more like a Windows program. Well, it actually supports both. The Command Set radio buttons let you toggle between a Windows-like IDE (CUA, or Common User Access) and a Turbo Pascal-like IDE (the Alternate set).

Speed Bar   The first time you use the Windows IDE, the speed bar appears across the top of the desktop, just below the menu bar. You can change this to have the speed bar down the left side of the desktop, or as a window that you can move anywhere.

Environment|Editor

The Options|Environment|Editor dialog box controls those options that affect editing. The Windows IDE version of this is shown in Figure 9-7.

Editor Options   Most of the editor options are self-explanatory, with a few exceptions:

- Persistent blocks—when checked, moving the cursor outside a block has no effect on the block; when not checked, moving the cursor outside the block deselects the block.

- Block overwrite—when checked, typing a character in a selected block deletes the block; when not checked, the character is simply inserted as part of the block.

- Find text at cursor—when checked, the word at the cursor location acts as the default string for Find or Replace (DOS IDE only).

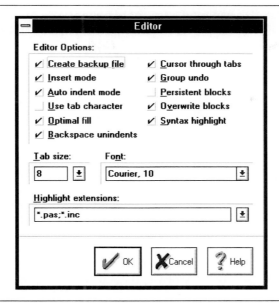

Figure 9-7. *Options\Environment\Editor dialog box in Windows IDE*

Tab Size   While the IDE normally sets Tab stops at 8 spaces, you can use the Tab size option to change this to a value from 2 to 16.

Highlight Extensions   Version 7.0 of the IDE supports syntax highlighting. If you use the IDE to edit a text file, however, the highlighting of reserved words might be distracting. The Highlight Extensions input box contains the file extensions where syntax highlighting is supported.

Font   In the Windows IDE, you can select the font that is used for the windows editor. Typically you use a fixed font (as opposed to a proportional font) so you can indent properly and line things up.

Some fonts display much slower than others. If you notice the windows editor refreshing slowly, you might try a different font.

Environment\Mouse

The Options\Environment\Mouse dialog box is primarily to allow you to control what happens when you hold down the CTRL key and press the right mouse button. As a default, this combination brings up help on the topic found at the current cursor location. You can change this so that it does nothing at all, or it brings up the object browser. In the DOS IDE you have a few more options: you can have it set a break-point, evaluate an expression, or add a variable to the watch window.

Environment|Startup

The options contained in the Options|Environment|Startup dialog box control the way the IDE sets up. This includes memory allocation, video interface preferences, and use of expanded memory.

Environment|Colors

The DOS IDE gives you full control over all the foreground and background colors used in the environment. To change a color, select the Options|Environment|Colors dialog box. Then choose the appropriate group (such as Desktop, Menus, or Dialogs) and item (such as normal text or selected text). Finally use the mouse or the cursor keys to select the colors for that item.

The Windows IDE gives you control over the colors used in syntax highlighting only.

Open

Once you have saved options in a disk file (using Options|Save), you can use the Options|Open dialog box to select an options file and load it into the IDE.

Save

Once you have set all your options the way you want them, you can save the configuration by selecting the Options|Save command. The options are saved using the current options file name, which appears as part of the menu. If you have selected the Auto Save feature, you need not use this command.

Save As

You can create different options files for specific situations. To save an options file under a new name, use the Options|Save As dialog box.

The Window Menu

As the mouse grows in popularity, fewer and fewer window commands are needed from menus. In fact, the Windows IDE requires a mouse, and does not supply many of the window commands included in the DOS IDE. See the "Getting Started" section of this chapter for hints on how to use your mouse to manipulate windows.

Tile

When you have more than one window open, you can use the Window|Tile command to rearrange them. This command resizes all windows so that they all fit on the screen at once.

Cascade

The Window|Cascade command is another way to order your windows. Instead of shrinking them, it cascades them in a way that causes the top line of each window to be visible.

Arrange Icons

In the Windows IDE, you can minimize an editor window, and it will appear as an icon on the desktop. When you use the Window|Arrange Icons command, the IDE will align all the icons along the bottom of the desktop.

Close All

When you are finished with a multiwindow program, and you want to start fresh, the easiest way is to use the Window|Close All command. This command removes all windows from the desktop.

Refresh Display

If, for whatever reason, the desktop display is wrong, you can use the Window|Refresh Display command, which simply repaints the entire screen.

Size/Move

When you select the Window|Size/Move command, you can move the active window around the screen using the arrow keys. To shrink or expand the size of the window, hold down the SHIFT key and use the arrow keys until the window is the size you desire.

This command, as well as the rest of the commands, are unavailable in the Windows IDE.

Zoom

Selecting Window|Zoom, or pressing F5, expands the active window to the size of the full screen. Selecting it again returns the window to its previous size and position.

Next

To move to the next window, based on window number, use F6 or Window|Next.

Previous

Pressing SHIFT-F6, or using Window|Previous changes the active window to the one with the previous number.

Close

The Window|Close command removes the active window from the screen. If the window contains a file that has been modified, you will be asked if you want to save the file before the window closes.

List

An easy way to select a desired window is to use the Window|List dialog box. This box displays a list of all windows currently loaded in the desktop. Selecting a window makes it the new active window.

Figure 9-8.   *The local menu for editor windows*

In the Windows IDE, each open (or minimized) window is displayed as a menu item. Selecting that item makes that window the active window.

The Help Menu

The online help included with the IDE is very extensive. To use help, select the appropriate option from the Help menu. This action will activate a help window. Once in a help window, you will usually see highlighted words called *help keywords*. A help keyword indicates that there is a help screen for that particular topic. To see that help screen, click the mouse on the help keyword. If you don't have a mouse, use the TAB key to highlight the keyword, then press ENTER.

Local Menus

Local menus are new to Version 7.0 of the IDE. In many windows, pressing the right mouse button, or pressing ALT-F10, brings up a menu with options that are applicable to the active window. Figure 9-8 shows the local menu for the editor window. There are also local menus for the Watch window, help windows, and Browser windows. All of the options in a local menu are also available from the main menu—the purpose of the local menu is to make the common options more easily available.

Chapter *10*

The Object Browser in DOS and Windows

Version 7 of the IDE includes a very powerful new feature: the ability to *browse* an executable program. Whenever you compile a program, the IDE generates not only the machine code necessary to run the program, but also a vast set of symbol tables that were used to help generate that machine code. Browsing a program means examining those symbol tables to understand the variables, constants, types, and subprograms that are part of the program, how they relate to one another, and how they relate back to the original Turbo Pascal source code. Obviously, browsing becomes much more useful as your programs grow in size.

If you use the TURBO command to invoke the DOS IDE, you will not be able to use the Object Browser. This feature is available only in the IDEs that have access to two megabytes of memory. For DOS this means you must use the TURBOX command with Turbo Pascal, or the BP command with Borland Pascal.

This chapter will introduce both the DOS and Windows versions of the Object Browser. Although these versions provide the same functionality, their user interfaces are very different.

The DOS Object Browser

The DOS Object Browser is based on one or more text windows called Browser windows. These windows act just like most of the other special windows, such as the Watch window. You can move them, size them, and close them easily with a mouse;

or almost as easily using the keyboard. For more information on windows, see Chapter 9.

Browsing Units

The Search|Units command displays a window that contains the set of units used to compile your program. As you can see in Figure 10-1, the units are sorted in alphabetical order. The program used in this example is the Flash Card program created in Chapter 17.

To browse a particular unit from the units list, click your mouse on the unit of interest. If you don't have a mouse, use the arrow keys to highlight the unit, and press ENTER. This will display another Browser window with a list of symbols defined in that unit. A sample Browser window for the FLCARD unit is shown in Figure 10-2.

The following commands are available from the Browser window of a unit:

Symbol Display

Near the top of the window is a horizontal line with the letters S and R. When the S is highlighted, you see a list of *symbols* declared in that unit. When the R is highlighted, you will see a list of locations where that unit is *referenced*.

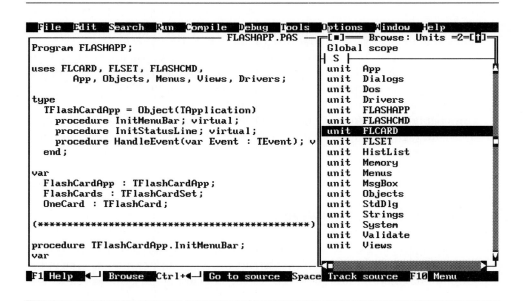

Figure 10-1.   *Browsing units in the DOS IDE*

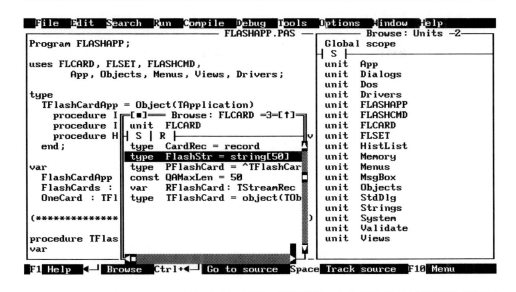

Figure 10-2. *Browsing one unit in the DOS IDE*

To change a Browser window to display the symbols, click your mouse on the letter S. If you don't have a mouse, use the CTRL-S key combination.

Referencer Display

When you click on the letter R, or press CTRL-R, you will display a list of reference locations. These locations are specified by a file name and a line number within that file.

Go To Source

When you see a declaration or reference in a Browser window, and want to see the actual code for that declaration, you have two options. The first is Go To Source, which appears in the status bar when a Browser window is active. When you click on Go To Source, the IDE will display an editor window with the declaration highlighted. You can also use CTRL-ENTER, or select the Go To Source command from the local menu.

If the current symbol in a Browser window is from a standard Borland unit, such as System or Crt, the Go To Source command will be disabled. You cannot browse the source of the standard units, only the symbols.

Track Source

The trouble with the Go To Source command is that it makes the Browser window inactive and the editor window active. If you just want to see the source but continue browsing, you can use the Track Source command. This command highlights the source in an editor window, but leaves the Browser window as the active window. The Track Source command is also available from the status bar, or the local menu, or the SPACEBAR hot key. Figure 10-3 is an example of using Track Source to find the declaration of the *FlashStr* type within the FLCARD unit.

You can also access Go To Source and Track Source from the global units list, such as the one in Figure 10-1.

Browse Symbol

In any Browser window, you can continue to browse in more detail by either clicking the mouse on an entry in the window, or using the arrow keys and pressing ENTER. Each time you do this the IDE will create another Browser window with the new information.

There is also an option to do all browsing within the same Browser window, as you will see later in this chapter. If you have selected this option, browsing a new symbol will display the new information in the same Browser window, instead of creating another window.

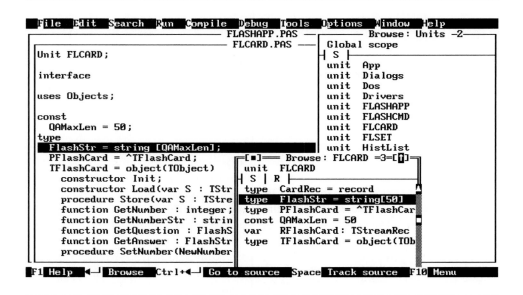

Figure 10-3.   *Tracking source code from the Browser*

Previous Browser

The Search|Previous Browser command from the main menu, or the Previous command in the Browser local menu, retrieves the previous Browser window. This feature is especially useful when you have chosen to use only one Browser window. In this case, the Previous command acts like a "rewind" tool, recalling the contents of the previous window.

Change Options

The Options command in the local menu displays the options that apply to the Object Browser. These options will be covered later in this chapter.

Browsing Objects

Although the Object Browser is nice for analyzing any declaration, it is especially useful for object declarations. The Browser window can display a complete object hierarchy as well as show inheritance information for any object.

To display the object hierarchy, select the Search|Objects command from the main menu. This command displays a Browser window such as the one in Figure 10-4. The lines in the hierarchy show the inheritance relationships among the objects. For

Figure 10-4. *Object hierarchy in the DOS IDE*

example, you can tell by Figure 10-4 that the TBufStream is a descendant of the TDosStream object, which is a descendant of the TStream object. If you scrolled to the top of the window, you would also see that TStream is a descendant of TObject.

If you want more information about a particular object definition, select that object from the hierarchy using the mouse or the ENTER key. When you do, you will see a new Browser window displaying the fields and methods of that object. Figure 10-5 shows the Browser window for the TFlashCard object.

All of the commands available in the unit displays are available for the object displays, including source tracking, reference information, and further browsing. In addition, there are several commands that are specific to object displays:

Inheritence Display

In object displays you will see an I in the top line along with the S and the R. When you click on the I, or press CTRL-I, you will see the ancestors and descendants of that object.

Hide Descendants

The object hierarchy display can often get too cluttered to be useful, especially when writing Turbo Vision applications. The IDE allows you to hide portions of the object

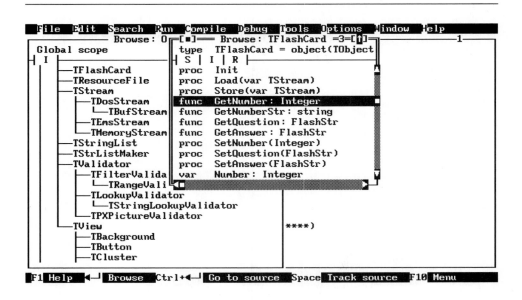

Figure 10-5.   *Browsing an object in the DOS IDE*

hierarchy to hide unwanted details. To hide the descendants of a particular object, click the mouse on the horizontal line just left of the object. If you don't have a mouse, use the arrow keys to highlight the object, then press the + (plus sign) key. When you do, a + will appear on the line indicating that there are hidden descendants.

Figure 10-6 displays the same object hierarchy that was in Figure 10-4, except many of the predefined objects in Turbo Vision have been hidden.

Show Descendants

To redisplay descendants that you hid previously, use the mouse to click on the + (plus sign) or type - (hyphen). This will cause the Browser window to display the immediate descendants of that object. You may need to do this repeatedly to show all descendants.

Browsing Globals

If you want to look for a declaration, but have no idea where it is located, you can start by selecting the Search|Globals command. The Browser window displayed by this command includes the names of every symbol defined by any unit in your program.

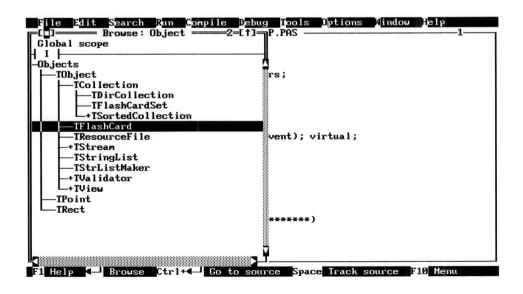

Figure 10-6.   *Browsing references in the DOS IDE*

This list of globals is usually very large, especially if you are writing Turbo Vision applications. To help you find a particular declaration, you can type the first few letters of the name of the declaration, and the IDE will scroll to the symbols that start with those letters. Figure 10-7 shows a global display after typing **PF**.

Searching for a Symbol

Another way to find a declaration, if you know the exact name of it, is to use the Search|Symbol dialog box. In this box you must type the full name of the symbol. If the IDE finds it, it displays a Browser window for that symbol. If it cannot find it, it displays an error in a dialog box.

Browser Options

There are three primary places where you can select options that control the behavior of the Browser window:

- The Options|Browser dialog box, which contains most of the options

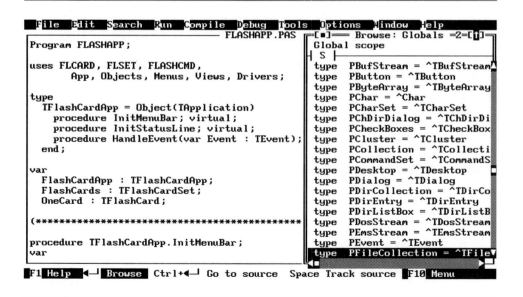

Figure 10-7.   Browsing globals in the DOS IDE

- The Options dialog box from the local menu of a Browser window, which contains a subset of the Options|Browser box that override the default options for a particular Browser window

- The Options|Environment|Preferences dialog box, which includes two options specific to the Object Browser

The rest of this section describes how each option affects the Object Browser.

Symbols

The Symbols option controls which symbols will be displayed in the Browser window. You can disable or enable the display of constants, variables, types, procedures, functions, and inherited fields and methods. Default values for this option are set in the Options|Browser dialog box, and local values are set in the local Options dialog box.

Display

There are two options in the Display group. The first, Qualified Symbols, controls whether the defining object name is included on any line showing a field or method. If you think this information does little besides clutter the display, you should disable this option.

The second Display option is called Sort Always. The Object Browser will always sort the displays that make sense, such as units and globals. If you want all displays to be sorted, select the Sort Always option.

Like the Symbols options, the Display options are set globally in Options|Browser, and locally in the local Options box.

Sub-browsing

As mentioned previously, the IDE allows you to use either one single Browser window, or multiple windows. The Sub-browsing option, part of the Options|Browser dialog box, can be set to either New Browser for multiple windows or Replace Current for a single window.

Preferred Pane

Most Browser windows let you alternate between the Symbol display and the Referencers display. The display that appears first is controlled by the Preferred Pane option, also part of Options|Browser.

Auto Track Source

Earlier in this chapter you learned how to use Track Source to locate the source code of a declaration. If you enable the Auto Track Source option in the Options|Environment|Preferences dialog box, you will see the source tracked every time you highlight a declaration. This option will not display new editor windows automatically, but if the editor window is visible, the source will be tracked.

Close on Go To Source

The Go To Source command changes the active window from the Browser window to the editor window containing the symbol. If you select the Close on Go To Source option (also in Options|Environment|Preferences) the IDE will close the Browser window. If this option is disabled, the editor window will become active, usually obscuring the Browser window, but the Browser window will not be closed.

The Windows Object Browser

Like the DOS version, the Windows Object Browser uses one or more Browser windows. These windows appear in the desktop just like any other window, with the ability to be sized, moved, and closed with a few clicks of the mouse. The text in this section assumes you are familiar with the Windows IDE. If you're not, be sure to study Chapter 9.

The Local Menu

To display a browser window, you select one of these commands: Search|Units, Search|Objects, Search|Globals, or Search|Symbols. When you do, the IDE will create a Browser window. If you click the right mouse button in a Browser window, you will bring up a local menu. The following paragraphs describe each of the commands in that menu.

Goto

One of the key features of the Browser window is that it can take you to the actual code for a symbol. The Goto command displays an editor window with the source code that includes the symbol highlighted in the Browser window. You can also use CTRL-G as an accelerator key.

If the current symbol in a Browser window is from a standard Borland unit, such as System or Crt, the Goto command will be disabled. You cannot browse the source of the standard units, only the symbols.

Browse

Most Browser windows contain a list of declarations. You can see more detail on a particular declaration by highlighting it and using the Browse command. An even easier method of browsing is to double-click the mouse on the declaration.

References

The IDE is capable of providing a list of all the places where a particular symbol is referenced, or used. When you select the References command, or press CTRL-R, you will display a list of reference locations.

Previous View

The Previous View command in the Browser local menu acts like a "rewind" tool, recalling the contents of the previous Browser window. This feature is enabled only when you have chosen to use only one Browser window (see the Window Mode command later in this section).

Overview

When you select the Overview command, or use CTRL-O, the IDE will display a Browser window with the complete object hierarchy. You will see an example of this window later in the chapter.

Print

If you want to print the contents of a Browser window, simply execute the Print command.

Window Mode

There are times when you don't want a bunch of Browser windows cluttering up your desktop. On the other hand, you may want more than one window to make comparisons. The Window Mode command toggles between one Browser window and many windows.

Options

The Options command is the same as the Options|Browser dialog box in the main menu. The specific options in this box will be covered at the end of the chapter.

The Speed Bar

The local menu for a Browser window is almost as convenient as you can get; however, there is also a speed bar at the top of each Browser window. The icons that are available for a particular window vary with the type of information in that window. Table 10-1 gives you a cross-reference between the icons in the speed bar and the commands in the local menu.

Browsing Units

The Search|Units command displays a window that contains the set of units used to compile your program. As you can see in Figure 10-8, the units are sorted in alphabetical order. The program used as an example for the rest of the chapter is the Flash Card program created in Chapter 18.

To browse a particular unit from the units list, double-click your mouse on the unit of interest. This will display another Browser window, replacing the existing window, with a list of symbols defined in that unit. A sample Browser window for the FLASHCRD unit is shown in Figure 10-9.

Typically the next step is to locate a specific declaration, and go to the source code. When you press CTRL-G, or use the Goto command from the local menu, the Object Browser will bring up an editor window with the selected declaration highlighted. Figure 10-10 shows the IDE after using Goto for the *FlashStr* type.

All of the commands in the local menu are at your disposal from this window. In addition, there are two other options:

Symbol	Equivalent Command
Question mark	Help
Document with arrow	Goto
Magnifying glass	Browse
Reference book	References
Left arrows	Previous View
Hierarchy diagram	Overview
One or three rectangles	Window Mode
Printer	Print

Table 10-1.   *Object Browser Speed Bar Reference*

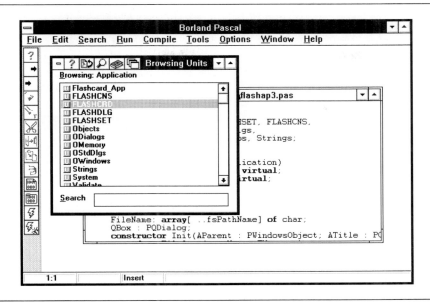

Figure 10-8.   *Browsing units in the Windows IDE*

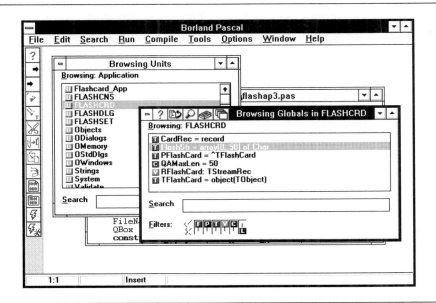

Figure 10-9.   *Browsing one unit in the Windows IDE*

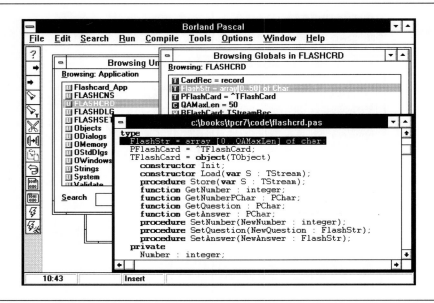

Figure 10-10.   *Using Go To to access source code from the Browser*

Search

Towards the bottom of the Browser window is a Search field. If there are too many declarations to display on the screen at once, you will see scroll bars in the window. If the number of declarations is extremely large, you may find it faster to enter the first few letters of the declaration of interest in the Search field. As you type the letters, the Browser window will automatically scroll to that area of the window.

Filters

Below the Search field are a set of filters that give you more control over which declarations appear in the Browser window. Each filter has a letter indicating the type of declaration being displayed. If the letter is pushed up, those declarations will appear in the Browser window. If the letter is pushed down, the declarations of that kind will be hidden. Table 10-2 indicates the letters used for filters and their meaning.

Browsing Objects

For the most part the Windows Object Browser is text-based, so there is little difference between it and the DOS version. The one major exception to this is the object overview. When you select Search|Objects from the menu bar, the Object

Letter	Meaning
L	Label
C	Constant
T	Type
V (Roman)	Variable
F	Function
P (Roman)	Procedure
V (Script)	Virtual declarations
P (Script)	Private declarations
I	Inherited declarations

Table 10-2.   *Filter Legend*

Browser gives you a pictorial overview of all of the objects in your program. Figure 10-11 shows the objects in the Flash Card program.

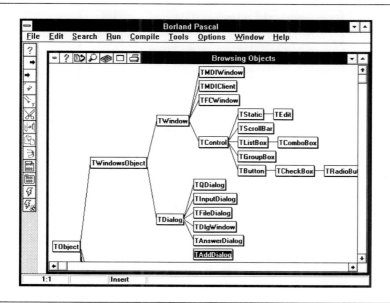

Figure 10-11.   *Object hierarchy in the Windows IDE*

As you look from left to right, the objects are displayed from ancestor to descendant. When you click on an object in the hierarchy, the Browser highlights the lines to the object's ancestor and descendants in red. This feature is especially helpful when you use more and more objects. There is no way to hide the descendants of an object like you can in the DOS Browser.

When you locate an object that you wish to browse, double-click on the name of the object. The new Browser window, such as the one in Figure 10-12, will be similar to a Browser window for a unit. The available filters are different because objects contain different kinds of declarations than units.

One major addition to the Browser window for an object is the connections to ancestor and descendants. To the left of the symbol display is a line and the name of the object's ancestor. To the right is a line and a list of the descendants. You can browse any of these objects by double-clicking on their names.

If you have a particular interest in an object's field or method declaration, double-click on the name of the declaration. This will bring up a Browser window for the symbol. From there you can go to the source code, show the references of the symbol, or any of the other available options. Figure 10-13 displays a typical display of references, in this case those for the Ok method within the *TAddDialog* object.

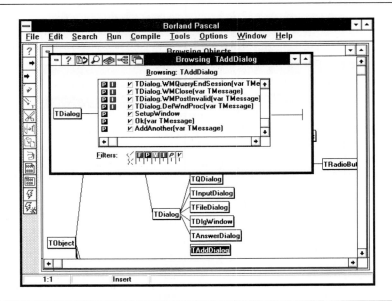

Figure 10-12. *Browsing an object in the Windows IDE*

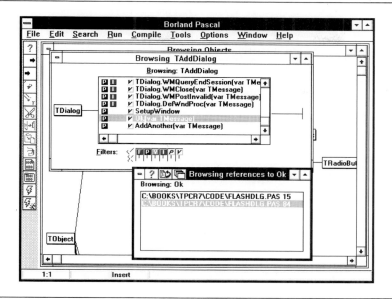

Figure 10-13. *Browsing references in the Windows IDE*

Browsing Globals

The Search|Globals command displays a Browser window with all of the declarations in your program. This includes all of the declarations in the standard units that are in one or more **uses** clauses. Obviously this list can become quite large. The Search and Filter areas at the bottom of the window are especially useful for the global declarations. These options were described previously in this chapter.

In Figure 10-14, the programmer has typed **PF** in the Search area. The Browser window has scrolled to include only the symbols that start with those letters.

Browsing a Symbol

If you know the exact name of a declaration you wish to browse, you can use the Search|Symbol dialog box. In this box you must type the full name of the symbol. If the IDE finds it, it displays a Browser window for that symbol. If it cannot find it, it displays an error in a dialog box.

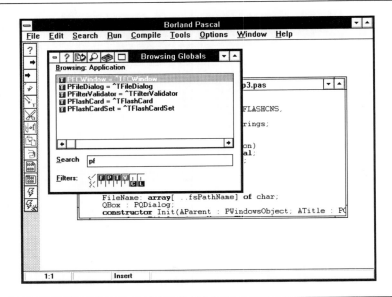

Figure 10-14. *Browsing globals in the Windows IDE*

Browser Options

The options for the Windows Object Browser appear in a dialog box that is accessible using either Options|Browser from the menu bar or Options from a Browser local menu. There are two sets of options in this box:

Symbols

The nine Symbols check boxes represent the nine kinds of filters available in the Object Browser. When a box is checked, new Browser windows will display symbols of that kind. When a box is blank, those symbols will be hidden. Think of these check boxes as being the default settings for the symbols—you can always use the filters to make changes within a particular Browser window.

Sub-browsing

The Sub-browsing option determines the default value for the Window Mode. You set this option to either New Browser for multiple windows, or Replace Current for a single Browser window. Again, you can override this by clicking on the appropriate icon in the speed bar.

Chapter **11**

The Resource
Workshop

The Windows IDE is one of the best environments for creating Windows programs. However, the IDE alone is not sufficient for developing most applications—it must be used in conjunction with the Resource Workshop.

This chapter will take you step by step through the creation of resources used in an actual application (the Flash Card program in Chapter 18). You can follow along on your computer as you develop a menu, a set of accelerators, and a dialog box. In addition, this chapter includes descriptions of the menu commands found throughout in the Resource Workshop.

What is a Resource?

A *resource* is a piece of the user interface of a Windows program. There are eight standard types of resources: menus, dialog boxes, accelerators, cursors, icons, bitmaps, font definitions, and string tables. Creating your user interface using Windows resources has several advantages over creating it as part of your Turbo Pascal program:

- Resources can be created interactively, making them easier to design and test.

- Resources are decoupled from your application, meaning you can alter part of the user interface without recompiling the program.

- Resources are easier to change than Turbo Pascal code.

- Resources are easier to reuse across multiple Windows applications.

Creating a Project

The collection of resources for a specific purpose is called a *project*. Before you can create any resource you must associate that resource with a project. The first time you use the Resource Workshop you probably have no existing projects, so you must create a new one.

To create a project, select the File|New Project dialog box. In this box you must choose the type of project. The default type is an .RC, or resource compiler file. A resource compiler file stores the resource information in text form, making it easy to edit both interactively and textually. It can also include other resource files of any type. This project type is the most versatile, and the one you'll use most often. The other project types will be covered later in this chapter.

When you press ENTER, or click on the Ok button, the Workshop will create a project called UNTITLED.RC. You may also notice that the screen flashes a few times and new menu items appear on the menu bar. The Resource Workshop creates and destroys menus based on what windows are currently active. When you first invoke the Workshop, only the File and Help menus appear. Once you create or load a project, the Edit, Resource, View, and Window menus are added. The Workshop also adds and removes items from individual menus.

Once a project is created or loaded, the *Project window* appears on the right side of the screen. The Project window contains the names of the resources contained in the current project. When there are multiple resources in a project, you can edit one of them by double-clicking on the entry in the Project window. When you first create a project, however, the Project window is blank.

Adding an Identifier Unit

When designing resources, always remember that the resources will eventually interact with your Pascal program. For instance, when the user selects a command from the menu bar, your program must interpret that command and take the appropriate action. With this in mind, you should always use a Pascal unit to store the identifiers used in the resources. You'll see how these identifiers are used as the chapter progresses.

The Resource Workshop cannot use any Pascal file for identifiers; the file must follow a very specific syntax. The only Pascal files that can act as resource identifiers are units that contain only constant declarations. The declarations must be in the **interface** section, and the **implementation** section must be empty. Any additional

declarations in the unit may compile under Turbo Pascal, but they won't compile in
the Resource Workshop.

Rather than creating the unit in the IDE, and switching back and forth all the
time, you can create the unit inside the Workshop. This is a three-step process:

1. Select File|Add to Project dialog box.

2. Change the File Type field to "PAS pascal constant unit."

3. Enter the name of the new unit in the File Name field.

Once you do these steps, the Workshop will attempt to find the file on your disk.
When it doesn't, it will ask you if you want to create it. If you do, click the Yes button
in the dialog box.

The Flash Card program uses a unit called FLASHCNS. Follow the above steps to
create this unit. When you do, the dialog boxes will disappear, but the screen will be
unchanged. To verify that you successfully created the unit, execute the View|By File
command. This command alters the display of the Project window so it shows the
names of the files included in the project. If you created the FLASHCNS unit
successfully, your screen will look like Figure 11-1.

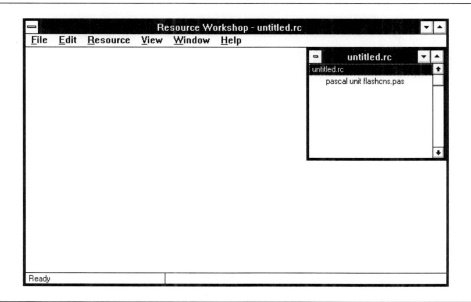

Figure 11-1.   *The By File display of the Project window*

Saving your work

At this stage your project is still called UNTITLED.RC, and your work is not saved. Even though there is very little in your project so far, it's always better to save your work often. To save your project, select either File|Save Project or File|Save File As. Since your project is called UNTITLED, the Workshop will automatically display the File|Save File As dialog box from either command. For the Flash Card program, let's call the project FLASH.RC.

There is one save option that you will want to set right away, called the multi-save option. With this option you can tell the Workshop to not only save the .RC file, but also to compile the file and store it as a .RES file. The .RES file is the one required by Turbo Pascal. To set the multi-save option, bring up the File|Preferences dialog box. Click on the .RES box in the Multi-save group, and a check mark will appear. From now on, whenever you save the project, the Workshop will save both FLASH.RC and FLASH.RES.

The next time you use the Resource Workshop, you will need to load the FLASH.RC project. To do this, select the File|Open Project dialog box. This box, shown in Figure 11-2, includes a list of the projects in the current directory. To load one of them, simply double-click on the filename. As it loads the file, it compiles the ASCII text into editable resources.

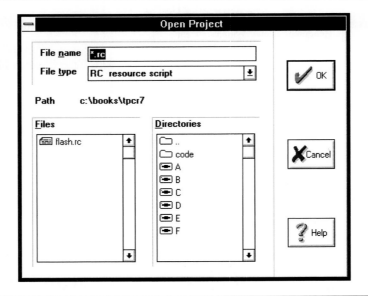

Figure 11-2. *The Open Project dialog box*

Creating a Menu

Once you have your project file and your identifier unit in place, you can create your first resource. For this project, we'll create the menu bar first.

To create a resource, execute the Resource|New command. This command displays a dialog box where you select the type of resource. Use the scroll bar to find the Menu type, then double-click on that type. The Workshop will add a menu to the project, using the default name MENU_1.

The name of the menu is used in Object Windows applications when the menu is loaded into your program. For this reason, you will want to change the name and use an identifier. To do this, select the Resource|Rename dialog box. Then enter the name of the menu, in this case *MenuBar*, in the New Name field. When you press ENTER or click Ok, the Workshop will search its list of identifiers for the name *MenuBar*. When it doesn't find it, it will ask if you want to create it. Press the Yes button, and enter the integer value of the identifier in the Value field of the New Identifier dialog box. For this example use the value 200. The Workshop will automatically add a constant declaration to the FLASHCNS unit, using proper Turbo Pascal syntax.

The Menu window has three main areas called *panes*. On the left side is the Dialog pane, where you can alter the attributes of a menu item. In the top of the right side is the Test Menu pane, which displays your menu as it will appear in your application. The rest of the right side is the Outline pane, which displays all of the items in the menu in outline form.

Changing Items

When the Workshop creates a menu resource, it includes one pop-up menu called "Pop-up" with one item called "Item," as shown in Figure 11-3. Your first task will be to change these defaults to the values you'll want in your program.

Item Text

The Item Text field in the Dialog pane contains the text that appears in the menu. To change the text of a menu item, find the item in the Outline pane and click it with your mouse. Then double-click on the Item Text field and type in the new value.

The & character is used to underline a letter in the menu item. When a letter is underlined the user can press that letter to select a command rather than clicking it with the mouse. For the first pop-up menu, change the pop-up text to **&File**, which will underline the F in the word File.

You may also choose to display an accelerator next to the menu item. To do this, add a \t (tab character) to the end of the text and type the accelerator value. The first item in the File menu should be **&Open\tF3**, which indicates that the F3 key is an accelerator for File|Open. Note that this does not create the accelerator; it only help the user to identify it. You will create the actual accelerator later in this chapter.

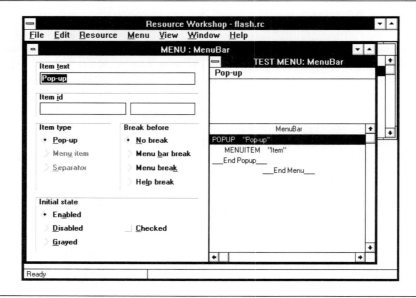

Figure 11-3.   *The Menu Resource window*

Item Id

The Item Id field contains the number or identifier of the command to execute when the user selects that menu item. Remember, you want to use identifiers as much as possible to keep your resources consistent with your application code. The command for File|Open is *cmFileOpen*. When you type this name in the Item Id field, you will be asked if you want to create the identifier. Create it, and use the value 201.

 Identifiers are case sensitive so that they will be compatible with C programs, which also run under the Resource Workshop. Be sure to capitalize your identifiers properly.

Item Type

Normally you set the menu item type when you create it. Thus the Item Type field usually serves as information only. In most circumstances, rather than changing the value in the Item Type field, you will want to delete the old menu item and create a new one of the proper type. In rare instances, such as converting an item to a separator, you might use the Item Type field to change the type.

Break Before

A *break* defines where the next menu item appears. The Workshop sets the most common values for these, and altering them is an advanced feature. Refer to *Windows 3.1 Programming* by Murray and Pappas (Osborne McGraw-Hill, 1992). The one change you might make is changing a pop-up menu from Menu Break to Help Break, which moves the menu to the far right side of the menu bar.

Initial State

The Initial State radio buttons determine the status of the menu item when your program begins: Enabled, meaning the command will work; Disabled, meaning the command will appear but won't work; and Grayed, meaning the command will be grayed out and the user will not be able to select it. There is also a check box called Checked, which adds a check mark next to the menu item.

Creating Items

Unless your menu bar has only one pop-up menu with one item you will need to create additional items. The commands to create items appear in the Menu menu. This menu will appear in the menu bar only when the Menu window is active.

New Pop-up

To add a new pop-up menu, first move the highlighted line in the Outline pane to just after where you want the new menu. For example, to add a second pop-up menu to the *MenuBar* menu, you must click on the "__End Menu__" line. Then either select Menu|New Pop-up, or press the CTRL-P accelerator. The Workshop will create a new pop-up menu with the same default values as the original one.

New Menu Item

Inserting new menu items follows the same paradigm—the insertion takes place just before the highlighted line. To add a second item to the File menu, highlight the first "__End Pop-up__" line. Then use either Menu|New Menu Item or the INS key. Once it is created, change the Item Text and Item ID to the desired values.

If you will be implementing the Flash Card program, add the rest of the menu items, using Table 11-1 as a guide. If done properly, the Menu window should look like Figure 11-4.

Menu Item	Item Text	Item ID	ID value
File|Open	&Open\tF3	cmFileOpen	201
File|Save	&Save\tF2	cmFileSave	202
File|Exit	E&xit\tALT-X	cmQuit	203
Card|Add	&Add	cmCardAdd	211
Card|Change	&Change	cmCardChange	212
Card|Delete	&Delete	cmCardDelete	213
Card|Random	&Random\tF8	cmCardRandom	214
Card|Next	&Next\tF9	cmCardNext	215

Table 11-1.   *Menu Items Associated with the MenuBar Resource*

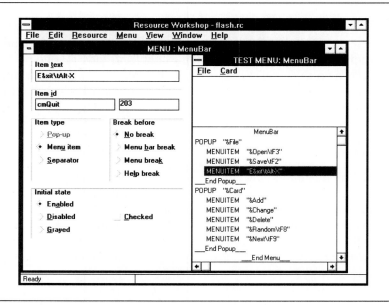

Figure 11-4.   *The Menu Bar for the Flash Card program*

New Separator

A *separator* is a horizontal line that separates one set of menu items from another. To insert a separator, highlight the menu item that will appear after the separator; then use Menu|New Separator or CTRL-S.

Standard Pop-ups

To promote consistency among applications, the Resource Workshop provides three "standard" pop-up menus. These menus have a complete set of menu items and associated commands. The commands do not use identifiers, but you can add them individually. To insert a standard pop-up, use one of the these commands: Menu|New File Pop-up, Menu|New Edit Pop-up, or Menu|New Help Pop-up.

Testing the Menu

The Test Menu pane lets you see what the menu will look like in your application. Click on an item in the pane, and the menu items will appear below it. As you move around in the Test Menu pane, the values in the other panes will be changed to reflect the current item.

Creating Accelerators

The menu bar created in the previous section included names of accelerators as part of the menu items. To create the actual accelerators, you must define an accelerator resource.

The process of creating an accelerator resource is the same as the one used for the menu. First, use Resource|New to bring up the New Resource dialog box. Then highlight the word ACCELERATORS and click the Ok button. This will create an Accelerator window with the default name ACCELERATORS_1. Finally, use Resource|Rename to create an identifier for the resource; in this case use the word *AccelKeys* and the value 299.

The Accelerator window has two panes: an Outline pane on the right that shows all of the accelerators defined in the active resource; and a Dialog Box pane that lets you change the attributes of an accelerator.

Changing an Accelerator

The resource created by the Workshop includes one line for the first accelerator. Here's how to change the default values.

Command

The Command field holds the identifier or number associated with the accelerator. Since you've already created the identifiers for the menu, you should use the same ones for the accelerators. For the first accelerator set the command to *cmFileOpen*.

Key

In addition to the command, you must define the key associated with an accelerator. There are two types of keys: ASCII and virtual. An ASCII key is any key that is part of the ASCII character set. In other words, ASCII keys are those that appear on a standard typewriter. Virtual keys are those that don't appear on the typewriter, such as the function keys and the arrow keys. You can also add modifiers to the key, such as SHIFT, ALT, or CTRL.

The easiest way to define the key is to use the Accelerator|Key Value command. When you select this command you will see the following in the Outline pane:

```
Use the keyboard to select a key.
Click the mouse or press ALT-ESC when done
```

When you see this message, press the accelerator as if you were doing it in the application. Then click the mouse. The Workshop will set the Key, Key Type, and Modifiers fields to the appropriate values based on the key sequence you used.

Adding an Accelerator

To add another accelerator use Acclerator|New Item or the INS key. The order of accelerators is not important, so don't worry about which line is highlighted in the Outline pane. If you add the rest of the accelerators defined by the menu, your window should look like Figure 11-5.

Creating a Dialog Box

The dialog box is by far the most complex resource you can create. Each part of a dialog box, called a control, must be specified individually. Also, you must define any relationships among the controls.

The Flash Card program includes five dialog boxes. The resources for two of them, "Open File" and "Save File," are already predefined in Object Windows. The other three are all very similar, so this section will take you through the creation of just one, "Add Card."

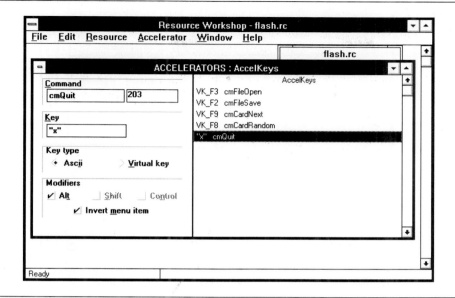

Figure 11-5. *The Accelerators for the Flash Card program*

The process for creating a Dialog resource is the same as that for any resource: select Resource|New, highlight the DIALOG line, and click Ok. For the "Add Card" box you should also rename the resource using the identifier *dlgAddCard* with a value of 240.

The Dialog Window

The Dialog window can be overwhelming, with four child windows and over thirty icons displayed at the same time. Refer to Figure 11-6 as you study the following text.

The Resource Window

The dialog box on the left side of the Dialog window is the resource itself. This is the dialog box that you are creating.

The Caption Window

In the top-right corner of the Dialog window is the Caption window. To change the caption, or title, of the dialog box, or one of its controls, use the mouse to select the resource or item. The current caption will appear in the Caption window. Double-click the title in the Caption window, then enter the new caption.

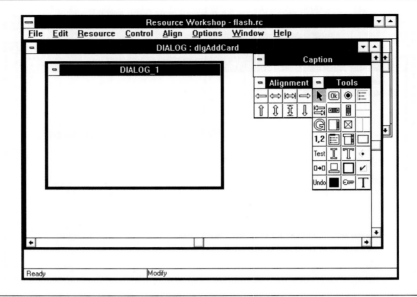

Figure 11-6.   *The Dialog window*

The Alignment Window

The Alignment window assists you in lining up the controls inside the dialog resource. This window, also called a palette, contains eight icons with arrows pointing in various directions. You will see how to use these icons later in the chapter.

The Tools Window

The Tools window is a palette of 28 icons. The first column of icons changes the edit mode of the window. The other three columns change the type of control to be created. Table 11-2 provides a cross reference between the Tools palette and the menu commands. The items in the last column, representing the Borland Custom Controls, do not have menu equivalents.

If you don't plan to use some of these child windows, you can either close them using their control boxes, or use a command from the Options menu, Options|Hide Tools, Options|Hide Alignment, and Options|Hide Caption.

Adding a Push Button

The general sequence for adding any type of control to your dialog box is the same:

1. Click on the type of control to create, or use its menu equivalent.

2. Move the mouse to the location of the new control.

3. Click the mouse to create the control.

4. Drag the control to its desired position and size.

5. Change its attributes in the Style dialog box.

Icon	(col,row)	Equivalent Menu Command
Cursor arrow	1,1	Options|Modify Controls
Arrows with stops	1,2	Options|Set Tabs
Large G	1,3	Options|Set Groups
Bold 1,2	1,4	Options|Set Order
Test	1,5	Options|Test Dialog
Square, square	1,6	Edit|Duplicate
Undo	1,7	Edit|Undo
Ok button	2,1	Control|Push Button
Scroll bar	2,2	Control|Horizontal Scroll Bar
Box with scroll bar	2,3	Control|List Box
Box around controls	2,4	Control|Group Box
Edit cursor	2,5	Control|Edit Text
Square & rectangle	2,6	Control|Icon
Dark square	2,7	Control|Black Rectangle
Black circle inside white one	3,1	Control|Radio Button
Scroll bar	3,2	Control|Vertical Scroll Bar
X in square	3,3	Control|Check Box
Combo box	3,4	Control|Combo Box
Large T	3,5	Control|Static Text
Large square	3,6	Control|Black frame
Key	3,7	Control|Custom

Table 11-2.   Tool Palette Icon Summary

To see how this process works, let's add a push button to the "Add Card" dialog box. Start by clicking your mouse on the Ok button in the Tools window. You'll see the cursor change from an arrow to a little push button. Now move the cursor to where you want the button to appear, near the lower-left corner of the dialog box, and click the mouse. You should now see a push button with the word "Text" inside. The mouse should return to its normal arrow, too.

At this point the new push button is selected, as indicated by a gray frame around the control. This means you can drag the button around in the dialog box in case it's not exactly where you want it. You can also change the size of the button by dragging the appropriate edge of the gray frame.

The final step to creating the push button is to change the features of the button. This is done with the help of a Style dialog box. To display this box, either double-click the mouse in the control, or use the Control|Style command. There are fields in this box to change the text of the push button, the identifier associated with that button, and various other attributes. Figure 11-7 shows the Style dialog box.

To create the "Add Card" dialog box, you need a total of three push buttons, with these values:

Caption	Control ID	ID Value	Button Type
A&dd Another	dlgAddAnother	241	Default Push Button
&OK	IDOK	1	Push Button
&Cancel	IDCANCEL	2	Push Button

The identifiers for the other two buttons are predefined, so you won't need to add them to the identifier unit.

Application programs do not care about the locations of controls within a dialog box, only their identifiers.

Adding More Controls

The "Add Card" dialog box also includes two edit controls where the user will enter the question and answer for the flash card. To create an edit control, click the mouse on the large edit icon, the one that looks like an I. Then click the mouse where the control will go, and expand its width by dragging the right edge. Finally, use the Control|Style dialog box to set the proper identifier. For the question control, use *dlgQuestion* with a value of 242. For the answer control, use *dlgAnswer* and 243.

The rest of the controls in the dialog box are static text. As you can see by Figure 11-8, there is static text to represent the card number, and to help identify the edit controls. To add static text, follow the same process that you did for all other controls. In general, static text controls do not have identifiers associated with them, since the application does not need to communicate with them. The exception is static text

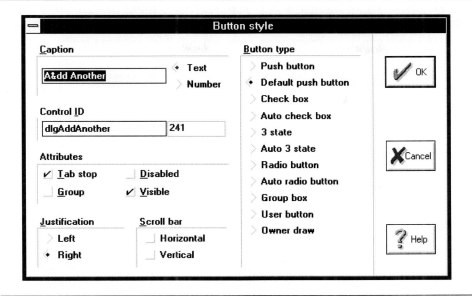

Figure 11-7. *The Style dialog box for a button control*

such as the card number, which the application must change in real time. For the
static text associated with the number "0," set the identifier to *dlgCardNum,* and use
the value 244.

Do not be concerned if your dialog box does not look exactly like the one in Figure
11-8. One of the key advantages of resources is that they're flexible. As long as you
have the three push buttons, the two edit controls, and at least one static text for the
card number, your dialog box will work with the Flash Card program.

Aligning the Controls

Once you have all the controls defined in your dialog box, you may wish to align them
for better appearance. The Align menu has four commands, each of which bring up
a different dialog box. Here is a description of each box:

Size

The Align|Size dialog box contains options to match the controls so that they all
have the same height or width. To use this box, you must first select multiple controls
by clicking on the first control, then holding down the SHIFT key and clicking on
the additional controls.

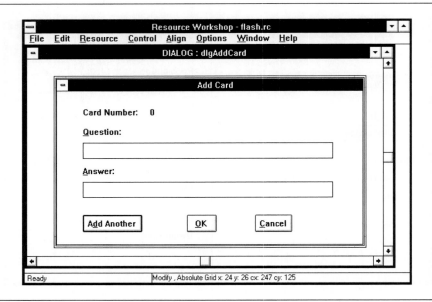

Figure 11-8.   *The final "Add Card" dialog box*

To align the three push buttons in the "Add Card" dialog box, place a frame around all three by selecting them. Then choose the Grow to Largest field in the Vertical group. When you click the OK button, the buttons will all be the same size.

Align

In addition to aligning the positions of controls, you can also align their sizes. The Align|Align dialog box lets you move controls around so that one or more of their sides are in line. The commands in this dialog box do not affect the sizes of controls, only their positions. For the three push buttons, use the Centers option in the Vertical group to make all the buttons aligned.

Array

The Align|Array dialog box is for controls that form a table of a certain number of rows and columns. This dialog box changes the layout of those controls.

Grid

The Align|Grid dialog box places a grid in the dialog box, and "snaps" the controls so that they are aligned with the grid lines. Select the size of the grid squares, and then check the Show Grid field to display it.

Setting the Order

The order of the controls in a dialog box is important because it defines the order in which you can use TAB to get from one control to another. As a default the controls are ordered based on the order you create them. Normally you will need to change this so they are ordered somewhat top to bottom.

The Options|Set Order command changes the display of your dialog resource so that you see only outlines of the controls and their ordinality. The cursor changes to a crosshair with a **1,2** next to it. To change the order, click the mouse on each control in the order you wish to see them. Figure 11-9 shows the final order of the "Add Card" dialog box.

Setting the Tabs

For each control in your dialog box you must decide whether it makes sense to allow the user to use TAB to get to that control. The Resource Workshop usually creates the proper defaults, setting the tabs for most controls except static text.

To verify the tab settings use the Options|Set Tabs command. The dialog box display will change so that the controls with tabs set are outlined in thick gray, and the controls with tabs disabled are outlined in thin black. Click the mouse on a control to toggle the tab setting.

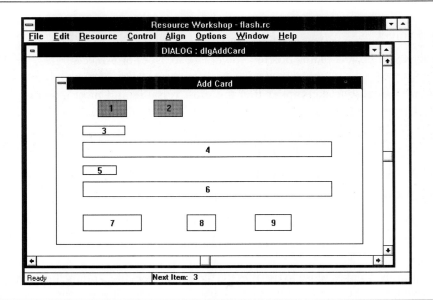

Figure 11-9.   *Ordering the controls in a dialog box*

Setting the Groups

You are accustomed to seeing groups for sets of radio buttons and check boxes. You can also set groups for combinations of static text and edit control. For example, by grouping the "Question:" static text with the edit control for the question, you let the user press ALT-Q to get to the edit control.

To set groups, use the Options|Set Groups command. The dialog resource display will place gray outlines around the controls that start groups. Click the mouse on a control to toggle the group setting.

Common Operations

As mentioned earlier in this chapter, the Resource Workshop uses a rather unusual approach to its menu bar, in that the menus vary based on what window is active. The previous sections covered the menus that were specific to menus, accelerators, and dialog boxes. The rest of the chapter is a reference of those menus and menu items that are common to all window types.

The File Menu

The File menu is one of those that starts small, and grows once you've opened or created a project. Here are the commands of the larger version of the File menu.

New Project

The File|New Project dialog box lets you create six types of projects:

- .RC—a resource compiler file; the most versatile and most general project type.

- .RES—a binary resource file; a compiled version of a .RC file; required by Object Windows applications.

- .CUR—a binary file that contains one cursor bitmap.

- .ICO—a binary file that contains one or more icon bitmaps.

- .BMP—a binary file that contains a bitmap.

- .FNT—a binary file that contains a font definition.

In most cases it makes sense to use the .RC file as a project file, and include the other types, which can be stand-alone, as necessary. For instance, if you create an icon as a separate .ICO file, you would add that to the .RC project.

Open Project

To restore an existing project into the Workshop you use the File|Open Project dialog box. If you know the name of the file to open you can type the name in the File Name field. Otherwise, select the type of file in the File Type field. The dialog box will display a list of the files that match the extension in a list box. Double-click on the file to load.

Save Project

If you have made changes to a project, you should save it periodically using the File|Save Project command. If you try to save a new project that has no name, the Workshop will take you to the File|Save File As dialog box.

Save File As

The File|Save File As dialog box lets you change the name of a project or name a new one. You may browse directories or files within a directory.

Close All

The File|Close All command closes all open windows in the Workshop. If you have made changes to any file, you will be given the opportunity to save those changes.

Add To Project

As your projects get larger, you may find it easier to split the projects into several files. Some programmers even prefer to place each resource in a separate file. When you need to create a project that is a combination of many files, you can use the File|Add To Project dialog box to bring them together. This dialog box is similar in appearance to the Open Project box; however, instead of opening a new file, this box will insert a file into the current one.

Remove From Project

If you have added several files to the project, and now wish to remove one, first select the file in the Project window. Then use the File|Remove From Project command to delete it.

Preferences

If you followed all the information in this chapter you have already seen the File|Preferences dialog box, in the "Saving Your Work" section of this chapter. There are six options in this box:

Undo Levels   By default, the Workshop stores 10 changes that can be reverted using the Edit|Undo command. If you expect to make more mistakes, and have plenty of memory, you can increase this value.

Text Editor   Since resource compiler (.RC) files are ASCII, you can edit them using any text editor. When the Workshop compiles your file and finds an error, it will automatically transfer you to the editor of your choice to fix the problem. The default editor is NOTEPAD.EXE, a simple word processor that comes standard with Windows.

Include Path   The Include Path field defines where the Workshop will search for include files.

Save .RES   One of the two multi-save options, this option tells the Workshop to save your project not only as a .RC ASCII file, but as a compiled (binary) .RES file as well.

Save .EXE   If you are modifying resources for a specific executable file (.EXE or .DLL), you can set this multi-save option so that when you save your changes, they are placed in the executable file also.

Make Backups   You should always save backup versions of your work, in case something goes wrong. If for some reason you cannot spare the disk space, you can disable this option.

Exit

The File|Exit command exits the Resource Workshop. If you have made changes to the project without saving it, the Workshop will give you the opportunity to do so.

The Edit Menu

Most Windows applications use an Edit menu to support clipboard operations. The Resource Workshop can cut and paste text, but more importantly, it can cut and paste entire resource items. This section will explain how it works, in addition to the other commands in the Edit menu.

Undo

Any time you change a resource, such as adding a button to a dialog box, or changing a menu item, the Workshop remembers the change. If you decided you don't like the change, you can execute the Edit|Undo command. The Workshop will "rewind" your changes to their previous state. You can set the Undo Levels option in the File|Preferences dialog box to allow you to use the Undo command multiple times (the default is 10 times).

Redo

The Edit|Redo command is the opposite of the Undo command. Suppose you use Edit|Undo eight times, and realize that you "undid" your resource too far. Use Edit|Redo to "fast-forward" your changes as if you did them manually.

Cut

The Edit|Cut command removes an item from a resource, and stores it in the clipboard.

Copy

The Edit|Copy command copies an item from a resource to the clipboard.

Paste

To copy a resource item from the clipboard into the resource, you use the Edit|Paste command. For example, suppose you need to move a menu item from one pop-up menu to another. The easiest way is to follow these steps:

1. Bring the menu into a Menu window by selecting it from the Project window.

2. Select the item to move in the Outline pane.

3. Execute the Edit|Cut command.

4. Highlight the menu item below where you want to paste the item in the clipboard.

5. Execute the Edit|Paste command.

Delete

The Edit|Delete command removes an item from a resource without placing a copy in the clipboard. If you accidently delete an item, use Edit|Undo to retrieve it.

Duplicate

If you have a resource item that you want to copy many times, you can use the Edit|Duplicate dialog box. This box lets you create a set of items in a row, in a column, or in a table of rows and columns.

To use the Duplicate tool, use the mouse to highlight the item to duplicate. In the Edit|Duplicate dialog box select the number of rows and columns you want. You can also specify the amount of spacing between the items. When you click the OK button, the selected item will be duplicated in your resource. Use the mouse to move the items to the location you desire.

Select All

If you want to use Copy or Cut on an entire resource, start with the Edit|Select All command. Once all the items are selected, use the appropriate clipboard command.

The Resource Menu

The Resource menu contains the commands to create and modify resources. The following are the items in the Resource menu:

New

The Resource|New dialog box lets you create a new resource within the current project. Use your mouse to highlight the type of resource you wish to create, and click OK.

Edit

When you use the Resource|Edit command, the Workshop will create a resource window based on which resource is highlighted in the Project window. A shortcut for this command is to double-click the resource in the Project window.

Edit as Text

If you want to modify the ASCII text that makes up a resource, select the Resource|Edit as Text command. However, you will find the interactive editor much more friendly.

View

The Resource|View command is similar to Resource|Edit, except you cannot make changes to the resource in the window.

Save Resource As

As you create a resource in a particular project, you may decide that the resource will be useful in other projects as well. When you do, use the Resource|Save Resource As dialog box to create a separate file for that resource. You can later add the resource to other projects as needed.

Rename

If you have created any resources using the techniques outlined in this chapter, then you have already used the Resource|Rename dialog box. It is in this box where you change the name of a resource, and associate the resource with an identifier.

Identifiers

The Resource|Identifiers dialog box lets you create, change, and remove identifiers used in your project.

The View Menu

The View menu actually changes based on which resource window is active. There is View menu for Menu windows and for bitmap windows. This section covers the third and most common View menu, which contains commands that affect the Project window.

By Type

When you select the View|By Type command, the Project window will sort the resources by their type, putting all dialog boxes together, all menus together, and so on.

By File

The View|By File option sorts the resources in the Project window by the files that contain them.

Show Identifiers

The Project window can also show the identifiers defined in your project. To avoid cluttering up the window, you will usually want to disable the resource display.

Show Resources

The View|Show Resources option is the default for the Project window. When this option is enabled, the window will show the resources defined by the project. When disabled, the Project window can be used to display files and identifiers, based on the other options selected.

Show Items

The typical way to see more detail for a resource is to open a resource window. Alternatively, you can select the View|Show Items command, which will expand the display in the Project window to show all of the items for each resource. Like the identifier display, this tends to provide more clutter than value.

Show Unused Types

By default, the View|By Type display only shows resource types when a resource of that type is defined. You can display the resource types that are unused as well by selecting the View|Show Unused Types command.

The Window Menu

In an application that is filled with windows, the Window menu is surprisingly sparse. The first two commands let you Tile and Cascade the open windows, just like you can in most Windows applications. The rest of the Window menu is a list of the windows that are open in the Workshop. To activate a window, select the item that matches its name.

The Help Menu

The Help menu is very typical of Borland's products. Each of the commands in this menu brings up a Help window with the on-line help for the Workshop. The only difference among the commands is which screen is displayed in the Help window.

Chapter *12*

Debugging in DOS and Windows

As a general rule, programs do not run correctly the first time. Unfortunately, they often don't run correctly the tenth time, either. Tracking down and fixing program bugs can be time-consuming, painful, and unproductive. Fortunately, Turbo Pascal now includes both an integrated debugger and a stand-alone debugger that can help you spot problems in seconds and make your programming more rewarding.

The Integrated Debugger

Debuggers have been around for a long time. One of the first, DEBUG.COM, was included with the PC operating system. With DEBUG, a programmer could trace through a program one assembly-language instruction at a time, view segments of memory, and uncover bugs through a painstaking process. While useful in its own right, DEBUG suffered from several shortcomings. First, you could only see your program in assembler, a real limitation if you wrote the program in C, Pascal, or another high-level language. Second, variables were shown as addresses and offsets. Tracing a specific variable throughout a program was difficult, to say the least.

Programmers needed a better debugger—one that showed variables by name and could match source code to the underlying assembler instructions. Microsoft packaged a symbolic debugger—SYMDEB—with their assembler, and other software developers soon offered products of their own with additional desirable features. Recently, Borland introduced its own stand-alone debugger, Turbo Debugger, with a wide array of powerful features. Yet, as powerful as they are, all of these debuggers have one disadvantage—you have to get out of Turbo Pascal to use them.

While it lacks the advanced features you will find in Turbo Debugger, Turbo Pascal's integrated debugger does provide an easy-to-use way to track down all but the most subtle software bugs. Best of all, you don't need to leave the integrated development environment to use it. Even if you've never used a debugger before, you'll find the integrated debugger a pleasure. With it you can watch how variables change as you move through your program a line at a time, or you can set break points and jump from place to place in your program. The integrated debugger, combined with fast compilation, makes Turbo Pascal perhaps the most productive programming environment available.

Getting Ready to Debug

Before you debug a program, there are several things you must do. First, you must enable the $D compiler directive either by adding the compiler directive $D+ to your source code, or by enabling the Debug Information selection on the Options| Compiler dialog box. This tells Turbo Pascal to store program information that links a program's source code to its object code. If your program uses local variables, you should also enable the $L compiler directive by either including the $L+ compiler directive to your source code or by enabling the Local Symbols selection on the Options|Compiler dialog box. When this directive is enabled, Turbo Pascal stores information about local variables, allowing you to view them by name.

Finally, before you compile your program, you must be sure to enable the Integrated Debugging selection on the Options|Debugger dialog box. With this option enabled, the resulting executable code will contain debug information. If you do not intend to debug a program and you need extra RAM, disable this feature. With these details attended to, you can proceed to debug your program.

Debugger Features

Now that you know how to prepare to debug a program, you are ready to get started. The integrated debugger gives you complete control over the execution of your program. You can set break points, trace from line to line, watch variables change, and more. The important point is that you'll never have to guess what your program is doing—you'll be able to watch every step.

The Execution Bar

When you are debugging a program, the execution bar highlights the program statement that will execute next. You can move the cursor around the source file, and even load other source files into the editor, but the integrated debugger will always keep track of the execution bar. The execution bar remains active until the program terminates or until you end the debugging session by selecting the Run| Program Reset command.

Go to Cursor

The Go to Cursor feature lets you specify a temporary stopping point for your program. To use this feature, place the cursor on a line of code in your program and either press F4 or select Run|Go to Cursor. Turbo Pascal will execute your program until it reaches the program line containing the cursor, at which point control will be returned to you. This feature is especially handy if you want to go directly, rather than step by step, to a spot deep within your program.

To see how Go to Cursor works, consider the program shown in Figure 12-1. The execution bar is the first **begin** statement in the program, and the cursor is four lines down. When you press F4, the program executes the first two statements, skips the blank line, and halts execution at the line where the cursor is (see Figure 12-2).

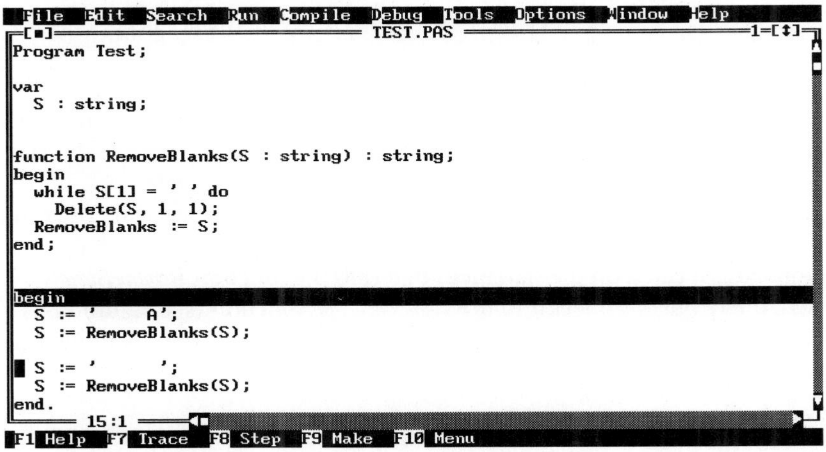

Figure 12-1. *Program at start of execution*

```
 File  Edit  Search  Run  Compile  Debug  Tools  Options  Window  Help
[■]════════════════════════ TEST.PAS ══════════════════════1═[↕]═
Program Test;

var
  S : string;


function RemoveBlanks(S : string) : string;
begin
  while S[1] = ' ' do
     Delete(S, 1, 1);
  RemoveBlanks := S;
end;


begin
  S := '     A';
  S := RemoveBlanks(S);

  S := '        ';
  S := RemoveBlanks(S);
end.
══════ 19:1 ═════
 F1 Help  F7 Trace  F8 Step  F9 Make  F10 Menu
```

Figure 12-2.   *After using Go to Cursor*

While Go to Cursor is like a breakpoint, it is less restrictive. Breakpoints have to be set and remain set until removed, while Go to Cursor relies only on the current position of the cursor. Note, however, that when you use this feature, the program will return control only if it reaches the line you selected. If, on the other hand, your program never executes that line, you will not receive control.

Trace Into

A fundamental feature of any debugger is the ability to execute one statement at a time. The Run|Trace Into command, also activated by the F7 key, executes the statement highlighted by the execution bar, moves the bar to the next statement, and returns control to you. If the execution bar is at a function or procedure call, Trace Into will jump to that part of the program and continue executing from there. In Figure 12-3, the execution bar is located on the statement that calls the function *RemoveBlanks*. When F7 is pressed, the debugger traces into the *RemoveBlanks* function (see Figure 12-4).

If you are not interested in tracing into a procedure call, but wish to execute the procedure and move to the next line, use the Step Over feature.

Step Over

Like Trace Into, the Step Over feature executes one line of code at a time. Step Over, however, will not trace into function or procedure calls. Instead, it executes the

```
 File  Edit  Search  Run  Compile  Debug  Tools  Options  Window  Help
┌─[■]────────────────────── TEST.PAS ═══════════════════════1=[↕]─┐
│Program Test;                                                    ▲│
│                                                                  │
│var                                                               │
│  S : string;                                                     │
│                                                                  │
│                                                                  │
│function RemoveBlanks(S : string) : string;                       │
│begin                                                             │
│  while S[1] = ' ' do                                             │
│    Delete(S, 1, 1);                                              │
│  RemoveBlanks := S;                                              │
│end;                                                              │
│                                                                  │
│                                                                  │
│begin                                                             │
│  S := '    A';                                                   │
│  S := RemoveBlanks(S);                                           │
│                                                                  │
│  S := '    ';                                                    │
│  S := RemoveBlanks(S);                                           │
│end.                                                             ▼│
└══ 17:1 ═══◄█──────────────────────────────────────────────►─────┘
 F1 Help  F7 Trace  F8 Step  F9 Make  F10 Menu
```

Figure 12-3.   *Before executing a function*

```
 File  Edit  Search  Run  Compile  Debug  Tools  Options  Window  Help
┌─[■]────────────────────── TEST.PAS ═══════════════════════1=[↕]─┐
│Program Test;                                                    ▲│
│                                                                  │
│var                                                               │
│  S : string;                                                     │
│                                                                  │
│                                                                  │
│function RemoveBlanks(S : string) : string;                       │
│begin                                                             │
│  while S[1] = ' ' do                                             │
│    Delete(S, 1, 1);                                              │
│  RemoveBlanks := S;                                              │
│end;                                                              │
│                                                                  │
│                                                                  │
│begin                                                             │
│  S := '    A';                                                   │
│  S := RemoveBlanks(S);                                           │
│                                                                  │
│  S := '    ';                                                    │
│  S := RemoveBlanks(S);                                           │
│end.                                                             ▼│
└══ 8:1 ═══◄█───────────────────────────────────────────────►─────┘
 F1 Help  F7 Trace  F8 Step  F9 Make  F10 Menu
```

Figure 12-4.   *After tracing into a function*

procedure or function as a single statement, moves the execution bar to the next statement, and returns control to you at that point. This feature is useful for avoiding procedures and functions that do not need to be debugged.

To see how this works, consider Figure 12-3, where the execution bar is positioned on the statement that calls the function *RemoveBlanks*. When you press F8, the debugger executes the entire statement, including the function call, at one time and moves the bar forward to the next statement (see Figure 12-5).

Evaluate and Modify

Pressing CTRL-F4 or selecting Debug|Evaluate/Modify pops up the Evaluate and Modify dialog box, a special window that lets you evaluate a variable or expression or modify the value of a variable. This window contains three input fields—Expression, Result, and New value (see Figure 12-6). In the Expression field you type the name of a variable, an expression, or a numeric value. For example, if you enter a hexadecimal number in the Expression field and press ENTER, the decimal equivalent will appear in the Result field (see Figure 12-7). You can also use the Evaluate and Modify window to change the value of a variable. For example, in Figure 12-8, the string variable *S* is found to contain only space characters. Use the TAB key to move to the New value field and type the letters **ABC.** Now the value of "*S*" has been modified to include the character string 'ABC'. Modifying the value of a variable is an easy way to test how your program reacts to a variety of situations.

```
  File  Edit  Search  Run  Compile  Debug  Tools  Options  Window  Help
 ─[■]═══════════════════════ TEST.PAS ═══════════════════════1═[↕]═
 Program Test;

 var
   S : string;


 function RemoveBlanks(S : string) : string;
 begin
   while S[1] = ' ' do
     Delete(S, 1, 1);
   RemoveBlanks := S;
 end;


 begin
   S := '    A';
   S := RemoveBlanks(S);
   S := '      ';
   S := RemoveBlanks(S);
 end.
 ══ 19:1 ══
  F1 Help  F7 Trace  F8 Step  F9 Make  F10 Menu
```

Figure 12-5. *After stepping over a function*

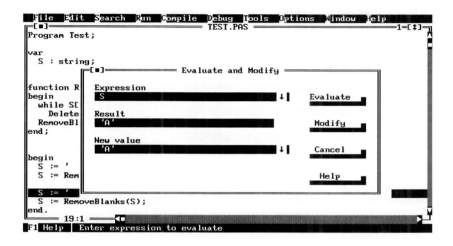

Figure 12-6.   *The Evaluate and Modify window*

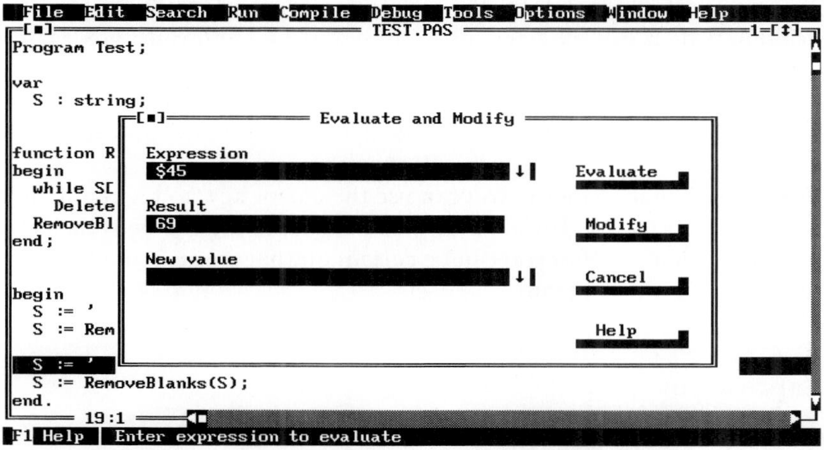

Figure 12-7.   *Converting a hexadecimal value*

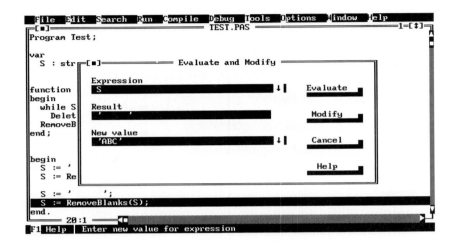

Figure 12-8.   *Modifying a variable*

Call Stack Window

In large programs, it is easy to lose track of the function and procedure calls that preceded a particular point in the program. The Call Stack window provides an easy way to find out how you got to the current location in your program. When you press CTRL-F3 (or select Call Stack from the Debug menu), Turbo Pascal opens the Call Stack window, which lists all active procedure and function calls. For example, in Figure 12-9, the Call Stack window shows four entries—*Proc3, Proc2, Proc1,* and *Test,* which is the name of the program itself. If a procedure takes parameters, the Call Stack window will display the values of those parameters along with the name of the procedure.

Inside the Call Stack window, you can use the cursor keys to highlight any of the entries. If you press ENTER, Turbo Pascal will take you to the source code location of the highlighted routine. Now you can be certain of what events brought you to your current position in the program.

Watch Expressions

A *watch expression* is a variable or expression you wish to observe while debugging a program. The ability to watch variables is one of the most important features of the integrated debugger. A program bug is almost always related to or signaled by an

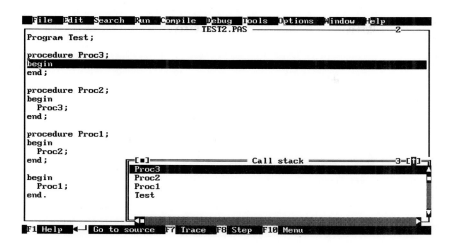

Figure 12-9. *The Call Stack window*

unexpected value in a variable. Watch expressions are displayed in the Watch window. You can open the Watch window by selecting Watch from the Debug menu.

The Watch window has its own local menu, which has six options. You can pop up this window by pressing the right mouse button, or ALT-F10.

Add

There are two ways to add a watch expression to the watch window. The first is by selecting the Debug|Add Watch dialog box. You can also display this box by pressing CTRL-F7.

The Add Watch dialog box is shown in Figure 12-10. If the cursor in your source file happened to be positioned on a symbol, that symbol will automatically appear in the Watch expression field. If this symbol is the correct one, simply press ENTER to add it to the watch list. Otherwise, enter the expression you want to watch. The symbol and its current value immediately appear in the Watch window (Figure 12-11). As you trace through your program, you can see how the variable changes. If the variable changes in a way that you don't expect, you may have found a bug.

Once you have created a Watch window, you can add new variables to it by activating the Watch window (by using the F6 key or the mouse) and selecting Add from the local menu, or pressing INS. When the Debug|Add Watch dialog box pops up, you type in the name of the variable you wish to add. Press ENTER to complete the process.

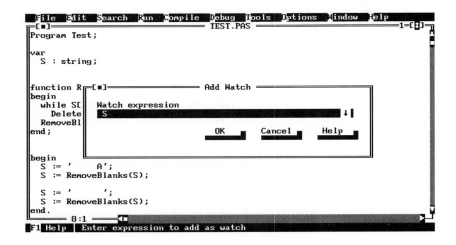

Figure 12-10. *Adding a variable to the Watch window*

```
  File  Edit  Search  Run  Compile  Debug  Tools  Options  Window  Help
 ┌─[■]═══════════════════════ TEST.PAS ════════════════════1═[↕]─┐
 Program Test;

 var
   S : string;

 function R┌─[■]═══════════════ Add Watch ═══════════════┐
 begin      │                                              │
    while S[  │ Watch expression                            │
      Delete  │ S                                        ↓ │ │
    RemoveBl  │                                              │
 end;         │         ┌──────┐  ┌────────┐  ┌──────┐      │
              │         │  OK  │  │ Cancel │  │ Help │      │
 begin        │         └──────┘  └────────┘  └──────┘      │
    S := '    └──────────────────────────────────────────────┘
    S := RemoveBlanks(S);

    S := '        ';
    S := RemoveBlanks(S);
 end.
 ═══ 8:1 ══════◄───────────────────────────────────────────►
 F1 Help │ Enter expression to add as watch
```

Figure 12-11. *A variable in the Watch window*

```
  File  Edit  Search  Run  Compile  Debug  Tools  Options  Window  Help
 ┌═══════════════════════════ TEST.PAS ═══════════════════1────┐
 begin
    while S[1] = ' ' do
      Delete(S, 1, 1);
    RemoveBlanks := S;
 end;


 begin
   S := '    A';
   S := RemoveBlanks(S);

   S := '        ';
   S := RemoveBlanks(S);
 end.
 ┌─[■]══════════════════════════ Watches ═══════════════════2═[↑]─┐
 │ S: '    A'                                                     ▲ │
 │                                                                  │
 │                                                                  │
 │ ◄─────────────────────────────────────────────────────────►    │
 F1 Help  F7 Trace  F8 Step  ◄┘ Edit  Ins Add  Del Delete  F10 Menu
```

Figure 12-11. *A variable in the Watch window*

You can add as many variables as you want to the Watch window or display a single variable in a number of different ways. For example, in Figure 12-12, the variable *S* is displayed both as a string and as the first character of the string.

Delete

As you debug your program, adding variables to the Watch window as you go, you may want to remove unneeded variables from the Watch window. The easiest way to do this is to activate the Watch window, move the highlight bar to the variable you want to remove, and select Delete from the local menu or press the DEL key.

Modify

You can also change the way you view a variable in the Watch window by highlighting the desired variable and pressing ENTER (or selecting Modify from the local menu). You can now change the variable or expression as desired. Press ENTER again to save the change.

Clear All

If you want to remove all variables from the Watch window, use the Clear All command from the local menu.

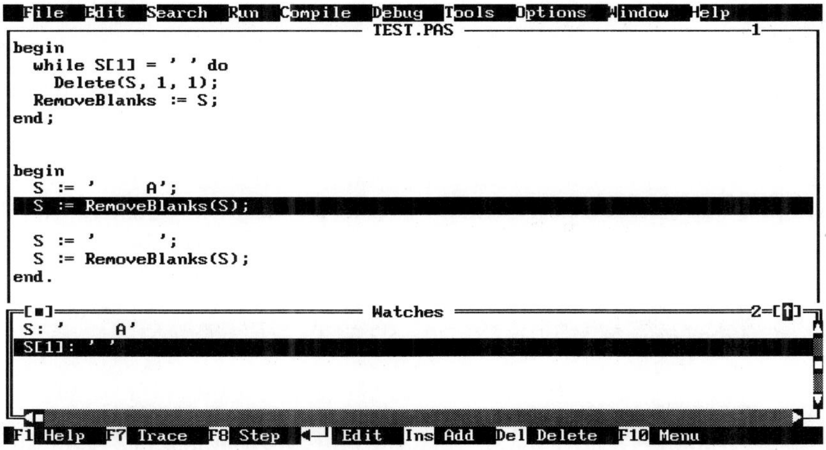

```
  File  Edit  Search  Run  Compile  Debug  Tools  Options  Window  Help
┌─────────────────────────────── TEST.PAS ───────────────────────────1─┐
│begin                                                                  │
│   while S[1] = ' ' do                                                 │
│     Delete(S, 1, 1);                                                  │
│   RemoveBlanks := S;                                                  │
│end;                                                                   │
│                                                                       │
│                                                                       │
│begin                                                                  │
│   S := '    A';                                                       │
│█S :=█RemoveBlanks(S);█████████████████████████████████████████████████│
│                                                                       │
│   S := '       ';                                                     │
│   S := RemoveBlanks(S);                                               │
│end.                                                                   │
┌─[■]──────────────────────── Watches ───────────────────────2─[↕]─┐
│S: '    A'                                                         ↑ │
│█S[1]: ' '█████████████████████████████████████████████████████████│
│                                                                   │
│                                                                 ↓ │
└─◄■──────────────────────────────────────────────────────────────►┘
 F1 Help  F7 Trace  F8 Step  ◄┘ Edit  Ins Add  Del Delete  F10 Menu
```

Figure 12-12.   *Two variables in the Watch window*

Disable

The Disable command in the local menu temporarily halts the updates of a watch expression.

Enable

The Enable command re-enables a watch expression that was previously disabled.

Breakpoints

A *breakpoint* is a flag attached to a line of source code that tells the IDE to stop execution when it reaches that line. Using breakpoints can be more efficient than tracing when you have a good idea of the location of the bug.

There are two types of breakpoints in the debugger: *unconditional* and *conditional*. When the IDE encounters an unconditional breakpoint, it always halts execution. When it hits a conditional breakpoint, it will halt only if certain conditions are true. You can also set a *pass count,* which tells the IDE to halt the program after executing a line a certain number of times.

Always set breakpoints on lines that contain an executable statement. Do not set breakpoints on blank lines, comment lines, compiler directives, data declarations, or other non-executable parts of your program.

Breakpoints are displayed in the Debug|Breakpoints dialog box. This box has six buttons: OK, Edit, Delete, View, Clear All, and Help. OK and Help are self-explanatory; the others are described here:

Edit

The Edit button allows you to change an existing breakpoint or add a new one. One line in the dialog box will appear in a different color. If that line is blank, pressing Edit will bring up the Add Breakpoint dialog box. If the highlighted line is on an existing breakpoint, pressing Edit will allow you to change it.

A simpler way to add a new breakpoint is to position the cursor on the line at which to break and press CTRL-F8, or select the Debug|Add Breakpoint command.

Delete

Once a breakpoint for a line has been set, it can be removed by repeating the same sequence used to set it; place the cursor on the line with the breakpoint and press CTRL-F8. Breakpoints are also cleared when you end your debugging session, and they are not made part of the .EXE program file.

View

If you use a lot of breakpoints in a program, it is easy to lose track of them. To locate breakpoints, select the View button in the Breakpoints dialog box. Turbo Pascal will find the break point, load the appropriate source file, and position the cursor on the line at which the breakpoint has been set.

Clear All

To clear all the breakpoints you have set in a program, choose Clear All from the Breakpoints dialog box.

CTRL-BREAK

You can halt your program's execution at any point by pressing CTRL-BREAK, which halts the program and positions the execution bar at the next statement to be executed. When you break a program from the outside, you cannot always be sure where you will be placed in the program. Still, this technique is useful for jumping in and out of a program at random points and is especially good for terminating endless loops.

A Debugging Example

As with most things, debugging is best learned by example. To see how the debugger can help uncover subtle errors in program code, consider the following program that consists of two parts. The first is a unit called UNIT1:

```
Unit Unit1;
{$D+,L+}

interface

procedure Proc1;

implementation

procedure Proc1;
var
  I : integer;
begin
  WriteLn('This is Proc1');
  while I < 2 do
    begin
```

```
      WriteLn('I = ', I);
      Inc(I, 1);
    end;
end;

end.
```

The second is a main program file (BUG.PAS):

```
Program Bug;
{$D+,L+}

uses Crt, UNIT1;

var
  W : integer;
  R1, R2 : real;

begin
  ClrScr;

  Proc1;

  R1 := 1.0E+38;
  for W := 1 to 10 do
    begin
      R2 := R1 + 1.0;
      WriteLn(R1, ' + 1.0 = ', R2);
      R1 := R2;
    end;

  WriteLn;
  Write('Press ENTER...');
  ReadLn;
end.
```

Before you read on, take a look at the previous listings and see if you can find the two bugs contained in them.

If you couldn't find the bugs, don't be too concerned. That's why we have debuggers in the first place. In fact, after using a debugger for a while, you will become much more adept at avoiding bugs altogether.

Starting Up

Type in and compile the program and unit just given. (Before compiling, check the Options|Debug dialog box to be sure that integrated debugging is on.) When you are ready, load the main program file into the editor, place the cursor on the call to *Proc1*, and press F4. The IDE will begin executing your program (performing a Make first, if needed) and stop with the execution bar highlighting the call to *Proc1* (see Figure 12-13). At this point, you can do several things. You can press F8 to step over the call to *Proc1;* you can press F7 to trace into *Proc1;* you can go to another point in the program and press F4 again; you can press CTRL-F2 to reset the program to the beginning; or you can press CTRL-F9 to let the program run. Let's press F7 to trace into *Proc1.*

Adding Watch Variables

When you trace into *Proc1*, the execution bar is placed on the first **begin** (see Figure 12-14). Notice that the variable *I* has been added to the Watch window and that its value is -31910. By now you may have spotted the bug in this procedure. As the following listing shows, the procedure assumes that *I* will start out at a more reasonable value, like 0 or 1.

```
while I < 2 do
  begin
    WriteLn('I = ', I);
    Inc(I, 1);
  end;
```

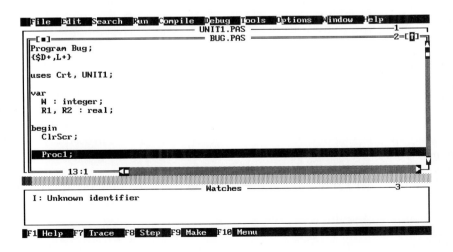

Figure 12-13.   *Starting a debugging session*

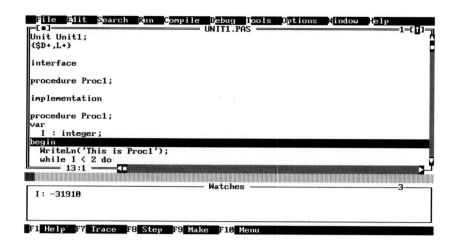

Figure 12-14.   *Tracing into Proc1*

Notice that *I* is never initialized, so you cannot know in advance what value *I* will have when the procedure executes. In this case, *I* has a value far below 2, so the loop will execute many more times than you probably expected. The next time you run this program, *I* might start with a value much greater than 2, and you would see nothing on the screen. In this case the Watch expression would save you a lot of time tracking down this little bug.

More on the Watch Window

Continue pressing F7 until you are back at the main program file. Position the cursor on the WriteLn statement and press F4 (see Figure 12-15). At the bottom you can see that the Watch window now has three variables—*I*, *R1*, and *R2*. Notice that *I* is now called an unknown identifier. Why? The variable *I* was local to procedure *Proc1*. We are now outside that procedure and beyond the scope of the variable, which is why the identifier is unknown.

If, on the other hand, a global variable *I* had been declared, the Watch window would reflect the value of the global variable. The Watch window can display the value of variables only within the variable's scope.

Looking at the Watch window, you might have been surprised to find that *R1* and *R2* have the same value, despite the fact that *R2* was assigned the value of *R1* plus 1.0.

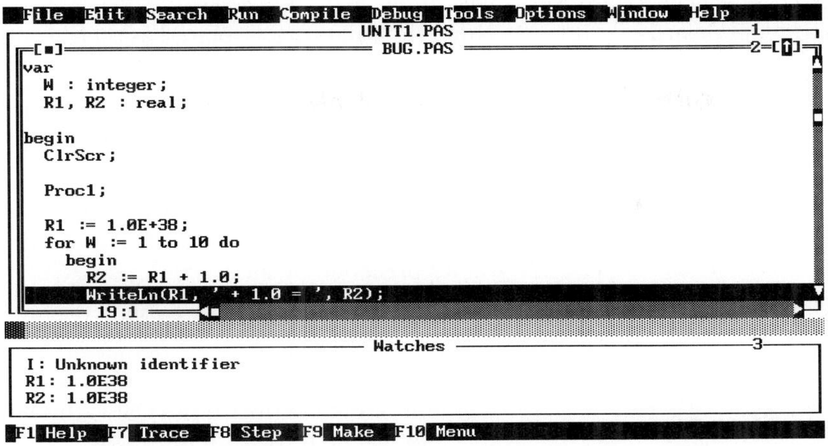

Figure 12-15. *Checking variables in the Watch window*

Here is the second bug. What happened? Floating-point variables retain only a fixed number of significant digits. When the number gets large, it will not reflect additions of small values. So, while you might expect *R1* to increase in value with each loop, the Watch window shows that this is not the case.

Display Format

You can use the Watch window to display the contents of any data type. If you do not specify otherwise, data is displayed in a default format (see Table 12-1). The Watch window, however, allows you to use format specifiers that alter the way the data is displayed. For example, you can view a value in hexadecimal format or as a raw memory dump. Table 12-2 lists the format specifiers and describes how they work.

Using format specifiers is fairly simple. When you add a variable to the Watch window, simply add a comma and list the format specifiers you want to use. For example, if you want to view an **integer** *I* in hexadecimal format, you would enter **I, x.** The following example program declares a variety of data types. Figure 12-16 shows how these variables look when displayed using format specifiers. Notice in the figure that a typecast is used to display the *Ch* variable as a decimal value. Using typecasts in the Watch window is a powerful method of viewing your data in a variety of ways.

Data Type	Default Display Format
Bytes, Integers, Words	Numeric scalars are displayed as their decimal value.
Reals	Floating-point variables are displayed in decimal format without exponents, if possible.
Characters	Characters from ASCII code 32 and up are displayed as themselves. Control characters, ASCII codes 0 to 31, are displayed as decimal values preceded by the # sign.
Booleans	Displayed as either True or False.
Pointers	Pointers are displayed as segments and offsets. If the segment portion matches the code segment or data segment, the CSEG or DSEG specifier will be displayed. Addresses are displayed in hexadecimal format.
Strings	Strings are displayed as concatenated characters, enclosed in quotes. Control characters are displayed as decimal numbers preceded by the # sign.
Arrays	Array contents are displayed within parentheses, separated by commas. If the array is multidimensional, nested parentheses are used.
Records	The contents of records are displayed as lists surrounded by parentheses. Elements in the record are separated by commas. Nested records are shown as nested lists.

Table 12-1.   *Default Display Formats*

```
Program BugTest;

uses Crt;

var
  Rec : record
    I : integer;
    B : byte;
  end;

  Ch : char;
  I : integer;
```

```
  R : real;
  S : string;
  P : pointer;
  D : (Zero, One, Two, Three);

begin
  ClrScr;

  R := 123;
  I := 123;
  Ch := 'A';
  S := '123' + #1 + 'ABC';
  P := @Ch;
  Rec.I := 1;
  Rec.B := 2;
  FillChar(D, SizeOf(D), 1);

  WriteLn;
  Write('Press ENTER...');
  ReadLn;
end.
```

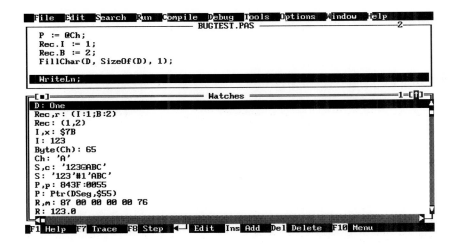

Figure 12-16.   *The Watch window*

Format Specifier	Result
$, H, X	Displays scalars.
C	Displays special characters as their ASCII graphic value instead of as decimal values.
D	Displays scalars as decimal values.
Fn	Displays a floating-point number with n significant digits. The value of n can range from 2 to 18; the default is 11.
M	Displays a memory dump of a variable as hex bytes. Adding the **D** specifier causes the dump to be shown in decimal, and the **C** or **S** specifier displays the dump as a string of ASCII and special characters.
P	Displays pointer in segment-and-offset format with both values in four-digit hex format.
R	Displays the record's field names along with their values.
S	Displays a string using ASCII and special characters. Normally, special characters are shown as decimal values.

Table 12-2.   *Watch Window Format Specifiers*

Programming for Debugging

When writing your program, keep in mind that the integrated debugger can only debug one statement per line. For example, Turbo Pascal allows you to write the following line of code:

```
S := 1 * Z; Z := I div Trunc(Sqrt(S)); S := Z Div 0;
```

This single line contains three statements. If an error occurs in any of the three, the integrated debugger will not be able to tell you which statement caused the error. In this case, it would be better to code as follows:

```
S := 1 * Z;
Z := I div Trunc(Sqrt(S));
S := Z div 0;
```

Now when an error occurs, you will know exactly which statement caused the error.

On the other hand, if you have sections of code that you are certain are correct, you might consider lumping them into one line to save time when tracing through the program. For example, the following code is efficient because you can trace past it in one step instead of four:

```
S := 1; X := 2; I := 3; J := 4;
```

This particular situation doesn't occur very often in your code, but it's nice to have the flexibility to combine lines when it makes sense.

Another important programming point is not to get sloppy just because you have the integrated debugger. It's always better to avoid problems by using proper programming techniques than to catch the problems afterward with the debugger.

As much as is possible and practical, break up programs into modules, rely on parameters rather than on global variables, and test modules as much as possible before integrating them into your programs.

Memory Requirements and Limitations

The integrated debugger requires memory and, with large programs, you might find that too little is left over to run a debugging session. You can maximize the use of memory through several techniques. First, if you have expanded memory installed in your computer, make sure that at least 64K is available; Turbo Pascal will use this memory to store the editor file.

If your program allocates more stack-and-heap memory than it uses, you can reduce the size of these data areas, freeing memory for the debugger. Removing RAM-resident programs, like SideKick, will also give the debugger more memory to work with.

When you compile your program, turn off error-checking compiler directives, such as the $S and $R directives. These directives increase the size of your programs. Where local symbols will not be watched, use the $L- compiler directive to reduce the size of the local symbol table.

You can also save memory by organizing your program into overlays. This will slow down your program, but give you more memory for debugging. As much as possible, test procedures and functions separately from the main program. This will speed up your testing and provide memory for debugging.

Finally, you can gain memory by modifying the TURBO.TPL file. Use the TPUMOVER program to remove any unused units from TURBO.TPL. This method, however, is a bit drastic and should be used only as a last resort.

While the integrated debugger is powerful, it does have some limitations. It will not, for example, trace into any of the standard Turbo Pascal units, including those in Turbo Vision and Object Windows. Of course, these units are supplied by Borland and do not require any debugging.

The integrated debugger will not trace into external procedures, interrupt procedures, procedures that are written entirely in inline code, any procedure not compiled with the $D+ compiler directive, any procedure for which the source code is not available, or any procedure set up as an exit procedure. In short, the integrated debugger will help you in 99% of the situations most programmers run into. If, however, you absolutely need to trace through every part of your program, consider using the Turbo Debugger, which is more powerful than the integrated debugger built into Turbo Pascal.

The Stand-Alone Debugger for Windows

The Windows IDE does not have the luxury of an integrated debugger. Instead you get the next best thing—a stand-alone debugger called Turbo Debugger that is easily accessible from the IDE. Turbo Debugger is available for all versions of the IDE, and basic features of each version are the same.

The easiest way to invoke Turbo Debugger from the Windows IDE is from the speed bar: select the last icon in the speed bar, a lightning bolt with a bug in the corner. When you do, the IDE will compile the program and pass the executable code

```
≡  File  Edit  View  Run  Breakpoints  Data  Options  Window  Help      READY
┌[■]═Module: TEST File: TEST.PAS 15═════════════════════════════1═[↑][↓]═┐
│  Program Test;                                                          │
│                                                                         │
│  var                                                                    │
│    S : string;                                                          │
│                                                                         │
│  function RemoveBlanks(S : string) : string;                            │
│  begin                                                                  │
│    while S[1] = ' ' do                                                  │
│      Delete(S, 1, 1);                                                   │
│    RemoveBlanks := S;                                                   │
│  end;                                                                   │
│                                                                         │
│► begin                                                                  │
│    S := '       A';                                                     │
│    S := RemoveBlanks(S);                                                │
│                                                                         │
├─────Watches──────────────────────────────────────────────────2────────┤
│                                                                         │
└─────────────────────────────────────────────────────────────────────────┘
 F1-Help F2-Bkpt F3-Mod F4-Here F5-Zoom F6-Next F7-Trace F8-Step F9-Run F10-Menu
```

Figure 12-17.   *Stand-alone debugger at start of execution*

to the debugger. You should then see a screen similar to Figure 12-17. As you can see, Turbo Debugger runs in text mode, not as a true Windows program.

The Turbo Debugger environment is very similar to the DOS IDE. It has a menu bar at the top, a status bar with hot keys on the bottom, and a series of windows in between. The window that fills up most of the screen is called a Module window. This window contains the source code of the module being debugged. The lower window is the Watch window, similar to the one in the integrated debugger.

The rest of this chapter will explain how to use the features of Turbo Debugger that are parallel to those in the integrated debugger. Study the on-line (Help feature) documentation if you need to use the more advanced features.

Controlling Program Execution

Borland has also been careful to maintain many of the same hot keys in the two debuggers. For instance F7 is still Trace Into, and F8 is still Step Over. In addition you can still press F4 to operate Execute to Cursor. These commands can also be found in the Run menu.

To run your program until you hit a breakpoint, or the program completes, press F9. This is slightly different from the hot key in the integrated debugger—CTRL-F9.

Watch Expressions

The Watch window is almost exactly the same in the two debuggers. To add a watch expression use Data|Add Watch. To activate the Watch window, select View|Watches.

One unique feature of Turbo Debugger is the Inspector window. This window is similar in function to the Watch window, but provides much more detail. Figure 12-18 shows a **string** variable viewed in both the Watch window and an Inspector window. Inspector windows are especially useful for complex data types like records and objects. To inspect a variable, use the Data|Inspect command.

Breakpoints

Breakpoints have the same purpose in Turbo Debugger as they do in the integrated debugger. To set a breakpoint, move the cursor to the desired line and either select Breakpoints|Add or press F2. An even easier way to set a breakpoint is to click your mouse on one of the first two columns of the desired line. When you set a breakpoint, the line is changed to a different color.

To see what breakpoints you have set, use the View|Breakpoints dialog box. As you can see in Figure 12-19, this box displays the breakpoints by module name and line number. If you have set any conditions on the breakpoint they are displayed in the right half of the dialog box.

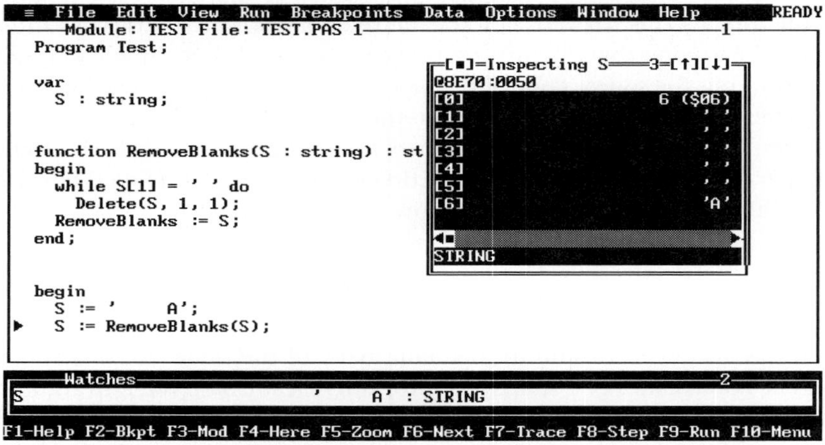

Figure 12-18. *Inspector window in stand-alone debugger*

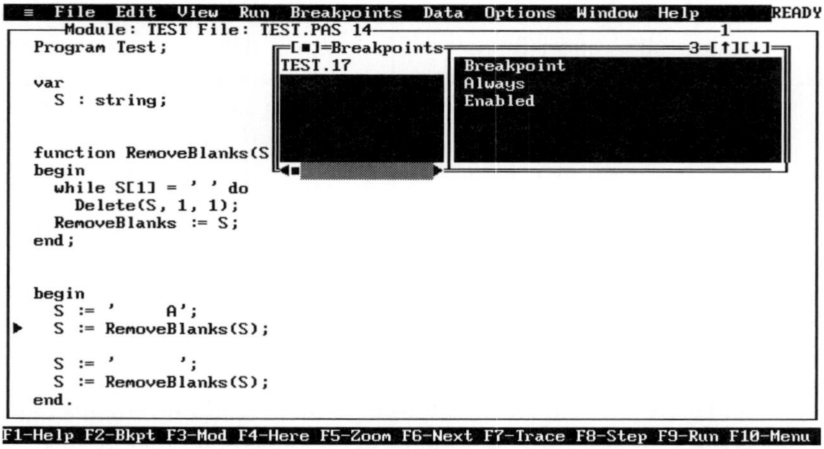

Figure 12-19. *Viewing beakpoints in the stand-alone debugger*

Evaluating and Modifying Expressions

You can examine and change variables using the Data|Evaluate/Modify dialog box. Although the appearance of the box is slightly different from the one on the integrated debugger (see Figure 12-20), the functionality is the same. To evaluate an expression, enter it in the top input area; the result will appear in the middle box. To change that result in your program, enter the new value in the bottom input area.

Bugs are a natural part of programming. No matter how carefully you code, you simply can't avoid errors in logic. Tracking down and correcting bugs used to be time-consuming and clumsy. With its built-in and stand-alone debuggers, the IDE greatly increases your programming productivity and will help you produce better programs.

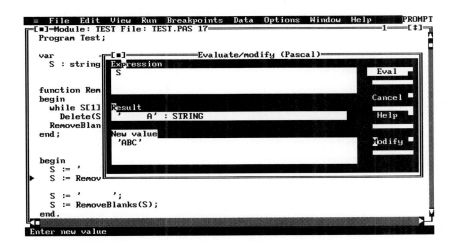

Figure 12-20. *Evaluating and modifying expressions*

Part *III*

Standard Turbo Pascal Libraries

Chapter **13**

The System Unit

Some programmers use Turbo Pascal for years without realizing that there is a System unit. This unit is automatically associated with all programs, so it is not included in the **uses** clause. It would be impossible to write any meaningful program that does not use the System unit.

Each of the chapters in Part I of this book covered portions of the System unit. This chapter is primarily a reference for all of the functions and procedures in the unit. These routines are grouped by subject, and special attention is given to subprograms that manipulate strings.

String Routines

The Turbo Pascal **string** data type (which is described in Chapter 3, "Complex Data Types") is a powerful and frequently used data structure. While it is most commonly used to hold words and messages, a string can perform far more interesting tasks.

As you may recall, a string consists of a length byte followed by as many bytes as are defined in the string declaration. For example, **string[4]** declares a 5-byte data type: one length byte followed by four character bytes.

One of the reasons that the **string** type is so powerful is that it can be processed in two different ways: by directly manipulating its individual elements or by using one of the Turbo Pascal standard functions and procedures for strings. Both methods (each of which are discussed in this chapter) have advantages, depending on the circumstances.

Using Standard Routines

Because they require a great many character manipulations, string-handling procedures are sometimes difficult to write. Turbo Pascal eliminates the need to write these character-by-character manipulations by providing powerful standard functions, making string manipulation an easy job.

Chr

The standard function Chr accepts an **integer** parameter and returns its equivalent ASCII value. For example, because ASCII code 65 represents the character "A", the statement Chr(65) returns **A.**

While it is not a **string** procedure, the Chr function is frequently used with **string** statements, especially those with unusual characters. For example, the following program writes out a string with a double exclamation point, a character represented by ASCII code 19.

```
Program DoubleExclamation;

uses Crt;

var
  S : string[20];

begin
  ClrScr;
  S := 'Wow' + Chr(19);
  Writeln(S);

  Writeln;
  Write('Press ENTER...');
  Readln;
end.
```

Upcase

Upcase, another character-level function, accepts a single lowercase alphabetic character from "a" to "z" and returns its uppercase equivalent. If the character is not lowercase and alphabetic, Upcase returns the character unchanged.

Concat

Concatenation is the combination of several strings into a single string. Turbo Pascal offers two ways to concatenate strings: Concat and the plus (+) operator.

The standard function Concat accepts any number of strings as parameters and returns them as one string. This program shows how to use this function:

```
Program Concatenate;

uses Crt;

var
  S1, S2, S3 : string[80];

begin
  ClrScr;
  S1 := 'This is the beginning -';
  S2 := '- This is the end.';
  S3 := Concat(S1, S2);
  Writeln(S3);

  Writeln;
  Write('Press ENTER...');
  Readln;
end.
```

In this example, strings *S1* and *S2* are passed into Concat, where they are combined and assigned to *S3*. When *S3* is written out, the message displayed is

This is the beginning—This is the end.

Most programmers prefer to use the + operator to concatenate their strings, primarily because it is simpler to use and produces more readable code, as shown here:

```
Program Concat;

uses Crt;

var
  S1, S2, S3, S4: string[80];

begin
  ClrScr;
  S1 := 'This is ';
  S2 := 'all one ';
  S3 := 'sentence.';
  S4 := S1 + S2 + S3;
  Writeln(s4);
```

```
    Writeln;
    Write('Press ENTER...');
    Readln;
end.
```

The statement

```
S4 := S1 + S2 + S3;
```

produces the same result as

```
S4 := Concat(S1, S2, S3);
```

but the + operator is more intuitive.

With both Concat and the + operator, the concatenated string is truncated when the total length of the concatenated strings exceeds the maximum length of the receiving string.

Copy

The standard function Copy extracts a substring from a larger string. To use Copy, you must know where in the larger string you want to start copying and how many characters you want to copy. For example, the statement

```
Copy(S, 12, 3);
```

tells Turbo Pascal to return three characters from string *S* starting with character 12.

The following program uses the Copy function to write a long string as a column ten characters wide.

```
Program DoCopy;

uses Crt;

var
  S : string[80];
  I : integer;

begin
  ClrScr;
  S := 'This is a long line that will be written out in a column.';
  I := 1;

  while I < Length(S) do
    begin
```

```
      WriteLn(Copy(S, I, 10));
      I := I + 10;
    end;

  WriteLn;
  Write('Press ENTER...');
  ReadLn;
end.
```

When you run this program, the output looks like this:

```
This is a
long line
that will
be written
 out in a
column.

Press ENTER...
```

Each line in the output, except the last line, contains ten characters, including blank characters. The last line contains only seven characters because this is all that remained at the end of the string. If you attempt to copy beyond the end of the string, you get either a partial result or no characters at all, but Turbo Pascal does not generate an error.

Delete and Insert

The Delete procedure removes characters from a string. As with Copy, you must specify the starting point in the string and the number of characters to delete. For example, the statement

```
Delete(S, 5, 3);
```

tells Turbo Pascal to delete three characters from string *S* starting at the fifth character.

The Insert procedure inserts one string into another string. Three parameters are passed into Insert: the string to insert, the string which will contain the inserted string, and the position of the insertion. For example, the statement **Insert(S1, S2, 4)** tells Turbo Pascal to insert string *S1* into *S2* starting at the fourth character. This sample program illustrates both Delete and Insert:

```
Program TestInsert;

uses Crt;

var
  S1, S2 : string[80];
```

```
begin
  ClrScr;
  S1 := 'A';
  S2 := '1234567890';
  WriteLn('Insert ',S1,' into ',S2);
  Insert(S1, S2, 3);
  WriteLn(S2);

  WriteLn('Remove ',S1,' from ',S2);
  Delete(S2, 3, 1);
  WriteLn(S2);

  WriteLn;
  Write('Press ENTER...');
  ReadLn;
end.
```

This program displays the string '12A34567890', showing that "A" has been inserted into the third character in the string. The statement **Delete(S2,3,1)** then removes the "A" from the string and displays it once again.

Length

The standard function Length returns the number of characters currently held in a **string** variable. Thus, if a string S is equal to

```
'This is a string. '
```

then **Length(S)** will be equal to 20. The blanks at the end of the string are counted as part of the string.

Pos

When you want to know if one string is contained in another, Turbo Pascal can tell you this with the standard function Pos. Consider the following example.

```
Program TestPos;

uses Crt;

var
  S : string[80];

begin
  ClrScr;
```

```
S := 'This is a test string';
WriteLn('The position of "test" in "', S, '" is: ',
        Pos('test', S));
WriteLn('The position of "TEST" in "', S, '" is: ',
        Pos('TEST', S));

WriteLn;
Write('Press ENTER...');
ReadLn;
end.
```

This program displays the following messages:

```
The position of "test" in "This is a test string" is: 11
The position of "TEST" in "This is a test string" is: 0

Press ENTER...
```

The first message confirms that the word "test" is located at the 11th character of the larger string. The second message simply shows that Pos returns zero when a match is not found. It should be evident from this program that Pos is case-sensitive.

Str and Val

Str and Val, two closely related standard procedures, are frequently used in programs that process numerical input and output. Str converts a number into a string, and Val converts a string into a number.

Str makes two parameters: a number (integer or real) and a **string** variable. The number can be formatted according to Turbo Pascal conventions. Examples of Str statements and their results are shown in Figure 13-1.

The first Str statement—**Str(10,S)**—converts an **integer** to a **string** with no formatting. The statement **Str(10:4, S),** on the other hand, is formatted as right-justified in a field four spaces wide. The resulting string, therefore, consists of two blank characters before the number 10.

Formatting **real** numbers is a bit more complicated. When a **real** number is unformatted, Str produces a string in scientific notation. For example, the statement

```
Str(3.2, S);
```

sets *S* equal to ' 3.2000000000E+00'. Note that a string begins with a blank character and contains all significant digits. If the number is negative, the leading blank is replaced with a minus sign.

If the **real** is formatted to a field width of 0—**Str(3.2:0, S)**—the result is '3.2E+00'. Only the essential digits are present, and no blanks are added to the string. The final

```
var
  s : String[20];
```

Statement	Result
Str(10,s);	'10'
Str(10:4,s);	' 10'
Str(3.2,s);	' 3.2000000000E+00'
Str(3.2:0,s);	'3.2E+00'
Str(3.2:15:3,s);	' 3.200'

Figure 13-1. *Results of the Str procedure*

example, **Str(3.2:15:3, S),** creates a 15-character string with three decimal places:
'   3.200'.

The Val procedure accepts three parameters: the string to convert into a number, the numeric variable to receive the value, and an **integer** variable used to flag errors. The following sample program shows how to use the Val procedure:

```
Program StringToNumber;

{$P+}

uses Crt;

(*********************************************)

procedure WriteNumber(S : string);
var
  R : real;
  Code : integer;
begin
  Val(S, R, Code);
  if Code = 0 Then
    WriteLn(R:0:3)
  else
    WriteLn('Error in numeric conversion');
end;

(*********************************************)


begin
  ClrScr;
```

```
WriteLn('Below is the conversion of 123.23');
WriteNumber('123.23');
WriteLn;

WriteLn('Below is the conversion of s123.23');
WriteLn;
WriteNumber('s123.23');

WriteLn;
Write('Press ENTER...');
ReadLn;
end.
```

At the heart of the sample program is the statement **Val(S, R, Code),** which attempts to convert string *S* into a valid **real** number. If *S* contains a valid number in the correct format, the conversion will be successful and code will set to zero; if *S* contains a non-numeric character, code will be set to a nonzero value.

To be valid for numeric conversions, a string must meet these conditions:

1. It must contain a number in integer, real, or scientific notation.

2. It must not contain any alphabetic or other characters not used in numeric representation. The "E" used in scientific notation is an exception.

3. It must not contain any trailing blanks—leading blanks are acceptable.

Table 13-1 shows examples of both valid and invalid strings for numeric conversion. As you can see, a string must be in a proper form before it can be converted.

A final point on converting strings to numbers: if you try to convert a string that contains a valid real number (for example, 1.32) into an integer, Turbo Pascal generates an error. The safest approach in such cases is to convert all numeric strings into reals and then convert the real to an integer with the Round or Trunc functions. (These two functions are described later in this chapter.)

Valid	Invalid	Reason
'12'	'1x2'	String contains a non-numeric character
'3.2E+100'	'3.2E+00 '	String contains a trailing blank character

Table 13-1.   *Valid and Invalid Strings for Numeric Conversion*

Direct Manipulation of Characters

While the Turbo Pascal string procedures are powerful, they do have limitations. For
example, to change a string to all uppercase characters, you must process the string
yourself. This is not a difficult task; a **string** variable, after all, is nothing more than
an array of characters with a length byte in position zero. The following program
shows how you can process strings. It contains the function *UpCaseStr*, which accepts
a **string** parameter, changes all lowercase letters to uppercase, and then returns the string.

```
Program UpperCase;

{$P+}

uses Crt;

var
  S : string[80];

(**************************************)

function UpCaseStr(S : string) : string;
var
  I : integer;

begin
  for I := 1 to Length(S) do
    S[I] := Upcase(S[I]);
  UpCaseStr := S;
end;

(**************************************)

begin
  ClrScr;
  S := 'abc';
  WriteLn(S);
  WriteLn('Change to uppercase.');
  WriteLn(UpCaseStr(S));

  WriteLn;
  Write('Press ENTER...');
  ReadLn;
end.
```

The main part of the function *UpCaseStr* processes the incoming string from the first character to the last. A character that is referred to individually in a string (for example, S[2]) can be substituted for a variable of type **char** in any expression. Thus, the standard Upcase procedure, which takes a parameter of type **char,** can accept individual characters from a string.

```
for I := 1 to Length(S) do
  S[I] := Upcase(S[I]);
```

When all characters in the string are uppercase, the function passes the altered string back to the program.

Manipulating the Length Byte

You can play some tricks with strings by altering the value of the length byte (byte 0). This lets you lengthen or shorten a string without assigning a new value. For example, consider this block of code:

```
S := 'ABCDEFG';
S[0] := Chr(3);
WriteLn(S);
```

When the string 'ABCDEFG' is assigned to variable *S*, Turbo Pascal sets the length to ASCII code 7. The next line, however, changes the length byte to ASCII code 3. The Chr function is used because Turbo Pascal considers the length byte to be a character. Thus, when the statement **WriteLn(S)** is executed, the output is ABC. In Turbo Pascal, changing the length byte changes the string.

On the other hand, changing characters in the string directly does not change the length byte, as illustrated by this code segment:

```
S := 'ABC';
S[4] := 'D';
S[5] := 'E';
WriteLn(S);
```

The first statement assigns the string 'ABC' to the variable *S* and sets the length byte to ASCII code 3. The next two statements change the value in positions 4 and 5 of the string, but this does not affect the length byte. Therefore, the statement **WriteLn(S)** displays ABC, not ABCDE.

Direct manipulation of strings has many practical uses, such as creating strings for special text displays. For example, the following program uses an 80-character string that contains the double horizontal line character (ASCII code 205) to split the screen in half:

```
Program SplitScreen;

uses Crt;

var
   Divider : string[255];

begin
   ClrScr;
   FillChar(Divider, Sizeof(Divider), 205);
   Divider[0] := Chr(80);

   GotoXY(1,14);
   Write(Divider);

   GotoXY(1,7);
   Write('This is the upper portion of the screen.');

   GotoXY(1,21);
   Write('This is the lower portion of the screen.');

   WriteLn;
   Write('Press ENTER...');
   ReadLn;
end.
```

The first statement in the procedure,

```
FillChar(Divider, SizeOf(Divider), 205);
```

fills the entire string, from position 0 to position 255, with the ASCII value 205. To make the string fill one line of the screen, however, the length byte must be 80. Therefore, the length byte is set to 80 with the statement

```
Divider[0] := Chr(80);
```

Now the string can be written to the screen, providing an attractive divider. In other places in the program, you might want to use the same string, but in shorter lengths, perhaps only 10 or 20 characters. Just change the length byte according to your needs; you do not have to change the characters because they are already set properly.

String Routines   **System Unit**

Chr

```
function Chr(I : integer) : char;
```

Returns the ASCII character that corresponds to I.

Concat

```
function Concat(S1, S2, ... : string) : string;
```

Combines any number of strings and returns them as a single string. If the length of the concatenated string is greater than 255, Turbo Pascal generates a run-time error.

Copy

```
function Copy(S : string; Start, Len : integer) : string;
```

Returns a portion of string S, which starts at character number Start and contains Len characters.

Delete

```
procedure Delete(S : string; Start, Len : integer);
```

Removes Len characters from string S starting with character number Start.

Insert

```
procedure Insert(Source : string; var Target : string;
                 Index : integer);
```

Inserts string Source into string Target at position Index.

Length

```
function Length(S : string) : integer;
```

Returns the length of string S.

Pos

```
function Pos(SubS, S : string) : integer;
```

Returns the position of SubS in S. If SubS is not found in S, Pos returns 0.

Str

```
procedure Str(I : integer{:Length}; var S : string);
procedure Str(R : real{:Length{:Decimals}}; var S : string);
```

Converts a real or integer number into a string.

Upcase

```
function Upcase(C : char) : char;
```

Return the uppercase value of C if C is a lowercase letter; otherwise, it simply returns C.

Val

```
procedure Val(S : string; var R : real; var Code : integer);
procedure Val(S : string; var I : integer; var Code : integer);
```

Attempts to convert S into a numerical value (R or I). If the conversion is successful, Turbo Pascal sets Code equal to zero. If unsuccessful, Code contains the position in the string at which the error occurred.

I/O Routines

Chapter 7, "Files," described files in great detail. All of the procedures and functions discussed in Chapter 7 are in the System unit. The only I/O routines not mentioned are the ones that manipulate files without opening them: Rename and Erase.

Sophisticated file management requires the ability to rename and erase files without going back to the DOS prompt. Turbo Pascal provides two procedures to do just that. To rename a file, first assign a file to a file variable, then call the Rename procedure with the new name specified:

```
Assign(F, 'FILE.OLD');
Rename(F, 'FILE.NEW');
```

The Erase procedure works essentially the same way. Assign the disk file to a file identifier and then call the Erase procedure.

```
Assign(F, 'FILE.OLD');
Erase(F);
```

The following program provides a simple method for renaming and erasing files. When you start the program, three choices are presented: rename a file, erase a file, or quit.

```
Program FileControl;

uses Crt;

var
  File1 : file;
  Name1,
  Name2 : string[255];
  Choice : char;

begin
  ClrScr;
  repeat
    Write('R)ename, E)rase, Q)uit: ');
    ReadLn(Choice);
    case Upcase(Choice) of
      'R':
        begin
          Write('Name of file to rename: ');
          ReadLn(Name1);
```

```
        Write('New name for the file: ');
        ReadLn(Name2);
        Assign(File1,Name1);
        Rename(File1,Name2);
      end;
    'E':
      begin
        Write('Name of file to erase: ');
        ReadLn(Name1);
        Assign(File1,Name1);
        Erase(File1);
      end;
  end; { of case }
  until Upcase(Choice) = 'Q';
end.
```

Make a selection by typing **R, E,** or **Q** and pressing ENTER. When renaming a file, enter the name of the existing file as well as the new name for the file. Erasing a file requires only that you enter the name of the file to be erased.

I/O Routines   System Unit

Append

```
procedure Append(var F: text);
```

Opens a text file for writing and positions the file pointer at the end of the file.

Assign

```
procedure Assign(var F : file; Name : string);
```

Links the file variable F to the file named in Name.

BlockRead

```
procedure BlockRead(var F : file; var B; NumRecs : integer;
                    var RecsRead : integer);
```

Attempts to read NumRecs records from untyped file F into buffer B. RecsRead indicates the number of records actually read.

BlockWrite

```
procedure BlockWrite(var F : file; var B; NumRecs : integer);
```

Writes NumRecs records from buffer B to untyped file F.

ChDir

```
procedure ChDir(S : string);
```

Changes the current directory to that in S.

Close

```
procedure Close(var F : file);
```

Flushes the buffer for file F and closes the file.

Eof

```
function Eof(F : file) : boolean;
```

Returns True when the file pointer in F reaches the end of the file.

Eoln

```
function Eoln(F : file) : boolean;
```

Returns True when the file pointer in F reaches either the end of a line (indicated by a carriage return and line feed) or the end of the file.

Erase

```
procedure Erase(F : file);
```

Deletes disk file F and removes its information from the directory.

FilePos

```
function FilePos(F : file) : integer;
```

Returns the record number at which the file pointer in typed file F is located.

FileSize

```
function FileSize(F : file) : integer;
```

Returns the number of records currently contained in typed file F.

Flush

```
procedure Flush(var F : text);
```

Sends to disk all buffered output for file F.

GetDir

```
procedure GetDir(D : byte; var S : string);
```

Gets the current directory for the drive specified by D. The directory is returned in S. If D is zero, GetDir searches the default drive.

IOResult

```
function IOResult : word;
```

Reports an error code when input/output operations are performed. If IOResult is not equal to zero, an error occurred.

MkDir

```
procedure MkDir(S : string);
```

Makes a directory with the name stored in string S. S should contain both drive and directory names.

Read and Readln

```
procedure Read({var F : file;} Parameters);
procedure Readln({var F : file;} Parameters);
```

Read receives input from either the standard input device or the file specified by F. Readln, which can be used only on text files, receives input in the same way that Read does, but after reading in the data, Readln moves the file pointer forward to just after the next carriage return/line feed delimiter.

Rename

```
procedure Rename(var F : file; S : string);
```

Changes the name of file F to that contained in S.

Reset

```
procedure Reset(var F : file {; I : integer});
```

Opens the file F for reading. If the file is untyped, you can specify the record size in I.

Rewrite

```
procedure Rewrite(var F : file {; I : integer});
```

Prepares a file to be written. If the file does not exist, Turbo Pascal creates it. If the file does exist, its contents are destroyed. If the file is untyped, you can specify the record size in I.

RmDir

```
procedure RmDir(S : string);
```

Removes the directory specified in S.

Seek

```
procedure Seek(var F : file; P : integer);
```

Moves the file pointer to the beginning of the record numbered P in file F.

SeekEof

```
function SeekEof(var F : file) : boolean;
```

Similar to Eof, except that it skips blanks, tabs, and end-of-line markers (CR/LF) before it tests for an end-of-file marker.

SeekEoln

```
function SeekEoln(var F : file) : boolean;
```

Similar to Eoln, except that it skips blanks and tabs before it tests for an end-of-line marker.

SetTextBuf

```
procedure SetTextBuf(var F : text; var Buf {; Size : word});
```

Assigns text file F to buffer Buf. If size is not specified, the buffer's size is that of Buf. Size can be used to override the default buffer size.

Truncate

```
procedure Truncate(var F);
```

Forces end of file to be the current position of the file pointer. Contents of the file beyond the file pointer are lost.

Write and Writeln

```
procedure Write({var F : file;} Parameters);
procedure Writeln({var F : file;} Parameters);
```

Write accepts a list of parameters, which it writes to the default output device. When the first parameter is a file variable, output is directed to that file. Writeln, which can be used only on text files, operates in the same way as Write, but it adds a carriage return and line feed at the end of the output.

Math Routines

Part of the System unit is a rich set of standard arithmetic functions that give easy access to complex computations. These functions are identified in the box at the end of this section.

You can also write your own numeric functions. The following listing contains two valuable numerical functions; the first computes the cumulative normal probability density function of a number and the second raises a number to a power.

```
Program NumberFunctions;

{$N+,E+}

uses Crt;

{$IFOPT N+}
type
  Float = double;
{$ELSE}
  Float = real;
{$ENDIF}

(**************************************************)

function N(X : Float) : Float;
  (* Computes the Cumulative Normal *)
```

```
  (* Probability Density Function  *)
var
  X2, T, Y1, Y2, Y3, Y4, Y5, Z, R : Float;

begin
  Y1 := 1.0 / (1.0 + (0.2316419*Abs(X)));
  Y2 := Y1 * Y1;
  Y3 := Y2 * Y1;
  Y4 := Y3 * Y1;
  Y5 := Y4 * Y1;
  X2 := X * X;

  Z := 0.3989423 * Exp(-X2/2.0);

  R := (1.330274*Y5) -
       (1.821256*Y4) +
       (1.781478*Y3) -
       (0.356538*Y2) +
       (0.3193815*Y1);

  T := 1.0 - (Z*R);

  if X > 0 then
    N := T
  else
    N := 1-T;
  end;

(*************************************************************)

function X_To_Y(X, Y : Float) : Float;
var
  R : float;
begin
  R := Y*Ln(X);
  X_To_Y := Exp(R);
end;

(*************************************************************)

begin
  ClrScr;
  Writeln('3 to power of 2 is: ', X_To_Y(3, 2):0:4);
  Writeln;

  Writeln('Cumulative normal probability of 1.96 = ',
          N(1.96):0:4);

  Writeln;
```

```
  Write('Press ENTER...');
  Readln;
end.
```

Notice the use of conditional compilation in this example program. If the $N+ directive is present (activating the 8087 mode), the data type *Float* represents a **double** data type. If, however, the $N+ is not present, the *Float* type is declared to be a standard type **real.** This use of conditional compilation lets you choose the degree of numerical precision throughout a program simply by changing a compiler directive.

Math Routines   **The System Unit**

Abs

```
function Abs(R : real) : real;
function Abs(I : integer) : integer;
```

Returns the absolute value of the parameter passed to it. The function result is the same type (**real** or **integer**) as the parameter.

Arctan

```
function ArcTan(R : real) : real;
```

Computes the arctangent of the parameter, in radians.

Cos

```
function Cos(R : real) : real;
```

Returns the cosine of R.

Exp

```
function Exp(R : real) : real;
```

Computes the exponential of R. When using standard real numbers with no 8087, Exp produces an overflow error when R is greater than 88 or less than -88.

Frac

```
function Frac(R : real) : real;
```

Returns the noninteger portion of R.

Int

```
function Int(R : real) : integer;
```

Returns the integer portion of R.

Ln

```
function Ln(R : real) : real;
```

Returns the natural logarithm of R.

Odd

```
function Odd(I : integer) : boolean;
```

Returns True when I is odd and False when I is even.

Ord

```
function Ord(S : (any scalar type)) : integer;
```

Returns the integer value of any scalar variable.

Pi

```
function Pi : real;
```

Returns the value of the mathematical constant Pi. The precision of the number depends on whether 8087 mode is activiated.

Random

```
function Random (I : word) : word;
function Random : real;
```

Returns a number randomly generated by Turbo Pascal. If you pass an integer expression, Random returns an interger greater than or equal to zero and less than the value of the parameter. Without a parameter, Random returns a real value greater than or equal to zero and less than one.

Randomize

```
procedure Randomize;
```

Initializes the seed value of the random-number generator. The seed value is stored in a **longint** variable RandSeed.

Round

```
function Round (R : real) : longint;
```

Returns the rounded integer value of R.

Sin

```
function Sin(R : real) : real;
```

Returns the sine of R.

Sqr

```
function Sqr(R : real) : real;
```

Returns the square of R.

Sqrt

```
function Sqrt(R : real) : real;
```

Returns the square root of R.

Trunc

```
function Trunc(R : real) : integer;
```

Returns the integer portion of R. The result must be within the legal range of an integer.

Pointer Routines

Chapter 6, "Pointers, Dynamic Memory, and Polymorphism," contains a detailed discussion of procedures and functions related to pointers. The summaries of these routines are included here for convenience.

Pointer Routines   System Unit

Addr

```
function Addr(var AnyVar) : pointer;
```

Returns the address of a variable, typed constant, or procedure. The result is a pointer type.

Assigned

```
function Assigned(P : pointer) : boolean;
```

Determines the state of a pointer or procedure variable. Assigned returns True if the pointer is not **nil.**

Cseg

```
function Cseg : word;
```

Returns the segment address of the program's code segment.

Dispose

```
procedure Dispose(P : pointer);
```

Frees heap memory allocated to a pointer variable. Dispose is used in conjunction with the New command.

Dseg

```
function Dseg : word;
```

Returns the segment address of the program's data segment.

FreeMem

```
procedure FreeMem(var P : pointer; I : integer);
```

Frees I bytes of heap memory associated with variable P, which must have been previously allocated by GetMem.

GetMem

```
procedure GetMem(var P : pointer; I : integer);
```

Reserves I bytes on the heap and stores the starting address in variable P.

Mark

```
procedure Mark(P : pointer);
```

Stores the top-of-heap address in pointer P.

MaxAvail

```
function MaxAvail : longint;
```

Returns the size of the largest block of unallocated memory on the heap.

MemAvail

```
function MemAvail : longint;
```

Returns the total amount of unallocated memory on the heap.

New

```
procedure New(var P : pointer);
```

Allocates memory on the heap for pointer P. After memory is allocated, the variable is referred to as P^.

Ofs

```
function Ofs(AnyVar) : integer;
```

Returns the memory-address offset for any variable, typed constant, or subprogram.

Ptr

```
function Ptr(Segment, Offset : word) : pointer;
```

Accepts two numbers that contain a segment and an offset, and returns a single 32-bit pointer value.

Release

```
procedure Release(var P : pointer);
```

Reclaims memory that has been allocated since the Mark command. P contains the top-of-heap address.

Seg

```
function Seg(AnyVar) : integer;
```

Returns the memory-address segment for any variable, typed constant, or subprogram.

SPtr

```
function SPtr : word;
```

Returns the current value of the stack pointer (SP) register.

SSeg

```
function SSeg : word;
```

Returns the current value of the stack segment (SS) register.

Other Routines

The final set of subprograms in the System unit are grouped in the category "Other Routines." This includes functions and procedures that modify program control, convert types, manipulate bytes, and other miscellaneous actions.

Other Routines   **System Unit**

Break

```
procedure Break;
```

Stops execution of a loop. Program control resumes at the first statement after the current loop.

Continue

```
procedure Continue;
```

Forces a program to branch to the first statement at the start of the current loop.

Dec

```
procedure Dec(var X {; N : longint});
```

Decrements scalar variable X by N. If you omit N, X will be decremented by 1.

Exclude

```
procedure Exclude (var S : set of SomeType; I : SomeType);
```

Removes a member I from set S. If I is not in the set, this procedure will do nothing.

Exit

```
procedure Exit;
```

Causes the program to leave the block currently being executed.

FillChar

```
procedure FillChar(var AnyVar; Count : word; Code : Scalar);
```

Fills Count bytes of memory with the value Code, which may be of any scalar type, starting at the address of AnyVar.

Halt

```
procedure Halt;
```

Terminates a program.

Hi

```
function Hi(I : integer) : byte;
```

Returns the high-order byte from integer I.

High

```
function High(X : array of AnyType) : Scalar;
```

Returns the index of the last element in an array or string.

Inc

```
procedure Inc(var X {; N : longint});
```

Increments the value of scalar X by N. If N is omitted from the parameter list, X is incremented by 1.

Include

```
procedure Include (var S : set of SomeType; I : SomeType);
```

Adds a member I to set S. If I is already in the set, this procedure will do nothing.

Lo

```
function Lo(I : integer) : byte;
```

Returns the low-order byte of integer I.

Low

```
function Low(X : array of AnyType) : Scalar;
```

Returns the index of the first element in an array or string.

Move

```
procedure Move(var V1, V2; I : integer);
```

Copies I bytes of memory from the location of variable V1 to the location of variable V2.

ParamCount

```
function ParamCount : word;
```

Returns the number of command-line parameters entered.

ParamStr

```
function ParamStr(I : word) : string;
```

Returns a parameter that was entered on the command line. For example, ParamStr(1) returns the first parameter. ParamStr (0) returns the path and filename of the executed file.

Pred

```
function Pred(var S : Scalar) : Scalar;
```

Decrements any scalar variable. The result type is the same as the parameter type.

RunError

```
procedure RunError(ErrorCode : byte);
```

Terminates a program using the run-time error code given as a parameter.

SizeOf

```
function SizeOf(AnyVar) : word;
```

Returns the number of bytes required by a variable or data type.

Succ

```
function Succ(S : Scalar) : Scalar;
```

Increments any scalar value. The result type is the same as the parameter type.

Swap

```
function Swap(I : integer) : integer;
```

Reverses the positions of the low- and high-order bytes of an integer or word. For example, if I equals 00FFh, Swap returns FF00h.

TypeOf

```
function TypeOf(AnyObject) : pointer;
```

Returns a pointer to an object type's virtual method table (VMT). The function takes a single parameter which can be either an object type identifier or an instance of an object. The primary use of TypeOf is to determine whether two objects (or an object type and an object instance) are the same type.

Chapter 14

The Crt and WinCrt Units

People often judge programs primarily by the quality of their video display. Screen presentation is so important that often programs are successful simply because they "look like" other popular programs. Your computer is capable of producing screen displays that are both attractive and helpful. This chapter discusses these capabilities and how you can control them with Turbo Pascal.

PC Text Display

Personal computers have two fundamental video modes: Text and Graphics (the Graphics mode is covered in Chapter 16). When in Text mode, a personal computer can display any of the 256 standard ASCII characters it supports. These characters are locked permanently in the computer's memory, so your PC always knows how to draw them.

To display characters, your computer uses a video adapter, which is a circuit board that connects the CPU to a monitor. Today, most computers have video graphics array (VGA) monitors. Monochrome adapters, color graphics adapters (CGA), and enhanced graphics adapters (EGA) are quickly becoming obsolete. This chapter will show you how to display text with any of these monitors.

The Video Adapter and Display Memory

A CGA monitor can display up to 80 characters horizontally on 25 lines, or a total of 2,000 characters in an entire screen. In addition, EGA monitors have a 43-line mode, and VGA monitors have a 50-line mode. Each character has its own foreground and background color. The foreground color is the color of the character itself; the background color is the color of the space around the character.

Your computer stores characters and color information in a special part of memory known as the *display memory*. This is what tells your computer which characters and colors to display. Although it is located on the video adapter card, the display memory is considered to be part of RAM. The first byte of the display memory contains the first character on your monitor, which appears in the upper-left corner.

Thus, if the first byte in the display memory contains the value 41h (the hexadecimal ASCII value for the letter "A"), the monitor displays the letter "A" in the upper-left corner of the monitor. The second byte in display memory contains the *attribute byte* for the first character. Attribute bytes control the color and other display information for each character.

This pattern—character, attribute, character, attribute—is repeated for all 2,000-4,000 characters that appear on the monitor. Thus, the contents of a single screen require 4,000-8,000 bytes of video memory.

The Attribute Byte

A color monitor in Text mode is capable of displaying 16 different colors, each of which consists of up to four elements: blue, red, green, and brightness. The color your computer displays depends on the particular combination of these elements. For example, the color black uses no elements, while light cyan uses the blue, green, and brightness elements. Video adapters also support a blinking element that makes the character flash on and off and has no effect on color.

An attribute byte stores the foreground and background color for the preceding character byte. Figure 14-1 shows how each bit in the attribute byte contributes to the color of the character and its background.

The first three bits (0, 1, and 2) in the attribute byte control a character's foreground color, while the fourth bit (bit 3) adds brightness to the color. You can combine these four elements to create 16 different foreground colors. Bits 4, 5, and 6 determine a character's background color, and bit 7, when on, makes the character blink. Because the blinking bit replaced the brightness bit, only eight colors are available for the background color.

On the monochrome monitor, the attribute byte can create only five display formats: hidden, normal, bright, underlined, and reverse. As with the color adapters, brightness is controlled by bit 3 and blinking is controlled by bit 7.

Characters are hidden when both the foreground and background colors are set to the same color. The brightness and blinking bits have no effect with hidden characters.

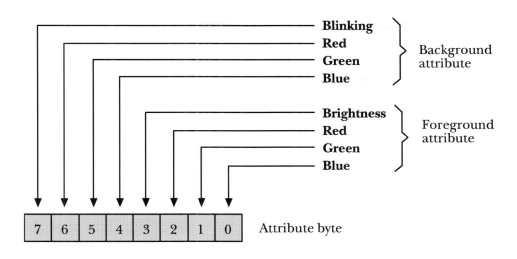

Figure 14-1.   *Mapping the attribute byte*

PC Text Modes

Personal computers support up to ten different text display modes. These modes, listed in Table 14-1, control both the size of the characters and the colors in a display. Mode 0, for example, displays large characters (40 per line) in shades of gray.

The first four display modes, 0 through 3, work only with color adapters, most of which can switch between the four modes. Mode 7, on the other hand, is used only by the monochrome adapter. Mode 256 is used in conjunction with Modes 0 to 3 (using the **or** operator) to provide 43- or 50-line displays.

You can change your computer's text mode with the Turbo Pascal command TextMode. This command always clears the screen before changing the mode.

Controlling Color with Turbo Pascal

Turbo Pascal allows you to select the foreground and background colors for your text with the commands TextColor and TextBackground. The color adapters provide 16 colors to choose from, as shown in Table 14-2. TextColor, which sets the foreground color (the color of the character), can use all 16 colors. TextBackground, which sets the background color, can use only the dark colors.

Turbo Pascal provides a standard constant called Blink, which when added to the foreground color causes the character to blink. Here are some examples of how to use Turbo Pascal's color commands:

Mode	Constant Name(s)	Size	Colors/Adapter
0	BW40	40x25	Black and White
1	CO40	40x25	Color
2	BW80	80x25	Black and White
3	CO80	80x25	Color
7	Mono	80x25	Monochrome adapter
256	Font8x8	80x43/50	EGA/VGA only

Table 14-1.   *Text Mode Constants*

```
TextBackground(Blue);

TextColor(Cyan);

TextColor(Cyan+Blink);
```

Once invoked, the new colors take effect with the next characters you display; the characters already on the screen retain their current colors.

Using Screen Coordinates

Like a map, your computer monitor has locations that are defined by coordinates. Screen coordinates are commonly referred to as X and Y, where X is the column

Dark Colors	Light Colors
0: Black	8: DarkGray
1: Blue	9: LightBlue
2: Green	10: LightGreen
3: Cyan	11: LightCyan
4: Red	12: LightRed
5: Magenta	13: LightMagenta
6: Brown	14: Yellow
7: LightGray	15: White

Table 14-2.   *Turbo Pascal Color Constants*

position and Y is the row position. (Coordinates are displayed in X,Y format.) Thus, the upper left corner of the monitor has coordinate position 1,1, while the lower right corner is at coordinate 80,25.

You can move the cursor to any coordinate location on your monitor with the Turbo Pascal command GotoXY. For example, the command **GotoXY(1,10)** positions the cursor at column 1 of row 10. If you want to know the coordinates for the cursor's current position, use the Turbo Pascal functions WhereX and WhereY. WhereX returns an integer that represents the cursor column; WhereY does the same for the cursor row.

Turbo Pascal's standard screen commands give you the control you need to create attractive and informative screen displays. The following program demonstrates how to create a simple data-entry routine with all of the commands described thus far: TextMode, TextColor, TextBackground, GotoXY, WhereX, and WhereY.

```
Program Box;

uses Crt;

var
   I, Code,
   X, Y : integer;
   S : string[20];

(***************************************************)

procedure DrawBox(X1, Y1, X2, Y2, FGround, BGround : integer);
var
  I : byte;
begin
  TextColor(FGround);
  TextBackground(BGround);
  for I := (X1+1) to (X2-1) do
    begin
      GotoXY(I, Y1);
      Write(#205);
      GotoXY(I, Y2);
      Write(#205);
    end;

  for I := (Y1+1) to (Y2-1) do
    begin
      GotoXY(X1,I);
      Write(#186);
      GotoXY(X2,I);
      Write(#186);
    end;

  GotoXY(X1,Y1);
```

```
   Write(#201);
   GotoXY(X2,Y1);
   Write(#187);
   GotoXY(X1,Y2);
   Write(#200);
   GotoXY(X2,Y2);
   Write(#188);
end;

(*********************************************)

procedure GetNumber;
begin
   DrawBox(5, 14, 35, 16, White, Black);

   GotoXY(7,15);
   Write('Enter a number (1-10):  ';
   X := WhereX;
   Y := WhereY;
   repeat
     GotoXY(X,Y);
     S := '    ';
     Write(S);
     GotoXY(X,Y);
     Readln(S);
     Val(S, I, Code);
   until (I > 0) and (I < 11) and (Code = 0);
end;

(*********************************************)

begin
   ClrScr;
   TextMode(CO40);
   GetNumber;

   ClrScr;
   TextMode(CO80);
   GetNumber;

   GotoXY(1,20);
   Writeln;
   Write('Press ENTER...');
   Readln;
end.
```

Text Display Routines **Crt Unit**

GotoXY

```
procedure GotoXY(X, Y : integer);
```

Places the cursor at a given screen location, where X is the desired column number, from 1 to 80, and Y is the desired line number, from 1 to (possibly) 50.

HighVideo

```
procedure HighVideo;
```

Enables the high-intensity video display.

LowVideo

```
procedure LowVideo;
```

Sets the video display to low intensity.

NormVideo

```
procedure NormVideo;
```

Restores the default screen attributes to those that were present when the program started.

TextBackground

```
procedure TextBackground(Color : byte);
```

Changes the background color of future character output to that specified by Color, a value from 0 to 7. See Table 14-2 for valid constants.

TextColor

```
procedure TextColor(Color : byte);
```

Changes the foreground color of future character output to that specified by Color, a value from 0 to 15. See Table 14-2 for valid constants.

TextMode

```
procedure TextMode(Mode : word);
```

Changes the text mode of the monitor. See Table 14-1 for valid modes. If the parameter is omitted, the monitor will be set to the previous text mode (presumably from some graphics mode).

WhereX

```
function WhereX : byte;
```

Determines the current column number of the cursor, from 1 to 80.

WhereY

```
function WhereY : byte;
```

Determines the current line number of the cursor from 1 to (possibly) 50.

The procedure *DrawBox* uses standard ASCII graphics characters to draw a rectangle anywhere on the screen. The procedure defines a data-entry portion on the screen.

Using Video Memory

The standard Turbo Pascal command Write uses a BIOS interrupt to send characters to the monitor. You can bypass BIOS, however, and write characters directly to display memory. In these days of 20Mhz to 50Mhz clock speeds, working faster than the BIOS is not nearly as important as it was several years ago; however, it may still be important to you. This chapter provides several Pascal and assembler routines that give your programs that extra burst of speed.

Another issue associated with the standard Turbo Pascal routines is that the Write command always moves the cursor to the next position on the screen. So, if you write a character to the lower-right corner of the screen, the display scrolls up one line. This makes it impossible to write out entire screens using Turbo Pascal statements. The remainder of this section will go into the technical details of your computer's video display and show how you can harness its power for your programs.

Before you can use your computer's display memory, you must know where to find it. On a monochrome adapter, the display memory starts at segment B000h, while on the color graphics adapter, it starts at B800h. Because each adapter uses different locations for video memory, you must determine which adapter is in use. One way to determine the adapter in use is shown here:

```
function VidSeg : word;
begin
  if Mem[$0000:$0449] = 7 then
    VidSeg := $B000
  else
    VidSeg := $B800;
end;
```

The *VidSeg* function checks the memory location at segment 0000h and offset 0449h, where DOS stores the video adapter code. If the byte at this location is equal to 7, the adapter is monochrome; if not, it is safe to assume the adapter is color graphics (CGA/EGA/VGA).

Once you know the type of video adapter in use, it is easy to bypass BIOS and write characters directly to the display memory. The program shown here determines the type of adapter used, and then fills the display memory with the letter "A" in white letters on a black background:

```
{$R-,S-}
Program FillScreen;

uses Crt;

var
   CharAtt,
   I, J,
   VS  : word;

(*********************************************************)

function VidSeg : word;
begin
```

```
   if Mem[$0000:$0449] = 7 then
     VidSeg := $B000
   else
     VidSeg := $B800;
end;

(*****************************************************)

begin
  ClrScr;
  VS := VidSeg;

  J := 0;

  (* $41 is the character 'A' *)
  (* $70 is White on Black *)

  CharAtt := ($70 Shl 4) + $41;

  for I := 1 to 2000 do
    begin
      MemW[VS:j] := CharAtt;   (* Write character and attribute *)
      Inc(J, 2);               (* Point to next video character *)
    end;

  GotoXY(1,1);
  Write('Press ENTER...');
  Readln;
end.
```

The program uses the function *VidSeg* to store the video display memory segment in the **integer** variable *VS*. The **for-do** loop uses the standard array MemW to move the character and attribute byte to video memory. Because MemW operates on a full word (16 bytes), both the attribute byte and character byte must be combined into a single word. The character is set to 41h, the ASCII code for the letter "A", and the attribute byte is set to 70h, which produces a white letter on a black background. The variable *J* holds the offset in display memory and is incremented by 2 after each character and attribute are written.

With the following procedure, *FastWrite*, you can write strings directly to display memory at specific X and Y coordinates, as well as set the color attributes.

```
procedure FastWrite(X, Y : byte;
                    Ch : char;
                    FGround, BGround : byte);
var
   W : word;
   I, ColAtr : byte;
```

```
begin
  ColAtr := (BGround shl 4) + FGround;     (* create att byte *)
  W := ((Y-1)*80 + (X-1)) * 2;             (* calculate offset *)

  MemW[VS:W] := (ColAtr shl 8) + Ord(Ch);
end;
```

The procedure first creates the attribute byte (*ColAtr*) by shifting the background color left four bits and adding the foreground color. Next, the procedure computes the starting offset in display memory with the following formula:

X := ((Y-1)*80 + (Xx-1)) * 2;

In each iteration of the loop, the Turbo Pascal array MemW sets the character byte and the attribute byte at the same time. The procedure combines them by shifting the color byte to the left eight bits and adding the character byte. Notice that this puts the attribute byte in the high-order portion of the word, yet the attribute byte should be placed after the character byte in display memory. Once again, Intel's backward storage method forces you to think in reverse when operating with words.

Simple Windows

Normally, your programs will take advantage of the PC's entire 80x25 video display. There are times, however, when it is desirable to restrict output to just a portion of your monitor, using the Turbo Pascal command Window. For example, the command

```
Window(11, 11, 20, 15);
```

restricts your program's display to a 10 by 5 rectangle starting at column 11 and row 11; the remainder of the display is off limits to the Write command. (Note that the *FastWrite* procedure pays no attention to Turbo Pascal and can write outside the active window.) When you want to return to the full screen, the command

```
Window(1, 1, 80, 25)
```

returns the monitor to normal operation.

The Window command's most useful feature is its ability to realign the screen coordinates so that they fit the active window; that is, screen coordinates refer only to the active window, not to the entire screen. Thus, the command

```
GotoXY(1, 1);
```

positions the cursor at the upper-left corner of the active window, not the entire screen. In fact, Turbo Pascal treats the window as if it were the entire screen: when text runs off the bottom of the window, the screen scrolls up one line.

Pop-Up Windows

While useful in its own right, the Turbo Pascal Window command is simply not powerful enough to create professional-looking pop-up windows. The problem is that a Turbo Pascal window wipes out the portion of the screen it uses. Most people expect windows to act the way they do in Microsoft Windows; that is, when a window disappears, the text that was on the screen "beneath" the window reappears.

To create true pop-up windows, save the contents of the screen before you open the window and then restore the screen when you close the pop-up window.

To save a screen, define a variable that can store all the information contained in the screen: 2,000 characters, 2,000 color attributes, and the X and Y coordinates of the cursor. The following data structure, *ScreenType*, provides all you need.

```
type
  ScreenType = record
    Pos : array [1..80, 1..25] of record
      Ch : char;
      At : byte;
    end;
    CursX,
    CursY : byte;
  end;
```

ScreenType, a nested record data type, stores characters and attributes in the array named *Pos*, which has dimensions that match the coordinates of your monitor. Thus, to refer to the character in column 10 and row 20, you would use the following statement:

```
Screen.Pos[10,20].Ch
```

The **byte** variables *CursX* and *CursY* are used to store the cursor position.

The *ScreenType* data type is quite powerful. You can use it not only to store a screen's contents, but also to change the contents of the variable in memory, and then move it directly to video display, updating an entire video display in one shot.

There are several ways you can use a *ScreenType* variable to save and restore video images. One way to do this is to declare the variable **absolute** at the display memory location. If you have a color graphics adapter, you would use this declaration:

```
var
  Screen : ScreenType absolute $B800;
```

Unfortunately, this approach requires you to choose the address in advance, which means you can service only one type of video adapter (unless you define separate screens for monochrome and color). A better approach is to define the screen as a pointer variable. The program then sets the pointer to the correct offset in display memory, depending on the adapter in use. The following program demonstrates this technique:

```pascal
Program WindowPointer;

uses Crt;

const
  MaxWin = 5;

type
  ScreenPtr = ^ScreenType;
  ScreenType = record
    Pos : array [1..80, 1..25] of record
      Ch : char;
      At : byte;
    end;
    CursX, CursY : byte;
  end;

var
    Screen : ScreenPtr;

(******************************************************)

function VidSeg : word;
begin
  if Mem[$0000:$0449] = 7 then
    VidSeg := $B000
  else
    VidSeg := $B800;
end;

(******************************************************)

begin
  ClrScr;
  Screen := Ptr(VidSeg,$0000);
  Screen^.Pos[1,1].Ch := 'A';
  Screen^.Pos[80,25].Ch := 'Z';
  GotoXY(40, 12);
  Readln;
end.
```

The program begins by clearing the screen and then uses the Ptr function to point the *Screen* variable to the correct location in the display memory. Because of this repositioning, any changes made to the variable *Screen* will show up on your monitor.

When you use this method, do not use the Dispose command on the *Screen* variable, or Turbo Pascal will try to deallocate memory from the display adapter, most likely crashing your program. For a review of pointers, see Chapter 6.

Multiple Logical Screens and Pop-Up Windows

Your program can have as many screen variables as its memory will hold. Screens that are held in memory, and not displayed, are often called logical screens to distinguish them from the physical screen (the computer monitor). A program can write to a logical screen without disturbing the display on the physical screen. Then, when you want to display the logical screen, simply move its contents into the physical screen.

The use of logical screens is best explained by an example. This program uses one physical screen variable (Screen) and three logical screen variables (Screen1, Screen2, and Screen3). By typing 1, 2, or 3 on the keyboard, you can display any of the three logical screens.

```
Program FastScreenDemo;

uses Crt;

const
   MaxWin = 5;

type
  ScreenPtr = ^ScreenType;
  ScreenType = record
    Pos : array [1..80, 1..25] of record
      Ch : char;
      At : byte;
    end;
    CursX, CursY : byte;
  end;

var
   Screen,
   Screen1,
   Screen2,
   Screen3 : ScreenPtr;
   Ch : char;
   I, J : byte;

(**************************************************)
```

```
function VidSeg : word;
begin
  if Mem[$0000:$0449] = 7 then
    VidSeg := $B000
  else
    VidSeg := $B800;
end;


(**********************************************)

begin
  New(Screen1);
  New(Screen2);
  New(Screen3);

  for I := 1 to 80 do
    for J := 1 to 25 do
      begin
        Screen1^.Pos[I,J].Ch := '1';
        Screen2^.Pos[I,J].Ch := '2';
        Screen3^.Pos[I,J].Ch := '3';
        Screen1^.Pos[I,J].At := $07;
        Screen2^.Pos[I,J].At := $07;
        Screen3^.Pos[I,J].At := $07;
      end;

  ClrScr;
  Screen := Ptr(VidSeg,$0000);

  repeat
    GotoXY(1,1);
    Write('Press 1,2,3 to change screens or 0 to exit.');

    Ch := ReadKey;
    case Ch of
      '1' : Screen^ := Screen1^;
      '2' : Screen^ := Screen2^;
      '3' : Screen^ := Screen3^;
    end;
  until Ch = '0';
end.
```

Screen, which is superimposed on the display memory, acts as the physical device. The program changes the display memory by setting the physical device variable *Screen* equal to one of the logical screens. The transfer is fast, and the entire screen updated in one statement. A program can also move the contents of the physical screen to a logical screen with a statement like this:

```
PhysicalScreen^ := LogicalScreen^;
```

Manipulating logical screens is the technique you need to create pop-up windows. Before you open a pop-up window, save a copy of the physical screen in a logical screen variable. Then, when you close the window, restore the screen to its original appearance. Thus, your windows seem to pop up from nowhere and, when no longer needed, disappear without a trace.

The following program uses an array of logical screens to create up to five pop-up windows. When you run the program, you will see how windows can overlap without causing problems.

```pascal
Program WindowDemo;
{$R-}

uses Crt;

const
  MaxWin = 5;

type
  ScreenType = record
    Pos : array [1..80,1..25] of record
      Ch : Char;
      At : byte;
    end;
    CursX,
    CursY : byte;
  end;

  WindowPtr = ^WindowType;
  WindowType = record
    Scr : ScreenType;
    WinX1,
    WinY1,
    WinX2,
    WinY2 : byte;
  end;

var
  Ch : char;
  I : integer;
  VS : word;
  ActiveWin : WindowPtr;
  Windows : array [0..MaxWin] Of WindowPtr;
```

```
  CurrentWindow : integer;

(**************************************************)

function VidSeg : word;
begin
  if Mem[$0000:$0449] = 7 then
    VidSeg := $B000
  else
    VidSeg := $B800;
end;

(**************************************************)

procedure FastWrite(X, Y : byte;
                    Ch : char;
                    FGround, BGround : byte);
var
  W : word;
  I, ColAtr : byte;
begin
  ColAtr := (BGround shl 4) + FGround;      (* create attr byte *)
  W := ((Y-1)*80 + (X-1))*2;                (* calculate offset *)

  MemW[VS:W] := (ColAtr shl 8) + Ord(Ch);
end;

(**************************************************)

procedure FastBox(X1, Y1, X2, Y2, FGround, BGround : byte);
var
  I : byte;
  S : char;
begin
  TextColor(FGround);
  TextBackground(BGround);

  S := #205;
  for I := (X1+1) to (X2-1) do
    begin
      FastWrite(I, Y1, S, FGround, BGround);
      FastWrite(I, Y2, S, FGround, BGround);
    end;

  S := #186;
  for I := (Y1+1) to (Y2-1) do
    begin
      FastWrite(X1, I, S, FGround, BGround);
      FastWrite(X2, I, S, FGround, BGround);
```

```
      end;

  S := #201;
  FastWrite(X1, Y1, S, FGround, BGround);
  S := #187;
  FastWrite(X2, Y1, S, FGround, BGround);
  S := #200;
  FastWrite(X1, Y2, S, FGround, BGround);
  S := #188;
  FastWrite(X2, Y2, S, FGround, BGround);
end;

(*****************************************)

procedure SetUpWindows;
var
  I : integer;
begin
  New(ActiveWin);
  for I := 0 to MaxWin do
    New(Windows[I]);

  with ActiveWin^ do
    begin
      WinX1 := 1;
      WinY1 := 1;
      WinX2 := 80;
      WinY2 := 25;
      with Scr do
        begin
          CursX := WhereX;
          CursY := WhereY;
        end;
    end;

  ActiveWin := Ptr(VidSeg, $0000);
  CurrentWindow := 0;
  with Windows[CurrentWindow]^ do
    begin
      WinX1 := 1;
      WinY1 := 1;
      WinX2 := 80;
      WinY2 := 25;
      with Scr do
        begin
          CursX := 1;
          CursY := 1;
        end;
    end;
```

```
  end;

(******************************************)

procedure OpenWindow;
begin
  if CurrentWindow < MaxWin then
    begin
      Windows[CurrentWindow]^.Scr := ActiveWin^.Scr;
      Windows[CurrentWindow]^.Scr.CursX := WhereX;
      Windows[CurrentWindow]^.Scr.CursY := WhereY;

      CurrentWindow := CurrentWindow + 1;
      with Windows[CurrentWindow]^ do
        begin
          WinX1 := CurrentWindow * 10;
          WinY1 := CurrentWindow * 2;
          WinX2 := WinX1 + 20;
          WinY2 := WinY1 + 5;

          with Scr do
            begin
              CursX := 1;
              CursY := 1;
            end;

          Window(WinX1, WinY1, WinX2, WinY2);
          FastBox(WinX1-1, WinY1-1, WinX2+1, WinY2+1, Yellow, Black);
          TextColor(Yellow);
          TextBackGround(Black);
          ClrScr;
        end;
    end;
end;

(******************************************)

procedure CloseWindow;
begin
  if CurrentWindow > 0  then
    begin
      Windows[CurrentWindow]^.Scr.CursX := WhereX;
      Windows[CurrentWindow]^.Scr.CursY := WhereY;

      CurrentWindow := CurrentWindow - 1;
      ActiveWin^.Scr := Windows[CurrentWindow]^.Scr;
      with Windows[CurrentWindow]^ do
        begin
          Window(WinX1, WinY1, WinX2, WinY2);
```

```
            GotoXY(Scr.CursX, Scr.CursY);
        end;
     end;
end;

(*****************************************)

procedure FillWindow;
var
  Ch : Char;
begin
  Ch := ReadKey;
  repeat
    Write(Chr(Random(80)+30));
    Delay(20);
  until KeyPressed;
end;

(*****************************************)

begin
  ClrScr;
  VS := VidSeg;
  SetUpWindows;

  TextColor(Yellow+Blink);
  GotoXY(1, 25);
  Write('Press any key to open/close windows...');
  GotoXY(1, 1);

  TextColor(Yellow);
  FillWindow;
  for I := 1 to MaxWin do
    begin
      OpenWindow;
      FillWindow;
    end;

  for I := 1 to MaxWin do
    begin
      CloseWindow;
      FillWindow;
    end;
end.
```

The output from this program (after partial execution) appears in Figure 14-2.

These fast, clean screen procedures make your windows look professional. Now you can spend your time on filling the windows with useful information and tools

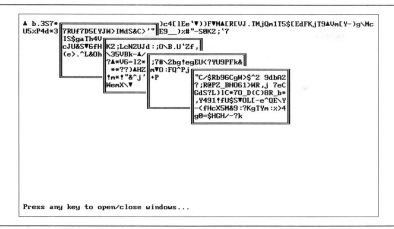

Figure 14-2.   Sample output from WindowDemo program

(calendars, calculators, note pads, and so on) and not on getting the windows started in the first place. If you are willing to spend some extra time learning, you can create even more professional windows using Turbo Vision. See Chapter 17 for all the details.

Screen Control Routines   **Crt Unit**

ClrEol

```
procedure ClrEol;
```

Clears the current screen line from the cursor position to the right edge of the screen (or window).

ClrScr

```
procedure ClrScr;
```

Clears the screen (or window) and positions the cursor at location (1,1).

DelLine

```
procedure DelLine;
```

Deletes the line of the screen (or window) on which the cursor is located. Lines below the deleted line scroll up one line.

InsLine

```
procedure InsLine;
```

Inserts a blank line on the screen (or window) at the current cursor position.

Window

```
procedure Window(X1, Y1, X2, Y2 : byte);
```

Restricts the active screen to the rectangle defined by coordinates X1,Y1 (upper left) and X2,Y2 (lower right). The upper-left corner of the window becomes coordinate 1,1.

Avoiding Vertical Retrace

Earlier in this chapter you studied the *FastWrite* procedure, which is much faster for text output than Write. However, this approach is complicated by vertical retrace, which creates a "snow" effect on CGA adapters. If you want your program to write directly to video memory, you must take special steps to eliminate snow. Try running the following program, which uses the *FastWrite* procedure to display a large "V" on your monitor.

```
Program CGASnowDemo;

{$R-}

uses Crt;

var
  VS : word;
  I, J : byte;
  S : string;

(*******************************************************)

function VidSeg : word;
begin
  if Mem[$0000:$0449] = 7 then
    VidSeg := $B000
```

```
    else
      VidSeg := $B800;
end;


(*****************************************************)


procedure FastWrite(X, Y : byte;
                    var S : string;
                    FGround, BGround : byte);
var
  W : word;
  I, ColAtr : byte;

begin
  ColAtr := (BGround shl 4) + FGround;    (* create attr byte *)
  W := ((Y-1)*80 + (X-1)) * 2;      (* calculate offset *)

  for I := 1 to Length(S) do
    begin
      MemW[VS:W] := (ColAtr shl 8) + Ord(S[I]);
      Inc(W, 2);
    end;
end;



(*****************************************************)


begin
  ClrScr;
  VS := VidSeg;
  S := 'XXXXXXX';
  J := 5;

  for I := 1 to 25 do
    begin
      FastWrite(J, I, S, Yellow, Black);
      Inc(J, 1);
    end;

  for I := 25 downto 1 do
    begin
      FastWrite(J, I, S, Yellow, Black);
      Inc(J, 1);
    end;

  GotoXY(1, 24);
  Write('Press ENTER...');
  Readln;
end.
```

When you run this program with a CGA adapter, you will notice some "snow" on your screen. This is caused by the vertical retrace, a process that updates your screen from display memory many times per second (each vertical retrace takes approximately 1.25 milliseconds). If you move bytes directly to display memory while a vertical retrace is in progress, you will get snow.

The only way to avoid snow is to write to display memory between vertical retraces; in other words, the program must wait until the retrace has ended and then write the characters to display memory before the next retrace begins. Turbo Pascal is simply not fast enough to do this; you must use an external assembler procedure, inline code, or the **asm** statement.

The following listing is an assembler procedure that writes out a string to video memory without generating snow. The assembler listing uses the special features of the Turbo Assembler, so you must use TASM.EXE to assemble it.

```
.MODEL TPASCAL

.DATA

VIDTYPE DB ?

.CODE

FastWrite PROC FAR x:BYTE, y:BYTE, s:DWORD, fg:BYTE, bg:BYTE

            PUBLIC      FASTWRITE

FASTSTR:

;------------------------------------------------------------
; Compute offset into display memory—((y-1)*80 + (x-1)) * 2
;------------------------------------------------------------


            PUSH    DS
            XOR     BX,BX
            XOR     AX,AX
            MOV     BL,x            ; Get x from stack;
            MOV     AL,y            ; Get y from stack;
            DEC     BX              ; Decrement x and y to get
            DEC     AX              ;   correct offset.
            MOV     CX,0080         ; Multiply y (in AX) by
            MUL     CX              ;   80 (in CX).
            ADD     AX,BX           ; Add x to y;
            MOV     CX,0002         ; Multiply the
            MUL     CX              ;   sum by 2.
            MOV     DI,AX           ; Store starting offset in DI.
```

```
;-----------------------------------------------------------
; Create the attribute byte
;-----------------------------------------------------------

            MOV     BL,bg       ; Get the background color.
            MOV     AL,fg       ; Get the foreground color.
            MOV     CL,4        ; Shift the foreground color
            SHL     BX,CL       ;   into the high nybble.
            ADD     BX,AX       ; Add in the foreground.
            XCHG    BL,BH       ; Move into the upper byte.
            MOV     DX,3DAH     ; Load CRT port address in DX.


;-----------------------------------------------------------
; Get the monitor type
;-----------------------------------------------------------

            XOR     AX,AX       ; Assign 0000h to ES.
            MOV     ES,AX

            MOV     AX,0449h    ; Assign offset of
            MOV     SI,AX       ; video type location.

            MOV     AX,ES:[SI]  ; If video type is 7
            CMP     AL,7        ; then monitor is

            JZ      MONO        ; monochrome.

            MOV     AX,0B800H   ; Load the color
            MOV     ES,AX       ;   segment into ES.
            MOV     VIDTYPE,1
            JMP     CHKSTR      ; Continue.

MONO:
            MOV     AX,0B000H   ; Load the monochrome
            MOV     ES,AX       ;   segment into ES.
            MOV     VIDTYPE,0


;-----------------------------------------------------------
; Load the string and check for zero length
;-----------------------------------------------------------


CHKSTR:     LDS     SI,S        ; Load string address into DS:SI.
            MOV     CL,[SI]     ; Move string length into CL.
            CMP     CL,0        ; If string length is zero,
            JZ      ENDSTR      ;   exit procedure.
            CLD                 ; Clear direction flag.


NEXTCHAR:   INC     SI          ; Point to next character.
```

```
            MOV     BL,[SI]     ; Move it into BL.
            CMP     VIDTYPE,0   ; If monochrome, don't check
            JE      MOVECHAR    ; for retrace.

WLOW:       IN      AL,DX       ; Get CRT status.
            TEST    AL,1        ; Is retrace off?
            JNZ     WLOW        ; If off, wait for it to start.
            CLI                 ; No interrupts, please.

WHIGH:      IN      AL,DX       ; Get CRT status.
            TEST    AL,1        ; Is retrace on?
            JZ      WHIGH       ; If on, wait for it to stop.

MOVECHAR:   MOV     AX,BX       ; Move color and character to AX.
            STOSW               ; Move color/character to screen.
            STI                 ; Interrupts are now allowed.

LOOP        NEXTCHAR            ; Done yet?

ENDSTR:     POP     DS
            RET

FASTWRITE   ENDP
CODE        ENDS
            END
```

The *FastWrite* procedure checks the adapter I/O port number 3DAh for a status bit known as the vertical sync signal. When this status bit is on, a vertical retrace is in progress. The procedure first checks to see if the monitor is between retraces (the status bit equals 0). If so, the loop repeats until a retrace begins. The procedure then waits for the retrace to end.

As soon as the retrace ends, the procedure moves characters to the display memory. Because the procedure waited until the very end of a retrace, there should be ample time to move the characters before the next retrace begins.

Use TASM, the Turbo Assembler, to assemble this code to an object file (FASTWRIT.OBJ) and declare the external routine as shown in the program listed here:

```
Program CGANoSnowDemo;

{$R-,F+}

uses Crt;

var
  I, J : byte;
  S : string;
```

```
{$L FASTWRIT}
procedure FastWrite(X, Y : byte;
                    var S : string;
                    FGround, BGround : byte); external;

begin
  ClrScr;
  S := 'XXXXXXX';
  J := 5;

  for I := 1 to 25 do
    begin
      FastWrite(J, I, S, Yellow, Black);
      Inc(J, 1);
    end;

  for I := 25 downto 1 do
    begin
      FastWrite(J, I, S, Yellow, Black);
      Inc(J, 1);
    end;

  GotoXY(1, 24);
  Write('Press ENTER...');
  Readln;
end.
```

The *WindowDemo* program, shown previously in this chapter, also creates snow on CGA monitors. There is just no way to avoid it with code written in Turbo Pascal. An external procedure written in assembler, however, can eliminate the snow while making the screen update even faster. Listed here are two assembler procedures you can use as external procedures. The first moves a logical screen to video memory. The second moves the screen currently in video memory to a logical screen. In both cases, snow is eliminated. Be sure to use the Turbo Assembler to assemble this listing.

```
.MODEL TPASCAL

.DATA

VIDTYPE DB ?

.CODE

PUBLIC READSCR
PUBLIC WRITESCR

WRITESCR PROC FAR s:DWORD
```

```
;-----------------------------------------------------------
; Save registers.
;-----------------------------------------------------------

          PUSH      DS

;-----------------------------------------------------------
; Get the monitor type.
;-----------------------------------------------------------


          XOR       AX,AX       ; Assign 0000h to ES.

          MOV       ES,AX

          MOV       AX,0449h    ; Assign offset of
          MOV       SI,AX       ; video type location.

          MOV       AX,ES:[SI]  ; If video type is 7
          CMP       AL,7        ; then monitor is
          JZ        MONO1       ; monochrome.

          MOV       AX,0B800H   ; Load the color
          MOV       ES,AX       ;   segment into ES.
          MOV       VIDTYPE,1
          JMP       CONT1       ; Continue.

MONO1:
          MOV       AX,0B000H   ; Load the monochrome
          MOV       ES,AX       ;   segment into ES.
          MOV       VIDTYPE,0


;-----------------------------------------------------------
; Load buffer to screen.
;-----------------------------------------------------------

CONT1:    LDS       SI,s        ; Load buffer address in DS:SI.
          MOV       DI,0        ; Point to start of memory.

          MOV       CX,2000     ; Move 2000 characters.
          CLD                   ; Clear direction flag.

          MOV       DX,3DAh     ; Load CRT port address.

NEXTCHAR1: CMP      VIDTYPE,0   ; If monochrome, don't check
          JE        MOVECHAR1   ; for retrace.

WLOW1:    IN        AL,DX       ; Get CRT status.
          TEST      AL,1        ; Is retrace off?
```

```
              JNZ       WLOW1      ; If off, wait for it to start.
              CLI                  ; No interrupts, please.

WHIGH1:       IN        AL,DX      ; Get CRT status.
              TEST      AL,1       ; Is retrace on?
              JZ        WHIGH1     ; If on, wait for it to end.

MOVECHAR1:    LODSW                ; Get word from buffer to AX.
              STOSW                ; Move word from AX to screen.
              STI                  ; Interrupts are allowed.
              LOOP      NEXTCHAR1  ; Done yet?

ENDSTR1:

;----------------------------------------------------------
; Restore registers.
;----------------------------------------------------------

              POP       DS

              RET

WRITESCR      ENDP

READSCR   PROC FAR s:DWORD

;----------------------------------------------------------
; Save registers.
;----------------------------------------------------------

              PUSH      DS

;----------------------------------------------------------
; Get the monitor type
;----------------------------------------------------------

              XOR       AX,AX      ; Assign 0000h to ES.
              MOV       ES,AX

              MOV       AX,0449h   ; Assign offset of
              MOV       SI,AX      ; video type location.

              MOV       AX,ES:[SI] ; If video type is 7
              CMP       AL,7       ; then monitor is
              JZ        MONO2      ; monochrome.


              MOV       VIDTYPE,1
```

```
              MOV     AX,0B800H  ; Load the color
              MOV     DS,AX      ;   segment into DS.
              JMP     CONT2      ; Continue.


MONO2:
              MOV     VIDTYPE,0
              MOV     AX,0B000H  ; Load the monochrome
              MOV     DS,AX      ;   segment into DS.


CONT2:
              LES     DI,s       ; Load buffer address in ES:DI.
              MOV     SI,0       ; Point to start of memory.
              MOV     CX,2000    ; Characters in screen.
              CLD                ; Clear direction flag.


;-----------------------------------------------------------
; Transfer display memory to buffer.
;-----------------------------------------------------------


              MOV     DX,3DAh    ; Load CRT port address into DX.

NEXTCHAR2:    CMP     ES:VIDTYPE,0 ; If monochrome, don't check
              JE      MOVECHAR2    ; for retrace.

WLOW2:        IN      AL,DX      ; Get CRT status.

              TEST    AL,1       ; Is retrace off?
              JNZ     WLOW2      ; If off, wait for it to start.
              CLI                ; No interrupts please.

WHIGH2:       IN      AL,DX      ; Get CRT status.
              TEST    AL,1       ; Is retrace on?
              JZ      WHIGH2     ; If on, wait for it to end.

MOVECHAR2:    LODSW              ; Move word from screen to AX.
              STOSW              ; Move AX to buffer.
              LOOP    NEXTCHAR2  ; Done yet?
              STI                ; Interrupts are allowed.


ENDSTR2:

;-----------------------------------------------------------
; Restore registers.
;-----------------------------------------------------------

              POP     DS

              RET
```

```
READSCR        ENDP

CODE           ENDS

               END
```

The assembler listing just given contains two procedures, *WriteScr* and *ReadScr*. You can use these two procedures in the program WindowDemo as shown here:

```
Program WindowDemoCGA;

{$R-}

uses Crt;

const
  MaxWin = 5;

type
  ScreenType = record
    Pos : array [1..80,1..25] of record
      Ch : Char;
      At : byte;
    end;
    CursX,
    CursY : byte;
  end;

  WindowPtr = ^WindowType;
  WindowType = record
    Scr : ScreenType;
    WinX1,
    WinY1,
    WinX2,
    WinY2 : byte;
  end;

var
  Ch : char;
  I : integer;
  VS : word;
  Windows : array [0..MaxWin] Of WindowPtr;
  CurrentWindow : integer;

(**************************************************)

{$L FASTWRIT}
procedure FastWrite(X, Y : byte;
```

```
                    S : string;
                    FGround, BGround : byte); external;

{$L FASTSCR}
procedure WriteScr(var S : ScreenType); external;
procedure ReadScr(var S : ScreenType); external;

(***************************************************)

procedure FastBox(X1, Y1, X2, Y2, FGround, BGround : byte);
var
  I : byte;
  S : string[1];
begin
  TextColor(FGround);
  TextBackground(BGround);

  S := #205;
  for I := (X1+1) to (X2-1) do
    begin
      FastWrite(I, Y1, S, FGround, BGround);
      FastWrite(I, Y2, S, FGround, BGround);
    end;

  S := #186;
  for I := (Y1+1) to (Y2-1) do
    begin
      FastWrite(X1, I, S, FGround, BGround);
      FastWrite(X2, I, S, FGround, BGround);
    end;

  S := #201;
  FastWrite(X1, Y1, S, FGround, BGround);
  S := #187;
  FastWrite(X2, Y1, S, FGround, BGround);
  S := #200;
  FastWrite(X1, Y2, S, FGround, BGround);
  S := #188;
  FastWrite(X2, Y2, S, FGround, BGround);
end;

(*****************************************)

procedure SetUpWindows;
var
  I : integer;
begin
  for I := 0 to MaxWin do
    begin
```

```
      New(Windows[I]);
      FillChar(Windows[I]^, SizeOf(Windows[I]^), 0);
    end;

  CurrentWindow := 0;
  with Windows[CurrentWindow]^ do
    begin
      WinX1 := 1;
      WinY1 := 1;
      WinX2 := 80;
      WinY2 := 25;
      with Scr do
        begin
          CursX := 1;
          CursY := 1;
        end;
      end;
  end;

(*****************************************)

procedure OpenWindow;
begin
  if CurrentWindow < MaxWin then
    begin
      ReadScr(Windows[CurrentWindow]^.Scr);
      Windows[CurrentWindow]^.Scr.CursX := WhereX;
      Windows[CurrentWindow]^.Scr.CursY := WhereY;

      CurrentWindow := CurrentWindow + 1;
      with Windows[CurrentWindow]^ do
        begin
          WinX1 := CurrentWindow * 10;
          WinY1 := CurrentWindow * 2;
          WinX2 := WinX1 + 20;
          WinY2 := WinY1 + 5;

          with Scr do
            begin
              CursX := 1;
              CursY := 1;
            end;

          Window(WinX1, WinY1, WinX2, WinY2);
          FastBox(WinX1-1, WinY1-1, WinX2+1, WinY2+1, Yellow, Black);
          TextColor(Yellow);
          TextBackGround(Black);
          ClrScr;
        end;
```

```
      end;
end;

(*****************************************)

procedure CloseWindow;
begin
  if CurrentWindow > 0  then
    begin
      Windows[CurrentWindow]^.Scr.CursX := WhereX;
      Windows[CurrentWindow]^.Scr.CursY := WhereY;

      CurrentWindow := CurrentWindow - 1;
      WriteScr(Windows[CurrentWindow]^.Scr);
      with Windows[CurrentWindow]^ do
        begin
          Window(WinX1, WinY1, WinX2, WinY2);
          GotoXY(Scr.CursX, Scr.CursY);
        end;
    end;
end;

(*****************************************)

procedure FillWindow;
var
  Ch : Char;
begin
  Ch := ReadKey;
  repeat
    Write(Chr(Random(80)+30));
    Delay(20);
  until KeyPressed;
end;

(*****************************************)

begin
  ClrScr;
  SetUpWindows;

  TextColor(Yellow+Blink);
  GotoXY(1, 25);
  Write('Press any key to open/close windows...');
  GotoXY(1, 1);

  TextColor(Yellow);
  FillWindow;
  for I := 1 to MaxWin do
```

```
    begin
      OpenWindow;
      FillWindow;
    end;

  for I := 1 to MaxWin do
    begin
      CloseWindow;
      FillWindow;
    end;
end.
```

Today there are fewer CGA monitors still in use. However, programmers that still use them should not need to suffer with slow I/O or snow.

Other Crt Subprograms

The remainder of the subprograms in the Crt unit are summarized in the following section. These routines are no less important or useful than the other routines; however, they need much less explanation.

Miscellaneous Crt Routines   **Crt Unit**

AssignCrt

```
procedure AssignCrt(var F : text);
```

Allows the user to send output to the video display by writing to file F.

Delay

```
procedure Delay(Ms : word);
```

Suspends program execution for Ms milliseconds.

KeyPressed

```
function KeyPressed : boolean;
```

Returns True when a key has been pressed.

NoSound

```
procedure NoSound;
```

Stops any tone currently being generated by the PC's speaker.

ReadKey

```
function ReadKey : char;
```

Reads a character from the keyboard without echo. If the result is #0, then a special key has been pressed and you must call ReadKey again to capture the second part of the key code. See Appendix C, "The PC Keyboard," for these special codes.

Sound

```
procedure Sound(Freq : word);
```

Generates a tone from the PC's speaker at a frequency specified by Freq. The tone continues until the NoSound procedure is executed.

The WinCrt Unit

The primary purpose of the WinCrt unit is to ease your transition from DOS to Windows programming. Most of the subprograms that enhance a nongraphic program, such as modifying colors and sounds, are not included in WinCrt. Therefore, if you want to improve the look of programs that use WinCrt you will need to progress to using Object Windows. Object Windows is introduced in the latter part of Chapter 16, "Graphics," and covered in more detail in Chapter 18, "Object Windows."

Using WinCrt Windows

To a non-Windows programmer, even the simplest of Turbo Pascal Windows programs can be frustrating at first. Take the traditional "Hello World" program, for instance:

```
Program HelloWorld1;

begin
  Writeln ('Hello World');
end.
```

When you run this in Windows, you get run-time error number 105, which means a file is not open. File? What file?

Actually in this case the file is a device: the CRT. In Windows programming, you must create an area for input and output to take place, called a *window*. Setting up a window can be a difficult task. The WinCrt unit, however, greatly simplifies the process. It automatically creates a window and redirects all Turbo Pascal CRT I/O to that window.

To show how simple it really is, here's the WinCrt version of the "Hello World" program:

```
Program HelloWorld2;

uses WinCrt;

begin
  Writeln ('Hello World');
end.
```

The output of this program is shown in Figure 14-3.

Obviously the **uses** clause must do much more than allow you access to routines in the WinCrt unit, and it does. In the initialization section of the WinCrt unit is the code that assigns the standard input and output file variables to a WinCrt window. This window is then opened either explicitly, through a call to InitWinCrt, or implicitly, through calls to Read(ln) or Write(ln).

When the window is opened, the following takes place:

1. The title is set to the full path and filename of the program that is running, in this case C:\BP\HELLO.EXE.

2. The location and size of the window are determined, normally based on default values.

3. A control menu is included in the upper-left corner, mostly to allow the user to close the window.

Once the window is created, you can modify it just like any other window—move it, size it, minimize it, and so on.

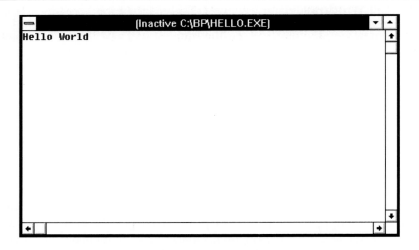

Figure 14-3.   *"Hello World" after execution*

When the program finishes, the window is placed in the *inactive* state. This is indicated by the change in title, as shown in Figure 14-3. Once inactive, the contents of the window will not change. The user can scroll though the window (if any of the output is outside the window boundaries), observe any data that is needed, then close it. If you don't want to give the user this luxury, you can close the window as part of your program using DoneWinCrt.

One other WinCrt procedure, TrackCursor, is worth special mention. When you call this procedure within your program, Borland Pascal will make sure that the current cursor location will always be visible. Thus if you output multiple pages of text, the most recent part will always be within the boundaries of the WinCrt window. If you need to see other parts of the output, you can use the scroll bars. If you do not call TrackCursor, the origin (coordinate 0,0) will remain in the upper-left corner, and you may need to use the scroll bars to see the most recent output.

WinCrt Subprogram Reference

The best way to detail the WinCrt unit is to compare it to its Crt counterpart. Table 14-3 shows you which routines are exactly the same, which cannot be found in WinCrt, and which are unique to WinCrt. Only those in the third column need further elaboration.

Same for both	Unique to Crt	Unique to WinCrt
AssignCrt	Delay	CursorTo
ClrEol	DelLine	DoneWinCrt
ClrScr	HighVideo	InitWinCrt
GotoXY	InsLine	ReadBuf
KeyPressed	LowVideo	ScrollTo
ReadKey	NormVideo	TrackCursor
WhereX	NoSound	WriteBuf
WhereY	Sound	WriteChar
	TextBackground	
	TextColor	
	TextMode	
	Window	

Table 14-3.   *Comparison of the Crt and WinCrt Units*

Routines Unique to WinCrt

CursorTo

```
procedure CursorTo(X, Y : integer);
```

Places the cursor at a give X, Y coordinate. This procedure is the same as GotoXY, except the origin is based on 0,0 instead of 1,1.

DoneWinCrt

```
procedure DoneWinCrt;
```

Closes the WinCrt window. Without using this procedure, the window will go to the "inactive" state, and the user must close the window.

InitWinCrt

```
procedure InitWinCrt;
```

Creates the WinCrt window. This is called automatically whenever your program calls Read(ln) or Write(ln).

ReadBuf

```
function ReadBuf(Buffer: PChar; Count : word) : word;
```

Gets a null-terminated string from the user.

ScrollTo

```
procedure ScrollTo(X, Y : integer);
```

Moves the contents of the WinCrt window so that the upper-left corner contains the X, Y coordinate.

TrackCursor

```
procedure TrackCursor;
```

Tells the program to scroll the window to keep the cursor position visible at all times.

WriteBuf

```
function WriteBuf(Buffer : PChar; Count : word) : word;
```

Displays the first Count characters of a null-terminated string.

WriteChar

```
procedure WriteChar(Ch : char);
```

Displays a single character at the current cursor location in the WinCrt window.

Chapter *15*

The Dos and WinDos Units

Your PC consists of various physical devices: a keyboard, a monitor, disk drives, a printer, and so on. The Disk Operating System (DOS) and Basic Input Output System (BIOS) are comprised of software routines that control these devices, making sure data comes and goes to the right place without errors.

Your Turbo Pascal programs are constantly using DOS and BIOS services for such activities as writing to a disk file, displaying information on the monitor, getting the current time and date, and more. Because Turbo Pascal does all the work for you, you don't normally need to know anything about the DOS and BIOS services that are being called into play. Still, there are two reasons why you should know about these services and how to use them.

First, while Turbo Pascal gives you access to many services, it does not use them all. If you want complete control over your PC, you will have to learn to harness the power of DOS and BIOS services. Second, even if you never need to use these services, learning about them will greatly increase your understanding of personal computers and operating systems.

Turbo Pascal 7.0 provides a standard unit named Dos which contains routines that call specific DOS and BIOS services as well as the data structures and procedures you need to call services on your own. For Windows programming, Borland Pascal has the WinDos unit. With these routines you can get information on files, get a directory listing, set time and date for the system and individual files, and more. This chapter describes these subprograms and how you use them.

Date and Time Routines

The system clock keeps track of the current date and time. You can get the date and time from the system clock with the GetTime and GetDate procedures. Likewise, you can set the time and date of the system clock with SetTime and SetDate.

Files have their own date stamp, a single long integer that contains both the time and date the file was created or last updated. You can get the time stamp for any file with GetFTime. Before you can interpret the file's time stamp, you must pass it through UnPackTime, which produces a date and time. You can reverse this process with PackTime, which takes a time and date and returns a long integer that you can use in SetFTime to set a file's time and date.

The following unit demonstrates getting and setting dates for both the system clock and DOS files:

```
Unit DATES;
interface

procedure GetSystemDateTime;
procedure SetSystemDateTime;
procedure GetFileDateTime(FileName : string);
procedure SetFileDateTime;


implementation

uses Dos;

const
  DayName: array [0..6] of String[10] =
    ('Sunday', 'Monday', 'Tuesday', 'Wednesday',
     'Thursday', 'Friday', 'Saturday');

var
  Year, Month, Day, DayOfWeek,
  Hour, Minute, Second, Sec100 : word;
  F : file;
  T : longint;
  TimeStamp : DateTime;

procedure GetSystemDateTime;
begin
  WriteLn('Current date and time.');
  GetDate(Year, Month, Day, DayOfWeek);
  WriteLn('System Date = ',DayName[DayOfWeek],' ',Month,'/',Day,
           '/',Year);
  GetTime(Hour, Minute, Second, Sec100);
  WriteLn('System time = ',Hour,':',Minute,':',Second,':',Sec100);
  WriteLn;
```

```
end;

procedure SetSystemDateTime;
begin
  WriteLn('Set current date and time.');
  Write('Enter year (1980 or later): ');
  ReadLn(Year);
  Write('Enter month: ');
  ReadLn(Month);
  Write('Enter day: ');
  ReadLn(Day);
  Write('Enter hour: ');
  ReadLn(Hour);
  Write('Enter minute: ');
  ReadLn(Minute);
  Second := 0;
  Sec100 := 0;
  SetDate(Year, Month, Day);
  SetTime(Hour, Minute, Second, Sec100);

  { Display new date and time }
  GetSystemDateTime;
end;

procedure GetFileDateTime(FileName : string);
begin
  WriteLn('Get date and time for a file.');
  if FileName = '' then
    begin
      Write('Enter file name: ');
      ReadLn(FileName);
    end;
  Assign(F, FileName);
  Reset(F);
  GetFTime(F, T);
  UnPackTime(T, TimeStamp);
  with TimeStamp do
    begin
      WriteLn('File name: ', FileName);
      WriteLn('Date: ', Month, '/', Day, '/', Year);
      WriteLn('Time: ', Hour, ':', Min, ':', Sec);
    end;
  Close(F);
end;

procedure SetFileDateTime;
var
  FileName : string;
begin
```

```
  WriteLn('Set file date and time.');
  Write('Enter file name: ');
  ReadLn(FileName);
  Assign(F, FileName);
  Reset(F);
  with TimeStamp do
    begin
      Write('Year: ');
      ReadLn(Year);
      Write('Month: ');
      ReadLn(Month);
      Write('Day: ');
      ReadLn(Day);
      Write('Hour: ');
      ReadLn(Hour);
      Write('Minute: ');
      ReadLn(Minute);

      Second := 0;
    end;

  PackTime(TimeStamp, T);
  SetFTime(F, T);
  Close(F);
  GetFileDateTime(FileName);
end;

end.
```

Date and Time Routines	**DOS Unit**

GetDate

```
procedure GetDate(var Year, Month, Day, DayOfWeek : word);
```

Returns the date as stored in the system clock.

GetFTime

```
procedure GetFTime(var F; var Time : longint);
```

Returns in Time the time stamp for the file F. File F must be assigned and opened before using this procedure. The variable Time is a packed value and must be unpacked with the UnpackTime procedure.

GetTime

```
procedure GetTime(var Hour, Minute, Second, Sec100 : word);
```

Returns the time as stored in the system clock.

PackTime

```
procedure PackTime(var DT : DateTime; var Time : longint);
```

Accepts the variable DT, which contains date and time information, and returns Time, which contains the same information in packed form.

SetDate

```
procedure SetDate(Year, Month, Day : word);
```

Updates the system clock to the date passed as parameters. For example, the command SetDate(1997, 12, 1) sets the date to December 1, 1997.

SetFTime

```
procedure SetFTime(Var F; Time : longint);
```

Sets the time stamp of file F to the value of Time, which is a packed representation of the time and date. Time is created with the procedure PackTime.

SetTime

```
procedure SetTime(Hour, Minute, Second, Sec100 : word);
```

Sets the system clock according to the values passed as parameters.

UnpackTime

```
procedure UnpackTime(Time : longint; var DT : DateTime);
```

Decodes the variable Time and returns the results in DT.

Related Type

```
DateTime = record    { TDateTime in WinDos }
  Year, Month, Day,
  Hour, Min, Sec : integer;
end;
```

Used with GetTime and SetTime to read and set the time and date of the system clock.

Disk and File Routines

The Dos unit contains two disk-status routines: DiskFree and DiskSize. DiskFree returns the number of free bytes on a disk, and DiskSize returns the total number of used and unused bytes on a disk.

Some of the most useful routines in the Dos unit are those that operate on disk files. Two routines, FindFirst and FindNext let you read the files in any directory. FindFirst, as the name implies, reads information on the first file in the directory while FindNext gets information on each subsequent file. You can use the DOS wildcard characters in your search and even specify the type of file to search for (for example, archive, system, hidden).

If you want to know the attributes for a specific file, you can use GetFAttr, which returns the file attribute byte for the named file. SetFAttr, on the other hand, allows you to set the value of a file's attribute byte. The FExpand function takes a filename as a parameter and returns the complete file spec, including the disk drive, path, and filename. FSplit does just the opposite, taking a complete file spec and returning its components: path, name, and extension. FSearch looks for a file within a list of directories. If the file is found, FSearch returns the complete file spec; if not, it returns a blank string.

The FILES unit, shown here, demonstrates the use of Dos unit routines that manipulate files, directories, and disks:

```
Unit FILES;

interface

procedure DiskStatus;
procedure DisplayDirectory;
procedure FileSearchAndReport;

implementation

uses Dos;

procedure DiskStatus;
var
  Space : longint;
begin
  WriteLn('Disk status.');
  Space := DiskFree(0);
  WriteLn('Free space on disk = ', Space,' bytes/ ',
          Space div 1024, ' Kbytes');
  Space := DiskSize(0);
  WriteLn('Total space on disk = ', Space, ' bytes/ ',
          Space Div 1024, ' Kbytes');
  WriteLn;
end;

function PadRight(S : string; L : word) : string;
 {
 This function adds blank characters to
 a String until it reaches length L. If
 the String is longer than L to begin with,
 this function truncates the String.
 }
begin
  if Length(S) > L then
    S[0] := Chr(L);
  while Length(S) < L do
    S := S + ' ';
  PadRight := S;
end;


procedure DisplayDirectory;
var
  Srec : SearchRec;
```

```
  TimeStamp : DateTime;
  DS : DirStr;
  FN : NameStr;
  EN : ExtStr;
  FullName : PathStr;

begin
  WriteLn('Directory listing:');
  FindFirst('*.*', AnyFile, Srec);
  while DosError = 0 do
    begin
      with Srec do
        begin
          UnPackTime(Time, TimeStamp);
          with TimeStamp do
            begin
              FullName := FExpand(Name);
              FSplit(FullName, DS, FN, EN);
              WriteLn(PadRight(DS,20), ' ',
                      PadRight(FN,9), ' ',
                      PadRight(EN,5), ' ',
                      Size:7, ' ', Year);
            end;
        end;
      FindNext(Srec);
    end;
end;

procedure FileSearchAndReport;
var
  Attr : word;
  TheFile : file;
  DS, S : string;
begin
  WriteLn('Search for a file by name.');
  repeat
    Write('Enter file name: ');
    ReadLn(S);
    Write('Enter directory: ');
    ReadLn(DS);
    S := FSearch(S, DS);
    if S = '' then WriteLn('File not found...');
  until S > '';


  Assign(TheFile, S);
  GetFAttr(TheFile, Attr);

  if (Attr and ReadOnly) > 0 then
```

```
    WriteLn('File is read only')
  else
    WriteLn('File is not read only');

  if (Attr and Hidden) > 0 then
    WriteLn('File is hidden')
  else
    WriteLn('File is not hidden');

  if (Attr and SysFile) > 0 then
    WriteLn('File is system file')
  else
    WriteLn('File is not system file');

  if (Attr and VolumeID) > 0 then
    WriteLn('File is Volume ID')
  else
    WriteLn('File is not Volume ID');

  if (Attr and Directory) > 0 then
    WriteLn('File is Directory')
  else
    WriteLn('File is not Directory');

  if (Attr and Archive) > 0 then
    WriteLn('File is Archive')
  else
    WriteLn('File is not Archive');
end;

end.
```

Disk and File Routines   DOS Unit

DiskFree

```
function DiskFree(Drive : word) : longint;
```

Returns the amount of free disk space, in bytes, on drive Drive (1 = A, 2 = B, 0 = default drive).

DiskSize

```
function DiskSize(Drive : word) : longint;
```

Returns the size, in bytes, of drive Drive (1 = A, 2 = B, 0 = default drive).

FExpand

```
function FExpand(P : PathStr) : PathStr;
```

Accepts a filename P and returns the filename with its complete path structure, including drive.

FindFirst

```
procedure FindFirst(Path : string; Attr : word;
        var S : SearchRec);
```

Returns information on the first file found in directory Path whose attributes match Attr. The standard values of Attr are in defined in the Related Constants section.

FindNext

```
procedure FindNext(var S : SearchRec);
```

Returns information on the next file found in the directory Path defined in FindFirst whose attributes match Attr defined in FindFirst. If the search is successful, the value of DosError will be zero.

FSearch

```
function FSearch(Path : PathStr; DirList : string) : PathStr;
```

Searches in the list of directories included in DirList for a filename that matches Path. If the file is found, the result is returned as a string. If not found, the function returns an empty string.

FSplit

```
procedure FSplit(Path : PathStr; var Dir : DirStr;
          var Name : NameStr; var Ext : ExtStr);
```

Accepts a filename Path and returns its components. The types used in this procedure are defined in the Related Types section.

GetFAttr

```
procedure GetFAttr(var F; var Attr : word);
```

Returns the file attribute for file F. Before calling this procedure, F must be assigned but not opened. See the Related Constants section for possible values of Attr.

SetFAttr

```
procedure SetFAttr(var F; Attr : word);
```

Sets the attribute byte of file F to Attr. File F must be assigned but not opened before calling this procedure.

Related Types

```
SearchRec = record
  Fill : array [1..21] of byte;
  Attr : byte;
  Time : longint;
  Size : longint;
  Name : string[12];
end;
```

This type is used internally by FindFirst and FindNext.

```
DirStr = string[67];
ExtStr = string[3];
NameStr = string[8];
PathStr = string[79];
```

These types are strings of different lengths used by FSplit and other procedures.

Related Constants

```
ReadOnly = $01;
Hidden   = $02;
SysFile  = $04;
VolumeID = $08;
Directory= $10;
Archive  = $20;
AnyFile  = $3F;
```

These are the various bits that can be set for file attributes.

Process Routines

Exec and Keep are two of the more advanced routines in the Dos unit. Exec allows you to execute programs or the DOS shell from within a program, while Keep terminates a program, but keeps it resident in memory. The SwapVectors routine, when used with Exec, provides some margin of safety. When you use Exec to run a child program from within your Turbo Pascal program, you run the risk that the child program will permanently alter the interrupt vector table. By calling SwapVectors before and after the call to Exec, you can make sure that the interrupt vectors will be restored to their original state. One final process-control routine is DosExitCode, which provides a DOS error result upon program termination. This code can be used by other programs or by a batch file.

DOS maintains an area in memory that contains information about the computer's environment (for example, the number of file handles, the location of COMMAND.COM, and so on). This information is contained in a number of environment strings. The function EnvCount returns the number of environment strings in memory, and the function EnvStr returns a specified environment string. A third routine, GetEnv, returns the environment string for a specific environment element (for example, FILES, COMSPEC, PATH).

Finally, the Dos unit contains a number of miscellaneous routines that provide information and control over the computer. The DosVersion routine returns an *integer* whose high and low bytes contain the version of DOS in use. The personal computer also has two features—control-break checking and disk-write verification—that can be turned on or off. The CTRL-BREAK key combination is used to terminate programs. When control-break checking is disabled, DOS checks for CTRL-BREAK only during console, printer, or communications I/O; when it is enabled, DOS checks for CTRL-BREAK at every system call. The GetCBreak routine returns a boolean value that indicates if control-break checking is on or off. SetCBreak accepts a boolean value that turns control-break checking on or off. Similarly, the GetVerify routine returns a boolean value that indicates if disk-write verification is on or off, while SetVerify accepts a boolean value that turns disk-write verification on or off. When disk-write verification is enabled, DOS verifies every disk write; when it is disabled, DOS performs no verification.

The following unit demonstrates how each of these routines can be used:

```
Unit PROCESS;

interface

procedure SystemInfo;

implementation

uses Dos;

procedure DosShell;
begin
  WriteLn('DOS SHELL: Type EXIT to return to program...');
  SwapVectors;
  Exec(GetEnv('COMSPEC'), '');
  WriteLn('DosExitCode = ', DosExitCode);
  SwapVectors;
end;


(*******************************************************)

procedure SystemInfo;
var
  I : integer;
  YN : Char;
  DosVer : Word;
  Verify,
  CBreak : Boolean;
begin
 WriteLn('System info: ');
{ WriteLn('Number of Environment Strings = ', EnvCount);
 for I := 1 to EnvCount do
   WriteLn(I:2,': ',EnvStr(I));
 WriteLn;
}
 WriteLn('COMSPEC = ',GetEnv('COMSPEC'));
```

```
WriteLn('PATH = ',GetEnv('PATH'));
WriteLn;
DosVer := DosVersion;
WriteLn('DOS Version: ', Lo(DosVer),'.', Hi(DosVer));
WriteLn;

GetCBreak(CBreak);
if CBreak then
  begin
    WriteLn('CTRL-Break checking is ON.');
    Write('Turn CTRL-Break checking OFF? Y/N: ');
    ReadLn(YN);
    if UpCase(YN) = 'Y' then
      SetCBreak(FALSE);
  end
else
  begin
    WriteLn('CTRL-Break checking is OFF.');
    Write('Turn CTRL-Break checking ON? Y/N: ');
    ReadLn(YN);
    if UpCase(YN) = 'Y' then
      SetCBreak(TRUE);
  end;

GetVerify(Verify);
if Verify then
  begin
    WriteLn('Disk write verification is ON.');
    Write('Turn disk write verification OFF? Y/N: ');
    ReadLn(YN);
    if UpCase(YN) = 'Y' then
      SetVerify(FALSE);
  end
else
  begin
    WriteLn('Disk write verify is OFF.');
    Write('Turn disk write verification ON? Y/N: ');
    ReadLn(YN);
    if UpCase(YN) = 'Y' then
      SetVerify(TRUE);
  end;

WriteLn;
GetCBreak(CBreak);
if CBreak then
  WriteLn('CTRL-Break checking is ON.')
else
  WriteLn('CTRL-Break checking is OFF.');
```

```
  GetVerify(Verify);
  if Verify then
    WriteLn('Disk write verification is ON.')
  else
    WriteLn('Disk write verify is OFF.');

end;

end.
```

Process Routines   DOS Unit

DosExitCode

```
function DosExitCode : word;
```

Returns the exit code of a subprocess (0 = normal termination, 1 = termination by CTRL-C, 2 = termination by device error, 3 = termination by Keep procedure.

DosVersion

```
function DosVersion : word;
```

Returns the version of the operating system. The major release number is in the high-order byte, and minor version number is in the low-order byte.

EnvCount

```
function EnvCount : integer;
```

Returns the number of strings defined in the DOS environment.

EnvStr

```
function EnvStr(I : integer) : string;
```

Returns the environment string based on the index *I*.

Exec

```
procedure Exec(Path, CmdLine : string);
```

Executes the file named in Path with command-line parameters defined in CmdLine.

GetCBreak

```
procedure GetCBreak(var Break : boolean);
```

Returns the current state of CTRL-BREAK checking in DOS. When Break is False, DOS checks for CTRL-BREAK during console, printer or serial I/O. When it is True, DOS checks for CTRL-BREAK at every system call.

GetEnv

```
function GetEnv(EnvVar : string) : string;
```

Returns the environment string for the environment variable specified in EnvVar.

GetVerify

```
procedure GetVerify(var Verify : boolean);
```

Returns the status of write-verification in DOS. When Verify is True, DOS verifies all disk writes.

Keep

```
procedure Keep(ExitCode : word);
```

Terminates the program, but keeps it resident. The procedure passes ExitCode as a standard DOS error code.

SetCBreak

```
procedure SetCBreak(Break : boolean);
```

Turns CTRL-BREAK on (when Break is True) or off (when Break is False).

SetVerify

```
procedure SetVerify(Verify : boolean);
```

Turns disk-write verification on (when Verify is True) or off (when Verify is False).

SwapVectors

```
function SwapVectors;
```

Exchanges the current values of the interrupt vector table with those that were saved when the program started executing.

System Services Routines

The interrupt support routines give you the tools to call any DOS or BIOS service or install your own interrupt service routines. GetIntVec returns the current address for the routine executed by a particular interrupt; SetIntVec replaces the existing interrupt routine with one of your own. The Intr procedure executes any interrupt service, while MsDos executes only DOS services. Using these services requires some knowledge of the CPU registers. After an introduction to these registers, this section will give you some samples of using system services that are not provided by explicit subprograms in the Dos unit.

The 8088 Registers

The 8088 family of microprocessors (which includes the 8086, 80286, 80386 and 80486) includes a standard set of 14 registers, or internal memory locations, which the CPUs use to execute commands. These registers are shown in Figure 15-1.

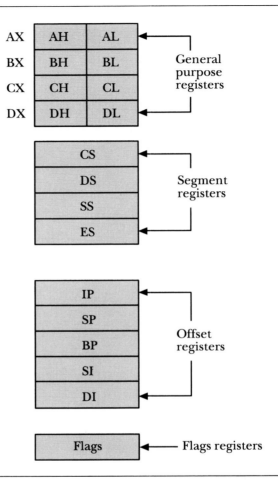

Figure 15-1.   *The 8088 CPU registers*

The first four registers—AX, BX, CX, and DX—are general-purpose areas that temporarily store data used in computations, comparisons, and other operations. Assembly-language programmers use these registers in the same way Pascal program-mers use variables. Each of the general-purpose registers is divided into two one-byte registers; thus AX consists of AH and AL. These general registers are the ones most commonly used to call DOS and BIOS services.

The 8088 also has four segment registers: CS, DS, SS, and ES. CS stores the program's segment, DS contains the data segment, SS holds the stack segment, and ES holds temporary segments for special operations. The CS and SS registers hold critical data that is changed only at great risk to the program's integrity. Therefore, Turbo Pascal does not allow you to access these registers for DOS or BIOS calls, but DS and ES are used occasionally to pass segment addresses.

A memory address consists of a segment and an offset, and the 8088 contains five offset registers: IP, SP, BP, SI, and DI. These are used in conjunction with the segment registers to address specific locations in memory. Turbo Pascal allows access only to SI, DI, and BP; IP and SP are never used in DOS or BIOS calls.

Finally, the Flags register contains information about the status of the instruction last executed. Individual bits in the flag byte indicate specific conditions that result from CPU operations, although not all bits are used. The Flags register is used primarily to identify error conditions. While it can be used in Turbo Pascal, the Flags register is generally not necessary for DOS and BIOS calls, as they usually return error codes in one of the general registers.

The Registers data type is the key to unlocking the power of DOS and BIOS services. This type, passed to both MsDos and Intr, includes fields that match most of the 8088's registers:

```
type
  Registers = record
    case integer of
      0 : (AX, BX, CX, DX, BP, SI, DI, DS, ES, Flags : word);
      1 : (AL, AH, BL, BH, CL, CH, DL, DH : byte);
  end;
```

The Registers data type contains only those CPU registers that are used in BIOS and DOS services. The record has two variant parts: one part consists of **word** variables representing whole registers; the other part consists of bytes that define the high and low portions of the general registers. For example, the two **byte** variables AL and AH refer to the same memory location that contains AX. The low-order byte (AL) precedes the high-order byte (AH) because the 8088 microprocessor stores bytes within words in reverse order. Therefore, if the integer 1 is stored in AX, it appears in memory as follows:

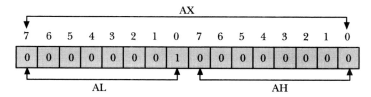

Before you can call MsDos or Intr, you must set the register-set variable to specific values that tell the computer which service you want and how you want to execute it. For example, to select a DOS service, place the code for the service in the AH register. DOS service 2Bh, which sets the system date, is shown here:

```
Program SetTime;

uses Dos, Crt;

var
  Regs : Registers;

begin
  ClrScr;
  FillChar(Regs, SizeOf(Regs), 0);
  with Regs do
    begin
      AH := $2B;
      DH := 12;    (* Month *)
      DL := 31;    (* Date  *)
      CX := 1997;  (* Year  *)
    end;

  MsDos(Regs);    (* Call the DOS service *)

  if Regs.AL <> 0 then
    WriteLn('Error!')
  else
    WriteLn('Date has been set.');

  WriteLn;
  Write('Press ENTER...');
  ReadLn;
end.
```

The procedure first initializes the register set to zero with the statement

```
FillChar(Regs, SizeOf(Regs), 0);
```

and then puts 2Bh, the code for setting the system date, in AH. Next, registers DH, DL, and CX are filled with date information.

MsDos accepts the register-set variable as a parameter and calls the DOS procedure that updates the system date to December 31, 1997. If the DOS service detects an error, it returns the register set with the error code in AL. The statement

```
if Regs.AL > 0 then
  WriteLn('Error!');
```

checks this code; if it is not equal to zero, an error occurs. Of course, it's much easier to call the SetDate procedure that is part of the Dos or WinDos units.

While the MsDos procedure is used for DOS services, the Intr procedure is used for BIOS services. Intr accepts two variables: the interrupt number and the register-set variable. For example, the BIOS call that prints the contents of a screen is invoked by setting register AH to 5 and calling interrupt 5, as follows:

```
FillChar(Regs, SizeOf(Regs), 0);
Regs.AH := 5;
Intr(5, Regs);
```

The first parameter is the interrupt number. The example above calls interrupt 5, which can be used to do many things. Setting Regs.AH to 5, however, specifies the print-screen service (the same service invoked by pressing the SHIFT and PRINT SCREEN keys at the same time). In this service, no error indicator is returned in the register set.

The use of DOS and BIOS services greatly increases what you can do with Turbo Pascal, but learning to use them properly takes some time. The remainder of this chapter deals with procedures that incorporate the most useful of the DOS and BIOS services not supported by the Dos and WinDos units and provides examples of how to use them.

Setting the Cursor Size

At times in a program, it is best not to show the cursor. At other times, a large cursor makes more sense than a small one. Typically, a cursor consists of two scan lines. A color graphics adapter, however, can display a cursor with as many as 8 scan lines, and a monochrome adapter can go up to 14. The more scan lines used, the larger the cursor; if no scan lines are used, the cursor disappears.

To set the cursor size, use BIOS interrupt 10h with register AH set equal to 1. Put the number of the starting scan line in register CH and the ending scan line in CL. The color graphics adapter uses 8 scan lines (0 to 7); the monochrome adapter uses 14 lines (0 to 13). The lower scan lines appear toward the top of the screen. For example, a small cursor on a color graphics monitor consists of scan lines 6 and 7, the bottom two scan lines.

```
Program Cursor;

uses Dos, Crt;

(***********************************************************)

procedure CursorSize(Stype, Size : char);
var
  Regs : Registers;
  I : integer;
begin
  Size := UpCase(Size);
  if UpCase(Stype) = 'M' then
    I := 6
```

```
    else
       I := 0;

    Regs.AH := $01;

    case Size of
       'O' :
         begin
           Regs.CH := $20;
           Regs.CL := $20;
         end;
       'B' :
         begin
           Regs.CH := $0;
           Regs.CL := $7+I;
         end;
       'S' :
         begin
           Regs.CH := $6+I;
           Regs.CL := $7+I;
         end;
       end;

    Intr($10, Regs);
  end;

  (*******************************************************)

  begin
    ClrScr;
    WriteLn('Big cursor');
    CursorSize('C', 'B');
    WriteLn;
    Write('Press ENTER...');
    ReadLn;

    WriteLn;
    WriteLn;
    WriteLn('No cursor');
    CursorSize('C', 'O');
    WriteLn;
    Write('Press ENTER...');
    ReadLn;

    WriteLn;
    WriteLn;
    WriteLn('Small cursor');
    CursorSize('C', 'S');
    WriteLn;
```

```
    Write('Press ENTER...');
    ReadLn;

end.
```

This procedure sets the cursor size according to the parameters you pass to it. The parameter Stype can be equal to M for monochrome or C for color graphics. The parameter size can take three values: B for big, S for small, or O for off.

If the computer uses a monochrome adapter, the variable *I* is set equal to 6; otherwise it is set to 0. The cursor is turned off by simply setting both CH and CL to 20h, while a large cursor is created by setting CH to 0, and CL to 7 for color-graphics adapters or 13 for monochrome adapters. For a small cursor, CH and CL are set to 6 and 7 for color graphics adapters or 12 and 13 for monochrome adapters.

Reporting Key State

Turbo Pascal is unable to directly read some of the most powerful keys on the PC: NUM LOCK, SCROLL LOCK, CTRL, ALT, the two shift keys, CAPS LOCK, and Ins. BIOS interrupt 16h, which reports the status of these keys, increases your control over the keyboard.

To check the status of these special keys, use interrupt 16h with register AH set to 2. After interrupt 16h is done, it returns a status byte in register AL. Each bit in this byte indicates the status for one of the eight special keys.

In the following procedure, interrupt 16h checks on the status of the eight special keys:

```
Program Shift;

uses Crt, Dos;

var
  Ins,
  CapsLock,
  NumLock,
  ScrollLock,
  Alt,
  Ctrl,
  LeftShift,
  RightShift : boolean;


(*********************************************************)


procedure ShiftStatus(var Ins,
                          CapsLock,
                          NumLock,
                          ScrollLock,
```

```
                              Alt,
                              Ctrl,
                              LeftShift,
                              RightShift : boolean);

var
   Regs : Registers;

begin
  Regs.AH := 2;
  Intr($16, Regs);

  RightShift        := (Regs.AL and $01) > 0;
  LeftShift         := (Regs.AL and $02) > 0;
  Ctrl              := (Regs.AL and $04) > 0;
  Alt               := (Regs.AL and $08) > 0;
  ScrollLock        := (Regs.AL and $10) > 0;
  NumLock           := (Regs.AL and $20) > 0;
  CapsLock          := (Regs.AL and $40) > 0;
  Ins               := (Regs.AL and $80) > 0;

end;

(********************************************************)

begin
  ClrScr;
  WriteLn('Press Ins and then Ctrl to stop...');

  repeat
    ShiftStatus(Ins,CapsLock,NumLock,ScrollLock,
               Alt,Ctrl,LeftShift,RightShift);

    GotoXY(1,4);
    WriteLn('Ins.........', Ins, ' ');
    WriteLn('CapsLock....', CapsLock, ' ');
    WriteLn('NumLock.....', NumLock, ' ');
    WriteLn('ScrollLock..', ScrollLock, ' ');
    WriteLn('Alt.........', Alt, ' ');
    WriteLn('Ctrl........', Ctrl, ' ');
    WriteLn('LeftShift...', LeftShift, ' ');
    WriteLn('RightShift..', RightShift, ' ');
  until (Ins and Ctrl);

  WriteLn;
  Write('Press ENTER...');
  ReadLn;
end.
```

The procedure *ShiftStatus,* which accepts a **boolean** parameter for each of the eight special keys, checks each bit in the byte returned in register AL. Thus, the eight parameters are set according to the individual bits in the status byte.

System Services Routines   **DOS Unit**

GetIntVec

```
procedure GetIntVec(IntNo : byte; var Vector : pointer);
```

Returns in Vector the current contents of interrupt vector number IntNo.

Intr

```
procedure Intr(Func : byte; var Regs : Registers);
```

Calls BIOS interrupt Func with registers defined by Regs.

MsDos

```
procedure MsDos(var Regs : Registers);
```

Executes DOS services using the values set in Regs.

SetIntVec

```
procedure SetIntVec(IntNo : byte; Vector : pointer);
```

Places the value of Vector at the interrupt IntNo in the interrupt vector table.

Related Type

```
Registers = record
  case integer of
    0 : (AX, BX, CX, DX, BP, SI, DI, DS, ES, Flags : word);
    1 : (AL, AH, BL, BH, CL, CH, DL, DH : word);
end;
```

Contains the CPU registers that are used in BIOS and DOS services.

The WinDos Unit

When you are writing applications that will run in the Windows environment, you should use the WinDos unit instead of the Dos unit. Almost all of routines in Dos are available in WinDos, as you can see in Table 15-1. Also, no routines are available only in WinDos—the ones listed in the "Unique to WinDos" column have equivalents in

Same (or Similar)	Unique to Dos	Unique to WinDos
DiskFree	DosExitCode	CreateDir
DiskSize	EnvCount	FileExpand
DosVersion	EnvStr	FileSearch
FindFirst	Exec	FileSplit
FindNext	FExpand	GetArgCount
GetCBreak	FSearch	GetArgStr
GetDate	FSplit	GetCurDir
GetEnvVar(GetEnv)	Keep	RemoveDir
GetFAttr	SwapVectors	SetCurDir
GetFTime		
GetIntVec		
GetTime		
GetVerify		
Intr		
MsDos		
PackTime		
SetCBreak		
SetDate		
SetFAttr		
SetIntVec		
SetTime		
SetVerify		
UnpackTime		
SetFTime		

Table 15-1.   *Comparison of the Dos and WinDos Units*

either Dos or System, but under a different name. You can learn about these differences in the section "Routines Unique to WinDos" at the end of the chapter.

The creators of the WinDos unit chose to conform to the standards of Windows functions rather than trying to match its Dos counterpart. For this reason many types and constants have slightly different names. For instance, the SearchRec type in the Dos unit is the TSearchRec in the WinDos unit. Constant names start with a unique prefix. For example, file attributes like Hidden and ReadOnly in Dos are faHidden and faReadOnly in WinDos.

The major differences in the functions and procedures is the conversion of parameter types to their WinDos equivalents. This includes changing string parameters to PChar parameters. Thus the FindFirst procedure, declared like this in Dos,

```
procedure FindFirst(Path : string; Attr : word;
          var S : SearchRec);
```

is declared like this in WinDos:

```
procedure FindFirst(Path : PChar; Attr : word;
          var S : TSearchRec);
```

This explains why the first column in Table 15-1 is titled "Same (or Similar)."

Earlier in this chapter you studied a unit called FILES which demonstrated the use of file, disk, and directory routines in the Dos unit. The following listing is the same unit converted to work for Windows, called FILESW:

```
Unit FILESW;

interface

procedure DiskStatus;
procedure DisplayDirectory;
procedure FileSearchAndReport;

implementation

uses WinDos, WinCrt, Strings;

procedure DiskStatus;
var
  Space : longint;
begin
  WriteLn('Disk status.');
  Space := DiskFree(0);
  WriteLn('Free space on disk = ', Space,' bytes/ ',
          Space div 1024, ' Kbytes');
  Space := DiskSize(0);
```

```
  WriteLn('Total space on disk = ', Space, ' bytes/ ',
            Space Div 1024, ' Kbytes');
  WriteLn;
end;


function PadRight(Str : PChar; L : word) : string;
 {
 This function adds blank characters to
 a String until it reaches length L. If
 the String is longer than L to begin with,
 this function truncates the String.
 }
var
  S : string;
begin
  S := StrPas(Str);
  if Length(S) > L then
    S[0] := Chr(L);
  while Length(S) < L do
   S := S + ' ';
  PadRight := S;
end;


procedure DisplayDirectory;
var
  Srec : TSearchRec;
  TimeStamp : TDateTime;
  DS, FN, EN,
  FullName : array [0..79] of char;

begin
  WriteLn('Directory listing:');
  FindFirst('*.*', faAnyFile, Srec);
  while DosError = 0 do
    begin
      with Srec do
        begin
          UnPackTime(Time, TimeStamp);
          with TimeStamp do
            begin
              FileExpand(FullName, Name);
              FileSplit(FullName, DS, FN, EN);
              WriteLn(PadRight(DS,20), ' ',
                      PadRight(FN,9), ' ',
                      PadRight(EN,5), ' ',
                      Size:7, '  ', Year);
            end;
        end;
    end;
```

```
      FindNext(Srec);
    end;
end;

procedure FileSearchAndReport;
var
  Attr : word;
  TheFile : file;
  DS, S : array [0..79] of char;
begin
  WriteLn('Search for a file by name.');
  repeat
    Write('Enter file name: ');
    ReadLn(S);
    Write('Enter directory: ');
    ReadLn(DS);
    FileSearch(S, S, DS);
    if S = '' then WriteLn('File not found...');
  until S > '';


  Assign(TheFile, S);
  GetFAttr(TheFile, Attr);

  if (Attr and faReadOnly) > 0 then
    WriteLn('File is read only')
  else
    WriteLn('File is not read only');

  if (Attr and faHidden) > 0 then
    WriteLn('File is hidden')
  else
    WriteLn('File is not hidden');

  if (Attr and faSysFile) > 0 then
    WriteLn('File is system file')
  else
    WriteLn('File is not system file');

  if (Attr and faVolumeID) > 0 then
    WriteLn('File is Volume ID')
  else
    WriteLn('File is not Volume ID');

  if (Attr and faDirectory) > 0 then
    WriteLn('File is Directory')
  else
    WriteLn('File is not Directory');
```

```
  if (Attr and faArchive) > 0 then
    WriteLn('File is Archive')
  else
    WriteLn('File is not Archive');
end;

end.
```

If you compare this listing to the FILES unit listing, you will notice only subtle differences. For one, the local variables in the *DisplayDirectory* procedure are now null-terminated strings.

To test this unit, you can write a simple driver:

```
Program FilesTest;

uses FILESW, WinCrt;

begin
  DiskStatus;
  DisplayDirectory;
  FileSearchAndReport;
end.
```

See the last section of Chapter 14 for information on writing Windows applications with the WinCrt unit.

Routines Unique to WinDos The WinDos Unit

CreateDir

```
procedure CreateDir(Dir : PChar);
```

Creates a directory with the specified name. This procedure is similar to MkDir in the System unit.

FileExpand

```
function FileExpand(Dest, Name : PChar) : PChar;
```

Accepts a filename Name and returns the filename with its complete path structure, including drive. The Dest parameter is actually the return value. This function is similar to the FExpand procedure in the Dos unit.

FileSearch

```
function FileSearch(Dest, Name, List : PChar) : PChar;
```

Searches in the list of directories included in List for a filename that matches Name. If the file is found, the result is returned as a null-terminated string. If not found, the function returns an empty string. The Dest parameter is actually the return value. This function is similar to the FSearch procedure in the Dos unit.

FileSplit

```
function FileSplit(Path, Dir, Name, Ext: PChar) : PChar;
```

Accepts a filename Path and returns its components. The Dir, Name, and Ext parameters are actually the return values. This function is similar to the FSplit procedure in the Dos unit.

GetArgCount

```
function GetArgCount : integer;
```

Returns the number of arguments in the program call. This function is similar to ParamCount in the System unit.

GetArgStr

```
function GetArgStr(Dest : PChar; Index : integer;
                   MaxLen : word) : PChar;
```

Returns a specific argument in the program call. This function is similar to ParamStr in the System unit.

GetCurDir

```
function GetCurDir(Dir : PChar; Drive : byte) : PChar;
```

Returns the current directory on a given drive. The Dir parameter is actually the return value. This function is similar to GetDir in the System unit.

RemoveDir

```
procedure RemoveDir(Dir : PChar);
```

Removes the specified directory. This procedure is similar to RmDir in the System unit.

SetCurDir

```
procedure SetCurDir(Dir : PChar);
```

Changes the current directory to that specified by Dir. This procedure is similar to ChDir in the System unit.

Chapter *16*

Graphics in DOS and Windows

Your computer's graphics capability is one of its strongest features. Using graphics you can create drawings, charts, multi-font text, or anything that can be drawn. But using graphics requires far more work than using the PC's Text mode. You must develop methods for drawing lines and characters and be able to scale them in the proper perspective. What's more, there are now more than ten commonly available graphics adapters comprising more than two dozen different graphics modes. Fortunately, Turbo Pascal provides an exceptionally rich set of graphics routines that can make graphics programming much easier.

Borland's support for graphics comes in two variations:

- The BGI (Borland Graphics Interface), a complete set of tools for graphics in the DOS environment.

- The GDI (Graphics Device Interface), the portion of the Windows API that lets you display graphics.

This chapter covers some of the basics of programming graphics using both the BGI and the GDI.

Setting Up the BGI

Compared with the Graphics mode, the PC's Text mode is easy to use. Displaying information on the screen is as simple as placing ASCII characters in specific memory locations. The text screen is neatly divided into 80 columns and 25 rows, and your computer already knows how to draw the ASCII characters, sparing you most of the headaches.

The Graphics mode requires a completely different orientation. Instead of characters and attribute bytes, you have pixels, the smallest picture element on your computer's display. A single character on your computer's screen is made up of many pixels arranged in a pattern that forms a character. In the Graphics mode, you can light pixels anywhere on your display. The program listed here, which demonstrates some fundamental graphics programming techniques, lights pixels at random locations on your screen.

```
Program DemoPixel;

uses Crt, Graph;

var
  X, Y,
  ErrorCode,
  GraphMode,
  GraphDriver : integer;

begin
  (* Initiate the CGA high resolution mode. *)
  GraphDriver := CGA;
  GraphMode := CGAhi;
  InitGraph(GraphDriver, GraphMode, 'C:\BP\BGI');
  ErrorCode := GraphResult;
  if ErrorCode <> grOK then
    begin
      WriteLn('Graphics error: ', GraphErrorMsg(ErrorCode));
      Halt;
    end;

  repeat
    X := Random(640); (* CGA high resolution coordinates *)
    Y := Random(200); (* 640 X 200 *)
    PutPixel(X, Y, White);
    Delay(100);
  until KeyPressed;
```

```
   CloseGraph;
end.
```

The preceding program not only demonstrates the concept of the pixel, but also highlights some of the difficulties involved in writing graphics programs. The program begins by initializing the Turbo Pascal CGA graphics driver. It does this by first specifying the type of adapter and the graphics mode and then calling InitGraph. You must also tell InitGraph where to look for the .BGI file that corresponds to the adapter. A .BGI file contains information on a specified graphics adapter. This information is needed to draw a graph properly. In the example, this file is found in the C:\BP\BGI directory.

```
GraphDriver := CGA;
GraphMode := CGAhi;
InitGraph(GraphDriver, GraphMode, 'C:\BP\BGI');
```

After calling InitGraph, the program calls GraphResult, a function that returns a status code. If the code is not equal to grOK, you know that an error occurred. (grOK is a constant defined in the Graph unit and has a value of zero.) If an error is detected, the program passes the error code to the GraphErrorMsg function, which then returns a string that describes the error condition.

```
ErrorCode := GraphResult;
if ErrorCode <> grOK then
  begin
     WriteLn('Graphics error: ', GraphErrorMsg(ErrorCode));
     Halt;
  end;
```

While checking for graphics errors is not required, it is a good idea. Nearly every graphics procedure and function can produce serious errors when used improperly. Always remember, though, to store the value of GraphResult in a variable because once the function is called, it will thereafter return the value 0 until another error occurs.

Specifying the display adapter in your program is fine if you know in advance what adapter will be used. If you're wrong, however, the program won't run. Notice also that the screen coordinate limits (640 and 200) are hard-coded into the program. If your computer uses a graphics adapter that has a different coordinate system, the program will not work properly. To make a graphics program truly useful, it must be able to run on any graphics adapter and, ideally, would use that adapter's advanced features as much as possible.

Graphics Adapters and Coordinate Systems

Your graphics screen consists of pixels arranged in horizontal and vertical lines. This is true of all computer graphics modes; the major difference is the size of the pixel. In CGA's Low-resolution mode, the pixels are quite large, so only 320 fit horizontally and 200 fit vertically. The VGA adapter, a relatively new video display controller, has a high-resolution mode with pixels so small that 640 fit horizontally and 480 fit vertically. The smaller the pixel, the more pixels per image, and the higher the quality of the graphics display.

Each adapter has one or more graphics modes, and each mode has an associated coordinate system. The coordinate system for high-resolution CGA graphics is 320 × 200, as shown in Figure 16-1. Graphics coordinates begin at position (0,0), which is located at the upper-left corner of the screen. The rightmost pixel is number 319 and the bottommost is number 199. By referring to pixels by coordinates, you can light the pixels you want for your graphics image.

Now you can see why it is so important to know what graphics adapter is installed and which mode is active. Screen coordinate systems vary from adapter to adapter and from mode to mode. For example, the CGA adapter supports high- and low-resolution modes, each having different coordinate systems. If you want to light a pixel at the lower-right corner of the screen, you must know what the screen coordinates are. Fortunately, Turbo Pascal provides the answer with two Graph unit functions, GetMaxX and GetMaxY, which return the maximum X and Y coordinates

Figure 16-1. *CGA high-resolution coordinates*

for the active graphics display adapter and mode. Here is the program given earlier, but updated to be used on any graphics adapter:

```
Program DemoPixel2;

uses Crt, Graph;

var
  MaxX,
  MaxY,
  X, Y,
  ErrorCode,
  GraphMode,
  GraphDriver : integer;

begin
  GraphDriver := Detect;
  InitGraph(GraphDriver, GraphMode, 'C:\BP\BGI');
  ErrorCode := GraphResult;
  if ErrorCode <> grOK then
    begin
      WriteLn('Graphics error: ', GraphErrorMsg(ErrorCode));
      Halt;
    end;

  MaxX := GetMaxX;
  MaxY := GetMaxY;

  repeat
    X := Random(MaxX) + 1;
    Y := Random(MaxY) + 1;
    PutPixel(X, Y, White);
    Delay(100);
  until KeyPressed;

  CloseGraph;
end.
```

This program demonstrates how complicated even simple graphics programs can be. Given the rich set of tools that the Turbo Pascal graphics unit provides, the possibilities could fill a book on their own. The remainder of this chapter will touch on the important aspects of graphics programming and how to use the basics of the Graph unit.

| **Set-up Routines** | **Graph Unit** |

ClearDevice

```
procedure ClearDevice;
```

Clears the graphics screen.

ClearViewPort

```
procedure ClearViewPort;
```

Clears the current viewport.

CloseGraph

```
procedure CloseGraph;
```

Restores the video display to the mode that existed prior to entering graphics mode. The procedure also frees memory used by the graphics system.

DetectGraph

```
procedure DetectGraph(var GD, GM : integer);
```

Returns the detected graphics driver (GD) and graphics mode (GM) for the installed display adapter.

GetAspectRatio

```
procedure GetAspectRatio(var Xasp, Yasp : word);
```

Returns in Xasp and Yasp the effective resolution of the graphics screen. The aspect ratio is computed as Xasp divided by Yasp.

GetDriverName

```
function GetDriverName : string;
```

Returns the name of the current graphics driver.

GetGraphMode

```
function GetGraphMode : integer;
```

Returns the current graphics mode. The numeric value of the graphics mode must be interpreted in combination with the graphics driver.

GetMaxMode

```
function GetMaxMode : word;
```

Returns a value that indicates the highest-resolution graphics mode for the installed adapter.

GetMaxX

```
function GetMaxX : integer;
```

Returns the maximum horizontal coordinate for the current graphics mode.

GetMaxY

```
function GetMaxY : integer;
```

Returns the maximum vertical coordinate for the current graphics mode.

GetModeName

```
function GetModeName(ModeNumber : word) : string;
```

Returns a string describing the graphics mode denoted in ModeNumber.

GetModeRange

```
procedure GetModeRange(GraphDriver : integer;
          var LoMode, HiMode : integer);
```

Returns the highest (HiMode) and lowest (LoMode) resolution modes for the graphics driver denoted by GraphDriver.

GetViewSettings

```
procedure GetViewSettings(var VP : ViewPortType);
```

Returns in VP the current viewport settings. See "Related Types" later in this section for a description of ViewPortType.

GraphDefaults

```
procedure GraphDefaults;
```

Resets the graphics settings to their default values.

GraphErrorMsg

```
function GraphErrorMsg(Code : integer) : string;
```

Returns an error message corresponding to the error condition denoted by Code.

GraphResult

```
function GraphResult : integer;
```

Returns an error code for the last graphics procedure.

InitGraph

```
procedure InitGraph(var GraphDriver : integer;
          var GraphMode : integer; DriverPath : string);
```

Initializes the graphics environment to the graphics driver GraphDriver and mode GraphMode. If GraphDriver is zero, the procedure automatically detects the display adapter and sets the mode to the highest resolution. The procedure will look for .BGI files in the path defined by DriverPath.

InstallUserDriver

```
function InstallUserDriver(Name : string;
          AutoDetectPtr : pointer) : integer;
```

Installs a non-Borland graphics driver. Name contains the name of the file that contains the driver, and AutoDetectPtr is a pointer to an optional autodetect function. The driver must be in .BGI format.

RegisterBGIDriver

```
function RegisterBGIDriver(Driver : pointer) : integer;
```

Allows the user to load a .BGI driver file (read from disk onto the heap or linked into the program using BINOBJ) and register the driver with the graphics system. Driver is a pointer to the location of the .BGI driver. If an error occurs, the function returns a value less than zero; otherwise, it returns the assigned driver number.

RestoreCRTMode

```
procedure RestoreCRTMode;
```

Restores the video display to the mode that existed before graphics was initialized.

SetActivePage

```
procedure SetActivePage(Page : word);
```

For display adapters that support multiple pages, this procedure changes the active page.

SetAspectRatio

```
procedure SetAspectRatio(Xasp, Yasp : word);
```

Changes the aspect ratio used to display graphics to Xasp divided by Yasp.

SetGraphBufSize

```
procedure SetGraphBufSize(BufSize : word);
```

Sets the size of the graphics buffer.

SetGraphMode

```
procedure SetGraphMode(Mode : integer);
```

Sets the current graphics mode to that specified by Mode.

SetViewPort

```
procedure SetViewPort(X1, Y1, X2, Y2 : integer;
                      Clip : boolean);
```

Selects a rectangular portion of the graphics screen to use as the active screen. When Clip is True, drawings are clipped at the borders of the viewport.

SetVisualPage

```
procedure SetVisualPage(Page : word);
```

Selects the graphics page to display.

Related Types

```
ViewPortType = record
  X1, Y1, X2, Y2 : integer;
  Clip : boolean;
end;
```

Used by GetViewSettings to provide information on the current viewport.

Drawing Shapes

The primary reason for a graphics interface is to allow you to draw shapes. The BGI includes procedures for drawing both simple shapes, such as lines and circles, and more complex shapes, such as three-dimensional bars and pie slices. Once you master the simpler shapes you will have little difficulty moving to the more complex ones. This section details the drawing of lines and circles.

Lines

A fundamental task in graphics is drawing a line between two points. The Graph unit provides a Line procedure that does this. Still, you may find it useful to understand how such a routine works because, as you do more complicated graphics programming, you will probably decide to write your own specialized graphics routines.

Drawing horizontal or vertical lines is easy—you simply hold one coordinate value fixed and plot pixels along the other coordinate. Once you begin to slant the line, however, the process becomes much more complicated. Somehow, you must determine which pixels to light. This is done with an algorithm that computes one coordinate given a value of the other coordinate.

Graphics systems based on algorithms (as opposed to fixed bit maps) are the basis of nearly all graphics and provide a great deal of flexibility because an algorithm need not be tied to a particular scaling factor. This means that you can use the same algorithm to draw a small box or a large box, a circle or an ellipse, a thick line or a thin line. The algorithm for drawing a straight line is fairly straightforward.

The straight-line algorithm is based on the algebraic equation for a straight line:

$$Y = A + BX$$

where Y is the vertical coordinate, X is the horizontal coordinate, A is a constant factor, and B is the slope of the line. Once you have determined the value of A and B, drawing the line is easy.

To compute A and B, you need two coordinate pairs. In the code extract shown here, X1,Y1 and X2,Y2 are pairs of coordinates representing points on the graphics screen.

```
DX := (X2 - X1);
DY := (Y2 - Y1);
if DX <> 0 Then
   B := DY / DX
else
   B := 0;
A := Y1 - X1 * b;
```

The *B* variable is defined as the difference between the X coordinates divided by the difference between the Y coordinates. If *X1* equals *X2*, then *B* is defined as zero. Once *B* is calculated, *A* is easily calculated using one of the two coordinate pairs.

With *A* and *B* both defined, the algorithm is complete. To draw the line, you need only trace along the X axis, compute the corresponding Y coordinate, and plot the pixel. One problem with this approach, however, is that lines will become very sparse when the range between the X coordinates is small compared to the range of the Y coordinates. To compensate for this, the line-drawing procedure must compare the distances between the vertical coordinates and between the horizontal coordinates. If the gap between the Y coordinates is greater than the gap between the X coordinates, tracing should move along the vertical axis. The complete line-drawing process is contained in the procedure *PlotLine*, in the following program:

```
Program LineDemo;

uses Crt, Graph;

var
  MaxX,
  MaxY,
  ErrorCode,
  GraphMode,
  GraphDriver : integer;

(**********************************************************)

procedure PlotLine(X1, Y1, X2, Y2, Color : integer);
var
  A,B   : real;
  Dx, Dy,
  X, Y, I : integer;
```

```
  (********************************************************)

  procedure Switch(var X, Y : integer);
  var
    T : word;
  begin
    T := X;
    X := Y;
    Y := T;
  end;

(********************************************************)

begin
  if Abs(X1-X2) > Abs(Y1-Y2) then
    begin
      { Gap between X's is greater than Y's.
        Trace horizontally }
      if X1 > X2 then
        begin
          Switch(X1, X2);
          Switch(Y1, Y2);
        end;

      Dx := (X2 - X1);
      Dy := (Y2 - Y1);
      if Dx <> 0 then
        B := Dy / Dx
      else
        B := 0;
      A := Y1 - X1*B;
      for X := X1 to X2 do
        begin
          Y := Round(A + X*B);
          PutPixel(X, Y, Color);
        end;
    end
  else
    begin
      { Gap between Y's is greater than X's.
        Trace vertically. }
      if Y1 > Y2 then
        begin
          Switch(Y1, Y2);
          Switch(X1, X2);
        end;
```

```
      Dx := (X2 - X1);
      Dy := (Y2 - Y1);

      if Dx <> 0 then
        B := Dy / Dx
      else
        B := 0;
      A := Y1 - X1*B;

      for Y := Y1 to Y2 do
        begin
          if B <> 0 then
            X := Round((Y-A) / B)
          else
            X := 0;
          PutPixel(X, Y, Color);
        end;
    end;
end;

(********************************************************)

begin
  GraphDriver := Detect;
  InitGraph(GraphDriver, GraphMode, 'C:\BP\BGI');
  ErrorCode := GraphResult;
  if ErrorCode <> grOK then
    begin
      WriteLn('Graphics error: ', GraphErrorMsg(ErrorCode));
      Halt;
    end;

  MaxX := GetMaxX;
  MaxY := GetMaxY;

  repeat
    PlotLine(Random(MaxX),
             Random(MaxY),
             Random(MaxX),
             Random(MaxY),
             White);
  until KeyPressed;

  CloseGraph;
end.
```

This program draws lines between random points on the computer screen (see Figure 16-2). To stop the program, simply press any key.

Figure 16-2.   *Drawing lines with BGI*

If you find drawing a straight line is difficult, imagine the difficulty in writing complete graphics routines for drawing polygons, ellipses, pie charts, and, perhaps most difficult, text characters. The Graph unit is a tremendous asset to all graphics programmers.

The procedure Line in the Graph unit, does exactly the same thing that *PlotLine* did, only much faster. Line takes four parameters in the form of coordinate pairs. The statement

```
Line(MaxX div 2, 0, MaxX div 2, MaxY);
```

draws a line that runs down the center of the screen, from top to bottom. Using *MaxX* **div** 2 to determine the center of the horizontal axis makes the statement independent of the coordinate system in use.

Here is the same line program using the Line procedure:

```
Program LineDemo2;

uses Crt, Graph;

var
  MaxX,
  MaxY,
  ErrorCode,
```

```
   GraphMode,
   GraphDriver : integer;

begin
   GraphDriver := Detect;
   InitGraph(GraphDriver, GraphMode, 'C:\BP\BGI');
   ErrorCode := GraphResult;
   if ErrorCode <> grOK then
     begin
       WriteLn('Graphics error: ', GraphErrorMsg(ErrorCode));
       Halt;
     end;

   MaxX := GetMaxX;
   MaxY := GetMaxY;

   repeat
     Line(Random(MaxX),
          Random(MaxY),
          Random(MaxX),
          Random(MaxY));
   until KeyPressed;

   CloseGraph;
end.
```

Circles

The procedure Circle takes three parameters. The first two form a coordinate pair that determines the center of the circle, while the third parameter is the radius of the circle in horizontal pixels—Circle computes the appropriate number of vertical pixels to maintain the proper proportions. The ratio of vertical to horizontal pixels is known as the *aspect ratio*. Each graphics driver has an aspect ratio that determines the scaling of graphics images. While Turbo Pascal allows you to alter the aspect ratio, you will probably never need to do so.

As an example, the statement

```
Circle(MaxX div 2, MaxY div 2, 10);
```

draws a circle at the center of the screen with a radius of ten horizontal pixels. You can increase the size of the radius to a point where parts of the circle run off the edge of the screen. When this occurs, the image is *clipped*, or truncated, to protect you from writing into memory outside that allocated for graphics images.

The example program listed here demonstrates the use of the Line and Circle procedures as well as some other important graphics techniques. The program begins by drawing lines that intersect at the center of the screen and then draws concentric circles from the edge of the screen toward the center (see Figure 16-3).

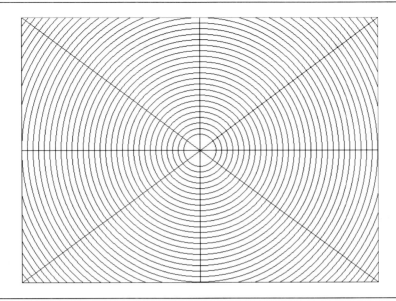

Figure 16-3. *Drawing circles with BGI*

Then the program saves a rectangular area around the center of the screen and flashes it in reverse and normal colors.

```
Program CircleDemo;

uses Crt, Graph;

var
  MaxX,
  MaxY,
  I,
  ErrorCode,
  GraphMode,
  GraphDriver : integer;
  Size : word;
  P : pointer;

begin
  GraphDriver := Detect;
  InitGraph(GraphDriver, GraphMode, 'C:\BP\BGI');
  ErrorCode := GraphResult;
  if ErrorCode <> grOK then
    begin
      WriteLn('Graphics error: ', GraphErrorMsg(ErrorCode));
      Halt;
```

```
     end;

  MaxX := GetMaxX;
  MaxY := GetMaxY;

  { Draw lines on screen }
  Line(MaxX div 2, 0, MaxX div 2, MaxY);
  Line(0, MaxY div 2, MaxX, MaxY div 2);
  Line(0, 0, MaxX, MaxY);
  Line(MaxX, 0, 0, MaxY);

  { Draw concentric circles }
  I := MaxY;
  while i > 20 do
    begin
      Circle(MaxX div 2, MaxY div 2, I);
      I := I - 10;
    end;

  { Save a portion of the screen }
  Size := ImageSize(Round(MaxX * 0.25),
                    Round(MaxY * 0.25),
                    Round(MaxX * 0.75),
                    Round(MaxY * 0.75));

  GetMem(P, Size);
  GetImage(Round(MaxX * 0.25),
           Round(MaxY * 0.25),
           Round(MaxX * 0.75),
           Round(MaxY * 0.75), P^);

  { Flash a portion of the screen }
  for I := 1 to 6 do
    begin
      PutImage(Round(MaxX * 0.25),
               Round(MaxY * 0.25),
               P^, NotPut);

      GetImage(Round(MaxX * 0.25),
               Round(MaxY * 0.25),
               Round(MaxX * 0.75),
               Round(MaxY * 0.75), P^);
    end;

  Readln;
  CloseGraph;
end.
```

The use of GetImage and PutImage is covered later in this chapter.

Drawing Routines   Graph Unit

Arc

```
procedure Arc(X, Y : integer;
            StAngle, EndAngle, Radius : word);
```

Draws a portion of a circle centered around coordinates X and Y with a radius of Radius. The circle begins drawing clockwise from StAngle and stops at EndAngle.

Bar

```
procedure Bar(X1, Y1, X2, Y2 : integer);
```

Draws a filled-in rectangular area of the screen, based on the current fill pattern.

Bar3D

```
procedure Bar3D(X1, Y1, X2, Y2 : integer;
              Depth : word; Top : boolean);
```

Draws a filled-in three-dimensional rectangular area of the screen. The rectangle is drawn Depth pixels deep. If Top is True, the procedure draws a three-dimensional top on the rectangle.

Circle

```
procedure Circle(X, Y : integer; Radius : word);
```

Draws a circle with a radius of Radius centered at the coordinate X, Y.

DrawPoly

```
procedure DrawPoly(NumPoints : word; var PolyPoints);
```

Draws a polygon defined by NumPoints points. The array PolyPoints contains the coordinates for the points of the polygon.

GetArcCoords

```
procedure GetArcCoords(var ArcCoords : ArcCoordsType);
```

Returns the coordinates used by the most recently used Arc or Ellipse command. See "Related Types" for the structure of ArcCoordsType.

GetPixel

```
function GetPixel(X, Y : integer) : word;
```

Returns the color of the pixel at coordinates X,Y.

GetX

```
function GetX : integer;
```

Returns the horizontal coordinate of the current position.

GetY

```
function GetY : integer;
```

Returns the vertical coordinate of the current position.

Line

```
procedure Line(X1, Y1, X2, Y2 : integer);
```

Draws a line from X1,Y1 to X2,Y2.

LineRel

```
procedure LineRel(DX, DY : integer);
```

Draws a line from the current position to a point defined by DX and DY. For example, if the current position is 1,2 the command LineRel(100, 100) will draw a line from 1,2 to 101,102.

LineTo

```
procedure LineTo(X, Y : integer);
```

Draws a line from the current position to X,Y.

MoveRel

```
procedure MoveRel(DX, DY : integer);
```

Moves the current position DX pixels horizontally and DY pixels vertically.

MoveTo

```
procedure MoveTo(X, Y : integer);
```

Moves the current position to the pixel at X,Y.

PieSlice

```
procedure PieSlice(X, Y : integer;
                   StAngle, EndAngle, Radius : word);
```

Draws a slice of a pie chart centered at X,Y, with a radius of Radius, starting at StAngle and ending at EndAngle.

PutPixel

```
procedure PutPixel(X, Y : integer; Pixel : word);
```

Plots a single point of color, defined by Pixel, at position X,Y.

Rectangle

```
procedure Rectangle(X1, Y1, X2, Y2 : integer);
```

Draws a rectangle with its upper-left corner at X1,Y1 and lower-right corner at X2,Y2.

Sector

```
procedure Sector(X, Y : integer; StAngle, EndAngle,
                 XRadius, YRadius : word);
```

Draws a sector (part of an ellipse) centered at X,Y, starting at StAngle, ending at EndAngle, with horizontal radius XRadius and vertical radius YRadius.

SetWriteMode

```
procedure SetWriteMode(WriteMode : integer);
```

Selects one of two modes for drawing lines. In CopyPut mode (0) lines are drawn using assembler MOV command. In XORPut mode (1) lines are drawn using the XOR command.

Related Types

```
ArcCoordsType = record
  X, Y : integer;
  XStart, YStart : integer;
  XEnd, YEnd : integer;
end;
```

Used by GetArcCoords to provide information on the most recently drawn arc.

Using Colors and Patterns

Once you understand how to draw shapes, you are ready to spice up those shapes with colors and patterns. The Graph unit includes over twenty subprograms that alter (or retrieve) colors and patterns.

Earlier in this chapter you studied a program that draws concentric circles. This next program uses the same circles, but fills the sectors of the circles with a random selection of colors and patterns (see Figure 16-4).

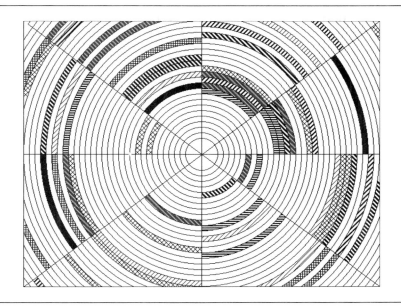

Figure 16-4.   *Filling with colors and patterns using BGI*

```
Program PatternDemo;

uses Crt, Graph;

var
  Palette : PaletteType;
  MaxX,
  MaxY,
  I,
  ErrorCode,
  GraphMode,

  GraphDriver : integer;
  Size : word;
  P : pointer;

begin
  GraphDriver := Detect;
  InitGraph(GraphDriver,GraphMode,'C:\BP\BGI');
  ErrorCode := GraphResult;
  if ErrorCode <> grOK then
```

```
    begin
      WriteLn('Graphics error: ',GraphErrorMsg(ErrorCode));
      Halt;
    end;

  MaxX := GetMaxX;
  MaxY := GetMaxY;

  { Draw lines on screen }
  Line(MaxX div 2, 0, MaxX div 2, MaxY);
  Line(0, MaxY div 2, MaxX, MaxY div 2);
  Line(0, 0, MaxX, MaxY);
  Line(MaxX, 0, 0, MaxY);

  { Draw concentric circles }
  I := MaxY;
  while I > 20 do
    begin
      Circle(MaxX div 2, MaxY div 2, I);
      I := I - 10;
    end;

  GetPalette(Palette);

  { Fill in portions of the graphic image }
  repeat
    SetFillStyle(Random(9), Random(Palette.Size)+1);
    FloodFill(Random(MaxX), Random(MaxY), White);
  until KeyPressed;

  CloseGraph;
end.
```

The last part of this program fills the graphic with different colors and patterns. This process begins with the GetPalette procedure, which returns information about the color capabilities of the current graphics driver and mode. GetPalette takes a single parameter of type PaletteType, which is defined as follows:

```
type
  PaletteType = record
    Size : byte;
    Colors : array[0..MaxColors] of shortint;
```

The Size field contains the number of colors currently available, and Colors contains the numeric codes that correspond to the colors. With a single call to GetPalette you know exactly what you have to work with in terms of graphic colors.

The procedures that do the hard work—drawing different patterns in varying colors—are SetFillStyle and FloodFill. The Graph unit defines 12 different patterns to use as filler in graphics. The procedure SetFillStyle lets you choose the pattern you want to use and the color you want to display it in. FloodFill "paints" the inside of a polygon or circle using the pattern and color you defined using SetFillStyle. To do its job, FloodFill needs two pieces of information: (1) the location of a pixel inside the area to fill and (2) the color of the boundary of the area. The boundary color is the only way FloodFill can determine where to stop filling.

A few procedures in the Graph unit fill in shapes as they draw them. One such procedure is FillPoly. The FillPoly procedure creates a polygon with any number of sides and fills it with a color and pattern you define with the SetFillStyle procedure.

To use the FillPoly procedure you must first define a variable array of PointType, a record type defined in the Graph unit that contains an X and Y coordinate. The following example program shows how this is done.

```pascal
Program ColorDemo;

uses Crt, Graph;

type
  TriType = array [1..3] of PointType;

var
  Tri : TriType;
  S : string;
  MaxX,
  MaxY,
  X1, Y1,
  ErrorCode,
  GraphMode,
  GraphDriver : integer;
  Palette : PaletteType;

begin
  GraphDriver := Detect;
  InitGraph(GraphDriver, GraphMode, 'C:\BP\BGI');
  GraphMode := GetMaxMode;
  InitGraph(GraphDriver, GraphMode, 'C:\BP\BGI');
  ErrorCode := GraphResult;
  if ErrorCode <> grOK then
    begin
      WriteLn('Graphics error: ', GraphErrorMsg(ErrorCode));
      Halt;
    end;
```

```
  MaxX := GetMaxX;
  MaxY := GetMaxY;

  GetPalette(Palette);
  SetFillStyle(3, 3);

  while not Keypressed do
    begin
      SetFillStyle(Random(13), Random(Palette.Size) + 1);
      Tri[1].X := Random(MaxX);
      Tri[1].Y := Random(MaxY);
      Tri[2].X := Random(MaxX);
      Tri[2].Y := Random(MaxY);
      Tri[3].X := Random(MaxX);
      Tri[3].Y := Random(MaxY);

      FillPoly(3,Tri);
      Delay(100);

      X1 := X1 + (MaxX div 12);
      Y1 := Y1 + (MaxY div 12);
    end;

  CloseGraph;
end.
```

The example program uses the FillPoly procedure to draw triangles. Since a triangle is completely defined by three points, the following definition is sufficient:

```
type
  TriType = array [1..3] of PointType;
```

A variable named *Tri* is declared as *TriType*. To create a triangle, the program first defines the three coordinate pairs in *Tri*. The call to FillPoly passes the number of points in the polygon (three in this case) and the variable *Tri,* which contains the coordinates. As the following listing shows, the triangle's coordinates are determined randomly.

```
Tri[1].X := Random(MaxX);
Tri[1].Y := Random(MaxY);
Tri[2].X := Random(MaxX);
Tri[2].Y := Random(MaxY);
Tri[3].X := Random(MaxX);
Tri[3].Y := Random(MaxY);

FillPoly(3, Tri);
```

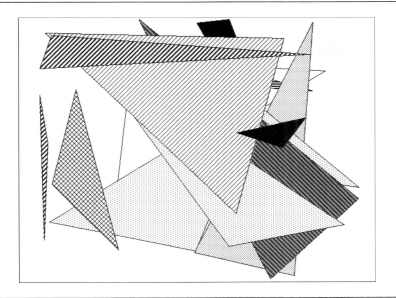

Figure 16-5.   *Filling triangles with colors and patterns using BGI*

For each triangle drawn, colors and patterns are also selected randomly using SetFillStyle, as shown here:

```
SetFillStyle(Random(13), Random(Palette.Size) + 1);
```

This statement randomly selects one of the 12 fill patterns defined in the Graph unit and also randomly selects a color from the video mode palette (see Figure 16-5). Thus, when you run this program, you will see randomly generated triangles with randomly selected patterns and colors.

Color and Pattern Routines   **Graph Unit**

FillEllipse

```
procedure FillEllipse(X, Y : integer;
                      Xradius, Yradius : word);
```

Draws an ellipse centered at coordinates X,Y with a vertical radius of Yradius and a horizontal radius of Xradius. The ellipse is filled with the current fill color and fill style, and the border is drawn with the current color.

FillPoly

```
procedure FillPoly(NumPoints : word; var PolyPoints);
```

Draws a polygon with NumPoints points. The array PolyPoints contains the coordinates for the points of the polygon.

FloodFill

```
procedure FloodFill(X, Y : integer; Border : word);
```

Fills an enclosed area of the graphics display with the current color and pattern. The area must be completely enclosed by the color Border, and the X,Y coordinates must lie within the area to be filled.

GetBkColor

```
function GetBkColor : word;
```

Returns the index for the current palette of the current background color.

GetColor

```
function GetColor : word;
```

Returns the current drawing color in the graphics mode.

GetDefaultPalette

```
procedure GetDefaultPalette(var Pal : PaletteType);
```

Returns in Pal the default palette for the current graphics driver. See "Related Types" for the structure of PaletteType.

GetFillPattern

```
procedure GetFillPattern(var FP : FillPatternType);
```

Returns in FP the definition of the current fill pattern. See "Related Types" for the structure of FillPatternType.

GetFillSettings

```
procedure GetFillSettings(var FS : FillSettingsType);
```

Returns in FS the current fill pattern and color. See "Related Types" for the structure of FillSettingsType.

GetLineSettings

```
procedure GetLineSettings(var LST : LineSettingsType);
```

Returns in LST the current settings for line style, pattern, and thickness. See "Related Types" for the structure of LineSettingsType.

GetMaxColor

```
function GetMaxColor : word;
```

Returns the highest value that represents a color in the current palette.

GetPalette

```
procedure GetPalette(var P : PaletteType);
```

Returns in P the current palette. See "Related Types" for the structure of PaletteType.

GetPaletteSize

```
function GetPaletteSize : word;
```

Returns the maximum number of palette entries that the current graphics mode can support.

SetAllPalette

```
procedure SetAllPalette(var Palette);
```

Changes all palettes to the definition contained in Palette.

SetBkColor

```
procedure SetBkColor(Color : word);
```

Sets the default background color for the graphics mode using entry Color of the current palette.

SetColor

```
procedure SetColor(Color : word);
```

Sets the current drawing color to Color, an index in the palette.

SetFillPattern

```
procedure SetFillPattern(Pattern : FillPatternType;
                         Color : word);
```

Defines the graphic pattern used to fill portions of the screen with commands such as FillPoly and FloodFill.

SetFillStyle

```
procedure SetFillStyle(Pattern : word; Color : word);
```

Sets the pattern used to fill areas of a graphics display.

SetLineStyle

```
procedure SetLineStyle(LineStyle : word; Pattern : word;
                       Thickness : word);
```

Determines the style, pattern, and thickness of lines drawn in graphics mode.

SetPalette

```
procedure SetPalette(ColorNum : word; Color : shortint);
```

Sets color number ColorNum of the active palette to Color.

SetRGBPalette

```
procedure SetRGBPalette(ColorNum, RedValue,
                        GreenValue, BlueValue : integer);
```

Sets palette entry ColorNum to consist of a particular combination of red, green, and blue.

Related Types

```
FillPatternType = array [1..8] of byte;
```

Used by GetFillPattern and SetFillPattern to retrieve and modify the fill pattern.

```
FillSettingsType = record
  Pattern : word;
  Color : word;
end;
```

Used by GetFillSettings to describe the most recently used color and pattern.

```
LineSettingsType = record
  LineStyle : word;
  Pattern : word;
  Thickness : word;
end;
```

Used by GetLineSettngs to describe the most recently used line style, pattern, and thickness.

```
PaletteType = record
  Size : byte;
  Colors : array [0..MaxColor] of shortint;
end;
```

Used by GetPalette, GetDefaultPalette, and SetAllPalette to retrieve and modify the size and colors in the palette.

Working with Images

The example program in the Circles section demonstrates how you can save a portion of a graphics screen and redisplay it in an altered form. The process of saving a graphics image requires three steps:

1. Determine how much memory you will need to store the graphics image.

2. Allocate a buffer of that size.

3. Save the image in the buffer.

This is accomplished with the following code:

```
Size := ImageSize(Round(MaxX * 0.25),
                  Round(MaxY * 0.25),
                  Round(MaxX * 0.75),
                  Round(MaxY * 0.75));

GetMem(P, Size);

GetImage(Round(MaxX * 0.25),
         Round(MaxY * 0.25),
         Round(MaxX * 0.75),
         Round(MaxY * 0.75), P^);
```

The first statement uses the function ImageSize to calculate the amount of memory required to store a rectangular image defined by two coordinate pairs defining upper-left and lower-right points on the screen. The amount of memory will vary dramatically with the display adapter and graphics mode in use, but cannot exceed 64K. The GetMem procedure then allocates memory from the heap to pointer variable *P*. Finally, the procedure GetImage moves the image defined by the coordinate pairs to the buffer that *P* points to.

Once you have saved a graphics image, you can retrieve it any time. In the example program, this is done with the procedure PutImage:

```
PutImage(Round(MaxX * 0.25),
         Round(MaxY * 0.25),
         P^, NotPut);
```

PutImage takes four parameters. The first two are a coordinate pair that indicate where the upper-left corner of the saved image should appear on the screen. The third parameter is the pointer to the buffer where the image is stored. The fourth

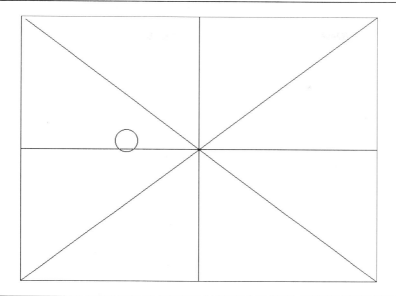

Figure 16-6.   *Dragging a circle using BGI*

parameter is the most interesting because it determines how the image will appear. The example above uses the constant NotPut, which uses a bitwise negation process (in which the value of individual bits is reversed) to reverse the colors of the image, producing a reverse video effect.

The PutImage procedure can also be used to "drag" an image across the screen. The important quality of dragging an image is that when the image moves, it does not disturb the pixels "underneath" the image. Anyone who has worked with desktop publishing or other "paint" programs is familiar with the dragging concept.

To drag an image, you must do two things. First, the image to be dragged must be stored in a buffer separate from the underlying image. Second, you must use the procedure PutImage with XORPut as the third parameter. The following sample program demonstrates how this is done. It saves the image of a circle, draws lines on the screen, and then drags the circle around the screen (see Figure 16-6).

```
Program DragDemo;

uses Crt, Graph;

var
  Direction : (Up, Down, Right, Left);
  XX,YY,
```

```
    MaxX,
    MaxY,
    ErrorCode,
    GraphMode,
    GraphDriver : integer;
    Size : word;
    P : pointer;

begin
  GraphDriver := Detect;
  InitGraph(GraphDriver, GraphMode, 'C:\BP\BGI');
  ErrorCode := GraphResult;
  if ErrorCode <> grOK then
    begin
      WriteLn('Graphics error: ', GraphErrorMsg(ErrorCode));
      Halt;
    end;

  MaxX := GetMaxX;
  MaxY := GetMaxY;

  { Draw a circle, save it, and clear the screen. }

  Circle(MaxX div 2, MaxY div 2, 20);

  XX := Round(MaxX * 0.45);
  YY := Round(MaxY * 0.45);
  Size := ImageSize(XX, YY,
                    Round(MaxX * 0.55),
                    Round(MaxY * 0.55));
  GetMem(P, Size);
  GetImage(XX, YY,
           Round(MaxX * 0.55),
           Round(MaxY * 0.55), P^);

  ClearViewPort;

  { Draw lines on screen }
  Line(MaxX div 2, 0, MaxX div 2, MaxY);
  Line(0, MaxY div 2, MaxX, MaxY div 2);
  Line(0, 0, MaxX, MaxY);
  Line(MaxX, 0, 0, MaxY);

  { Start dragging the circle. }

  Direction := Down;
  PutImage(XX, YY, P^, XORPut);
  repeat
```

```
     PutImage(XX, YY, P^, XORPut);
     case Direction of
       Down :
         begin
           YY := YY + 5;
           if YY > (MaxY * 0.75) then
             Direction := Left;
         end;

       Left :
         begin
           XX := XX - 5;
           if XX < (MaxX * 0.25)  then
             Direction := Up;
         end;

       Up :
         begin
           YY := YY - 5;
           if YY < (MaxY * 0.25)  then
             Direction := Right;
         end;

       Right :
         begin
           XX := XX + 5;
           if XX > (MaxX * 0.75)  then
             Direction := Down;
         end;
     end;

     PutImage(XX, YY, P^, XORPut);
  until KeyPressed;

  CloseGraph;
end.
```

The dragging is accomplished with the statement

```
PutImage(XX, YY, P^, XORPut);
```

This statement is used twice for each step in the movement. The first time it is used, PutImage erases the circle; the second time, it redraws it at the new location. As the circle moves around the screen, the lines are left undisturbed. An important point in using this technique is to define the smallest possible buffer to store the dragged image—the larger the buffer, the longer it takes to update the image, and the slower the dragging will seem.

Image Routines   **Graph Unit**

GetImage

```
procedure GetImage(X1, Y1, X2, Y2 : integer;
                   var BitMap);
```

Stores a rectangular portion of the graphics screen, defined by X1,Y1 and X2,Y2, in BitMap.

ImageSize

```
function ImageSize(X1, Y1, X2, Y2 : integer) : word;
```

Returns the number of bytes required to store the bitmap for the portion of the screen defined by X1,Y1 and X2,Y2.

PutImage

```
procedure PutImage(X, Y : integer; var BitMap;
                   BitBlt : word);
```

Displays the contents of BitMap starting at X,Y. BitBlt specifies the process to use to display the bitmap. See "Related Constants" for valid values of BitBlt.

Related Constants

```
CopyPut = 0;
XORPut  = 1;
OrPut   = 2;
AndPut  = 3;
NotPut  = 4;
```

Used by PutImage to define the logical operator used when displaying an image.

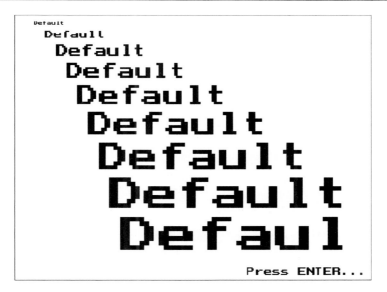

Figure 16-7.   *A bit-mapped font*

Graphical Text

Graphics wouldn't be much use without text. The ability to combine text and graphics is the foundation of the desktop publishing industry. The Graph unit contains five fonts: one bitmapped font and four "stroked" fonts. A bitmapped font is one that is created from a static number of elements. When it is enlarged, the bitmapped characters become "blocky" because their definition is not changed to match their larger size (see Figure 16-7).

Stroked fonts, on the other hand, create characters by means of an algorithm. Because the algorithms are insensitive to scale, stroked fonts actually become more precise as they are enlarged (see Figure 16-8). The program listed here demonstrates the difference between bitmapped and stroked fonts. It displays each of the five Graph fonts, starting with the default bitmapped font, in increasing size.

```
Program TextDemo;

uses Crt, Graph;

const
  CharType : array [0..4] of string[20] =
```

```
                      ('Default', 'Triplex', 'Small',
                       'Sans Serif', 'Gothic');

var
  S : string;
  MaxX,
  MaxY,
  I, J, K,
  ErrorCode,
  GraphMode,
  GraphDriver : integer;

begin
  GraphDriver := Detect;
  InitGraph(GraphDriver, GraphMode, 'C:\BP\BGI');
  GraphMode := GetMaxMode;
  InitGraph(GraphDriver, GraphMode, 'C:\BP\BGI');
  ErrorCode := GraphResult;
  if ErrorCode <> grOK then
    begin
      WriteLn('Graphics error: ', GraphErrorMsg(ErrorCode));
      Halt;
    end;

  MaxX := GetMaxX;
  MaxY := GetMaxY;

  for I := 0 To 4 do
    begin
      K := 0;
      for J := 1 To 10 do
        begin
          SetTextStyle(I, HorizDir, J);
          OutTextXY(J*20, K, CharType[I]);
          K := K + TextHeight(CharType[I]) + 10;
        end;

      SetTextStyle(0, HorizDir, 2);
      S := 'Press ENTER...';
      OutTextXY(MaxX - TextWidth(S), MaxY - TextHeight(S), S);
      ReadLn;
      ClearDevice;
    end;

  CloseGraph;
end.
```

To select a font, use the procedure SetTextStyle, which takes three parameters. The first parameter is the font, and can range from 0 (default) to 4 (Gothic). The

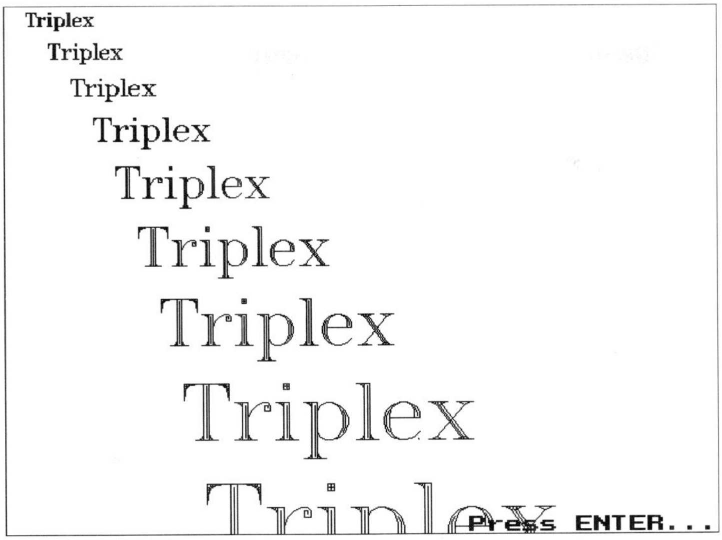

Figure 16-8.   *A stroked font*

second parameter is the direction in which the text is to be written. You have two choices here: 0 (horizontal) or 1 (vertical). The third parameter controls the size of the characters. The normal font size is 1 for the default font and 4 for the stroked fonts, but these can be increased to ten times the normal size.

Once you have selected a font, you can display text with the OutTextXY procedure, which displays a string starting at coordinates you supply as parameters. Notice that in the example program, OutTextXY is used in conjunction with the function TextHeight to determine where the next line of text should be placed. TextHeight is necessary because each font has a different scale. If you wish to place one line of text below another, you must determine the height of the current text and use that number to calculate the distance you have to move down in order to write the next line. In the program, the statement

```
K := K + TextHeight(CharType[I]) + 10;
```

moves the next line of text down by the size of the current line plus ten pixels. As you can see, using text in the Graphics mode is not easy, even when the fonts are defined for you.

Graphical Text Routines   **Graph Unit**

GetTextSettings

```
procedure GetTextSettings(var TS : TextSettingsType);
```

Returns in TS the current text settings. See "Related Types" for the structure of TextSettingsType.

InstallUserFont

```
function InstallUserFont(FontFileName : string) : integer;
```

Installs a non-Borland font, based on the contents of the file named by FontFileName.

OutText

```
procedure OutText(TextString : string);
```

Displays the string TextString using the current settings for fonts, justification, height, and width.

OutTextXY

```
procedure OutTextXY(X, Y : integer; TextString : string);
```

Displays the string TextString at position X,Y using the current settings for fonts, justification, height, and width.

RegisterBGIFont

```
function RegisterBGIFont(Font : pointer) : integer;
```

Loads a .BGI font driver file (read from disk onto the heap or linked into the program using BINOBJ) and registers the font with the graphics system. Font is a pointer to the location of the .BGI driver. If an error occurs, the function returns a value less than zero; otherwise, it returns the assigned font number.

SetTextJustify

```
procedure SetTextJustify(Horiz, Vert : word);
```

Defines the display format used by OutText and OutTextXY.

SetTextStyle

```
procedure SetTextStyle(Font : word; Direction : word;
                       CharSize : word);
```

Defines how characters will be displayed in graphics mode. The characteristics include the font, the direction in which the writing takes place, and the size of the characters.

SetUserCharSize

```
procedure SetUserCharSize(MultX, DivX, MultY, DivY : word);
```

Changes the width and height proportions for stroked fonts. For example, if MultX is 1 and DivX is 2, then characters will be displayed with one-half the width they would normally have.

TextHeight

```
function TextHeight(TextString : string) : word;
```

Determines how much vertical space TextString will require given the current font and multiplication factor.

TextWidth

```
function TextWidth(TextString : string) : word;
```

Returns the width in pixels required to display TextString given the current font and multiplication factor.

Related Types

```
TextSettingsType = record
  Font : word;
  Direction : word;
  CharSize : word;
  Horiz : word;
  Vert : word;
end;
```

Used by GetTextSettings to describe the most recently used text attributes.

Graphics in Windows

The GDI for Windows is even more powerful for graphics than the BGI, as you might imagine. All programs written to run in Windows use the GDI. In Turbo Pascal for Windows, the GDI is part of the WinTypes and WinProcs units. As their names imply, WinTypes contains all the type definitions of the Windows API, and WinProcs contains all the subprograms. There are over 500 routines in the WinProcs unit, so a discussion of every one is impractical. This section will get you started using the GDI by creating the same programs done for the BGI, except this time they will run in Windows.

Introducing Object Windows

It is possible to write any Windows program using only the routines in the WinProcs unit; however, many calls are required to set up a window and interact with other windows. Borland's ObjectWindows simplifies these tasks by providing an object-oriented framework for any Windows application. Although Chapter 18 will cover ObjectWindows in detail, this section will give you enough to start writing graphics programs.

The main object of any ObjectWindows program is the *application*. To create an application, you must create a descendent of the type TApplication. The primary purpose of an application object is to control the *main window* of the application. The main window is the root window of the application, and it controls any child windows that might be part of your program. In simple programs, such as those created in this chapter, the main window is the only window. A main window usually requires a new object declaration, which is a descendent of the TWindow object.

The following listing is a template for any program that outputs graphics to a single window:

```
Program Template;

uses WinTypes, WinProcs, OWindows;

type
  PTheWindow = ^TTheWindow;
  TTheWindow = object(TWindow)
    procedure Paint(PaintDC: HDC;
                     var PaintInfo: TPaintStruct); virtual;
  end;

  TTheApplication = object(TApplication)
    procedure InitMainWindow; virtual;
  end;

procedure TTheWindow.Paint;
begin
  {draw the graphics here}
end;

procedure TTheApplication.InitMainWindow;
begin
  MainWindow := New(PTheWindow, Init(nil, 'A Program'));
end;

var
  TheApp: TTheApplication;

begin
  TheApp.Init('A Program');
  TheApp.Run;
  TheApp.Done;
end.
```

If you run this program, you will see a blank window, which you must close using the window's control box.

A few lines in this program deserve special attention. The first step in creating a graphics program is to create a window object. This object is a descendent of the TWindow object. The TWindow object itself has no functionality, so you must create descendents. In the previous listing, the new object type is called *TTheWindow*.

Whenever a window object is displayed or redisplayed, its contents must be recreated. In most ObjectWindows programs this will include a combination of menus, dialog boxes, and child windows. In simple graphics programs, however, you need only to override the Paint method. In the Paint method you will draw your shapes and text.

The first procedure call in the main program,

```
TheApp.Init('A Program');
```

initializes the application. The string in the call provides a name for the application. Although this string is not used by ObjectWindows, it is traditionally set to be the same as the window name.

The Init method of the TApplication object is responsible for calling the InitMainWindow method. In this method you assign the main window to be the window of your choice. The call to New includes the descendent type of the window and the name of the window.

You can actually run the previous program, and you will see a nice, blank window. If you are new to Windows programming, you should type in this program, and verify that you can move, size, and close the window.

Drawing Lines and Shapes

Drawing in Windows has many similarities to drawing using the BGI. In the BGI you used GetMaxX and GetMaxY to draw shapes relative to the current coordinate system. This is even more important in Windows, when you never know how large or small the drawing area will be. In this section you will see how to draw lines and shapes that are independent of window size.

To draw a line in a Windows window, you need two procedures: MoveTo and LineTo. MoveTo moves the graphics pointer to a particular coordinate pair. LineTo draws a line from the current position to a new position. You can think of drawing lines in Windows like writing with a pen: moving to a location with the pen up, then drawing a line with the pen down.

 The coordinate system in Windows is similar to BGI's: The upper-left corner is 0,0, and the lower-right corner depends on the size of the window.

The following program draws random lines in a window, similar to the LineDemo program described earlier in this chapter. Study the program so you can pick out the differences between it and the *Template* program (shown previously).

```
Program LinesWin;

uses WinTypes, WinProcs, OWindows;
```

```
type
  PLineWindow = ^TLineWIndow;
  TLineWindow = object(TWindow)
    procedure Paint(PaintDC: HDC;
                    var PaintInfo: TPaintStruct); virtual;
  end;

  TLineApplication = object(TApplication)
    procedure InitMainWindow; virtual;
  end;

procedure TLineWindow.Paint;
var
  Bounds : TRect;
  I : integer;
begin
  RandSeed := 11111;
  GetClientRect(HWindow, Bounds);
  for I := 1 to 100 do
    begin
      MoveTo(PaintDC, Random(Bounds.Right),
             Random(Bounds.Bottom));
      LineTo(PaintDC, Random(Bounds.Right),
             Random(Bounds.Bottom));
    end;
end;

procedure TLineApplication.InitMainWindow;
begin
  MainWindow := New(PLineWindow, Init(nil, 'Lines'));
end;

var
  LineApp: TLineApplication;

begin
  LineApp.Init('Lines');
  LineApp.Run;
  LineApp.Done;
end.
```

Obviously the primary change is the implementation of the Paint method. This method determines the size of the current window, then draws one hundred lines within the window boundaries.

The Paint method includes a parameter called PaintDC, which contains the *display context* of the window. A display context is a logical drawing surface. When the program calls the Paint method, it associates the actual window with a display context. Within the method you "draw" on the display context, and it appears in the window.

The GetClientRect procedure is what you use to keep your program from assuming a specific window size. GetClientRect returns a value in *Bounds,* which is a record containing the bounds of the rectangular window. *Bounds.Left* and *Bounds.Top* will always be 0, and *Bounds.Right* and *Bounds.Bottom* will define the lower-right corner of the display context.

The most puzzling statement of all to you may be this one:

```
RandSeed := 11111;
```

What's the point of using random numbers if you always use the same ones? The answer lies in the purpose of the Paint method, which includes redrawing part or all of the display when necessary. Suppose you run the *LinesWin* program, which creates the window shown in Figure 16-9. Then you pop up some other window which hides a portion of the *Lines* window. When you remove that window, Windows calls Paint to redraw only the portion of the window that was obscured. If you draw different lines on that portion of the screen, you will get unexpected results.

Always make sure that Paint draws the same window. Use other methods to alter the window display.

To draw a circle in a window, you must use either the Ellipse function or the Arc function—there is no Circle routine. To specify an ellipse you define the rectangle that is just large enough to contain the ellipse. In other words the ellipse would touch the rectangle at the center of each side of the rectangle. The following illustration demonstrates the ellipse created within rectangle bound by 0,0 and 15,20.

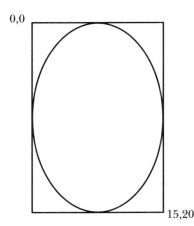

The following program uses the Ellipse function to draw concentric circles.

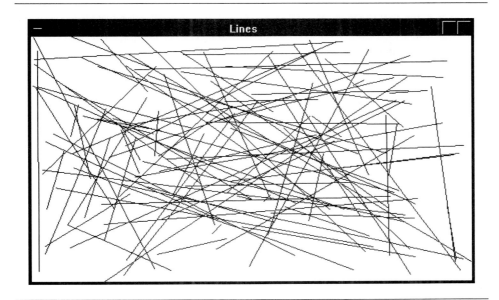

Figure 16-9.   *Drawing lines in Windows*

```
Program CirclesWin;

uses WinTypes, WinProcs, OWindows;

type
  PCircWindow = ^TCircWIndow;
  TCircWindow = object(TWindow)
    procedure Paint(PaintDC: HDC;
                    var PaintInfo: TPaintStruct); virtual;
  end;

  TCircApplication = object(TApplication)
    procedure InitMainWindow; virtual;
  end;

procedure TCircWindow.Paint;
var
  Bounds : TRect;
  I : integer;
  CenterX, CenterY : integer;
begin
  GetClientRect(HWindow, Bounds);
  CenterX := Bounds.Right div 2;
  CenterY := Bounds.Bottom div 2;
```

```
{ Draw concentric circles }
I := CenterX;
while I > 10 do
  begin
    Ellipse(PaintDC,
        CenterX - I, CenterY - I,
        CenterX + I, CenterY + I);
    I := I - 10;
  end;

{ Add lines on screen }
MoveTo(PaintDC, CenterX, 0);
LineTo(PaintDC, CenterX, Bounds.Bottom);
MoveTo(PaintDC, 0, CenterY);
LineTo(PaintDC, Bounds.Right, CenterY);
MoveTo(PaintDC, 0, 0);
LineTo(PaintDC, Bounds.Right, Bounds.Bottom);
MoveTo(PaintDC, Bounds.Right, 0);
LineTo(PaintDC, 0, Bounds.Bottom);
end;

procedure TCircApplication.InitMainWindow;
begin
  MainWindow := New(PCircWindow, Init(nil, 'Circles'));
end;

var
  CircApp: TCircApplication;

begin
  CircApp.Init('Circles');
  CircApp.Run;
  CircApp.Done;
end.
```

Notice that the circles are drawn from the outside in. This is required because, by default, all ellipses are filled in with a white brush. Figure 16-10 shows the output of the program.

It is common practice in Windows programming to call functions as if they were procedures, ignoring the return value. See Chapter 4, "Subprograms," for more details.

Patterns in Windows

When drawing shapes, Windows uses two special tools to create patterns: pens and brushes. A pen controls the color, thickness, and style of a line. A brush controls the

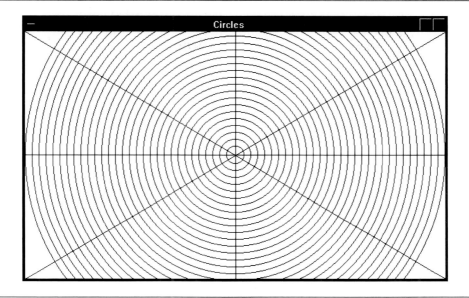

Figure 16-10. *Drawing circles in Windows*

color, pattern, and style of solid shapes. One pen and one brush are always active. The default pen is a thin, black, continuous line; the default brush is a solid white fill.

To recreate the patterned arcs done for BGI in Figure 16-4, you need a brush style called a hatched brush. A hatched brush fills a shape with one of six predefined hatch patterns: horizontal lines, vertical lines, upward diagonal lines, downward diagonal lines, crossed lines that form squares, and crossed lines that form diamonds.

The following program uses a hatched brush with a random pattern and color to demonstrate the FloodFill function. Its output appears in Figure 16-11.

```
Program PatternsWin;

uses WinTypes, WinProcs, OWindows;

type
  PPatternWindow = ^TPatternWIndow;
  TPatternWindow = object(TWindow)
    procedure Paint(PaintDC: HDC;
                    var PaintInfo: TPaintStruct); virtual;
  end;

  TPatternApplication = object(TApplication)
    procedure InitMainWindow; virtual;
  end;
```

```
procedure TPatternWindow.Paint;
var
  Bounds : TRect;
  HatchBrush : HBrush;
  I : integer;
  CenterX, CenterY : integer;
begin
  RandSeed := 11111;
  GetClientRect(HWindow, Bounds);
  CenterX := Bounds.Right div 2;
  CenterY := Bounds.Bottom div 2;

  { Draw lines on screen }
  MoveTo(PaintDC, CenterX, 0);
  LineTo(PaintDC, CenterX, Bounds.Bottom);
  MoveTo(PaintDC, 0, CenterY);
  LineTo(PaintDC, Bounds.Right, CenterY);
  MoveTo(PaintDC, 0, 0);
  LineTo(PaintDC, Bounds.Right, Bounds.Bottom);
  MoveTo(PaintDC, Bounds.Right, 0);
  LineTo(PaintDC, 0, Bounds.Bottom);

  { Draw concentric circles }
  I := CenterX;
  while I > 10 do
    begin
      Arc(PaintDC,
          CenterX - I, CenterY - I,
          CenterX + I, CenterY + I,
          CenterX, CenterY - I,
          CenterX, CenterY - I);
      I := I - 10;
    end;

  { Fill in portions of the graphic image }
  for I := 1 to 100 do
    begin
      HatchBrush := CreateHatchBrush(Random(6),
                    RGB(Random(256), Random(256), Random(256)));
      SelectObject(PaintDC, HatchBrush);
      FloodFill(PaintDC, Random(Bounds.Right),
                Random(Bounds.Bottom), $00000000);
      DeleteObject(HatchBrush);
    end;
end;

procedure TPatternApplication.InitMainWindow;
begin
  MainWindow := New(PPatternWindow, Init(nil, 'Patterns'));
```

```
end;

var
  PatternApp: TPatternApplication;

begin
  PatternApp.Init('Patterns');
  PatternApp.Run;
  PatternApp.Done;
end.
```

Let's examine the four primary routines that accomplish the pattern fill: CreateHatchBrush, SelectObject, FloodFill, and DeleteObject.

To change the current brush, you must first create a new brush handle. The CreateBrush function accepts one of the six hatch patterns plus a color, and returns a handle of type HBrush. The color is often set by calling the RGB function, which accepts three byte values that reflect the red intensity, green intensity, and blue intensity of the color.

Once you have created a brush handle, you must associate it with the display context. The SelectObject function accepts a brush handle, pen handle, or font handle, and uses it to replace the current tool in the display context. Once you are finished drawing with that tool, you should call DeleteObject to free the memory associated with the handle.

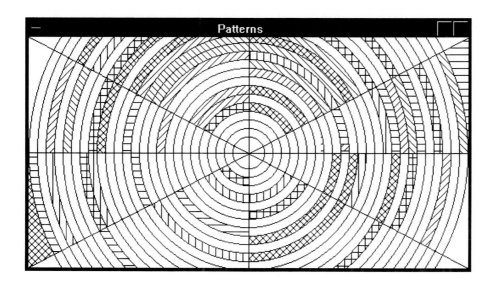

Figure 16-11. *Filling with colors and patterns in Windows*

The FloodFill function itself requires the display context and the X and Y coordinates of the starting point for flooding. The last parameter is the color that serves as the boundary for the flood. In the previous listing, a **longint** constant is used to specify the color, as an alternative to calling the RGB function. Since black has no color intensity, its color value is 0.

The previous program used FloodFill to fill existing shapes with a brush. The more common approach in Windows is to fill each shape as you draw it. This next listing shows you how to call the Polygon function to draw and fill a series of triangles:

```
Program PolygonsWin;

uses WinTypes, WinProcs, OWindows;

type
  PPolyWindow = ^TPolyWIndow;
  TPolyWindow = object(TWindow)
    procedure Paint(PaintDC: HDC;
                    var PaintInfo: TPaintStruct); virtual;
  end;

  TPolyApplication = object(TApplication)
    procedure InitMainWindow; virtual;
  end;

procedure TPolyWindow.Paint;
type
  TTriangle = array [1..3] of TPoint;
var
  Bounds : TRect;
  HatchBrush : HBrush;
  Tri : TTriangle;
  I : integer;
begin
  RandSeed := 11111;
  GetClientRect(HWindow, Bounds);

  { Create Triangles }
  for I := 1 to 100 do
    begin
      HatchBrush := CreateHatchBrush(Random(6),
                 RGB(Random(256), Random(256), Random(256)));
      SelectObject(PaintDC, HatchBrush);
      Tri[1].X := Random(Bounds.Right);
      Tri[1].Y := Random(Bounds.Bottom);
      Tri[2].X := Random(Bounds.Right);
      Tri[2].Y := Random(Bounds.Bottom);
      Tri[3].X := Random(Bounds.Right);
      Tri[3].Y := Random(Bounds.Bottom);
```

```
        Polygon(PaintDC, Tri, 3);
        DeleteObject(HatchBrush);
    end;
end;

procedure TPolyApplication.InitMainWindow;
begin
  MainWindow := New(PPolyWindow, Init(nil, 'Polygons'));
end;

var
  PolyApp: TPolyApplication;

begin
  PolyApp.Init('Polygons');
  PolyApp.Run;
  PolyApp.Done;
end.
```

To call Polygon, you must create an array of type TPoint, and pass that array along with the number of points to use. The output of this program is shown in Figure 16-12.

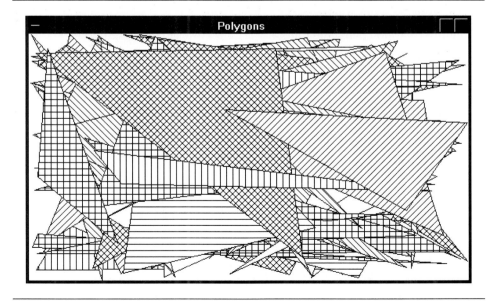

Figure 16-12. *Creating filled triangles in Windows*

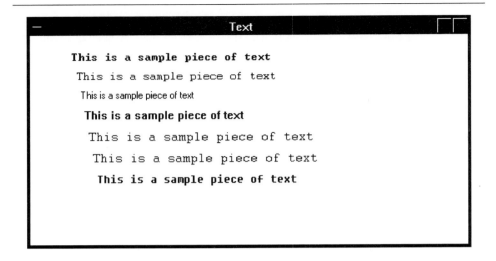

Figure 16-13.   *The stock fonts in Windows*

Drawing Graphical Text

Fonts in Windows are defined by the Control Panel in the Program Manager. This makes all fonts consistent throughout all the Windows Applications you have. When you change a font using WinProcs, you are actually making a font request—Windows will make the actual font change based on the fonts that are loaded at the time.

The easiest way to change fonts to select a *stock tool*. A stock tool is a set of predefined brushes, pens, and fonts that are already loaded into Windows. There are six different fonts in the stock tool set. The following program demonstrates all six, and produces the output in Figure 16-13.

```
Program TextWin;

uses WinTypes, WinProcs, OWindows, Strings;

type
  PTextWindow = ^TTextWIndow;
  TTextWindow = object(TWindow)
    procedure Paint(PaintDC: HDC;
                    var PaintInfo: TPaintStruct); virtual;
  end;

  TTextApplication = object(TApplication)
    procedure InitMainWindow; virtual;
  end;

procedure TTextWindow.Paint;
```

```
const
  TestString : PChar = 'This is a sample piece of text';
var
  Bounds : TRect;
  TheFont : HFont;
  X, Y : integer;
begin
  GetClientRect(HWindow, Bounds);
  Y := 20;
  for X := OEM_FIXED_FONT to SYSTEM_FIXED_FONT do
    begin
      TheFont := GetStockObject(X);
      SelectObject(PaintDC, TheFont);
      TextOut(PaintDC, X*5, Y, TestString, StrLen(TestString));
      Y := Y + Hiword(GetTextExtent(PaintDC, 'T', 1)) + 10;
    end;
end;

procedure TTextApplication.InitMainWindow;
begin
  MainWindow := New(PTextWindow, Init(nil, 'Text'));
end;

var
  TextApp: TTextApplication;

begin
  TextApp.Init('Text');
  TextApp.Run;
  TextApp.Done;
end.
```

The names of the fonts are listed in the "Related Constants" section of the GDI summary box at the end of the chapter.

The *TextWin* program calls three new routines: GetStockObject, TextOut, and TextExtent. GetStockObject is a simple function that creates a handle based on a stock tool constant. The handle can then be used as the input to SelectObject.

Do not use DeleteObject to remove stock objects from memory—they remain resident throughout the Windows session.

The TextOut function is the primary method of outputting text to a window. It does not use the current position, so you must supply X and Y coordinates for the upper-left corner of the text. The final parameter to TextOut is the number of characters to display.

To obtain the amount of space required for a string you call TextExtent. This program uses TextExtent to determine where to place the next line of text so that there is no overlap. The return value of TextExtent is a **longint** number, where the upper word is the length and the lower word is the height.

If you want a font other than the stock fonts, you need to create a *logical font*. A logical font is a record that defines the characteristics of a desired font. Once you are satisfied with the record fields, you call CreateFontIndirect to associate the logical font with a font handle.

This next program not only creates logical fonts, but it also introduces another method of the TWindow object: WMLButtonDown. This method is called whenever the user pushes down on the left mouse button. By default, this method does nothing. The *TextWin2* program overrides this method to change fonts when the user clicks the left mouse button.

```
Program TextWin2;

uses WinTypes, WinProcs, OWindows, Strings;

type
  PTextWindow = ^TTextWIndow;
  TTextWindow = object(TWindow)
    Family : byte;
    constructor Init(AParent : PWindowsObject; ATitle : PChar);
    procedure Paint(PaintDC : HDC;
                    var PaintInfo : TPaintStruct); virtual;
    procedure WMLButtonDown(var Msg : TMessage);
                virtual wm_First + wm_LButtonDown;
    procedure ShowFont(PaintDC : HDC);
  end;

  TTextApplication = object(TApplication)
    procedure InitMainWindow; virtual;
  end;

const
  FontFamilies : array [0..3] of byte =
      (ff_Roman, ff_Swiss, ff_Script, ff_Modern);
  NormalText : TLogFont =
      (lfHeight : 10;          lfWidth : 0;
       lfEscapement : 0;       lfOrientation : 0;
       lfWeight : fw_Normal;   lfItalic : 0;
       lfUnderline : 0;        lfStrikeOut : 0;
       lfCharSet : ANSI_CharSet;
       lfOutPrecision : Out_Default_Precis;
       lfClipPrecision : Clip_Default_Precis;
       lfQuality : Default_Quality;
       lfPitchAndFamily : Default_Pitch or ff_Script);

constructor TTextWindow.Init;
```

```
begin
  inherited Init(AParent, ATitle);
  Family := 0;
end;

procedure TTextWindow.ShowFont(PaintDC : HDC);
const
  TestString : PChar = 'This is a sample piece of text';
var
  Bounds : TRect;
  TheFont : HFont;
  LogFont : TLogFont;
  X, Y : integer;
begin
  GetClientRect(HWindow, Bounds);
  Y := 6;
  for X := 1 to 10 do
    begin
      LogFont := NormalText;
      LogFont.lfHeight := 10 + Y*2;
      LogFont.lfPitchAndFamily := Default_Pitch or
             FontFamilies[Family];
      TheFont := CreateFontIndirect(LogFont);
      SelectObject(PaintDC, TheFont);
      TextOut(PaintDC, X*20, Y, TestString,
             StrLen(TestString));
      Y := Y + Hiword(GetTextExtent(PaintDC, 'T', 1)) + 4;
      DeleteObject(TheFont);
    end;
end;

procedure TTextWindow.Paint;
begin
  ShowFont(PaintDC);
end;

procedure TTextWindow.WMLButtonDown;
var
  PaintDC : HDC;
  Region : HRgn;
  Bounds : TRect;
begin
  PaintDC := GetDC(HWindow);
  GetClientRect(HWindow, Bounds);
  Region := CreateRectRgnIndirect(Bounds);
  PaintRgn(PaintDC, Region);
  Family := (Family + 1) mod 4;
  ShowFont(PaintDC);
  ReleaseDC(HWindow, PaintDC);
```

```
end;

procedure TTextApplication.InitMainWindow;
begin
  MainWindow := New(PTextWindow, Init(nil, 'Text'));
end;

var
  TextApp: TTextApplication;

begin
  TextApp.Init('Text');
  TextApp.Run;
  TextApp.Done;
end.
```

Notice that all the drawing is done in a new procedure, *ShowFont,* instead of in Paint. This makes the drawing available to other methods.

In the Paint method, the display context is passed as a parameter to the method. WMLButtonDown has no such parameter, so you must retrieve the display context. This is accomplished through a call to GetDC. Once you are finished drawing, you make the display context available to other windows by calling ReleaseDC.

Before WMLButtonDown can display the next font, it clears the entire window. It calls GetClientRect to get the bounds of the window, and uses them to create a region handle. Finally it calls PaintRgn to fill the window using the default white brush.

The output of the window after two mouse clicks is shown in Figure 16-14.

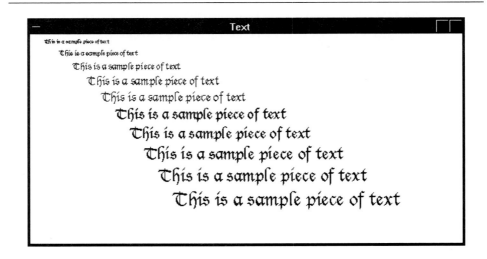

Figure 16-14.   *A logical font in Windows*

Selected Graphics Routines   **WinProcs unit**

Arc

```
function Arc(DC : HDC;
             X1, Y1, X2, Y2, X3, Y3, X4, Y4 : integer) : Bool;
```

Draws an arc based on a bounding rectangle. The corners of the rectangle are defined by X1,Y1 and X2,Y2. The starting point of the arc is based on a line that passes from the center of the rectangle through the point X3,Y3. The stopping point is based on a line through X4,Y4.

CreateFontIndirect

```
function CreateFontIndirect(var LogFont : TLogFont) : HFont;
```

Defines a font handle based on a logical font definition. See "Related Types" for the record structure of TLogFont.

CreateHatchBrush

```
function CreateHatchBrush(Index : integer;
                          Color : TColorRef) : HBrush;
```

Defines a brush handle based on a hatch index and a color. See "Related Constants" for valid values of Index. See "Related Types" for the definition of TColorRef.

CreateRectRgnIndirect

```
function CreateRectRgnIndirect(var Rect: TRect) : HRgn;
```

Creates a rectangular region handle based on the coordinates in Rect.

DeleteObject

```
function DeleteObject(Handle : THandle) : Bool;
```

Frees memory associated with a drawing handle.

Ellipse

```
function Ellipse(DC : HDC; X1, Y1, X2, Y2 : integer) : Bool;
```

Draws an ellipse just inside a bounding rectangle. The corners of the rectangle are defined by X1,Y1 and X2,Y2.

FloodFill

```
function FloodFill(DC : HDC; X, Y : integer;
                   Color : TColorRef) : Bool;
```

Fills any bounded area including X,Y with the current brush pattern. The bounded area must be in the color Color.

GetClientRect

```
procedure GetClientRect(Wnd : HWnd; var Rect : TRect);
```

Returns the rectangle that is defined by the given window handle.

GetDC

```
function GetDC(Wnd : HWnd) : HDC;
```

Retrieves a display context that is associated with the given window handle.

GetStockObject

```
function GetStockObject(Index : integer) : THandle;
```

Gets one of several predefined drawing handles. See "Related Constants" for valid values of Index.

GetTextExtent

```
function GetTextExtent(DC : HDC; Str : PChar;
                            Count : integer) : longint;
```

Determines the pixel height and width of the string Str based on the current font. The height is in the high word and the width is in the low word.

LineTo

```
function LineTo(DC : HDC; X, Y : integer) : Bool;
```

Draws a line from the current position to the one defined by X,Y.

MoveTo

```
function MoveTo(DC : HDC; X, Y : integer) : Bool;
```

Moves the current position to that defined by X,Y.

PaintRgn

```
function PaintRgn(DC : HDC; Rgn : HRgn) : Bool;
```

Fills a given region using the current brush.

Polygon

```
function Polygon(DC : HDC; var Points; Count : integer) : Bool;
```

Draws a polygon based on the array of points in Points.

ReleaseDC

```
function ReleaseDC(Wnd : HWnd; DC : HDC) : integer;
```

Releases a device context, currently used by the Wnd window, for use by other applications.

SelectObject

```
function SelectObject(DC : HDC; HObject : THandle) : THandle;
```

Selects a brush, font, or pen to be used in the display context.

TextOut

```
function TextOut(DC : HDC; X, Y : integer;
                 Str: PChar; Count : integer) : Bool;
```

Displays the text Str at the location X,Y.

Related Types

```
HBrush = THandle;  { THandle is a word }
```

Defines a brush handle.

```
HDC = THandle;
```

Defines the handle of a display context.

```
HFont = THandle;
```

Defines a font handle.

```
HRgn = THandle;
```

Defines a region handle.

```
TColorRef = longint;
```

Defines a color based on red, green, and blue intensities. A value of this type should be in the form $00BBGGRR, where BB is the blue intensity, GG is the green intensity, and RR is the red intensity. White would be defined as $00FFFFFF.

```
TLogFont = record
  lfHeight,
  lfWidth,
  lfEscapement,
  lfOrientation,
  lfWeight : integer;
  lfItalic,
  lfUnderline,
  lfStrikeOut,
  lfCharSet,
  lfOutPrecision,
  lfClipPrecision,
  lfQuality,
  lfPitchAndFamily : byte;
  lfFaceName : array [0..lf_FaceSize - 1] of byte;
end;
```

Defines a logical font.

```
TPoint = record
  X : integer;
  Y : integer;
end;
```

Defines the X and Y coordinates of a point.

```
TRect = record
  Left,
  Top,
  Right,
  Bottom : integer;
end;
```

Defines a rectangle, using the X and Y coordinates of the upper-left and lower-right corners.

Related Constants

```
hs_Horizontal = 0;
hs_Vertical = 1;
```

```
hs_FDiagonal = 2;
hs_BDiagonal = 3;
hs_Cross = 4;
hs_DiagCross = 5;
```

Shows valid hatch styles for hatch brushes.

```
White_Brush = 0;
LtGray_Brush = 1;
Gray_Brush = 2;
DkGray_Brush = 3;
Black_Brush = 4;
Hollow_Brush = 5;
Null_Brush = 5;
White_Pen = 6;
Black_Pen = 7;
Null_Pen = 8;
OEM_Fixed_Font = 10;
ANSI_Fixed_Font = 11;
ANSI_Var_Font = 12;
System_Font = 13;
Device_Default_Font = 14;
Default_Palette = 15;
System_Fixed_Font = 16;
```

Shows valid stock objects used by GetStockObject.

Chapter *17*

Turbo Vision

Sometimes you find a program that is so easy to use, you wish you could write your own programs to look just like it. The Turbo Pascal IDE is one such program—easy to use, full mouse support, pull-down menus, and so on. Turbo Vision, now in its second version, gives you the ability to write programs that work just like the DOS IDE.

Turbo Vision is a set of very large units, and much of the code is primarily for internal use. This chapter attempts to break Turbo Vision into meaningful portions and then covers those portions enough so that you can write complex programs. The chapter goes through the development of one complete example, so each section flows into the next. Shortly after an object type is introduced and explained, you will find a summary of methods and related subprograms and constants defined for that object. The methods are divided between primary methods, which you will use often, and other methods, which are either internal or seldom-required methods. With this organization, you can read the chapter from beginning to end once and then use the summary areas later as a reference.

The largest benefit of Turbo Vision is that it becomes a huge collection of reusable software. The next time you need to create a menu, for example, you'll simply define an object variable of type TMenuBox and insert the menu items into the object. If TMenuBox doesn't quite handle a specific capability, you can create a new object type that inherits all the functionality of TMenuBox but adds the new capability.

Turbo Vision is extremely flexible. A side effect of this flexibility is that it is also fairly complicated. You will find yourself calling Turbo Vision methods and procedures without any idea of why you're calling them—you're simply copying an example. This is fine; the details will make sense as you gain experience. Some details are never unveiled, but that is the wonder of OOP. By the way, Turbo Vision is entirely built around the concepts of inheritance and polymorphism. If you aren't familiar with these terms, study the discussion of objects in Chapters 3, 4, and 6.

Creating and Using Flash Cards

Throughout this chapter you will follow the development of a single application. Each example will, therefore, have a context, making it easier to understand. The application being developed is a program that allows you to create and use flash cards on the screen. As with all Turbo Vision programs, this application has the same look and feel as the Turbo Pascal environment.

As a user of this program, you would start by entering data for the flash cards. Each card has a question "side" and an answer "side." For simplicity, each side can contain only one 50-character line of text. The following illustration shows the screen used to enter a card:

Notice that it looks exactly like the dialog boxes you use in the IDE.

Once the data for each card is entered, you can save those cards to a file on disk. Then you can run through the cards, either in random or sequential order. First, the question side of the card is displayed, as you can see here:

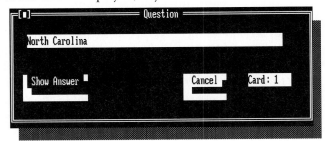

Once you read the question side, you can either look at the answer side or go directly to the next card. Figure 17-1 shows a screen in which both sides of a flash card are displayed. You can leave the program at any time by selecting a menu option or status-line command or by pressing a predefined hot key, in this case ALT-X. Many other commands are also bound to hot keys.

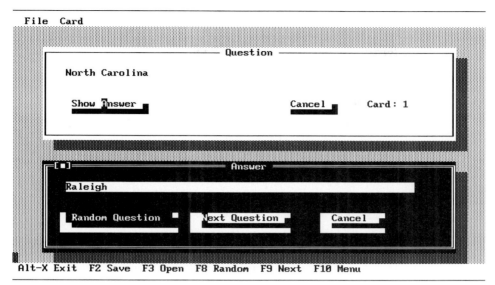

Figure 17-1.   *Dialog box to display the answer side of a flash card*

Now that you understand what the *Flashcard_App* program does, you are ready to learn how it was made. The rest of this chapter takes you step by step through the development of this program. This will help you to create your own programs using Turbo Vision.

Creating an Application Object

When you first decide to tackle a large programming effort, you will probably find it difficult to determine a starting place. Often, if you start by prototyping your user interface, you can iron out the functionality of your application. Turbo Vision makes it easy for you to start this way. It allows you to achieve visual results of your efforts almost immediately.

The first step in creating a Turbo Vision application is to create a descendent of the TApplication object type. You can start by creating a simple descendant, with no new data fields and no overridden virtual methods. This gives you the following program:

```
Program Just_an_Application;

uses App;
```

```
type
  TFlashCardApp = object(TApplication)
  end;

var
  FlashCardApp : TFlashCardApp;

begin
  FlashCardApp.Init;
  FlashCardApp.Run;
  FlashCardApp.Done;
end.
```

After declaring the new object type, the preceding program creates a variable of that type and calls three inherited methods.

Figure 17-2 shows the screen displayed when you run this simple program. The top line, blank at the moment, will contain the menu bar. The entire middle of the screen is called the desktop. Finally, the status line takes up the bottom line, which contains hints and hot keys. The default status line includes a single entry, ALT-X, which enables you to exit the application. You should already be familiar with these terms from the Turbo Pascal IDE.

`Alt-X Exit`

Figure 17-2.   *Display of the default application desktop*

To run any Turbo Vision application, you must call three methods: Init, Run, and Done. The Init method initializes all the internal structures required by Turbo Vision. You may choose to override this to include your own initializations. If you do, be sure to call the parent method, TApplication.Init. The Run method executes the application based on the way you set it up. Finally, Done cleans everything up.

TApplication Object Summary   **APP.TPU**

Heritage

TApplication ➡ TProgram ➡ TGroup ➡ TView ➡ TObject

Primary Methods

```
constructor Init;
```

Initializes internal Turbo Vision subsystems; must be called by every application.

```
procedure Cascade;
```

Cascades all windows that are tileable (normally this excludes dialog boxes).

```
destructor Done; virtual;
```

Cleans up internal Turbo Vision subsystems; should be called by every application.

```
procedure DosShell;
```

Clears the screen and starts a DOS Shell.

```
procedure Tile;
```

Tiles all windows that are tileable (normally this excludes dialog boxes).

Primary Inherited Methods

Inherited from TProgram (see TProgram summary):

```
procedure InitMenuBar; virtual;
procedure InitStatusLine; virtual;
procedure Run; virtual;
```

Inherited from TView (see TView summary):

```
procedure GetExtent(var Extent : TRect);
```

Other Methods

```
procedure GetTileRect(var R : TRect); virtual
```

Can be overridden to change the tile/cascade area to something other than the entire desktop.

```
procedure HandleEvent(var Event: TEvent); virtual;
```

Used internally to handle the TApplication-specific events: DOS shell, cascade, and tile.

```
procedure WriteShellMsg; virtual;
```

Creating Event Commands

Once you have the outline for your application, you need to determine the commands that will be available. By convention, these commands should be defined as constants and should start with the letters "cm". Turbo Vision reserves all constants from 0 to 99 and from 256 to 999. This leaves you with the values 100 to 255 and 1,000 to 65,535 for your own commands. The vast majority of the reserved commands are handled internally by Turbo Vision, so you need not be concerned about them. The few exceptions are covered in later discussions.

For the flash card application, the following commands are defined initially:

```
const
  { valid event commands }

  cmCardAdd     = 211;
```

```
cmCardChange = 212;
cmCardDelete = 213;
cmCardNext   = 214;
cmCardRandom = 215;
```

Other commands will also be used, but these are already provided by Turbo Vision. The numbering scheme used for these commands reflects the menu structure that will support the commands. There is no requirement to use any specific values, other than using only nonreserved values.

Creating a Menu Bar

You can use Turbo Vision to create menus in two forms: horizontal and vertical. Their associated object types are TMenuBar and TMenuBox, respectively. Turbo Vision creates a global variable, MenuBar, for the menu bar associated with the main application. To assign menu items to this global variable, you must override the virtual method TApplication.InitMenuBar.

Here is the definition of the menu bar for the flash card application:

```
procedure TFlashCardApp.InitMenuBar;
var
  R : TRect;
begin
  GetExtent(R);
  R.B.Y := 1;
  MenuBar := New (PMenuBar, Init (R, NewMenu(
      NewSubMenu('~F~ile', hcNoContext, NewMenu (
        StdFileMenuItems(nil)),
      NewSubMenu ('~C~ard', hcNoContext, NewMenu (
        NewItem ('~A~dd', '', 0, cmCardAdd, hcNoContext,
        NewItem ('~C~hange', '', 0, cmCardChange, hcNoContext,
        NewItem ('~D~elete', '', 0, cmCardDelete, hcNoContext,
        NewItem ('~R~andom', 'F8', kbF8, cmCardRandom, hcNoContext,
        NewItem ('~N~ext', 'F9', kbF9, cmCardNext, hcNoContext,
        nil)))))),
    nil)))));
end;
```

The first step in creating a menu is to define its dimensions. This is done by first calling method GetExtent for the application object. All dimension rectangles are given relative to the view, so they all include (0,0) as their first corner. Since the menu bar takes only one line, you should set the bottom line to 1. Note that a menu's dimensions are for the main part of the menu only, not for any of its submenus.

The global variable MenuBar is actually a pointer to a menu, so it must be assigned a value using the procedure New. Using the extended form of this procedure, the second parameter to New is a call to TMenuBar.Init. Init is a fairly complex **constructor** because it must handle menus of any size. It requires the dimension rectangle and the menu items as parameters.

When you define the menu items, you are actually inserting them into a linked list. The functions NewMenu, NewSubMenu, and NewItem are required to define the list. The last parameter in each of these functions is a pointer to the next menu item (or submenu item), which will be **nil** for the last item.

Each menu entry contains five parts: the name of the entry, the name of a shortcut key for that entry (if applicable), the key code for the shortcut key, the command to be executed, and a help context key. The entry name can include a character enclosed by tilde (~) characters; this defines the letter that can be pressed to access that menu entry. For now, set all help context keys to the global constant hcNoContext, which defines no related help. The key codes are all defined as constants in the Drivers unit, and all start with the letters "kb".

The File menu in this program is one of three standard menus supplied by Turbo Vision. The other two, Edit and Window, are not applicable to this program since it doesn't use a clipboard or multiple windows. You should consider using these standards to save you time and promote consistency across applications. The names of the standard menu functions and the commands they generate are listed in the TMenuBar summary box.

TMenuBar Object Summary   **MENUS.TPU**

Heritage

TMenuBar → TMenuView → TView → TObject

Primary Method

```
constructor Init(var Bounds : TRect; AMenu : PMenu);
```

Creates a menu bar in the given rectangle.

Related Subprograms

```
function NewMenu(Items: PMenuItem): PMenu;
```

Creates the entries for a menu bar or menu box.

```
function NewSubMenu(Name : TMenuStr;  AHelpCtx : word;
         SubMenu : PMenu; Next : PMenuItem) : PMenuItem;
```

Creates a submenu within a menu bar or menu box.

```
function NewItem(Name, ShortCutName : TMenuStr;
         ShortCutKeyCode, ShortCutCommand : word;
         AHelpCtx : word; Next : PMenuItem) : PMenuItem;
```

Defines an item within a menu or submenu.

```
function NewLine(Next : PMenuItem) : PMenuItem;
```

Adds a horizontal line within a menu box.

```
function StdFileMenuItems(Next : PMenuItem) : PMenuItem;
```

Creates menu items for the standard file menu: New, Open, Save, Save As, Save All, Change Dir, DOS Shell, and Exit.

```
function StdEditMenuItems(Next : PMenuItem) : PMenuItem;
function StdWindowMenuItems(Next : PMenuItem) : PMenuItem;
```

Related Types

```
TMenu = record
  Items : PMenuItem;
  Default : PMenuItem
end;
```

Defines a menu, including its entries and which entry is the default.

```
PMenuItem = ^TMenuItem;
TMenuItem = record
  Next : PMenuItem;
  Name : PString;              { PString = ^String }
  Command : word;
  Disabled : boolean;
  KeyCode, HelpCtx : word;
  case integer of
    0 : (Param : PString);
    1 : (SubMenu : PMenu);
  end;
end;
```

Defines a menu entry.

```
TMenuStr = String[31];
```

The maximum length for a menu entry is 31 characters.

Related Constants

```
cmQuit = 1;
cmClose = 4;
cmZoom = 5;
cmResize = 6;
cmNext = 7;
cmPrevious = 8;
cmCut = 20;
cmCopy = 21;
cmPaste = 22;
cmUndo = 23;
cmClear = 24;
cmTile = 25;
cmCascade = 26;
cmNew = 30;
cmOpen = 31;
cmSave = 32;
cmSaveAs = 33;
cmSaveAll = 34;
cmChangeDir = 35;
cmDosShell = 36;
cmCloseAll = 37;
```

Commands generated from the standard menu items.

Other Methods

```
procedure Draw; virtual;
```

Called internally to display the menu bar.

```
procedure GetItemRect(Item : PMenuItem;
          var R : TRect); virtual;
```

Called internally to determine if a mouse click occurred in the menu box.

TMenuBox Object Summary   **MENUS.TPU**

Heritage

TMenuBox → TMenuView → TView → TObject

Primary Methods

```
constructor Init(var Bounds : TRect; AMenu : PMenu;
          AParentMenu : PMenuView);
```

Creates a menu box, often as a submenu.

Related Subprograms

See list in TMenuBar summary.

Other Methods

See list in TMenuBar summary.

kb*XXXX* Constant Summary   DRIVERS.TPU

Primary Values

```
kbF1 .. kbF10, kbCTRLF1 .. kbCTRLF10,
kbShiftF1 .. kbShiftF10, kbAltF1 .. kbAltF10,
kbAlt1 .. kbAlt0,
kbAltA .. kbAltZ,
kbEnter, kbEsc, kbTab, kbCtrlEnter,
kbUp, kbDown, kbLeft, kbRight,
kbHome, kbEnd, kbPgUp, kbPgDn,
kbCtrlLeft, kbCtrlRight,
kbCtrlHome, kbCtrlEnd, kbCtrlPgUp, kbCtrlPgDn,
kbIns, kbDel, kbShiftIns, kbShiftDel, kbCtrlIns, kbCtrlDel
```

Keyboard keys used to specify hot keys.

TRect Object Summary   OBJECTS.TPU

Heritage
None.

Primary Method

```
procedure Assign(XA, YA, XB, YB : integer);
```

Assigns values to the corners of the rectangle.

Related Types

```
TPoint = object
  X, Y : integer;
end;
```

Defines a point on the screen.

Other Methods

```
function Contains(P : TPoint): boolean;
```

Determines whether the point is inside the rectangle.

```
procedure Copy(R : TRect);
```

Assigns the values in R to the values in the object.

```
function Empty: boolean;
```

Determines whether any characters can fit in the rectangle.

```
function Equals(R : TRect) : boolean;
```

Determines whether the two rectangles are equal.

```
procedure Grow(ADX, ADY : integer);
```

Changes the size of the rectangle using the deltas.

```
procedure Intersect(R : TRect);
```

Reduces the size of the rectangle to become the intersection with the R rectangle.

```
procedure Move(ADX, ADY : integer);
```

Adds the deltas to both dimensions of the rectangle.

```
procedure Union(R : TRect);
```

Increases the size of the rectangle to become the union with the R rectangle.

Creating a Status Line

Defining the status line is similar to defining menus. This is the code that defines the status line for the flash card application:

```
procedure TFlashCardApp.InitStatusLine;
var
  R : TRect;
begin
GetExtent(R);
R.A.Y := R.B.Y - 1;
StatusLine := New (PStatusLine, Init (R,
    NewStatusDef (0, $FFFF,
      NewStatusKey ('~ALT-X~ Exit', kbAltX, cmQuit,
      NewStatusKey ('~F2~ Save', kbF2, cmSave,
      NewStatusKey ('~F3~ Open', kbF3, cmOpen,
      NewStatusKey ('~F8~ Random', kbF8, cmCardRandom,
      NewStatusKey ('~F9~ Next', kbF9, cmCardNext,
      NewStatusKey ('~F10~ Menu', kbF10, cmMenu,
      nil)))))),
    nil)));
end;
```

As with the menu bar, this method starts by assigning a rectangle to the dimensions of the status line (at the bottom of the screen, this time). Then it initializes the pointer StatusLine with a call to Init, which requires a list of status key items.

Each status key has three parts: the string entry that normally includes the key name and the command name, the code for the hot key, and the command to be executed. The key name is normally enclosed in tilde characters, so it appears in a highlighted color.

TStatusLine Object Summary   MENUS.TPU

Heritage

TStatusLine ➡ TView ➡ TObject

Primary Method

```
constructor Init(var Bounds: TRect; ADefs: PStatusDef);
```

Creates a status line in the given rectangle.

Related Subprograms

```
function NewStatusDef(AMin, AMax : word;
          AItems : PStatusItem;
          ANext : PStatusDef) : PStatusDef;
```

Creates the entries for a status line. AMin and AMax represent valid values for help contexts.

```
function NewStatusKey(AText : String; AKeyCode : word;
        ACommand : word;
        ANext : PStatusItem) : PStatusItem;
```

Creates a single entry for a status line, including the key name, key code, and command name.

Related Types

```
PStatusDef = ^TStatusDef;
TStatusDef = record
  Next : PStatusDef;
  Min, Max : word;
  Items : PStatusItem;
end;
```

Defines a status line, including the help context range.

```
PStatusItem = ^TStatusItem;
TStatusItem = record
  Next : PStatusItem;
  Text : PString;
  KeyCode : word;
  Command : word;
end;
```

Defines an item on the status line.

Other Methods

```
destructor Done; virtual;
```

Releases memory containing the status line; normally called internally.

```
procedure Draw; virtual;
```

Called internally to draw the status line on the screen.

```
function GetPalette : PPalette; virtual;
```

Can be overridden to change the color scheme.

```
procedure HandleEvent(var Event : TEvent); virtual;
```

Called internally to handle status line events.

```
procedure Hint(AHelpCtx : word): String; virtual;
```

Must be overridden to provide a one-line help message in the status line.

```
constructor Load(var S : TStream);
```

Called internally to load a status line from a stream.

```
procedure Store(var S : TStream);
```

Called internally to store the status line to a stream.

```
procedure Update;
```

Redraws the status line based on the help context.

Creating the Event Handler

The final piece in the outer layer of each application object is the event handler. You can create an event handler by overriding the method TProgram.HandleEvent.

Any event handler must first call its ancestor's event handler. The rest of the structure is easier to copy as a template than to understand. For the flash card application, the event handler looks like this:

```
procedure TFlashCardApp.HandleEvent(var Event: TEvent);
begin
  TApplication.HandleEvent(Event);
  if Event.What = evCommand then
    begin
      case Event.Command of
        cmOpen        : OpenFile(FlashCards);
        cmSave        : SaveFile(FlashCards);
```

```
        cmCardAdd    : AddCard(FlashCards);
        cmCardChange : ChangeCard;
        cmCardDelete : DeleteCard(FlashCards);
        cmCardNext   : NextCard(FlashCards);
        cmCardRandom : RandomCard(FlashCards);
        else
          Exit;
        end;
      ClearEvent(Event);
    end;
end;
```

All event handlers should have the same **case** statement nested inside the **if-then** statement. The options for the **case** statement are the applications commands.

Notice that when a command is received, the event handler simply calls a procedure to process the command. For prototyping purposes, you might consider calling MessageBox for each command processor. Here are the stubs for the flash card commands:

```
Unit FLCMD1;

interface

const
(* application event commands *)
  cmCardAdd    = 211;
  cmCardChange = 212;
  cmCardDelete = 213;
  cmCardNext   = 214;
  cmCardRandom = 215;

procedure OpenFile;
procedure SaveFile;
procedure AddCard;
procedure ChangeCard;
procedure DeleteCard;
procedure NextCard;
procedure RandomCard;

implementation

uses MsgBox;

procedure OpenFile;
begin
  MessageBox('Open File not implemented yet', nil, mfOkButton);
end;
```

```
procedure SaveFile;
begin
  MessageBox('Save File not implemented yet', nil, mfOkButton);
end;


procedure AddCard;
begin
  MessageBox('Add Card not implemented yet', nil, mfOkButton);
end;


procedure ChangeCard;
begin
  MessageBox('Change Card not implemented yet', nil, mfOkButton);
end;


procedure DeleteCard;
begin
  MessageBox('Delete Card not implemented yet', nil, mfOkButton);
end;


procedure NextCard;
begin
  MessageBox('Next Card not implemented yet', nil, mfOkButton);
end;


procedure RandomCard;
begin
  MessageBox('Random Card not implemented yet', nil, mfOkButton);
end;


end.
```

The MessageBox procedure is a simple dialog box that has your message plus an OK button. Later each of these procedures will be implemented and tested, and the call to MessageBox removed.

Given the three methods just defined, you can create the final definition of the *TFlashCardApp* object:

```
type
  TFlashCardApp = object(TApplication)
    procedure InitMenuBar; virtual;
```

```
      procedure InitStatusLine; virtual;
      procedure HandleEvent(var Event : TEvent); virtual;
   end;
```

Almost every application you write will override these three methods. You may also choose to override TApplication.Init to include program initialization code, although it's usually better to keep them separate. The following listing shows the flash card application as it is completed so far:

```
Program Flashcard_App1;

uses FLCMD1,
      App, Menus, Objects, Views, Drivers;

type
  TFlashCardApp = Object(TApplication)
    procedure InitMenuBar; virtual;
    procedure InitStatusLine; virtual;
    procedure HandleEvent(var Event : TEvent); virtual;
  end;

var
  FlashCardApp : TFlashCardApp;

(*************************************************)

procedure TFlashCardApp.InitMenuBar;
var
  R : TRect;
begin
  GetExtent(R);
  R.B.Y := 1;
  MenuBar := New (PMenuBar, Init (R, NewMenu(
     NewSubMenu('~F~ile', hcNoContext, NewMenu
               (StdFileMenuItems(nil)),
       NewSubMenu ('~C~ard', hcNoContext, NewMenu (
       NewItem ('~A~dd', '', 0, cmCardAdd, hcNoContext,
       NewItem ('~C~hange', '', 0, cmCardChange, hcNoContext,
       NewItem ('~D~elete', '', 0, cmCardDelete, hcNoContext,
       NewItem ('~R~andom', 'F8', kbF8, cmCardRandom, hcNoContext,
       NewItem ('~N~ext', 'F9', kbF9, cmCardNext, hcNoContext,
       nil)))))),
     nil)))));
end;

(*************************************************)

procedure TFlashCardApp.InitStatusLine;
```

```
var
  R : TRect;
begin
GetExtent(R);
R.A.Y := R.B.Y - 1;
StatusLine := New (PStatusLine, Init (R,
    NewStatusDef (0, $FFFF,
      NewStatusKey ('~ALT-X~ Exit', kbAltX, cmQuit,
      NewStatusKey ('~F2~ Save', kbF2, cmSave,
      NewStatusKey ('~F3~ Open', kbF3, cmOpen,
      NewStatusKey ('~F8~ Random', kbF8, cmCardRandom,
      NewStatusKey ('~F9~ Next', kbF9, cmCardNext,
      NewStatusKey ('~F10~ Menu', kbF10, cmMenu,
      nil)))))),
    nil)));
end;

(************************************************)

procedure TFlashCardApp.HandleEvent(var Event: TEvent);
begin
  TApplication.HandleEvent(Event);
  if Event.What = evCommand then
    begin
      case Event.Command of
        cmOpen       : OpenFile;
        cmSave       : SaveFile;
        cmCardAdd    : AddCard;
        cmCardChange : ChangeCard;
        cmCardDelete : DeleteCard;
        cmCardNext   : NextCard;
        cmCardRandom : RandomCard;
        else
          Exit;
        end;
      ClearEvent(Event);
    end;
end;

(************************************************)

begin
  FlashCardApp.Init;
  FlashCardApp.Run;
  FlashCardApp.Done;
end.
```

TProgram Object Summary   APP.TPU

Heritage

TProgram → TGroup → TView → TObject

Primary Methods

```
procedure HandleEvent(var Event : TEvent); virtual;
```

Overridden to allow for event handling in each application. Any method that overrides this should call this method as its first statement. Without an override, it handles only internal events.

```
procedure InitMenuBar; virtual;
```

Overridden to create a menu bar at the top of the screen. Without an override, it creates an empty menu bar.

```
procedure InitStatusLine; virtual;
```

Overridden to create a status line at the bottom of the screen. Without an override, it creates a status line with the ALT-X Quit command only.

```
procedure Run; virtual;
```

Called internally to start the application's event handler.

Related Global Variables

```
Application : PApplication = nil;
```

Stores a pointer to the main application object.

```
DeskTop : PDeskTop = nil;
```

Stores a pointer to the desktop for the application.

```
MenuBar : PMenuView = nil;
```

Stores a pointer to the main menu (bar or box) for the application.

```
StatusLine : PStatusLine = nil;
```

Stores a pointer to the status line for the application.

Related Types

```
TEvent = record
  What : word;
  case word of
    {...}
    evMessage: (Command : word {...} );
end;
```

Defines an event (internal information has been omitted).

Other Methods

```
Destructor Done;
```

Called internally to dispose of the desktop, main menu, and status line.

```
procedure GetEvent(var Event : TEvent); virtual;
```

Called internally to see if an event has occurred.

```
procedure GetPalette : PPalette; virtual;
```

Can be overridden to change the color schemes for the entire application.

```
procedure Idle; virtual;
```

Can be overridden to accomplish tasks in background mode while no events have occurred.

```
constructor Init;
```

Called internally to initialize internal variables.

```
procedure InitScreen; virtual;
```

Called internally to change the screen mode.

```
procedure OutOfMemory; virtual;
```

Can be overridden to handle the inability of the program to access enough memory. By default, it does nothing.

```
procedure PutEvent(var Event : TEvent); virtual;
```

Called internally to store the current event in an internal buffer.

```
procedure SetScreenMode(Mode : word);
```

Sets the screen mode. Valid constants are smCO80, smBW80, and smMono. For extended line mode, smFont8x8 can also be included.

```
function ValidView(P : PView) : PView;
```

Called internally to check the validity of a view and make sure there was enough memory to create it.

TDeskTop Object Summary   **APP.TPU**

Heritage

TDeskTop → TGroup → TView → TObject

Primary Inherited Methods

Inherited from TGroup (see TGroup summary):

```
procedure Delete(P : PView);
function ExecView(P : PView): word;
procedure Insert(P : PView);
```

Other Methods

```
procedure Cascade(var R: TRect);
```

Cascades all windows that are tileable (normally this excludes dialog boxes).

```
procedure HandleEvent(var Event : TEvent); virtual;
```

Called internally to handle events in the desktop.

```
constructor Init(var Bounds : TRect);
```

Called internally to create the desktop.

```
function NewBackground : PView; virtual;
```

Can be overridden to change the default background.

```
procedure Tile(var R : TRect);
```

Tiles all windows that are tileable (normally this excludes dialog boxes).

```
procedure TileError; virtual;
```

Called internally when an error has occurred attempting to tile. By default, it does nothing.

TGroup Object Summary   VIEWS.TPU

Heritage

TGroup → TView → TObject

Primary Methods

```
procedure Delete(P : PView);
```

Removes a view from the group.

```
function ExecView(P : PView) : word;
```

Executes a modal view. Control stays in that view until an appropriate command exits the view. The exit command is returned by the function.

```
procedure Insert(P : PView);
```

Adds a view to the group. This normally causes the view to appear on the screen.

Other Methods

Group objects are almost never created explicitly, so their internal methods are of little value. See the methods for each descendant object type.

Writing Support Code

Until now you have watched the development of an application prototype that can support any Turbo Vision program. Once you are satisfied with the design and the interface, you must start on the implementation of the "meat" of the program. In this section, you will see the lowest level of the flash card application, an object that represents a single flash card. The next sections build on this object until the application is complete.

In the spirit of OOP, the rest of the design revolves around two objects: *TFlashCard,* which models a single flash card, and *TFlashCardSet,* which represents a group of flash cards. The implementation of *TFlashCard* is straightforward. As you can see by the FLCARD unit, the flash card object is similar in form to the *TPerson* object that you studied in Chapter 4, "Subprograms":

```
Unit FLCARD;

interface

uses Objects;
```

```
const
  QAMaxLen = 50;
type
  FlashStr = string [QAMaxLen];
  PFlashCard = ^TFlashCard;
  TFlashCard = object(TObject)
    constructor Init;
    function GetNumber : integer;
    function GetNumberStr : string;
    function GetQuestion : FlashStr;
    function GetAnswer : FlashStr;
    procedure SetNumber(NewNumber : integer);
    procedure SetQuestion(NewQuestion : FlashStr);
    procedure SetAnswer(NewAnswer : FlashStr);
  private
    Number : integer;
    Question : FlashStr;
    Answer : FlashStr;
  end;


implementation

constructor TFlashCard.Init;
begin
  Question := ' ';
  Answer := ' ';
end;

(************************************************)

function TFlashCard.GetNumber : integer;
begin
  GetNumber := Number;
end;

(************************************************)

function TFlashCard.GetNumberStr : string;
var
  CNumStr : string[3];
begin
  Str(GetNumber, CNumStr);
  GetNumberStr := CNumStr;
end;

(************************************************)

function TFlashCard.GetQuestion : FlashStr;
```

```
begin
  GetQuestion := Question;
end;


(************************************************)


function TFlashCard.GetAnswer : FlashStr;
begin
  GetAnswer := Answer;
end;


(************************************************)


procedure TFlashCard.SetNumber(NewNumber : Integer);
begin
  Number := NewNumber;
end;


(************************************************)


procedure TFlashCard.SetQuestion(NewQuestion : FlashStr);
begin
  Question := NewQuestion;
end;


(************************************************)


procedure TFlashCard.SetAnswer(NewAnswer : FlashStr);
begin
  Answer := NewAnswer;
end;

end.
```

You may have noticed that *TFlashCard* is a descendent of TObject. All objects you create to run in Turbo Vision should be created from TObject. That way you can easily create collections and streams of the objects, as you will see later in this chapter.

TObject Object Summary   **OBJECTS.TPU**

Heritage

None.

Primary Methods

```
constructor Init;
```

Allocates the space for an object and initializes all fields (sets them to zeros).

```
procedure Free;
```

Disposes of an object.

Other Method

```
destructor Done; virtual;
```

Called internally by Free to handle memory cleanup for an object.

Creating Collections

How many times have you written code to support arrays or linked lists? Every time you create a new record structure, you find yourself writing more code to support collections of that structure. With Turbo Vision, you may never have to write array support software again.

Turbo Vision includes an object type called TCollection, as well as a few descendant object types. These collection objects are independent of the user interface software, so they can be used easily in any application. Even more advantageous is that collections are polymorphic: Used properly, they can store different objects in the same set. If you want the collection to stay sorted at all times, use TSortedCollection. Be aware, however, that sorted collections do not support duplicate entries. If you need this ability, you must create your own descendant.

A Turbo Vision collection is a list of pointers. Therefore, to use a collection object, you do not need to create a descendant object type. For proper encapsulation, however, you will often create descendants anyway, to refine the functionality of the object type.

To make this clearer, look at the definition of the *TFlashCardSet* object in the FLSET unit:

```
Unit FLSET;

interface
```

```
uses Objects, FLCARD;

type
  PFlashCardSet = ^TFlashCardSet;
  TFlashCardSet = object(TCollection)
    constructor Init;
    function NewCard : PFlashCard;
    procedure Replace(ACard : PFlashCard);
    procedure Delete(ACard : PFlashCard);
    function NextCard : PFlashCard;
    function AnyCard : PFlashCard;
  private
    CurrentCard : integer;
  end;
```

This object definition provides complete functionality for a set of flash cards.

Now, examine each method of *TFlashCardSet* in more detail. The initialization is done primarily through a call to TCollection.Init:

```
constructor TFlashCardSet.Init;
begin
  TCollection.Init(10, 5);
  CurrentCard := -1;
  Randomize;
end;
```

Init requires two parameters: the initial size of the collection and the amount the collection will grow when the initial size is exceeded. The growth process takes a relatively long time when the collections get large, so choose these numbers carefully. The call to Randomize is to support the ability to select flash cards at random.

Normally, when you want to add an object to a collection, you enter the data and then insert the pointer into the collection. From an object oriented sense, however, the flash card method works more like this: "Give me a new blank card, let me fill in both sides, and replace it in the set." Here is the *NewCard* method:

```
function TFlashCardSet.NewCard : PFlashCard;
var
  BlankCard : PFlashCard;
begin
  New(BlankCard, Init);
  TCollection.Insert(BlankCard);
  BlankCard^.SetNumber(Count);
  NewCard := BlankCard;
end;
```

Collections number their entries from 0 to N-1, just like most computer science applications. Flash cards, however, are used by everyone, so it makes more sense to number them from 1 to N (where N is the number of cards). This number-shifting is evident in the *Replace* and *Delete* methods, shown here:

```
procedure TFlashCardSet.Replace(ACard : PFlashCard);
begin
  TCollection.AtPut(ACard^.GetNumber - 1, ACard);
end;

(************************************************)

procedure TFlashCardSet.Delete(ACard : PFlashCard);
begin
  TCollection.AtDelete(ACard^.GetNumber - 1);
end;
```

The final two methods (actually you'll see a few more later in the chapter) retrieve cards from the set, either in sequential order or in random order:

```
function TFlashCardSet.NextCard : PFlashCard;
var
  ACard : PFlashCard;
begin
  CurrentCard := CurrentCard + 1;
  if CurrentCard = Count then
    CurrentCard := 0;
  ACard := TCollection.At(CurrentCard);
  if ACard <> nil then
    ACard^.SetNumber(CurrentCard+1);
  NextCard := ACard;
end;

(************************************************)

function TFlashCardSet.AnyCard : PFlashCard;
var
  ACard : PFlashCard;
begin
  CurrentCard := Random(Count);
  ACard := TCollection.At(CurrentCard);
  ACard^.SetNumber(CurrentCard + 1);
  AnyCard := ACard;
end;
```

Notice that both of these methods set the number of a flash card, even though the number is stored in the collection. The reason is that, when the collection deletes an object, it doesn't know anything about numbering of the objects, so it can't make any updates. Therefore, the flash card numbers stored in the collection are not necessarily correct.

TCollection Object Summary   **OBJECTS.TPU**

Heritage

TCollection ➞ TObject

Primary Field

```
Count : integer;
```

The only way to determine current size of the collection is to access this data field.

Primary Methods

```
constructor Init(ALimit, ADelta : integer);
```

Creates a collection object with the desired initial size. When that size is exceeded, the collection will grow based on ADelta.

```
function At(Index : integer) : pointer;
```

Gets a pointer to the *n*th entry in the collection.

```
procedure AtDelete(Index : integer);
```

Deletes the *n*th entry in the collection.

```
function AtInsert(Index : integer; Item : pointer);
```

Inserts the new entry at the *n*th position. Entry positions beyond Index are incremented by one.

```
function AtPut(Index : integer; Item : pointer);
```

Replaces the nth entry in the collection.

```
procedure Delete(Item : pointer);
```

Deletes a specific entry in the collection.

```
procedure DeleteAll;
```

Deletes all entries in the collection.

```
destructor Done; virtual;
```

Disposes the entire collection.

```
function FirstThat(Test : pointer): pointer;
```

Searches for a specific entry in the collection. Test is the address of the boolean function that defines the condition. That function must be local to the subprogram that requires it and must be declared as a **far** function.

```
procedure ForEach(Action : pointer);
```

Executes the specified procedure for every entry in the collection. Action is the address of a procedure that performs on a single entry. That procedure must be local to the subprogram that requires it and must be declared as a **far** function.

```
function IndexOf(Item : pointer) : integer; virtual;
```

Determines the index of an entry in the collection.

```
procedure Insert(Item : pointer); virtual;
```

Inserts an entry at the end of the collection.

```
function LastThat(Test : pointer) : pointer;
```

Searches in reverse for a specific entry in the collection. Test is the address of the boolean function that defines the condition. That function must be local to the subprogram that requires it and must be declared as a **far** function.

Other Methods

```
procedure Error(Code, Info : integer); virtual;
```

Called internally to handle errors. By default, the procedure causes a run-time error.

```
function GetItem(var S : TStream) : pointer; virtual;
```

Called internally to retrieve an entry from the stream. Must be overridden only if the entry type is not a descendant of TObject.

```
constructor Load(var S : TStream);
```

Called internally to load the collection from a stream.

```
procedure Pack;
```

Removes all entries that point to **nil.**

```
procedure PutItem(var S : TStream; Item : pointer); virtual;
```

Called internally to write an entry to the stream. Must be overridden only if the entry type is not a descendant of TObject.

```
procedure SetLimit(ALimit : integer); virtual;
```

Changes the size of the collection. Although the collection will grow automatically, you may want this to shrink the collection after many entries have been deleted. It actually copies the collection into a smaller one, so it takes a long time.

```
procedure Store(var S : TStream);
```

Called internally to write the collection to the stream.

TSortedCollection Object Summary   **OBJECTS.TPU**

Heritage

TSortedCollection ➔ TCollection ➔ TObject

Primary Methods

```
function Compare(Key1, Key2 : pointer) : integer; virtual;
```

Must be overridden with a function that compares the two keys, and returns -1, 0, or 1 based on the comparison.

```
function IndexOf(Item : pointer) : integer; virtual;
```

Searches for an entry and returns its index. If the entry is not in the collection, it returns the value -1.

```
procedure Insert(Item : pointer); virtual;
```

Adds an entry to the collection in the proper place.

Primary Inherited Methods

From TCollection (see TCollection summary):

```
Count : integer;    {a data field}
constructor Init(ALimit, ADelta);
function FirstThat(Test : pointer): pointer;
procedure ForEach(Action : pointer);
function LastThat(Test : pointer): pointer;
```

Other Methods

```
function KeyOf(Item : pointer): pointer; virtual;
```

Can be overridden if the Item is not the entire key.

```
function Search(Key : pointer; var Index: integer) :
          boolean; virtual;
```

Called internally to search for a key in the collection.

TStringCollection Object Summary   **OBJECTS.TPU**

Heritage

TStringCollection ➞ TSortedCollection ➞ TCollection ➞ TObject

Primary Inherited Methods

From TSortedCollection (see TSortedCollection summary):

```
function IndexOf(Item : pointer) : integer; virtual;
procedure Insert(Item : pointer); virtual;
```

From TCollection (see TCollection summary):

```
Count : integer;    {a data field}
constructor Init(ALimit, ADelta);
function FirstThat(Test : pointer): pointer;
procedure ForEach(Action : pointer);
function LastThat(Test : pointer);
```

Other Methods

```
function Compare(Key1, Key2 : pointer) : integer; virtual;
```

A pure ASCII string comparison; may be overridden to sort using a different comparison.

```
procedure FreeItem(Item : pointer); virtual;
```

Called internally to dispose of a string in the collection.

```
function GetItem(var S : TStream); pointer; virtual;
```

Called internally to read a string from the stream.

```
procedure PutItem(var S : TStream;  Item : pointer); virtual;
```

Called internally to write a string to the stream.

Creating a Simple Dialog Box

Being familiar with the Turbo Pascal environment, you already know how dialog boxes operate, and what types of I/O can be represented. Creating your own dialog box is a matter of initializing an empty box and then inserting the pieces you want.

To ease you into the methods of dialog box design, consider the creation of a very simple box. This box will have one button on it. When the box is displayed on the screen, a user must press that button in order to continue.

Study the code for the procedure that creates this simple dialog box:

```pascal
procedure NotApplicableBox(Name : string);
var
  Dialog : PDialog;
  R : TRect;
  Control : word;
begin
  R.Assign(20, 9, 55, 15);
  Dialog := New(PDialog, Init(R, Name));
  with Dialog^ do
    begin
      R.Assign(4, 2, 29, 4);
      Insert(New(PButton, Init(R, '(not applicable)',
            cmOK, bfDefault)));
    end;
  Control := DeskTop^.ExecView(Dialog);
end;
```

The first step in creating a dialog box is to assign the area of the screen where the box will appear. For this you use R.Assign, just like you did for menus and status lines. Then you allocate memory to a dialog pointer, using New. This creates a blank dialog box with the title taken from a parameter.

The next step is to insert one or more standard objects. In this case a button was chosen. After you assign a rectangular area for the button, Insert is called with an initialization of the button. This initialization includes the text that will appear and the event that will be generated when the button is pressed.

When you've completely defined the dialog box, you make a call to ExecView. This function displays the dialog box and accepts no commands other than the ones defined by the box itself. This exclusiveness makes this dialog box a modal view. Later in this chapter, you will see how to make nonmodal dialog boxes.

The MessageBox procedure is an excellent tool to display a simple dialog box, but it only supports four types of buttons: OK, Cancel, Yes, and No. If you need a button with text other than those four, you need to write your own. You will learn about writing more complex dialog boxes in the next section.

TDialog Object Summary **DIALOGS.TPU**

Heritage

TDialog → TWindow → TGroup → TView → TObject

Primary Method

```
constructor Init(var Bounds : TRect;  ATitle : TTitleStr);
```

Creates a dialog box with the given dimensions and title.

Related Constants

```
cmOK = 10;
```

Event set when user presses the OK button or presses ENTER.

```
cmCancel = 11;
```

Event set when user presses the Cancel button or presses ESCAPE.

```
cmYes = 12;
```

Event set when user presses the Yes button, if there is one.

```
cmNo = 13;
```

Event set when user presses the No button, if applicable.

Primary Inherited Method

Inherited from TGroup (see TGroup summary):

```
procedure Insert(P : PView);
```

Inherited from TView (see TView summary):

```
procedure GetData(var Rec); virtual;
procedure SetData(var Rec); virtual;
```

Other Methods

```
procedure HandleEvent(var Event : TEvent); virtual;
```

Called internally to handle cmOK, cmCancel, cmYes, and cmNo. All other events are raised to the parent object.

```
function GetPalette : PPalette; virtual;
```

Can be overridden to change the dialog box colors.

```
function Valid(Command : word) : boolean; virtual;
```

Called internally to determine if the command is valid.

TView Object Summary   VIEWS.TPU

Heritage

TView ➡ TObject

Primary Methods

```
procedure GetData(var Rec); virtual;
```

Copies a number of bytes from its internal structure to the parameter, based on the size of the parameter.

```
procedure GetExtent(var Extent : TRect);
```

Returns a rectangle, with a (0,0) origin, that matches the current size of the view.

```
procedure SetData(var Rec); virtual;
```

Copies a number of bytes from the parameter to its internal structure, based on the size of the parameter.

Other Methods

View objects are almost never created explicitly, so their internal methods are of little value. See the methods for each descendant object type.

Creating More Complex Dialog Boxes

Until now, you have seen the skeleton user interface and the internal mechanisms for the flash card application. In this section, you will see how to put everything together to create a working program. The procedures in this section are part of the FLASHCMD unit; it has an interface like this:

```
Unit FLASHCMD;

interface

uses FLSET;

const
(* application event commands *)
  cmCardAdd    = 211;
  cmCardChange = 212;
  cmCardDelete = 213;
  cmCardNext   = 214;
  cmCardRandom = 215;
  cmShowAnswer = 231;

procedure NewFile;
procedure OpenFile(var NewSet : TFlashCardSet);
procedure SaveFile(var TheSet : TFlashCardSet);
procedure AddCard(var ToSet : TFlashCardSet);
procedure ChangeCard;
procedure DeleteCard(var FromSet : TFlashCardSet);
procedure NextCard(var TheSet : TFlashCardSet);
procedure RandomCard(var TheSet : TFlashCardSet);
procedure ShowAnswer;
procedure RemoveBoxes;

implementation
```

```
uses FLCARD,
      StdDlg, Dialogs, Views, App, MsgBox, Objects, Dos;
```

Most of the commands involve the use of dialog boxes so you can see more examples of dialog box entries. The first example is the AddCard procedure:

```
procedure AddCard(var ToSet : TFlashCardSet);
type
  TEditData = record
    Ans : FlashStr;
    Quest : FlashStr;
  end;
var
  Dialog : PDialog;
  R : TRect;
  Control : word;
  Q, A : PView;
  CardNumber : string;
  EditData : TEditData;
  ACard : PFlashCard;
begin
  (* repeat as long as the user wants to make additions *)
  repeat

    (* create the dialog box *)
    R.Assign(20, 6, 55, 20);
    Dialog := New(PDialog, Init(R, 'Add Card'));
    with Dialog^ do
      begin

        (* insert the card number as static text *)
        New(ACard, Init);
        ACard := ToSet.NewCard;
        Str(ACard^.GetNumber, CardNumber);
        R.Assign(3, 2, 29, 3);
        Insert(New(PStaticText,
            Init(R, 'Card Number : '+ CardNumber)));

        (* insert the answer InputLine with a label *)
        R.Assign(2, 8, 29, 9);
        A := New(PInputLine, Init(R, QAMaxLen));
        Insert(A);
        R.Assign(2, 7, 12, 8);
        Insert(New(PLabel, Init(R, 'Answer:', A)));

        (* insert the Ok command as a button *)
        R.Assign(5, 11, 15, 13);
        Insert(New(PButton,
```

```
                Init(R, '~O~K', cmOK, bfDefault)));

          (* insert the Cancel command as a button *)
          R.Assign(18, 11, 28, 13);
          Insert(New(PButton,
              Init(R, 'Cancel', cmCancel, bfNormal)));

          (* insert the question InputLine with a label *)
          R.Assign(2, 5, 29, 6);
          Q := New(PInputLine, Init(R, QAMaxLen));
          Insert(Q);
          R.Assign(2, 4, 12, 5);
          Insert(New(PLabel, Init(R, 'Question:', Q)));

          (* give values to the input lines *)
          EditData.Quest := ACard^.GetQuestion;
          EditData.Ans := ACard^.GetAnswer;
          SetData(EditData);
        end;

    (* execute the dialog box *)
    Control := DeskTop^.ExecView(Dialog);

    if Control <> cmCancel then
      begin

        (* save the information entered *)
        Dialog^.GetData(EditData);
        ACard^.SetQuestion(EditData.Quest);
        ACard^.SetAnswer(EditData.Ans);
        ToSet.Replace(ACard);
      end
    else

      (* ignore the information entered and remove the card *)
      ToSet.Delete(ACard);
  until Control = cmCancel;
end;
```

This procedure starts by creating a dialog box. It then adds seven objects to the box. The first is the card number. Because this number cannot be changed by the user, the PStaticText object is used.

The last two objects actually go near the top of the dialog box. They are added last because they are the default items. These objects consist of a TInputLine, used to enter data, and a TLabel, which is a label for the input line. The label is linked to the input line object so that when the user tabs to that item, the label is highlighted. The rest of the objects are another input line and label pair, and two buttons.

Once you define a dialog box that requires data entry, you must assign initial values to entry areas. This process requires the definition of the TEditData record. After you assign values to the fields in this record, a call to the SetData method stores the data in the internal structures of the dialog box.

The ExecView method is called after the data values are set. This method does all of the I/O for the dialog box. It terminates only when the user presses one of the two buttons. The value of the button pressed is returned as the value of the function.

If the user presses the OK button, the GetData method is called to retrieve the values entered. Those values are then used in a call to the *Replace* method of the flash card set. The entire sequence is placed in a repeat loop to allow the user to enter multiple cards.

For the display of the flash cards, a different methodology was selected. Since there is one dialog box for the question and one for the answer, the two must work together. One way to accomplish this is to define global variables for the dialog boxes and process events outside the dialog boxes rather than within them. Here are the required global variables:

```
var
  TheCard : PFlashCard;

const
  QBox : PDialog = nil;
  ABox : PDialog = nil;
```

The first dialog box of the pair is the one that displays the question side of a flash card. Its dialog box looks like this:

```
procedure ShowQuestion;
var
  R : TRect;
  Control : word;
  CardNumber : string;
begin

  (* create the dialog box *)
  R.Assign(5, 2, 75, 11);
  QBox := New(PDialog, Init(R, 'Question'));
  with QBox^ do
    begin

      (* insert the question as static text *)
      R.Assign(4, 2, 63, 3);
      Insert(New(PStaticText, Init(R, TheCard^.GetQuestion)));

      (* include a Cancel button to allow user to stop *)
      R.Assign(40, 5, 50, 7);
```

```
        Insert(New(PButton,
            Init(R, 'Cancel', cmCancel, bfNormal)));

        (* include a Show Answer button for that command *)
        R.Assign(3, 5, 18, 7);
        Insert(New(PButton, Init(R, 'Show ~A~nswer',
                        cmShowAnswer, bfDefault)));

        (* insert the card number as static text *)
        R.Assign(55, 5, 65, 6);
        Str(TheCard^.GetNumber, CardNumber);
        Insert(New(PStaticText, Init(R, 'Card: '+ CardNumber)));
    end;

  (* add the dialog box to the desktop (don't make it modal) *)
  Desktop^.Insert(QBox);
end;
```

The dialog box itself has no new types of items—it has two static texts and two buttons. The user cannot enter any data, so much of the code in the previous dialog box is not required. You may have noticed a new command constant: *cmShowAnswer*. There is no menu or status line entry for this command, but it is required for the implementation.

Instead of calling ExecView to add the dialog box to the desktop, this procedure calls Insert. The Insert method adds the dialog box, but it allows events to occur outside of the box. This is the nonmodal form of a dialog box. In this case, it was required because you don't want the question box to be erased when the answer is displayed. Modal views are closed before control is passed back to the caller.

If the user selects the Show Answer button, the program displays the answer side of the flash card. The following procedure does this:

```
procedure ShowAnswer;
var
  R : TRect;
  Control : word;
begin

  (* create the dialog box *)
  R.Assign(5, 13, 75, 22);
  ABox := New(PDialog, Init(R, 'Answer'));
  with ABox^ do
    begin

      (* insert the answer as static text *)
      R.Assign(4, 2, 63, 3);
      Insert(New(PStaticText, Init(R, TheCard^.GetAnswer)));
```

```
      (* include a Next Question button *)
      R.Assign(25, 5, 42, 7);
      Insert(New(PButton, Init(R, '~N~ext Question',
                          cmCardNext, bfNormal)));

      (* include a Cancel button *)
      R.Assign(47, 5, 58, 7);
      Insert(New(PButton,
          Init(R, 'Cancel', cmCancel, bfNormal)));

      (* include a Random Question button *)
      R.Assign(3, 5, 23, 7);
      Insert(New(PButton, Init(R, '~R~andom Question',
                          cmCardRandom, bfDefault)));
    end;

  (* add the dialog box to the desktop *)
  DeskTop^.Insert(ABox);
end;
```

The dialog box itself presents nothing new. The logic is defined by the events that
will occur when the user presses any of the various buttons.

Before examining that logic, study the last three command procedures:

```
procedure NextCard(var TheSet : TFlashCardSet);
begin
  TheCard := TheSet.NextCard;
  RemoveBoxes;
  ShowQuestion;
end;

(***********************************************)

procedure RandomCard(var TheSet : TFlashCardSet);
begin
  TheCard := TheSet.AnyCard;
  RemoveBoxes;
  ShowQuestion;
end;

(***********************************************)

procedure RemoveBoxes;
begin
  Desktop^.Delete(ABox);
  if ABox <> nil then
    begin
      Dispose(ABox, Done);
```

```
      ABox := nil;
    end;
  Desktop^.Delete(QBox);
  if QBox <> nil then
    begin;
      Desktop^.Delete(QBox);
      Dispose(QBox, Done);
      QBox := nil;
    end;
end.-
```

The last procedure, *RemoveBoxes,* is also not part of the main menu, but it was added to support the nonmodal dialog boxes.

Here is how the commands work together:

1. The user starts by selecting Random Card or Next Card. Either of these clears the desktop and displays a question.

2. If the user wants to see the answer, that user presses the button, generating the *cmShowAnswer* event, which displays the answer.

3. If the user does not want to see the answer, the user can do one of three things:

    • Press the Cancel button, which clears the desktop.

    • Enter F8 or the Random Card menu command, which displays another question without showing the answer.

    • Enter F9 or the Next Card menu command, which displays the next question without showing the answer. Presumably the user would use one of these last two options when the answer is obvious.

4. Once the answer side of the card is displayed, the user has the same three options, but these options are all included as buttons in the dialog box.

TButton Object Summary   **DIALOGS.TPU**

Heritage

TButton ➡ TView ➡ TObject

Primary Method

```
constructor Init(var Bounds : TRect; ATitle: TTitleStr;
          ACommand : word; AFlags : Byte);
```

Creates a button object for insertion into a dialog box. Each button has a name and an event command (raised if the button is "pushed").

Related Constants

```
bfNormal = $00;
```

Flag for non-default, centered buttons.

```
bfDefault = $01;
```

Flag for default, centered buttons.

```
bfLeftJust = $02;
```

Flag for non-default, left-justified buttons.

```
bfDefault + bfLeftJust
```

Combination for default, left-justified buttons.

Other Methods

```
destructor Done; virtual;
```

Disposes of the fields for the button.

```
procedure Draw; virtual;
```

Called internally to display the button.

```
function GetPalette: PPalette; virtual;
```

Can be overridden to change the button's color scheme.

```
procedure HandleEvent(var Event : TEvent); virtual;
```

Called internally to determine if the button was pressed.

```
constructor Load(var S : TStream);
```

Called internally to load a button from the stream.

```
procedure MakeDefault(Enable : boolean);
```

Can be called to make this button the default (or take away the default attribute).

```
procedure SetState(AState : word; Enable : boolean; virtual;
```

Called internally to change the state of the button.

```
procedure Store(var S : TStream);
```

Called internally to send the button to the stream.

TInputLine Object Summary   DIALOGS.TPU

Heritage

TInputLine ➞ TView ➞ TObject

Primary Method

```
constructor Init(var Bounds : TRect; AMaxLen: integer);
```

Creates an input line object that will allow input up to AMaxLen characters.

Other Methods

```
function DataSize : word; virtual;
```

Called internally to get the maximum size of the input line. Can be overridden when creating a descendant object that handles other data types.

```
destructor Done; virtual;
```

Disposes of the input line object.

```
procedure Draw; virtual;
```

Called internally to display the input line. Can be overridden when creating a descendant object that handles other data types.

```
procedure GetData(var Rec); virtual;
```

Can be used to convert a data type to a string suitable for editing.

```
function GetPalette : PPalette; virtual;
```

Can be used to change the input line's color scheme.

```
procedure HandleEvent(var Event : TEvent); virtual;
```

Called internally to recognize events inside the input line.

```
constructor Load(var S : TStream);
```

Called internally to load an input line from the stream.

```
procedure SelectAll(Enable : boolean);
```

Highlights the entire input line, or unhighlights it.

```
procedure SetData(var Rec); virtual;
```

Can be used to convert the input string into a user-defined data type.

```
procedure SetState(AState : word; Enable : boolean); virtual;
```

Called internally to change the state of the input line.

```
procedure Store(var S : TStream);
```

Called internally to send an input line to the stream.

TLabel Object Summary   DIALOGS.TPU

Heritage

TLabel ➞ TStaticText ➞ TView ➞ TObject

Primary Method

```
constructor Init(var Bounds : TRect; AText : String;
            ALink : PView);
```

Creates a label object that will be highlighted when the ALink view is selected.

Other Methods

```
destructor Done; virtual;
```

Disposes of the label object.

```
procedure Draw; virtual;
```

Called internally to display the label.

```
function GetPalette : PPalette; virtual;
```

Can be used to change the label's color scheme.

```
procedure HandleEvent(var Event : TEvent); virtual;
```

Called internally to recognize events inside the label.

```
constructor Load(var S : TStream);
```

Called internally to load a label from the stream.

```
procedure Store(var S : TStream);
```

Called internally to send a label to the stream.

TStaticText Object Summary DIALOGS.TPU

Heritage

TStaticText ➡ TView ➡ TObject

Primary Method

```
constructor Init(var Bounds : TRect; AMaxLen: integer);
```

Creates a line of static (nonselectable, nonchangeable) text.

Other Methods

```
destructor Done; virtual;
```

Disposes of the static text object.

```
procedure Draw; virtual;
```

Called internally to display the static text.

```
function GetPalette : PPalette; virtual;
```

Can be used to change the input line's color scheme.

```
procedure GetText(var S : String); virtual;
```

Called internally to obtain the stored string.

```
constructor Load(var S : TStream);
```

Called internally to load static text from the stream.

```
procedure Store(var S : TStream);
```

Called internally to send static text to the stream.

TCheckBoxes Object Summary   DIALOGS.TPU

Heritage

TCheckBoxes → TCluster → TView → TObject

Primary Inherited Method

Inherited from TCluster (see TCluster summary):

```
constructor Init(var Bounds : TRect;  AStrings : PSItem);
```

Other Methods

```
procedure Draw; virtual;
```

Called internally to display the check boxes.

```
function Mark(Item : integer) : boolean; virtual;
```

Called internally to see if an item is checked.

```
procedure Press(Item : integer); virtual;
```

Called internally to toggle an item.

TRadioButtons Object Summary   DIALOGS.TPU

Heritage

TRadioButtons → TCluster → TView → TObject

Primary Inherited Method

Inherited from TCluster (see TCluster summary):

```
constructor Init(var Bounds : TRect;  AStrings : PSItem);
```

Other Methods

```
procedure Draw; virtual;
```

Called internally to display the radio buttons.

```
function Mark(Item : integer) : boolean; virtual;
```

Called internally to see if the *n*th item is selected.

```
procedure MovedTo(Item : integer); virtual;
```

Called internally to tab over to the *n*th item.

```
procedure Press(Item : integer); virtual;
```

Called internally when a button is pressed.

```
procedure SetData(var Rec); virtual;
```

Called internally to copy button information into internal fields.

TCluster Object Summary   **DIALOGS.TPU**

Heritage

TCluster ➡ TView ➡ TObject

Primary Method

```
constructor Init(var Bounds : TRect;  AStrings : PSItem);
```

Creates a cluster object. Clusters are abstract objects used to define check boxes and radio buttons.

Related Data Types

```
PSItem = ^TSItem;
TSItem = record
  Value : PString;     { PString = ^String }
  Next : PSItem;
end;
```

Defines a linked list of strings for cluster objects.

Related function

```
function NewSItem(Str : String;  ANext : PSItem) : PSItem;
```

Allocates memory and assigns a string for inclusion into a TSItem record.

Other Methods

```
function DataSize : word; virtual;
```

Called internally to get the number of items in the cluster.

```
destructor Done; virtual;
```

Disposes of the cluster object.

```
procedure DrawBox; virtual;
```

Called internally to display the box next to an item.

```
procedure GetData(var Rec); virtual;
```

Called internally to copy cluster information from internal fields.

```
function GetHelpCtx : word; virtual;
```

Allows for different help contexts based on which cluster item is selected.

```
function GetPalette : PPalette; virtual;
```

Can be used to change the cluster's color scheme.

```
procedure HandleEvent(var Event : TEvent); virtual;
```

Called internally to recognize events inside the cluster.

```
constructor Load(var S : TStream);
```

Called internally to load a cluster from the stream.

```
function Mark(Item : integer): boolean; virtual;
```

Called internally to see which items are marked.

```
procedure MovedTo(Item : integer); virtual;
```

Called internally to tab over to the *n*th item.

```
procedure Press(Item : integer); virtual;
```

Called internally to select the *n*th item.

```
procedure SetData(var Rec); virtual;
```

Called internally to copy cluster information into internal structures.

```
procedure SetState(AState : word; Enable : boolean); virtual;
```

Called internally to change the state of the cluster.

```
procedure Store(var S : TStream);
```

Called internally to send a cluster to the stream.

TListBox Object Summary   **DIALOGS.TPU**

Heritage

TListBox → TListViewer → TView → TObject

Primary Methods

```
constructor Init(var Bounds : TRect; ANumCols : word;
           VScrollBar : PScrollBar);
```

Creates a list box with a given size and number of columns. Can include an optional vertical scroll bar.

```
procedure NewList(AList : PCollection); virtual;
```

Assigns the items in a collection to the list box. See discussion of collections earlier in this chapter.

Other Methods

```
function DataSize : word; virtual;
```

Called internally to get the current size of the list box.

```
destructor Done; virtual;
```

Disposes of the list box object.

```
procedure GetData(var Rec); virtual;
```

Called internally to copy list items from internal structures.

```
function  GetText(Item, : integer;
           MaxLen : integer) : string; virtual;
```

Called internally to get the *n*th item in the list.

```
constructor Load(var S : TStream);
```

Called internally to load a list box from the stream.

```
procedure SetData(var Rec); virtual;
```

Called internally to copy list items to internal structures.

```
procedure Store(var S : TStream);
```

Called internally to send a list box to the stream.

THistory Object Summary   DIALOGS.TPU

Heritage

THistory $\longrightarrow$ TView $\longrightarrow$ TObject

Primary Method

```
constructor Init(var Bounds : TRect;
            ALink : PInputLine; AHistoryID : word);
```

Creates a pick-list associated with a given input line. The AHistoryID parameter allows multiple input lines to share the same history list. The list appears as a single icon (down arrow) until the icon is selected.

Other Methods

```
procedure Draw; virtual;
```

Called internally to display the history icon.

```
function GetPalette : PPalette; virtual;
```

Can be used to change the history icon's color scheme.

```
constructor Load(var S : TStream);
```

Called internally to load a history list from the stream.

```
procedure Store(var S : TStream);
```

Called internally to send a history list to the stream.

TFileDialog Object Summary   STDDLG.TPU

Heritage

TFileDialog ➞ TDialog ➞ TWindow ➞ TGroup ➞ TView ➞ TObject

Primary Methods

```
constructor Init(AWildCard : WildStr;
            ATitle : string;  InputName : string;
            Buttons : word;  HistoryId : byte);
```

Creates a dialog box with a list box for files, a history list, and one or more standard buttons.

```
procedure GetFileName(var S : PathStr);
```

Returns the name of the file chosen by the user.

Related Type

```
WildStr = Dos.PathStr;
```

Defines the initial value of the filename, which normally includes wildcard characters.

Related Constants

```
fdOkButton = 1;
```

Flag to include an OK button.

```
fdOpenButton = 2;
```

Flag to include an Open button.

```
fdReplaceButton = 4;
```

Flag to include a Replace button.

```
fdClearButton = 8;
```

Flag to include a Clear button.

Other Methods

```
destructor Done; virtual;
```

Disposes of the file dialog box.

```
procedure GetData(var Rec); virtual;
```

Called internally to retrieve data from internal structures.

```
procedure HandleEvent(var Event : TEvent); virtual;
```

Called internally to handle events within the file dialog box.

```
constructor Load(var S : TStream);
```

Called internally to read a file dialog box from the stream.

```
procedure Store(var S : TStream);
```

Called internally to write file dialog box data to the stream.

```
function Valid(Command : word) : boolean; virtual;
```

Called internally to determine which commands are valid.

Using Streams

The major commands remaining are those that save cards to a file and reload them. Turbo Vision provides an extremely powerful object, called a stream, to support this. A stream is a path that an object can follow to or from another location. The primary support for streams is for DOS files and EMS memory. Streams are as polymorphic as collections, allowing you to use the same stream for different object types.

The flash card application uses a buffered DOS file stream. This object type is called TBufStream. In order to use this stream in objects you create, you must register the objects into Turbo Vision. The first step in registration is to define a registration record. Here is the record for a flash card:

```
const
(* for Stream registration *)
  RFlashCard : TStreamRec = (
    ObjType: 150;
    VmtLink: Ofs(TypeOf(TFlashCard)^);
    Load: @TFlashCard.Load;
    Store: @TFlashCard.Store);
```

The first field of the registration record is a unique object ID. The valid values go from 100 to 65,535. The second field points to the VMT of the object. The final two fields are the addresses of the procedures that access streams for this object type.

The implementation of the *Load* and *Store* procedures, which become part of the *TFlashCard* object definition, is shown here:

```
constructor TFlashCard.Load(var S : TStream);
begin
  S.Read(Number, SizeOf(Number));
```

```
    S.Read(Question, SizeOf(Question));
    S.Read(Answer, SizeOf(Answer));
end;

(************************************************)

procedure TFlashCard.Store(var S : TStream);
begin
  S.Write(Number, SizeOf(Number));
  S.Write(Question, SizeOf(Question));
  S.Write(Answer, SizeOf(Answer));
end;
```

These procedures are implemented primarily by calling TStream.Read and TStream.Write for each data field in the object type. If the object is a descendant of another object, these overridden methods must call the respective procedures of their ancestors.

The *TFlashCardSet* object type also requires stream registration and support procedures:

```
const
(* for Stream registration *)
  RFlashCardSet: TStreamRec = (
    ObjType: 140;
    VmtLink: Ofs(TypeOf(TFlashCardSet)^);
    Load: @TFlashCardSet.Load;
    Store: @TFlashCardSet.Store);


(************************************************)

constructor TFlashCardSet.Load(var S : TStream);
begin
  TCollection.Load(S);
  CurrentCard := -1;
  Randomize;
end;

(************************************************)

procedure TFlashCardSet.Store(var S : TStream);
begin
  TCollection.Store(S);
end;
```

Once you have set up each object in your application hierarchy, you must register the streams. This is often done in a single procedure at the start of the application. All object types that will be used in the stream must be registered. For the flash card application, registration is required for types *TFlashCard, TFlashCardSet,* and TCollection:

```
procedure RegisterStreams;
begin
  RegisterType(RCollection);
  RegisterType(RFlashCard);
  RegisterType(RFlashCardSet);
end;
```

In the flash card program, streams are used for the Save File and Open File commands. Only files that were saved using the application can be read into the application.

Turbo Vision provides the entire dialog box used in the IDE for use in your own program. This object type, TFileDialog, was summarized earlier in the chapter. Writing a procedure to use this dialog box is fairly simple:

```
procedure SaveFile(var TheSet : TFlashCardSet);
var
  SaveBox : PFileDialog;
  FCStream : TBufStream;
  Control : word;
begin
  (* use the standard Save File dialog box *)
  New(SaveBox, Init(TheFileName, 'Save File As',
      'Save File Name', fdOkButton, 1));
  Control := DeskTop^.ExecView (SaveBox);
  if Control <> cmCancel then
    begin

      (* save the set using a buffered stream *)
      SaveBox^.GetFileName(TheFileName);
      FCStream.Init(TheFileName, stCreate, 512);
      FCStream.Put(@TheSet);
      FCStream.Done;
    end;
end;
```

This procedure assumes that a global variable *TheFileName* has been declared. The dialog box created by this code is shown in Figure 17-3.

The *SaveFile* procedure starts by creating the dialog box. Required parameters for this initialization are the default filename, the title of the dialog box, a label for the filename, a list of buttons to be used, and a history list ID. The dialog box is then executed, and it returns an event based on the button pressed by the user.

Assuming the user wants to save the card set to the stream, the procedure gets the name of the file, opens the file as a stream, and calls TBufStream.Put with the address

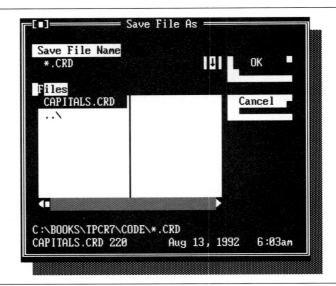

Figure 17-3.   *Dialog box created by global variable TheFileName*

of the flash card set. The Put method calls the *Store* procedure for the *TFlashCardSet* object type, which in turn calls the *Store* procedure for each flash card.

Loading data from the stream follows a very similar process. First a dialog box obtains the filename. Second, a stream is created based on the filename. Finally, the data is loaded from the stream. Here is the code for opening a flash card file:

```
procedure OpenFile(var NewSet : TFlashCardSet);
var
  OpenBox : PFileDialog;
  FCStream : TBufStream;
  Control : word;
  PFCSet : PFlashCardSet;
begin

  (* use the standard Open File dialog box *)
  New(OpenBox, Init('*.CRD', 'Open File', 'Card File Name',
      fdOkButton + fdOpenButton, 1));
  Control := DeskTop^.ExecView (OpenBox);
  if Control <> cmCancel then
    begin

      (* read the file as a buffered stream *)
      OpenBox^.GetFileName(TheFileName);
```

```
        FCStream.Init(TheFileName, stOpenRead, 512);
        PFCSet := PFlashCardSet(FCStream.Get);
        NewSet := PFCSet^;
        FCStream.Done;
    end;
end;
```

The final step in making the entire flash card application work is to modify the main application methods to support the actual commands.

First you need a few variables:

```
var
  FlashCardApp : TFlashCardApp;
  FlashCards : TFlashCardSet;
  OneCard : TFlashCard;
```

Next, you must add the required parameters to the event commands and add support for the new commands discussed earlier:

```
procedure TFlashCardApp.HandleEvent(var Event: TEvent);
begin
  TApplication.HandleEvent(Event);
  if Event.What = evCommand then
    begin
      case Event.Command of
          cmOpen        : OpenFile(FlashCards);
          cmSave        : SaveFile(FlashCards);
          cmCardAdd     : AddCard(FlashCards);
          cmCardChange  : ChangeCard;
          cmCardDelete  : DeleteCard(FlashCards);
          cmCardNext    : NextCard(FlashCards);
          cmCardRandom  : RandomCard(FlashCards);
          cmShowAnswer  : ShowAnswer;
          cmCancel      : RemoveBoxes;
          else
             Exit;
          end;
      ClearEvent(Event);
    end;
end;
```

Finally, you must add any other required initializations to the main program. The final program code will look like this:

```
begin
  FlashCards.Init;
  RegisterStreams;
```

```
    FlashCardApp.Init;
    FlashCardApp.Run;
    FlashCardApp.Done;
end.
```

You can now probably take any or all of this flash card application and use it to help you develop your own applications. Remember that many things (like error checking) were removed from the program to maintain simplicity. Also keep in mind that there are many other ways this same application could have been developed. Feel free to improve it in any way you wish.

TBufStream Object Summary   OBJECTS.TPU

Heritage

TBufStream → TDosStream → TStream → TObject

Primary Methods

```
constructor Init(FileName : FNameStr;  Mode, Size : word);
```

Creates or opens a file as a stream, using the given file mode and buffer size.

```
destructor Done; virtual;
```

Closes the file and flushes the buffer.

Primary Inherited Methods

Inherited from TStream (see TStream summary):

```
function Get : PObject;
procedure Put(P : PObject);
```

Related Constants

```
stCreate = $3C00;
```

Mode for creating or overwriting a file.

```
stOpenRead = $3D00;
```

Mode for opening a file as read-only.

```
stOpenWrite = $3D01;
```

Mode for opening a file as write-only.

```
stOpen = $3D02;
```

Mode for opening a file as read/write.

Related Types

```
FNameStr = string[79];
```

Limits filenames to 79 characters.

Other Methods

```
procedure Flush; virtual;
```

Called internally to flush the file buffer.

```
function GetPos : Longint; virtual;
```

Called internally to determine the file position.

```
function GetSize : Longint; virtual;
```

Called internally to determine the file size.

```
procedure Read(var Buf; Count : word); virtual;
```

Called internally to read bytes from the file.

```
procedure Seek(Pos : Longint); virtual;
```

Called internally to go to a file position.

```
procedure Truncate; virtual;
```

Called internally to delete to the end of the file.

```
procedure Write(var Buf; Count : word); virtual;
```

Called internally to write bytes to the file.

TEmsStream Object Summary   OBJECTS.TPU

Heritage

TEmsStream ➞ TStream ➞ TObject

Primary Methods

```
constructor Init(MinSize : Longint);
```

Creates an EMS stream using the given number of bytes.

```
destructor Done; virtual;
```

Must be called to release EMS memory.

Primary Inherited Methods

Inherited from TStream (see TStream summary):

```
function Get : PObject;
procedure Put(P : PObject);
```

Other Methods

```
function GetPos : Longint; virtual;
```

Called internally to determine the current EMS address.

```
function GetSize : Longint; virtual;
```

Called internally to determine the size of the EMS stream.

```
procedure Read(var Buf; Count : word); virtual;
```

Called internally to read bytes from EMS memory.

```
procedure Seek(Pos : Longint); virtual;
```

Called internally to go to a specific address in EMS memory.

```
procedure Truncate; virtual;
```

Called internally to remove all data past the current EMS address.

```
procedure Write(var Buf; Count : word); virtual;
```

Called internally to write bytes to EMS memory.

TStream Object Summary   OBJECTS.TPU

Heritage

TStream ➡ TObject

Primary Methods

```
function Get : PObject;
```

Reads an object from the stream by calling the Load constructor for each part of the object.

```
procedure Put(P : PObject);
```

Writes an object to the stream by calling the Store procedure for each part of the object.

```
procedure Read(var Buf; Count: word); virtual;
```

Reads a variable of a given size from the stream. Called by each Load procedure.

```
procedure Write(var Buf; Count : word); virtual;
```

Writes a variable of a given size to the stream. Called by each Store procedure.

Related Procedure

```
procedure RegisterType(var S: TStreamRec);
```

Allows an object type inherited from TObject to be loaded and saved using streams.

Related Types

```
PStreamRec = ^TStreamRec;
TStreamRec = record
  ObjType : word;              (* unique id (> 100) *)
  VmtLink : word;         (* offset of the object type *)
  Load : pointer;       (* address of the Load method *)
  Store : pointer;    (* address of the Store method *)
  Next : word;                    (* internal use *)
end;
```

Defines the stream characteristics of an object.

Other Methods

Stream objects are almost never created explicitly, so their internal methods are of little value. See the methods for each descendant object type.

Other Turbo Vision Objects

The final four Turbo Vision major objects are useful for development of applications but were not used in the flash card program.

When you want to display a large amount of text or allow the user to enter a large amount of text, you should create a descendant of TWindow. Windows are special cases of groups: They are enclosed in a frame, numbered, and often have scroll bars to support traversal using a mouse. If the information in the window will not fit on the screen at once, a view object of type TScroller must be inserted into the window. The physical scroll bars are type TScrollBar. For an example of a scrollable window, study the TVGUID08.PAS program in the \TVISION subdirectory of your Turbo Pascal directory.

A resource is a special case of a buffered DOS stream. It is used to store and retrieve user-interface objects such as menus and dialog boxes. You can place the code that creates these objects into a separate program that also writes the objects to a resource file. Your main application program would then simply read the objects from the resource file. This makes your programs more modular and also decreases the size of your main executable program.

TWindow Object Summary   **VIEWS.TPU**

Heritage

TWindow → TGroup → TView → TObject

Primary Methods

```
constructor Init(var Bounds : TRect; ATitle: TTitleStr;
                 ANumber : integer);
```

Creates a window in the given location, with the given title and window number.

```
function StandardScrollBar (AObjects : word) : PScrollBar;
```

Creates and inserts a scroll bar in the window.

Related Constants

```
wfMove = 1;
```

Allows the window to be moved around the desktop.

```
wfGrow = 2;
```

Allows the window to be resized.

```
wfClose = 4;
```

Adds a close icon to the upper-left corner of the window.

```
wfZoom = 8;
```

Adds a zoom icon to the upper-right corner of the window.

Other Methods

```
procedure Close; virtual;
```

Called internally to close the window.

```
destructor Done; virtual;
```

Disposes of a window object.

```
function GetPalette : PPalette; virtual;
```

Can be overridden to change the window's colors.

```
function GetTitle(MaxSize : integer): TTitleStr; virtual;
```

Called internally to get the window title.

```
procedure HandleEvent(var Event : TEvent); virtual;
```

Called internally to handle events that occur within the window, such as moving, sizing, and zooming.

```
procedure InitFrame; virtual;
```

Called internally to create a window frame.

```
constructor Load(var S : TStream);
```

Called internally to read a window from the stream.

```
procedure SetState(AState : word; Enable : boolean); virtual;
```

Called internally to change the state of the window.

```
procedure SizeLimits(var Min, Max : TPoint); virtual;
```

Changes the size limits of the window.

```
procedure Store(var S : TStream);
```

Called internally to write a window to the stream.

```
procedure Zoom; virtual;
```

Called internally to zoom the window.

TScroller Object Summary   **VIEWS.TPU**

Heritage

TScroller ➔ TView ➔ TObject

Primary Methods

```
constructor Init(var Bounds : TRect; AHScrollBar,
            AVScrollBar : PScrollBar);
```

Creates a scroller within a window with optional scroll bars.

```
procedure SetLimit(X, Y : integer);
```

Sets the size of the data inside the scroll area (not the region of the scroller itself).

Primary Inherited Methods

From TView (see TView summary):

```
procedure Draw; virtual;
```

Other Methods

```
procedure ChangeBounds(var Bounds : TRect); virtual;
```

Called internally to change the size of the scroller.

```
function GetPalette : PPalette; virtual;
```

Can be overridden to change the scroller's colors.

```
procedure HandleEvent(var Event : TEvent); virtual;
```

Called internally to handle scroller events.

```
constructor Load(var S : TStream);
```

Called internally to read a scroller object from the stream.

```
procedure ScrollDraw; virtual;
```

Called internally to redraw the scroller.

```
procedure ScrollTo(X, Y : integer);
```

Called internally to scroll to a different part of the view.

```
procedure SetState(AState : word; Enable : boolean);
```

Called internally to change the state of the scroller.

```
procedure Store(var S : TStream);
```

Called internally to write a scroller to the stream.

TScrollBar Object Summary   **VIEWS.TPU**

Heritage

TScrollBar ➝ TView ➝ TObject

Related Constants

```
sbHorizontal = 0;
```

Allows a horizontal scroll bar to be included.

```
sbVertical = 1;
```

Allows a vertical scroll bar to be included.

```
sbHandleKeyboard = 2;
```

Allows support of keyboard commands for scrolling.

Other Methods

Objects of type TScrollBar are almost always created using the method TWindow.StandardScrollBar.

TResourceFile Object Summary   **OBJECTS.TPU**

Heritage

TResourceFile ➝ TObject

Primary Methods

```
constructor Init(AStream : PStream);
```

Initializes the resource file with a buffered DOS stream.

```
function Get(Key : String): PObject;
```

Retrieves an object from the resource file.

```
procedure Put(Item : PObject; Key : String);
```

Writes an object to a resource file, and assigns a key to the object.

Other Methods

```
function Count : integer;
```

Determines the number of objects in the resource file.

```
procedure Delete(Key : String);
```

Deletes an object stored in a resource file.

```
destructor Done; virtual;
```

Disposes of a resource file after flushing the buffer.

```
procedure Flush;
```

Flushes the buffer for the resource file if any changes were made.

```
function KeyAt(I : integer): string;
```

Can be used to determine the contents of a resource file.

```
function SwitchTo(AStream : PStream; Pack : boolean) : PStream;
```

Switches the resource file from one stream to another, packing the new file if desired.

Chapter **18**

Using Object Windows

In Chapter 16, you studied some graphics programs that used a small piece of Object Windows. These programs relied on Object Windows to create a window that looked just like any other Windows application, including borders that could be sized, moved, minimized and maximized, all with very little effort on your part.

The present chapter will show you how to use Object Windows to write more complex applications, including menus, accelerators, and dialog boxes. Like Turbo Vision, Object Windows is extremely large and sometimes confusing. This chapter will key in on the fundamental concepts to help you transition to writing complete Windows applications. This chapter relies heavily on the Resource Workshop presented in Chapter 11.

This chapter will walk you through the creation of an application that creates, saves, and displays flash cards. This is functionally the same program that was developed using Turbo Vision in Chapter 17. If you have used Turbo Vision and want to transition to Object Windows, use the two programs in these chapters to help determine the differences between the two libraries, and in turn help you determine what changes you'll need to make. If you have not used Turbo Vision before, it is certainly not a prerequisite. With the exception of a few common concepts (collections and streams), you will find a thorough explanation of the application without needing to search through Chapter 17.

Creating an Application Object

Any program that uses Object Windows to support user interaction must start with an object of type TApplication. This object controls the creation of the main window of the program, as well as any application-specific initializations. You must always create a descendant object from the TApplication type to supply the necessary parameters for the main window.

To demonstrate the use of TApplication, consider the following program. This program can act as a template for starting any Object Windows application:

```
Program Just_An_Application;

uses OWindows;

type
  TFlashCardApp = object(TApplication)
    procedure InitMainWindow; virtual;
  end;

var
  FlashCardApp : TFlashCardApp;

(************************************************)

procedure TFlashCardApp.InitMainWindow;
begin
  MainWindow := New(PWindow, Init(nil, 'Flash Cards'));
end;

begin
  FlashCardApp.Init('Flash Cards');
  FlashCardApp.Run;
  FlashCardApp.Done;
end.
```

The program defines a descendant object called *FlashCardApp*. This object overrides the *InitMainWindow* method, which is called internally by the TApplication.Init method.

The implementation *TFlashCardApp.InitMainWindow* is essentially one statement that creates the window. This statement,

```
MainWindow := New(PWindow, Init(nil, 'Flash Cards'));
```

initializes the MainWindow field, which is inherited from the TApplication object. The Init method called is part of the TWindow object, which supplies the name that will appear at the top of the window. In this case the window will contain "Flash Cards."

You can actually run this program, and a window will appear with the proper title. All keystrokes and mouse operations will be ignored by the program because you have not defined any event handlers. The window will contain a standard Windows control box, which allows you to move, size, and close the window.

Defining Menu Commands

Almost all Windows applications include a menu bar. The combination of Object Windows and the Resource Workshop make it easy for you to create menus that are customized for your application.

The first step in creating a menu is to determine the names of each menu option. As you design your application, you'll probably write out the menu on paper to avoid wasted effort on the computer. Table 18-1 shows the design of the Flash Card menu bar in table form. The options in the two menus provide all of the functionality included in the application:

- The ability to add, change, and delete cards in the current set

- The ability to display cards in numeric or random order

- The ability to save the cards to a file for later retrieval

Once you have the design of the menu in mind, you need to define constants that represent the commands associated with each menu item. These constants are placed in their own unit, which can then be accessed by the Resource Workshop.

The FLASHCNS unit, shown here, defines all of the constants needed to support the Flash Card program. The constants numbered 201 through 215 are used for the commands associated with the menu options described in the previous section. The remaining constants will be discussed as they are used elsewhere in the application.

```
Unit FLASHCNS;

interface

const
  MenuBar      = 200;
```

File Menu	Card Menu
Open	Add
Save	Change
Quit	Delete
	Next
	Random

Table 18-1.   *Flash Card Menu Design*

```
    cmFileOpen    = 201;
    cmFileSave    = 202;
    cmQuit        = 203;
    cmCardAdd     = 211;
    cmCardChange  = 212;
    cmCardDelete  = 213;
    cmCardNext    = 214;
    cmCardRandom  = 215;
    cmShowAnswer  = 231;

    dlgAddCard    = 240;
    dlgAddAnother = 241;
    dlgQuestion   = 242;
    dlgAnswer     = 243;
    dlgCardNum    = 244;

    dlgRandom     = 250;
    dlgNext       = 251;

    AccelKeys     = 299;

implementation

end.
```

The format of a unit that contains constants used by the Resource Workshop is very strict. This unit must contain only constants in the **interface** section of the unit, and the **implementation** section must be empty.

Creating and Loading a Menu Bar

To create a menu bar you have three choices:

- Interactively, using the Resource Workshop, or
- Using a text editor to create a resource file that can be compiled by the Resource Workshop
- Programmatically, using various procedures in the WinProcs unit

The first option is the easiest, and offers the greatest flexibility. The second is best when you are copying a resource from another source, such as this book. The third is better for changing menus on the fly while an application is running.

The following lines are the first part of the FLASH.RC file, which will contain all of the resources used in the Flash Card program. You can enter these lines in any text editor, including the Windows IDE.

```
#include "flashcns.pas"
MenuBar MENU
BEGIN
 POPUP "&File"
 BEGIN
   MENUITEM "&Open\tF3", cmFileOpen
   MENUITEM "&Save\tF2", cmFileSave
   MENUITEM "&Quit\tALT-X", cmQuit
 END

 POPUP "&Card"
 BEGIN
   MENUITEM "&Add", cmCardAdd
   MENUITEM "&Change", cmCardChange
   MENUITEM "&Delete", cmCardDelete
   MENUITEM "&Random\tF8", cmCardRandom
   MENUITEM "&Next\tF9", cmCardNext
 END

END
```

C and C++ programmers will recognize much of the syntax of a resource file. Since Windows is written in C, the Resource compiler was originally designed to support C applications. Borland has expanded the Resource Workshop to support Turbo Pascal applications, but has left the syntax of the resource files alone.

The first line uses a **#include** command to retrieve the constants from the FLASHCNS unit. This accomplishes the same task as the File|Add to Project command in the Resource Workshop. The second line starts the menu definition, using the constant MenuBar as the menu number. The rest of the listing defines the two menus and their options.

Each MENUITEM line includes the string that will appear in the menu and the command that will be generated when the user selects that command. The ampersand indicates the letter that will be underlined in the menu. The user has the option of typing that letter to select a command rather than using the mouse. The \t is a tab, which separates the command from its accelerator key. (Accelerators are covered in the next section.)

Once you have entered these lines in an editor, you should load them in as a project in the Resource Workshop. The Workshop will compile the lines to verify the syntax, and load the menu into the Workshop editor. When you select the menu line, you will bring up the menu editor, which should display the menu as in Figure 18-1. When you are satisfied with the menu, save the file using the multi-save option that also creates a compiled .RES file. If you are unfamiliar with this process, see Chapter 11.

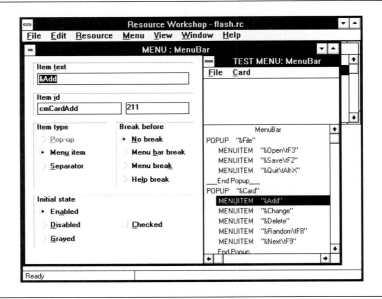

Figure 18-1. *The menu bar in the Resource Workshop*

Alternatively, you can use the interactive method to create the menu bar in the Resource Workshop. Chapter 11 takes you step by step through the creation of this same menu bar.

To add the menu to your application, you must first create a descendant of the TWindow object. This object will be defined in full in a later section. For now it will include only a new constructor, called *Init*.

```
TFCWindow = object(TWindow)
  constructor Init(AParent : PWindowsObject; ATitle : PChar);
end;
```

The implementation of the *Init* constructor must call the LoadMenu function in the WinProcs unit to load the menu from the resource file. Here's how it works:

```
constructor TFCWindow.Init;
begin
  TWindow.Init(AParent, ATitle);
  Attr.Menu := LoadMenu(HInstance, PChar(MenuBar));
end;
```

One of the fields inherited by *TFCWindow* is Attr, which is a variant record. The Menu field of Attr contains a handle to the actual menu. When you call LoadMenu you must supply the window handle, called HInstance, and the number of the resource.

This resource number must be of type PChar, which is why you see the typecast **PChar(MenuBar)**.

Creating and Loading Accelerators

An *accelerator* is the Windows term for a hot-key: it allows you to use a key combination instead of the menus to execute a command. Accelerators are defined in a resource file. The simplest way by far to create an accelerator is to use the Resource Workshop; however, it's much more difficult to identify the steps on paper. Instead, you can add the following lines to the FLASH.RC files:

```
AccelKeys ACCELERATORS
BEGIN
  VK_F3, cmFileOpen, VIRTKEY
  VK_F2, cmFileSave, VIRTKEY
  VK_F9, cmCardNext, VIRTKEY
  VK_F8, cmCardRandom, VIRTKEY
  "x", cmQuit, ASCII, ALT
END
```

This section of the file starts with a resource number definition, using one of the constants in the FLASHCNS unit, *AccelKeys*. Then it defines five accelerators. The first four are called virtual keys because they are keys that are not included in the ASCII character set. The identifier VK_F3 is a predefined constant that represents the F3 function key. The last accelerator is the ASCII character "x" plus the ALT key, or ALT-X. Each line defines not only the key sequence, but also the command that will be executed when the sequence is pressed. These commands do not necessarily have menu equivalents (although all of the above ones do).

You should now load the file into the Resource Workshop to verify that the syntax is correct. You can bring up the accelerator editor, and you should see the definitions that appear in Figure 18-2.

Again, the best way to create accelerators on your own is to use the Resource Workshop as an interactive tool. Chapter 11 demonstrates this process.

Loading accelerators into an application is done in a similar fashion to loading the menu bar. In this case you call the LoadAccelerators function, and place the returned handle in the HAccTable field of the application object. The best place for this is in an overridden method called *InitInstance*:

```
procedure TFlashCardApp.InitInstance;
begin
  HAccTable := LoadAccelerators(HInstance, PChar(AccelKeys));
  inherited InitInstance;
end;
```

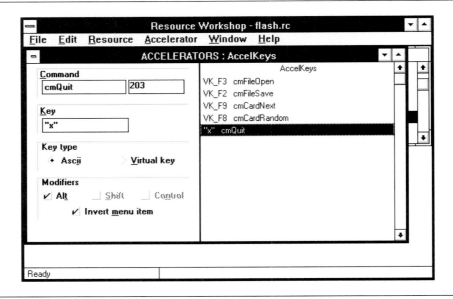

Figure 18-2.   *Accelerators loaded into the Resource Workshop*

The *InitInstance* method is called internally every time users attempt to start their application. If your application allows more than one main window at any given time, this method would be called once for each instance of the application. Like most overridden methods, *TFlashCardApp.InitInstance* does its unique piece and then calls its inherited method.

Completing the Skeletal Application

One of the distinct advantages of an integrated development environment is the ease of continually testing your program. With the IDE you can write a small program, try it, fix it, and then write some more. If you try to create an entire application before doing any testing, you will find it much more difficult to find the bugs.

Object Windows makes this process of continuous development even easier, since all of the underlying architecture is already in place. Thus once you have a menu bar and some accelerators in place, you are ready to try your program.

Before you do, however, you should probably add some code that verifies that the proper commands are sent when a user selects a menu option or presses an accelerator. To do this, you must add one method to the *TFCWindow* object for every command. Here's a simplified version with only one command handler:

```
type
  TFCWindow = object(TWindow)
    constructor Init(AParent : PWindowsObject; ATitle : PChar);
    procedure FileOpen(var Msg : TMessage);
      virtual cm_First + cmFileOpen;
  end;
```

The *FileOpen* procedure will be called every time the user selects the *cmFileOpen* command, either from the menu or by pressing F3. The syntax of the method declaration is a little unusual, with an integer expression appearing after the word **virtual**. This expression represents an index into an internal method table. These methods are called dynamic methods, and are used for objects that contain a large number of virtual methods.

You will find the complete implementation of the *FileOpen* procedure later in this chapter. For now you can use a stub, or placeholder. The MessageBox subprogram, part of the WinProcs unit, makes writing stubs easy:

```
procedure TFCWindow.FileOpen;
begin
  MessageBox(HWindow, 'Not Implemented Yet', 'Open File', mb_OK);
end;
```

The parameters to MessageBox are the window handle, the title of the box, the text in the box, and the buttons for the box. The constant mb_OK specifies that the box should include just an OK button. This call will produce the dialog box shown in Figure 18-3.

All that's left for the skeletal version of the Flash Card program is to write a stub for every command. Here is the complete program:

Figure 18-3. *A sample call to MessageBox*

```
Program Flashcard_App;

{$R FLASH.RES}

uses FLASHCNS,
     OWindows, WinProcs, WinTypes;

type
  TFlashCardApp = object(TApplication)
    procedure InitMainWindow; virtual;
    procedure InitInstance; virtual;
  end;

  PFCWindow = ^TFCWindow;
  TFCWindow = object(TWindow)
    constructor Init(AParent : PWindowsObject; ATitle : PChar);
    procedure FileOpen(var Msg : TMessage);
      virtual cm_First + cmFileOpen;
    procedure FileSave(var Msg : TMessage);
      virtual cm_First + cmFileSave;
    procedure Quit(var Msg : TMessage);
      virtual cm_First + cmQuit;
    procedure EditAdd(var Msg : TMessage);
      virtual cm_First + cmCardAdd;
    procedure EditChange(var Msg : TMessage);
      virtual cm_First + cmCardChange;
    procedure EditDelete(var Msg : TMessage);
      virtual cm_First + cmCardDelete;
    procedure NextCard(var Msg : TMessage);
      virtual cm_First + cmCardNext;
    procedure RandomCard(var Msg : TMessage);
      virtual cm_First + cmCardRandom;
  end;

var
  FlashCardApp : TFlashCardApp;

(************************************************)

constructor TFCWindow.Init;
begin
  inherited Init(AParent, ATitle);
  Attr.Menu := LoadMenu(HInstance, PChar(MenuBar));
end;

procedure TFCWindow.FileOpen;
begin
  MessageBox(HWindow, 'Not Implemented Yet', 'Open File', mb_OK);
end;
```

```
procedure TFCWindow.FileSave;
begin
  MessageBox(HWindow, 'Not Implemented Yet', 'Save File', mb_OK);
end;

procedure TFCWindow.Quit;
begin
  Done;
end;

procedure TFCWindow.EditAdd;
begin
  MessageBox(HWindow, 'Not Implemented Yet', 'Add Card', mb_OK);
end;

procedure TFCWindow.EditChange;
begin
  MessageBox(HWindow, 'Not Implemented Yet', 'Change Card', mb_OK);
end;

procedure TFCWindow.EditDelete;
begin
  MessageBox(HWindow, 'Not Implemented Yet', 'Delete Card', mb_OK);
end;

procedure TFCWindow.NextCard;
begin
  MessageBox(HWindow, 'Not Implemented Yet', 'Next Card', mb_OK);
end;

procedure TFCWindow.RandomCard;
begin
  MessageBox(HWindow, 'Not Implemented Yet', 'Random Card', mb_OK);
end;

procedure TFlashCardApp.InitMainWindow;
begin
  MainWindow := New(PFCWindow, Init(nil, 'Flash Cards'));
  if HAccTable = 0 then
    MessageBox(MainWindow^.HWindow,
        'Accelerators not loaded', 'Error', mb_OK);
end;

procedure TFlashCardApp.InitInstance;
begin
  HAccTable := LoadAccelerators(HInstance, PChar(AccelKeys));
  inherited InitInstance;
end;
```

```
begin
  FlashCardApp.Init('FlashCards');
  FlashCardApp.Run;
  FlashCardApp.Done;
end.
```

The line following the program header is a $R compiler directive. This directive supplies the name of the resource file that contains the menu bar and the accelerators.

TApplication Object Summary   **OWindows Unit**

Heritage

TApplication ➡ TObject

Primary Methods

```
constructor Init(AName : PChar);
```

Initializes the application object, primarily by calling InitApplication, InitInstance, and InitMainWindow.

```
destructor Done; virtual;
```

Disposes of the application object.

```
function ExecDialog(ADialog : PWindowsObject) : integer; virtual;
```

Executes a modal dialog box.

```
procedure InitApplication; virtual;
```

Overridden to perform any initializations to be done only when the first instance is created.

```
procedure InitInstance; virtual;
```

Overridden to perform any initializations to be done for every instance of the application.

```
procedure InitMainWindow; virtual;
```

Overridden to initialize the main window of the application.

```
function MakeWindow(AWindowsObject : PWindowsObject)
                        : PWindowsObject; virtual;
```

Creates a window or a modeless dialog box.

Primary Fields

```
HAccTable : THandle;
```

Holds the handle to the accelerator table.

```
MainWindow : PWindowsObject;
```

Holds a pointer to the main window.

Related Subprograms

```
function LoadAccelerators(Instance : THandle;
                        TableName : PChar) : THandle;
```

Loads the accelerators defined by TableName from the resource file into the application.

TWindow Object Summary   OWindows Unit

Heritage

TWindow ➡ TWindowsObject ➡ TObject

Primary Methods

```
constuctor Init(AParent : PWindowsObject; ATitle : PChar);
```

Initializes a window, setting the window title to ATitle.

```
constructor InitResource(AParent : PWindowsObject;
                         ResourceID : word);
```

Initializes a window (usually a control) based on a resource object.

```
procedure Paint(PaintDC : HDC;
                var PaintInfo : TPaintStruct); virtual;
```

Overridden to display the content of a window, other than child windows and dialog boxes.

```
procedure SetupWindow; virtual;
```

Overridden to initialize window characteristics.

```
procedure WMLButtonDown(var Msg : TMessage);
                virtual wm_First + wm_LbuttonDown;
```

Overridden to respond to the click of a left mouse button.

Primary Inherited Method

Inherited from TWindowsObject:

```
function CanClose: boolean; virtual;
```

See the TWindowsObject summary box.

Primary Field

```
Attr : TWindowAttr;
```

Holds the attributes of the window. See "Related Types" for a description of the TWindowAttr type.

Related Types

```
TWindowAttr = record
  Title : PChar;
  Style : longint;
  ExStyle : longint;
  X, Y, W, H : integer;
  Param : pointer;
  case integer of
    0: (Menu : HMenu);
    1: (Id : integer);
```

Most fields are for internal use. You must set the Menu field to associate a menu with the window.

Related Subprograms

```
function LoadMenu(Instance : THandle; MenuName : PChar) : HMenu;
```

Loads the menu pointed to by MenuName from the resource file into the window pointed to by Instance.

TWindowsObject Object Summary   OWindows Unit

Heritage

TWindowsObject ➜ TObject

Primary Methods

```
function CanClose : boolean; virtual;
```

Overridden to determine whether the user can close the window. Often this checks to make sure files are saved, and so on.

Primary Fields

```
HWindow : HWnd;
```

Holds the handle to the associated window.

Writing Support Code

Until now you have watched the development of an application prototype that can support any Object Windows program. Once you are satisfied with the design and the interface, you must start on the implementation of the "meat" of the program. In this section, you will see the lowest level of the program, an object that represents a single flash card. The next sections build on this object until the application is complete.

The design revolves around two objects: *TFlashCard*, which models a single flash card, and *TFlashCardSet*, which represents a group of flash cards. The implementation of *TFlashCard* is straightforward. As you can see by the FLASHCRD unit, the flash card object is almost exactly the same as the Turbo Vision version shown in Chapter 17:

```
Unit FLASHCRD;

interface

uses Objects, Strings;

const
  QAMaxLen = 50;
type
  FlashStr = array [0..QAMaxLen] of char;
  PFlashCard = ^TFlashCard;
  TFlashCard = object(TObject)
    constructor Init;
    constructor Load(var S : TStream);
    procedure Store(var S : TStream);
    function GetNumber : integer;
    function GetNumberPChar : PChar;
    function GetQuestion : PChar;
    function GetAnswer : PChar;
    procedure SetNumber(NewNumber : integer);
    procedure SetQuestion(NewQuestion : FlashStr);
    procedure SetAnswer(NewAnswer : FlashStr);
  private
```

```
      Number : integer;
      Question : FlashStr;
      Answer : FlashStr;
      end;

  CardRec = record    {for transfers}
    CardNum : array [0..3] of char;
    Question : FlashStr;
    Answer : FlashStr;
  end;

const
(* for Stream registration *)
  RFlashCard : TStreamRec = (
    ObjType: 150;
    VmtLink: Ofs(TypeOf(TFlashCard)^);
    Load: @TFlashCard.Load;
    Store: @TFlashCard.Store);


implementation

constructor TFlashCard.Init;
begin
  StrPCopy(Question, ' ');
  StrPCopy(Answer, ' ');
end;

(*************************************************)

constructor TFlashCard.Load(var S : TStream);
begin
  S.Read(Number, SizeOf(Number));
  S.Read(Question, SizeOf(Question));
  S.Read(Answer, SizeOf(Answer));
end;

(*************************************************)

procedure TFlashCard.Store(var S : TStream);
begin
  S.Write(Number, SizeOf(Number));
  S.Write(Question, SizeOf(Question));
  S.Write(Answer, SizeOf(Answer));
end;

(*************************************************)

function TFlashCard.GetNumber : integer;
```

```
begin
  GetNumber := Number;
end;


(**************************************************)


function TFlashCard.GetNumberPChar : PChar;
var
  CNumStr : string;
  CNumPChar : array [0..3] of char;
begin
  Str(GetNumber, CNumStr);
  StrPCopy (CNumPChar, CNumStr);
  GetNumberPChar := @CNumPChar;
end;


(**************************************************)


function TFlashCard.GetQuestion : PChar;
begin
  GetQuestion := @Question;
end;


(**************************************************)


function TFlashCard.GetAnswer : PChar;
begin
  GetAnswer := @Answer;
end;


(**************************************************)


procedure TFlashCard.SetNumber(NewNumber : integer);
begin
  Number := NewNumber;
end;


(**************************************************)


procedure TFlashCard.SetQuestion(NewQuestion : FlashStr);
begin
  Question := NewQuestion;
end;


(**************************************************)


procedure TFlashCard.SetAnswer(NewAnswer : FlashStr);
begin
  Answer := NewAnswer;
```

```
end;

end.
```

The major difference between the Turbo Vision version and the Object Windows version is the switch from standard Turbo Pascal strings to null-terminated strings, using the type PChar. If you are still unfamiliar with null-terminated strings, see Chapter 6. The subprograms that display strings in Windows applications accept PChar parameters, so it is easier to use PChars throughout the application.

Borland has simplified the manipulation of null-terminated strings with the Strings unit. Strictly speaking, this unit is part of the standard set of units and not part of Object Windows; however, it is rarely used independently of Object Windows. The statement

```
StrPCopy(CNumPChar, CNumStr);
```

converts a standard string to a null-terminated string. Note that StrPCopy is actually defined as a function; however, since its return value is not useful, it is usually called as a procedure. See Chapter 4 for more information on the extended syntax that allows functions to be called like procedures.

Another unique feature to this version is the *CardRec* data type. This type will be used by the dialog boxes to pass data about a flash card from the application to the dialog box and back:

```
type
  CardRec = record
    CardNum : array [0..3] of char;
    Question : FlashStr;
    Answer : FlashStr;
  end;
```

The card number is stored in the record as a null-terminated string so that the dialog boxes don't need to worry about conversion to and from **integer**. Although this type is not used in the FLASHCRD unit itself, it makes more sense to define it here since it is so dependent on the fields of the *TFlashCard* object.

Turbo Vision and Object Windows have one unit in common—the Objects unit. This unit contains the definitions for TObject, TCollection, and TStream. Thus a collection used in a Turbo Vision application can be used in an Object Windows application without any changes. If you did not study all of Chapter 17, you need to read at least the "Using Collections" and "Using Streams" sections of that chapter.

The only difference between the FLSET unit in Chapter 17 and the FLASHSET unit shown here is that they use different versions of the TFlashCard object. Therefore the FLASHSET unit includes the FLASHCRD unit in its **uses** clause, instead of FLCARD.

```
Unit FLASHSET;

interface

uses Objects, FLASHCRD;

type
  PFlashCardSet = ^TFlashCardSet;
  TFlashCardSet = object(TCollection)
    Constructor Init;
    Constructor Load(var S : TStream);
    procedure Store(var S : TStream);
    function NewCard : PFlashCard;
    procedure Replace(ACard : PFlashCard);
    procedure Delete(ACard : PFlashCard);
    function NextCard : PFlashCard;
    function AnyCard : PFlashCard;
  private
    CurrentCard : Integer;
    end;

const
(* for Stream registration *)
  RFlashCardSet: TStreamRec = (
    ObjType: 140;
    VmtLink: Ofs(TypeOf(TFlashCardSet)^);
    Load: @TFlashCardSet.Load;
    Store: @TFlashCardSet.Store);

implementation

constructor TFlashCardSet.Init;
begin
  TCollection.Init(10, 5);
  CurrentCard := -1;
  Randomize;
end;


(**************************************************)

constructor TFlashCardSet.Load(var S : TStream);
begin
  TCollection.Load(S);
  CurrentCard := -1;
  Randomize;
end;
```

```
(************************************************)

procedure TFlashCardSet.Store(var S : TStream);
begin
  TCollection.Store(S);
end;

(************************************************)

function TFlashCardSet.NewCard : PFlashCard;
var
  BlankCard : PFlashCard;
begin
  New(BlankCard, Init);
  TCollection.Insert(BlankCard);
  BlankCard^.SetNumber(Count);
  NewCard := BlankCard;
end;

(************************************************)

procedure TFlashCardSet.Replace(ACard : PFlashCard);
begin
  TCollection.AtPut(ACard^.GetNumber - 1, ACard);
end;

(************************************************)

procedure TFlashCardSet.Delete(ACard : PFlashCard);
begin
  TCollection.AtDelete(ACard^.GetNumber - 1);
end;

(************************************************)

function TFlashCardSet.NextCard : PFlashCard;
var
  ACard : PFlashCard;
begin
  CurrentCard := CurrentCard + 1;
  if CurrentCard = Count then
    CurrentCard := 0;
  ACard := TCollection.At(CurrentCard);
  ACard^.SetNumber(CurrentCard+1);
  NextCard := ACard;
end;
```

```
(************************************************)

function TFlashCardSet.AnyCard : PFlashCard;
var
  ACard : PFlashCard;
begin
  CurrentCard := Random(Count);
  ACard := TCollection.At(CurrentCard);
  ACard^.SetNumber(CurrentCard + 1);
  AnyCard := ACard;
end;

end.
```

Strings Unit Summary

StrCat

```
function StrCat(Dest, Source : PChar) : PChar;
```

Concatenates the string pointed to by Source to the end of the string pointed to by Dest. The string is returned in Dest. No length checking is done, so memory will be corrupted if Dest has not allocated enough space.

StrComp

```
function StrComp(Str1, Str2 : PChar) : integer;
```

Compares two strings; returns a positive number if Str1 > Str2, a negative number if Str1 < Str2, and zero if they are the same.

StrCopy

```
function StrCopy(Dest, Source : PChar) : PChar;
```

Copies the string pointed to by Source to the string pointed to by Dest. No length checking is done, so memory will be corrupted if Dest has not allocated enough space.

StrDispose

```
procedure StrDispose(Str : PChar);
```

Frees the memory associated with Str.

StrECopy

```
function StrECopy(Dest, Source : PChar) : PChar;
```

Copies the string pointed to by Source to the string pointed to by Dest; also returns a pointer to the end of Dest. No length checking is done, so memory will be corrupted if Dest has not allocated enough space.

StrEnd

```
function StrEnd(Str : PChar) : PChar;
```

Returns a pointer to the end of Str, which is the first null character.

StrIComp

```
function StrIComp(Str1, Str2 : PChar) : integer;
```

Same as StrComp, except case insensitive.

StrLCat

```
function StrLCat(Dest, Source : PChar; MaxLen : word) : PChar;
```

Same as StrCat, except the copy is limited to MaxLen characters.

StrLComp

```
function StrLComp(Str1, Str2 : PChar; MaxLen : word) : integer;
```

Same as StrComp, except only the first MaxLen characters are compared.

StrLCopy

```
function StrLCopy(Dest, Source : PChar; MaxLen : word) : PChar;
```

Same as StrCopy, except the copy is limited to MaxLen characters.

StrLen

```
function StrLen(Str : PChar) : word;
```

Returns the length of the string pointed to by Str.

StrLIComp

```
function StrLIComp(Str1, Str2 : PChar; MaxLen : word) : integer;
```

Same as StrIComp, except only the first MaxLen characters are compared.

StrLower

```
function StrLower(Str : PChar) : PChar;
```

Changes Str so that all characters are lowercase.

StrMove

```
function StrMove(Dest, Source : PChar; Count : word) : PChar;
```

Moves Count characters from the location of Source to the location of Dest.

StrNew

```
function StrNew(Str : PChar) : PChar;
```

Allocates enough memory to fit Str and returns a copy of Str.

StrPas

```
function StrPas(Str : PChar) : string;
```

Converts a null-terminated string to a standard string.

StrPCopy

```
function StrPCopy(Dest : PChar; Source : string) : PChar;
```

Converts a standard string to a null-terminated string. The new string is pointed to by Dest.

StrPos

```
function StrPos(Str1, Str2 : PChar) : PChar;
```

Returns the location of the first occurrence of Str2 within Str1.

StrRScan

```
function StrRScan(Str : PChar; Ch : char) : PChar;
```

Returns the location of the last occurrence of Ch within Str.

StrScan

```
function StrScan(Str : PChar; Ch : char) : PChar;
```

Returns the location of the first occurrence of Ch within Str.

StrUpper

```
function StrUpper(Str : PChar) : PChar;
```

Changes Str so that all characters are uppercase.

Creating Dialog Boxes

Until now you have created the main window, the menu bar, the accelerators, and the support code. All that remains is the code that executes each menu command. Most of the command implementations given in this section involve the use of dialog boxes so you can learn how to create your own dialog boxes.

For the Flash Card program, all dialog box implementations will be placed in one unit called FLASHDLG:

```
Unit FLASHDLG;

interface

{$R FLASH.RES}

uses FLASHCRD, FLASHSET, FLASHCNS,
     Objects, ODialogs, OWindows,
     WinProcs, WinTypes, Strings;

var
  TheSet : PFlashCardSet;
  OneCard : PFlashCard;
```

Notice that this unit will use two global variables, *TheSet* and *OneCard*, to avoid the burden of passing them around as parameters from method to method. These variables must be initialized in the initialization section of the unit:

```
begin
  OneCard := New(PFlashCard, Init);
  TheSet := New(PFlashCardSet, Init);
end.
```

Add Card Dialog Box

The creation of a dialog box usually begins in the Resource Workshop. Using this tool you design how the dialog box will appear to the user. You also associate buttons in the box with commands that will be handled by your Turbo Pascal code. The following listing is the resource code for the first dialog box, called "Add Card:"

```
dlgAddCard DIALOG 24, 26, 247, 125
STYLE WS_POPUP | WS_CAPTION | WS_SYSMENU
CAPTION "Add Card"
BEGIN
  LTEXT "Card Number:", -1, 21, 13, 50, 8,
    WS_CHILD | WS_VISIBLE
```

```
  LTEXT "&Question:", -1, 21, 29, 35, 8
    WS_CHILD | WS_VISIBLE | WS_GROUP
  EDITTEXT dlgQuestion, 21, 42, 202, 13, ES_LEFT | WS_CHILD |
    WS_VISIBLE | WS_BORDER | WS_TABSTOP
  LTEXT "&Answer:", -1, 21, 61, 28, 8
    WS_CHILD | WS_VISIBLE | WS_GROUP
  EDITTEXT dlgAnswer, 21, 74, 202, 13, ES_LEFT | WS_CHILD |
    WS_VISIBLE | WS_BORDER | WS_TABSTOP
  DEFPUSHBUTTON "A&dd Another", dlgAddAnother, 21, 101, 48, 14,
    WS_CHILD | WS_VISIBLE | WS_TABSTOP
  PUSHBUTTON "&OK", IDOK, 105, 101, 24, 14
    WS_CHILD | WS_VISIBLE | WS_TABSTOP
  PUSHBUTTON "&Cancel", IDCANCEL, 160, 101, 30, 14
    WS_CHILD | WS_VISIBLE | WS_TABSTOP
  CONTROL "0", dlgCardNum, "EDIT", ES_LEFT | WS_CHILD |
    WS_VISIBLE, 75, 13, 16, 10
END
```

This dialog box appears in Figure 18-4. As you can see there is a static text for the card number, edit controls for the question and answer, and three push buttons. The card number is determined by the software. The user enters the question for that card, presses TAB to move to the next field, and enters the answer. Then the user has three choices:

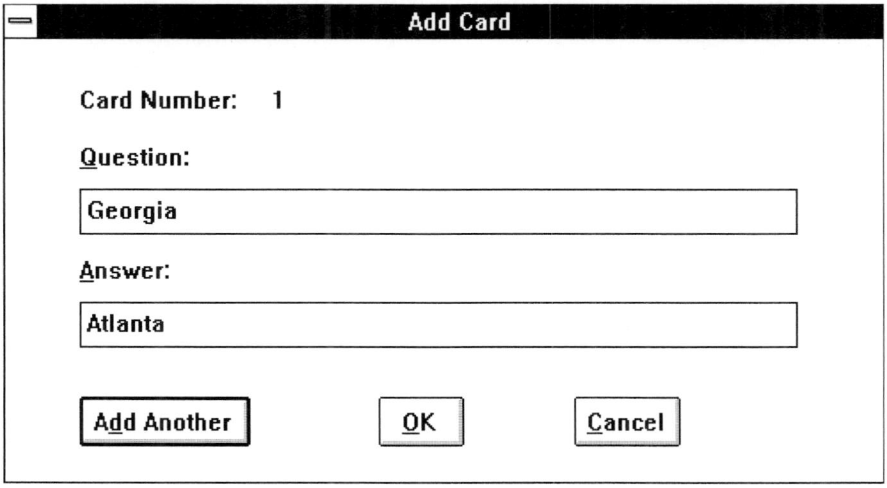

Figure 18-4. *The Add Card dialog box*

- Press the Add Another button to increment the card number and add another card.

- Press the OK button to save the current card but exit the dialog box.

- Press the Cancel button to not add this card.

If the user presses Add Another, the program automatically moves the cursor back to the Question field to enter the next question.

Dialog boxes are implemented using the TDialog object, part of the ODialogs unit. Very seldom do you use the TDialog type without creating a descendant object type. Based on the above description, it is obvious that the "Add Card" dialog box will require some extra logic.

The Turbo Pascal portion of the implementation starts with the object declaration, *TAddDialog*:

```
type
  PAddDialog = ^TAddDialog;
  TAddDialog = object(TDialog)
    procedure SetupWindow; virtual;
    procedure Ok(var Msg : TMessage);
      virtual id_First + id_Ok;
    procedure AddAnother(var Msg : TMessage);
      virtual id_First + dlgAddAnother;
  end;
```

The methods *Ok* and *AddAnother* are dynamic methods, similar to those used in the *TFCWindow* object type. The expression after the word **virtual** tells the compiler that this method will be called in response to a dialog box command.

The *SetupWindow* method does any initializations necessary before the dialog box is displayed. For the "Add Card" dialog box, the method looks like this:

```
procedure TAddDialog.SetupWindow;
begin
  inherited SetupWindow;
  OneCard := TheSet^.NewCard;
  SetDlgItemText(HWindow, dlgCardNum, OneCard^.GetNumberPChar);
end;
```

After calling its ancestor, the method creates a new card for the set by calling the *NewCard* method of the *TFlashCardSet* object. The call to SetDlgItemText changes the text associated with the *dlgCardNum* resource to the string returned by *GetNumberPChar*. This is how the dialog box displays the number of the card being added.

When the user presses the OK button, you need to retrieve the strings entered for Question and Answer. This is done with the complement of SetDlgItemText, called GetDlgItemText:

```
procedure TAddDialog.Ok;
var
  Temp : FlashStr;
  TempSize : integer;
begin
  GetDlgItemText(HWindow, dlgQuestion, Temp, TempSize);
  OneCard^.SetQuestion(Temp);
  GetDlgItemText(HWindow, dlgAnswer, Temp, TempSize);
  OneCard^.SetAnswer(Temp);
  TheSet^.Replace(OneCard);
  EndDlg(id_Ok);
end;
```

The GetDlgItemText function retrieves a string based on the resource identifier, in this case *dlgQuestion* and *dlgAnswer*. As it retrieves these values, the *Ok* method inserts them into the current card, and then replaces the card in the set. The call to the EndDlg method closes the dialog box and sets the return code to the given identifier.

The final method in TAddDialog allows the user to continue to add cards quickly and easily. As you can see, in many ways the *AddAnother* method works like a combination of the *Ok* and *SetupWindow* methods:

```
procedure TAddDialog.AddAnother;
var
  Temp : FlashStr;
  TempSize : integer;
  Handle : word;
begin
  GetDlgItemText(HWindow, dlgQuestion, Temp, TempSize);
  OneCard^.SetQuestion(Temp);
  GetDlgItemText(HWindow, dlgAnswer, Temp, TempSize);
  OneCard^.SetAnswer(Temp);
  TheSet^.Replace(OneCard);
  OneCard := TheSet^.NewCard;
  SetDlgItemText(HWindow, dlgCardNum, OneCard^.GetNumberPChar);
  SendDlgItemMsg(dlgQuestion, em_SetSel, 0,
          MakeLong(0, QAMaxLen));
  SetFocus(GetItemHandle(dlgQuestion));
end;
```

Like *Ok*, this method retrieves the question and answer entered by the user, and replaces the card in the set. Like *SetupWindow*, it creates a new card and changes the card number displayed in the dialog box.

The two additional calls at the end of *AddAnother* make life a little easier for the user. The call to SendDlgItemMsg using the em_SetSel constant tells the resource associated with *dlgQuestion* to highlight itself. This way the user can enter the next question without manually deleting the old one. The call to the SetFocus function tells the dialog box to move the cursor to the resource associated with *dlgQuestion*. This keeps the user from having to use the TAB key or mouse to move back to the Question field.

The only step remaining is to modify the stub of *TFCWindow.CardAdd* so that it executes a *TAddDialog* dialog box:

```
procedure TFCWindow.CardAdd;
var
  AddCard : PAddDialog;
begin
  AddCard := New(PAddDialog, Init(@Self, PChar(dlgAddCard)));
  if Application^.ExecDialog(AddCard) = id_Cancel then
    TheSet^.Delete(OneCard);
end
```

Executing a dialog box is a two-step process. First, you must create an object of the proper TDialog (or descendant) type. The call to Init inside the New statement associates the dialog box object with the resource identified by dlgAddCard. The second step is to call TApplication.ExecDialog, which will set up the dialog box, display it, allow the user to enter the data, and close it. When this step closes the dialog box it returns a value representing the last button pushed. If that button is the Cancel button, you need to delete the last card that was added.

Question Dialog Box

The second dialog box in the program displays a flash card question. This box is displayed whenever the user selects either Card|Random or Card|Next. There are no edit fields in this dialog box. Once the card number and the question appear, the user can press one of these two buttons: Show Answer, which displays the answer in another dialog box, or Cancel, which closes the dialog box without showing the answer. You can see an example of this box in Figure 18-5.

The first step in implementing this dialog box is with the Resource Workshop, as was the case for the "Add Card" box. Usually you would create the dialog box interactively; this time you can merely enter this text:

```
dlgQuestion DIALOG 18, 18, 219, 60
STYLE WS_POPUP | WS_CAPTION | WS_SYSMENU
CAPTION "Question"
BEGIN
  CONTROL "0", dlgCardNum, "EDIT", ES_LEFT | WS_CHILD |
    WS_VISIBLE, 197, 42, 16, 12
  CONTROL "", dlgQuestion, "EDIT", ES_CENTER | WS_CHILD |
    WS_VISIBLE, 11, 8, 202, 12
```

```
    PUSHBUTTON "Show &Answer", 1, 17, 40, 48, 14
    PUSHBUTTON "&Cancel", 2, 101, 40, 29, 14, WS_CHILD |
      WS_VISIBLE | WS_TABSTOP
    LTEXT "Card:", -1, 175, 42, 22, 8
END;
```

The two controls identified by *dlgCardNum* and *dlgQuestion* have been created so that the program can change their values, but the user cannot (the WS_TABSTOP attribute has been removed). The only controls accessible by the user are the two push buttons.

Returning to the FLASHDLG unit, the implementation of the "Question" dialog box actually requires two object definitions:

```
type
  PAnswerDialog = ^TAnswerDialog;
  TAnswerDialog = object(TDialog)
    procedure SetupWindow; virtual;
    procedure Next(var Msg : TMessage);
      virtual id_First + dlgNext;
    procedure Random(var Msg : TMessage);
      virtual id_First + dlgRandom;
  end;

  PQDialog = ^TQDialog;
  TQDialog = object(TDialog)
    ABox : PAnswerDialog;
    procedure SetupWindow; virtual;
    procedure Ok(var Msg : TMessage);
      virtual id_First + id_OK;
  end;
```

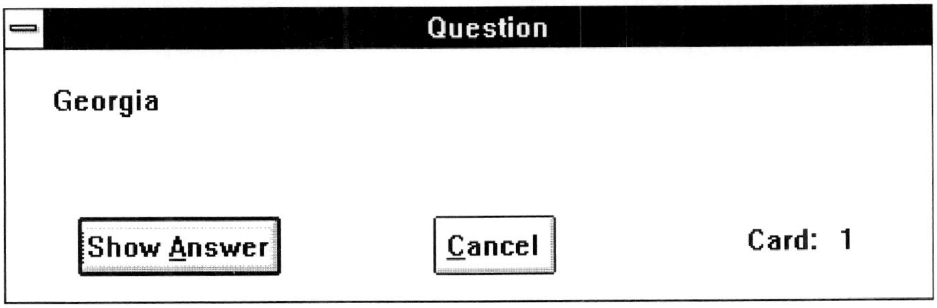

Figure 18-5. *The Question dialog box*

You'll find more discussion on the *TAnswerDialog* type later in the chapter. For now you should notice that the *TQDialog* object includes a field called ABox that points to a *TAnswerDialog* object.

The *TQDialog* type is a fairly simple descendant of TDialog. It includes a *SetupWindow* method to set the Card Number and Question fields, and an *Ok* method to do the special processing required when the user presses the Show Answer push button. Why is the method called *Ok* when the button is named Show Answer? The reason is that the resource associates the button with the number 1, which is the Ok command. Since the method is a dynamic method, you cannot change its name. An alternative solution would be to add a new constant to the FLASHCNS unit, use that constant in the resource, and create a new dynamic method indexed by that constant.

Here are the implementations of the two methods:

```
procedure TQDialog.SetupWindow;
begin
  inherited SetupWindow;
  SetDlgItemText(HWindow, dlgCardNum, OneCard^.GetNumberPChar);
  SetDlgItemText(HWindow, dlgQuestion, OneCard^.GetQuestion);
end;

procedure TQDialog.Ok;
var
  DlgStatus : word;
begin
  ABox := new(PAnswerDialog, Init(@Self, PChar(dlgAnswer)));
  DlgStatus := Application^.ExecDialog(ABox);
  EndDlg(DlgStatus);
end;
```

The *Ok* method is responsible for executing the "Answer" dialog box. When the user presses the Show Answer button, this method displays the answer in a box. That box returns a status, which the *Ok* method passes on to its caller. You'll see how the value is set later.

That brings us to the final step—executing the dialog box. As mentioned earlier, this dialog box will be displayed from two commands: Card|Random and Card|Next. To eliminate code duplication, you can create a new method that executes the dialog box. The *NextCard* and *RandomCard* methods in the *TFCWindow* object would then call the new method as needed. To see how this works, study this listing:

```
procedure TFCWindow.ShowQuestion(Action : word);
begin
  repeat
    if Action = dlgNext then
      OneCard := TheSet^.NextCard
    else
      OneCard := TheSet^.AnyCard;
    QBox := new(PQDialog, Init(@Self, PChar(dlgQuestion)));
```

```
      Action := Application^.ExecDialog(QBox);
   until Action = id_Cancel;
end;

procedure TFCWindow.NextCard;
begin
   ShowQuestion(dlgNext);
end;

procedure TFCWindow.RandomCard;
begin
   ShowQuestion(dlgRandom);
end;
```

The new method is called *ShowQuestion*. This method contains a **repeat-until** loop that allows the user to go through many flash cards without selecting a command from the menu bar. Based on an initial command, *ShowQuestion* selects either the next card in sequence or a card at random. Then it creates a dialog box and calls ExecDialog. That function returns a status, which represents the next command, either displaying the next card (*dlgNext*), displaying a random card (*dlgRandom*), or ending display of cards (*id_Cancel*).

Answer Dialog Box

The last dialog box in the Flash Card program is the "Answer" box. This box displays the answer to the flash card once the user has seen the question. Figure 18-6 depicts the entire screen when the "Answer" dialog box is active. The box has three buttons: Random Question, Next Question, and Cancel. Near the top of the box is the answer to the flash card. Once users have read the answer, they can either see another card, or stop the display process.

Once again the artistic portion of the dialog box is done in the Resource Workshop. Here is the resource code that helped create Figure 18-6:

```
dlgAnswer DIALOG 6, 97, 219, 62
STYLE WS_POPUP | WS_CAPTION | WS_SYSMENU
CAPTION "Answer"
BEGIN
  CONTROL "", dlgAnswer, "EDIT", ES_CENTER | WS_CHILD |
    WS_VISIBLE, 11, 8, 202, 12
  DEFPUSHBUTTON "&Random Question", dlgRandom, 17, 42, 66, 14,
    WS_CHILD | WS_VISIBLE | WS_TABSTOP
  PUSHBUTTON "&Next Question", dlgNext, 98, 42, 58, 14,
    WS_CHILD | WS_VISIBLE | WS_TABSTOP
  PUSHBUTTON "&Cancel", 2, 171, 42, 29, 14,
    WS_CHILD | WS_VISIBLE | WS_TABSTOP
END
```

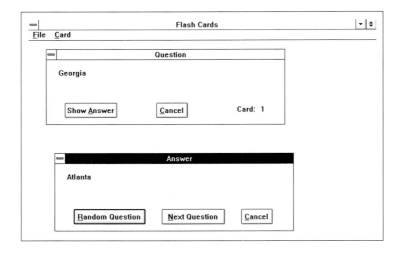

Figure 18-6.   *The Answer dialog box*

Like the "Question" box, this box includes a control (identified by *dlgAnswer*) that is modifiable by the program, but not the user.

You saw the definition of the *TAnswerDialog* object in the previous section. This descendant of TDialog has three methods:

- *SetupWindow*, which supplies the flash card answer to the box for display

- *Random*, which is executed when the user presses the Random Question button, and

- *Next*, which is executed when the user presses Next Question

All three of these methods have simple implementations:

```
procedure TAnswerDialog.SetupWindow;
begin
  inherited SetupWindow;
  SetDlgItemText(HWindow, dlgAnswer, OneCard^.GetAnswer);
end;

procedure TAnswerDialog.Random;
begin
  EndDlg(dlgRandom);
```

```
end;

procedure TAnswerDialog.Next;
begin
  EndDlg(dlgNext);
end;
```

The *Random* and *Next* methods close the dialog box, passing back the *dlgRandom* or *dlgNext* constants as status values. The *TQDialog* box passes these constants back to *TFCWindow.ShowQuestion*, which uses the value to determine its next course of action.

File Dialogs

Up to now you have seen the code that implements all of the commands in the Card menu. With that code you can create and view flash cards. To make the program truly useful, however, you must also be able to store and retrieve card sets. Object Windows uses streams to simplify saving and reading files that contain objects. If you are unfamiliar with streams, study the Using Streams section of Chapter 17.

Object Windows also includes a standard dialog object for saving and opening files. This object, called TFileDialog, is located in the OStdDlgs unit. Using this object not only saves you hours of development time, but also makes your dialog boxes consistent with those used in the IDE. Figure 18-7 shows the "File Open" dialog box for the Flash Card program.

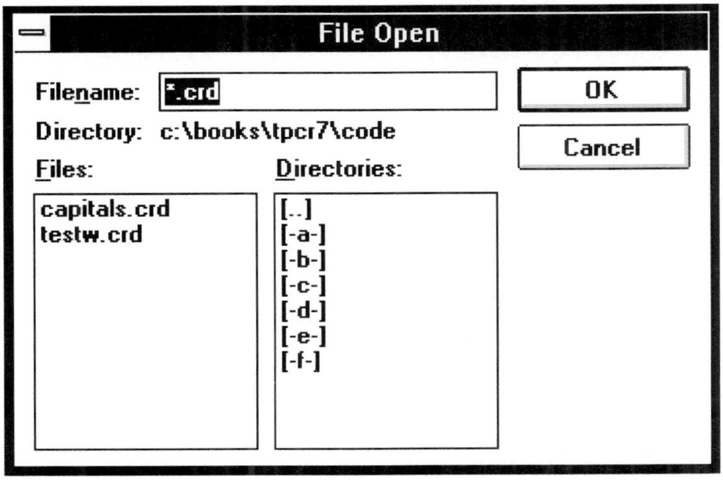

Figure 18-7.   The File Open dialog box

Creating a file dialog box can be done with just one call to ExecDialog:

```
procedure TFCWindow.FileOpen;
var
  FCStream : TBufStream;
begin
  if Application^.ExecDialog(New(PFileDialog,
          Init(@Self, PChar(sd_FileOpen),
          StrCopy(FileName, '*.CRD')))) = id_Ok then
    begin
      FCStream.Init(FileName, stOpenRead, 512);
      TheSet := PFlashCardSet(FCStream.Get);
      FCStream.Done;
    end;
end;
```

Part of the call to ExecDialog is a call to TFileDialog.Init, which includes a parameter for the type of file dialog (in this case sd_FileOpen), and a parameter for the name of the file, called FileName. If the initial value of the filename parameter includes a wildcard specification, the dialog box will display a list of files with that specification.

Loading the flash cards from the file is accomplished by initializing the file as a stream and loading the data from the stream. The data read is converted to a flash card set with this call:

```
TheSet := PFlashCardSet(FCStream.Get);
```

Putting It All Together

With the exception of a few *TFCWindow* methods, all of the code you have studied in this "Creating Dialog Boxes" section belongs in the FLASHDLG unit. All that remains are the final touches to the main program.

The following listing is the complete code for the Flashcard_App program. When you combine it with the code for the four supporting units, you have a complete, working Object Windows application.

```
Program Flashcard_App;

uses FLASHDLG, FLASHCRD, FLASHSET, FLASHCNS,
     Objects, OWindows, OStdDlgs,
     WinProcs, WinTypes, WinDos, Strings;

type
  TFlashCardApp = object(TApplication)
    procedure InitMainWindow; virtual;
    procedure InitInstance; virtual;
  end;
```

```
  PFCWindow = ^TFCWindow;
  TFCWindow = object(TWindow)
    FileName: array[0..fsPathName] of char;
    QBox : PQDialog;
    constructor Init(AParent : PWindowsObject; ATitle : PChar);
    procedure FileOpen(var Msg : TMessage);
      virtual cm_First + cmFileOpen;
    procedure FileSave(var Msg : TMessage);
      virtual cm_First + cmFileSave;
    procedure Quit(var Msg : TMessage);
      virtual cm_First + cmQuit;
    procedure CardAdd(var Msg : TMessage);
      virtual cm_First + cmCardAdd;
    procedure CardChange(var Msg : TMessage);
      virtual cm_First + cmCardChange;
    procedure CardDelete(var Msg : TMessage);
      virtual cm_First + cmCardDelete;
    procedure NextCard(var Msg : TMessage);
      virtual cm_First + cmCardNext;
    procedure RandomCard(var Msg : TMessage);
      virtual cm_First + cmCardRandom;
    procedure ShowQuestion(Action : word);
  end;

var
  FlashCardApp : TFlashCardApp;

(************************************************)

procedure RegisterStreams;
begin
  RegisterType(RCollection);
  RegisterType(RFlashCard);
  RegisterType(RFlashCardSet);
end;

(************************************************)

constructor TFCWindow.Init;
begin
  inherited Init(AParent, ATitle);
  Attr.Menu := LoadMenu(HInstance, PChar(MenuBar));
end;

procedure TFCWindow.FileOpen;
var
  FCStream : TBufStream;
begin
```

```
    if Application^.ExecDialog(New(PFileDialog,
            Init(@Self, PChar(sd_FileOpen),
            StrCopy(FileName, '*.CRD')))) = id_Ok then
    begin
      FCStream.Init(FileName, stOpenRead, 512);
      TheSet := PFlashCardSet(FCStream.Get);
      FCStream.Done;
    end;
end;

procedure TFCWindow.FileSave;
var
  FCStream : TBufStream;
begin
  if Application^.ExecDialog(New(PFileDialog,
            Init(@Self, PChar(sd_FileSave),
            StrCopy(FileName, '*.CRD')))) = id_Ok then
    begin
      FCStream.Init(FileName, stCreate, 512);
      FCStream.Put(TheSet);
      FCStream.Done;
    end;
end;

procedure TFCWindow.Quit;
begin
  Done;
end;

procedure TFCWindow.CardAdd;
var
  AddCard : PAddDialog;
begin
  AddCard := New(PAddDialog, Init(@Self, PChar(dlgAddCard)));
  if Application^.ExecDialog(AddCard) = id_Cancel then
    TheSet^.Delete(OneCard);
end;

procedure TFCWindow.CardChange;
begin
  MessageBox(HWindow, 'Not Implemented Yet', 'Change Card', mb_OK);
end;

procedure TFCWindow.CardDelete;
begin
  MessageBox(HWindow, 'Not Implemented Yet', 'Delete Card', mb_OK);
end;

procedure TFCWindow.ShowQuestion(Action : word);
```

```
begin
  repeat
    if Action = dlgNext then
      OneCard := TheSet^.NextCard
    else
      OneCard := TheSet^.AnyCard;
    QBox := new(PQDialog, Init(@Self, PChar(dlgQuestion)));
    Action := Application^.ExecDialog(QBox);
  until Action = id_Cancel;
end;

procedure TFCWindow.NextCard;
begin
  ShowQuestion(dlgNext);
end;

procedure TFCWindow.RandomCard;
begin
  ShowQuestion(dlgRandom);
end;


procedure TFlashCardApp.InitMainWindow;
begin
  MainWindow := New(PFCWindow, Init(nil, 'Flash Cards'));
  if HAccTable = 0 then
    MessageBox(MainWindow^.HWindow, 'Accelerators not loaded',
        'Error', mb_OK);
end;

procedure TFlashCardApp.InitInstance;
begin
  HAccTable := LoadAccelerators(HInstance, PChar(AccelKeys));
  inherited InitInstance;
end;

begin
  RegisterStreams;
  FlashCardApp.Init('FlashCards');
  FlashCardApp.Run;
  FlashCardApp.Done;
end.
```

Actually, calling this program "complete" is a little misleading. First, two of the methods, *CardChange* and *CardDelete* are still stubs. Second, there are plenty of enhancements that can be done to make this program even more useful. If you see a need for this program, or something similar, challenge yourself to type it in, make it work, and build on it. That's what Object Windows is all about.

TDialog Object Summary   **ODialogs Unit**

Heritage

TDialog → TWindowsObject → TObject

Primary Methods

```
constructor Init(AParent : PWindowsObject; AName : PChar);
```

Initializes the dialog box.

```
procedure Cancel(var Msg : TMessage);
            virtual id_First + id_Cancel;
```

Overridden to process the dialog box when the user presses the Cancel button.

```
procedure EndDlg(ARetValue : integer); virtual;
```

Destroys the dialog box and returns the given value to the procedure that called
Execute.

```
function Execute : integer; virtual;
```

Executes the dialog box.

```
procedure Ok(var Msg : TMessage); virtual id_First + id_OK;
```

Overridden to process the dialog box when the user presses the OK button.

```
function SendDlgItemMsg(DlgItemID : integer; AMsg, WParam : word;
                    LParam : longint) : longint;
```

Sends a message to a control within the dialog box.

Related Subprograms

```
function GetDlgItemText(Dlg : HWnd; IDDlgItem : integer;
             Str : PChar; MaxCount : integer) : integer;
```

Gets the contents of an edit control identified by IDDlgItem and returns it in Str.

```
procedure SetDlgItemText(Dlg : HWnd; IDDlgItem : integer;
                         Str : PChar);
```

Sets the contents of an edit control identified by IDDlgItem to the string Str.

```
function SetFocus(Wnd : HWnd) : HWnd;
```

Moves the cursor (or other focus mechanism) to the window referenced by Wnd.

TControl Object Summary   ODialogs Unit

Heritage

TControl ➡ TWindow ➡ TWindowsObject ➡ TObject

Primary Methods

```
constructor Init(AParent : PWindowsObject; AnId : integer;
             ATitle : PChar; X, Y, W, H : integer);
```

Creates a control window at a given location within its parent window.

```
constructor InitResource(AParent : PWindowsObject;
                         ResourceID : word);
```

Creates a control window that is associated with the given resource.

TButton Object Summary   **ODialogs Unit**

Heritage

TButton → TControl → TWindow → TWindowsObject → TObject

Primary Methods

```
constructor Init(AParent : PWindowsObject; AnId : integer;
                 ATitle : PChar; X, Y, W, H : integer;
                 IsDefault : boolean);
```

Creates a push button at a given location within its parent window. If IsDefault is True, the button will be highlighted to indicate it is the default.

```
constructor InitResource(AParent : PWindowsObject;
                         ResourceID : word);
```

Creates a push button that is associated with the given resource.

TCheckBox Object Summary   **ODialogs Unit**

Heritage

TCheckBox → TButton → TControl → TWindow → TWindowsObject → TObject

Primary Methods

```
constructor Init(AParent : PWindowsObject; AnId : integer;
                 ATitle : PChar; X, Y, W, H : integer;
                 AGroup : PGroupBox);
```

Creates a check box at a given location within its parent window. If AGroup is not **nil**, the check box is associated with the given group.

```
constructor InitResource(AParent : PWindowsObject;
                         ResourceID : word);
```

Creates a check box that is associated with the given resource.

```
function GetCheck : word; virtual;
```

Returns zero if the box is unchecked; non-zero if it is checked. You can also use the constants described in "Related Constants."

```
procedure SetCheck(CheckFlag : word); virtual;
```

Sets the state of the check box. CheckFlag should be one of the constants shown in "Related Constants."

```
procedure Toggle; virtual;
```

Toggles the state of the check box.

Related Constants

```
bf_Unchecked = 0;
bf_Checked = 1;
bf_Grayed = 2;
```

The various states available for a check box.

TRadioButton Object Summary   ODialogs Unit

Heritage

TRadioButton ➞ TCheckBox ➞ TButton ➞ TControl ➞
TWindow ➞ TWindowsObject ➞ TObject

Primary Methods

```
constructor Init(AParent : PWindowsObject; AnId : integer;
                 ATitle : PChar; X, Y, W, H : integer;
                 AGroup : PGroupBox);
```

Creates a radio button at a given location within its parent window. If AGroup is not **nil**, the radio button is associated with the given group.

Primary Inherited Methods

Inherited from TCheckBox:

```
function GetCheck : word; virtual;
constructor InitResource(AParent : PWindowsObject;
                         ResourceID : word);
procedure SetCheck(CheckFlag : word); virtual;
procedure Toggle; virtual;
```

TStatic Object Summary   ODialogs Unit

Heritage

TStatic ➡ TControl ➡ TWindow ➡ TWindowsObject ➡ TObject

Primary Methods

```
constructor Init(AParent : PWindowsObject; AnID : integer;
                 ATitle : PChar; X, Y, W, H : integer;
                 ATextLen : word);
```

Creates a static control at a given location within its parent window. The text to display is ATitle, and its length is ATextLen.

```
constructor InitResource(AParent : PWindowsObject;
                         ResourceID, ATextLen : word);
```

Creates a static control that is associated with the given resource.

```
procedure Clear; virtual;
```

Deletes the text of a static control.

```
function GetText(ATextString : PChar;
                 MaxChars : integer) : integer;
```

Retrieves the current contents of the static control. The string itself is returned in ATextString. This function is used primarily by TEdit objects.

```
procedure SetText(ATextString : PChar); virtual;
```

Changes the text of a static control to that in ATextString.

```
function Transfer(DataPtr : pointer;
                  TransferFlag : word) : word; virtual;
```

Transfers text between the static control and the given memory location.

TEdit Object Summary   ODialogs Unit

Heritage

TEdit → TStatic → TControl → TWindow → TWindowsObject → TObject

Primary Methods

```
constructor Init(AParent : PWindowsObject; AnID : integer;
                 ATitle : PChar; X, Y, W, H : integer;
                 ATextLen : word; MultiLine : boolean);
```

Creates an edit control at a given location within its parent window. The text to display is ATitle, and its length is ATextLen. If MuliLine is true, the control will be a multi-line edit control; otherwise it will be single-line.

```
function GetLine(ATextString : PChar; StrSize : integer;
                 LineNumber : integer) : boolean; virtual;
```

Retrieves one line from a multi-line edit control. The string is returned in ATextString.

```
function GetLineLength(LineNumber : integer) : integer; virtual;
```

Returns the number of characters in a given line of a multi-line edit control.

```
function GetNumLines: integer; virtual;
```

Returns the current number of lines of a multi-line edit control.

```
function IsModified : boolean; virtual;
```

Returns True if the user changed the contents of an edit control.

Primary Inherited Methods

Inherited from TStatic:

```
procedure Clear; virtual;
function GetText(ATextString : PChar;
                MaxChars : integer) : integer;
procedure SetText(ATextString : PChar); virtual;
```

TListBox Object Summary   ODialogs Unit

Heritage

TListBox → TControl → TWindow → TWindowsObject → TObject

Primary Methods

```
constructor Init(AParent : PWindowsObject; AnId : integer;
                 X, Y, W, H : integer);
```

Creates a list box control at a given location within its parent window.

```
function AddString(AString : PChar) : integer; virtual;
```

Adds a string to the list box. The strings are sorted, and the position of the added string is returned.

```
function DeleteString(Index : integer) : integer; virtual;
```

Removes the string at the specified Index from the list box.

```
function GetCount : integer; virtual;
```

Returns the current number of strings in the list box.

```
function GetSelIndex : integer; virtual;
```

Returns the index of the string that has been selected.

```
function GetString(AString : PChar;
                   Index : integer) : integer; virtual;
```

Returns in AString the string specified by Index.

```
function SetSelIndex(Index : integer) : integer; virtual;
```

Selects (highlights) the string specified by Index.

TComboBox Object Summary   **ODialogs Unit**

Heritage

TComboBox ➡ TListBox ➡ TControl ➡ TWindow ➡
TWindowsObject ➡ TObject

Primary Methods

```
constructor Init(AParent : PWindowsObject; AnID : integer;
                 X, Y, W, H : integer;
                 AStyle, ATextLen : word);
```

Creates a "combo" box, or combination list box, control at a given location within its parent window. The length of the edit control is ATextLen. See "Related Constants" for valid values of AStyle.

```
constructor InitResource(AParent : PWindowsObject;
                         ResourceID, ATextLen : word);
```

Creates a combo box that is associated with the given resource.

Primary Inherited Methods

From TListBox:

```
function AddString(AString : PChar) : integer; virtual;
function DeleteString(Index : integer) : integer; virtual;
function GetCount : integer; virtual;
function GetSelIndex : integer; virtual;
function GetString(AString : PChar;
                  Index : integer) : integer; virtual;
function SetSelIndex(Index : integer) : integer; virtual;
```

Related Constants

```
cbs_Simple = 1;          {list box always visible}
cbs_DropDown = 2;        {list box displayed when selected}
cbs_DropDownList = 3;    {drop down with no edit control}
```

Used to specify the style of the combo box.

TScrollBar Object Summary   **ODialogs Unit**

Heritage

TScrollBar → TControl → TWindow → TWindowsObject → TObject

Primary Methods

```
constructor Init(AParent : PWindowsObject; AnID : integer;
                 X, Y, W, H : integer; IsHorizontal : boolean);
```

Creates a scroll bar control at a given location within its parent window. IsHorizontal determines whether it is a horizontal or vertical scroll bar.

```
function GetPosition: integer;
```

Returns the current position in the scroll bar.

```
procedure SetRange(LoVal, HiVal : integer); virtual;
```

Sets the lower and upper bounds of the scroll bar.

Primary Fields

```
LineMagnitude : integer;
```

The number of lines to scroll when the user presses the arrows in the scroll bar.

```
PageMagnitude : integer;
```

The number of lines to scroll when the user clicks the mouse in the thumb area of the scroll bar.

TGroupBox Object Summary   ODialogs Unit

Heritage

TGroupBox → TControl → TWindow → TWindowsObject → TObject

Primary Methods

```
constructor Init(AParent : PWindowsObject; AnID : integer;
                 AText : PChar; X, Y, W, H : integer);
```

Creates a group box at a given location within its parent window, setting the associated text to AText.

```
constructor InitResource(AParent : PWindowsObject;
                         ResourceID : word);
```

Creates a group box that is associated with the given resource.

```
procedure SelectionChanged(ControlID : integer); virtual;
```

Overridden to handle application-specific actions when one of the child controls has changed.

Primary Field

```
NotifyParent : boolean;
```

Indicates whether the group box should be notified when one of the child controls has changed.

TDlgWindow Object Summary   ODialogs Unit

Heritage

TDlgWindow → TDialog → TWindowsObject → TObject

Primary Methods

```
constructor Init (AParent :  PWindowsObject;AName : PChar);
```

Creates a dialog window within its parent window, based on the resource identified by AName.

```
procedure GetWindowClass(var AWndClass : TWndClass); virtual;
```

Overridden to provide a new window class with its associated menu, icon, and cursor.

Primary Inherited Methods

All primary methods from the TDialog object are used for the TDlgWindow object.

TFileDialog Object Summary   **OStdDlg Unit**

Heritage

TFileDialog ➝ TDialog ➝ TWindowsObject ➝ TObject

Primary Method

```
constructor Init(AParent : PWindowsObject;
                 AFileName, AMask : PChar; IsOpen : boolean);
```

Creates a file dialog box within its parent window. The default wildcard specification is taken from AMask, and the file name chosen by the user is placed in

Part IV

Writing Applications in Turbo Pascal

Chapter *19*

Procedure and Function Library

Good programmers are pack rats; they store every function and procedure they come across because they know that sooner or later they will use them. Putting together a good library of procedures and functions takes years of coding, testing, and swapping information with other programmers. You can get a head start on your library with the procedures and functions in this chapter.

String Routines

In Chapter 3, "Complex Data Types," you were introduced to the data type **string,** and in Chapter 13, "The System Unit," you studied the standard routines and how to manipulate strings. In this section you will put this knowledge to use to solve some of the more common programming problems that can be resolved by creatively using strings.

All of the routines in this chapter will be contained in units. Units are a great way to store reusable code because you know exactly where to look for a routine. The string routines are in the STRNGUTL unit:

```
Unit STRNGUTL;

{$P+}

interface
```

```
procedure ReplaceString (FindString, ReplaceString : string;
                              var BigString : string);

procedure WritelnWithName (Strg, Name : string);

function ReadInteger(Prompt : string) : integer;

procedure StripLeadingBlanks(var Strg: string);
procedure StripTrailingBlanks(var Strg: string);

procedure Demo;
```

Replacing Strings

The first utility is used to replace a part of a string with another string:

```
procedure ReplaceString (FindString, ReplaceString : string;
                              var BigString : string);
var
  I : integer;
begin
  I := Pos(FindString, BigString);
  if I > 0 then
    begin
      Delete(BigString, I, Length(FindString));
      Insert(ReplaceString, BigString, I);
    end;
end;
```

This procedure uses four standard routines: Pos, Delete, Insert, and Length. First you locate the string you wish to remove within the larger string using Pos. The statement

```
I := Pos(FindString, BigString);
```

stores the location of the first character of the unwanted string.

Now that you know where in the larger string the substring is located, you can remove it with Delete. This is accomplished with the following statement:

```
Delete(BigString, I, Length(FindString));
```

The first parameter, *BigString*, contains the string to delete; the second parameter, *I*, indicates the position of *FindString* in *BigString*. *Length(FindString)*, the third parameter, uses the standard function Length to tell the program how many characters to delete.

Finally, the following statement inserts the second substring (*ReplaceString*) in *BigString* at exactly the same position as the other string.

```
Insert(ReplaceString, BigString, I);
```

This tells Turbo Pascal to insert *ReplaceString* into the *BigString* at position *I*.

Now that you know how the program works, you should be able to guess how it will look when it runs. The statements

```
BigStr := 'Tell Steve to pay me the five dollars he owes me.';
WriteLn(BigStr);
ReplaceString ('Steve', 'John', BigStr);
WriteLn(BigStr);
```

first write out *BigStr* in its original form. They then substitute 'John' for 'Steve' and write *BigStr* out again, as shown here:

Tell Steve to pay me the five dollars he owes me.
Tell John to pay me the five dollars he owes me.

Thus, by combining four of the string-processing procedures, you are able to perform a rather complex piece of programming with only a few lines of code.

Personalizing Messages

The ReplaceString procedure, shown previously, can be put to some clever uses. For example, suppose you want to add a personal touch to a program by inserting the user's name into some of the messages your computer displays. To do this, you need to know the user's name, in what strings it is to be inserted, and where it goes in those strings.

First, set a general rule: the @ character in a string indicates where the user's name should be placed. If the name is "John," the string 'Hello, @' would become 'Hello, John'. You can place the @ character anywhere you want the name to appear. The following procedure *WritelnWithName* demonstrates how to do this:

```
procedure WritelnWithName(Strg, Name : string);
var
  I : integer;
begin
  ReplaceString ('@', Name, Strg);
  Writeln(Strg);
end;
```

One problem with this routine is that every time it encounters the @ character in a message, it replaces it with the user's name. For example, in the message 'This is the @ character, @.', you would want the first @ to print as is and the second @ to change the individual's name. WritelnWithName will change the first @ and leave the second unchanged. Therefore, you should choose a character that will not be used in its literal form in messages. You could also choose a sequence of characters, such as @@, which would enable you to use a single @ as part of the text.

Error-Free Data Entry

Converting strings to numbers has one very important application: checking for errors in numbers entered by a user. For example, the code for a program that asks a user to enter his or her age may look like this:

```
var
  Age : integer;
begin
  Write('Enter age: ');
  ReadLn(Age);
end.
```

The problem with this code is that if a user enters invalid characters or numbers with spaces, Turbo Pascal generates a run-time error and aborts the program. Avoid this situation by having the user enter the number into a string and then convert the string into a number. If the conversion fails, the user entered an invalid number, and you can ask for input again. The following function implements this method:

```
function ReadInteger(Prompt : string) : integer;
var
  Num, Code : integer;
  NumString : string[20];
begin
  repeat
    Write(Prompt);
    ReadLn(NumString);
    Val(NumString, Num, Code);
    if Code <> 0 then
      Write(^g);              (* Make the computer beep *)
  until Code = 0;
  ReadInteger := Num;
end;
```

In *ReadInteger*, when the user enters his or her age into the **string** variable *NumString*, the program attempts to convert *NumString* into the **integer** *Num*. If the conversion fails, the **integer** variable *Code* is set to a value other than zero. When this occurs, the program writes the character ^g, which makes the terminal beep, and continues the loop until the user enters a valid number.

Removing Blanks

Blank characters at the end of a numeric string cause a numeric conversion to fail. The string '10 ', for example, cannot be converted to a numeric value unless the blank character at the end is removed. Unwanted blanks can be removed with the procedures *StripLeadingBlanks* and *StripTrailingBlanks,* as shown here:

```
procedure StripLeadingBlanks(var Strg: string);
begin
  while (Length(Strg) > 0) and (Strg[1] = ' ') do
    Delete(Strg, 1, 1);
end;

procedure StripTrailingBlanks(var Strg: string);
begin
  while Strg[Length(Strg)] = ' ' do
    Delete(Strg, Length(Strg), 1);
end;
```

A calling program would pass a string into StripLeadingBlanks or StripTrailingBlanks as a reference parameter, so whatever changes are made to the string are retained after the procedure ends.

StripTrailingBlanks consists of a **while-do** loop that controls a Delete statement:

```
while Strg[Length(Strg)] = ' ' do
  Delete(Strg, Length(Strg), 1);
```

This loop removes blanks from the end of a string by repeatedly deleting the last character from the string: the expression **Strg[Length(Strg)]** points to the last character in the string *Strg*. If the last character is blank, that character is removed with the Delete procedure.

These are just a few examples of how strings can be used to solve tricky programming problems. As you program, you will discover many more.

The final procedure in the STRNGUTL unit demonstrates each of the other routines in the unit. If you get into the habit of including demos in your units, you are less likely to forget how to use any of the routines. A sample output of this program appears in Figure 19-1.

```
OLD: Tell Steve to pay me the five dollars he owes me.
NEW: Tell John to pay me the five dollars he owes me.

Enter your name: Kimberly
Hello, Kimberly
This message is unchanged.
This message, Kimberly, has been changed.

Enter your age: 24
I wish I was 24

string = <       20      >
string = <       20>
Value is: 20

Press ENTER...
```

Figure 19-1.   *Sample output from string demo procedure*

```
procedure Demo;
var
  Str, FindStr, ReplaceStr : string[80];

  BigStr : string[255];
  Message1,
  Message2,
  Message3 : string[255];
  Name : string[20];
  I, Code,
  Age : integer;

begin
  ClrScr;
  FindStr := 'Steve';
  ReplaceStr := 'John';
  BigStr := 'Tell Steve to pay me the five dollars he owes me.';
  WriteLn('OLD: ', BigStr);
  ReplaceString (FindStr, ReplaceStr, BigStr);
  WriteLn('NEW: ', BigStr);
  WriteLn;

  Message1 := 'Hello, @';
  Message2 := 'This message is unchanged.';
  Message3 := 'This message, @, has been changed.';

  Write('Enter your name: ');
  ReadLn(Name);

  WritelnWithName(Message1, Name);
  WritelnWithName(Message2, Name);
  WritelnWithName(Message3, Name);
```

```
  Writeln;

  Age := ReadInteger('Enter your age: ');
  Writeln ('I wish I was ', Age);
  Writeln;

  Str := '    20    ';
  WriteLn('string = <', Str, '>');
  StripTrailingBlanks(Str);
  WriteLn('string = <', Str, '>');
  Val(Str, I, Code);
  WriteLn('Value is: ', I);
  WriteLn;

  Write('Press ENTER...');
  ReadLn;
end;
```

Big Strings

Turbo Pascal limits strings to a maximum of 255 characters. While this is long enough for most strings, there are times when you will need longer strings. The object defined in this section, *BigString*, allows you to define strings up to 32,767 characters long. The object includes an **integer** field, which keeps track of the string length, and an array of characters. Here is the full object declaration:

```
const
  MaxLen = 1000;

type BigString = object
  Length : integer;
  Chars : array [1..MaxLen] of char;
  procedure Init(Str : string);
  procedure WriteStr;
  procedure Concat(OtherStr : BigString);
  procedure Insert(StrToInsert : BigString; At : integer);
  procedure Delete(First, Count : integer);
  function Pos(StrToFind : BigString) : integer;
  procedure Copy(FromStr : BigString; First, Count : integer);
end;
```

A variable of type *BigString* can hold up to 1,000 characters, and it can be easily extended by changing the value of *MaxLen*.

The methods defined for this object mimic the standard Turbo Pascal string commands; they use the same names and similar syntax, but begin with the object name. For example, the equivalent of Turbo Pascal's Insert command is the BigString.Insert method.

Init

Init initializes a big string to a value specified in parameter *Str.*

```
procedure BigString.Init(Str : string);
var
  I : integer;
begin
  Length := System.Length(Str);
  for I := 1 to Length do
    Chars[I] := Str[I];
end;
```

WriteStr

WriteStr displays a big string in the screen, similar to how Write displays a standard string.

```
procedure BigString.WriteStr;
var
  I : integer;
begin
  for I := 1 to Length do
    Write(Chars[I]);
end;
```

Concat

Big strings cannot use the Turbo Pascal concatenation operator +. You can, however, simulate the Concat command, as shown in the procedure *BigString.Concat,* which concatenates *OtherStr* to the one stored by the object.

```
procedure BigString.Concat(OtherStr : BigString);
var
  I : integer;
begin
  Move(OtherStr.Chars[1], Chars[Length+1], OtherStr.Length);
  Length := Length + OtherStr.Length;
end;
```

Insert

Insert inserts one big string into the one stored by the object, starting at character *At.*

```
procedure BigString.Insert(StrToInsert : BigString;
                           At : integer);
var
  TempStr : BigString;
```

```
begin
  Move(Chars[1], TempStr.Chars[1], At-1);
  Move(StrToInsert.Chars[1], TempStr.Chars[At],
        StrToInsert.Length);
  Move(Chars[At], TempStr.Chars[At+StrToInsert.Length],
        Length-At+1);
  TempStr.Length := StrToInsert.Length + Length;
  if TempStr.Length > MaxLen then
    TempStr.Length := MaxLen;

  Move(TempStr.Length, Length, TempStr.Length+2);
end;
```

Delete

Delete removes characters from the object starting at character *First*. It deletes as many characters as specified in the parameter *Count*.

```
procedure BigString.Delete(First, Count : integer);
var
  TempStr : BigString;
begin
  Move(Chars[1], TempStr.Chars[1], First-1);
  Move(Chars[First+Count], TempStr.Chars[First],
        Length-(First+Count)+1);
  TempStr.Length := Length - Count;

  Move(TempStr.Length, Length, TempStr.Length+2);
end;
```

Pos

The function *BigString.Pos* returns the position of one *BigString* inside the object's string. To indicate the position, Pos returns a positive number; if no match is found, it returns 0.

```
function BigString.Pos(StrToFind : BigString) : integer;
var
  Found : boolean;
  I, J, StopFlag : integer;
begin
  StopFlag := Length - StrToFind.Length + 1;
  for I := 1 to StopFlag do
    begin
      Found := True;
      J := 1;

      repeat
```

```
      if Chars[I+J-1] <> StrToFind.Chars[J] then
        begin
          Found := False;
          Break;
        end;
      J := J + 1;
    until J = StrToFind.Length;

    if Found then
      begin
        Pos := I;
        Exit;
      end;
  end;

  Pos := 0;
end;
```

Copy

Because the Turbo Pascal string function Copy cannot be directly duplicated for large strings (Turbo Pascal cannot define a function using an object data type) you must use *BigString.Copy,* which provides a result in the form of a procedure. This method takes Count characters from FromStr, starting from character First, and assigns them to the object.

```
procedure BigString.Copy(FromStr : BigString;
                         First, Count : integer);
begin
  Move(FromStr.Chars[First], Chars[1], Count);
  Length := Count;
end;
```

Math Routines

Most of the numerical procedures and functions your programs need are available in Turbo Pascal and were summarized in Chapter 13, "The System Unit." There are a few others, however, that are handy in some situations. Your math library can start with the routines in the MATHUTL unit:

```
Unit MATHUTL;

interface

type
```

```
   BinStr = string[8];

function Real_To_Frac(R : real; Denom : integer) : string;
function Frac_To_Real(Frac : string;
                         var Code : integer) : real;

function Binary(b : byte) : Binstr;
procedure SetBit(Position, Value : byte;
                    var ChangeByte : byte);
function BitOn(Position, TestByte : byte) : boolean;
procedure BinaryDemo;

function Compute_Formula(var P : integer;
                           Strg : string;
                           var Error : boolean) : real;
procedure Calculator;
```

The implementation of the unit will be complete at the end of the following sections.

Real_To_Frac

Real_To_Frac converts a decimal value into a fraction stored in a string. The function accepts two parameters: *R*, the value to convert, and *Denom*, the denominator of the desired fraction. The function returns a string that contains the integer portion of the fraction, as well as the fractional portion. The two are separated by a space.

```
function Real_To_Frac(R : real; Denom : integer) : string;
var
  IntStr, NumerStr, DenomStr,
  S1, S2 : string[20];
  R2, IntPart, FracPart : real;
  Code, P, Numer : integer;

begin
  if R = 0 then
    begin
      Real_To_Frac := '0';
      Exit;
    end;

  IntStr := '0';
  DenomStr := '0';
  NumerStr := '0';

  Str(R:0:8, S2);
  P := Pos('.', S2);
  if P > 0 then
```

```
  S1 := Copy(S2, 1, P-1);

Delete(S2, 1, P-1);
Val(S1, IntPart, Code);
Str(IntPart:0:0, IntStr);

Val(S2, FracPart, Code);
if FracPart > 0.0 then
  begin
    Numer := 0;
    repeat
      Numer := Numer+1;
      R2 := Numer/Denom;
    until R2 >= FracPart;
    if (R2-FracPart) > (1.0/(Denom*2.0)) then
      Numer := Numer-1;

    while (not Odd(Numer)) and (Numer > 0) do
      begin
        Numer := Numer div 2;
        Denom := Denom div 2;
      end;
    Str(Numer:0, NumerStr);
    Str(Denom:0, DenomStr);
  end;

if (NumerStr = '1') and (DenomStr = '1') then
  begin
    NumerStr := '0';
    Val(IntStr, R2, Code);
    R2 := R2 + 1;
    Str(R2:0:0, IntStr);
  end;

if (IntStr = '0') and (NumerStr = '0') then
  Real_To_Frac := '0'
else if NumerStr = '0' then
  Real_To_Frac := IntStr
else if IntStr = '0' then
  begin
    if (NumerStr = '1') and (DenomStr = '1') then
      Real_To_Frac := '1'
    else
      Real_To_Frac := NumerStr + '/' + DenomStr;
  end
else
  Real_To_Frac := IntStr + ' ' + NumerStr + '/' + DenomStr;
end;
```

Frac_To_Real

Frac_To_Real, a function of type **real,** converts a string that contains a fraction into a real number. The routine takes two parameters: *Frac,* the string that contains the fraction, and *Code,* an integer that indicates an error in conversion. If *Code* is equal to zero, no error occurred; if it is not equal to zero, an error did occur. The fraction is formed by an integer, a space, the numerator, a slash, and a denominator. The following are all legal fractions:

```
14 1/2
3/16
29
```

As you can see, both the whole number and the fractional portion are optional.

```
function Frac_To_Real(Frac : string;
                      var Code : integer) : real;
var
  Numer, Denom, IntPart : real;
  NumerStr, DenomStr, IntStr : string[8];
  P_slash, P_space,
  P, J : integer;

begin
  while (Frac[1] = ' ') and (Length(Frac) > 0) do
    Delete(Frac, 1, 1);
  if Frac = '' then
    begin
      Frac_To_Real := 0;
      Exit;
    end;

  P_slash := Pos('/', Frac);
  P_space := Pos(' ', Frac);

  IntStr := '';
  NumerStr := '';
  DenomStr := '';

  if (P_slash > 0) and (P_space > 0) then
    begin (* slash and space *)
      for J := 1 to P_space-1 do
        IntStr := IntStr + Frac[J];
      for J := P_space+1 to P_slash-1 do
        NumerStr := NumerStr + Frac[J];
      for J := P_slash+1 to Length(Frac) do
        DenomStr := DenomStr + Frac[J];
```

```
      Val(IntStr, IntPart, Code);
      Val(NumerStr, Numer, Code);
      Val(DenomStr, Denom, Code);

      Frac_To_Real := IntPart + Numer / Denom;
   end

  else if P_slash > 0 then
    begin (* slash and no space *)
      for J := P_space+1 to P_slash-1 do
        NumerStr := NumerStr + Frac[J];
      for J := P_slash+1 to Length(Frac) do
        DenomStr := DenomStr + Frac[J];

      Val(NumerStr, Numer, Code);
      Val(DenomStr, Denom, Code);

      Frac_To_Real := Numer / Denom;
    end

  else if P_space > 0 then
    begin (* no slash and space *)
      for J := 1 to P_space-1 do
        IntStr := IntStr + Frac[J];

      Val(IntStr, IntPart, Code);
      Frac_To_Real := IntPart;
    end

  else
    begin (* no slash and no space *)
      IntStr := IntStr + Frac;
      Val(IntStr, IntPart, Code);
      Frac_To_Real := IntPart;
    end;
end;
```

Bit Manipulation

While they are considered arithmetic in nature, bit-manipulation operators are not often used for computations. More often, they test or set specific bit values. The following listing contains several procedures that use these bit-manipulation operators.

```
function Binary(b : byte) : Binstr;
 {
 This function accepts a byte parameter and returns
```

```
  a string of eight ones and zeros indicating the binary
  form of the byte.
  }

var
  I : integer;
  bt : byte;
  Str : Binstr;
begin
  bt := $01;
  Str := '';
  for I := 1 to 8 do
    begin
      if (b and bt) > 0 then
        Str := '1' + Str
      else
        Str := '0' + Str;
      {$R-}
      bt := bt shl 1;
      {$R+}
    end;
  Binary := Str;
end;

(***********************************************************)

procedure SetBit(Position, Value : byte;
                 var ChangeByte : byte);
  {
  This procedure sets a particular bit in the byte ChangeByte
  to either 1 or 0. The bit is specified by Position, which
  can range from 0 to 7.
  }
var
  bt : byte;
begin
  bt := $01;
  bt := bt shl Position;
  if Value = 1 then
    ChangeByte := ChangeByte or bt
  else
    begin
      bt := bt xor $FF;
      ChangeByte := ChangeByte and bt;
    end;
end;

(***********************************************************)
```

```
function BitOn(Position, TestByte : byte) : boolean;
 {
 This function tests if a bit in TestByte is turned on
 (equal to one). The bit to test is indicated by the parameter
 Position, which can range from 0 (right-most bit) to 7
 (left-most bit). if the bit indicated by Position is
 turned on, then BitOn returns True.
 }
var
  bt : byte;
begin
  bt := $01;
  bt := bt shl Position;
  BitOn := (bt and TestByte) > 0;
end;
```

Function *Binary* converts a byte value into a string of ones and zeros that represent the bits. Procedure *SetBit* turns on or off any individual bit in a byte. The last routine, the **boolean** function *BitOn,* tests whether a particular bit in a byte is turned on.

The following procedure demonstrates the use of the bit-manipulation subprograms:

```
procedure BinaryDemo;
type
  Binstr = string[8];
var
  I : integer;
  b : byte;
begin
  ClrScr;
  WriteLn;
  WriteLn('Demonstrate binary conversion.');
  Write('Enter a number (0 - 255): ');
  ReadLn(b);
  WriteLn('Binary equivalent is: ', Binary(b));
  WriteLn;
  WriteLn;

  WriteLn('Demonstrate SetBit procedure.');
  b := 0;
  for I := 0 to 7 do
    begin
      SetBit(I, 1, b);
      WriteLn(binary(b));
    end;

  for I := 0 to 7 do
```

```
    begin
      SetBit(I, 0, b);
      WriteLn(binary(b));
    end;
  WriteLn;
  WriteLn;

  Write('Enter a number (0 - 255): ');
  ReadLn(b);
  WriteLn('Binary value is ',binary(b));
  if BitOn(0,b) then
    WriteLn('Bit 0 is on.')
  else
    WriteLn('Bit 0 is off.');
  WriteLn;
  Write('Press ENTER...');
  ReadLn;
end;
```

An Interactive Calculator

In Chapter 4 "Subprograms," you learned about recursion, where a subprogram can call itself, or multiple subprograms can call each other. In most cases you want to avoid recursion because it adds a tremendous amount of confusion. On the other hand, some algorithms are so naturally adapted to a recursive structure that forcing them into a nonrecursive form just does not make sense. A good example of such an algorithm is a function that evaluates a mathematical expression stored in a string. The following function shows how the recursive process follows the flow of the underlying algorithm. Study it carefully.

```
function Compute_Formula(var P : integer;
                         Strg : string;
                         var Error : boolean) : real;
var
  R : real;
  I,
  BreakPoint : integer;
  Ch : char;

(*******************)

  procedure Eval(var Formula : string;
                 var Value : real;
                 var BreakPoint : integer);
  const
    Numbers : set of char = ['0'..'9','.'];
  var
    P, I : integer;
```

```
  Ch : char;

(*********************)

  procedure NextP;
  begin
    repeat
      P := P + 1;
      if P <= Length(Formula) then
        Ch := Formula[P]
      else
        Ch := #13;
    until (Ch <> ' ');
  end;

(*******************)

  function Expr : real;
  var
    E : real;
    Operator : char;

(******************)

    function SmplExpr : real;
    var
      S : real;
      Operator : char;

(*****************)

    function Term : real;
    var
      T : real;

(**************)

      function S_Fact : real;

(**************)

        function Fct : real;
        var
          fn : string[20];
          l, start: integer;
          F : real;

(************)
```

```
procedure Process_As_Number;
var
  Code : integer;
begin
  Start := P;
  repeat
    NextP;
  until not(Ch in Numbers);

  if Ch = '.' then
    repeat
      NextP;
    until not(Ch in Numbers);

  if Ch = 'E' then
    begin
      NextP;
      repeat
        NextP;
      until not(Ch in Numbers);
    end;

  Val(Copy(Formula, Start, P-Start), F, Code);
end;

(*************)

procedure Process_As_New_Expr;
begin
  NextP;
  F := Expr;
  if Ch = ')' then
    NextP
  else
    BreakPoint := P;
end;

(*************)

procedure Process_As_Standard_Function;

(***********)

  function Fact(I : integer) : real;
  begin
    if I > 0 then
      Fact := I * Fact(I-1)
    else
      Fact := 1;
```

```
      end;

 (***********)

 begin {Process_As_Standard_Function}
   if Copy(Formula, P, 3) = 'ABS' then
     begin
       P := P + 2;
       NextP;
       F := Fct;
       f := Abs(f);
     end
   else if Copy(Formula, P, 4) = 'SQRT' then
     begin
       P := P + 3;
       NextP;
       F := Fct;
       f := Sqrt(f);
     end
   else if Copy(Formula, P, 3) = 'SQR' then
     begin
       P := P + 2;
       NextP;
       F := Fct;
       f := Sqr(f);
     end
   else if Copy(Formula, P, 3) = 'SIN' then
     begin
       P := P + 2;
       NextP;
       F := Fct;
       f := Sin(f);
     end
   else if Copy(Formula, P, 3) = 'COS' then
     begin
       P := P + 2;
       NextP;
       F := Fct;
       f := Cos(f);
     end
   else if Copy(Formula, P, 6) = 'ARCTAN' then
     begin
       P := P + 5;
       NextP;
       F := Fct;
       f := ArcTan(f);
     end
   else if Copy(Formula, P, 2) = 'LN' then
     begin
```

```
                        P := P + 1;
               NextP;
               F := Fct;
               f := Ln(f);
             end
          else if Copy(Formula, P, 3) = 'EXP' then
             begin
               P := P + 2;
               NextP;
               F := Fct;
               f := Exp(f);
             end
          else if Copy(Formula, P, 4) = 'FACT' then
             begin
               P := P + 3;
               NextP;
               F := Fct;
               f := fact(Trunc(f));
             end
          else
             BreakPoint := P;
        end;


   (***************)


   begin { Fct }
     if Ch in Numbers then
        Process_As_Number
     else if Ch = '(' then
        Process_As_New_Expr
     else
        Process_As_Standard_Function;
     Fct := F;
   end;


(****************)


begin {S_Fact}
   if Ch = '-' then
     begin
        NextP;
        S_Fact := -Fct;
     end
   else
     S_Fact := Fct;
end;


(******************)
```

```pascal
    begin {Term}
      T := S_Fact;
      while Ch = '^' do
        begin
          NextP;
          t := Exp(Ln(t) * S_Fact);
        end;
      Term := t;
    end;

  (*********************)

  begin {SmplExpr}
    S := term;
    while Ch in ['*', '/'] do
      begin
        Operator := Ch;
        NextP;
        case Operator of
          '*' : S := S*term;
          '/' : S := S/term;
        end;
      end;
    SmplExpr := s;
  end;

(*********************)

begin {Expr}
  E := SmplExpr;
  while Ch in ['+', '-'] do
    begin
      Operator := Ch;
      NextP;
      case Operator of
        '+' : e := e+SmplExpr;
        '-' : e := e-SmplExpr;
      end;
    end;
  Expr := E;
end;

(*********************)

begin {Eval}
  for I := 1 to Length(Formula) do
    Formula[I] := Upcase(Formula[I]);
  if Formula[1] = '.' then
    Formula := '0' + Formula;
```

```
   if Formula[1] = '+' then
     Delete(Formula, 1, 1);
   P := 0;
   NextP;
   Value := Expr;

   if Ch = #13 then
     Error := False
   else
     Error := True;
   BreakPoint := P;
  end;

(********************)

begin {Compute_Formula}
  Eval(Strg, R, P);
  Compute_Formula := R;
end;
```

This function evaluates a **string** equation through a series of recursive calls. If successful, the result is passed back to the program; if not, the **boolean** parameter *Error* is set to True, and the **integer** parameter *P* indicates the point in the string at which the error was detected.

Coding this same procedure in a nonrecursive manner is possible, but given the nature of the algorithm, which lends itself to the recursive approach, it is undesirable.

In the following program, you will be asked to enter an equation, which the program stores in a string and passes to the function *Compute_Formula*.

```
procedure Calculator;
 var
   I : integer;
   Formula : string[80];
   P : integer;
   Result : real;
   Error : boolean;

(********************)

begin
 ClrScr;
   repeat
   Write('Enter Formula: ');
   Read(Formula);
   if Formula <> '' then
     begin
     Result := Compute_Formula(P,Formula,Error);
     if Error then
```

```
     begin
     WriteLn;
     WriteLn('Error!');
     WriteLn(Formula);
     for I := 1 to P-1 do Write(' ');
     WriteLn('^');
     end
   else
     WriteLn(' = ',Result:0:2);
   end;
 ReadLn;
 until Formula = '';
end;
```

I/O and File Routines

Both TurboVision and ObjectWindows include several routines and objects that make input and output more user friendly. There may be cases, however, when you want more control over the I/O processes. The INOUTUTL unit gives you procedures to get complete input from a user. Also included are routines for file encryption.

```
Unit INOUTUTL;

interface

type
  KeyType = (NullKey, F1, F2, F3, F4, F5, F6, F7, F8, F9, F10,
             CarriageReturn, Tab, ShiftTab, Bksp,
             UpArrow, DownArrow, RightArrow, LeftArrow,
             DeleteKey, InsertKey, HomeKey, EndKey, PgUp, PgDn,
             Esc, TextKey, NumberKey, Space);

procedure FastWrite(X, Y : byte;
                    Ch : char;
                    FGround, BGround : byte);

procedure InKey(var IsSpecial : boolean;
                var SpecialKey : KeyType;
                var Ch : char);

procedure InputStringShift(var S : string;
                           WindowLength,
                           MaxLength,
                           X,Y : integer;
                           FT : char;
                           BackgroundChar : integer);
```

```
procedure EncodeFile(FileName, Password : string);
procedure DecodeFile(FileName, Password : string);
```

Fast Write

The fastest way to display text is to write directly to video memory. The *FastWrite* procedure, introduced in Chapter 8, "External Procedures and Inline Code," speeds up output to monochrome, EGA, and VGA terminals. For CGA monitors, see Chapter 8.

```
var
  VS : word;

function VidSeg : word;
begin
  if Mem[$0000:$0449] = 7 then
    VidSeg := $B000
  else
    VidSeg := $B800;
end;


(************************************************)


procedure FastWrite(X, Y : byte;
                    Ch : char;
                    FGround, BGround : byte);
var
  W : word;
  I, ColAtr : byte;
begin
  ColAtr := (BGround shl 4) + FGround;   (* create
                                            attribute byte *);
  W := ((Y-1)*80 + (X-1))*2;             (* calculate
                                            Offset *)

  MemW[VS:W] := (ColAtr shl 8) + Ord(Ch);
end;
```

To make *FastWrite* work as quickly as possible, you need to determine the proper location of video memory at initialization time, instead of during every call. Thus, you want to add the following code at the bottom of the unit:

```
begin
  VS := VidSeg;
end.
```

Generating Sound

The Turbo Pascal commands Sound and NoSound control the PC's sound generator. Sound takes an **integer** parameter that specifies the pitch of the tone. The tone continues until you issue the NoSound command. By using the Delay command, you can produce a tone that lasts a specified amount of time. The procedure *Beep*, presented here, uses these three commands to create a tone of a certain pitch and duration. The parameter *Freq* determines the pitch, and *Time* specifies the duration in milliseconds.

```
procedure Beep(Freq, Time: integer);
begin
  Sound(Freq);
  Delay(Time);
  NoSound;
end;
```

InKey

Turbo Pascal's input procedures Read and ReadLn are quite limited in some ways. When entering data, you can only delete backward with the BACKSPACE key. There is no direct way to know if a function key has been pressed. The next two procedures, *InKey* and *InputStringShift*, extend your ability to control the keyboard.

Each time you press a function key, the PC generates a scan code along with a character. For example, function key F1 generates a scan code (#0) followed by ASCII character 59, the semicolon. The procedure *InKey* checks for the scan code when a key is pressed. If the code is present, *InKey* sets the parameter *IsSpecial* to True. The procedure relies heavily on the definition of the type *KeyType*, shown earlier in the unit interface section.

You can use the *KeyType* type definition to easily program control loops by testing for a specific key, as shown here:

```
repeat
  InKey(IsFkey, Fkey, Ch);
until Fkey = F1;
```

In this example, the program keeps accepting keyboard input until you press the F1 key. The complete *InKey* procedure is shown here:

```
procedure InKey(var IsSpecial : boolean;
                var SpecialKey : KeyType;
                var Ch : char);
begin
  IsSpecial := False;
  Ch := ReadKey;
```

```
  if (Ch = #0) then
    begin
      IsSpecial := True;
      Ch := ReadKey;
    end;

  if IsSpecial then
    case Ord(Ch) of
       15:   SpecialKey := ShiftTab;
       72:   SpecialKey := UpArrow;
       80:   SpecialKey := DownArrow;
       75:   SpecialKey := LeftArrow;
       77:   SpecialKey := RightArrow;
       73:   SpecialKey := PgUp;
       81:   SpecialKey := PgDn;
       71:   SpecialKey := HomeKey;
       79:   SpecialKey := EndKey;
       83:   SpecialKey := DeleteKey;
       82:   SpecialKey := InsertKey;
       59:   SpecialKey := F1;
       60:   SpecialKey := F2;
       61:   SpecialKey := F3;
       62:   SpecialKey := F4;
       63:   SpecialKey := F5;
       64:   SpecialKey := F6;
       65:   SpecialKey := F7;
       66:   SpecialKey := F8;
       67:   SpecialKey := F9;
       68:   SpecialKey := F10;
    end
  else
    case Ord(Ch) of
        8:   SpecialKey := Bksp;
        9:   SpecialKey := Tab;
       13:   SpecialKey := CarriageReturn;
       27:   SpecialKey := Esc;
       32:   SpecialKey := Space;
       45..46, 48..57:    SpecialKey := NumberKey;
       else SpecialKey := TextKey;
    end;

end;
```

InputStringShift

A good input procedure allows you to use all the keys on the PC keyboard to delete characters with both the BACKSPACE and DEL keys, move back and forth with RIGHT

ARROW and LEFT ARROW keys, and switch between Insert and Overwrite modes by pressing the INS key.

InputStringShift provides your program with all these features. This procedure also lets you enter a string that is longer than the space on the screen you provided for input. For example, even if you set aside only 10 spaces on the screen for input, you still can accept strings as long as 255 characters. *InputStringShift* shifts the string back and forth in the input window as you type or use the arrow and DEL keys.

InputStringShift takes seven parameters, which are shown here:

```
procedure InputStringShift(var S : string;
                           WindowLength,
                           MaxLength,
                           X, Y : integer;
                           FT : char;
                           BackgroundChar : integer);
```

S, a string variable, accepts the input; *WindowLength* specifies the size of the data-entry field (from 1 to 255); *MaxLength* is the maximum length of the string (from 1 to 255); and *X* and *Y* are the screen coordinates of the first character of the input field. *FT* specifies the field type and can be either "T" for text or "N" for numeric. When the field is empty, blank spaces are filled with a character specified by the parameter *BackgroundChar.* Character 176 is a good choice because it creates a lightly shaded background.

```
procedure InputStringShift(var S : string;
                           WindowLength,
                           MaxLength,
                           X, Y : integer;
                           FT : char;
                           BackgroundChar : integer);
var
  XX, I, J, P : integer;
  Ch : char;
  InsertOn,
  IsSpecial : boolean;
  TheKey : KeyType;
  Offset : integer;

  procedure XY(X, Y : integer);
  var
    Xsmall : integer;
  begin
    repeat
      Xsmall := X - 80;
      if Xsmall > 0 then
```

```
         begin
           Y := Y+1;
           X := Xsmall;
         end;
     until Xsmall <= 0;
     GotoXY(X, Y);
  end;

  (*************************************)

  procedure SetString;
  var
    I : integer;
  begin
    I := Length(S);
    while S[I] = char(BackgroundChar) do
      I := I-1;
    S[0] := char(I);
  end;

  (*************************************)

begin {InputStringShift}
  J := Length(S)+1;
  for I := J to MaxLength do
    S[I] := char(BackgroundChar);
  S[0] := char(MaxLength);

  for I := 1 to WindowLength do
    FastWrite(X+I-1, Y,S[I], Yellow, Black);
  P := 1;
  Offset := 0;
  InsertOn := True;

  repeat
    XX := X+(P-Offset);
    if (P-Offset) = WindowLength then
      XX := XX-1;
    XY(XX, Y);

    InKey(IsSpecial, TheKey, Ch);

    if (FT = 'N') then
      begin
        if (TheKey = TextKey) or
           ((Ch = '-') and ((P > 1) or (S[1] = '-'))) then
          begin
            Beep(100, 250);
            TheKey := NullKey;
```

```
          end
      else if (Ch = '.') then
        begin
          if not((Pos('.', S) = 0) or (Pos('.', S) = P)) then
            begin
              Beep(100, 250);
              TheKey := NullKey;
            end
          else if (Pos('.', S) = P) then
            Delete(S, P, 1);
        end;
    end;

  case TheKey of
    NumberKey, TextKey, Space :
      if Length(S) = MaxLength then
        begin
          if P = MaxLength then
            begin
              Delete(S, MaxLength, 1);
              S := S + Ch;
              if P = WindowLength+Offset then
                Offset := Offset+1;
                for I := 1 to WindowLength do
                  FastWrite(X+I, Y, S[I+Offset],
                                    Yellow, Black);
            end
          else
            begin
              if InsertOn then
                begin
                  Delete(S, MaxLength, 1);
                  Insert(Ch, S, P);
                  if P = WindowLength + Offset then
                    Offset := Offset + 1;
                  if P < MaxLength then
                    P := P + 1;
                  for I := 1 to WindowLength do
                    FastWrite(X+I, Y, S[I+Offset],
                                      Yellow, Black);
                end
              else      (* overwrite *)
                begin
                  Delete(S, P, 1);
                  Insert(Ch, S, P);
                  if P = WindowLength + Offset then
                    Offset := Offset + 1;
                  if P < MaxLength then
                    P := P + 1;
```

```
                for I := 1 to WindowLength do
                  FastWrite(X+I, Y, S[I+Offset],
                               Yellow, Black);
              end;
          end;
      end
    else {not the last character}
      begin
        if InsertOn then
          Insert(Ch, S, P)
        else
          begin
            Delete(S, P, 1);
            Insert(Ch, S, P);
          end;
        if P = WindowLength+Offset then
          Offset := Offset+1;
        if P < MaxLength then
          P := P+1;
        for I := 1 to WindowLength do
          FastWrite(X+I, Y, S[I+Offset],
                     Yellow, Black);
      end;

Bksp :
  if P > 1 then
    begin
      P := P-1;
      Delete(S, P, 1);
      S := S + Char(BackgroundChar);
      if Offset > 1 then
        Offset := Offset-1;
      for I := 1 to WindowLength do
        FastWrite(X+I, Y, S[I+Offset],
                   Yellow, Black);
      Ch := ' ';
    end
  else
    begin
      beep(100,250);
      Ch := ' ';
      P := 1;
    end;

LeftArrow :
  if P > 1 then
    begin
      P := P-1;
      if P < Offset then
```

```
                    begin
                       Offset := Offset-1;
                       for I := 1 to WindowLength do
                          FastWrite(X+I, Y, S[I+Offset],
                                        Yellow, Black);
                    end;
              end
           else
              begin
                SetString;
                Exit;
              end;

   RightArrow :
      if (S[P] <> char(BackgroundChar)) and
         (P < MaxLength) then
         begin
           P := P+1;
           if P = (WindowLength+Offset) then
              begin
                 Offset := Offset+1;
                 for I := 1 to WindowLength do
                    FastWrite(X+I, Y, S[I+Offset],
                                  Yellow, Black);
              end;
         end
      else
         begin
           SetString;
           Exit;
         end;

   DeleteKey :
     begin
       Delete(S, P, 1);
       S := S + char(BackgroundChar);
       for I := 1 to WindowLength do
          FastWrite(X+I, Y, S[I+Offset],
                       Yellow, Black);
     end;

   InsertKey :
     if InsertOn then
       InsertOn := False
     else
       InsertOn := True;

   else
     if not(TheKey in [CarriageReturn, UpArrow, DownArrow,
```

```
                        PgDn, PgUp, NullKey, Esc, Tab,
                     F1, F2, F3, F4, F5, F6,
                     F7, F8, F9, F10]) then
        Beep(100,250);
    end;

  until (TheKey in [CarriageReturn, UpArrow, DownArrow, PgUp,
                    PgDn, Esc, Tab, F1, F3, F4, F5, F6, F7,
                    F8, F9, F10]);
  SetString;
end;
```

File Encryption

Protecting letters, data, and programs is a common task. The only sure protection is to encode the file itself. The procedures presented here do this, and offer some extra features as well.

EncodeFile

The Encode program encrypts a file based on a password you provide. To encrypt a file, call *EncodeFile* with the filename and a password. If you enter the name of a file that does not exist, the program will abort with the message "File not found." The program also checks to see whether the file was already encrypted. Files encrypted with *EncodeFile* contain the word "LOCKED" in the first six bytes. When *EncodeFile* finds these letters, it aborts and displays the message "File already locked." This protection is necessary to keep you from encrypting the same file twice.

Note also that this routine overwrites the original file with binary zeros and then erases the file. This keeps out snoopers who might browse through your disk with a special program for this purpose.

The password can be up to six characters long. It generates two seed values, which control the encryption. Encode stores these two seed values in the encrypted file so that the file can never be decoded with an incorrect password.

```
procedure EncodeFile(FileName, Password : string);
const
  MaxBuf = 30000;
var
  Seed1,
  Seed2 : byte;
  Source,
  Dest : file;
  Buffer : array [1..MaxBuf] of byte;
  BytesRead : real;
  I : integer;
  I1,I2 : byte;
```

```pascal
RR : integer;

(*************************************)

procedure OpenFiles;
const
  S : array [1..6] of char = ('L','O','C','K','E','D');
begin
  Assign(Source, FileName);
  {$I-}
  Reset(Source, 1);
  {$I+}
  if IOresult <> 0 then
    begin
      WriteLn('file not found.');
      Halt;
    end;

  BlockRead(Source,Buffer,6);

  if (Buffer[1] = ord('L')) and
     (Buffer[2] = ord('O')) and
     (Buffer[3] = ord('C')) and
     (Buffer[4] = ord('K')) and
     (Buffer[5] = ord('E')) and
     (Buffer[6] = ord('D')) then
    begin
      WriteLn('file already locked.');
      Halt;
    end;

  Reset(Source, 1);
  Assign(Dest, '$$$$.$$');
  Rewrite(Dest, 1);
  BlockWrite(Dest, S, 6);
  BlockWrite(Dest, Seed1, 1);
  BlockWrite(Dest, Seed2, 1);
end;

(*************************************)

procedure GetSeed;
var
  I, J : integer;
begin
  Seed1 := 0;
  Seed2 := 0;

  J := Length(password);
```

```
    for I := 1 to Length(password) do
      begin
        Seed1 := Seed1 + (Ord(password[I]) * I);
        Seed2 := Seed2 + (Ord(password[I]) * J);
        J := J - 1;
      end;
  end;


  (*************************************)


  procedure CloseFiles;
  var
    I : integer;
  begin
    Rewrite(Source, 1);
    FillChar(Buffer, MaxBuf, 0);
    while BytesRead > 0 do
      begin
        if BytesRead > MaxBuf then
          BlockWrite(Source, Buffer, MaxBuf)
        else
          begin
            I := Trunc(BytesRead);
            BlockWrite(Source, Buffer, I)
          end;
        BytesRead := BytesRead - MaxBuf;
      end;
    Close(Source);
    Close(Dest);
    Erase(Source);
    Rename(Dest,FileName);
  end;

(*************************************)

begin {EncodeFile}
  GetSeed;
  OpenFiles;
  I1 := Seed1;
  I2 := Seed2;
  BlockRead(Source, Buffer, MaxBuf, RR);
  BytesRead := RR;
  while RR > 0 do
    begin
      for I := 1 to RR do
        begin
          I1 := I1 - I;
          I2 := I2 + I;
          if odd(I) then
```

```
                  Buffer[I] := Buffer[I] - I1
             else
                  Buffer[I] := Buffer[I] + I2;
           end;
       BlockWrite(Dest, Buffer, RR);
       BlockRead(Source, Buffer, MaxBuf, RR);
       BytesRead := BytesRead + RR;
     end;
   CloseFiles;
end;
```

DecodeFile

DecodeFile restores files that have been encrypted with the *EncodeFile* procedure.
DecodeFile first checks to see if the file is locked; locked files have the letters "LOCKED"
in the first six bytes. Next it uses the password to generate two seed values and
compares those to the seed values stored in the encrypted file. If the seed values
match, the program continues; if not, it displays the message "Wrong password" and
stops.

```
procedure DecodeFile(FileName, Password : string);
const
  MaxBuf = 30000;
var
  Source,
  Dest    : file;
  Buffer  : array [1..MaxBuf] of byte;
  BytesRead : real;
  Seed1,
  Seed1x,
  Seed2,
  Seed2x : byte;
  I : integer;
  I1,I2 : byte;
  RR : integer;

  (**************************************)

  procedure OpenFiles;
  begin
    Assign(Source, FileName);
    {$I-}
    Reset(Source, 1);
    {$I+}
    if IOresult <> 0 then
      begin
        WriteLn('file not found.');
```

```
        Halt;
      end;

    BlockRead(Source, Buffer, 6);
    if (Buffer[1] <> ord('L')) or
       (Buffer[2] <> ord('O')) or
       (Buffer[3] <> ord('C')) or
       (Buffer[4] <> ord('K')) or
       (Buffer[5] <> ord('E')) or
       (Buffer[6] <> ord('D')) then
      begin
        WriteLn('File not locked.');
        Halt;
      end;

    BlockRead(Source,Seed1x,1);
    BlockRead(Source,Seed2x,1);

    if ((Seed1 <> Seed1x) or (Seed2 <> Seed2x)) then
      begin
        WriteLn('Wrong password.');
        Halt;
      end;

    Assign(Dest, '$$$$$.$$');
    Rewrite(Dest, 1);
  end;

(*************************************)

procedure GetSeed;
var
  I, J : integer;
begin
  Seed1 := 0;
  Seed2 := 0;

  J := Length(password);
  for I := 1 to Length(password) do
    begin
      Seed1 := Seed1 + (ord(password[I]) * I);
      Seed2 := Seed2 + (ord(password[I]) * J);
      J := J - 1;
    end;
end;

(*************************************)

procedure CloseFiles;
```

```pascal
  var
    I : integer;
  begin
    Rewrite(Source, 1);
    FillChar(Buffer, MaxBuf, 0);
    while BytesRead > 0 do
      begin
        if BytesRead > MaxBuf then
          BlockWrite(Source, Buffer, MaxBuf)
        else
          begin
            I := Trunc(BytesRead);
            BlockWrite(Source, Buffer, I)
          end;
        BytesRead := BytesRead - MaxBuf;
      end;
    Close(Source);
    Close(Dest);
    Erase(Source);
    Rename(Dest, FileName);
  end;

(***************************************)

begin {DecodeFile}
  GetSeed;
  OpenFiles;
  I1 := Seed1;
  I2 := Seed2;
  BlockRead(Source, Buffer, MaxBuf, RR);
  BytesRead := RR;
  while RR > 0 do
    begin
      for I := 1 to RR do
        begin
          I1 := I1 - I;
          I2 := I2 + I;
          if odd(I) then
            Buffer[I] := Buffer[I] + I1
          else
            Buffer[I] := Buffer[I] - I2;
        end;
      BlockWrite(Dest, Buffer, RR);
      BlockRead(Source, Buffer, MaxBuf, RR);
      BytesRead := BytesRead + RR;
    end;
  CloseFiles;
end;
```

Chapter 20

Complex Data Structures

Chapter 6, "Pointers, Dynamic Memory, and Polymorphism," introduced complex data structures by implementing a linked list. This chapter demonstrates three more complex structures: the doubly linked list, the stack, and the binary tree.

This chapter will also demonstrate how to write data structures so that they are reusable. In other words, the traditional way to use a data structure is to copy an existing example and change the records it operates upon. This method can easily lead to errors that are difficult to find. Also if you find a mistake in an algorithm, you will need to correct that mistake in many places. A better way is to write the data structure so that it can adapt to any record type, and therefore not require any changes for new programs. If you find a mistake in the structure, you only need to change it in one place. The stack and binary tree objects in this chapter are examples of reusable structures.

Doubly Linked Lists

Doubly linked lists maintain links in both directions, allowing you to process the list backward or forward. This requires an additional pointer field (*Prev*) added to the record used in the singly linked list:

```
type
  CustPtr = ^CustRec;
  CustRec = record
```

```
  Name : string[20];
  Address : string[40];
  City : string[20];
  State : string[2];
  Prev,
  Next : CustPtr;
end;
```

The *Prev* pointer keeps track of the link preceding the current one, while the *Next* pointer keeps track of the next link.

While they are more powerful than singly linked lists, doubly linked lists require you to write even more code. You were introduced to a singly linked list in Chapter 6. Now look closely at Figure 20-1 where a doubly linked list is shown. Adding the backward-referencing pointer doubles the number of linkages to maintain.

Doubly linked lists require position pointers to keep track of both the beginning and the end of the list. When a new link is created, you must keep track of the location of the first record, the last record, the current record, and the record prior to the current record. The following program segment illustrates this process:

```
if FirstCust = nil then
  begin
    New(CurrentCust);
    EnterData;
    CurrentCust^.Next := nil;
    CurrentCust^.Prev := nil;
    FirstCust := CurrentCust;
    LastCust := CurrentCust;
  end
else
  begin
    PrevCust := LastCust;
    New(CurrentCust);
    EnterData;
    PrevCust^.Next := CurrentCust;
    CurrentCust^.Next := nil;
    CurrentCust^.Prev := PrevCust;
    LastCust := CurrentCust;
  end;
```

When *FirstCust* is equal to **nil,** the program creates the first element in the linked list and sets its pointers, *Prev* and *Next,* to **nil.** The other position pointers, *FirstCust* and *LastCust,* are set equal to *CurrentCust.*

The next time through, the program branches to the **else,** where it sets PrevCust equal to *LastCust* before creating the new link. When it creates the new link, the program sets the *Prev* pointer to *PrevCust* and the *Next* pointer in *PrevCust* to *CurrentCust,* establishing the double link to allow processing in either direction.

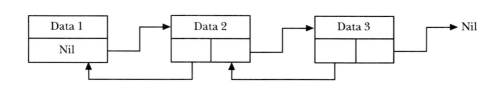

Figure 20-1.   *A doubly linked list*

The following program uses doubly linked lists to manage a list of names and addresses. Two important features are the ability to sort the list and to write out the list in reverse order.

```
Program DoubleLink;

uses Crt;

type
  CustPtr = ^CustRec;
  CustRec = record
    Name : string[20];
    Address : string[40];
    City : string[20];
    State : string[2];
    Prev,
    Next : CustPtr;
  end;

var
  FirstCust,
  LastCust,
  PrevCust,
  CurrentCust : CustPtr;

  Ch : char;

(*************************************)

procedure AddRecord;

  (*************************************)

  procedure EnterData;
  begin
    with CurrentCust^ do
      begin
```

```
        Write('Enter customer name: ');
        ReadLn(Name);
        Write('Enter address: ');
        ReadLn(Address);
        Write('Enter city: ');
        ReadLn(City);
        Write('Enter state: ');
        ReadLn(State);
      end;
  end;

  (************************************)

begin
  ClrScr;
  if FirstCust = nil then
    begin
      New(CurrentCust);
      EnterData;
      CurrentCust^.Next := nil;
      CurrentCust^.Prev := nil;
      FirstCust := CurrentCust;
      LastCust := CurrentCust;
    end
  else
    begin
      PrevCust := LastCust;
      New(CurrentCust);
      EnterData;
      PrevCust^.Next := CurrentCust;
      CurrentCust^.Next := nil;
      CurrentCust^.Prev := PrevCust;
      LastCust := CurrentCust;
    end;
end;

(************************************)

procedure ListRecords;
var
  Ch : char;

  (************************************)

  procedure ListForwards;
  begin
    CurrentCust := FirstCust;
    while CurrentCust <> nil do
      begin
```

```
          with CurrentCust^ do
            WriteLn(Name,', ',Address,', ',City,', ',State);
          CurrentCust := CurrentCust^.Next;
        end;
    end;

  (*************************************)

  procedure ListBackwards;
  begin
    CurrentCust := LastCust;
    while CurrentCust <> nil do
      begin
        with CurrentCust^ do
          WriteLn(Name,', ',Address,', ',City,', ',State);
        CurrentCust := CurrentCust^.Prev;
      end;
  end;

  (*************************************)

begin
  repeat
    Write('F)orwards or B)ackwards, Q)uit: ');
    Ch := ReadKey;
    if Ch = #0 then
      Ch := ReadKey;
    WriteLn;
    Ch := UpCase(Ch);
  until (Ch in ['F','B','Q']);

  if Ch = 'F' then
    ListForwards
  else if Ch = 'B' then
    ListBackwards;
  WriteLn;
  Write('Press ENTER...');
  ReadLn;
end;

(*************************************)

procedure SortRecords;
var
  NextRec,FarCust : CustPtr;
  SortDone : boolean;
begin
  repeat
    CurrentCust := FirstCust;
```

```
      PrevCust := nil;
      SortDone := True;

   while CurrentCust^.Next <> nil do
     begin
       NextRec := CurrentCust^.Next;

       if CurrentCust^.Name > NextRec^.Name then
         begin
           SortDone := False;

           if NextRec^.Next <> nil then
             begin
               FarCust := NextRec^.Next;
               FarCust^.Prev := CurrentCust;
             end
           else
             FarCust := nil;

           if CurrentCust^.Prev = nil then
             begin
               FirstCust := NextRec;
               PrevCust := nil;
             end
           else
             begin
               PrevCust := CurrentCust^.Prev;
               PrevCust^.Next := NextRec;
             end;

           CurrentCust^.Next := FarCust;
           CurrentCust^.Prev := NextRec;

           NextRec^.Next := CurrentCust;
           NextRec^.Prev := PrevCust;

           CurrentCust := FirstCust;
         end
       else
         CurrentCust := CurrentCust^.Next;
   end;

  until SortDone;

  LastCust := CurrentCust;
  WriteLn;
  Write('Sort completed. Press ENTER...');
  ReadLn;
end;
```

```
(***********************************)

begin
  FirstCust := nil;

  repeat
    ClrScr;
    repeat
      Write('A)dd a customer, L)ist customers, S)ort, Q)uit: ');
      Ch := ReadKey;
      if Ch = #0 then
         Ch := ReadKey;
      WriteLn;
      Ch := Upcase(Ch);
    until Ch in ['A','L','S','Q'];

    if Ch = 'A' then
      AddRecord
    else if Ch = 'L' then
      ListRecords
    else if Ch = 'S' then
      SortRecords;

  until Ch = 'Q';
end.
```

Dynamic memory allocation is a powerful tool. It allows you to expand your program's data space while opening the door to linked lists and other dynamic data structures. But there is a price to pay. Linked lists maximize the efficient use of memory, but impose some overhead and require much more time to develop.

Stacks as Reusable Objects

The burden of developing dynamic data structures is especially high when you must reinvent them for every application. With object technology, however, you can develop a general solution for a dynamic data structure, then reuse that structure for multiple applications.

Consider the *stack* data structure. This data structure acts just like the stack of trays at a typical cafeteria. You can only place new trays on the top of the stack, and you can only take off the top tray. The stack is also known as a last-in-first-out, or LIFO, structure.

The easiest way to implement a general solution for a stack is to use pointers. If all of the items in the stack are merely pointers to the actual objects, then the stack can be used for items of any size or complexity. The items can even be different, giving you polymorphism. Figure 20-2 depicts the stack object.

Here is the interface portion of the STACKS unit, which includes the definition of the *TStack* object:

```
Unit STACKS;

interface

type
  PEntry = ^TEntry;
  TEntry = record
    Item : pointer;
    Next : PEntry;
  end;

  TStack = object
    procedure Push(AnItem : pointer);
    function Pop : pointer;
    function IsEmpty : boolean;
  private
    Top : PEntry;
  end;
```

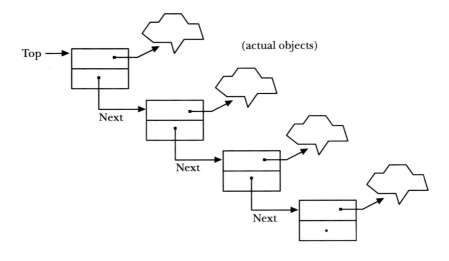

Figure 20-2.   *A reusable stack structure*

Following the rule of encapsulation (defined in Chapter 3, "Complex Data Types"), the stack is accessible only through its methods. The *TEntry* type is used to maintain pointers to the item being stored and the next entry in the stack. This type is only for internal use; programs that use the *TStack* object will not need to use the *TEntry* type.

The implementations of these methods are actually pretty straightforward. The *TStack.Push* method creates a new entry, points the *Item* field to the data being stored, points the *Next* field to the top of the stack, and moves the *Top* pointer. The *Pop* method retrieves the top data item, moves the *Top* pointer down, and disposes of the old pointers. The following listing is the implementation of the STACKS unit:

```
implementation

procedure TStack.Push;
var
  Temp : PEntry;

begin
  New(Temp);
  Temp^.Item := AnItem;

  {link the new record to the top of the stack}
  Temp^.Next := Top;

  {set the top of the stack to the new record}
  Top := Temp;
end;


{************************************************************}

function TStack.Pop;
var
  Temp : PEntry;
begin
  if Top = nil then
    Pop := nil
  else
    begin
      Pop := Top^.Item;

      {remember the old entry so it can be disposed}
      Temp := Top;

      Top := Top^.Next;
      Dispose(Temp);
    end;
```

```
end;

{**********************************************************}

function TStack.IsEmpty;
begin
  IsEmpty := Top = nil;
end;

end.
```

To use the *TStack* object you only need to call *Push* to store data and *Pop* to retrieve it. The most difficult part is creating pointers to each of the items being stored. Here is a program that uses *TStack* to store and retrieve **integers**:

```
Program TestStacks;

uses STACKS, Crt;

type
  PInteger = ^integer;

var
  TheStack : TStack;
  P : PInteger;
  Ptr : pointer;
  I : integer;

begin
  ClrScr;
  Randomize;
  for I := 1 to 7 do
    begin
      New(P);
      P^ := Random(100);
      Writeln('Pushing ', P^);
      TheStack.Push(P);
    end;
  Writeln;

  while not TheStack.IsEmpty do
    begin
      P := PInteger(TheStack.Pop);
      Writeln('Popping ', P^);
    end;

  Writeln;
  Write('Press ENTER...');
```

```
   Readln;
end.
```

In the **for-do** loop, the program calls New to reserve memory for each item. You might be tempted to call New only once and reuse the same pointer; however, you must realize that the *TStack* object must have a new memory location every time you call *Push*.

The **while-do** loop retrieves each item off the stack. The statement

```
P := PInteger(TheStack.Pop);
```

calls the *Pop* function to retrieve a pointer from *TheStack*, then uses type casting to convert it to the *PInteger* pointer type before assigning the pointer to *P*. The type cast guarantees that *P^* will be the proper type (in this case **integer**). See Chapter 2, "Primitive Data Types," for more on type casting.

The output of this program is shown in Figure 20-3. Notice how the first **integer** off the stack is indeed the last one that was placed on it.

Binary Trees as Abstract Objects

A stack is relatively easy to make reusable because the stack always keeps the items in the same order. As your data structures get more complex, however, you will find it harder to develop reusable objects.

Take the *binary tree* structure, for example. As you can see in Figure 20-4, a binary tree is usually pictured upside-down from a tree found in nature. The top entry (or

```
Pushing 39
Pushing 8
Pushing 13
Pushing 18
Pushing 29
Pushing 37
Pushing 0

Popping 0
Popping 37
Popping 29
Popping 18
Popping 13
Popping 8
Popping 39

Press ENTER...
```

Figure 20-3.   *Output from the TestStacks program*

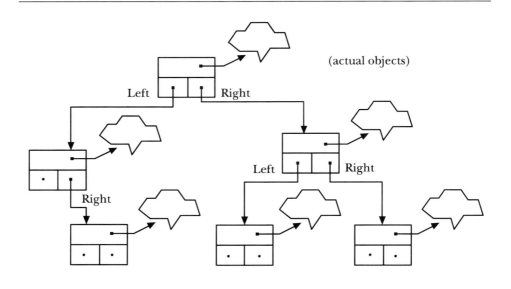

Figure 20-4.   *Pictorial representation of a binary tree*

node) of the tree is called the *root*. Each node has zero, one or two *branches*. If a node has no branches, it can be called a *leaf*. Binary trees are stored in a very specific order so that the nodes are always sorted. You can retrieve data much faster with a binary tree than with most other data structures.

Implementing the Tree Structure

To implement a binary tree object, you must know how to keep the entries sorted. But in order to sort the entries, you must understand the nature of the entries (strings, records, numbers, and so on). So how can an object know about the entries and still be reusable? Well, essentially it can't.

To get around this dilemma you can create an *abstract object*. An abstract object contains most of the logic to implement the structure, but leaves out the entry-specific logic. You must then create a descendent object which fills in the missing logic based on the data type being stored. Both Turbo Vision and ObjectWindows include several examples of abstract objects. One of these, TSortedCollection, is described in Chapter 21, "Merging, Searching, and Sorting."

You will understand the concept of abstract objects better by looking at the definition of the *TTree* object:

```
Unit TREES;
```

```
interface

type
  PNode = ^TNode;
  TNode = record
    Item : pointer;
    Left : PNode;
    Right: PNode;
  end;
  NodeProc = procedure(ANode : pointer);

  TTree = object
    constructor Init;
    function IsEqual(Key1, Key2 : pointer) : boolean; virtual;
    function IsLessThan(Key1, Key2 : pointer) : boolean; virtual;
    procedure Insert(NewNode : pointer);
    procedure ForEach(DoSomething : NodeProc);
    procedure Delete(AKey : pointer; var Found : boolean);
    function FindNode(AKey : pointer) : pointer;
    function Size : word;
    function Depth : word;
  private
    Root : PNode;
    TheSize : word;
  end;
```

What make *TTree* an abstract object are the two virtual methods *IsEqual* and *IsLessThan*. These are the two functions that require specific knowledge of the data in each entry. Thus *IsEqual* and *IsLessThan* are merely placeholders. You must create a descendant of *TTree* and override these methods to be able to use the data structure. (You will see this later in the chapter.)

The other unusual feature of this object definition is the use of a *procedural type*. Turbo Pascal lets you pass procedures as parameters, and the type of the parameter is called a procedural type. The definition

```
NodeProc = procedure(ANode : pointer);
```

shows that all procedures passed to a subprogram of type *NodeProc* must include exactly one pointer parameter. The method

```
procedure ForEach(DoSomething : NodeProc);
```

gives the *TTree* object the flexibility to traverse the tree, passing each node to a procedure. The called procedure can then operate on that node, such as printing its value to the screen.

The implementation of the *TTree* object is somewhat complex. The advantage of an abstract object, however, is that you can use it again and again without understanding how it works (only how to use it). Many of the routines use recursion, so it might help to review that concept by rereading Chapter 4, "Subprograms."

```
implementation

constructor TTree.Init;
begin
  Root := nil;
  TheSize := 0;
end;

{***********************************************************}

function TTree.IsEqual;
begin
  IsEqual := True;
end;

function TTree.IsLessThan;
begin
  IsLessThan := false;
end;

{***********************************************************}

procedure TTree.Insert;
var
  PSearch,
  PParent,
  PTemp : PNode;

begin
  PSearch := Root;

  {traverse the tree}
  while PSearch <> nil do
    begin
      PParent := PSearch;
      if IsLessThan(NewNode, PSearch^.Item) then
        PSearch := PSearch^.Left
      else
        PSearch := PSearch^.Right;
    end;

  {create a new node}
  New(PTemp);
```

```
  PTemp^.Item := NewNode;
  PTemp^.Left := nil;
  PTemp^.Right := nil;

  {insert the new node in the tree}
  if PSearch = Root then
    Root := PTemp
  else if IsLessThan(NewNode, PParent^.Item) then
    PParent^.Left := PTemp
  else
    PParent^.Right := PTemp;
  TheSize := TheSize + 1;
end;

{************************************************************}

function TTree.Size;
begin
  Size := TheSize;
end;

{************************************************************}

function TTree.Depth;
var
  LeftDepth,
  RightDepth : word;

  function NodeDepth(Node : PNode) : word;
  begin
    if Node = nil then
      NodeDepth := 0
    else
      begin
        LeftDepth := NodeDepth(Node^.Left);
        RightDepth := NodeDepth(Node^.Right);
        if LeftDepth > RightDepth then
          NodeDepth := LeftDepth + 1
        else
          NodeDepth := RightDepth + 1;
      end;
  end;

begin  {Depth}
  Depth := NodeDepth(Root);
end;

{************************************************************}
```

```pascal
function TTree.FindNode;
var
  PSearch : PNode;
  Found : boolean;
begin
  PSearch := Root;
  Found := False;

  while (PSearch <> nil) and not Found do
    if IsEqual(AKey, PSearch^.Item) then
      Found := true
    else if IsLessThan(AKey, PSearch^.Item) then
      PSearch := PSearch^.Left
    else
      PSearch := PSearch^.Right;

  if Found then
    FindNode := PSearch^.Item
  else
    FindNode := nil;
end;

{*************************************************************}

procedure TTree.ForEach;
  procedure DoNode(Node : PNode);
  begin
    if Node <> nil then
      begin
        DoNode(Node^.Left);
        DoSomething(Node^.Item);
        DoNode(Node^.Right);
      end;
  end;
begin
  DoNode(Root);
end;

{*************************************************************}

procedure TTree.Delete;
var
  PSearch,
  PParent,
  Temp : PNode;
begin
  PSearch := Root;
  Found := False;
  while (PSearch <> nil) and not Found do
```

```
     if IsEqual(AKey, PSearch^.Item) then
       Found := true
     else
       begin
         PParent := PSearch;
         if IsLessThan(AKey, PSearch^.Item) then
           PSearch := PSearch^.Left
         else
           PSearch := PSearch^.Right;
       end;

  if Found then
    begin
      if PSearch^.Left = nil then
        Temp := PSearch^.Right
      else
        begin
          Temp := PSearch^.Left;
          while Temp^.Right <> nil do
            Temp := Temp^.Right;
          Temp^.Right := PSearch^.Right;
        end;
      if PSearch = Root then
        Root := Temp
      else if PSearch = PParent^.Left then
        PParent^.Left := Temp
      else
        PParent^.Right := Temp;
      Dispose(PSearch);
    end;
end;

end.
```

Notice that the *IsEqual* and *IsLessThan* methods have a skeletal implementation, but they are essentially placeholders which will be overridden by descendant objects.

Using the Tree Structure

The critical concept needed to implement an actual binary tree is the *key*. A key is a portion of an item being stored that is used to sort the tree. You can also use the key when searching for data: you provide the key to the *FindNode* method, and it returns the remainder of the information associated with that key.

In this particular implementation, the key should be at the beginning of the item. For example, suppose you used the binary tree to store personnel data. Although there are many fields in a personnel record, only one (typically) acts as the key. So if you want the records sorted by Social Security number, you would define a record like this:

```
type
  Personnel = record
    SocSec : string[11];
    Name : string[30];
    Address : string[50];
    Income : real;
    Age : integer;
  end;
```

If you wanted to store the records sorted by name instead, you would change the order so that the *Name* field was first.

Let's create a simple program that uses the *TTree* object. First, we define types that will act as the nodes in the tree:

```
Program TreeTest;

uses TREES, Crt;

type
  PNameStr = ^TNameStr;
  TNameStr = string[20];

  PPerson = ^TPerson;
  TPerson = record
    Name : TNameStr;
    Phone : string[12];
  end;
```

This simple tree will use the *Name* field as the key, and have a *Phone* field as the only other data in each node.

Next we define an object type which is a descendant type of *TTree*:

```
TPersonTree = object(TTree)
  function IsEqual(Key1, Key2 : pointer) : boolean; virtual;
  function IsLessThan(Key1, Key2 : pointer) : boolean; virtual;
  procedure Insert(AName, APhone : string);
end;
```

The two functions are the abstract methods we must override to help *TTree* with its sorting. The *Insert* method simplifies adding items to the tree.

Now we implement each of these methods:

```
function TPersonTree.IsEqual;
begin
  IsEqual := PNameStr(Key1)^ = PNameStr(Key2)^;
end;

function TPersonTree.IsLessThan;
begin
  IsLessThan := PNameStr(Key1)^ < PNameStr(Key2)^;
end;

procedure TPersonTree.Insert;
var
  P : PPerson;
begin
  New(P);
  P^.Name := AName;
  P^.Phone := APhone;
  inherited Insert(P);
end;
```

Both *IsEqual* and *IsLessThan* are passed as pointers to the nodes, which also serve as pointers to the keys of those nodes (since they are co-located). The methods convert the **pointer** variables to *PNameStr* variables, then dereference the pointers and compare the keys. The *Insert* method creates a new node on the heap and passes the node pointer to *TTree.Insert*.

The last step before we can actually use the new object is to create a *NodeProc* procedure. In this case we need a procedure that displays the values of each field on screen. To do this, convert the **pointer** to a *PPerson* type; then display each field:

```
procedure WriteNode(ANode : pointer); far;
var
  APerson : PPerson;
begin
  APerson := PPerson(ANode);
  Writeln (APerson^.Name:20, APerson^.Phone:15);
end;
```

The **far** directive is required for all procedures that will act as parameters. This directive forces the compiler to use both the segment and offset values when leaving the procedure instead of assuming that the segment stays constant.

That's all the preparation that needs to be done. The rest of the program uses the *TPersonTree* object to add nodes, find keys, delete nodes, and so on:

```
var
  TheTree : TPersonTree;
```

```
   Key,
   APerson : PPerson;
   Found : boolean;

begin
  ClrScr;
  TheTree.Init;
  TheTree.Insert('Jones, Kris', '805-911-1361');
  TheTree.Insert('Smith, Kimmy', '716-200-9876');
  TheTree.Insert('Harbin, Vic', '414-555-3882');
  TheTree.Insert('Allison, Brenda', '714-400-2006');
  TheTree.Insert('Noel, Ashlyn', '800-123-4567');

  Writeln('Depth = ', TheTree.Depth);
  Writeln('Size = ', TheTree.Size);

  TheTree.ForEach(WriteNode);
  Writeln;

  New(Key);
  Key^.Name := 'Noel, Ashlyn';
  Writeln('Searching for Noel:');
  APerson := TheTree.FindNode(Key);
  if APerson <> nil then
    WriteNode(APerson)
  else
    Writeln('    not in tree');

  Key^.Name := 'Hughes, GQ';
  Writeln('Searching for Hughes:');
  APerson := TheTree.FindNode(Key);
  if APerson <> nil then
    WriteNode(APerson)
  else
    Writeln('    not in tree');


  Key^.Name := 'Lederman, Mimi';
  TheTree.Delete(Key, Found);
  Writeln('Lederman Deleted: ', Found);
  Key^.Name := 'Jones, Kris';
  TheTree.Delete(Key, Found);
  Writeln('Jones Deleted: ', Found);

  Writeln;
  TheTree.ForEach(WriteNode);
```

```
    Writeln;
    Write('Press ENTER...');
    Readln;
end.
```

When you run this program you will see the output shown in Figure 20-5.

```
Depth = 3
Size = 5
     Allison, Brenda    714-400-2006
        Harbin, Vic    414-555-3882
        Jones, Kris    805-911-1361
       Noel, Ashlyn    800-123-4567
       Smith, Kimmy    716-200-9876

Searching for Noel:
       Noel, Ashlyn    800-123-4567
Searching for Hughes:
   not in tree
Lederman Deleted: FALSE
Jones Deleted: TRUE

     Allison, Brenda    714-400-2006
        Harbin, Vic    414-555-3882
       Noel, Ashlyn    800-123-4567
       Smith, Kimmy    716-200-9876

Press ENTER...
```

Figure 20-5.   *Output from the TreeTest program*

Chapter 21

Merging, Searching, and Sorting

Some programming tasks are so common that over the years standardized, highly efficient algorithms have been developed to take care of them. Searching, sorting, and merging are three of the most common, turning up in nearly every book on computer programming. While entire books have been devoted to these subjects, this chapter touches on only the most practical algorithms and how they are implemented in Turbo Pascal.

Merging

Merging files refers to the process by which two ordered files are combined to form one large ordered file. For example, a master file of historical transactions might be updated by merging a file of daily transactions into it. Both files must be ordered in the same way (for example, by date or account number); the updated file then becomes the master file that will be updated the next day.

Of course, you could add the daily file to the end of the historical file and sort the whole thing at one time, but sorting takes far longer than merging.

The merge process is straightforward. It starts by reading the first record from each file, after which the program enters a loop. Inside the loop, the program compares the two records and writes the one with the lower value to the newly created file. Another record is then read from the input file.

This process continues until all records in one or both files have been processed. Usually, one of the input files runs out of records before the other. When this occurs, the procedure continues to read records from the remaining file and write them to the newly created file.

This process is illustrated in Figure 21-1, where two input files of integers are merged. File 1 contains three integer records—1, 4, and 6—and File 2 contains four integer records— 2, 3, 7, and 9. The procedure reads and compares the first records from File 1 and from File 2. The record from File 1 is then written to the merged file because it is lower in value than the record from File 2.

The procedure then reads a new record from File 1 and compares it to the record already in Record 2. Record 1 has a greater value than the value already in Record 2. Therefore, Record 2 is written to the merged file and another record is read from File 2.

This process continues until the procedure reaches the end of File 1, at which point the procedure reads all the records remaining in File 2 and writes them to the merge file. The procedure ends when it reaches the end of File 2.

While the merge procedure is simple in concept, it is not so simple to express in Turbo Pascal. The major complexity is in determining when a new record is needed from an input file and when an input file is empty. In the following program, input is controlled through two **boolean** functions, *GetItem1* and *GetItem2*:

```
Program MergeTest;

uses CRT;

type
```

	File 1	File 2	
	1	2	
	4	3	
	6	7	
		9	

Step 1: record 1 = 1   record 2 = 2 ⟶ Write record 1
Step 2: Read a new record 1
Step 3: record 1 = 4   record 2 = 2 ⟶ Write record 2
Step 4: Read a new record 2
Step 5: record 1 = 4   record 2 = 3 ⟶ Write record 2
Step 6: Read a new record 2
Step 7: record 1 = 4   record 2 = 7 ⟶ Write record 1
Step 8: Read a new record 1
Step 9: record 1 = 6   record 2 = 7 ⟶ Write record 1
Step 10: Read a new record 1— end of file
Step 11: record 1 = EOF   record 2 = 7 ⟶ Write record 2
Step 12: Read a new record 2
Step 13: record 1 = EOF   record 2 = 9 ⟶ Write record 2
Step 14: Read a new record 2— end of file
Step 15: Both input files are EOF:
        Procedure ends

Figure 21-1.   *Merging two sorted files*

```
    Str80 = String[80];

var
  File1,
  File2,
  File3 : Str80;

{************************************}

procedure Merge(Fname1, Fname2, Fname3 : Str80);
var
  Ok1, Ok2 : boolean;
  F1, F2, F3 : text;
  I1, I2 : integer;

{************************************}

  function GetItem1(var I : integer) : boolean;
  begin
    if not Eof(F1) then
      begin
        ReadLn(F1, I);
        GetItem1 := true;
      end
    else
      GetItem1 := false;
  end;

{************************************}

  function GetItem2(var I : integer) : boolean;
  begin
    if not Eof(F2) then
      begin
        ReadLn(F2, I);
        GetItem2 := true;
      end
    else
      GetItem2 := false;
  end;

{************************************}

begin
  Assign(F1, Fname1);
  Reset(F1);
  Assign(F2, Fname2);
  Reset(F2);
  Assign(F3, Fname3);
```

```
  Rewrite(F3);

Ok1 := GetItem1(I1);
Ok2 := GetItem2(I2);

while Ok1 or Ok2 do
  begin
    { if ok1 is true, then A record from File 1 is present. }
    { if ok2 is true, then A record from File 2 is present. }

    if Ok1 and Ok2 then      { records are present }
      begin                   { from both files.    }
        if I1 < I2 then
          begin
            WriteLn(F3, I1);
            Ok1 := GetItem1(I1);
          end
        else
          begin
            WriteLn(F3, I2);
            Ok2 := GetItem2(I2);
          end;
      end
    else if Ok1 then     { A record is present from }
      begin              { the first file only.     }
        WriteLn(F3, I1);
        Ok1 := GetItem1(I1);
      end
    else if Ok2 then     { A record is present from }
      begin              { the second file only.    }
        WriteLn(F3, I2);
        Ok2 := GetItem2(I2);
      end;
  end;
Close(F1);
Close(F2);
Close(F3);
end;

{*************************************}

begin
  ClrScr;
  Write('Enter name of first file: ');
  ReadLn(File1);
  Write('Enter name of second file: ');
  ReadLn(File2);
  Write('Enter name of merged file: ');
  ReadLn(File3);
```

```
   Merge(File1, File2, File3);
end.
```

GetItem1 and *GetItem2* read the next record from their respective files. If successful, the value True is returned along with the record read; if unsuccessful (that is, if it reaches the end of the file), False is returned. By isolating the input process in these two functions, the structure of the merge procedure is simplified.

When the procedure Merge begins, the **boolean** variables *Ok1* and *Ok2* are set with *GetItem1* and *GetItem2*. The loop controlled by the statement

```
while Ok1 or Ok2 do
```

executes as long as records are present from either file and terminates when the end is reached for both files.

Three program branches are contained in the **while-do** loop. The first is executed when input from both files is present. In this case, the procedure compares the two records, the record with the lower value is written to the merge file, and another record is read.

The two other branches execute when one of the input files reaches its end. When this occurs, the loop continues to read records from the remaining file and write them to the merged file. When the procedure reaches the end of the remaining file, the input files and the merged file are closed and the procedure ends.

Searching Methods

In programming, *searching* means finding a particular item within a group of items, for example, finding a particular **integer** in an array of **integers,** finding a person's name in an array of **strings,** and so forth. The two methods of searching presented here, sequential and binary, accomplish the same end with different means.

Sequential Search

The sequential search is so simple it practically needs no explanation. The program simply starts at the beginning of the array to be searched and compares each element with the value you are seeking. The process of finding the number 10 in an array of **integers** is shown in Figure 21-2. The search compares *X,* which is equal to 10, to the first element, then the second, and so on. As soon as the value finds a match in the array, it exits from the search process and returns the index of the element found, which in this example is 4.

The following program includes the function *SeqSearch,* which takes three parameters: the value to search for, the array to search through, and the number of elements in the array.

Variable x equals 10:

Index	Array	Comparison	Result
1	3	x = 3?	False
2	21	x = 21?	False
3	4	x = 4?	False
4	10	x = 10?	True
5	55		
6	31		
7	9		
8	12		
9	15		Exit from search: Return index value 4

Figure 21-2.   *Locating a number with a sequential search*

```
Program SequentialSearch;

type
  Int_Arr = Array [1..100] of integer;

var
  A : Int_Arr;
  I, J : integer;

{*****************************}

function SeqSearch(X : integer;
                   A : Int_Arr;
                   N : integer) : integer;
var
  I : integer;
begin
  for I := 1 to N do
    if X = A[I] then
      begin
        SeqSearch := I;
        exit;
      end;
  SeqSearch := 0;
end;

{*****************************}
```

```
begin
  for I := 1 to 100 do
    A[I] := Random(100);

  repeat
    Write('Enter A number to search for (0 to exit): ');
    ReadLn(I);
    J := SeqSearch(I, A, 100);
    if J = 0 then
      WriteLn('Number not in list.')
    else
      WriteLn(I, ' is element number ', J);
    WriteLn;
  until I = 0;
end.
```

When SeqSearch finds a matching value, it assigns the value to the function and exits. Because a sequential search processes the array element by element, the order of the list is unimportant—the search works equally well with random lists as with sorted lists.

Binary Search

The binary search is one of the most efficient searching methods known and a big improvement over the sequential search. With an array of 100 elements, for example, a sequential search requires an average of 50 comparisons to find a match; the binary search requires at most seven comparisons and as few as four to accomplish the same goal. As the list gets longer, the relative efficiency of the binary search increases.

To perform a binary search, a list must be in sorted order. The search begins by testing the target element against the middle element in the array. If the target element is higher than the middle element, the search continues in the upper half of the list; if the target value is lower than the middle element, the target element is in the lower half.

The binary search process is shown in Figure 21-3. The array is searched for the target value 10. The fifth element, which is equal to 12, is tested first. Since 10 is less than 12, the target value must be in the lower half of the array. The algorithm, therefore, selects element 2—midway between 1 and 4. The value of the second element is 4 (less than 10). The algorithm knows the target value must lie between elements 3 and 4. First, the algorithm tests element 3 and fails. This leaves element 4, which is equal to 10. The binary search now ends, returning a value of 4. Had element 4 been equal to 11, no match would have been found, and the function would have returned a zero.

Because the array in Figure 21-3 is so small, the benefit of the binary search is not fully illustrated. For example, a sequential search of a 1,000-element array requires 500 comparisons on average, whereas a binary search requires at most 10 comparisons.

Variable x equals 10:

Index	Array	Comparison	Result
1	3	5	Lower
2	4	2	Higher
3	9	3	Higher
4	10	4	Equal
5	12		
6	15		
7	21		
8	31		
9	55		

Figure 21-3.   *Searching a sorted array with the binary search alogrithm*

The following program uses the function *Bsearch* to perform a binary search on an array of **integers**:

```
Program BinarySearch;

type
  Int_Arr = array [1..100] of integer;

var
  A : Int_Arr;
  I, J : integer;

function Bsearch(X : integer;
                A : Int_Arr;
                N : integer) : integer;
var
  High, Low, Mid : integer;
begin
  Low := 1;
  High := N;
  while High >= Low do
    begin
      Mid := Trunc((High+Low) div 2);
      if X > A[Mid] then
        Low := Mid + 1
```

```
        else if X < A[Mid] then
            High := Mid - 1
        else
            High := -1;
      end;
  if High = -1 then
    Bsearch := Mid
  else
    Bsearch := 0;
end;


{****************************}

begin
  J := 2;
  A[1] := 1 + Random(5);
  for I := 2 to 100 do
    A[I] := A[I-1] + Random(5);

  repeat
    Write('Enter a number to search for: (0 to exit): ');
    ReadLn(I);
    J := Bsearch(I, A, 100);
    if J = 0 then
      WriteLn('Number not in list.')
    else
      WriteLn(I, ' is element number ', J);
    WriteLn;
  until I = 0;
end.
```

The code that fills the array,

```
A[1] := 1 + Random(5);
for I := 2 to 100 do
  A[I] := A[I-1] + Random(5);
```

is especially designed to guarantee that the array is sorted in ascending order. The first value in the array is assigned a random number between 1 and 5. Each additional value is assigned to be from 0 to 4 larger than the previous number. In many programs you will need to use a sorting algorithm, such as those given later in this chapter.

The main code of the binary search algorithm, contained in the function *Bsearch,* is as follows:

```
Low := 1;
High := N;
while High >= Low do
```

```
   begin
     Mid := Trunc((High+Low) div 2);
     if X > A[Mid] then
       Low := Mid + 1
     else if X < A[Mid] then
       High := Mid - 1
     else
       High := -1;
   end;
 if High = -1 then
   Bsearch := Mid
 else
   Bsearch := 0;
```

The variables *Low* and *High* keep track of the portion of the array being searched. At the beginning, the program sets *Low* equal to 1 and *High* equal to *N*, the number of elements in the array. Thus, the algorithm begins with the entire array.

The binary search loop is controlled by the statement

```
while High >= Low do
```

Each time the loop executes, either *High* is decremented or *Low* is incremented by the average of these variables plus 1, bringing them closer to each other. If *Low* becomes greater than *High,* the element you are searching for does not exist in the sorted array and *Bsearch* returns zero.

If, at any point, *A[Mid]* is equal to the value you are searching for, the program sets high equal to -1, causing the loop to terminate and the function to return the value of *Mid*.

Sorting Methods

Although many sorting algorithms have been developed over the years, three are the most frequently used: the bubble sort, the shell sort, and the quick sort.

The bubble sort is easy to write but terribly slow. The shell sort is moderately fast, but excels in its use of memory resources. The quick sort, the fastest of the three, requires extensive stack space for recursive calls. Knowing all three algorithms, and understanding why one is better than another, is important and illustrates the subtleties of good programming.

General Sorting Principles

The sorting algorithms presented in this section compare one element in an array to another, and, if the two elements are out of order, the algorithms switch their order in the array. This process is illustrated in this code segment:

```
if A[I] > A[I+1] then
  begin
    Temp := A[I];
    A[I]  := A[I+1];
    A[I+1] := Temp;
  end;
```

The first line of code tests if two elements of the array are out of order. Generally, arrays are in order when the current element is smaller than the next element. If the elements are not properly ordered, that is, when the current element is greater than the next element, their order is switched. The switch requires a temporary storage variable of the same type as that of the elements in the array being sorted.

The main difference between the three sorting algorithms is the method by which array elements are selected for comparison. The comparison method has a tremendous impact on the efficiency of the sort. For example, the bubble sort, which compares only adjacent array elements, may require half a million comparisons to sort an array, while the quick sort requires only three or four thousand.

Bubble Sort

To computer programmers, there are good methods, there are bad methods, and there are *kludges*. A kludge is a method that works, but slowly and inefficiently. The bubble sort is a good example of a kludge: given enough time, it will sort your data, but you might have to wait a day or two.

The bubble-sort alogorithm is simple: it starts at the end of the array to be sorted and works toward the beginning of the array. The procedure compares each element to the one preceding it. If the elements are out of order, they are switched. The procedure continues until it reaches the beginning of the array.

Because the sort works backward through the array, comparing each adjacent pair of elements, the lowest element will always "bubble" to the top after the first pass. After the second pass, the second lowest element will "bubble" to the second position in the array, and so on, until the algorithm has passed through the array once for every element in the array.

This code shows this process in Turbo Pascal:

```
for I := 2 to N do
  for J := N downto I do
```

```
if A[J-1] > A[J] then
  Switch(A[J], A[J-1]);
```

As you can see, the bubble-sort algorithm is compact; in fact, technically it is a single Turbo Pascal statement. The bubble sort receives two inputs: *A,* the array to be sorted, and *N,* the number of elements in the array. The inside loop, controlled by the statement

```
for J := N downto I do
```

performs all the comparisons in each pass through the array. The outside loop, controlled by the statement

```
for I := 2 to N do
```

determines the number of passes to execute. Notice that *J* executes from the end of the array (*N*) to *I* and that *I* decreases after every pass. Thus, each pass through the array becomes shorter as the bubble sort executes.

An example of how the bubble sort works is shown in Figure 21-4. An array of 10 integers is sorted in order of increasing value. The elements of the array are listed at the end of each pass. A pass consists of one complete execution of the inside **for-do** loop.

The order of the original array is shown in the row labeled "Start." The values range from 0 to 92, and they are distributed randomly throughout the array. The first

Pass	Position in Array									
	1	2	3	4	5	6	7	8	9	10
Start:	91	6	59	0	75	0	48	92	30	83
1	0	91	6	59	0	75	30	48	92	83
2	0	0	91	6	59	30	75	48	83	92
3	0	0	6	91	30	59	48	75	83	92
4	0	0	6	30	91	48	59	75	83	92
5	0	0	6	30	48	91	59	75	83	92
6	0	0	6	30	48	59	91	75	83	92
7	0	0	6	30	48	59	75	91	83	92
8	0	0	6	30	48	59	75	83	91	92
9	0	0	6	30	48	59	75	83	91	92

Figure 21-4.   *Sorting an array of integers with the bubble-sort algorithm*

pass through the array places the lowest value (0) in the first position in the array, and the number 91 is shifted from the first position into the second position. The other elements are still more or less randomly scattered.

With each step of the bubble sort, the next lowest number takes its proper place in the array, and the higher numbers get shifted to the right. By the end of the eighth pass, the array is completely sorted, yet the sort continues to make one more pass over the array.

The following program contains the bubble-sort algorithm, which takes an **integer** array and the number of elements in the array as parameters:

```
Program BubbleTest;

type
  Int_Arr = array [1..10] of integer;

var
  I : integer;
  A : Int_Arr;

{********************************************}

procedure Bubble(var A : Int_Arr;
                     N : integer);
var
  I, J : integer;

{********************************************}

  procedure Switch(var A, B : integer);
  var
    C : integer;
  begin
    C := A;
    A := B;
    B := C;
  end;

{********************************************}

begin
  for I := 2 to N do
    for J := N downto I do
      if A[J-1] > A[J] then
        Switch(A[J], A[J-1]);
end;

{********************************************}
```

```
begin
  A[1]  := 91;
  A[2]  := 06;
  A[3]  := 59;
  A[4]  := 0;
  A[5]  := 75;
  A[6]  := 0;
  A[7]  := 48;
  A[8]  := 92;
  A[9]  := 30;
  A[10] := 83;

  for I := 1 to 10 do
    Write(A[I]:4);
  WriteLn;
  Bubble(A, 10);

  for I := 1 to 10 do
    Write(A[I]:4);
  WriteLn;

  Write('Press ENTER...');
  ReadLn;
end.
```

The program begins by assigning random values to array A, and displays the values on your terminal. The procedure *Bubble* sorts the array. When the sort is finished, the array is displayed again.

The weakness of the bubble sort is that it compares only adjacent array elements. If the sorting algorithm first compared elements separated by a wide interval, and then focused on progressively smaller intervals, the process would be more efficient. This train of thought led to the development of the shell-sort and quick-sort algorithms.

Shell Sort

The shell sort is far more efficient than the bubble sort. It first puts elements approximately where they will be in the final order and determines their exact placement later. The strength of the algorithm lies in the method it uses to estimate an element's approximate final position.

The key concept in the shell sort is the *gap,* which is the distance between the elements compared. If the gap is 5, the first element is compared with the sixth element, the second with the seventh, and so on. In a single pass through the array, all elements within the gap are put in order. For example, the elements in this array are in order, given a gap of 2:

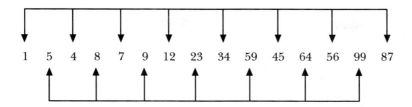

As you can see, the array is nearly completely sorted before the algorithm tests adjacent elements. In the next pass over this array, the gap is reduced to 1, which results in a completely sorted array. The initial value of the gap is arbitrary, although it is common to set it to one half the number of elements in the array (that is, *N div 2*).

The many versions of the shell sort vary in complexity and efficiency. The version presented in this chapter is extremely efficient, requiring few passes to complete the sort.

Unfortunately, there is no simple way to describe how this particular shell algorithm works. Efficient algorithms tend to be more complex than inefficient ones and are therefore harder to express in words. This is why poor algorithms are used so often. Figure 21-5 contains the essential code for the shell-sort algorithm. Review this code as you read the explanation.

```
                    while Gap > 0 do
                       begin
                         for I := (Gap + 1) to N do
                            begin
                              J := I - Gap;
                            while (J > 0) do
                                 begin
                                   K := J + Gap;
                                   if (A[J] <= A[K]) then
                                      J := 0
                                   else
                                     begin
                                       Switch(A[J], A[K]);
                                       J := J - Gap;
                                       end;
                                 end;
                            end;
                         Gap := Gap div 2;
                       end;
```

Outside loop   Inside loop

Figure 21-5.   *Essential code for the shell-sort algorithm*

The first line in the procedure sets the gap to *N div 2*. The outside loop in the shell sort, controlled by the statement

```
while Gap > 0 do
```

determines the number of passes made through the array. After each pass through the array, the gap is reduced by half for each pass until the gap reaches 0. For example, if there were ten elements in the array, the first gap would be 5, followed by 2, 1, and 0. Because **integer** division is used, *1 div 2* results in 0.

In each pass, three variables determine which elements to compare: *I, J,* and *K*. The variable *I* points to the far element, and *J* points to the near element. For example, if the gap is 5, *I* will equal 6 and *J* will equal 1. Before the comparison, *K* is set to the sum of *J* and *Gap,* which, for the first comparison, equals *I*.

The comparison uses *K* instead of *I* because it may be necessary to backtrack through the array. To backtrack, *J* is reduced by *Gap,* and *K* is also changed so that a new pair of elements is compared. Because *I* controls the inside loop, it should not be changed in this backtracking process.

Consider the example in Figure 21-6 where a ten-element array is being sorted. At step 1, *Gap* is 2, *J* is equal to 6, and *K* is equal to 8. Thus, the sixth and eighth elements in the array will be compared. Since element 6 is 85 and element 8 is 49, the two must be switched, as is shown in step 2.

Position in Array

	1	2	3	4	5	6	7	8	9	10
Step 1:	19	9	32	63	86	85	87	49	35	86
						↑ j		↑ k		
Step 2:	19	9	32	63	86	49	87	85	35	86
				↑ j		↑ k				
Step 3:	19	9	32	49	86	63	87	85	35	86
		↑ j		↑ k						
Step 4:	19	9	32	49	86	63	87	85	35	86
							↑ j		↑ k	

Figure 21-6.   *Sorting an array of integers with the shell-sort algorithm*

Next, the algorithm decreases *J* by *Gap*, in this case 4. Since *J* is greater than zero, the inside loop executes again. Because *J* has been reduced by 2, the fourth and sixth elements are compared. Again, the elements are out of order and need to be switched. As before, *J* is decreased by *Gap*, or 2, leading to step 3.

Elements 2 and 4 of the array are in the correct order, so rather than switching the elements, the program sets *J* to zero. Now, the result of *J - Gap* is negative 2. Since this is less than zero, the inner loop is terminated and *I* is incremented. Working downward, *J* is set to *I - Gap*, or 7, and *K* is set equal to *J + Gap*, or 9.

In short, *I* keeps track of the overall flow of the algorithm, while *K* backtracks when necessary. This tricky bit of logic increases the efficiency by about 300% over the most simple shell sort.

The following sample program includes the procedure *Shell*, which contains the shell-sort algorithm.

```
Program ShellTest;

uses CRT;

type
  Int_Arr = Array [1..10] of integer;

var
  I : integer;
  A : Int_Arr;

{***************************}

procedure Shell(var A : Int_arr;
                    N : integer);
var
  Gap,
  I, J, K, X : integer;

{****************************}

  procedure Switch(var A, B : integer);
  var
    C : integer;
  begin
    C := A;
    A := B;
    B := C;
  end;

{****************************}

begin
  Gap := N div 2;
```

```
    while Gap > 0 do
      begin
        for I := (Gap + 1) to N do
          begin
            J := I - Gap;
            while (J > 0) do
              begin
                K := J + Gap;
                if (A[J] <= A[K]) then
                  J := 0
                else
                  begin
                    Switch(A[J], A[K]);
                    J := J - Gap;
                  end;
              end;
          end;
        Gap := Gap div 2;
      end;
end;

{*********************}

begin
  ClrScr;
  A[1] := 19;
  A[2] := 9;
  A[3] := 32;
  A[4] := 63;
  A[5] := 86;
  A[6] := 85;
  A[7] := 87;
  A[8] := 49;
  A[9] := 35;
  A[10] := 86;

  for I := 1 to 10 do
    Write(A[I]:4);
  WriteLn;

  Shell(A, 10);

  for I := 1 to 10 do
    Write(A[I]:4);

  WriteLn;
  Write('Press ENTER...');
  ReadLn;
end.
```

Shell accepts the array to be sorted, including the number of elements in the array, and then returns the array in its sorted form. If you test this program against the bubble sort with an array of 1,000 elements, you will see an amazing difference in the time required to sort the array. Yet as efficient as the shell sort is, the quick sort is two or three times as efficient.

Quick Sort

The queen of all sorting algorithms is the quick sort: this algorithm is widely accepted as the fastest general-purpose sort available.

One of the pleasing aspects of the quick sort is that it sorts things in much the same way people do. It first creates large "piles," and then sorts those piles into smaller and smaller piles, eventually ending up with a completely sorted array.

The quick-sort algorithm begins by estimating a midrange value for the array. If the array consists of numbers 1 through 10, the midpoint could be 5 or 6. The midpoint's exact value is not crucial; the algorithm will work with a midpoint of any value. However, the closer the estimated midpoint is to the true midpoint of the array, the faster the sort.

The procedure calculates a midpoint by averaging the first and last elements in the portion of the array being sorted. Once the procedure selects a midpoint, it puts all the elements lower than the midpoint in the lower part of the array, and all the elements higher in the upper part. This is illustrated in Figure 21-7.

Mid-Point	1	2	3	4	5	6	7	8	9	10
Step 1: 55	86	3	10	23	12	67	59	47	31	24
Step 2: 35	24	3	10	23	12	31	47	59	67	86
Step 3: 27	24	3	10	23	12	31	47	59	67	86
Step 4: 18	24	3	10	23	12	31	47	59	67	86
Step 5: 11	12	3	10	23	24	31	47	59	67	86
Step 6: 6	10	3	12	23	24	31	47	59	67	86
Step 7: 23	3	10	12	23	24	31	47	59	67	86
Step 8: 72	3	10	12	23	24	31	47	59	67	86
Step 9: 63	3	10	12	23	24	31	47	59	67	86
Final order:	3	10	12	23	24	31	47	59	67	86

Figure 21-7. *The quick-sort algorithm*

In step 1, the midpoint is 55, which is the average of 86 and 24. In step 2, the segment being sorted is 24 through 47, leading to a midpoint of 35. Notice that the elements in the segment rarely split evenly around the midpoint. This does not harm the algorithm, but does decrease its efficiency somewhat.

At each step in the process, the quick sort orders the elements of an array segment around the midpoint value. As the segments get smaller and smaller, the array approaches the completely sorted order.

In this program, the procedure *Quick* contains the quick-sort algorithm:

```pascal
Program QuickTest;

uses CRT;

type
  Int_Arr = array [1..10] Of integer;

var
  InFile : text;
  I : integer;
  A : Int_Arr;

{***************************}

procedure Quick(var Item : Int_Arr;
                    Count : integer);

{***************************}

  procedure PartialSort(Left, Right : integer;
                        var A: Int_Arr);
  var
    II,
    L1, R1,
    I, J, K : integer;

{***************************}

    procedure Switch(var A, B : integer);
    var
      C : integer;
    begin
      if A <> B then
        begin
          C := A;
          A := B;
          B := C;
        end;
    end;
```

```
{*****************************}

  begin
    K := (A[Left] + A[Right]) div 2;
    I := Left;
    J := Right;
    repeat
      while A[I] < K do
        Inc(I,1);

      while K < A[J] do
        Dec(J,1);

      if I <= J then
        begin
          Switch(A[I],A[J]);
          Inc(I,1);
          Dec(J,1);
        end;
    until I > J;

    if Left < J then
      PartialSort(Left, J, A);
    if I < Right then
      PartialSort(I, Right, A);
  end;

{*********************}

begin
  PartialSort(1, Count, Item);
end;

{********************}

begin
  ClrScr;
  A[1]  := 86;
  A[2]  := 3;
  A[3]  := 10;
  A[4]  := 23;
  A[5]  := 12;
  A[6]  := 67;
  A[7]  := 59;
  A[8]  := 47;
  A[9]  := 31;
  A[10] := 24;
```

```
  for I := 1 to 10 do
    Write(A[I]:4);
  WriteLn;

  Quick(A, 10);

  for I := 1 to 10 do
    Write(A[I]:4);
  WriteLn;

  Write('Press ENTER...');
  ReadLn;
end.
```

The *Quick* procedure begins by calling the nested procedure *PartialSort,* which takes three parameters: the lower bound of the array segment, the upper bound, and the array itself. When first called, the lower bound passed to *PartialSort* is 1, and the upper bound is the number of elements in the array.

PartialSort computes a midpoint and orders the elements in the array segment accordingly. It then calls itself by passing new lower and upper boundaries, thereby focusing on progressively smaller segments of the array. When it reaches the lowest level of the array, the recursion ends, and the procedure passes the sorted array back to the program.

Comparing Sorting Algorithms

The number of comparisons required to sort a list is the universal measure by which all sorting algorithms are judged. The number of comparisons is expressed as a multiple of the number of elements in the list. For example, if you are sorting an array of N elements with the bubble sort, the program will have to perform $(N^2-N)/2$ comparisons. If N is 100, the number of comparisons is 4950.

This benchmark is fine for those with a theoretical bent, but most programmers find it easier to compare sorting methods by measuring the amount of time it takes for each method to sort the same array. Table 21-1 shows the results of tests performed using the bubble-sort, shell-sort, and quick-sort algorithms on arrays with 100, 500, and 1,000 random numbers. As the table shows, the bubble sort is a poor algorithm compared to the shell and quick sorts, taking from 6 to 68 times longer to sort an array. Between the shell sort and quick sort, the difference in time is also significant. The shell sort takes twice as long as the quick sort and requires nearly four times as many comparisons.

The only drawback to the quick sort is the amount of space it requires on the stack. Because quick sort is a recursive procedure, space on the stack must be allocated every time the procedure calls itself. If you are concerned about stack space, you might want to use the shell sort; otherwise, use the quick sort.

Size	Sort Type	Time	Comparisons
100	Bubble	0.66	4,950
100	Shell	0.11	849
100	Quick	0.06	232
500	Bubble	15.88	124,750
500	Shell	0.77	5,682
500	Quick	0.44	1,473
1,000	Bubble	63.66	499,500
1,000	Shell	1.87	13,437
1,000	Quick	0.93	3,254

Table 21-1.   *Relative Efficiency of Different Sorting Methods*

Using Sorted Collections

The object TSortedCollection is found in the Objects unit, which is part of both Turbo Vision and Object Windows. This object enables you to store collections in sorted order. Technically this object uses no sorting algorithm; rather, it uses a linked list to insert each item in the proper place. This way the collection is always sorted.

The TSortedCollection object is an abstract object. As you learned in Chapter 20, you must declare a descendant object to make an abstract object useful. Consider this definition:

```
type
  TIntArray = object(TSortedCollection)
    function Compare(Key1, Key2 : pointer) : integer; virtual;
  end;
```

The type *TIntArray* inherits all necessary methods from TSortedCollection, except for *Compare*. It overrides this function to tell the object how to determine the order of two items in the collection.

The method *TIntArray.Compare* returns one of three values: 1 if the first item is greater than the second, -1 if the first item is less than the second, and 0 if they are the same. To do this, the method must convert the pointers passed in as parameters to variables (such as **strings** or **integers**) which can be used for comparison. Here is the implementation of that method:

```
function TIntArray.Compare;
var
```

```
  Num1, Num2 : integer;
begin
  Num1 := PInteger(Key1)^;
  Num2 := PInteger(Key2)^;
  if Num1 > Num2 then
    Compare := 1
  else if Num1 < Num2 then
    Compare := -1
  else
    Compare := 0;
end;
```

To add an item to a sorted collection, you call the Insert method, which needs a pointer for an input parameter. To keep from having to create pointers outside the object, you can add a second method, *InsertInteger*:

```
procedure TIntArray.InsertInteger(Num : integer);
var
  P : PInteger;
begin
  P := New(PInteger);
  P^ := Num;
  Write(Num:4);
  Insert(P);
end;
```

This method accepts an **integer** value, creates a pointer, points it to the number, and calls Insert to add it to the collection.

The following program uses this object to sort ten numbers and display the sorted list:

```
Program SortedCollections;

uses Objects, Crt;

type
  PInteger = ^integer;
  TIntArray = object(TSortedCollection)
    function Compare(Key1, Key2 : pointer) : integer; virtual;
    procedure InsertInteger(Num : integer);
  end;

var
  A : TIntArray;
  I : integer;

{*********************************************}
```

```
procedure TIntArray.InsertInteger(Num : integer);
var
  P : PInteger;
begin
  P := New(PInteger);
  P^ := Num;
  Write(Num:4);
  Insert(P);
end;

{*******************************************}

function TIntArray.Compare;
var
  Num1, Num2 : integer;
begin
  Num1 := PInteger(Key1)^;
  Num2 := PInteger(Key2)^;
  if Num1 > Num2 then
    Compare := 1
  else if Num1 < Num2 then
    Compare := -1
  else
    Compare := 0;
end;

{*******************************************}

begin
  ClrScr;
  A.Init(10, 10);
  A.InsertInteger(91);
  A.InsertInteger(06);
  A.InsertInteger(59);
  A.InsertInteger(0);
  A.InsertInteger(75);
  A.InsertInteger(0);
  A.InsertInteger(48);
  A.InsertInteger(92);
  A.InsertInteger(30);
  A.InsertInteger(83);
  WriteLn;

  for I := 1 to A.Count do
    Write(PInteger(A.At(I-1))^:4);
  WriteLn;
```

```
   Write('Press ENTER...');
   ReadLn;
end.
```

When you execute this program you will see the output shown here.

```
91   6  59   0  75   0  48  92  30  83
 0   6  30  48  59  75  83  91  92
Press ENTER...
```

Study this output closely. If ten numbers were added to the collection, why are only nine displayed? Well, one of the features of the TSortedCollection object is that it removes any duplicates from the collection. Since two 0's were inserted in the collection, the second one was ignored.

If you don't want duplicates removed, you simply "tell" the object that there aren't any duplicates. You can accomplish this by modifying *Compare* so that it never returns a 0 (indicating that two items are equal):

```
function TIntArray.Compare;
var
  Num1, Num2 : integer;
begin
  Num1 := PInteger(Key1)^;
  Num2 := PInteger(Key2)^;
  if Num1 > Num2 then
    Compare := 1
  else
    Compare := -1;
end;
```

This second implementation of *Compare* returns a value of 1 if the first number is larger than the second, and returns -1 if the first number is less than or equal to the second. It is actually fooling the object into thinking that two numbers that are the same are actually different.

When you replace this method in the *SortedCollections* program, you will get the results shown here.

```
91   6  59   0  75   0  48  92  30  83
 0   0   6  30  48  59  75  83  91  92
Press ENTER...
```

Chapter **22**

Interrupts,
Telecommunications,
and Memory-Resident
Programs

Life is full of interruptions—and so is computing. In computer programming, interruptions are called interrupts. If you own a telephone, you will understand the concept of an interrupt. When your telephone rings, you stop what you are doing, answer the phone, and resume working when your conversation is over. In a way, computers have little telephones ringing inside the microprocessor that make it stop and do something else for a moment.

This chapter introduces the concept of interrupts and how they are used in Turbo Pascal. Interrupts are fundamental to the operation of your computer; and if you want to tap the full power of the personal computer, you must understand them. Because telecommunications commonly use interrupt programming, the concepts will be illustrated with examples from a Turbo Pascal communications program *CommX* given in this chapter.

Using Interrupts

Do you occasionally find it inconvenient when your telephone rings? Imagine how inconvenient it would be to have a telephone that does not ring. You would have to pick up the receiver from time to time to see if anyone were calling. Not only would this waste time, but you would run the risk of missing a call if someone called and hung up before you picked up the receiver.

Of course, our phones do ring, and so we can do other things and answer the telephone only when we know someone is calling. In similar fashion, interrupts allow your computer to work until something happens that requires your computer's attention.

One interrupt controls your computer's internal clock. About 18 times each second, this interrupt stops your microprocessor and asks it to increment the DOS time and date. You do not notice this because it happens so quickly. Other interrupts occur when you press a key on your keyboard or data comes into a serial port. In fact, interrupts occur all the time, but you do not notice them because they generally require the microprocessor to do very little work.

Hardware and Software Interrupts

Interrupts are of two types: hardware and software. Hardware interrupts, generated by such actions as pressing a key, a tick of the system clock, or data entering a serial port, originate in the computer's circuitry and are controlled by a special chip, the 8259 interrupt controller. When a hardware interrupt occurs, this chip acts as a traffic cop, making sure the interrupt goes in the correct direction. The 8259 receives an interrupt request, evaluates its priority, and routes the request to the procedure it needs.

Software interrupts are generated by programs that request special BIOS and DOS services. In Turbo Pascal, the commands Intr and MsDos create software interrupts (see Chapter 15, ("Dos and WinDos Units"). Whether hardware or software, all interrupts use the interrupt vector table.

The Interrupt Vector Table

The interrupt vector table is an array of memory addresses located at the lowest part of the PC's memory. The array is 1,024 bytes long and contains the addresses of all the routines that are triggered by interrupts. Because an address requires 4 bytes, the 1,024-byte interrupt vector table can hold a maximum of 256 interrupt addresses.

An interrupt, when initiated, fetches an address from the interrupt vector table, jumps to that memory location, and executes the routine located there. Each address in the interrupt vector table is used exclusively by a single interrupt. For example, Interrupt 8h, the clock timer, always fetches the address at offset 0020h. Table 22-1 contains the PC's eight hardware interrupts, numbers 8h through 0Fh, and their offsets in the interrupt vector table.

Of the hardware interrupts, the most useful to program are the clock tick (number 8h), the keyboard interrupt (number 9h), and the COM1 serial port (number 0Ch). Interrupt 0Ch is used for serial communications with other computers. Interrupts

Interrupt Number	Offset	Purpose
8h	0020h	System clock tick
9h	0024h	Keyboard interrupt
Ah	0028h	Not used
Bh	002Ch	Second serial port (COM2)
Ch	0030h	First serial port (COM1)
Dh	0034h	Hard-disk interrupt
Eh	0038h	Floppy-disk interrupt
Fh	003Ch	Printer interrupt

Table 22-1.   *Location of Hardware Interrupts in the Interrupt Vector Table*

8h and 9h are used for many purposes, including pop-up terminate-stay-resident (TSR) programs.

Replacing Interrupts

Each time you start your computer, DOS fills the interrupt vector table with addresses to standard interrupt routines. As soon as the computer is running, however, you can change addresses in the interrupt vector table to point to interrupt handling procedures that you have written; the interrupt will then execute your procedure instead of the default procedure. In short, by changing addresses in the interrupt vector table, you can usurp DOS and BIOS and take charge of your computer's basic functions.

Although programmers are not usually interested in altering the addresses of software interrupts, they are interested in changing hardware interrupt addresses. By changing the keyboard interrupt address, for example, a memory-resident program can intercept a keystroke and interpret it before it ever gets to the main program. This is how memory-resident programs such as SuperKey and SideKick work.

An interrupt address can be changed in two ways: by changing the interrupt vector table directly or by using a DOS service to do it for you. To change memory directly, you must overlay an array of addresses on the interrupt vector table, as follows:

```
var
  AsyncVector : pointer;
```

```
InterruptVector : array [0..$FF] of pointer
                    absolute $0000:$0000;
```

The example code just given uses the **pointer** data type. Pointers are 4-byte data types that hold a segment and offset that together constitute a memory address. The variable *InterruptVector*, an array of 256 (00h through FFh) addresses, is declared absolute at the very beginning of RAM, where the interrupt vector table resides. Since *InterruptVector* and the table share the same space, when you change a value in one, you also change it in the other. To change an address in the interrupt vector table, use the following statements:

```
AsyncVector := InterruptVector[$0C];
InterruptVector[$0C] := @AsyncInt;
```

The first statement stores the vector for Interrupt 0Ch in the variable *AsyncVector*. Saving the original address is important since you will need to restore it eventually. The second statement replaces the original vector with the address of a Turbo Pascal procedure named *AsyncInt*.

The Turbo Pascal operator @ returns a 4-byte address (segment and offset) of the procedure *AsyncInt*. The address is then loaded into the interrupt vector table. Now, when Interrupt 0Ch is triggered by data arriving at the serial port, *AsyncInt* will execute instead of the normal procedure.

When you are done using the interrupt vector, you must restore the original address that you saved in the pointer variable *AsyncVector*. If you do not restore the address, you may crash your computer and have to reboot. This single line of code is all you need to restore the original interrupt vector address:

```
InterruptVector[$0C] := AsyncVector;
```

With the interrupt vector now restored to its original value, your computer will operate normally.

It is simple to change interrupt addresses directly, but it is safer to use DOS services, which apply to a wider range of computers. DOS service 35h reports a vector's contents, and service 25h changes an address in the interrupt vector table. Fortunately, the Turbo Pascal DOS unit provides two routines—GetIntVec and SetIntVec—that do exactly what is needed. Both procedures take two parameters: the interrupt number (for example, 0Ch) and a pointer variable. The process of saving an interrupt vector and replacing it with a new vector is shown here:

```
GetIntVec($0C, AsyncVector);
SetIntVec($0C, @AsyncInt);
```

When you are done using the interrupt, you can restore the old interrupt address, as shown here:

```
SetIntVec($0C, AsyncVector);
```

Using the procedures from the DOS unit is safer than directly altering the interrupt vector table. But, now that you know how to change a vector to point to your own procedure, what does that procedure look like?

Writing the Interrupt Handler

Interrupt handler is a term that refers to the code that executes as the result of an interrupt. In the previous examples, the handler was a Turbo Pascal procedure named AsyncInt, which was attached to Interrupt 0Ch. Interrupt handlers are different from other types of procedures because you do not always control when they will execute. For example, Interrupt 0Ch is triggered when a byte is ready in COM1. You have no way of knowing when that will occur, so your interrupt handler must be extra cautious so as not to disturb the normal processing of the computer. In other words, a well-written interrupt handler is like a cat burglar: it enters when you least expect it, steals some computing time, and leaves without a trace.

The trick to writing interrupt handlers is leaving without a trace. To do this, the handler must save all the CPU's registers before executing and restore them when done. (The handler need not save the CS, IP, or Flags registers because DOS saves these for you prior to calling the interrupt.) But saving the CPU registers alone is not enough—you must also conquer the problem presented by the data segment.

Restoring the Data Segment

When an interrupt handler is invoked, only the code segment (CS) and instruction pointer (IP) registers are correctly set to the values your handler needs. The data segment (DS) register, on the other hand, contains the value used by the procedure being interrupted and may not contain the correct value for the interrupt handler. Without the correct data segment, your handler cannot refer to its own global variables. Your interrupt handler must, therefore, store its DS value someplace in the code segment, so that the correct DS can be set.

Turbo Pascal Interrupt Support

While all of this may seem a bit intimidating, Borland comes to the rescue. Turbo Pascal lets you write interrupt handler procedures that automatically save all registers, set up the DS register, and restore all registers when done. To declare a procedure as an interrupt handler, you need only append the **interrupt** directive to the end of the procedure declaration, as shown here:

```
procedure IntHandler; interrupt;
```

The **interrupt** directive instructs Turbo Pascal to insert the appropriate code to save registers, set up the DS register, restore registers, and issue an IRET (return from interrupt assembly language) command to terminate the procedure. You may optionally declare in your handler a list of pseudo-variables that represent the CPU registers:

```
procedure IntHandler(Flags, CS,IP, AX, BX, CX, DX,
                     SI, DI, DS, ES, BP); interrupt;

procedure IntHandler(SI, DI, DS, ES, BP); interrupt;
```

As you can see in the preceding listing, the parameter list can include all the CPU registers (Flags through BP) or a subset of the registers (for example, SI through BP). There are, however, two restrictions. First, you cannot change the order of the parameters. Second, if you delete parameters, you may only do so from the left. For example, if you want only the SI and DS registers, you must include SI, DI, DS, ES, and BP in your parameter list, in that order.

When your interrupt handler executes, you will have access to all the pseudo-parameters that you listed in the procedure heading. The values in the parameters will represent the contents of the CPU registers prior to the interrupt.

Note that the SP and SS registers are not included as pseudo-parameters. This means that your interrupt handler will be using the stack of the program it interrupted. This is a bit risky since you have no idea how large the stack of the interrupted program is. The safest approach is to avoid as much as possible using the stack in your interrupt handler. The next section of this chapter demonstrates how an interrupt handler can be used to create a telecommunications program.

PC Telecommunications

Telecommunications, the transmission of data from one computer to another via telephone lines, is simple in concept, but complicated in practice. In concept, the computer sends a byte to a serial port, which sends it on to the modem. The modem translates the bits into tones and sends the tones to another modem, which translates them back into bits. The translated bits are sent to the receiving serial port where they wait to be picked up by the software.

In practice, writing a program to do all these things is not so simple. The complexity is partly due to the number of hardware elements you must control: the RS-232 serial port, the INS8250 universal asynchronous receiver transmitter (UART), the 8259 interrupt controller, and the modem itself. In addition, there are many variations of modem speed, parity, stop bits, data bits, which serial port to use, and so on.

The Telecommunications Program

The following program, called *CommX*, provides a simple telecommunications capability using Interrupt 12. The program assumes you have a Hayes-compatible modem connected to your first serial port. Before you run the program, set the values in the *SelectModemSet* (included as part of *CommX*) procedure to those of the remote computer you want to call.

```
Program CommX;

{$S-,R-,I-,V-,F+}

uses Crt, Dos;

type
  ModemSetType = record
    ComPort,
    BPS,
    DataBits,
    StopBits         : integer;
    Parity           : char;
    PhoneNumber      : string;
  end;

const
  MainDseg : integer = 0;
  MaxBufLen  = 1024;
  CR         = #13;

  (*******************************)
  (* ISN8250 UART Registers.     *)
  (*******************************)
  DataPort = $03F8;

  (* Contains 8 bits to transmit or receive.   *)
  IER      = $03F9;

  (* Enables the serial port when set equal to 1. *)
  LCR      = $03FB;

  (* Sets communications parameters.            *)
  MCR      = $03FC;

  (* Bits 1, 2 and 4 are turned on to ready modem.*)
  LSR      = $03FD;

  (* When bit 6 is on, it is safe to send a byte. *)
  MDMMSR   = $03FE;
```

```
    (* Initialized to 80h when starting.            *)

  ENBLRDY  = $01;   (* Initial value for Port[IER].     *)
  MDMMOD   = $0B;   (* Initial value for Port[MCR].     *)
  MDMCD    = $80;   (* Initial value for Port[MDMMSR]. *)

  INTCTLR  = $21;   (* Port for 8259 Interrupt Controller. *)

var
  ModemSet         : ModemSetType;
  AsyncVector      : pointer;
  Regs             : Registers;
  Buffer           : array [1..MaxBufLen] of char;
  I,
  CharsInBuf,
  CircOut,
  CircIn           : word;
  Orig             : char;

(************************************************************)

procedure ClearBuffer;
begin
  CircIn := 1;
  CircOut := 1;
  CharsInBuf := 0;
  FillChar(Buffer, SizeOf(Buffer), 0);
end;

(************************************************************)

procedure SelectModemSet;
begin
  with ModemSet do
    begin
      ComPort     := 1;             (* Must be 1 in this program. *)

      repeat
        Write('BPS (1200,2400): ');
        ReadLn(BPS);
      until (BPS = 1200) or (BPS =2400);

      repeat
        Write('Data bits (7,8): ');
        ReadLn(DataBits);
      until DataBits in [7,8];

      repeat
```

```
          Write('Stop bits (0,1): ');
          ReadLn(StopBits);
        until StopBits in [0,1];

        repeat
          Write('Parity (N,E,O): ');
          ReadLn(Parity);
          Parity := UpCase(Parity);
        until Parity in ['N','E','O'];

        Write('Phone number: ');
        ReadLn(PhoneNumber);
      end;
end;

(****************************************************************)

procedure AsyncInt; interrupt;
begin
  Inline($FB);         (* STI *)

  if CharsInBuf < MaxBufLen then
    begin
      Buffer[CircIn] := char(Port[DataPort]);
      if CircIn < MaxBufLen then
        Inc(CircIn, 1)
      else
        CircIn := 1;
      Inc(CharsInBuf, 1);
    end;

  Inline($FA);         (* CLI *)
  Port[$20] := $20;
end;

(****************************************************************)


procedure SetSerialPort(ComPort,
                        BPS,
                        StopBits,
                        DataBits: integer;
                        Parity : char);
var
  Regs : Registers;
  Parameter : byte;
begin
  case BPS of
    1200 : BPS := 4;
```

```
   2400 : BPS := 5;
 end;

 if StopBits = 2 then
   StopBits := 1
 else
   StopBits := 0;

 if DataBits = 7 then
   DataBits := 2
 else
   DataBits := 3;

 Parameter := (BPS shl 5) + (StopBits shl 2) + DataBits;

 case Parity of
   'E' : Parameter := Parameter + 8;
   'O' : Parameter := Parameter + 24;
 end;

 with Regs do
   begin
     DX := ComPort - 1;
     AH := 0;
     AL := Parameter;
     Flags := 0;
   end;
 Intr($14, Regs);
end;

(************************************************************)

procedure EnablePorts;
var
 B : byte;
begin
 ClearBuffer;
 GetIntVec($0C, AsyncVector);
 SetIntVec($0C, @AsyncInt);

 B := Port[INTCTLR];
 B := B and $0EF;
 Port[INTCTLR] := B;

 B := Port[LCR];
 B := B and $7F;

 Port[LCR] := B;
 Port[IER] := ENBLRDY;
```

```
  Port[MCR] := $08 or MDMMOD;
  Port[MDMMSR] := MDMCD;
  Port[$20] := $20;
end;

(***********************************************************)

function GetCharInBuf : char;
begin
  if CharsInBuf > 0 then
    begin
      GetCharInBuf := Buffer[CircOut];
      if CircOut < MaxBufLen then
        Inc(CircOut, 1)
      else
        CircOut := 1;
      Dec(CharsInBuf,1);
    end;
end;

(***********************************************************)

function CarrierDetected : boolean;
var
  Ch : char;
  Timer  : integer;
begin
  CarrierDetected := False;
  Timer:=40;
  while (Port[MDMMSR] and $80) <> $80 do
    begin
      if KeyPressed then
        begin
          Ch := ReadKey;
          if Ch = #27 then
            Exit;
        end;
      if CharsInBuf > 0 then
        begin
          Ch := GetCharInBuf;
          Write(Ch);
          if Ch = CR then
            WriteLn;
        end;
      if Timer = 0 then
        Exit
      else
        begin
          Dec(Timer,1);
```

```
              Delay(1000);
          end;
      end;

  CarrierDetected := True;

end;


(*********************************************************)

procedure SendChar(B: byte);
begin
  while ((Port[LSR] and $20) <> $20) do
    begin
    end;
  Port[Dataport] := B;
end;

(*********************************************************)

procedure StringToPort(S : string);
var
  I : integer;
begin
  for I := 1 to Length(S) do
    SendChar(Ord(S[I]));
  SendChar(Ord(CR));
end;

(*********************************************************)

procedure DisablePorts;
var
  B : byte;
begin
  (* Turn off carrier signal. *)
  StringToPort('ATC0');

  (* Turn off the communication interrupt for COM 1. *)
  B := Port[INTCTLR];
  B := B or $10;
  Port[INTCTLR] := B;

  (* Disable 8250 Data Ready Interrupt. *)
  B := Port[LCR];
  B := B and $7F;
  Port[LCR] := B;
  Port[IER] := $0;
```

```
  (* Disable OUT2 on 8250. *)
  Port[MCR] := $0;

  Port[$20] := $20;

  SetIntVec($0C,AsyncVector);

end;

(*************************************************************)

function SuccessfulConnect(PhoneNumber : string) : boolean;
var
  S : string;
begin
  (* ATDT assumes touch-tone dial. *)
  S := 'ATDT'+PhoneNumber;
  StringToPort(S);
  Delay(300);
  if CarrierDetected then
    SuccessfulConnect:=True
  else
    begin
      Write('Error: Unable to Connect.');
      StringToPort('ATC0'); (* Turn off carrier signal. *)
      SuccessfulConnect:=False;
    end;
end;

(*************************************************************)

procedure SetHayesModem;
begin
  StringToPort('ATC0');         (* Turn off carrier signal.     *)
  Delay(1000);                  (* Wait a second.               *)
  StringToPort('ATZ');          (* Reset modem to cold-start.   *)
  Delay(1000);                  (* Wait a second.               *)
  StringToPort('ATF1');         (* Full Duplex.                 *)
  Delay(1000);                  (* Wait a second.               *)
  StringToPort('ATE0');         (* Do not echo in command state. *)
  Delay(1000);                  (* Wait a second.               *)
  StringToPort('ATV1');         (* Verbal result codes.         *)
  Delay(1000);                  (* Wait a second.               *)
  StringToPort('ATQ0');         (* Send result codes.           *)
  Delay(1000);                  (* Wait a second.               *)
end;

(*************************************************************)
```

```pascal
procedure StartCommunicating;
var
  OutChar,
  InChar : char;
begin
  ClearBuffer;

  repeat
    if (CharsInBuf > 0) then
      begin
        InChar := GetCharInBuf;

        if InChar in [#32..#126] then
          Write(InChar)
        else if (InChar = CR) then
          WriteLn;
      end;

    if KeyPressed then
      begin
        OutChar := ReadKey;
        if (OutChar <> #27) then
          begin
            SendChar(Ord(OutChar));
            if OutChar = CR then
              WriteLn
            else
              Write(OutChar);
          end;
      end;
  until OutChar = #27;
end;

(***********************************************************)

begin
  ClrScr;

  SelectModemSet;

  with ModemSet do
    SetSerialPort(ComPort, BPS, StopBits, DataBits, Parity);

  EnablePorts;

  SetHayesModem;

  if SuccessfulConnect(ModemSet.PhoneNumber) then
```

```
    StartCommunicating;

  WriteLn;
  Write('Logging off...');
  StringToPort('ATZ');        (* Reset modem to cold-start. *)
  Delay(1000);                (* Wait a second.             *)
  DisablePorts;
end.
```

The main block of this program calls several procedures and functions, and outlines the steps necessary to establish asynchronous communications. The first procedure called is *SelectModemSet*, which allows the user to specify the communications port to use, the bits per second, the number of stop and data bits, the parity, and the telephone number. (Note that this program is designed to use communications port number 1 (COM1) only.) These data items are stored in a record of type *ModemSetType*, which is defined in the following listing.

```
type
  ModemSetType = record
    ComPort,
    BPS,
    DataBits,
    StopBits         : integer;
    Parity           : char;
    PhoneNumber      : string;
  end;
```

After this record is initialized, its contents are passed to the procedure *SetSerialPort*, which uses BIOS Interrupt 14h to set the serial port to your parameters. To use this interrupt, you must set AH to 0, which tells BIOS to initialize a serial port, set AL to a parameter byte whose bits contain the communications settings, and set DX to 0 for COM1 or 1 for COM2.

The most difficult part of using Interrupt 14 is setting the bits in the parameter byte. Table 22-2 lists definitions of each bit in this byte.

Once the modem has been set, the interrupt is installed by procedure *EnablePorts*. This procedure saves the old interrupt vector address, installs the address of procedure *AsyncInt*, and prepares the INS8250 UART chip for communications.

The final step in preparation is to initialize the modem to the proper settings with the *SetHayesModem* procedure. While there are many modems available, the Hayes Smartmodem is the commonly accepted standard for personal computers. The modem commands used here should work on any modem compatible with the Hayes Smartmodem. Table 22-3 lists the commands available for the Hayes Smartmodem. For a full explanation of the internal operation of the Hayes Smartmodem, see the Smartmodem 1200 Hardware Reference Manual by Hayes Microcomputer Products,

7	6	5	4	3	2	1	0

Parameter	Bits Used	Bit Pattern	Meaning
Data Bits	Bits 0-1	00	5 data bits
		01	6 data bits
		10	7 data bits
		11	8 data bits
Stop Bits	Bit 2	0	1 stop bit
		1	2 stop bits
Parity	Bits 3-4	00	No parity
		01	Odd parity
		10	No parity
		11	Even parity
Speed (BPS)	Bits 5-7	000	100 BPS
		001	150 BPS
		010	300 BPS
		011	600 BPS
		100	1,200 BPS
		101	2,400 BPS
		110	4,800 BPS
		111	9,600 BPS

Table 22-2. *Contents of AL Register for BIOS Interrupt 14h*

Inc. If you use an incompatible modem, change this procedure to match your modem.

Now that the serial port is set, the interrupt is installed, and the modem is initialized, it is time to begin communications. The boolean function *SuccessfulConnect* dials the phone number passed to it and waits for a carrier-detect signal from the modem, indicating that the connection has been established, in which case the function returns True, and communications begin. If no carrier-detect signal is obtained, the function returns False and the program ends.

After the carrier-detect signal is received, control is passed to the procedure *StartCommunicating*, which transmits the characters you type and displays the characters received from the remote computer. This procedure continues until you press ESC, which produces an ASCII code 27.

Command	Parameters	Description
A	None	Modem answers a telephone call without waiting for a ring. This is used to change from Voice mode, where you speak to someone, to Data mode, where two computers communicate.
A/	None	Repeats the last command.
Cn	0,1	Transmitter off. When $n = 1$, the modem calls, answers, or connects to another modem. All other times, $n = 0$.
,(Comma)	None	Causes a two-second delay when dialing a telephone number.
Ds	Number	Puts the modem in the Originate mode and dials the telephone number represented by s.
En	0,1	When $n = 0$, the modem in the command state does not echo back characters; When $n = 1$, characters are echoed.
Fn	0,1	When $n = 0$, the modem operates in half-duplex; when $n = 1$, the modem operates in full-duplex.
Hn	0,1,2	This command controls your telephone's dial tone. When $n = 0$, the modem is "on-hook" and no dial tone is present. When $n = 1$, then modem is "off-hook" and the dial tone is present. The parameter 2 is used for special applications using amateur radio equipment.
In	0,1	This command requests the Smartmodem's three-digit product code. The first two digits indicate the product (for example, 12 indicates a Smartmodem 1200) and the third digit represents the revision number.
Mn	0,1,2	The **M** command controls the speaker. When $n = 0$, the speaker is always off. When $n = 1$, the speaker is on until a carrier is detected. When $n = 2$, the speaker is always on.
O	None	When the modem is on-line, the **O** command returns the modem to the Command state. In the Command state, any of the modem commands can be initiated.
P	None	Tells the modem to dial the telephone using pulses rather than tones.

Table 22-3. *Hayes Smartmodem Commands*

Command	Parameters	Description
Qn	0,1	The modem can send result codes that report the modem's status. The command **Q0** tells the modem to send status codes. **Q1** turns this feature off.
R	None	Put **R** at the end of a telephone number when calling an originate-only modem.
Sr?	1..16	Reads the contents of one of the 16 modem registers, specified by *r*.
Sr=n	r = 1..16	Sets modem register *r* to the value *n*.
;	None	Places a semicolon at the end of the dial command to force the modem back to the Command state after the modem connects with the remote modem.
T	None	Tells the modem to dial in Tone mode rather than Pulse mode.
Vn	0,1	The modem can return codes in numbers or words. **V0** selects numeric codes; **V1** selects words.
Xn	0,1	The modem can return a basic set of codes or an extended set. **X0** selects the basic set; **X1** selects the extended set.
Z	None	Sets the modem to its cold-start configuration, which is like turning the modem off and on.

Table 22-3.   *Hayes Smartmodem Commands* (continued)

The *DisablePorts* procedure, the final step, installs the original interrupt in the interrupt vector table and resets the UART chip.

The Circular Input Buffer

The *circular input buffer* is one of the central elements of an interrupt-driven communications program. Because data can arrive at the serial port at any time, the interrupt handler must be able to capture and process that data while the computer is busy doing something else. If the interrupt does not store the character in a buffer, the character will be lost before the program has time to capture it.

A circular buffer, which is an array of characters, resolves this problem by storing characters temporarily until your computer can catch up with the stream of input characters. The circular buffer is controlled by three **integer** variables: *CircIn, CircOut,* and *CharsInBuf*. *CircIn* points to the next character that the interrupt routine puts into the input buffer, and *CircOut* points to the next character to be taken out of the buffer. *CharsInBuf* is the number of characters waiting in the buffer.

When no characters are in the input buffer, *CircIn* and *CircOut* are equal and *CharsInBuf* is zero. When data comes into the serial port, the interrupt routine adds the incoming characters to the buffer and increments both *CircIn* and *CharsInBuf*. Note that when the end of the buffer is reached, *CircIn* is set to 1, the beginning of the buffer. This is why the buffer is called circular.

The procedure *GetCharInBuf* checks whether *CharsInBuf* is greater than zero, which indicates that characters are present in the buffer. If *CharsInBuf* is greater than zero, the character in the buffer is removed, *CharsInBuf* is decremented, and *CircOut* is incremented.

Thus, *CircOut* is constantly chasing *CircIn* to make sure that there are no characters in the input buffer.

Generally, your computer communicates at either 1,200 or 2,400 bits per second. This is fairly slow compared to the speed at which the 8088 processes data. Therefore, the circular buffer should never be full. The *AsyncCommunications* program uses a 1K buffer, which should be more than enough for most communications purposes.

Memory-Resident Programs

When Borland's SideKick program burst onto the software market in 1984, it seemed like magic. Anytime, anywhere, a key stroke could call up a notepad, calculator, and other useful utilities. SideKick could do this because it is a memory-resident program, that is, one that locks itself in memory and is always there even when you run other programs.

Now, years later, memory-resident programs are fairly common. Even so, they remain a mystery to most programmers. This section explains how you can write limited-function memory-resident programs using Turbo Pascal.

The Reentrance Issue

Memory-resident programs are often referred to as TSRs because they terminate but stay resident in your computer's memory. Locking a program into memory is easy; getting it to do something useful once it is there can be terribly complicated. Most of the problems have to do with the fact that DOS is not *reentrant*. If you are not familiar with the term reentrant, don't be too concerned; it is a technical term with a simple explanation.

DOS provides a rich set of services to the programmer. These services are used for disk I/O, controlling the video display, keyboard input, and more. The problem is that a DOS service will not work if it is interrupted by another DOS service. Normally, this will never occur because DOS executes only one program at a time.

With TSRs, however, the picture becomes more complicated. Consider this scenario: a program calls a DOS service to retrieve some data from a disk file. The DOS service begins executing, and at that moment, a TSR executes another DOS service. In short, the first DOS service is interrupted by the second. The result is disaster—the two DOS services collide and, most likely, your system crashes. That's what reentrance is all about.

There are two ways to deal with reentrance. The first approach is the easiest: make sure that your TSR never uses any DOS services. The second approach is more complicated: make sure that your TSR never executes a DOS service while another DOS service is active. With the second approach, your TSR has the full power of the PC at its disposal, but requires some very complex programming. This chapter will limit its scope to the easy way, avoiding the use of DOS services at all times.

Going Resident

Included in the Turbo Pascal DOS unit is a procedure named Keep, which terminates your program but keeps it resident. Keep takes a single **word** parameter, which is passed to DOS as an exit code. With the Keep procedure, making your program resident is the easiest, and last, step of the TSR process. Much has to be done before you get to the Keep command. For one thing, you have to decide how to activate your TSR once it is resident. You also have to install the interrupt handlers that will do the work of the TSR. Once you understand some basic concepts, you will be surprised how straightforward a TSR can be.

Activating the TSR

For a TSR to do anything, it has to be triggered. If you use SideKick, you know that the trigger is pressing the hot keys. In that case, the keyboard is the trigger. The computer's clock timer is another good trigger—one that is pulled about 18 times a second. In fact, the keyboard and the timer are the triggers used most often to activate TSRs. The one you select will depend on the application. The timer interrupt is great if you need to constantly check for something, like a value of a flag. The keyboard is better suited to TSRs that need to respond at the user's request. The program example given here uses both the timer and the keyboard to create a TSR that blanks your computer's screen after a certain amount of time has passed without keyboard activity. Pressing a key instantly restores the screen. Screen-blanking programs protect your monitor from "burn in," a problem that occurs when computers are left on, but unused, for long periods.

```
{$M 2000,0,0}
{$R-,S-,I-,D+,F+,V-,B-,N-,L+ }
Program SCRSAVE;
```

```
uses Dos;

const
  TimerInt = $08;            (* Timer interrupt *)
  KbdInt   = $09;            (* Keyboard interrupt *)
  TimeLimit : word = 5460; (* Wait 5 minutes before blanking *)

var
  Regs      : Registers;
  Cnt       : word;          (* Counts timer ticks         *)

  OldKbdVec   : pointer;
  OldTimerVec : pointer;

  Time : real;
  Code : word;

procedure SetActivePage(Page : integer);
begin
  with Regs do
    AX := $0500 + Page;
  Intr($10, Regs);
end;

(**************************************************************)

procedure STI;
inline($FB);

(**************************************************************)

procedure CLI;
inline($FA);

(**************************************************************)

procedure CallOldInt(Sub : pointer);
begin
  inline($9C/            { PUSHF                    }
         $FF/$5E/$06); { CALL DWORD PTR [BP+6] }
end;


(**************************************************************)

procedure Keyboard(Flags, CS, IP, AX, BX, CX, DX,
                   SI, DI, DS, ES, BP : word); interrupt;
begin
  CallOldInt(OldKbdVec);      (* Call original interrupt *)
```

```
   if Cnt >= TimeLimit then      (* Restore screen, if disabled *)
     SetActivePage(0);
   Cnt := 0;                      (* Reset counter *)
   STI;
end;

(*************************************************************)

procedure Clock(Flags, CS, IP, AX, BX, CX, DX,
                SI, DI, DS, ES, BP : word); interrupt;
begin
  CallOldInt(OldTimerVec);      (* Call original interrupt    *)
  if Cnt > TimeLimit then       (* if timer limit is reached, *)
    SetActivePage(1)            (* switch pages *)
  else
    Inc(Cnt,1);                 (* Otherwise, increment counter *)
  STI;
end;

(*************************************************************)

begin
  (* if user entered a number parameter, *)
  (* compute the delay factor.           *)
  if ParamCount = 1 then
    begin
      Val(ParamStr(1), Time, Code);
      if (Code = 0) and (Time > 0) and (Time < 11) then
        TimeLimit := Trunc(Time*18.2*60);
    end;

  (* Save original interrupts *)
  GetIntVec(KbdInt, OldKbdVec);
  GetIntVec(TimerInt, OldTimerVec);

  (* Install new interrupts *)
  SetIntVec(TimerInt, @Clock);
  SetIntVec(KbdInt, @Keyboard);

  Cnt := 0;  (* Initialize counter *)
  Keep(0);   (* Terminate and stay resident *)
end.
```

Notice that the listing just given begins with the following compiler directive:

{$M 2000,0,0}

This directive limits the stack segment to 2,000 bytes and allocates space for the heap. You must limit the amount of memory your TSR will use, especially the heap. If you do not limit the heap, your TSR will grab all available memory and leave none for any other programs.

Blanking the Screen

The TSR program just given relies on a useful feature that works only in text mode. This feature allows you to use multiple video pages to control the output of the screen. This TSR will only work in text mode, but it serves as an excellent example of how TSRs work.

How the TSR Works

Once installed, the TSR starts counting seconds. When the elapsed time passes a limit, the TSR blanks the screen. Time is counted from the last keystroke. Thus, if the limit is two minutes, the screen will go blank two minutes after the last keystroke. Once the screen is blank, pressing any key restores the screen, and the TSR begins counting time again.

This process depends on a counter that is continuously incremented. When a keystroke is detected, the counter is set back to zero and begins incrementing again. When the counter reaches a limit defined by the programmer, the TSR blanks the screen.

The Interrupt Handlers

The TSR relies on two interrupt handlers—*Keyboard* and *Clock*. The program attaches Keyboard to the keyboard interrupt ($09), so that anytime a key is pressed, *Keyboard* is activated. Likewise, *Clock*, the handler attached to the timer interrupt ($08), executes with every tick of the system clock. Notice that both handlers start out by calling the original interrupt (the one they replaced). This point is critical—your TSR must never interfere with the normal functioning of the keyboard and clock interrupts. The procedure *CallOldInt* is designed specifically for executing interrupts.

```
procedure Keyboard(Flags, CS, IP, AX, BX, CX, DX,
                   SI, DI, DS, ES, BP : word); interrupt;
begin
  CallOldInt(OldKbdVec);        (* Call original interrupt *)
  if (Cnt >= TimeLimit) then    (* Restore screen, if disabled *)
    Port[PortNum] := PortOn;
  Cnt := 0;                     (* Reset counter *)
  STI;
end;
```

```
(**********************************************************)

procedure Clock(Flags, CS, IP, AX, BX, CX, DX,
                SI, DI, DS, ES, BP : word); interrupt;
begin
  CallOldInt(OldTimerVec);    (* Call original interrupt *)
  if (Cnt > TimeLimit) then   (* if timer limit is reached, *)
    Port[PortNum] := PortOff   (* disable video            *)
  else
    Inc(Cnt,1);               (* Otherwise, increment counter *)
  STI;
end;
```

The *Clock* handler performs two tasks. First, it checks to see if the counter has passed the time limit. If so, the handler blanks the screen; if not, it increments the counter. The Keyboard handler does just the opposite. If the counter has passed the time limit, the handler restores the screen. In any case, the counter is reset to zero. As you can see, TSRs need not be complicated to be useful.

Installing the TSR requires four simple steps:

1. Save the original interrupts for the keyboard and timer.

2. Install your interrupt handlers.

3. Initialize the counter to zero.

4. Call Keep to terminate and stay resident.

```
(* Save original interrupts *)
GetIntVec(KbdInt, OldKbdVec);
GetIntVec(TimerInt, OldTimerVec);

(* Install new interrupts *)
SetIntVec(TimerInt, @Clock);
SetIntVec(KbdInt, @Keyboard);

Cnt := 0;   (* Initialize counter *)
Keep(0);    (* Terminate and stay resident *)
```

The SCRSAVE TSR program sets the default time limit at 5,460, about five minutes. When loading the TSR, the user can override the default by adding a number to the command line. The number indicates the number of minutes to wait before blanking the screen. For example, the command

SCRSAVE 1.5

sets the time interval to 90 seconds (1.5 minutes). You can specify any time limit up to ten minutes.

Interrupt processing is one of the most useful and challenging aspects of PC programming. With Turbo Pascal, you can easily write interrupt handlers for use in telecommunications and memory-resident programs. Though the concept of interrupts may be new to you, it is an area well worth exploring; mastery of the use of interrupts is a sign of a well-versed programmer.

Chapter ***23***

Optimizing Turbo Pascal Programs

At the very least, a program should be free from bugs. Users expect programs to work as advertised, from start to finish, day in and day out. But the fact that a program functions properly is not always enough: users also want programs that work quickly. Optimization is the process of making sure your program runs as fast as it can without compromising the basic functions it performs. This chapter suggests methods you can use to optimize your programs, streamline your code, and eliminate unnecessary bottlenecks.

Optimization: Perfection Versus Excellence

The cost of excellence is reasonable; the cost of perfection is exorbitant. Some programmers spend hours optimizing even unimportant sections of code. Good programmers, however, learn to select the code that can benefit most from optimization, and avoid wasting time on trivial improvements.

There are two criteria to consider when selecting the parts of a program to optimize. First, can the code be improved enough to make a difference? It's quite possible, especially if you are an experienced programmer, that you wrote the section optimally the first time. In most cases, however, even well-written sections can benefit from closer inspection.

Second, the improvements you make must be noticeable to the user. If the user will not notice the difference in speed, your efforts at optimization are wasted. If, however, you feel a section of code can be improved and that the improvement will be noticed by the user, start optimizing.

Approaches to Optimization

Speed is just one goal of optimization; others include minimizing code size and reducing the data space required. With RAM in plentiful supply, however, speed is by far the highest concern. Therefore, the suggestions presented in this chapter are directed to making your programs faster.

The most obvious way to speed up a program is to write sections in assembler using external procedures, inline code, or the **asm** statement. This approach, discussed in Chapter 8, "External Procedures and Inline Codes," requires time and an extensive knowledge of assembler. Before going to this extreme, you can gain a lot of speed simply by using Turbo Pascal more efficiently. A well-written Turbo Pascal procedure can run quite fast and is much easier to write, debug, and maintain than assembler code.

Timing Program Execution

You cannot optimize without having a way to measure just how much you gain or lose when you change a section of code. You may be surprised to find that a minor change can lead to a substantial increase in speed, while larger changes may do little to increase speed.

The guideline you need is contained in the procedures *ClockOn* and *ClockOff*, listed as follows in a unit named TIMER.

```
Unit TIMER;

interface

procedure ClockOn;
procedure ClockOff;

(************************************************************)
implementation
uses Dos;

var
  H, M, S, S100 : Word;
```

```
  StartClock,
  StopClock : real;

procedure ClockOn;
begin
  GetTime(H, M, S, S100);
  StartClock := (H * 3600) + (M * 60) + S + (S100 / 100);
end;

procedure ClockOff;
begin
  GetTime(H, M, S, S100);
  StopClock := (H * 3600) + (M * 60) + S + (S100 / 100);
  Writeln('Elapsed time = ', (StopClock - StartClock):0:2);
end;

end.
```

The TIMER unit uses the procedure GetTime from the Dos unit to get the time
from the system clock. The procedures *ClockOn* and *ClockOff* both call GetTime; both
use the result to calculate the current time in seconds. *ClockOn* stores its result in the
variable *StartClock,* while *ClockOff* computes the value of *StopClock,* subtracts *StartClock*
from it, and reports the elapsed time in seconds. The program named *TestLoop*
demonstrates how to use the procedures in the TIMER unit.

```
Program TestLoop;

uses Crt, TIMER;

var
  I, J : integer;

begin
  ClrScr;
  J := 0;

  ClockOn;     {Initialize value of StartClock}

  for I := 1 To MaxInt Do
    J := J + 1;

  ClockOff;              {Display elapsed time}
  Writeln;
  Write('Press ENTER...');
  Readln;
end.
```

TestLoop times the execution of a simple **for-do** loop by preceding it with a call to *ClockOn* and following it with a call to *ClockOff*. When you run this program, you will see the following message:

```
Elapsed time = 0.99

Press ENTER...
```

This message indicates that the **for-do** loop took 0.99 seconds to execute. All timings reported in this chapter are based on a PC-compatible computer running at 4.77 MHz. Your timings may differ, depending on the computer you use. The specific time you get, however, is unimportant. The value of the timing procedures is to evaluate the relative speed of different procedures that produce the same result. The program listed here demonstrates how to compare the speed of two similar routines.

```pascal
Program TestProcs;

uses Crt, TIMER;

const
  ArrLen = MaxInt;

type
  ArrType = array [1..ArrLen] of char;

var
  A : ArrType;
  I : integer;

procedure Init1(var A : ArrType;
                    L : integer);
begin
  FillChar(A, L, 0);
end;

procedure Init2(var A : ArrType;
                    L : integer);
var
  I : integer;
begin
  for I := 1 to L do
    A[I] := #0;
end;

begin
  ClrScr;
  ClockOn;
```

```
    Init1(A, ArrLen);
    ClockOff;

    ClockOn;
    Init2(A,ArrLen);
    ClockOff;

    Writeln;
    Write('Press ENTER...');
    Readln;
end.
```

The program just given uses two procedures, *Init1* and *Init2,* both of which initialize an array of characters to all binary zeros. *Init1* uses the Turbo Pascal standard procedure FillChar to initialize the array, while *Init2* accomplishes the same goal with a **for-do** loop.

The results of this program show that *Init1* takes 0.05 seconds to execute, while *Init2* requires 1.38 seconds. It is easy to see which is the better routine.

Optimizing Control Structures

When you optimize a program, control structures should be one of the first things you check. Because Turbo Pascal offers so many flexible control structures, it is easy to write control structures your first time through that are less than optimal.

Nested If-Then Statements

If-then statements evaluate boolean expressions, which can include numerous individual comparisons. When you optimize **if-then** statements, the goal is to minimize the number of comparisons the computer executes. The procedure listed here demonstrates a very poor use of **if-then** statements:

```
procedure BooleanTest1;
begin
   if (I = 1) then      { Comparison number 1 }
     begin
       A := '1';
     end;
   if (I = 2) then      { Comparison number 2 }
     begin
       A := '2';
     end;
   if (I = 3) then      { Comparison number 3 }
```

```
      begin
        A := '3';
      end;
    if (I = 4) then      { Comparison number 4 }
      begin
        A := '4';
      end;
    if (I <> 1) and (I <> 2) and
        (I <> 3) and (I <> 4) then    { Comparison number 5 }
      begin
        A := 'X';
      end;
end;
```

This routine executes one of five branches, depending on the value of variable *I*. Notice that all five comparisons are executed each time the code section is processed. This process can be made far more efficient with the following code:

```
procedure BooleanTest2;

begin
  if (I = 1) then            { Comparison number 1 }
    begin
      A := '1';
    end
  else if (I = 2) then     { Comparison number 2 }
    begin
      A := '2';
    end
  else if (I = 3) then     { Comparison number 3 }
    begin
      A := '3';
    end
  else if (I = 4) then     { Comparison number 4 }
    begin
      A := '4';
    end
  else
    begin
      A := 'X';
    end;
end;
```

Here, the **else-if** statement reduces the number of comparisons required. For example, if *I* equals 1, only one comparison is executed. At the other extreme, when *I* is less than 1 or greater than 4, all four comparisons are required.

While the **if-then-else** structure is clearly efficient, the **case** control structure is even more efficient. This code section shows how the **case** statement would replace the **if-then-else** structure:

```
procedure BooleanTest3;
begin
  case I of
    1 :
      begin
        A := '1';
      end;
    2 :
      begin
        A := '2';
      end;
    3 :
      begin
        A := '3';
      end;
    4 :
      begin
        A := '4';
      end;
    else
      begin
        A := 'X';
      end;
    end;
end;
```

While the **case** statement does not eliminate the number of potential comparisons, under certain circumstances, it does perform them a bit more efficiently. These three procedures are compared in the following program, which repeated each procedure 30,000 times.

```
Program BooleanTest;

uses Crt, TIMER;

var
  I, J : word;
  A : char;

{***************************************************}

procedure BooleanTest1;
```

```
begin
  if (I = 1) then       { Comparison number 1 }
    begin
      A := '1';
    end;
  if (I = 2) then       { Comparison number 2 }
    begin
      A := '2';
    end;
  if (I = 3) then       { Comparison number 3 }
    begin
      A := '3';
    end;
  if (I = 4) then       { Comparison number 4 }
    begin
      A := '4';
    end;
  if (I <> 1) and (I <> 2) and
     (I <> 3) and (I <> 4) then   { Comparison number 5 }
    begin
      A := 'X';
    end;
end;

{*****************************************************}

procedure BooleanTest2;

begin
  if (I = 1) then            { Comparison number 1 }
    begin
      A := '1';
    end
  else if (I = 2) then    { Comparison number 2 }
    begin
      A := '2';
    end
  else if (I = 3) then    { Comparison number 3 }
    begin
      A := '3';
    end
  else if (I = 4) then    { Comparison number 4 }
    begin
      A := '4';
    end
  else                       { Comparison number 5 }
    begin
      A := 'X';
    end;
```

```
end;

{*****************************************************}

procedure BooleanTest3;
begin
  case I of
    1 :
      begin
        A := '1';
      end;
    2 :
      begin
        A := '2';
      end;
    3 :
      begin
        A := '3';
      end;
    4 :
      begin
        A := '4';
      end;
    else
      begin
        A := 'X';
      end;
    end;
end;

{*****************************************************}

begin
  ClrScr;
  Writeln('Random values of I...');
  Writeln;
  RandSeed := 0;
  ClockOn;
  for J := 1 to 30000 do
    begin
      I := Random(7);
      BooleanTest1;
    end;
  ClockOff;

  RandSeed := 0;
  ClockOn;
  for J := 1 to 30000 do
    begin
```

```
      I := Random(7);
      BooleanTest2;
    end;
  ClockOff;

  RandSeed := 0;
  ClockOn;
  for J := 1 to 30000 do
    begin
      I := Random(7);
      BooleanTest3;
    end;
  ClockOff;

  Writeln;
  Writeln;
  Writeln('I = 1...');
  Writeln;

  I := 1;
  ClockOn;
  for J := 1 to 30000 do
    BooleanTest1;
  ClockOff;

  ClockOn;
  for J := 1 to 30000 do
    BooleanTest2;
  ClockOff;

  ClockOn;
  for J := 1 to 30000 do
    BooleanTest3;
  ClockOff;

  Writeln;
  Writeln;
  Writeln('I = 5...');
  Writeln;

  I := 5;
  ClockOn;
  for J := 1 to 30000 do
    BooleanTest1;
  ClockOff;

  ClockOn;
  for J := 1 to 30000 do
```

```
   BooleanTest2;
 ClockOff;

 ClockOn;
 for J := 1 to 30000 do
   BooleanTest3;
 ClockOff;

 Writeln;
 Write('Press ENTER...');
 Readln;
end.
```

This program produced the results shown in Table 23-1. Overall, the **if-then-else** statement is almost as efficient as the **case** statement, but both are much more efficient than the **if-then** statements.

Testing Values in Boolean Expressions

If-then statements, **repeat-until** loops, and **while-do** loops all require boolean expressions, expressions that compare a variable to one or more test values. These tests can take several forms, from chained comparisons to set comparisons. Which one is most efficient?

Perhaps some will be surprised that set comparisons, while more compact to write, are far less efficient in operation. For example, the following statement uses the **in** operator to test if a character variable *Ch* contains a letter in the set ['A', 'B', 'C']:

```
if Ch in ['A', 'B', 'C'] then
```

The same comparison is performed far more efficiently with the next chained comparison:

Procedure	I = Random	I = 1	I = 5
BooleanTest1	9.00	3.18	3.96
BooleanTest2	7.97	1.98	2.91
BooleanTest3	7.63	2.03	2.53

Table 23-1.   *Results of Boolean Test*

```
if (Ch = 'A') or (Ch = 'B') or (Ch = 'C') then
```

If that surprises you, try tracing through both statements using the Turbo Debugger. You will find that the chained comparison requires far less code.

The program called *TestChar* demonstrates the difference in speed between comparisons using the **in** operator and two similar forms of **if-then** statements.

```
Program TestChar;

uses Crt, TIMER;

var
  I : integer;
  Ch : Char;

begin
  ClrScr;
  Ch := 'A';

{ Set Inclusion Statement }

  ClockOn;
  for I := 1 to MaxInt do
    begin
      if Ch in ['A', 'B', 'C'] then
        begin
        end;
    end;
  ClockOff;

{ if-then Statement }

  ClockOn;
  for I := 1 to MaxInt do
    begin
      if (Ch = 'A') or (Ch = 'B') or (Ch = 'C') then
        begin
        end;
    end;
  ClockOff;

{ Nested if-then statement }

  ClockOn;
  for I := 1 to MaxInt do
    begin
      if (Ch = 'A') then
        begin
```

```
                    end
          else if (Ch = 'B') then
              begin
              end
          else if (Ch = 'C') then
              begin
              end;
        end;
  ClockOff;

  Writeln;
  Writeln;
  Writeln;

  Ch := 'C';

{ Set Inclusion Statement }

  ClockOn;
  for I := 1 to MaxInt do
    begin
        if Ch in ['A', 'B', 'C'] then
            begin
            end;
      end;
  ClockOff;

{ if-then Statement }

  ClockOn;
  for I := 1 to MaxInt do
    begin
        if (Ch = 'A') or (Ch = 'B') or (Ch = 'C') then
            begin
            end;
      end;
  ClockOff;

{ Nested if-then statement }

  ClockOn;
  for I := 1 to MaxInt do
    begin
        if (Ch = 'A') then
            begin
            end
        else if (Ch = 'B') then
            begin
            end
```

```
        else if (Ch = 'C') then
          begin
          end;
     end;
  ClockOff;

  Writeln;
  Write('Press ENTER...');
  Readln;
end.
```

When the character in question is 'A,' the loop using the **in** comparison requires 2.96 seconds to execute (Table 23-2), while the chained comparison and nested **if-then-else** statements require only 1.05 and 1.04 seconds, respectively. When the character is the last one tested (in this case the letter 'C'), the results are similar, though the performance of the **in** comparison degrades less than the other two.

Optimizing Arithmetic

The speed of your calculations depends largely on the type of variables involved (**integer** or **real**) and the type of operation involved (addition, subtraction, multiplication, or division). Integer computations always require much less time than computations with real variables. The following program, *MathComp*, compares the speed of integer and real computations for addition operations. You can change the program to test other operations.

```
Program MathComp;

uses Crt,TIMER;

var
  I,
  A, B, C : integer;
  X, Y, Z : real;

begin
  ClrScr;
  A := 1;
  B := 1;
  ClockOn;
  for I := 1 to 10000 do
    begin
      C := A + B;
    end;
  ClockOff;
```

```
X := 1.0;
Y := 1.0;
ClockOn;
for I := 1 to 10000 do
  begin
    Z := X + Y;
  end;
ClockOff;

Writeln;
Write('Press ENTER...');
Readln;
end.
```

Table 23-3 shows the execution times in seconds for **integer** and **real** variables for the four arithmetic operators. As you can see, **integer** computations are almost ten times faster than **real** computations across the board.

Division involving **real** variables is the slowest of all the computations, requiring over twice as much time as multiplication operations and four times as much as addition or subtraction.

In general, avoid using **reals** when **integers** will do. If you must use **reals**, avoid division when possible. For example, the equation

$X / 4.0$

can be changed to

$X * 0.25$

which is far faster.

Comparison	Ch = 'A'	Ch = 'C'
Set inclusion	2.96	3.13
Chained comparison	1.05	1.43
Nested if-then-else	1.04	1.54

Table 23-2. *Timings for Character Comparisons*

Operation	integer	real
Addition	0.33	2.03
Subtraction	0.33	3.19
Multiplication	0.60	4.89
Division	0.66	13.02

Table 23-3. *Timings for Various Arithmetic Operations*

Some programs that use a lot of calculations contain many complicated formulas. In such programs, optimization should be second to readability. If, in the process of optimization, you make a subtle change to a complicated formula, you may never find your error.

Optimizing File Operations

Even when you use a hard disk, disk file input and output are slow operations. This is especially true for Turbo Pascal text files. You can speed up your text-file operations by specifying a text buffer for the file. The process is demonstrated in the program listed here:

```
Program TestTextBuf;

uses Crt, TIMER;

var
  Buf1 : array [1..256] of char;
  Buf2 : array [1..1023] of char;
  Buf3 : array [1..1024] of char;
  Buf4 : array [1..4096] of char;
  T : Text;

{****************************************************}

procedure WriteFile;
var
  S : string;
  I : integer;
begin
  FillChar(S, SizeOf(S), 'A');
```

```
  S[0] := Chr(255);
  for I := 1 to 100 do
    Writeln(T, S);
end;

{****************************************************}

begin
  ClrScr;
  Assign(T, 'TEST.X');

  Rewrite(T);
  ClockOn;
  WriteFile;
  ClockOff;

  Rewrite(T);
  SetTextBuf(T, Buf1);
  ClockOn;
  WriteFile;
  ClockOff;

  Rewrite(T);
  SetTextBuf(T, Buf2);
  ClockOn;
  WriteFile;
  ClockOff;

  Rewrite(T);
  SetTextBuf(T, Buf3);
  ClockOn;
  WriteFile;
  ClockOff;

  Rewrite(T);
  SetTextBuf(T, Buf4);
  ClockOn;
  WriteFile;
  ClockOff;

  Close(T);
  Erase(T);

  Writeln;
  Write('Press ENTER...');
  Readln;
end.
```

Buffer size	Time
128 bytes (default)	5.38
256 bytes	5.16
1023 bytes	6.87
1024 bytes	2.20
4096 bytes	1.43

Table 23-4.   *Impact of Text Buffers of Various Sizes*

This program declares a text file named *T* and four buffers of different sizes: 256 bytes, 1,023 bytes, 1,024 bytes, and 4,096 bytes. If you do not specify a buffer to a text file, Turbo Pascal assigns a default buffer of 128 bytes.

Generally speaking, the larger the buffer, the faster your input and output operations will be. This is not strictly the case with Turbo Pascal text files, as Table 23-4 shows.

Output to the default 128-byte buffer is fairly slow (5.38 seconds) as is output to a 256-byte buffer (5.16 seconds). Surprisingly, a 1,023-byte buffer is actually slower than the default buffer. Yet, increasing the buffer by one byte, to 1,024 bytes, cuts the elapsed time to just 2.20 seconds. Increasing the buffer to 4,096 bytes brings the elapsed time down to 1.43 seconds.

As for the difference in time between the 1,023-byte buffer and the 1,024-byte buffer, why does adding one byte cause a significant increase in speed? Disks are organized into 512-byte sectors that are organized into clusters of 1,024 bytes for floppy disk and from 2,048 to 8,192 bytes for hard disks. When a buffer's size is set equal to the size of a cluster, the disk drive does less work with each read and write. In general, the best buffer sizes are multiples of 1,024 bytes.

Optimizing String Operations

The **string** data type is an important part of Turbo Pascal, largely due to the standard procedures provided for string manipulation. However, string procedures, especially concatenation, can be quite slow.

The program called *TestProcs* uses two procedures, each of which creates a string that contains 100 characters, all of which are 'A's.

```
Program TestProcs;

uses Crt, TIMER;
```

```
var
  I : integer;

{*****************************}

procedure Concat1;
var
  I : integer;
  S : string;
begin
  S := '';
  for I := 1 to 100 do
    S := S + 'A';
end;

{*****************************}

procedure Concat2;
var
  I : integer;
  S : string;
begin
  for I := 1 to 100 do
    S[I] := 'A';
  S[0] := Chr(100);    { Set string length }
end;

{*****************************}

begin
  ClrScr;
  ClockOn;
  for I := 1 to 100 do
    Concat1;
  ClockOff;

  ClockOn;
  for I := 1 to 100 do
    Concat2;
  ClockOff;

  Writeln;
  Write('Press ENTER...');
  Readln;
end.
```

Procedure *Concat1*, which uses the Turbo Pascal concatenation operator, requires 6.32 seconds, while procedure *Concat2*, which uses an index to the string's characters, needs only 0.27 second.

The Copy command can also be replaced to increase speed, as demonstrated by the *CopyString* program:

```pascal
Program CopyString;

uses Crt, TIMER;

var
  P, I, J : integer;
  S1, S2 : string;

begin
  ClrScr;

  S1 := 'ABCDEFGHIJKLMNOP';

  ClockOn;
  for I := 1 to 10000 do
    S2 := Copy(S1, 3, 5);     { Using the Copy command }
  ClockOff;

  ClockOn;
  for I := 1 to 10000 do
    begin
      Move(S1[3], S2[1], 5);    { Using the Move command }
      S2[0] := Chr(5);          { Set the length byte }
    end;
  ClockOff;

  Writeln;
  Write('Press ENTER...');
  Readln;
end.
```

In *CopyString*, the command

```pascal
S2 := Copy(S1, 3, 5);
```

is replaced by the statements

```pascal
Move(S1[3], S2[1], 5);
S2[0] := Chr(5);
```

The Move command copies a portion of *S1* into *S2*, while the second statement correctly sets the length of *S2*. The Copy command requires 2.58 seconds for 10,000 iterations, compared with only 1.32 seconds for the optimized code.

Compiler Directives

Compiler directives control error-checking features in Turbo Pascal. The three directives that have an impact on execution speed are the $R directive, which checks the range of indexes; the $S directive, which checks the stack errors; and the $B directive, which enables short-circuit boolean evaluation.

Range Checking

When enabled, the Range Checking ($R) compiler directive adds code that checks for out-of-range conditions when assigning numeric values or accessing array elements. This additional code significantly increases overhead in your program, with noticeable results.

```
{$R+}
Program DirectiveTest;

uses Crt, TIMER;

var
  I, J : integer;
  A : array [1..100] of byte;

begin
  ClrScr;
  Write('Range checking...');
  ClockOn;
  for I := 1 to 1000 do
    for J := 1 to 100 do
      A[J] := 1;
  ClockOff;

  Writeln;
  Write('Press ENTER...');
  Readln;
end.
```

When run with the {$R+} directive, this program takes 9.45 seconds; with {$R-}, it takes only 3.08 seconds. While range checking is essential during program development, you must disable this compiler directive to get the best performance for your program.

Stack Checking

The Stack Checking compiler directive ({$S+}) instructs the compiler to make sure that the stack has enough memory for local variables before calling a procedure. This is extremely important because stack errors are among the most difficult to trace. The program listed here demonstrates what effect stack checking can have on a program's performance.

```
{$S+}
Program DirectiveTest;

uses Crt, TIMER;

var
  I : integer;
  S : string;

{*******************************************************}

procedure Proc;
var
  X : array [1..5000] of word;
begin
end;

{*******************************************************}

begin
  ClrScr;
  S := 'AAAAAAAAAAAAAAAAAAAAAAAAAAAAAAAAAAAAAAAAAAAAAAAA';
  Write('Stack checking...');
  ClockOn;
  for I := 1 to 10000 do
    Proc;
  ClockOff;

  Writeln;
  Write('Press ENTER...');
  Readln;
end.
```

This program makes repeated calls to a procedure, *Proc*, that uses a large local array variable. When the stack-checking directive is enabled ({$S+}), the program executes in 0.88 second; when disabled ({$S-}), it executes in just 0.49 second. As with range checking, stack checking is essential during program development and testing. Once completed, however, the directive should be turned off to maximize performance.

Boolean Evaluation

Turbo Pascal supports two types of boolean evaluation: complete and short-circuit. Which one you choose can have a dramatic impact on the efficiency of your program. Consider the following boolean evaluation:

```
if (A = 1) or (A = 2) or (A = 3) then
```

If *A* is equal to 1, then there is no need to test any of the other conditions in the statement. Yet, under complete evaluation, that is exactly what happens. Short-circuit evaluation, as its name implies, jumps out of the boolean expression as soon as a condition is met that assures a correct answer. The program listed here demonstrates the impact of boolean evaluation on program performance.

```
{$B+}
Program DirectiveTest;

uses Crt, TIMER;

var
  A, I : integer;

{*********************************************************}

begin
  ClrScr;

  ClockOn;
  A := 1;
  for I := 1 to 10000 do
    begin
      if (A = 1) or (A = 2) or (A = 3) then
        begin
        end;
    end;
  ClockOff;

  Writeln;
  Write('Press ENTER...');
  Readln;
end.
```

When short-circuit evaluation is enabled ({$B-}), the program executes in 0.27 second; under complete evaluation ({$B+}), execution takes 0.71 second. Unless you have good reason to insist on complete evaluation, you should always select short-circuit evaluation for your programs.

Procedures and Functions

Pascal allows the programmer to break a program down into procedures and functions, providing a more orderly framework for the program. Unfortunately, every time a procedure is called, Turbo Pascal must perform housekeeping tasks to keep track of memory. You can easily increase the speed of a program by putting a procedure's code directly into the main body of another procedure or into the main program. The impact of declaring a separate procedure is demonstrated by *TestProc3*:

```
Program TestProc3;

uses Crt, TIMER;

var
  I, J : integer;

{******************************}

procedure DemoProc;
begin
  J := 0;
  J := 0;
  J := 0;
  J := 0;
end;

{******************************}

begin
  ClrScr;

  ClockOn;
  for I := 1 to 30000 do
    DemoProc;                      { Procedure call }
  ClockOff;

  ClockOn;
  for I := 1 to 30000 do
    begin
      J := 0;                      { No procedure call }
```

```
      J := 0;
      J := 0;
      J := 0;
    end;
  ClockOff;

  Writeln;
  Write('Press ENTER...');
  Readln;
end.
```

Procedure *DemoProc* in *TestProc3* sets the **integer** variable *J* equal to zero four times. The same process is also repeated in the main program block. When you run the program, the procedure requires 2.26 seconds for 30,000 iterations compared with only 1.48 seconds for the code in the program block.

Clearly, calling a procedure adds to a program's overhead. However, putting the code directly in the program has several disadvantages. First, if the procedure is called several times in the program, you must duplicate its code each time, adding to your program's code size. Second, when you want to change the procedure, you have to change it in each place it occurs. You must weigh these disadvantages against the speed you gain by removing the procedure call.

Reference Parameters Versus Value Parameters

When Turbo Pascal passes a reference parameter to a procedure, it passes the variable's address, not the value of the variable. Value parameters, on the other hand, pass the entire contents of the variable. If the value parameter is a 4,000-byte array, 4,000 bytes are passed to the procedure, compared with only 4 bytes when Turbo Pascal passes an address.

As the program *TestParams1* demonstrates, it takes longer to pass value parameters:

```
Program TestParams1;

uses Crt, TIMER;

type
  AType = array [1..2000] of integer;

var
  A : AType;
  I, J : integer;

{******************************}
```

```
procedure A1(var A : AType);
  begin
  end;

{******************************}

procedure A2(A : AType);
  begin
  end;

{******************************}

begin
  ClrScr;

  ClockOn;
  for I := 1 to 1000 do
    A1(A);
  ClockOff;

  ClockOn;
  for I := 1 to 1000 do
    A2(A);
  ClockOff;

  Writeln;
  Write('Press ENTER...');
  Readln;
end.
```

TestParams1 uses two procedures, *A1* and *A2*. Procedure *A1* accepts a reference parameter and *A2* accepts a value parameter. In both procedures, the parameter is an array of 2000 integers. When you run this program, you will find that procedure *A1* requires only 0.06 second for 1,000 iterations, while *A2* requires 15.32 seconds to complete the same number of iterations. If you want to maximize the performance of your programs, try substituting reference parameters for value parameters. But, be careful—reference parameters retain any changes you make to them inside the procedure.

Performance is a concern for all programmers. Fortunately, Turbo Pascal produces some of the fastest, most efficient code of any compiler available. By using Turbo Pascal creatively, taking advantage of all its power, you can create programs that really fly.

Speed is just one consideration, and it can work to the detriment of maintainability. Optimized code often uses tricks and special logic that you might not remember a year later. If you must optimize, make sure that the benefits are worth the effort, and document any code that is not straightforward.

Part V

Appendixes

Appendix *A*

Turbo Pascal Error Codes

Two types of errors may occur in Turbo Pascal programs: compiler errors, which prevent a file from being executable; and run-time errors, which occur while your program is running. Both are discussed in this appendix.

Compiler Error Messages

Compiler error messages refer to problems in your code or programming environment that prevent Turbo Pascal from producing an executable file. In the integrated development environment, Turbo Pascal will attempt to locate the source-code location of the error.

1	Out of memory
2	Identifier expected
3	Unknown identifier
4	Duplicate identifier
5	Syntax error
6	Error in real constant
7	Error in integer constant
8	String constant exceeds line

10	Unexpected end of file
11	Line too long
12	Type identifier expected
13	Too many open files
14	Invalid filename
15	File not found
16	Disk full
17	Invalid compiler directive
18	Too many files
19	Undefined type in pointer definition
20	Variable identifier expected
21	Error in type
22	Structure too large
23	Set base type out of range
24	File components may not be files or objects
25	Invalid string length
26	Type mismatch
27	Invalid subrange base type
28	Lower bound greater than upper bound
29	Ordinal type expected
30	Integer constant expected
31	Constant expected
32	Integer or real constant expected
33	Pointer type identifier expected
34	Invalid function result type
35	Label identifier expected
36	Begin expected
37	End expected
38	Integer expression expected
39	Ordinal expression expected
40	Boolean expression expected
41	Operand types do not match operator
42	Error in expression
43	Illegal assignment
44	Field identifier expected

45	Object file too large
46	Undefined external
47	Invalid object-file record
48	Code segment too large
49	Data segment too large
50	Do expected
51	Invalid Public definition
52	Invalid Extrn definition
53	Too many Extrn definitions
54	Of expected
55	Interface expected
56	Invalid relocatable reference
57	Then expected
58	To or Downto expected
59	Undefined forward
60	Too many procedures
61	Invalid typecast
62	Division by zero
63	Invalid file type
64	Cannot read or write variables of this type
65	Pointer variable expected
66	String variable expected
67	String expression expected
68	Circular unit reference
69	Unit name mismatch
70	Unit version mismatch
71	Internal stack overflow
72	Unit file format error
73	Implementation expected
74	Constant and case types do not match
75	Record or object variable expected
76	Constant out of range
77	File variable expected
78	Pointer expression expected
79	Integer or real expression expected

80	Label not within current block
81	Label already defined
82	Undefined label in preceding statement part
83	Invalid @ argument
84	Unit expected
85	";" expected
86	":" expected
87	"," expected
88	"(" expected
89	")" expected
90	"=" expected
91	":=" expected
92	"[" or "(." expected
93	"]" or ".)" expected
94	"." expected
95	".." expected
96	Too many variables
97	Invalid For control variable
98	Integer variable expected
99	Files are not allowed here
100	String length mismatch
101	Invalid ordering of fields
102	String constant expected
103	Integer or real variable expected
104	Ordinal variable expected
105	Inline error
106	Character expression expected
107	Too many relocation items
108	Overflow in arithmetic operation
109	No enclosing For, While, or Repeat statement
112	Case constant out of range
113	Error in statement
114	Cannot call an interrupt procedure
116	Must be in 8087 mode to compile this
117	Target address not found

118	Include files are not allowed here
119	No inherited methods are accessible here
120	Nil expected
121	Invalid qualifier
122	Invalid variable reference
123	Too many symbols
124	Statement part too large
126	Files must be Var parameters
127	Too many conditional symbols
128	Misplaced conditional directive
129	ENDIF directive missing
130	Error in initial conditional defines
131	Header does not match previous definition
132	Critical disk error
133	Cannot evaluate this expression
134	Expression incorrectly terminated
135	Invalid format specifier
136	Invalid indirect reference
137	Structured variables are not allowed here
138	Cannot evaluate without System unit
139	Cannot access this symbol
140	Invalid floating-point operation
141	Cannot compile overlays to memory
142	Pointer or procedural variable expected
143	Invalid procedure or function reference
144	Cannot overlay this unit
146	File access denied
147	Object type expected
148	Local object types are not allowed
149	Virtual expected
150	Method identifier expected
151	Virtual constructors are not allowed
152	Constructor identifier expected
153	Destructor identifier expected
154	Fail only allowed within constructors

155	Invalid combination of opcode and operands
156	Memory reference expected
157	Cannot add or subtract relocatable symbols
158	Invalid register combination
159	286/287 instructions are not enabled
160	Invalid symbol reference
161	Code generation error
162	Asm expected
163	Duplicate dynamic method index
164	Duplicate resource identifier
165	Duplicate or invalid export index
166	Procedure or function identifier expected
167	Cannot export this symbol
168	Duplicate export name
169	Executable file header too large

Run-time Error Messages

A run-time error is an error condition that occurs while your program is running. When such an error occurs, Turbo Pascal displays this message:

Run-time error *nnn* at *xxxx:yyyy*

where *nnn* is the numeric code for the run-time error, *xxxx* is the program segment in which the error occurred, and *yyyy* is the offset of the location of the error.

DOS Errors

1	Invalid function number
2	File not found
3	Path not found
4	Too many open files
5	File access denied
6	Invalid file handle
12	Invalid file access code

15	Invalid drive number
16	Cannot remove current directory
17	Cannot rename across drives
18	No more files

I/O Errors

100	Disk read error
101	Disk write error
102	File not assigned
103	File not open
104	File not open for input
105	File not open for output
106	Invalid numeric format

Critical Errors

150	Disk is write-protected
151	Unknown unit
152	Drive not ready
153	Unknown command
154	CRC error in data
155	Bad drive request structure length
156	Disk seek error
157	Unknown media type
158	Sector not found
159	Printer out of paper
160	Device write fault
161	Device read fault
162	Hardware failure

Fatal Errors

200	Division by zero
201	Range check error

202	Stack overflow error
203	Heap overflow error
204	Invalid pointer operation
205	Floating-point overflow
206	Floating-point underflow
207	Invalid floating-point operation
208	Overlay manager not installed
209	Overlay file read error
210	Object not initialized
211	Call to abstract method
212	Stream registration error
213	Collection index out of range
214	Collection overflow error
215	Arithmetic overflow error
216	General protection fault

ASCII Codes for the PC

Dec	Hex	ASCII Symbol	Control Code	Ctrl Key	Dec	Hex	ASCII Symbol	Control Code	Ctrl Key
0	00		NUL	^@	16	10	▶	DLE	^P
1	01	☺	SOH	^A	17	11	◀	DC1	^Q
2	02	☻	STX	^B	18	12	↕	DC2	^R
3	03	♥	ETX	^C	19	13	‼	DC3	^S
4	04	♦	EOT	^D	20	14	¶	DC4	^T
5	05	♣	ENQ	^E	21	15	§	NAK	^U
6	06	♠	ACK	^F	22	16	▬	SYN	^V
7	07	•	BEL	^G	23	17	↨	ETB	^W
8	08	◘	BS	^H	24	18	↑	CAN	^X
9	09	○	HT	^I	25	19	↓	EM	^Y
10	0A	◙	LF	^J	26	1A	→	SUB	^Z
11	0B	♂	VT	^K	27	1B	←	ESC	^[
12	0C	♀	FF	^L	28	1C	∟	FS	^\
13	0D	♪	CR	^M	29	1D	↔	GS	^]
14	0E	♫	SO	^N	30	1E	▲	RS	^ ^
15	0F	☼	SI	^O	31	1F	▼	US	^_

Dec	Hex	ASCII Symbol	Dec	Hex	ASCII Symbol
32	20		72	48	H
33	21	!	73	49	I
34	22	"	74	4A	J
35	23	#	75	4B	K
36	24	$	76	4C	L
37	25	%	77	4D	M
38	26	&	78	4E	N
39	27	'	79	4F	O
40	28	(	80	50	P
41	29	)	81	51	Q
42	2A	*	82	52	R
43	2B	+	83	53	S
44	2C	,	84	54	T
45	2D	-	85	55	U
46	2E	.	86	56	V
47	2F	/	87	57	W
48	30	0	88	58	X
49	31	1	89	59	Y
50	32	2	90	5A	Z
51	33	3	91	5B	[
52	34	4	92	5C	\
53	35	5	93	5D	]
54	36	6	94	5E	^
55	37	7	95	5F	_
56	38	8	96	60	`
57	39	9	97	61	a
58	3A	:	98	62	b
59	3B	;	99	63	c
60	3C	<	100	64	d
61	3D	=	101	65	e
62	3E	>	102	66	f
63	3F	?	103	67	g
64	40	@	104	68	h
65	41	A	105	69	i
66	42	B	106	6A	j
67	43	C	107	6B	k
68	44	D	108	6C	l
69	45	E	109	6D	m
70	46	F	110	6E	n
71	47	G	111	6F	o

Dec	Hex	ASCII Symbol	Dec	Hex	ASCII Symbol
112	70	p	152	98	ÿ
113	71	q	153	99	Ö
114	72	r	154	9A	Ü
115	73	s	155	9B	¢
116	74	t	156	9C	£
117	75	u	157	9D	¥
118	76	v	158	9E	Pt
119	77	w	159	9F	ƒ
120	78	x	160	A0	á
121	79	y	161	A1	í
122	7A	z	162	A2	ó
123	7B	{	163	A3	ú
124	7C	|	164	A4	ñ
125	7D	}	165	A5	Ñ
126	7E	~	166	A6	ª
127	7F	⌂	167	A7	º
128	80	Ç	168	A8	¿
129	81	ü	169	A9	⌐
130	82	é	170	AA	¬
131	83	â	171	AB	½
132	84	ä	172	AC	¼
133	85	à	173	AD	¡
134	86	å	174	AE	<<
135	87	ç	175	AF	>>
136	88	ê	176	B0	░
137	89	ë	177	B1	▒
138	8A	è	178	B2	▓
139	8B	ï	179	B3	│
140	8C	î	180	B4	┤
141	8D	ì	181	B5	╡
142	8E	Ä	182	B6	╢
143	8F	Å	183	B7	╖
144	90	É	184	B8	╕
145	91	æ	185	B9	╣
146	92	Æ	186	BA	║
147	93	ô	187	BB	╗
148	94	ö	188	BC	╝
149	95	ò	189	BD	╜
150	96	û	190	BE	╛
151	97	ù	191	BF	┐

Dec	Hex	ASCII Symbol	Dec	Hex	ASCII Symbol
192	C0	└	224	E0	α
193	C1	┴	225	E1	β
194	C2	┬	226	E2	Γ
195	C3	├	227	E3	π
196	C4	─	228	E4	Σ
197	C5	┼	229	E5	σ
198	C6	╞	230	E6	μ
199	C7	╟	231	E7	τ
200	C8	╚	232	E8	ϕ
201	C9	╔	233	E9	θ
202	CA	╩	234	EA	Ω
203	CB	╦	235	EB	δ
204	CC	╠	236	EC	∞
205	CD	═	237	ED	$\varnothing$
206	CE	╬	238	EE	$\in$
207	CF	╧	239	EF	$\cap$
208	D0	╨	240	F0	$\equiv$
209	D1	╤	241	F1	$\pm$
210	D2	╥	242	F2	$\geq$
211	D3	╙	243	F3	$\leq$
212	D4	╘	244	F4	$\lceil$
213	D5	╒	245	F5	$\rfloor$
214	D6	╓	246	F6	$\div$
215	D7	╫	247	F7	$\approx$
216	D8	╪	248	F8	$\circ$
217	D9	┘	249	F9	$\bullet$
218	DA	┌	250	FA	$\cdot$
219	DB	█	251	FB	$\sqrt{}$
220	DC	▄	252	FC	η
221	DD	▌	253	FD	^{2}
222	DE	▐	254	FE	■
223	DF	▀	255	FF	

Appendix C

The PC Keyboard

The computer keyboard produces codes that are associated with letters and symbols. One key, however, can produce a different set of codes when you press other keys at the same time. For example, the A key normally produces the letter "a" (ASCII code 97), but when pressed along with the SHIFT key, it produces the letter "A" (ASCII code 65). Two other keys—CTRL and ALT—produce even more codes.

Some keys, such as the function keys (F1 through F10), produce two codes: a scan code (#0) and another code that indicates the key pressed. To read keys that produce scan codes, use the following procedure:

```
procedure Inkey(var Ch : char;
                var FKey : boolean);
begin
  FKey := False;
  Ch := ReadKey;
  if Ch = #0 then
    begin
      FKey := True;
      Ch := ReadKey;
    end;
end;
```

This procedure uses ReadKey, which is found in the Crt unit. When **FKey** is True, a scan-code key has been pressed and the ASCII code for that key is returned in Ch. When **FKey** is False, a normal key has been pressed and the value is contained in Ch.

The following table lists the keys on the PC keyboard and the codes they return.

Key	Normal		SHIFT		CTRL		ALT	
F1	0	59	0	84	0	94	0	104
F2	0	60	0	85	0	95	0	105
F3	0	61	0	86	0	96	0	106
F4	0	62	0	87	0	97	0	107
F5	0	63	0	88	0	98	0	108
F6	0	64	0	89	0	99	0	109
F7	0	65	0	90	0	100	0	110
F8	0	66	0	91	0	101	0	111
F9	0	67	0	92	0	102	0	112
F10	0	68	0	93	0	103	0	113
LEFT ARROW	0	75		52	0	115		none
RIGHT ARROW	0	77		54	0	116		none
UP ARROW	0	72		56		none		none
DOWN ARROW	0	80		50		none		none
HOME	0	71		55	0	119		none
END	0	79		49	0	117		none
PGUP	0	73		57	0	132		none
PGDN	0	81		51	0	118		none
INS	0	82		48		none		none
DEL	0	83		46	0	255		none
ESC		27		27		27		none
BACKSPACE		8		8		127		none
TAB		9	0	15		none		none
ENTER		13		13		10		none
A		97		65		1	0	30
B		98		66		2	0	48
C		99		67		3	0	46
D		100		68		4	0	32
E		101		69		5	0	18
F		102		70		6	0	33
G		103		71		7	0	34
H		104		72		8	0	35
I		105		73		9	0	23
J		106		74		10	0	36

Key	Normal	SHIFT	CTRL		ALT	
K	107	75		11	0	37
L	108	76		12	0	38
M	109	77		13	0	50
N	110	78		14	0	49
O	111	79		15	0	24
P	112	80		16	0	25
Q	113	81		17	0	16
R	114	82		18	0	19
S	115	83		19	0	31
T	116	84		20	0	20
U	117	85		21	0	22
V	118	86		22	0	47
W	119	87		23	0	17
X	120	88		24	0	45
Y	121	89		25	0	21
Z	122	90		26	0	44
[	91	123		27		none
\	92	124		28		none
]	93	125		29		none
'	96	126		none		none
0	48	41		none	0	129
1	49	33		none	0	120
2	50	64	0	3	0	121
3	51	35		none	0	122
4	52	36		none	0	123
5	53	37		none	0	124
6	54	94		30	0	125
7	55	38		none	0	126
8	56	42		none	0	127
9	57	40		none	0	128
*	42	none	0	114		none
Keypad +	43	43		none		none
Keypad –	45	45		none		none
=	61	43		none	0	131

Key	Normal	SHIFT	CTRL	ALT	
/	47	63	none	none	
;	59	58	none	none	
-	45	95	31	0	130

Appendix **D**

Turbo Pascal Reserved Words

The following are Turbo Pascal reserved words. The term *reserved words* has been expanded to include standard directives and standard types.

Absolute

Declares a variable that resides at a specific memory location. For example:

```
var
  R : real;
  X : integer absolute R;        (* X shares memory with R *)
  Y : integer absolute 0000:0000; (* Y is located at segment 0 *)
                                 (*    at offset 0 *)
```

And

Combines two boolean expressions such that both must be True for the entire expression to be True. For example:

```
if (A > B) and (C > D) then ...
```

And also compares two bytes or integers and returns a third byte or integer. A bit in the resulting integer is turned on only if both bits in the same position are on in the first and second integers.

Array

Defines a data type that repeats its structure a specified number of times. For example:

```
var
   I : Array [1..20] Of Integer;
```

defines a data item that consists of 20 integers.

Asm

Indicates that the code that follows is to be interpreted as assembly language instructions.

Assembler

Indicates that a procedure contains just an **asm** statement.

Begin

Indicates the beginning of a block of code.

Boolean

An enumerated type with the values True and False; defined in the System unit.

Byte

An integer type with the range 0-255; defined in the System unit.

Case

A control structure that branches conditionally based on the value of a scalar. For example:

```
var
   I : integer;

begin
  I := Random(10);
  case I of
    1 :
      begin
        { Statements }
      end;

    2..3 :
      begin
        { Statements }
      end;
```

```
    4 :
      begin
        { Statements }
      end;

    else
      begin
        { Statements }
      end;

    end;
```

Char

An enumerated type that contains all ASCII values; defined in the System unit.

Comp

An 8087 data type for extremely large integers; defined in the System unit.

Const

Defines a data item as either a typed or untyped constant. For example:

```
const
  I = 100;              (* Untyped constant *)
  J : integer = 100; (* Typed constant *)
```

Constructor

Defines a method (in an object) that is used to initialize the virtual methods within an object.

Destructor

Defines a method (in an object) that is used to remove virtual methods from the virtual method table, usually before deallocating a dynamically allocated object.

Div

Performs integer division.

Do

Used with looping control structures. For example:

```
for I := 1 to 10 do ...

while I < 11 do ...
```

Double

An 8087 data type for real numbers with eight significant digits; defined in the System unit.

Downto

Used in **for-do** loops where the counter is decremented. For example:

```
for I := 100 downto 1 do ...
```

Else

Executes a block of code when an **if-then** statement is False. For example:

```
if A < B then
  begin
    { Statements }
  end
else
  begin
    { Statements }
  end;
```

End

Denotes the end of a block of code, the end of a case statement, the end of a record definition, or the end of a program or unit.

Export

Indicates that a procedure or function can be exported as part of a DLL.

Exports

Defines the indices of the subprograms exported as part of a DLL.

Extended

An 8087 data type for real numbers with 16 significant digits; defined in the System unit.

External

Tells Turbo Pascal to look in an object file for the executable code for a procedure. For example:

```
{$L ASM_PROC}
procedure ExtProc; external;
```

Far

Indicates that a far return is generated for a subprogram, meaning that both segment and offset are pushed on the stack.

File

A data type that stores data on a disk.

For

Used in **for-do** loops. For example:

```
for I := 1 to 100 do ...
```

Forward

Declares the heading of a procedure before the actual procedure is defined. The full heading is declared with the **forward** clause. Later, when the body of the procedure is declared, only the procedure name is used. For example:

```
procedure X(I, J : integer) : forward;

{ other declarations }

procedure X;

begin
  { Statements }
end;
```

Function

Declares a subroutine to be a function. Functions return values of a specific data type. For example:

```
function Add(A, B : integer) : integer;
begin
  Add := A + B;
end;
```

Goto

Transfers control to the location of the label contained in the **goto** statement. For example:

```
label
  EndProc; (* Label declaration *)

begin
```

```
for I := 1 to 1000 do
   begin
     J := J + 1;
     if J > 1000 then
        goto EndProc;
   end;

EndProc:
end;
```

If

Used in **if-then** statements. For example:

```
if A < B then ...
```

Implementation

Indicates the beginning of the implementation section of a unit.

In

Tests for set inclusion. For example:

```
procedure Check(Ch : char);
begin
   if Ch in ['A'..'Z'] then ...
```

Index

Defines the number that other programs will use to access a DLL subprogram.

Inherited

Used inside the body of a method to call the immediate ancestor of that method.

Inline

Tells Turbo Pascal to treat the code that follows as machine-language instructions. For example:

```
inline($1E/$06/$07/$1F);
```

Integer

A scalar type with a range −32,768 to 32,767; defined in the System unit.

Interface

Defines the beginning of the interface section of a unit.

Interrupt

Defines a procedure as an interrupt procedure. Interrupt procedures are used for writing interrupt service routines.

Label

Declares labels used with **goto** statements (see **Goto**).

Library

Defines a unit as a DLL.

Longint

An integer type with a range from −2,147,483,647 to 2,147,483,647; defined in the System unit.

Mod

Returns the remainder of integer division.

Name

Defines a name for a DLL export, in addition to its index.

Near

Indicates that a near return is generated for a subprogram, meaning that only the offset is pushed on the stack.

Nil

May be assigned to any pointer variable. Used in comparisons to test whether a pointer has a valid value. For example:

```
type
  Aptr = ^Arecord;
  Arecord = record
    I : integer;
    Next : Aptr;
  end;

var
  A : Aptr;

begin
  New(A);
  if A^.Next = nil then ...
```

Not

Reverses the result of a boolean expression. For example, if

```
A > B
```

is True, then

```
not (A > B)
```

is False.

Object
Used to define an object consisting of data elements and methods.

Of
Used in the **case** statement (see **Case**) and in declaration of a set or array data type.

Or
Combines boolean expressions such that the entire expression is True if either condition is True. For example:

```
if (A > B) or (C > D) then ...
```

is True if either the first or the second comparison (or both) is True. **Or** also compares two bytes or integers and returns a third byte or integer. A bit in the resulting integer is turned on if either or both bits in the same position are on in the first and second integers.

Packed
Declares arrays such that the arrays use less memory than they normally would. Turbo Pascal supports this reserved word, but it has no effect since all Turbo Pascal arrays are stored in packed format.

Pointer
A data type for any address. Most pointer types point to an address that contains data of a specific type—the **pointer** type is not type-specific. This type is defined in the System unit.

Private
Indicates that subsequent fields and methods in an object definition are unaccessible from other units or programs.

Procedure
Defines a block of code as belonging to a procedure.

Program

Defines a block of code as belonging to a program. This is the first statement in a program.

Public

Indicates that subsequent fields and methods in an object definition are accessible from other units and programs.

Real

The standard data type for floating-point numbers; defined in the System unit.

Record

Defines a complex data type that combines several simple or complex data types. For example:

```
type
  Student = record
    Name : string[20];
    Age : integer;
  end;

  Class = record
    Students : array [1..30] of Student;
    RoomNumber : integer;
  end;
```

Repeat

Used in **repeat-until** control structures. For example:

```
I := 1;
repeat
  { Statements }
  I := I + 1;
until I > 100;
```

Resident

Indicates that a DLL export will stay in memory as long as the DLL is loaded.

Set

Defines a set variable or type. For example:

```
var
  Letters : set of char;
```

Shl

Shifts the bits in a byte or integer one position to the left and sets the rightmost bit to zero.

Shortint

An integer type ranging from −128 to 127; defined in the System unit.

Shr

Shifts the bits in a byte or integer one position to the right and sets the leftmost bit to zero.

Single

An 8087 data type for real numbers with four significant digits; defined in the System unit.

String

Defines a string data type. A string can be defined from 1 to 255 characters long. If no length is specified, the length defaults to 255 characters. For example:

```
var
   S : string; (* Maximum 255 characters *)
```

Then

Used in **if-then** statements (see **If**).

To

Used in **for-do** loops (see **For**).

Type

Defines data types that can then be used to define variables. For example:

```
type
  PersonType = record
    Name : string[20];
    Address : string[50];
    Income : real;
  end;

var
  Person1, Person2 : PersonType;
```

Unit

Declares the source file to be a Turbo Pascal unit.

Until

Used in **repeat-until** loops (see **Repeat**).

Uses

Declares the use of one or more units. For example:

```
Program Test;

uses Crt, Dos;
```

Var

Defines variables or variable parameters. For example:

```
var
  I : integer;
  S : string;
```

Virtual

Used to define a method in an object as a virtual method.

While

Used in **while-do** loops. For example:

```
I := 0;
while I < 100 do
  begin
    { Statements }
    I := I + 1;
  end;
```

With

Used for implicit reference to a record variable. For example:

```
var
  Person : record
    Name : string;
    Age : integer;
  end;

begin
  with Person do
    begin
```

```
        ReadLn(Name);
        ReadLn(Age);
      end;
```

Word

An integer type ranging from 0 to 65,535; defined in the System unit.

Xor

Combines boolean expressions such that the entire expression is True if only one of two conditions is True. For example:

```
if (A > B) xor (C > D) then ...
```

is True if the first comparison is True or the second comparison is True, but not if both (or neither) are True. Xor also compares two bytes or integers and returns a third byte or integer. A bit in the resulting integer is turned on if either, but not both, bits in the same position is on in the first and second integers.

Index

A

$A compiler directive, 27
@ operator, 165-166
Abs function, 351
absolute clause, 374
Abstract object, 676, 709
Addr function, 354
Address, 154
Align Data directive. *See* $A compiler
    directive
and operator, 52
Append procedure, 183-184, 344
Arrays
        bounds of, 60
        defining, 59-60
        index type, 60
        multidimensional, 62-63
        of records, 71
Arc function, 493
Arc procedure, 453
ArcTan function, 351
ASCII codes, 775-778
ASCII value, 330
asm statement, 218-221
        advantages of, 219
Aspect ratio, 450
Assembler
        debugging, 221-226
        writing, 210-214

assembler clause, 219
Assign procedure, 183, 344
AssignCrt procedure, 397
Assigned function, 354
Assignment operator, 47

B

$B compiler directive, 27
        and execution speed, 761-762
Bar procedure, 453
Bar3D procedure, 453
begin, 117
        in blocks, 11
        in if-then statements, 124
BetTest program, 129-132
BigString object, 633-636
        Concat method, 634
        Copy method, 636
        Delete method, 635
        Init method, 634
        Insert method, 634-635
        Pos method, 635-636
        WriteStr method, 634
Binary tree, 675-685
BinarySearch program, 694-696
BIOS services, 422-427
Block, 11-14, 89
BlockRead procedure, 198-199, 344
BlockWrite procedure, 199, 344
boolean data type, 43

Boolean Evaluation directive. *See* $B compiler directive

Boolean expression, 120
    optimizing, 749-752

Boolean functions, 121-122

Borland Graphics Interface (BGI), 435-475
    colors and patterns, 456-465
    drawing shapes, 445-170
    graphical text, 471-476
    setting up, 436-445

Break procedure, 142-144, 357

Breakpoints
    defining, 312-313
    in Turbo Debugger, 323

Brush, 482-483

BubbleTest program, 699-700

byte data type, 41-42
    vs. char data type, 43
    structure of, 51

C

$C compiler directive, 35

Calculator procedure, 643-650

Callback routine, 29

case statement, 132-136
    optimizing, 745-749
    ranges in, 135-136

CGA adapters, 384-397

char data type, 43

ChDir procedure, 345

Chr function, 330, 341

Circle procedure, 450, 453

CircleDemo program, 451-452

CirclesWin program, 481-482

Circular Input Buffer, 730-731

ClearDevice procedure, 440

ClearViewPort procedure, 440

Close procedure, 184, 345

CloseGraph procedure, 440

ClrEol procedure, 383

ClrScr procedure, 383

Code segment, 153-156

Code Segment Attributes directive. *See* $C compiler directive

Colordemo program, 459-460

COM1 device, 204

COM2 device, 204

CommX program, 719-727

comp data type, 43

Compare function, 100-102

Compile Menu, 244-245
    Build, 244
    Clear Primary File, 245
    Compile, 244
    Destination, 244
    Information, 245
    Make, 244
    Primary File, 245
    Target, 245

Compiler directives, 25-39
    conditional, 37-39
    global, 26
    local, 27
    parameter, 35
    switch, 26

CON device, 203-204

Concat function, 330-332, 341

Condition statement, 119-122

Conditional branching, 122

const declaration, 7-8

Constant, 4

Continue procedure, 144-145, 358

Control structures, 117-151

Control variable, 137

constructor method, 109, 111-112
    with pointers, 174

Coordinate Systems, 438-445

Copy function, 332, 341, 758

Cos function, 351

CreateBrush function, 485

CreateDir procedure, 432

CreateFontIndirect function, 490, 493

CreateHatchBrush function, 493

CreateRectRgnIndirect function, 493

Crt unit, 363-398

CSeg function, 354

CursorSize procedure, 423-425
CursorTo procedure, 401

D

$D compiler directive
      for debugging, 27-28, 222, 302
      for executable files, 35
Data segmemt, 153-156
Date routine, 404-408
DATES unit, 404-406
Debug Information directive. *See* $D
compiler directive
Debug menu, 245-247
      Add Breakpoint, 247
      Add Watch, 246
      Breakpoints, 245
      Call Stack, 246
      Evaluate/Modify, 246
      Output, 246
      User Screen, 246
      Watch, 246
Debugger, integrated, 301-322
      breakpoints, 312-313
      call stack, 12;8
      evaluate/modify, 306-307
      example, 313-320
      execution bar, 303
      go to cursor, 303-304
      memory requirements, 321-322
      step, 304-305
      trace, 304
      watch expressions, 308-312
Debugger, stand-alone. *See* Turbo
  Debugger
Dec procedure, 358
Declarations, 5-11
Delay procedure, 397
Delete procedure, 333-334, 341
DeleteObject function, 485, 493-494
DelLine procedure, 383-384
destructor method, 174-175
DetectGraph procedure, 440
Devices, 202-204
Discriminated union, 70

Disk and file routines, 408-414
DiskFree function, 408, 411
DiskSize function, 408, 412
Display context, 479-480
Display memory, 364
Dispose procedure, 161-163, 175, 355
div operator, 47
DoneWinCrt procedure, 401
Dos unit, 403-427
DosError variable,
DosExitCode function, 414, 417
DosVersion function, 414, 417
double data type, 42
DoubleLink program, 667-671
Doubly linked lists, 665-671
DragDemo program, 467-469
DrawBox procedure, 367-368
DrawPoly procedure, 453
DSeg function, 355

E

$E compiler directive, 28
Early binding, 107
Edit Menu, 237-239
      Clear, 239
      Copy, 238
      Cut, 238
      Paste, 238-239
      Redo, 238
      Show Clipboard, 239
      Undo, 238
80x87 data type, 42-43
Elements, 3-5
Ellipse function, 480, 494
else clause
      in case statement, 136
      in if statement, 124-128
else-if statement, 126-128
Emulation directive. *See* $E compiler
  directive
Encapsulation, 76-77
end, 117
      in blocks, 11
      in if-then statements, 124

Enumerated types, 43-45
EnvCount function, 414, 417
EnvStr function, 414, 417
Eof function, 188, 345
Eoln function, 345
Erase procedure, 343-344, 345
Error messages, 767-774
Exclude procedure, 358
Exec procedure, 414, 418
Executable File Description directive.
   See $D compiler directive
Exit procedure, 146-148, 358
Exp function, 351
Expression, 46-47
extended data type, 42
Extended Syntax directive. *See* $X
   compiler directive
Extensibility, 113
external directive, 211
External procedure, 210-214
     advantages of, 210
     using global data and
       procedures, 212-214

F

$F compiler directive, 20, 28-29
     with external procedures, 208,
      214
Factorial function, 114
Far calls, 28
far clause, 683
FastScreenDemo, 376-377
FastWrite procedure, 372-373
FExpand function, 408, 412
File buffers, 190-191
     optimizing, 756
File Encryption, 659-664
File handle, 184
File Menu, 234-237
    Change Dir, 236
    DOS Shell, 237
    Exit, 237
    New, 234
    Open, 234-235

Print, 237
    Printer Setup, 237
    Recalling Files, 237
    Save, 235
    Save All, 236
    Save As, 236
File pointer, 183
FileExpand function, 432-433
FilePos function, 202, 346
Files, 181-202. *See also* Text files,
   Typed files, Untyped files
FILES unit, 409-411
FileSearch function, 433
FileSize function, 202, 346
FileSplit, 433
FILESW unit, 429-432
FillChar procedure, 358, 742-743
FillEllipse procedure, 461
FillPoly procedure, 459-460, 462
FindFirst procedure, 408, 412
FindNext procedure, 408, 412
Flags register, 421
Flash Card program
    in Object Windows, 582-611
    in Turbo Vision, 500-562
FLASHCMD unit, 537-543
FLASHCNS unit, 575-576
FLASHCRD unit, 588-591
FLASHDLG unit, 598-607
FLASHSET unit, 592-594
FLCARD unit, 523-525
FloodFill function, 483, 486, 494
FloodFill procedure, 459, 462
FLSET unit, 526-528
Flush procedure, 191, 346
for-do loops, 137-139
    constants in, 139
Force Far Calls directive. *See* $F
   compiler directive
forward declaration, 92
Frac function, 352
FreeMem procedure, 165, 355
Free union, 70
FSearch function, 408, 412

FSplit procedure, 408, 413
Functions
    called as procedures, 88-89
    vs. procedures, 87-88

G

$G compiler directive, 29
Generate 80286 Code directive. *See*
  $G compiler directive
GetArcCoords procedure, 454
GetArgCount function, 433
GetArgStr function, 433
GetAspectRatio procedure, 440
GetBkColor function, 462
GetCBreak procedure, 415, 418
GetClientRect procedure, 480, 494
GetColor function, 462
GetCurDir function, 434
GetDate procedure, 404, 406
GetDC function, 492, 494
GetDefaultPalette procedure, 462
GetDlgItemText function, 601
GetDir procedure, 346
GetDriverName function, 441
GetEnv function, 414, 418
GetFAttr procedure, 408, 413
GetFillPattern procedure, 462
GetFillSettings procedure, 463
GetFTime procedure, 404, 406-407
GetGraphMode function, 441
GetImage procedure, 466, 470
GetIntVec procedure, 419, 427, 716
GetLineSettings procedure, 463
GetMaxColor function, 463
GetMaxMode function, 440
GetMaxX function, 438-439, 440
GetMaxY function, 438-439, 440
GetMem procedure, 165, 355
GetModeName function, 442
GetModeRange procedure, 442
GetPalette procedure, 458, 463
GetPaletteSize function, 463
GetPixel function, 454
GetScreenType procedure,

GetStockObject funciton, 489, 494
GetTextExtent function, 495
GetTextSettings procedure, 474
GetTime procedure, 404, 407
GetVerify procedure, 415, 418
GetViewSettings procedure, 442
GetX function, 454
GetY function, 454
Global variable, 84
goto statement, 148-151
    restrictions, 150-151
GotoXY procedure, 367, 369
GraphDefaults procedure, 442
GraphErrorMsg function, 437, 442
Graphics. *See* Borland Graphics
  Interface, Graphics Device
  Interface
Graphics Device Interface (GDI),
  476-498
    drawing shapes, 478-482
    drawing text, 488-492
    patterns in, 482-487
Graphics mode, 436
GraphResult function, 437, 442

H

Halt procedure, 358
Hardware interrupts, 714
Hayes-compatible modem, 719
Headings, 5
Heap, 153-156
Hi function, 359
Hierarchy of operators, 120-121
High function, 96, 359
HighVideo procedure, 369

I

$I compiler directive
    for includes, 20, 36
    for input/output, 29, 183
Identifier, 4
if-then statement, 122-132
    nested, 128-132
    optimizing, 743-749

Images, 466-471
    clipping, 450
ImageSize function, 466, 470
implementation section, 18
Inc procedure, 359
#include command, 577
Include File directive. *See* $I compiler
    directive
Include procedure, 359
Includes, 19-20
Inheritance, 74-76, 112
inherited clause, 76
InitGraph procedure, 437, 443
InitWinCrt procedure, 402
Inline directive, 208-209
inline statement, 206-208
INOUTUTL unit, 650-664
    Beep procedure, 652
    DecodeFile procedure, 662-664
    EncodeFile procedure, 659-662
    FastWrite procedure, 651
    InKey procedure, 652-653
    InputStringShift procedure,
        19;30-659
Input/Output Checking directive. *See*
    $I compiler directive
Insert procedure, 333-334, 341
InsLine procedure, 384
InstallUserDriver function, 443
InstallUserFont function, 474
Int function, 352
Integer arithmetic, 49-50
integer data type, 41
    converting to strings, 335-337
    structure of, 51
Integrated Development
    Environment (IDE), 229-257
        active window, 232
        check box, 232
        close box, 231
        controls, 232
        desktop, 231
        dialog box, 232
        input box, 232

list box, 232
main menu, 230
push button, 232
radio button, 232
resize corner, 231
scroll bars, 231
speed bar, 233
status bar, 230
zoom box, 231
interface section, 18
interrupt directive, 717-718
Interrupt handler, 717-718
Interrupt vector table, 714-717
Interrupts, 713-718
    addresses, 716
    COM1 serial port, 714
    keyboard, 714
    pseudo-parameters, 718
    replacing, 715-717
    vectors, 714
Intr procedure, 419-427
IOResult function, 183, 346

K ───────────────────────

$K compiler directive, 29-30
Keep procedure, 414, 418, 732
Key state, 425-427
KeyPressed function, 397-398

L ───────────────────────

$L compiler directive
    for debugging, 30, 222, 302
    for linking, 36, 211, 216
label
    declaring, 10-11
    with goto statement, 148
Length function, 334, 342
Line procedure, 449-450, 454
LineDemo program, 446-448
LineRel procedure, 454
LinesWin program, 478-479
LineTo function, 478-480, 495
LineTo procedure, 455
Link buffer, 249

Link Object File directive. *See* $L compiler directive
Linked lists, 169-174
Ln function, 352
Lo function, 359
LoadAccelerators function, 579
LoadMenu function, 578
Local menus, 257
Local Symbol Information directive. *See* $L compiler directive
Logical font, 490
Logical operators, 57-58, 119-120
Logical screens, 376-378
longint data type, 42
LowVideo procedure, 369
Low function, 96, 359
LPT1 device, 204
Lst variable, 204

M

$M compiler directive, 36-37, 160
Map files, 249
Mark procedure, 163-165, 355
Math routines, 349-354
MATHUTL unit, 636-637
    Binary function, 640-641
    BitOn function, 642
    Frac_To_Real function, 639-640
    Real_To_Frac function, 637-638
    SetBit procedure, 641
MaxAvail function, 355
Mean function, 97
MemAvail function, 164, 356
Memory Allocation Sizes directive. *See* $M compiler directive
Memory-Resident Programs, 731-737
MemW array, 372-373
MergeTest program, 688-691
Merging, 687-691
MessageBox procedure (Object Windows), 581
MessageBox procedure (Turbo Vision), 515
Methods, 73-74, 103-114

constructor, 109, 111-112
    implementing, 103-106
    and private areas, 106-107
    static, 107-109
    and type compatibility, 112-114
    virtual, 108-114
MkDir function, 346
mod operator, 51
Move procedure, 360, 758
MoveRel procedure, 454
MoveTo function, 478-480, 495
MoveTo procedure, 454
MsDos procedure, 419-427

N

$N compiler directive, 30, 351
Near calls, 28
New procedure, 161-163, 175, 346
NewItem function, 506
NewMenu function, 506
NewSubMenu function, 506
NormVideo procedure, 369
NoSound procedure, 398
not operator, 57
NUL device, 204
Null character, 43, 167
Null-terminated strings, 61-62, 167
NumberFunctions program, 349-351
Numeric Processing directive. *See* $N compiler directive

O

$O compiler directive, 21,
    to include overlays, 30-31
    to specify an overlay, 37
Object hierarchy, 75
Object Browser (DOS IDE), 259-268
    globals, 265-266
    go to source, 261
    hide descendants, 264
    inheritance display, 264
    objects, 263-265
    options, 266-268
    previous browser, 263

referencer display, 261
search, 266
symbol display, 260-261
track source, 262
units, 260-263
Object Browser (Windows IDE),
    268-276
    browse, 269
    globals, 275
    goto, 268
    objects, 272-274
    options, 276
    overview, 269
    print, 269
    referencers, 269
    speed bar, 270
    symbols, 275
    units, 270-272
Object Windows
    accelerators, 579-580
    creating an application, 573-575
    dialog boxes, 598-607
    menu bar, 576-579
    menu commands, 575-576
    for simple graphice, 476-478
    skeletal applications, 580-581
Objects
    abstract, 676
    ancestor, 75
    defining, 71-78
    descendant, 75
    pointers in, 174-175
    reusable, 671-673
Odd function, 352
Ofs function, 154-158, 356
Open parameters, 96-98
Open Parameters directive. *See* $P
    compiler directive
Operators
    arithmetic, 46-47
    hierarchy of, 48-49
Optimization, 739-764
    approaches to, 740
    arithmetic, 752-754

control structures, 743-752
criteria, 739
file operations, 754
parameters, 763-764
string operations, 756-759
Options menu, 247-254
    Compiler, 247
    Debugger, 250
    Directories, 250
    Environment|Color, 254
    Environment|Editor, 252-253
    Environment|Mouse, 253-254
    Environment|Preferences,
        251-252
    Environment|Startup, 254
    Linker, 248-249
    Memory sizes, 247-248
    Open, 254
    Save, 254
    Save As, 254
    Tools, 251
or operator, 52-53
Ord function, 44-45, 352
OutText procedure, 474
OutTextXY procedure, 473, 474
Overflow Checking directive. *See* $Q
    compiler directive
Overlay Code Generation directive.
    See $O compiler directive
Overlay unit, 22
Overlays, 20-25
OvrClearBuf procedure, 25
OvrGetBuf procedure, 25
OvrInit procedure, 24
OvrInitEMS procedure, 25
OvrResult variable, 24
OvrSetBuf procedure, 25

P

$P compiler directive, 31, 98
PackTime procedure, 404, 407
PaintRgn function, 492, 495
ParamCount function, 360
Parameters, 84-87

constant, 86-87
different types, 94-95
literal values, 102
open, 96-98
reference, 85, 100
self, 112
set, 98-99
untyped, 99-102
value, 86
ParamStr function, 360
Pathname, 181
PatternDemo program, 457
PatternsWin program, 483-485
PChar Type, 167-168
with Object Windows, 591
Pen, 482
PERLIST unit, 176-178
PERSONS unit, 104-106
Pi function, 352
PieSlice procedure, 455
PlotLine procedure, 446-448
Pointers, 160-166
advantages of, 160
compatibility, 176
with complex data structures, 169-174
declaring, 169
to objects, 175-176
standard routines, 354-357
variables, 160
Polygon function, 495
PolygonsWin program, 486-487
Polymorphism, 176-180
in complex data structures, 672
and var parameters, 113-114
and virtual methods, 176
Polymorphism program, 179-180
Pop-up windows, 374-383
Pos function, 334-335, 342
Pred function, 360
Primitive data types, 41-58
Printer unit, 204
private clause, 77
PRN device, 204

Procedural type, 677
Procedures
defining, 83-84
PROCESS unit, 415-417
program, 3
Ptr function, 356
public clause, 77
PutImage procedure, 466, 470
PutPixel procedure, 455

Q
$Q compiler directive, 31-32
QuickTest program, 706-708

R
$R compiler directive, 32, 111
and execution speed, 759
for resource files, 584
Random access files, 199
Random function, 353
Randomize procedure, 353
Range Checking directive. *See* $R compiler directive
Read procedure, 347
with text files, 186
with typed files, 193
ReadBuf function, 402
ReadInteger function, 630
ReadKey function, 398
Readln procedure, 347
from the keyboard, 15-17
with test files, 185-186
Real arithmetic, 55-56
real data type, 42
converting to strings, 335-337
Records
defining, 63-67
variant, 67-70
Rectangle procedure, 455
Recursion, 114-115
Reentrant, 731
Reference parameters, 100
RegisterBGIDriver function, 443
RegisterBGIFont function, 474

Registers, 419-423
Registers data type, 421
Regular expression, 239
Release procedure, 163-165, 356
ReleaseDC function, 492, 495-496
RemoveDir procedure, 434
Rename procedure, 343-344, 347
repeat-until statement, 140-141
ReplaceString procedure, 628
Reserved words, 4, 783
Reset procedure, 183, 347
RestoreCRTMode procedure, 443
Rewrite procedure, 183, 347
    with typed files, 202
RmDir procedure, 347
Round function, 50, 353
Run Menu, 242-243
    Go To Cursor, 243
    Parameters, 243
    Program Reset, 243
    Run, 242-243
    Step Over, 243
    Trace Into, 243
RunError procedure, 360

S

$S compiler directive, 32
    and execution speed, 760
Scalar types, 43-45
Screen coordinates, 366-367
Screen swapping, 250
ScrollTo procedure, 402
SCRSAVE program, 732-735
Search Menu, 239-242
    Find, 239
    Find Error, 242
    Find Procedure, 242
    Go To Line Number, 241
    Replace, 240
    Search Again, 240
    Show Last Compiler Error,
        241-242
Searching, 691-696
    binary, 693-694

sequential, 691-693
Sector procedure, 456
Seek procedure, 202, 348
SeekEof function, 347
SeekEoln function, 347
Seg function, 154-158, 357
Segmented addressing, 154
Segments and offsets, 154-160
SelectObject function, 485, 496
Self parameter, 112
SequentialSearch program, 692-693
SetActivePage procedure, 443
SetAllPalette procedure, 463
SetAspectRatio procedure, 444
SetBkColor procedure, 464
SetCBreak procedure, 415, 419
SetColor procedure, 464
SetCurDir procedure, 434
SetDate procedure, 404, 407
SetDlgItemText procedure, 600
SetFAttr procedure, 408, 413
SetFillPattern procedure, 464
SetFillStyle procedure, 459-461, 464
SetFTime procedure, 404, 407
SetGraphBufSize procedure, 444
SetGraphMode procedure, 444
SetIntVec procedure, 419, 427, 716
SetLineStyle procedure, 464
SetPalette procedure, 464-465
SetRGBPalette procedure, 465
Sets
    character, 79
    defining, 78-81
    memory allocation, 79-81
    numeric, 78-79
    user-defined, 79
SetTextBuf procedure, 191, 348
SetTextJustify procedure, 475
SetTextStyle procedure, 472-473, 475
SetTime procedure, 404, 407-408
SetUserCharSize procedure, 475
SetVerify procedure, 415, 419
SetViewport procedure, 444
SetVisualPage procedure, 444

SetWriteMode procedure, 456
ShiftStatus procedure, 425-427
ShellTest program, 703-704
shl operator, 54
shortint data type, 41
shr operator, 54
Simple Link program, 171-173
Simple windows, 373-383
Sin function, 353
single data type, 42
SizeOf function, 198-199, 361
Smart Callbacks directive. *See* $K
    compiler directive
Software interrupts, 714
Sorting, 696-712
    bubble sort, 697-700
    comparison, 708-709
    principles, 697
    quick, 705-708
    shell, 700-705
    with TSortedCollection, 709-712
Sound procedure, 398
SortedCollections program, 710-712
SPtr function, 357
Sqr function, 353
Sqrt function, 353
SSeg function, 357
Stack Overflow Checking directive.
    See $S compiler directive
Stack segment, 153-156
Stacks, 671-675
STACKS unit, 672-675
Standard directives, 4
Standard input, 203-204
Standard output, 203-204
Stock tool, 488
Str procedure, 335-337, 342
StrCat function, 594
StrComp function, 594
StrCopy function, 594
StrDispose function, 595
Streams, 557-566
    registration, 558
StrECopy function, 595

StrEnd function, 595
StrIComp function, 595
Strings
    + operator for, 331
    character manipulation, 338-340
    converting to numbers, 335-337
    defining, 60-61
    length byte, 339-340
    literals, 102
    null-terminated, 61-62
    as open parameters, 98
    optimizing, 756
    standard routines, 329-342
    and typed files, 193-195
Strings unit, 591-597
StripLeadingBlanks procedure, 631
StripTrailingBlanks procedure, 631
StrLCat function, 595
StrLComp function, 595
StrLCopy function, 596
StrLen function, 596
StrLIComp function, 596
StrLower function, 596
StrMove function, 596
StrNew function, 596
STRNGUTL unit, 627-633
Strong typing, 9-10
StrPas function, 597
StrPCopy function, 597
StrPos function, 597
StrRScan function, 597
StrScan function, 597
Structured programming, xi-xii
StrUpper function, 597
STUDENTS unit, 106-107
Subprograms, 83-115
    nesting, 89-90
    precedence, 91
    scope of, 90
Succ function, 361
Swap function, 361
SwapVectors procedure, 414, 419
Symbol, 5

Symbol Reference Information
    directive. *See* $Y compiler directive
Syntax, 5
System unit, 329-361

T

$T compiler directive, 32-33, 166
Tag field, 69-70
TApplication object (Object
    Windows), 573-575
        ExecDialog method, 602
        HAccTable field, 579
        InitInstance method, 579
        InitMainWindow method, 574
        MainWindow field, 574
        object summary, 584-585
        for simple graphics, 476-477
TApplication object (Turbo Vision),
    501-502
        InitMenuBar method, 505
        InitStatusLine method, 512
        object summary, 503-504
TBufStream object, 557
        Get method, 561
        object summary, 562-564
        Put method, 559-560
TButton object (Object Windows),
    614
TButton object (Turbo Vision),
    543-545
TCheckBox object, 614-615
TCheckBoxes object, 549
TCluster object, 550-552
TCollection object, 526-527
        Init method, 527
        object summary, 529-531
TComboBox object, 619-620
TControl object, 613
TDeskTop object, 521-522
TDialog object (Object Windows),
    600-607
        object summary, 612-613
        SetupWindow method, 600
TDialog object (Turbo Vision), 534

ExecView method, 540
GetData method, 540
Insert method, 541
object summary, 535-536
SetData method, 540
TDlgWindow object, 622-623
TEdit object, 617-618
Telecommunications, 718-730
TEmsStream object, 564-565
Terminate-Stay-Resident (TSR)
    programs, 731-737
        triggering, 732
Text display, 363-370
        attribute byte, 364
        blinking, 364-366
        screen coordinates, 366-367
Text files, 182-191
        identifiers, 182-183
        reading numbers from, 186-188
        reading strings from, 185-186
        vs. typed files, 194-195
        writing, 189-190
Text mode, 363, 370
TextBackground procedure, 365-366,
    370
TextColor procedure, 365-366, 370
TextDemo program, 471-472
TextExtent function, 489
TextHeight function, 473, 475
TextMode procedure, 365
TextOut function, 489, 496
TextWidth function, 475-476
TextWin program, 488-489
TextWin2 program, 490-492
TFileDialog object (Object Windows),
    607
        object summary, 623
TFileDialog object (Turbo Vision),
    559
        object summary, 555-557
TGroup object, 522-523
TGroupBox object, 621-622
THistory object, 554-555
Time routines, 404-408

TIMER unit, 740-741
TInputLine object, 545-546
TLabel object, 547
TListBox object (Object Windows), 618-619
TListBox object (Turbo Vision), 553-554
TMenuBar object, 505-509
    Init method, 506
    object summary, 506-509
TMenuBox object, 509
TObject object, 525-526
TProgram object
    HandleEvent method, 514
    object summary, 519-521
TrackCursor procedure, 402
TRadioButton object, 615-616
TRadioButtons object, 549-550
TRect object, 510-511
Tree. *See* Binary tree
TREES unit, 676-681
TResourceFile object, 571-572
Trunc function, 50,
Truncate procedure, 348
TScrollBar object (Object Windows), 620-621
TScrollBar object (Turbo Vision), 571
TScroller object, 569-570
TSortedCollection object, 709
    Compare method, 709-712
    object summary, 532
    removing duplicates, 712
TStatic object, 616-617
TStaticText object, 548
TStatusLine object, 512-514
TStream object
    Read method, 558
    object summary, 565-566
    Write method, 558
TStringCollection object, 533
Turbo Assembler, 214-218
Turbo Debugger, 322-325
    for assembler, 221-226
    breakpoints, 323

controlling execution, 323
CPU window, 223
evaluating expressions, 325
register frame, 223
watch expressions, 323
Turbo Vision, 499-572
    collections, 526-534
    dialog boxes, 537-543
    event commands, 504-505
    event handler, 514-518
    menu bar, 505-506
    simple dialog boxes, 534
    status line, 511-512
    streams, 557-566
TView object, 536-537
TWindow object (Object Windows), 477
    Attr field, 578
    Init method, 574, 578
    object summary, 585-587
    Paint method, 478, 480
TWindow object (Turbo Vision), 567-569
TWindowsObject object, 587-588
Type casting, 45-46
Type compatibility, 42
    and methods, 112-114
type declarations, 8
Typed @ Operator directive. *See* $T compiler directive
Typed constants, 7-8
Typed files
    declaring, 191-192
    records and, 192-193
    with Rewrite, 202
    strings and, 193-195
    vs. text files, 194-195
TypeOf function, 361

U

UART, 718
Unary minus, 48-49
Units, 17-19
    advantages, 17

creating, 18-19
and objects, 77
using, 17-18
UnpackTime procedure, 404, 408
Unstructured branching, 148
Untyped constants, 7
Untyped files, 197-199
    with Reset statement, 198
    with Rewrite statement, 198
Untyped parameters, 99-102
Upcase function, 330, 342
    used in program, 338-339
uses clause, 18

V ─────────────────

$V compiler directive, 33-34, 95
Val procedure, 335-337, 342
Variables
    declaring, 9
    scope of, 92-94
Var-String Checking directive. *See* $V
    compiler directive
Vertical retrace, 384-397
Video memory, 370-373
    absolute clause with, 374
VidSeg function, 371
virtual clause, 109
Virtual methods, 108-114
    rules of, 110-111
Virtual method table, 111-114

W ─────────────────

$W compiler directive, 34
Watch expressions, 308-312
    adding, 309-310, 315
    clearing, 311
    deleting, 311
    disabling, 312
    display formats, 317-320
    enabling, 312
    modifying, 311
WhereX function, 367, 370
WhereY function, 367, 370
while-do statement, 141-142

WinCrt unit, 398-402
    creating a window, 399-400
    vs. Crt unit, 400-401
WinDos unit, 428-434
    vs. Dos unit, 428-429
Window menu, 254-257
    Arrange Icons, 255
    Cascade, 255
    Close, 256
    Close All, 255
    List, 256
    Next, 256
    Previous, 256
    Refresh Display, 255
    Size/Move, 255
    Tile, 255
    Zoom, 255
Window procedure, 373-374, 384
WindowDemo program, 378-382
Windows Stack Frames directive. *See*
    $W compiler directive
WinProcs unite, 476
WinTypes unit, 476
with statement, 64-67
word data type, 41-42
WordToHex function, 155-156
Write procedure, 349
    with text files, 189
    with typed files, 193
WriteBuf function, 402
WriteChar procedure, 402
Writeln procedure, 349
    to the screen, 15
    with text files, 189
WritelnWithName procedure, 629-630

X ─────────────────

$X compiler directive, 34-35, 89
xor operator, 52-53

Y ─────────────────

$Y compiler directive, 35